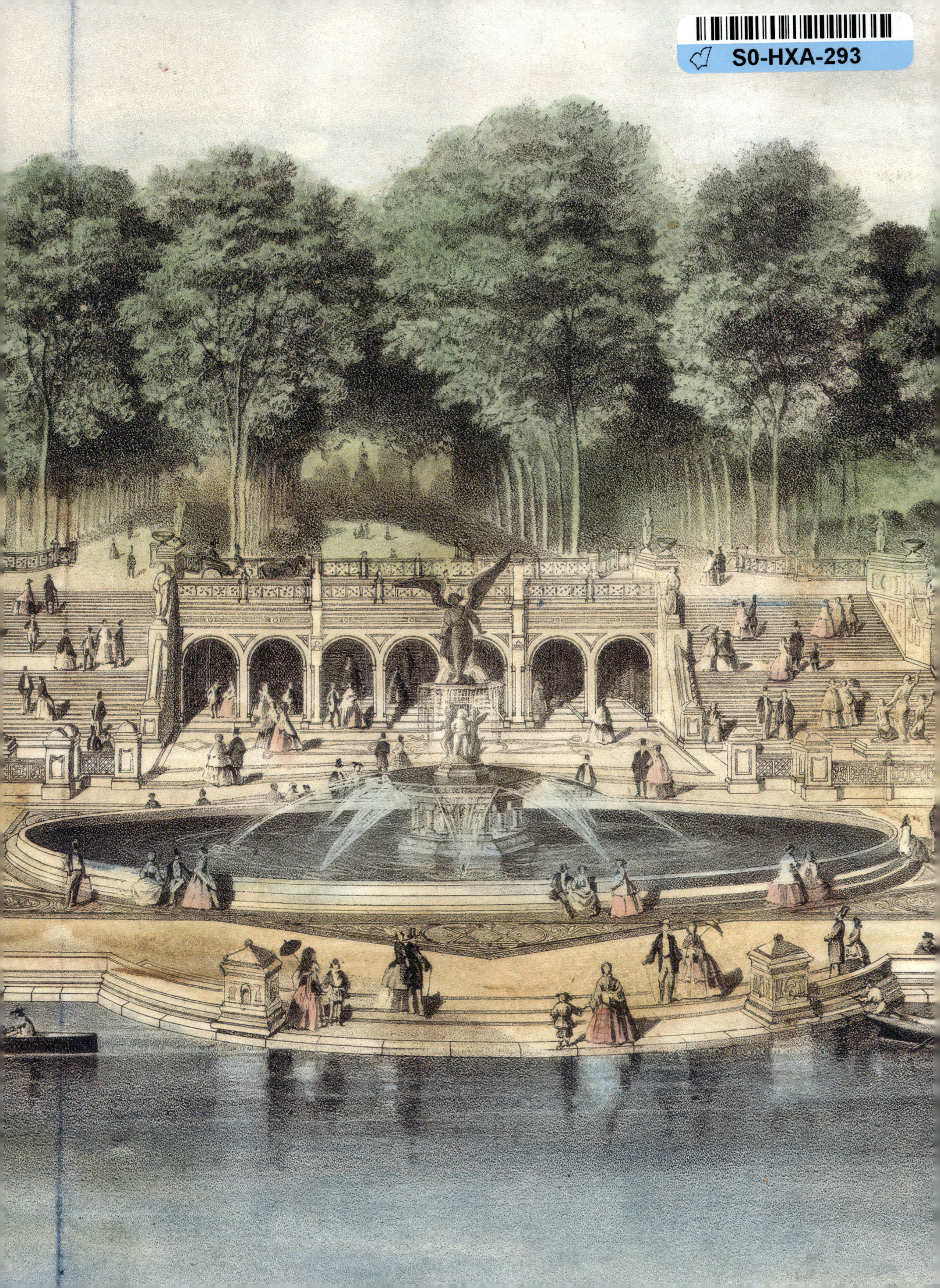

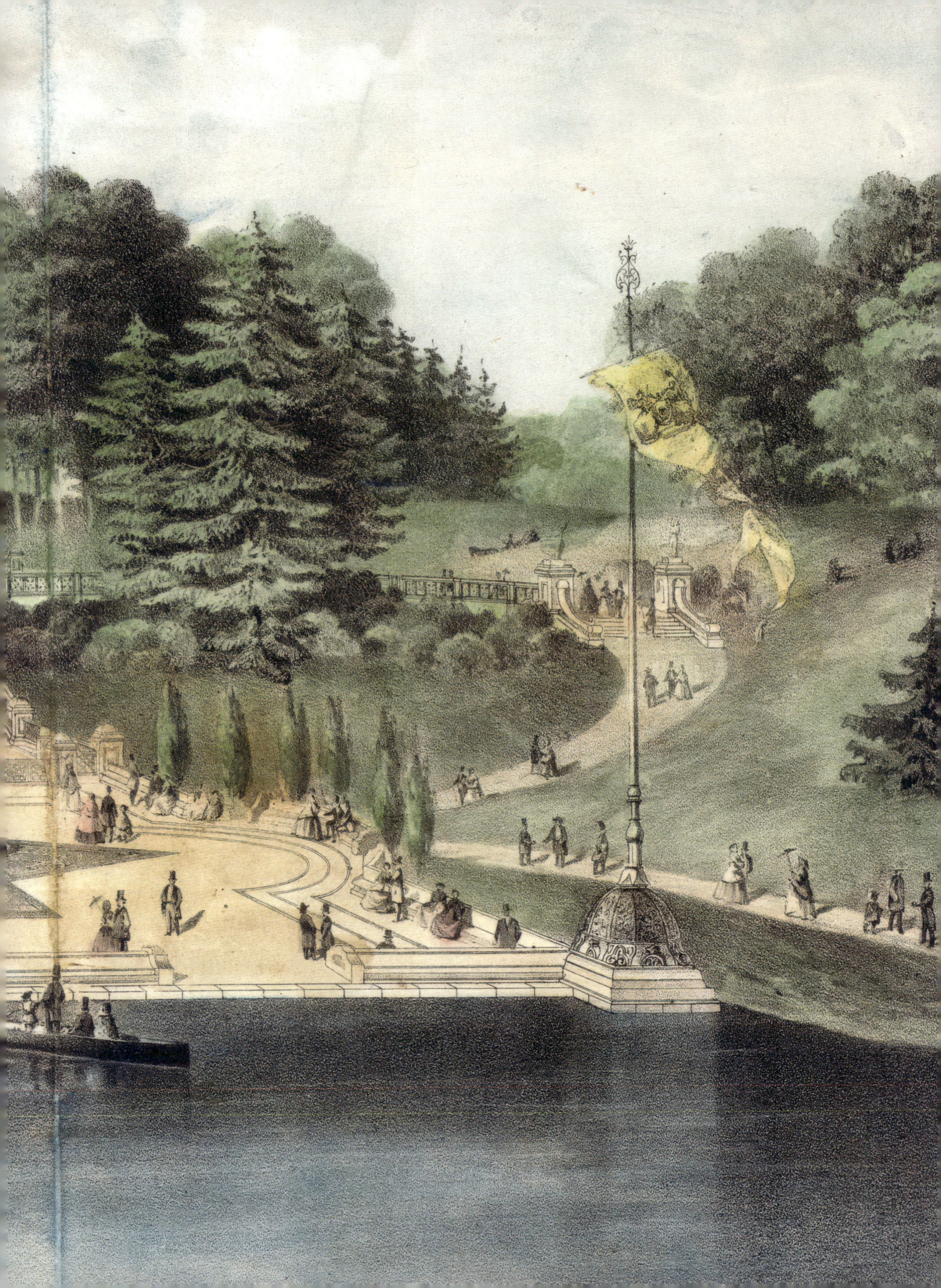

EMMA STEBBINS

Edited by Karli Wurzelbacher
Foreword by Tony Kushner

THE HECKSCHER MUSEUM OF ART

EMMA STEBBINS

CARVING OUT HISTORY

With essays by
Patricia Cronin
Ricky Flores
David J. Getsy
Melissa L. Gustin
Katrin Horn
and
Laura Turner Igoe

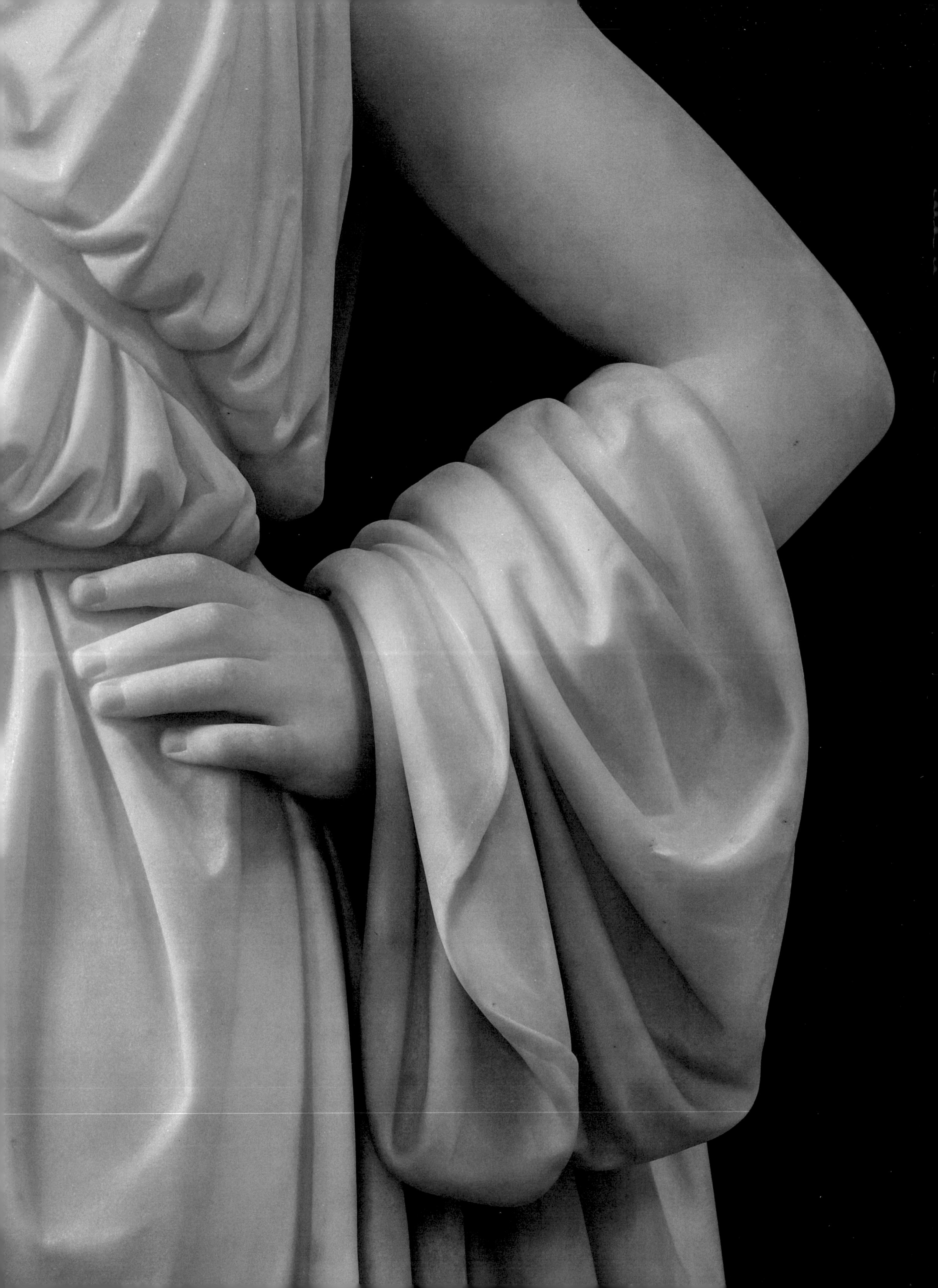

CONTENTS

FOREWORD

TONY KUSHNER

One New Year's Eve in the late 1970s or early 1980s—I apologize for imprecise dating but it was a long time ago—I went with friends to Central Park, hoping that on the Mall near the Naumburg Bandshell we might have an unobstructed view of the fireworks on the East River (I think it was the East River, maybe it was the Hudson, who knows?). I don't think we knew in advance that the *Bethesda Fountain* plaza had been turned for the night into a dance floor. The music was supplied primarily by loudspeakers, competing with many, many boom boxes that people had brought with them, each boom box broadcasting its owner's cassette mixtape. I also believe (unless I dreamed this or misremember it as happening on this and not some other night) there were several rowboats on the lake behind the plaza, in which instrumentalists contributed to the cacophony with chamber music. The crowd, of course, was enormous, dancing to whatever drummer they'd selected, as color-gelled klieg lights swept across the plaza, their beams reflected in a huge mirrored disco ball, twirling, suspended from the outstretched, benedictive right hand of the *Angel of the Waters* (see pl. 47).

According to my private personal mythology, that was the night I decided that *Bethesda Fountain* plaza was the Center of the Universe, at any rate the Center of *my* Universe, because, positioned at the center of this appropriately wheel-shaped Center of the Universe is Emma Stebbins's *Angel of the Waters*. If there's any sculpture in a more perfect and dynamic relationship to its architectural and natural circumstances, I'm unaware of it. Surely Stebbins's angel must be what Ezekiel saw in his vision: "the spirit of the living creature was within the wheel" (AV, Ezekiel 1:20). She is the living creature at the heart of Calvert Vaux's symmetrical wheel of a plaza; her vital asymmetrical presence sets the wheel spinning, revolving around her. She appears to be rising up from its revolving, as much as she appears to be alighting after descending from above. She's ascending and descending, both at once. She's a miracle of public art.

I've never read that Stebbins drew inspiration for the *Angel of the Waters* from the book of Ezekiel, although the prophet's vision was revealed in an aquatic setting, on the banks of the river Chebar while he was a captive in Babylon, and Ezekiel records that when the angels in his vision moved, he "heard the noise of their wings, like the noise of great waters" (AV, Ezekiel 1:24). Ezekiel also mentions that the tops of the heads of his angels were the color of the "terrible crystal" beryl—beryls come in many colors, but scholars agree that in the Holy Scriptures beryl was a shade of green. I realize it's unlikely that Stebbins anticipated her bronze *Angel of the Waters*'s acquisition of a verdigris cloak; I'm mentioning this only because it gives me the chance to complain about the recent stripping away of her gorgeous gray-green patina. The *Angel of the Waters* suffered this well-intended and probably necessary outrage in common with another great public artwork, the Statue of Liberty.

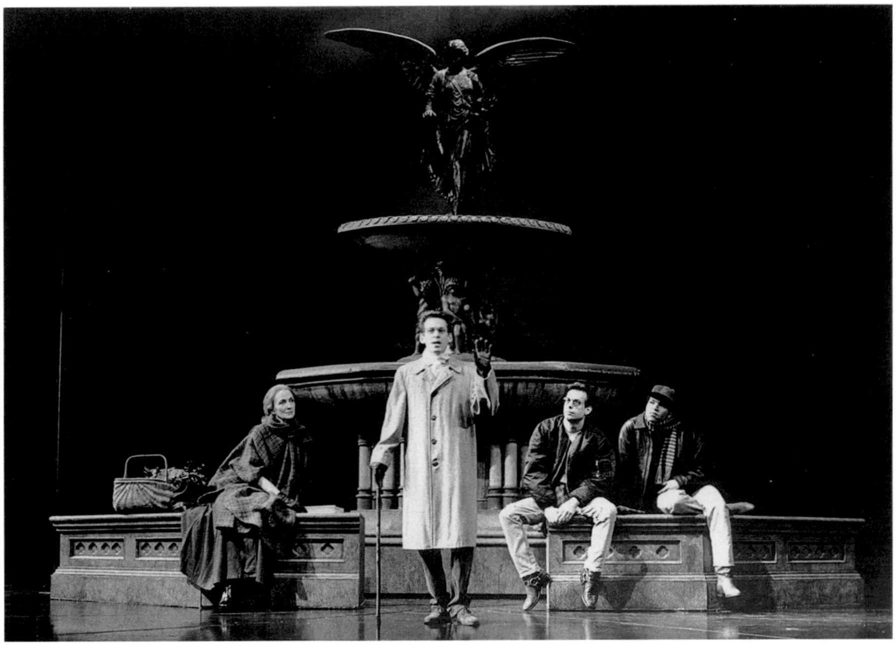

FIG. 1 Kathleen Chalfant, Stephen Spinella, Joe Mantello, and Jeffrey Wright in a scene from *Angels in America: Perestroika*, Walter Kerr Theatre, New York, NY, 1993–94.

The biblical text that directly inspired Stebbins is chapter five of the Gospel of John. Her sculpture commemorated the opening in 1842 of the Croton Aqueduct. It appears to have been Stebbins's idea, rather than that of her commissioners, to personify this new source of drinking water for the rapidly expanding city as the angel who, according to the evangelist, "troubled the waters" of a pool in Bethesda, giving them healing powers. It must have been Stebbins's decision to render the *Angel of the Waters* as a woman. In the Gospel, no reference is made to the gender of the angel of Bethesda; when they're assigned a gender, angels in the Bible are, I believe, always male.

Stebbins was among the first women in the United States to receive a commission for a public statue. In 1866, Congress approved Vinnie Ream as the sculptor of the Capitol Rotunda's statue of Abraham Lincoln (Mary Lincoln, who suspected Ream of flirting with Lincoln when he sat for her in 1865, claimed that Ream won the commission by leaning over the visitors' gallery railing during the senate's floor debate in a dress cut to display her décolletage). The rarity of an important commission going to a woman, and the misogyny enforcing the rarity, were evident in the hostile reception that greeted Stebbins's masterpiece. It was assumed that Stebbins was given the job by her brother, head of the Park's Statuary, Fountains, and Architectural Structures committee. How else to explain the dire results of hiring an artist so untalented and tasteless as to give an angel a flouncy skirt, an unruly hairdo, thick neck and limbs, and straps crisscrossing her breasts? She looked, one critic sneered, like a milkmaid.

She *could* be a milkmaid. With seriousness of purpose, a concentrated, experienced expression, with easeful grace, Stebbins's angel is performing a task, much as any milkmaid might do. She's working, she's a worker, same as all angels are in Holy Writ; "angel" is derived from *angelos*, the ancient Greek word for messenger, and in Hebrew, *malakh* is the word for earthly and heavenly messengers. Her humanity, rather than her divinity, is foremost, apart from her wings; I realize it's improbable,

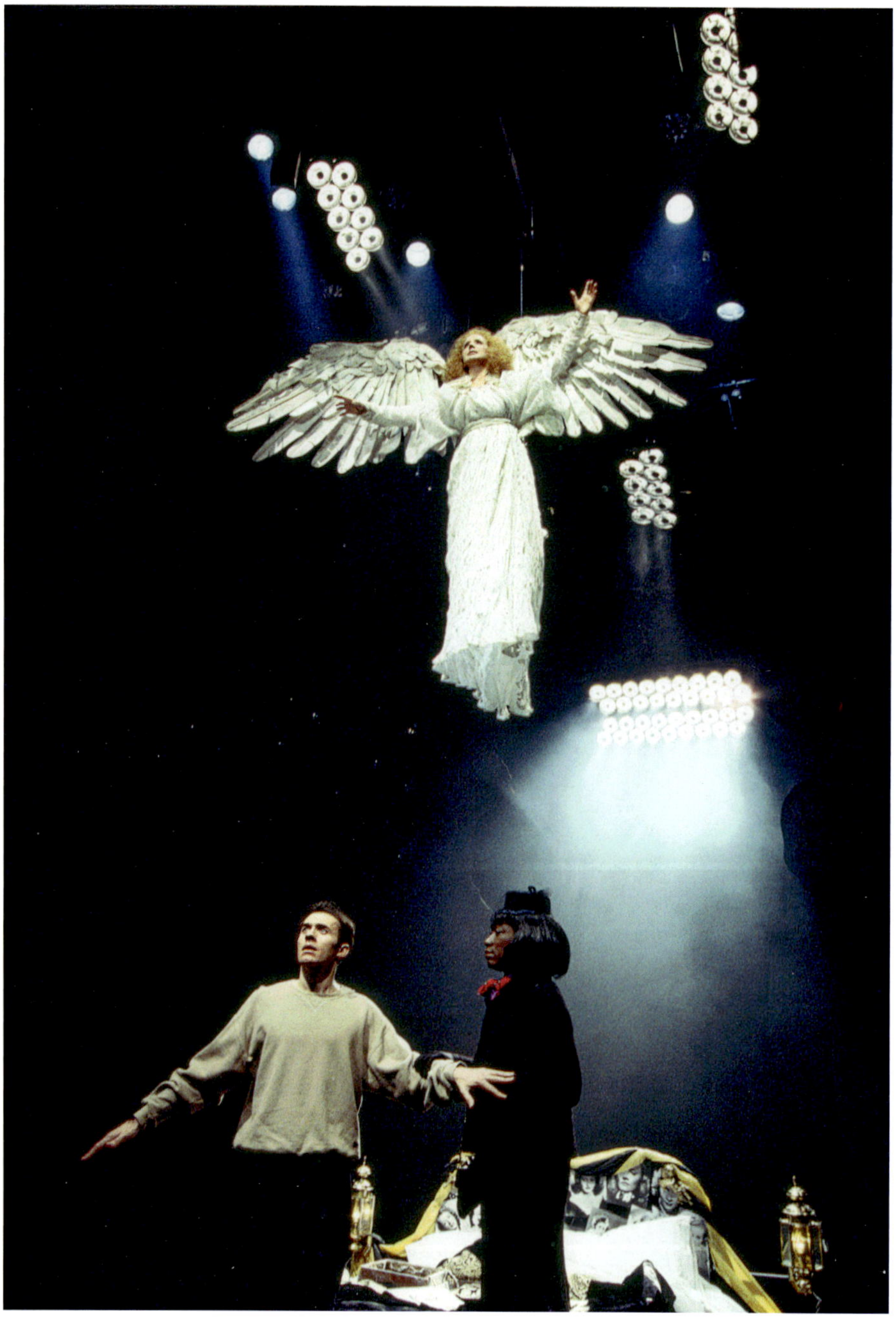

FIG. 2 Nancy Crane, Stephen Dillane, and Joseph Mydell in a scene from *Angels in America: Perestroika*, Cottesloe Theatre, National Theatre, London, UK, 1993.

but a determinedly agnostic/secular humanist/Brechtian reading of the sculpture might explain Stebbins's straps as the way a pair of costume wings are kept attached.

The *Angel of the Waters* has always seemed to me a uniquely democratic, American angel—especially those wings of hers, whether or not they're strapped on. Artists almost always depict the wings of angels, unless they're folded, with the leading edge of the wing and primary feathers pointing vertically. The wings of Stebbins's angel are horizontal. They lead the eye not upwards but outwards, not heavenwards but level with our earthbound surroundings. These wings are not annunciatory or admonitory exclamation marks, telling us to drop to our knees before a sovereign power. The Bethesda angel's horizontal wings gesture laterally towards expanded vision, they're a welcoming embrace.

In 1988, when I began work on my play *Angels in America*, I'd never heard of Emma Stebbins (see figs. 1, 2). I didn't know she was the artist responsible for my favorite angel. The subtitle of the play is *A Gay Fantasia on National Themes*, but I had no idea that the *Angel of the Waters* was sculpted by a lesbian, the lifelong partner of the great American actress Charlotte Cushman. I only knew that the play was going to conclude with a scene set at the base of the fountain on Bethesda plaza. I didn't know then that it'd take me three years to finish the play, nor that it'd require seven and a half hours of stage time to reach the final scene, but I knew from the start that the *Angel of the Waters* at the Center of the Center of the Universe was the direction in which I hoped I was heading.

I'm delighted that thanks to The Heckscher Museum of Art, we are being introduced, at very, very long last, to the body of work of Emma Stebbins. I'm honored to be a small part of this exhibition, and I feel blessed to be afforded the opportunity to express my deep admiration for and gratitude to this brilliant, important American artist.

PREFACE

HEATHER S. ARNET

The Heckscher Museum of Art is proud to present *Emma Stebbins: Carving Out History*, the first-ever museum exhibition and accompanying publication dedicated to the transatlantic career of neoclassical sculptor Emma Stebbins. Stebbins was a celebrated artist in her lifetime, and with her creation of the *Bethesda Fountain* she became the first woman to complete a public art commission in New York City. For over 150 years, Stebbins's *Bethesda Fountain* has been a global icon, yet she herself has been largely forgotten. Women and members of the LGBTQ+ community have been left out of the story and on the margins for too long. This revelatory project illuminates the full scope and impact of Stebbins's life and work, expanding our knowledge of American art history.

The Heckscher Museum of Art has a long relationship with Stebbins's work. Around 1859, Charles August Heckscher, an uncle of the museum's founder August Heckscher, commissioned two sculptures by Stebbins, *Industry* and *Commerce*. The pair have been part of the institution's collection since the 1920s. In recent years, guided by our Collection Stewardship Committee, we acquired three additional sculptures by the artist and now enjoy the privilege of stewarding the most extensive collection of Stebbins's work. It became clear that it was our responsibility to bring the depth and breadth of her groundbreaking career to the public through this exhibition and book.

Working in Rome from 1857 to 1870, Stebbins created marble and bronze sculptures and earned major public art commissions. She also met the love of her life, actress Charlotte Cushman, in Italy. They remained together until Cushman's death in 1876. Although Stebbins and Cushman could not legally wed, they considered themselves married. We timed the debut of *Emma Stebbins: Carving Out History* to coincide with the tenth anniversary of *Obergefell v. Hodges* (2015), the Supreme Court decision recognizing same-sex couples' right to marry in the United States. This presented the opportunity to engage with the LGBTQ+ community around exhibition design, interpretation, and programming, while underscoring the continued relevance of Stebbins's work and legacy. These initiatives build on the museum's ongoing strategic efforts to foster awareness of artists whose careers and life experiences can broaden our understandings of the past, foster community connections to the present, and inspire diverse possibilities for the future.

Developing this exhibition and book involved extensive research, national and international travel, a convening of scholars and curators, careful object conservation, new photography, and the commissioning of new scholarship. We are grateful for the generosity and foresight of exhibition campaign co-chairs Richard T. Cunniff Jr. and Robin T. Hadley, and leadership gifts from Priscilla and Robert Hughes and Andrea B. and Peter D. Klein. This exhibition would not have been possible without support from the Terra Foundation for American Art and the Henry Luce Foundation.

Major support for this publication was provided by the Wyeth Foundation for American Art and the Every Page Foundation. Additional support was provided by the Deborah Buck Foundation, the Stebbins Fund in memory of James F. Stebbins and Jane Stebbins Greenleaf, and the Gladys Krieble Delmas Foundation. Public support was provided by the National Endowment for the Arts, the New York State Council on the Arts, and the Town of Huntington, New York. Support for community engagement and public programming was provided by a distinguished Museums for America grant from the Institute of Museum and Library Services.

Tremendous thanks to the members of the staff and board of trustees of The Heckscher Museum of Art, especially Karli Wurzelbacher and the other members of our visionary curatorial department, and the dedicated development and communications teams who worked together to bring this project to fruition. The Museum is grateful to the many individuals who donated time, talent, and treasure to this project, with special thanks to Tony Kushner for his insightful foreword and to all of those who participated in the Accessibility, Youth, and Community Advisory groups, whose guidance and input was invaluable in helping to shape *Emma Stebbins: Carving Out History*.

Heather S. Arnet
Executive Director and CEO
The Heckscher Museum of Art

ACKNOWLEDGMENTS

KARLI WURZELBACHER

Hundreds of individuals and institutions played a part in the realization of the exhibition and publication *Emma Stebbins: Carving Out History*. The full staff of The Heckscher Museum of Art contributed, especially its greatest champion, Heather S. Arnet, Executive Director and CEO. I am immensely thankful for the partnership of Kerrilyn Blee, Registrar and Exhibitions Manager; Jessica Rosen, Curatorial Assistant; and Meredith A. Brown, Consulting Curator of Contemporary Art. Jessica Rosen and Curatorial Department volunteer Jacqueline Covey conducted invaluable research that informed my own work. Other colleagues helped to shape the exhibition, including Deborah Johnson, former Deputy Director and Director of Development; Kenneth Moss, Director of Facilities; Kristina Schaaf, Director of Visitor Experience; Joy Weiner, Director of Education and Public Programs; Lisa Raihana Sayedi, Manager of Community Engagement; and David Benner and Sandra Mossblad Luethi, Preparators.

I am grateful to authors Patricia Cronin, Ricky Flores, David J. Getsy, Melissa L. Gustin, Katrin Horn, Laura Turner Igoe, and Tony Kushner for their brilliant essays in this volume. *Emma Stebbins: Carving Out History* also benefited from insights generated during a scholarly convening that brought some of these writers into dialogue with Melissa Dabakis, Kenyon College; Ivan Gaskell, Bard Graduate Center; Shawnya L. Harris, Georgia Museum of Art; Karen Lemmey, Smithsonian American Art Museum; Jeffrey Richmond-Moll, Peabody Essex Museum; Thayer Tolles, the Metropolitan Museum of Art; and Stephanie Sparling Williams, Brooklyn Museum.

Other scholars, collectors, and Stebbins enthusiasts supported this project in various ways, including Pam Borman, Maria Teresa Cometto, Martha Edelheit, John and Mary McGuigan, Sara Cedar Miller, Elizabeth Milroy, Elizabeth Noble, Alison Tung, and Esther L. Hornik and Lystra A. Harris of the Charlotte Cushman Foundation. Staff members at each of the institutions listed in the figure captions and cited in the endnotes facilitated the research that underpins this book and show. I would also like to applaud photographers David Almeida, John Halpern, Rory Moore, Tony Rinaldo, and Jonathan Smith for their stunning new images of Stebbins's sculptures.

Paul Carlos, Urshula Barbour, and Giedre Kavalyauskas of Pure+Applied created the elegant and striking design of both the exhibition and this book. Laura Lesswing refined the ideas and writing throughout the publication through her tireless copyediting. Thanks as well to the team at Marquand Books, notably Gina Broze, Melissa Duffes, Tom Eykemans, Leah Finger, and Kestrel Rundle. I also appreciate the work of proofreader Carrie Wicks and indexer Enid Zafran.

The exhibition would not have been possible without the foresight of the private collectors and institutional leaders who care for Stebbins's work and so generously agreed to our loan requests. Thank you to Karen Bechtel and William Osborne; Tyler Elizabeth Burgess; Caroline Welling VanDeusen; James Rondeau and Sarah Kelly

Oehler at the Art Institute of Chicago; Adrienne Adair, Julie Reid, and Catherine Morrow at Belfast Central Library, Libraries NI; Anne Pasternak, Stephanie Sparling Williams, and Caroline Gillaspie at Brooklyn Museum; Lydah Pyles DeBin and Kristin Henley at the Center for Fiction; Erik Neil and Corey Piper at the Chrysler Museum of Art; Max Hollein and Thayer Tolles at the Metropolitan Museum of Art; and Kim Hewitt, Jill Martin Clements, and Elle Harms at Watertown Free Public Library.

Other lenders contributed artworks and archival material that brought Stebbins's story to life. Thanks to Anne Helmreich, Susan Cary, and Marisa Bourgoin at Archives of American Art, Smithsonian Institution; Eric Firestone and Jennifer Samet at Eric Firestone Gallery; Margaret Lynne Ausfeld and Pamela Bransford at Montgomery Museum of Fine Arts; Louise Mirrer and Heidi Nakashima at the New York Historical; and Petrina Jackson and Jenny Gotwals at Schlesinger Library, Radcliffe Institute, Harvard University.

In addition to the registrars and conservators at the institutions listed above, I would like to recognize the careful work of ArtCare Conservation, Brendan Catney, Quarto Conservation, and Tatti Art Conservation. I also appreciate the wizardry of Peter Fisher, Kira Lund, and Rasmus Degn Nielsen at Khora, who brought the *Bethesda Fountain* to the exhibition via augmented reality. Thank you to Betsy Smith, Salmaan Khan, Jessica Striebel MacLean, and Matt Reiley from the Central Park Conservancy for their help with this effort.

The national tour of *Emma Stebbins: Carving Out History* was organized and supported by the board and staff of the Art Bridges Foundation, especially Anne Kraybill, Andi Phillips, Laura Williams, and Chris Guerra. I am grateful to the leadership and colleagues at each of the museums presenting this exhibition for sharing Stebbins's life and work with their audiences.

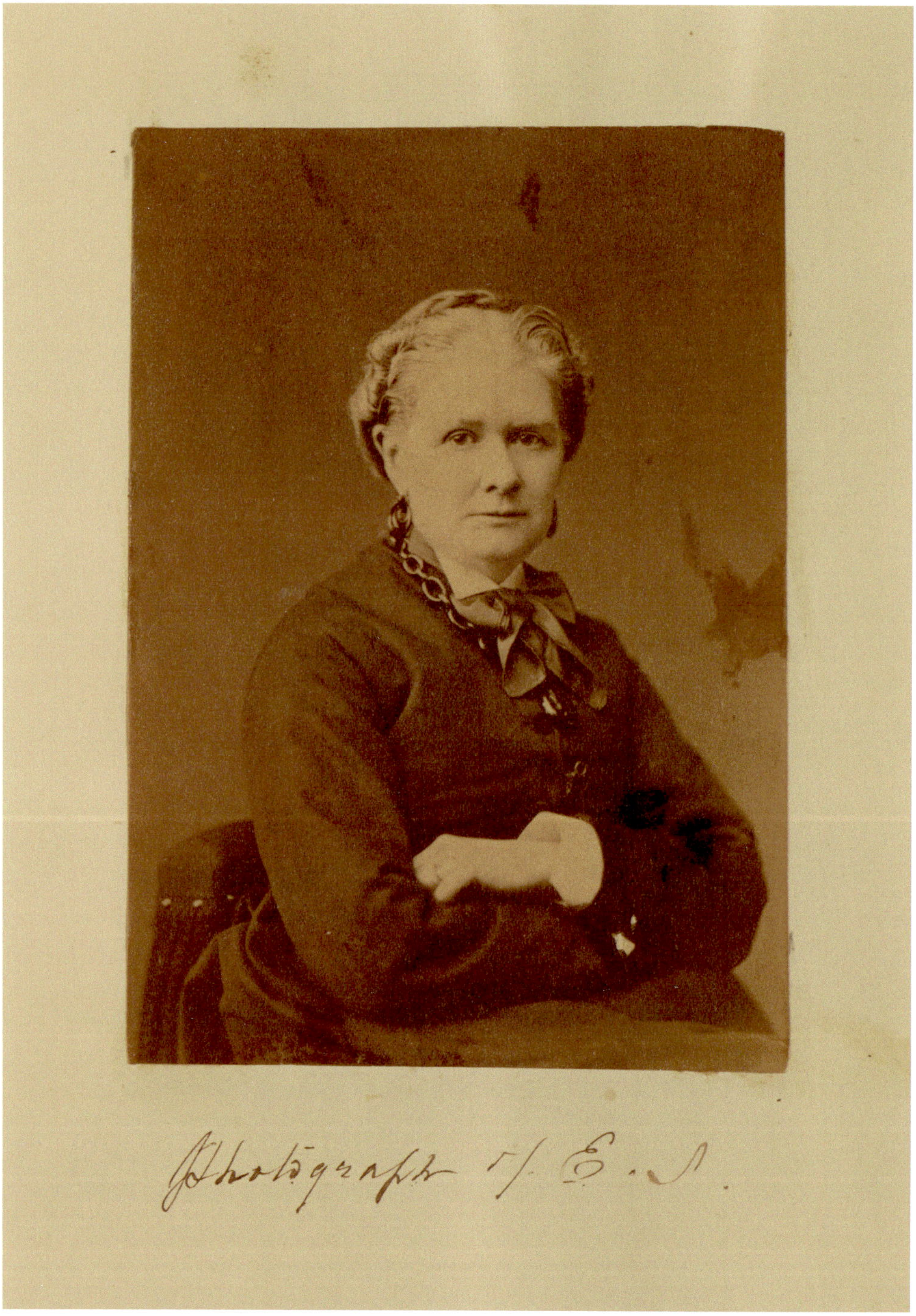

FIG. 1 *Emma Stebbins*. Albumen print from a glass negative, 5¾ × 4 in. (14.6 × 10.2 cm). From the Emma Stebbins scrapbook, 1858–82.

Archives of American Art, Smithsonian Institution, Washington, DC

KARLI WURZELBACHER

INTRODUCTION

Carving Out History

Emma Stebbins: Carving Out History examines the full scope of Stebbins's history-making career, asserting that she was one of the most significant American sculptors of the nineteenth century. From 1857 to 1870, she created innovative marble and bronze sculptures while living in Rome with her wife, renowned Shakespearean actress Charlotte Cushman. Stebbins modeled inventive and incisive interpretations of literary and biblical subjects as well as unprecedented allegories of American industry. With the *Bethesda Fountain* in 1863, she became the first woman to earn a commission for a public sculpture from the city of New York (pl. 47).[1] When Bostonians installed Stebbins's statue of educator Horace Mann on the grounds of the Massachusetts State House in 1865, she became the first woman in the country to complete an outdoor bronze monument (pl. 17).[2] Stebbins—a professional sculptor in a female marriage—reimagined what a woman's life could be in the mid-nineteenth century (see fig. 1).[3] Her art speaks to some of the most compelling issues of her time (and ours), including gender and sexuality, ecology and industry, and political conflict and public art.

STEBBINS'S PLACE IN ART HISTORY

Throughout her career, Stebbins enjoyed the patronage of prominent collectors, completed three high-profile public monuments, and exhibited her work to critical notice in Boston, Dublin, Liverpool, London, Munich, New York City, Philadelphia, and Rome. Her contemporaries lauded her as an example of "American capacity" in the arts and saw her work as "proof of the art capabilities of woman."[4] Stebbins figured in surveys of American art, including Henry T. Tuckerman's *Book of the Artists: American Artist Life* (1867), and in anthologies of women artists, including Elizabeth Fries Lummis Ellet's *Women Artists in All Ages and Countries* (1859; excerpted in

When quoting historical and archival documents, this book preserves the spelling, punctuation, and grammatical conventions of the original texts. In a few instances, minor adjustments were necessary for clarity.

this volume).[5] In 1878, Stebbins published a successful biography of Cushman that obliquely documented their life together (excerpted in this volume).

At the time of Stebbins's death in 1882, however, the *New-York Times* and several other major newspapers that had covered her career failed to report her passing. The *Brooklyn Daily Eagle* mistakenly identified her as the donor of the *Bethesda Fountain*, not its creator.[6] Suspecting that "the full extent of her accomplishments may not be known to the public," someone close to Stebbins sent an account of her life and art to the *New-York Tribune*.[7] The letter to the editor ran in lieu of an obituary, and Mary Stebbins Garland later expanded upon this information about her sister for the editor of *Appletons' Cyclopaedia of American Biography* (1888) (see Garland's historical text in this volume).

Like many historical women artists, Stebbins was largely forgotten for most of the twentieth century. With the exception of The Heckscher Museum of Art, which acquired two of her sculptures in the 1920s, there were no examples of her work in American art museums (see fig. 2).[8] Accounts of American sculpture recycled the limited information published in *Appletons' Cyclopaedia*, Ellet, and Tuckerman.[9] Beginning in the 1970s, however, new directions in the fields of American art history, feminist art history, and queer studies awakened scholarly interest in Stebbins's art and in the life and career of Cushman.[10] William H. Gerdts included Stebbins in his important publications and exhibitions on neoclassical American sculpture.[11] Works by Stebbins then entered the collections of the Brooklyn Museum and the Chrysler Museum of Art in the 1980s.[12] In the mid-1990s, Elizabeth Milroy published the first survey of the artist's oeuvre.[13] She relied on Cushman's correspondence at the Library of Congress, since few of Stebbins's own papers (such as letters or journals) survive. Milroy also uncovered an invaluable primary source: an annotated scrapbook compiled by Garland that contains photographs of the majority of Stebbins's sculptures.[14] Since 2014, Melissa Dabakis and Melissa L. Gustin have published on Stebbins's art, and Maria Teresa Cometto has authored a biography of her.[15]

Stebbins's artworks belong to the tradition of nineteenth-century neoclassical sculpture, the study of which has also been growing in recent decades.[16] Sculptors working within this international style emulated ancient Greek and Roman statuary in an effort to embody universal and eternal values in the form of the simplified, harmonious, and idealized nude figure.[17] In the US, neoclassical sculpture and architecture were associated with the democracy and culture of ancient Greece, and Dabakis has argued that these meanings remained potent when Stebbins was in Rome in the years leading up to and during the US Civil War and the Italian Risorgimento.[18] Scholars have also articulated how neoclassical marble sculptures reflect and produce understandings of class, sex, gender, sexuality, nationality, and race, including by giving form to ideologies and hierarchies that privilege whiteness as the ideal.[19]

Emma Stebbins: Carving Out History expands on existing scholarship and draws on additional primary sources and methodologies to present a comprehensive account of her career. It also contains the first sustained interpretations of some of her sculptures. Katrin Horn analyzes primary textual sources to locate Stebbins as a vital participant in the social and intellectual networks of artists, writers, activists, and politicians who shaped American culture at home and abroad. Laura Turner Igoe's ecocritical exploration of the sculptures *Industry* (pl. 10), *Commerce* (pl. 11), and the *Bethesda Fountain* connects Stebbins's work to nineteenth-century industries, the changing environment, and public health. Gustin considers the relation of Stebbins's representations of angels, especially *Sandalphon* (pl. 20), *Angel of the*

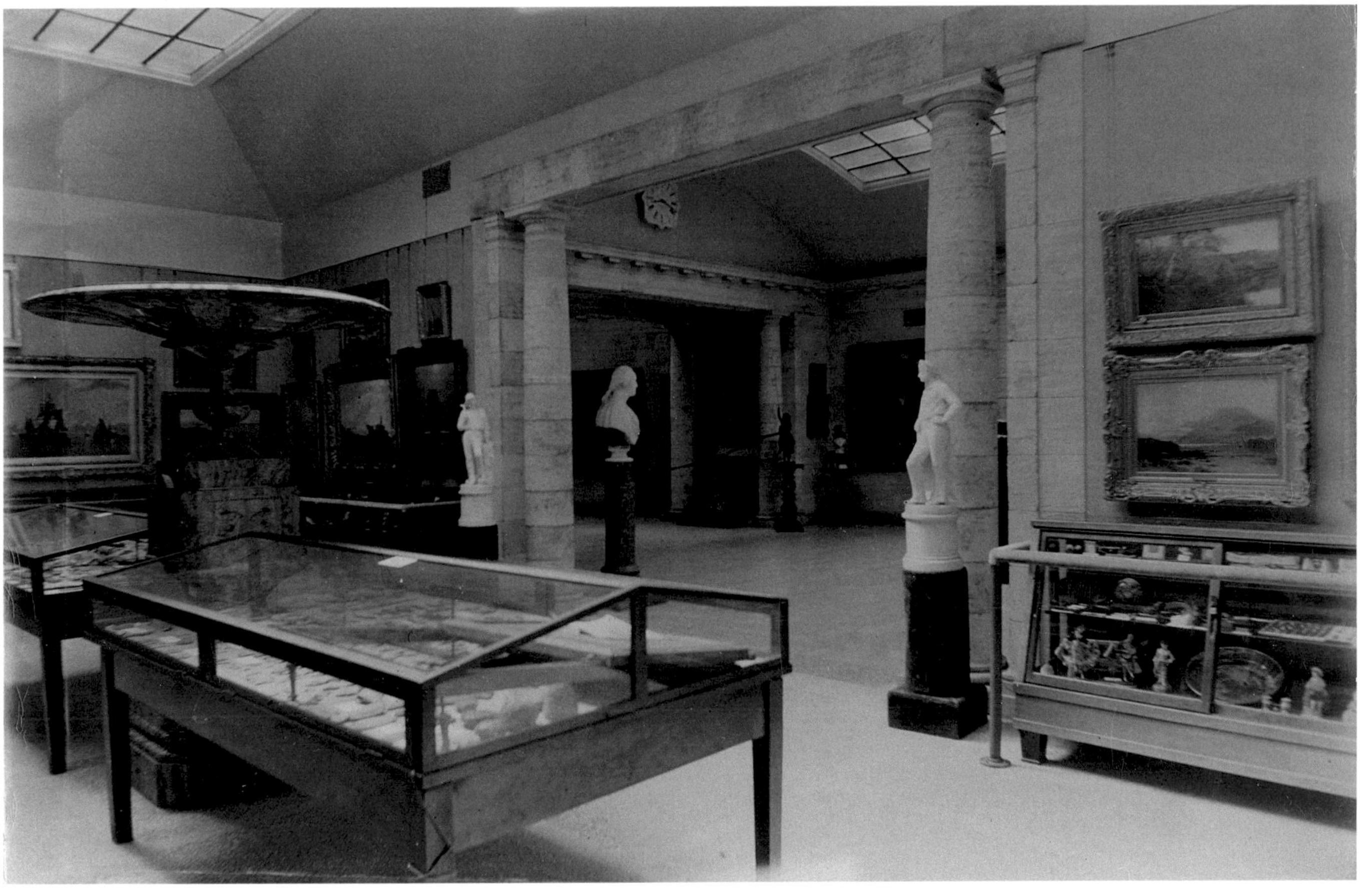

FIG. 2 Ben Conklin (American, 1873–1964), *Installation View of The Heckscher Museum of Art, Showing Two Sculptures by Emma Stebbins*, ca. 1945. Photograph, 6⅜ × 9 in. (16.2 × 22.9 cm).

Collection of the Huntington Historical Society, Huntington, NY, 76.2822

Waters (see pl. 47), and *Satan* (pl. 21), to their literary and visual sources to show how they disrupt normative gender ideas and ideals.

This book also includes three contemporary artists' essays on how Stebbins's work intersects with their own. In the foreword, Tony Kushner reflects on the role of the *Bethesda Fountain* within *Angels in America: A Gay Fantasia on National Themes*, the play he set in New York City during the HIV/AIDS epidemic of the 1980s.[20] Patricia Cronin describes how her own queer feminist artwork builds on the legacies of Stebbins and her peer Harriet Hosmer, who challenged society's expectations for women. Ricky Flores discusses the symbolism of *Angel of the Waters* and the Puerto Rican flag in his 1983 photograph, touching on the importance of faith and identity to his immigrant community.

The plates section represents the full breadth of Stebbins's sculptural production. It includes new photography of previously unlocated works, such as recent museum acquisitions and sculptures in private collections. It also incorporates images of Stebbins's three public monuments—*Horace Mann*, *Christopher Columbus*, and the *Bethesda Fountain*—as they appear in situ today. In addition, the plates section features nineteenth-century photographs, some of which document lost marble sculptures, as well as clay studies and plaster models that no longer exist, and which Stebbins never translated into stone or bronze. Beyond their documentary value for scholars today, photographs like these were critical to the circulation of her work in the nineteenth century. From Rome, Stebbins sent them to friends and patrons in the US. She also carried photographs of her sculptures when she traveled, showing them to journalists and others to promote her art. Several writers based their accounts of her sculptures on these images, rather than on the artworks themselves.

Emma Stebbins: Carving Out History also includes an extensive chronology gleaned from period correspondence and from the voluminous press coverage about Stebbins. It details her life and career with a focus on the creation, exhibition, and reception of her work. Three primary texts follow the chronology. Ellet's entry on Stebbins from *Women Artists in All Ages and Countries* is the only account of her early life in New York City. An excerpt from *Charlotte Cushman: Her Letters and Memories of Her Life* provides a glimpse of their home in Rome in Stebbins's own words. Published here for the first time, Garland's biographical manuscript, "Notes of the Art Life of Emma Stebbins," is a firsthand account of the artist's career. This book concludes with an afterword by David J. Getsy that reminds us that Stebbins had to live and work within the conventions of her time in order to subtly expand them.

ART LIFE: NEW YORK CITY, ROME, FAMILY

There are few records pertaining to the first four decades of Stebbins's life. She was born in 1815 in New York City to white American parents of English descent.[21] Little is known about her mother; her father worked as an accountant, as a "first teller" and "cashier" at banks, and as a broker on Wall Street. As a child, Stebbins lived with them and her seven siblings south of Canal Street. In her teenage years, the family rented a series of homes in the elite enclave of Hudson Square. Her father died in 1834, when she was nineteen years old.[22] Stebbins and her siblings were involved in New York City's economic and cultural development, and over a period of decades they elevated their family to a position of wealth and prominence.[23]

By the mid-1850s, Stebbins had earned a reputation as a professional artist of crayon portraits after studying privately with painter Henry Inman and with sculptor Edward Augustus Brackett. In her 1859 text, however, Ellet ignores the fact that Stebbins offered her work for sale and exhibited it publicly and instead positions her as an upper-class genteel amateur. Ellet, or the Stebbins family members who provided her with information, may have done this to differentiate Stebbins from women who pursued careers out of financial necessity, such as those who attended the New-York School of Design for Women. Established in the early 1850s, the school prepared middle-class women and girls for jobs in fields such as illustration and commercial design. Stebbins was one of the school's founders, whom historian April F. Masten has described as "reformers who linked the poverty of women to the degradation of workers in industrial society."[24] Little more is known about Stebbins's early political beliefs, but her contemporary, physician Elizabeth Blackwell, once described her as "full of noble aspirations for the spread of true art amongst the people."[25]

In May 1856, when she was forty years old, Stebbins traveled to Europe with her mother and her younger sister. Their stay in Rome stretched from the fall of that year to the spring of 1857. During this period, Stebbins decided to remain in Rome to resume her study of sculpture. Her knowledge of literature and the Bible and her previous involvement with contemporary art in America served her well as she began her new career.[26] Dozens of neoclassical sculptors from the US and Europe congregated in Rome, which offered a pleasant winter climate and beautiful countryside, along with ready access to ancient art; marble from Carrara and Seravezza; models, stone carvers, and other skilled workers for hire; and tourists eager to purchase art on their travels. The city also offered female American artists a degree of distance from their families and from the constraining norms of propriety. When Stebbins relocated to

Rome, she became the third female American sculptor working there, joining Hosmer and Louisa Lander, who were both more than ten years her junior.

Soon after arriving in Italy, Stebbins met Cushman, an American actress who was one of the most famous women in the US and Europe, and they decided to make a home together in Rome.[27] As Stebbins would later write, "from that time the current of their two lives ran, with rare exceptions, side by side."[28] Beginning in 1859, their household was a center of the expatriate community, and the two traveled together, were financially interdependent, cared for each other during severe illnesses, and supported each other's careers. Throughout *Emma Stebbins: Carving Out History*, the authors use various terms, including "lesbian," "queer," and "wife," in reference to Stebbins's sexuality and her relationship with Cushman.[29] Cushman herself sometimes used the language of marriage to describe their union.[30] As scholars Lisa Merrill and Sharon Marcus have demonstrated, the female marriage the two fashioned was not unique during their time, and it reflected a level of equality that women were not guaranteed in legally sanctioned heterosexual marriages.[31] Stebbins's life with Cushman in Rome made her career in sculpture possible, while Cushman's patronage of Stebbins and other artists kept her at the forefront of the cultural world during periods of retirement from the stage.

SCULPTING IN ROME AND EXHIBITING IN THE US, 1857–70

After arriving in Rome as a tourist, Stebbins spent her second year there, from fall 1857 through spring 1858, living with Hosmer and modeling *The Lotus Eater* in sculptor Paul Akers's studio (pl. 1). From them, and from Hosmer's mentor John Gibson, she learned the process for making a neoclassical marble sculpture. First, the artist devised a subject and composition in a small clay model, sometimes called a "sketch," or *bozzetto*. Hosmer explained that this was the time to determine "the proportions, and the general arrangement of the drapery, without regard to very careful finish of parts."[32] Approaching this initial step somewhat intuitively, Stebbins found it the most creatively rewarding. She once said, "our work must be something out of our inner selves, which we cannot lay out and determine beforehand."[33] Next, the artist produced a larger "perfectly finished" clay model, or *modello*, on top of a custom armature that assistants built up out of wood, wire, clay, and sometimes iron (which required a blacksmith). At this stage, Hosmer said, the sculptor "laboriously studies every part, corrects his ideal by comparison with living models, copies his drapery from actual drapery arranged . . . and gives . . . the last refinement of beauty," a process that might take several months. Then the artist's work "virtually ended." Workmen cast the clay sculpture in plaster, destroying the clay in the process. Using a pointing tool to transfer measurements from the plaster, "a science so perfect that to err is almost impossible," stone carvers could create marble replicas of the plaster to fill patrons' orders as needed. This final step could take three months or more.[34] Visits to sculptors' studios were part of the Grand Tour, and rather than buy a one-of-a-kind sculpture, some collectors were eager to own a version of an artwork that their friends might recognize from their own travels or from guidebooks and accounts in the press.[35]

In her thirteen-year career in Rome, Stebbins modeled at least thirty sculptures.[36] Of these, at least fourteen were realized in marble, and two were cast in bronze.[37] She primarily produced "ideal" sculptures—those that explored subjects from history, mythology, literature, or the Bible—as well as time-consuming civic commissions for public statuary.[38] For perspective, Stebbins's output was similar to Hosmer's in terms of the number of original compositions modeled.[39] However, Stebbins translated fewer compositions into marble, and she produced fewer multiples of each. Four marble copies of her *Charlotte Cushman* bust were created, making it one of her most popular works (pl. 14).[40] Meanwhile, Hosmer's studio filled at least thirty orders for her most popular work, the lighthearted "fancy piece" *Puck* (1855), and Hiram Powers's studio reproduced his bust of *Proserpine* (1844–49) in marble over 150 times.[41] Scholars have surmised that Stebbins's more limited production indicates that she chose to do her own marble carving.[42] Yet other factors explain her smaller body of work. For example, Stebbins eschewed portrait commissions, she rarely created the playful "fancy pieces" that many patrons preferred, and she almost never sculpted the nude female form, which was most popular of all.[43] Her "retiring, modest disposition" may have impeded her sales, and she held her work to impossibly high standards, with the result that she was "slow in producing."[44] Finally, like other Americans, Stebbins left Rome every summer, but she was often away from her studio for even longer periods.

At the beginning of 1859, Stebbins moved into 38 Via Gregoriana with Cushman and Hosmer and opened her own studio nearby. She worked throughout that spring and fall, and well into the spring of 1860. That May, she and Cushman left Italy for nearly a year and a half. Cushman returned to the US stage, and Stebbins debuted her sculptures in New York City, Boston, and Philadelphia. The four works she exhibited declared the range of her abilities. *The Lotus Eater*, an ideal male nude, displayed her erudition and her mastery of human anatomy. The *Charlotte Cushman* bust was a sensitive portrait that attested to Stebbins's connection to the famed actress and their joint place at the heart of expatriate Rome. In *Industry* and *Commerce*, she broke new artistic ground while working within the confines of a commission.

The Lotus Eater was the first male nude by a female American sculptor.[45] Although this fact was not explicitly remarked at the time, contemporary critics declared the work a success. In New York City, the dreamy figure was "worshiped" by "many a fair dame, and all the critics of the City."[46] Cognizant that women rarely had the opportunity to study from the nude model, one writer declared, "All over it are traces of so severe and [conscientious a] study of the human form, that . . . we should be disinclined to believe it the production of a woman."[47] The full-length and bust versions of *The Lotus Eater* reference an 1832 poem by Alfred, Lord Tennyson, which he based on an episode of Homer's *Odyssey* (see pls. 3–5). In the texts, travelers who consume the narcotic-like lotus plant lose interest in returning home. Milroy has linked the self-exile of these mythic characters to Stebbins's own position as an expatriate.[48] Dabakis has considered the subject and form of Stebbins's work in relation to the ancient Leaning Satyr (see fig. 7 in Igoe's essay in this volume), made famous by Nathaniel Hawthorne's novel *The Marble Faun* (1860), and to other sensuous male nudes by Akers and Hosmer. She proposes that the arcadian setting evoked by Stebbins's sculpture served as a counterpart to nineteenth-century Rome, which upper-class white Americans viewed as exotic, indolent, and premodern.[49] *The Lotus Eater*, like Stebbins's later sculpture *Autumn* (pl. 27), also alludes to imagery of Dionysus/Bacchus, the god of wine, and of Antinous, the same-sex lover of the Roman emperor Hadrian.[50] In her analysis of the sculpture, Gustin has argued that the "complexity and subtlety of Stebbins's selection of sources . . . and her rich, multivalent play between texts and images" constitutes "a quietly complex act of queer classical reception."[51] The queer valences of *The Lotus Eater* are also manifest in a

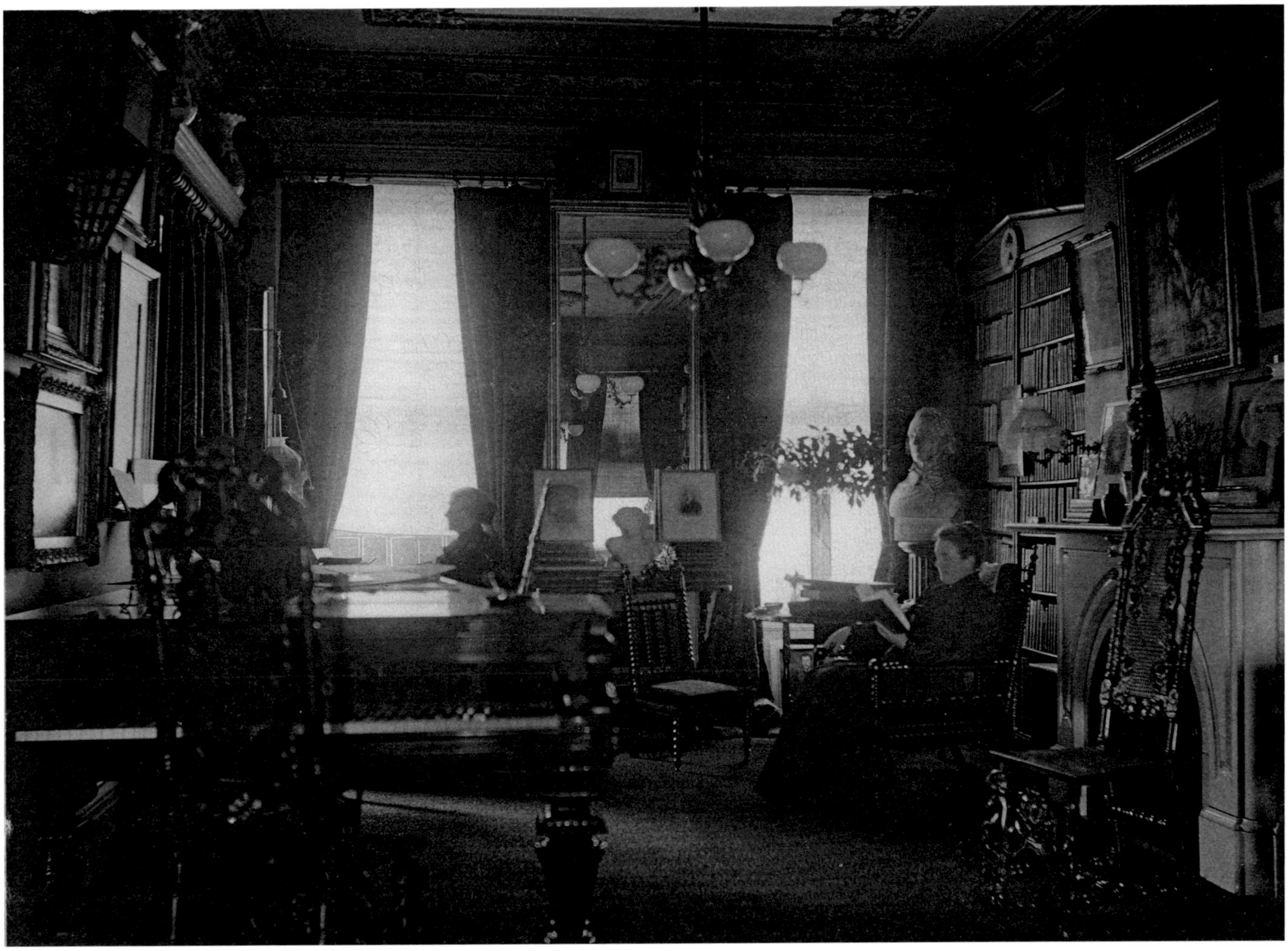

FIG. 3 *Annie Adams Fields and Sarah Orne Jewett, 148 Charles Street, Boston*, ca. 1881–1909. Photographic print, 6 × 7 15/16 in. (15.2 × 20.2 cm).

Boston Athenaeum, MA, Gift of Boylston A. Beale, May 1941, 1941.5 (no.4)

photograph that positions Stebbins's bust as the fulcrum of the Boston home of writers and romantic partners Annie Adams Fields and Sarah Orne Jewett (fig. 3).[52]

Commerce and *Industry* are the earliest known sculptural representations of industrial American laborers.[53] As Igoe discusses in this volume, the sailor and miner that Stebbins created for industrialist Charles August Heckscher elide the human toll and the ecological devastation of nineteenth-century mining and shipping. Stebbins did not challenge the social and economic hierarchies of the day with *Commerce* and *Industry*.[54] She did, however, test the limits of neoclassical sculpture. According to one writer, the subjects that Heckscher asked her to address—"mining and navigation"—offered "little opportunity . . . to exhibit imaginative power."[55] Nonetheless, Stebbins was able to create successful allegories while still depicting the two figures in realistic contemporary clothing, rather than in classical drapery or nude. This decision placed her at the vanguard of art's "innovating process, which declares that men and things may be represented as they really are."[56] Appraising *Industry* as "purely modern and American," one critic saw it as combining "every-day national truth, with the enduring and cosmopolite truth of art."[57] The pair and the positive reception they received may have influenced sculptor John Rogers, who overlapped with Stebbins in Rome.[58] Her works prefigure his painted plaster vignettes of everyday Americans, which became wildly popular with middle-class consumers in the 1860s.

Stebbins returned to Rome in the fall of 1861 with three pending monumental commissions: *Horace Mann* for Boston and the *Bethesda Fountain* for Central Park, which are discussed below, and a statue of Matthew Perry for Central Park, which she ultimately did not complete. In addition, in the spring of 1862, Stebbins began modeling sculptures in response to the US Civil War, which had begun the previous April while she was visiting the States. For example, *Sandalphon* and *Satan* capture the contrast between good and evil, a binary that other artists also explored to reflect the conflict between the North and South.[59] She completed the sculpture of the archangel in marble, but likely never translated *Satan*, the ultimate traitor, into marble or bronze. The subject of *Joseph the Dreamer*, also known as *Agriculture*, similarly connects to the war (pl. 24). In the book of Genesis, Joseph's brothers sell him into slavery in Egypt, where he eventually gains power after interpreting visions that directed the pharaoh to stockpile enough grain to sustain the world's population throughout seven years of famine. Stebbins's sculpture may allude to the North's use of science and mechanization to manage agricultural productivity, and to the fact that cotton from Egypt was supplanting the crop from the Confederate states.[60]

Stebbins's studio was busier than ever in 1863 and 1864. In 1863, she sold four copies of *The Lotus Eater* bust (see pl. 4), the commissioners of Central Park formalized their order for the *Bethesda Fountain*, and the same group was expressing interest in four additional bronze statues of the seasons for the Bethesda Terrace (pl. 28). By 1864, Stebbins had received two major commissions from collector Marshall O. Roberts: an over-life-size marble monument to Christopher Columbus (see pl. 39) and a relief of *Treaty of Hendrick Hudson with the Indians* (pl. 35). Also at this time, Hosmer was fighting the allegation that her sculpture *Zenobia in Chains* (1859) was "really executed by an Italian workman."[61] This debate over authorship hit home, given that Hosmer still lived at 38 Via Gregoriana. According to Cushman, Stebbins viewed it "as much an attack on her [Stebbins] as a woman worker as it was on Hattie [Hosmer] herself."[62] As a result, Stebbins attempted "to struggle along without the material help which all sculptors *must have*" and "to shuffle on to do *all* of her own work."[63] This statement may mean that Stebbins spent more time fashioning the large-scale clay models for her works, since the charge against Hosmer concerned the degree to which she sculpted her clay models.[64] It is hard to reconstruct from the available evidence what Stebbins's process initially entailed and how it might have changed in response to the Hosmer controversy and given shifts in her health, the volume of her commissions, and the size of her works.[65]

In December 1864, Hosmer published "The Process of Sculpture" to "correct the false, but very general impression, that the artist, beginning with the crude block, and guided by his imagination only, hews out his statue with his own hands."[66] Throughout the article, she differentiates between the "intellectual art" of the sculptor and the "mechanical art" of the skilled assistants and laborers who helped to build up the *modello*, make the plaster cast, and carve the stone. The discussions that Stebbins, Hosmer, and others were having about the nature of mental and physical labor may have informed Stebbins's undated sculptures *Machinist's Apprentice* and *Machinist* (pls. 6, 7).[67] However, her pair does not resolve into a simple dichotomy between intellectual creation and manual work. With matching furrowed brows and rolled-up sleeves, an older maker and a younger apprentice jointly produce metal gears for machines in multiple. The younger figure wields a writing implement in his right hand and a tool that might be a drafting compass or a blacksmith's wing divider in his left. Holding a forging hammer, the older figure stands at an anvil, evoking Hephaestus/Vulcan, the classical god who was a blacksmith and craftsman. He wears a frayed leather apron that has molded itself to his body over time, speaking to his years of experience. With his hat and facial hair, he calls to mind Stebbins's portraits of the artists she herself learned from, including Gibson (pl. 2) and Akers (see fig. 7 in the chronology in this volume).[68] The *Machinist* might also relate to Powers, who was described by one of his contemporaries as an "accomplished machinist" because he invented tools and devices to aid in the creation of his artwork.[69] The pair represented in *Machinist* and *Machinist's Apprentice* enacts a kind of labor that parallels that which produced the sculptures: beginning as clay that Stebbins formed with her mind and hands, they took shape in part through the work of the assistants she hired, who used tools and mechanical processes to realize her vision. Much as Stebbins's sailor and miner personify commerce and industry, *Machinist* and *Machinist's Apprentice* can be read as allegories for the relation of human ingenuity and mechanical innovation, or even for the neoclassical style, which positioned itself as the student and heir (or apprentice) to ancient art.

It is difficult to trace the specifics of Stebbins's production from the fall of 1865 through the spring of 1870 because there are far fewer primary sources to consult. She completed the *Bethesda Fountain*, the related sculptures of *Samuel*, for which her young nephew John Neal Tilton served as model (see pls. 42–44), and a posthumous bust of her brother, John Wilson Stebbins, who had died of cholera in 1837 (pl. 40). She may also have created some of the undated works documented in the Emma Stebbins scrapbook (see pls. 2, 12, 13, 29–34). Many sculptures that Stebbins had previously modeled were realized in marble in these years, including *Sandalphon*, two versions of *Christopher Columbus* (pls. 38, 39), and multiple busts of *The Lotus Eater* (see pl. 5) and *Charlotte Cushman*.

Stebbins's life in Rome and her career as a sculptor began to draw to a close in the spring of 1869, when Cushman discovered that she had breast cancer. The couple passed the remainder of the year traveling to seek treatment for her. After spending the spring of 1870 in Rome, they left the city for good that May to return to the US. Stebbins's retirement from Rome coincided with the waning of the neoclassical style and the antebellum worldview that had sustained it.[70] She spent the last years of her life first caring for her dying mother and her ailing wife and then struggling with her own health. Stebbins no longer sculpted, but she continued to exhibit her work sporadically. Central Park unveiled the *Bethesda Fountain* in 1873, and she showed her bust of Cushman at the Women's Pavilion of the Great Centennial Exposition in Philadelphia in 1876. That year, Cushman died in Boston at age fifty-nine; Stebbins died in New York City in 1882 at age sixty-seven.

PUBLIC MONUMENTS: *HORACE MANN*, *CHRISTOPHER COLUMBUS*, AND THE *BETHESDA FOUNTAIN*

To date, Stebbins's artistic legacy has been most tangible in three outdoor sculptures that remain part of the public landscape: *Horace Mann* in Boston, which belongs to the Massachusetts State House Art Collection, and *Christopher Columbus* in Brooklyn and the *Bethesda Fountain* in Manhattan, which belong to the New York City Department of Parks and Recreation. The histories of these three sculptures, which Stebbins created in the 1860s, shed light on who had the power to commission monuments, who had the opportunity to create them, and what merited commemoration at a time when Americans were just beginning to erect public sculptures.[71] Art historians including Harriet F. Senie hold that "it is the evolving ways that people use the works in our shared spaces that determine their meaning."[72] Over the course of more than 150 years, generations of viewers have reinterpreted and reshaped the meanings of

Stebbins's three statues. *Horace Mann* has been largely met with indifference, while *Christopher Columbus* has periodically catalyzed contention over competing narratives of the past. A broad and diverse public has continued to embrace the *Bethesda Fountain*, expanding and renewing its meanings of love, health, and peace.

The first monument that Stebbins completed was the bronze *Horace Mann* for the grounds of the Massachusetts State House in Boston (pl. 17). In the nearly nine-foot-tall sculpture, Stebbins portrays Mann in contemporary dress but enveloped in classical drapery. He stands before a stack of books, holds a tome in one arm, and extends his right hand. In 1859, just a few months after his death, a group of seven men appointed at a public meeting petitioned the legislature for space on the state house grounds to place a statue of Mann.[73] Women were also involved in commissioning the artwork, including Mann's widow, Mary Tyler Peabody Mann, and her sister, Elizabeth Palmer Peabody. While Mann had been a legislator and an abolitionist, his memorial was primarily meant to honor his work to create a universal secular public school system, which he believed was necessary in a democracy.[74] In addition to supporting education for girls, he helped to establish colleges to train women as professional teachers. To pay for *Horace Mann*, those commissioning it launched a subscription campaign to which schoolchildren and teachers throughout Massachusetts contributed. According to Garland, the head of the committee was "much interested that the statue of the Apostle of Female Education should be executed by a woman."[75] Stebbins's status as an exemplar of female achievement thus became part of the intended meaning of the work.[76]

Horace Mann continued to circulate as an emblem of education after its dedication on July 4, 1865. Between 1905 and 1949, at least four full-size copies in plaster and two in bronze were installed at schools and other educational institutions in Florida, Massachusetts, Missouri, Nebraska, Ohio, and Washington, DC.[77] In 1970, the original statue was mobilized when photojournalist Jeff Albertson captured an image of students gathered around it in protest of two events from that year: the National Guard's killing of four students at Kent State University in Ohio and the US invasion of Cambodia during the Vietnam War (fig. 4). However, Boston activists, including those fighting to end segregation in schools, have more often chosen to convene at Augustus Saint-Gaudens's well-known *Robert Gould Shaw and the 54th Regiment Memorial* (1884–97), which stands directly across the street from *Horace Mann*.[78] In the commemorative landscape of America, which is now estimated to include over fifty thousand public monuments, *Horace Mann* remains a rare tribute to an educator.[79] Yet the sculpture no longer seems to occupy a significant place in the nation's consciousness.

Scholars contend that public commemorative sculptures "not only spark debate; they require it."[80] This is especially true of the second monument that Stebbins sculpted: a seven-foot-tall marble *Christopher Columbus* for Marshall O. Roberts, a steamship magnate and art collector (pl. 39).[81] Completed in 1867, it shows Columbus pointing to a cross on his tunic and gripping the tiller of a ship. The original pedestal, now lost, included the date of America's "discovery" and a rendering of Columbus's signature. Roberts initially exhibited the artwork at the National Academy of Design, and in 1869 he donated *Christopher Columbus* to Central Park. It became New York City's first statue of the fifteenth-century Genoese navigator, colonizer, and enslaver. The parks department has since moved *Christopher Columbus* in and out of storage and displayed it in at least five locations, reflecting changing attitudes towards it.

It is difficult to ascertain Stebbins's personal view of Columbus as a historical figure, although Cometto has recently shown that James Russell Lowell's poem

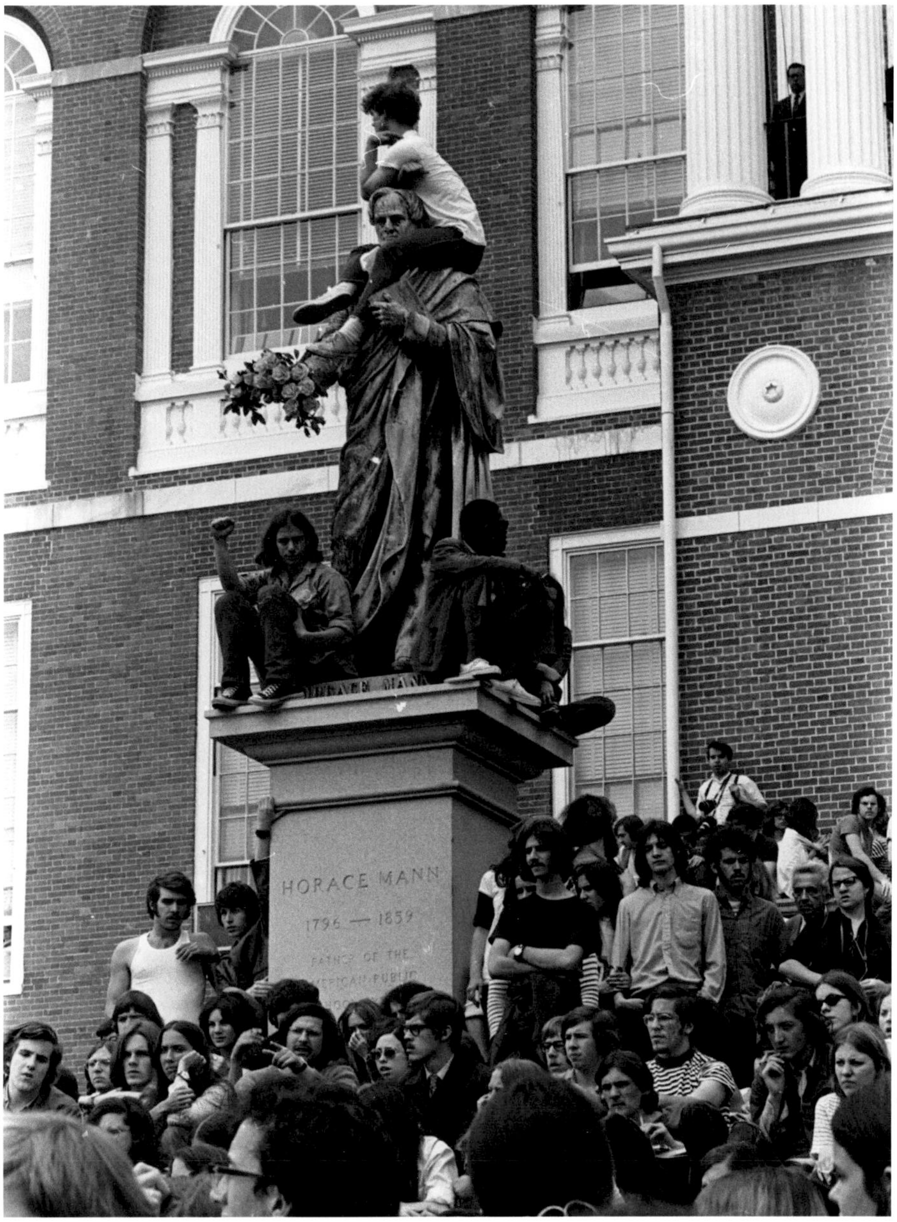

FIG. 4 Jeff Albertson (American, 1948–2007), *Demonstration at State House against the Killings at Kent State: Protesters on Statue of Horace Mann*, May 5, 1970. Scan from a 35 mm negative.

Jeff Albertson Photograph Collection, Robert S. Cox Special Collections and University Archives Research Center, University of Massachusetts Amherst Libraries

"Columbus" (1847) inspired her portrayal of him.[82] As Roberts described at the time of his gift, perhaps paraphrasing Stebbins's intentions, her sculpture positions Columbus at sea, "standing upon the deck of his ship, alone and at midnight, just before the land of the Western Continent burst upon his view. . . . the intrepid discoverer . . . looks eagerly, anxiously forward, piercing the darkness with his eye of faith."[83]

In the mid-nineteenth century, Americans in positions of power celebrated Columbus as a founding father who brought Christianity to the "New World." This mythmaking was especially useful at a time when the country was expanding westward by violently dispossessing Indigenous nations of their land. As art historian Vivien Green Fryd has explored, Columbus established a precedent for "using religion to justify conquest," and the US government commissioned multiple images of him for the Capitol building in Washington, DC.[84] In New York City, Stebbins's *Christopher Columbus* also became a symbol of commerce. Writing on behalf of the Central Park commissioners to accept Roberts's gift, the comptroller deemed it fitting that an "American merchant and promoter of maritime enterprise, has called upon the genius of the American sculptress" to complete the work.[85] The commissioners' appreciation of *Christopher Columbus* was fourfold: they saw it as the product of a "distinguished artist," a sign of Roberts's "munificent liberality," a marker of New York City's status as the "metropolis of the continent," and a "continual injunction to keep in memory the boundless benefaction that has accrued to humanity through the struggles and the trials of this great captain."[86]

Yet the city did not exhibit *Christopher Columbus* outdoors in Central Park as Roberts had intended. They failed to provide the marble with a "suitable glass house" to protect it from the elements, which was a condition of the gift.[87] Immediately following Roberts's donation, *Christopher Columbus* remained on view at the National Academy of Design. By 1871, the city had decided to present it, alongside a statue of George Washington, as part of the museum within the Arsenal building at 64th Street and 5th Avenue in Central Park.[88]

Twenty years later, in 1893, the parks department voted to relocate Stebbins's *Christopher Columbus* to McGown's Pass Tavern in Central Park at 102nd Street.[89] The business owner who leased the building from the city intimated that he accepted the statute "when no other disposal could be made of it."[90] According to the *New York Times*, *Christopher Columbus* "stood in the main restaurant . . . scarcely noticed by the crowds who assemble there. A dusty American flag has been stuck between the right arm and the body."[91] The timing of this move followed the four hundredth anniversary of Columbus's landing and the creation of another monument to Columbus for the southwest entrance of Central Park. Through the process of fundraising, commissioning, and inaugurating this new statue, leading Italian Americans intended to showcase their growing political power and to foster a sense of pan-ethnic Italian identity and community in the face of anti-immigrant discrimination.[92] Repurposing Stebbins's existing *Christopher Columbus*, which was created and donated to the public by deceased Americans of English descent, would not have served this purpose. Instead, the group ordered an iconographically similar sculpture, albeit one twice as large on an exponentially taller base, from Italian-born sculptor Gaetano Russo.

In 1912, the Knights of Columbus, a fraternal organization of Catholic men, "made a timely rediscovery" of Stebbins's "discoverer."[93] After realizing that *Christopher Columbus* was housed at the tavern, they wanted the city to transfer it to the new Columbus Park, formerly known as Mulberry Bend, in the working-class immigrant neighborhood of Five Points. This did not immediately come to pass, and after the tavern was razed in 1917, the parks department put *Christopher Columbus* in storage. It was found anew in 1934, when urban planner Robert Moses erected the sculpture in Columbus Park.[94] Architect Aymar Embury II designed a fourteen-foot-tall base and fluted shaft to replace the original pedestal. Fifteen thousand people, most of "Italian origin," attended the unveiling of Stebbins's monument on Columbus Day 1934 (see fig. 5).[95] With dictator Benito Mussolini in power in Italy and World War II on the horizon, New York City Mayor Fiorello La Guardia, himself of Italian and Jewish descent, used his remarks inaugurating the sculpture to "appeal to Europe to take a lesson from America in maintaining peace among diverse racial and religious elements."[96] Meanwhile, the "Columbus Day Anti-Fascist Committee," which included Italian American workers, demonstrated at Columbus Circle, declaring that the day's ceremonies were being used to popularize Fascism.[97] Thirty-seven years later, in 1971, the president of the Italian Historical Society of America and city officials felt that *Christopher Columbus* was being "overlooked and vandalized" in its Manhattan location.[98] They transferred the artwork to its present site in Brooklyn, which they renamed Columbus Park, in front of the New York State Supreme Court building.

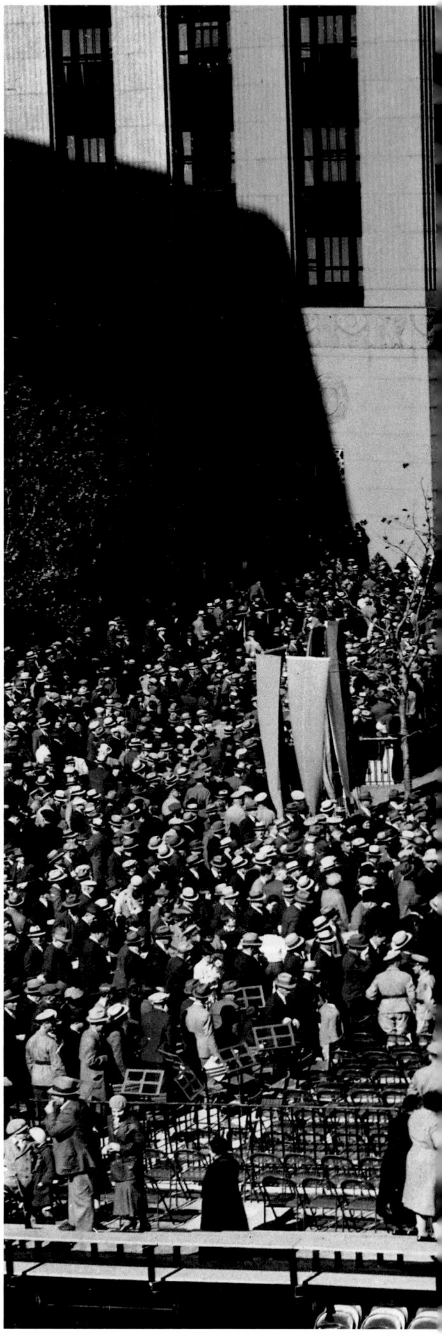

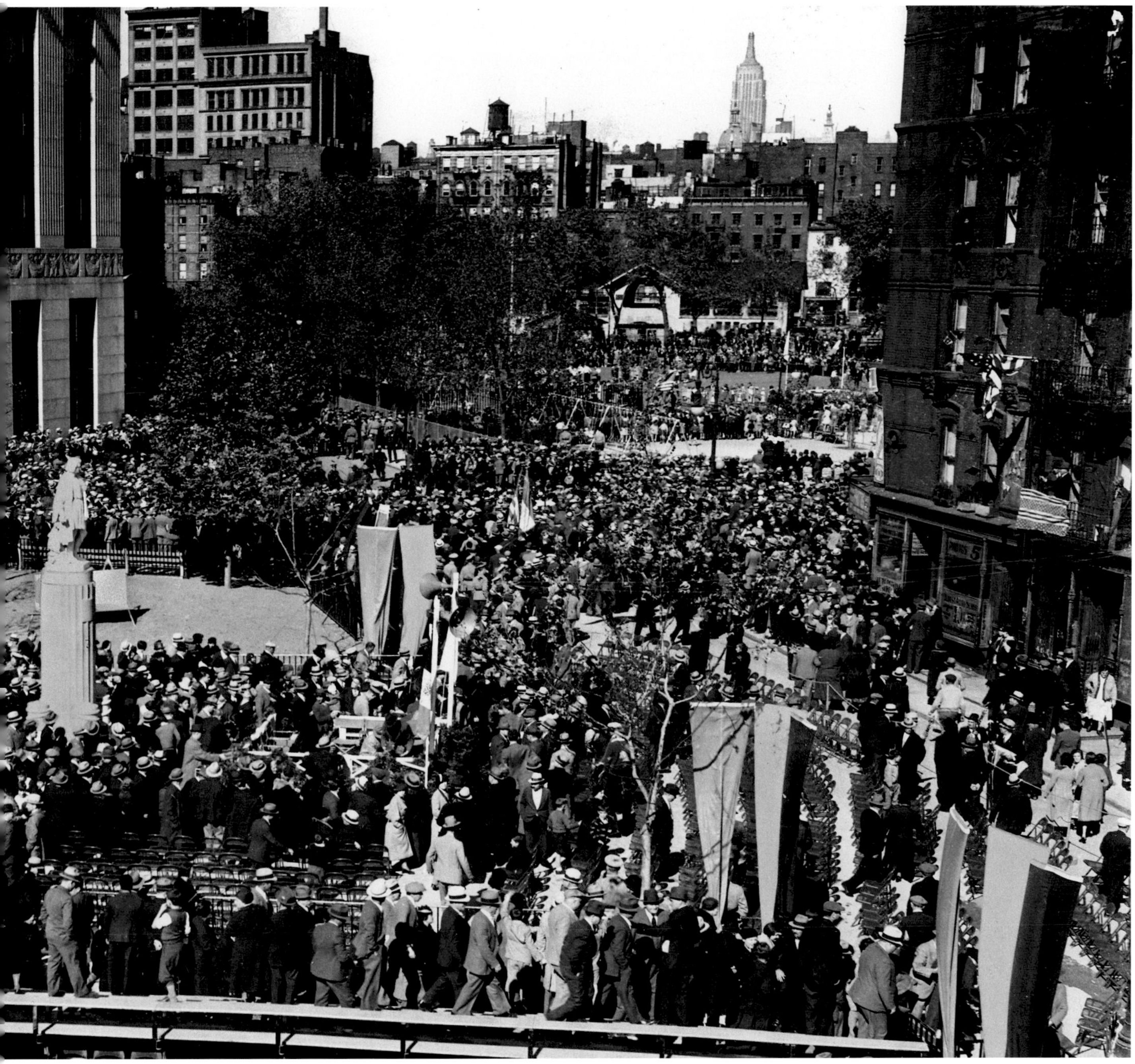

FIG. 5 Times Wide World Photo, *A General View of the Ceremony in Which Mayor La Guardia and Park Commissioner Moses Reopened Columbus Park*, October 12, 1934. From *New York Times*, October 13, 1934, 3. Image scanned from a negative.

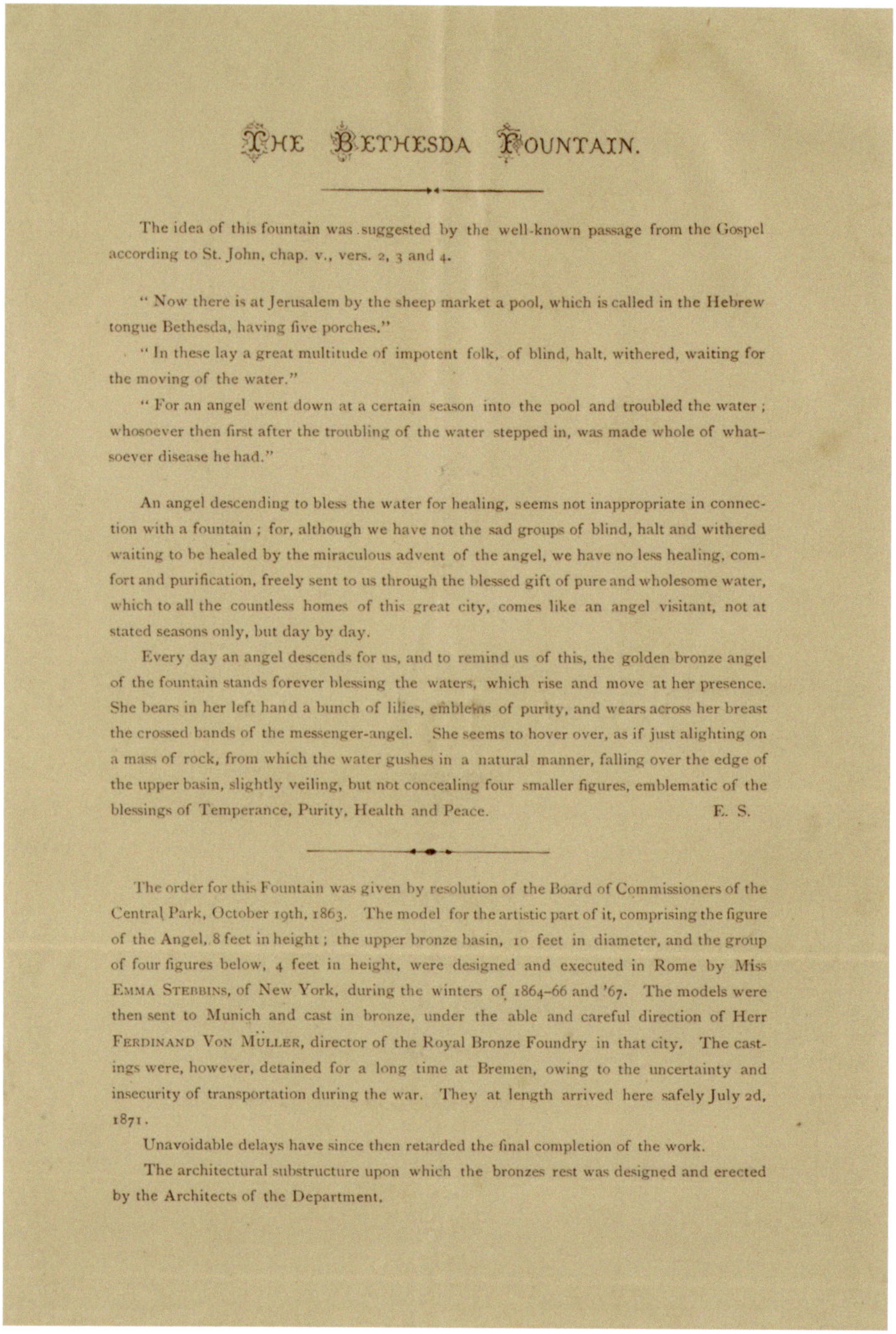

THE BETHESDA FOUNTAIN.

The idea of this fountain was suggested by the well-known passage from the Gospel according to St. John, chap. v., vers. 2, 3 and 4.

"Now there is at Jerusalem by the sheep market a pool, which is called in the Hebrew tongue Bethesda, having five porches."

"In these lay a great multitude of impotent folk, of blind, halt, withered, waiting for the moving of the water."

"For an angel went down at a certain season into the pool and troubled the water; whosoever then first after the troubling of the water stepped in, was made whole of whatsoever disease he had."

An angel descending to bless the water for healing, seems not inappropriate in connection with a fountain; for, although we have not the sad groups of blind, halt and withered waiting to be healed by the miraculous advent of the angel, we have no less healing, comfort and purification, freely sent to us through the blessed gift of pure and wholesome water, which to all the countless homes of this great city, comes like an angel visitant, not at stated seasons only, but day by day.

Every day an angel descends for us, and to remind us of this, the golden bronze angel of the fountain stands forever blessing the waters, which rise and move at her presence. She bears in her left hand a bunch of lilies, emblems of purity, and wears across her breast the crossed bands of the messenger-angel. She seems to hover over, as if just alighting on a mass of rock, from which the water gushes in a natural manner, falling over the edge of the upper basin, slightly veiling, but not concealing four smaller figures, emblematic of the blessings of Temperance, Purity, Health and Peace. E. S.

The order for this Fountain was given by resolution of the Board of Commissioners of the Central Park, October 19th, 1863. The model for the artistic part of it, comprising the figure of the Angel, 8 feet in height; the upper bronze basin, 10 feet in diameter, and the group of four figures below, 4 feet in height, were designed and executed in Rome by Miss EMMA STEBBINS, of New York, during the winters of 1864–66 and '67. The models were then sent to Munich and cast in bronze, under the able and careful direction of Herr FERDINAND VON MÜLLER, director of the Royal Bronze Foundry in that city. The castings were, however, detained for a long time at Bremen, owing to the uncertainty and insecurity of transportation during the war. They at length arrived here safely July 2d, 1871.

Unavoidable delays have since then retarded the final completion of the work.

The architectural substructure upon which the bronzes rest was designed and erected by the Architects of the Department.

FIG. 6 Program for the unveiling of the *Bethesda Fountain* in 1873. From the Emma Stebbins scrapbook, 1858–82. Printed sheet, 8⅛ × 5⅛ in. (20.6 × 13 cm).

Archives of American Art, Smithsonian Institution, Washington, DC

In 2017, following national discord about Confederate monuments, many began to critique statues of Columbus as symbols of genocide and slavery. Challenges to Columbus monuments accelerated in June 2020, in the wake of the systemic racism exposed by the murder of George Floyd by police officers in Minneapolis and the growth of the Black Lives Matter social justice movement.[99] In this context, Brooklyn leaders and residents debated whether to remove Stebbins's *Christopher Columbus*.[100] As of January 2025, the monument remains in place, although plans are underway to redesign and possibly rename the park.[101]

The third monument that Stebbins completed was the *Bethesda Fountain*, which rests at the heart of Central Park (pl. 47). More than twenty feet tall, it consists of the bronze *Angel of the Waters*, four bronze cherubs entitled *Temperance, Purity, Health and Peace*, and an octagonal stone basin supported by columns within a circular pool that is ninety-six feet in diameter. Stebbins began designing the artwork in 1861, formally received the order for it from the commissioners of Central Park in 1863, and sculpted it from 1864 to 1867. As she outlined in the program for its unveiling on May 31, 1873, Stebbins took inspiration from the Gospel of John, which describes an angel activating the water of a healing pool in Jerusalem (fig. 6). Sited in relation to the reservoirs of the Croton Aqueduct, the fountain celebrates the public infrastructure that brought clean water to the city following the cholera outbreak of the 1830s. The essays in this book consider the meanings of the *Bethesda Fountain* and its early reception in the context of Stebbins's personal experiences and nineteenth-century cultural ideas about ecology, health, and gender.

At the time of its creation and since, many have suggested that Stebbins received the fountain commission due to "flagrant nepotism," because her brother Henry G. Stebbins was a member of the Central Park Board of Commissioners.[102] However, Stebbins was already influential in her own right when she received the order. Her acclaim as an internationally renowned sculptor may have bolstered her brother's credibility in matters of culture. As she once described, Henry was "one of the 'City Fathers,'" but was not "profound nor esthetical."[103] Furthermore, large-scale figurative bronze fountains were unprecedented in the American landscape, meaning there was no one more qualified than Stebbins to complete the work.[104] The siblings' multiple transatlantic trips to visit each other likely proved beneficial for the project, assuring both parties that the commission would go forward despite ten years of challenges and delays caused by the Civil War and the Franco-Prussian War.

The *Bethesda Fountain* has continued to accrue meaning in relation to its original themes and as a symbol of New York City. Indeed, the volume and variety of visual representations of the sculpture, spanning the 1860s to the present, attest to its enduring power. At the turn of the century, the fountain appeared in stereographs and tourist postcards (see fig. 7), cementing its status as an icon of Central Park and the city itself. Paintings by such eminent artists as William Merritt Chase (see fig. 8) underscore the fountain's connection to the restorative powers of nature.[105] By the mid-1960s, the *Bethesda Fountain* was in disrepair, yet its worn appearance contributed to its appeal for some. It was "the center of gravity for the counterculture in the park," according to historian Vincent J. Cannato.[106] Street photographer Garry Winogrand photographed people frolicking in the pool (fig. 9), and artist Martha Edelheit reimagined the sculpture as an image that merges, almost like a tattoo,

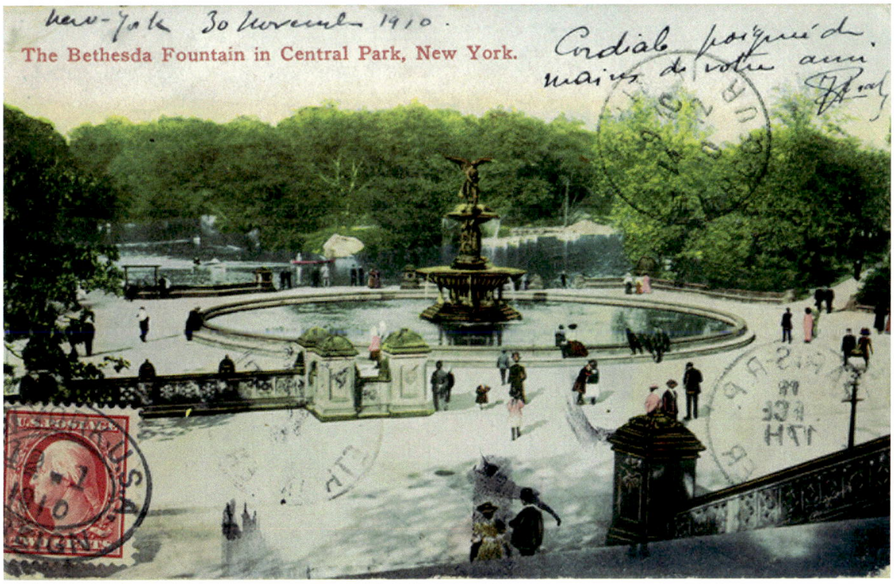

FIG. 7 Success Postal Card Co., *The Bethesda Fountain in Central Park, New York*, postmarked 1910. Photomechanical print, 3½ × 5½ in. (8.9 × 14 cm).

Stebbins research files, The Heckscher Museum of Art, Huntington, NY

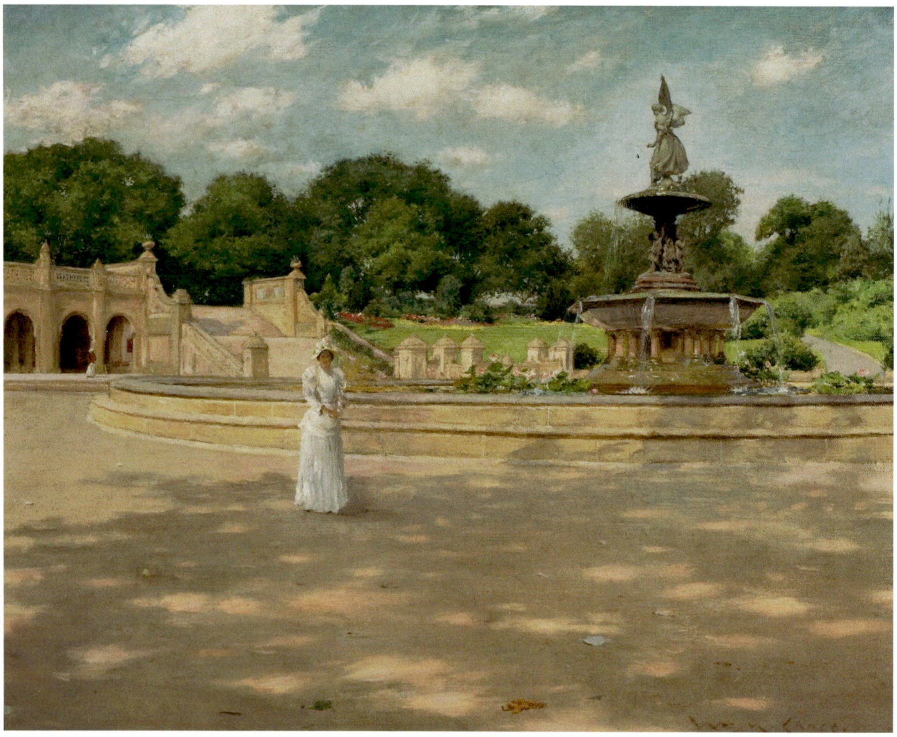

FIG. 8 William Merritt Chase (American, 1849–1916), *An Early Stroll in the Park*, 1890. Oil on canvas, 20 3/8 × 24 1/2 in. (51.8 × 62.2 cm).

Montgomery Museum of Fine Arts, Montgomery, AL, The Blount Collection, 1989.2.4

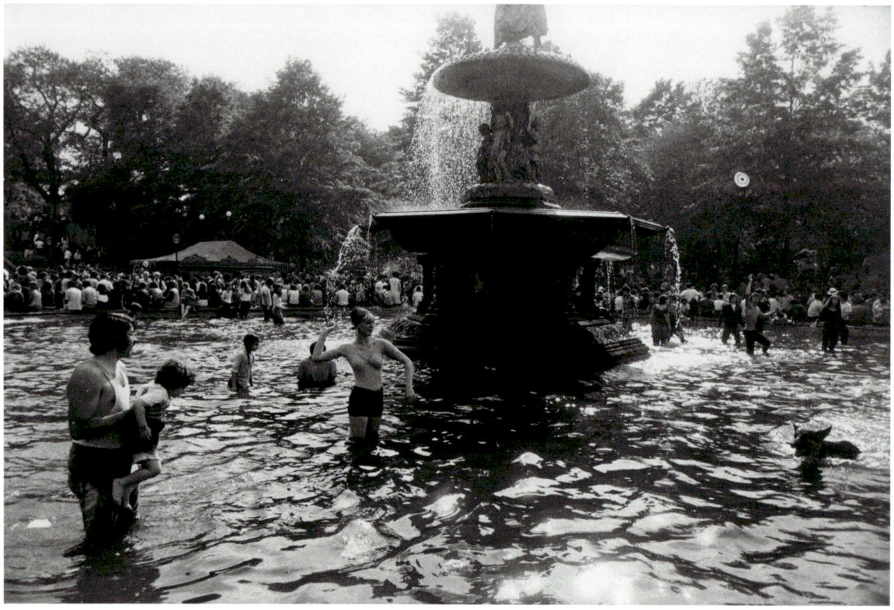

FIG. 9 Garry Winogrand (American, 1928–1984), *Untitled*, ca. 1970. Gelatin silver print, image: 8 7/8 × 13 1/4 in. (22.5 × 33.7 cm); sheet: 11 × 14 in. (27.9 × 35.6 cm).

Courtesy of Fraenkel Gallery, San Francisco, CA

with a nude figure lounging at the Bethesda Terrace in summertime (fig. 10). Riffing on her more realistic representation of the oxidized bronze in the upper-right corner, the monument in Edelheit's "tattoo" renders the angel nearly nude, with multicolored wings, supported by cherubs with different skin colors.[107] As Flores discusses in this volume, the *Bethesda Fountain* was also a place for the Puerto Rican immigrant community to claim visibility and belonging in the public sphere.[108] Beginning in the 1990s, Kushner's *Angels in America* reanimated the *Angel of the Waters* as a symbol of hope and commemoration. The fountain is a popular wedding venue, and its themes of clean water and health have also made it a site of environmental activism.[109] In 2020, during the COVID-19 pandemic, photographs of an empty Bethesda Terrace indexed quarantine before people gravitated to the outdoor site as a safe place to gather.[110]

FIG. 10 Martha Edelheit (American, b. 1931), *Bethesda Fountain*, 1973. Acrylic on canvas, 24 × 18 in. (61 × 45.7 cm).
Courtesy of Eric Firestone Gallery, New York, NY

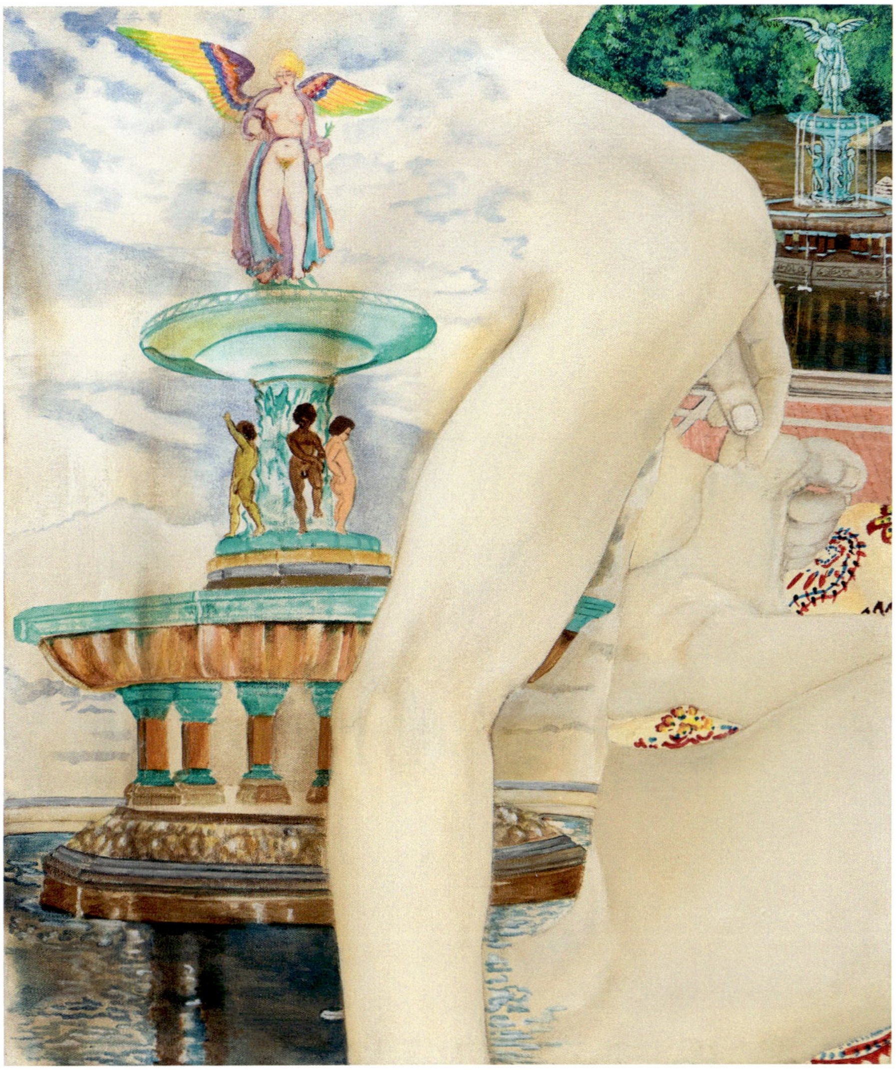

• • •

Stebbins carved out a career on two continents, shaping mid-nineteenth-century culture in ways that reverberate in the present day. The current of her life coursed through love, work, war, illness, fame, and obscurity. Initially recognized as a portraitist in New York City, Stebbins moved to Italy, became one of America's first female sculptors, and established a home with Cushman in Rome. She defied those who questioned her abilities as a "woman worker," and she eased the way for others through her early involvement with the New-York School of Design for Women. With her wife, she also formed a chosen family of artists and writers who sustained and challenged one another. From the queer history of Antinous to the labor of contemporary coal miners and sailors, Stebbins imbued her neoclassical marble sculptures with new content and forms. Now more than 150 years old, her two bronze monuments are testaments to women's contributions to civic life. With the *Bethesda Fountain*, Stebbins achieved her aspirations for spreading art "amongst the people," connecting a vast public, across generations, to an expansive message of love, peace, and healing.

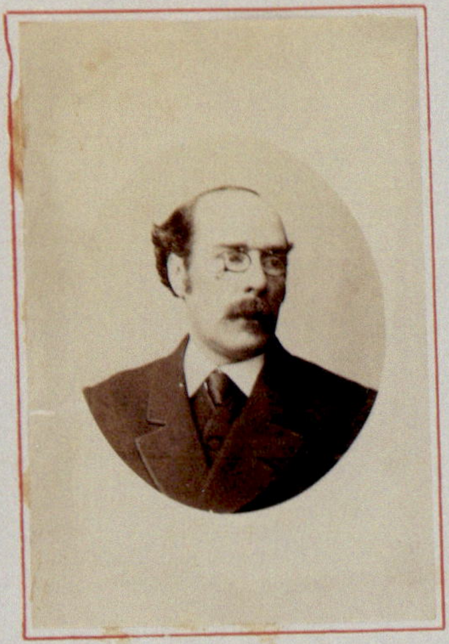

H. G. Wild

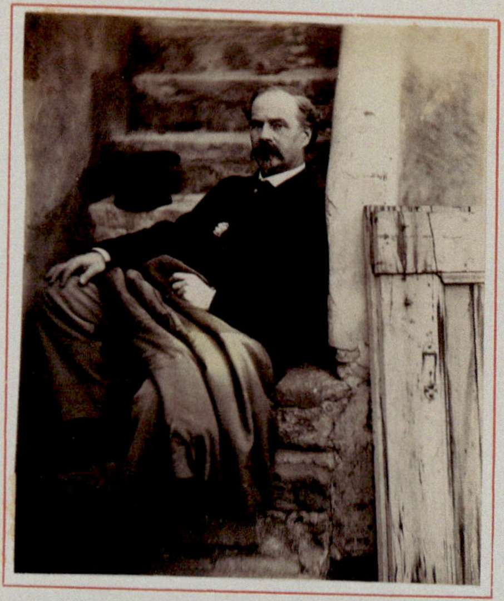

Story

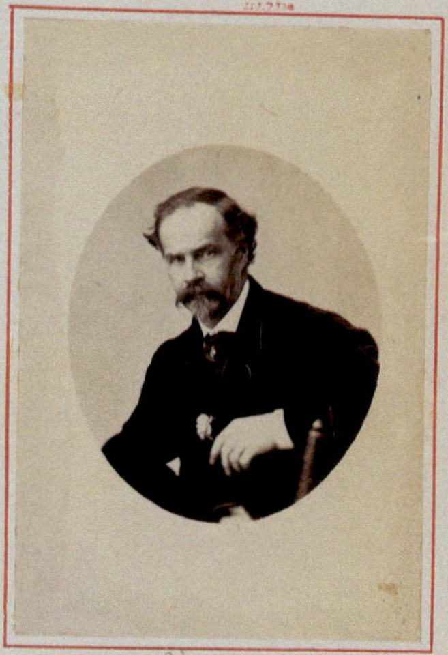

Story

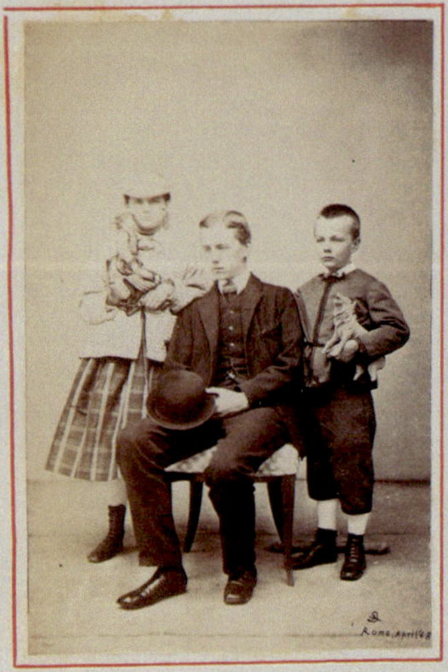

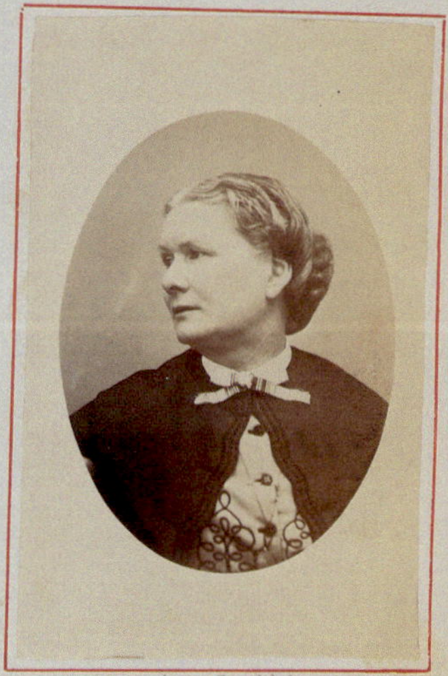

Miss Stebbins

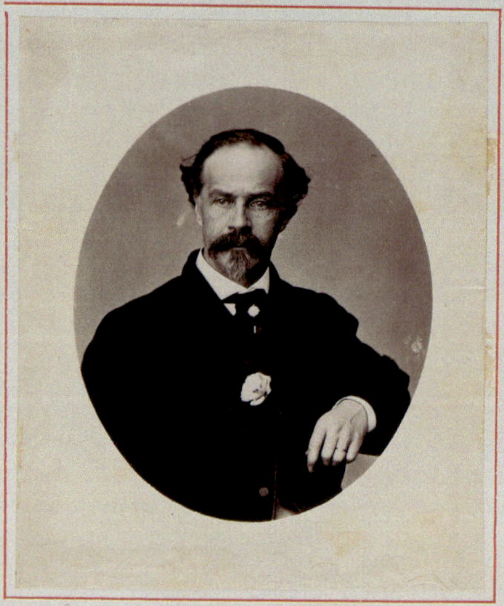

Story

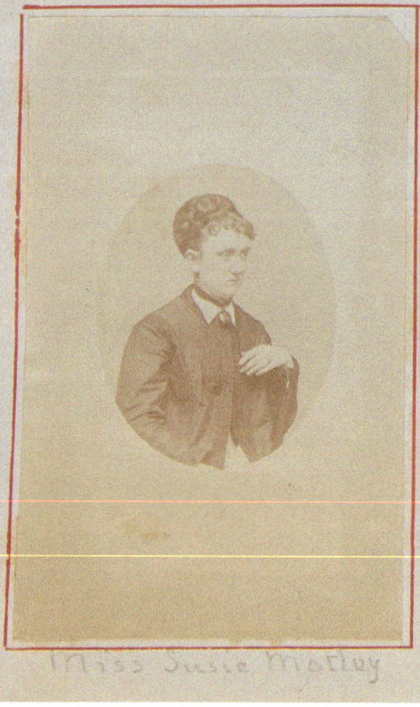

Miss Susie Motley

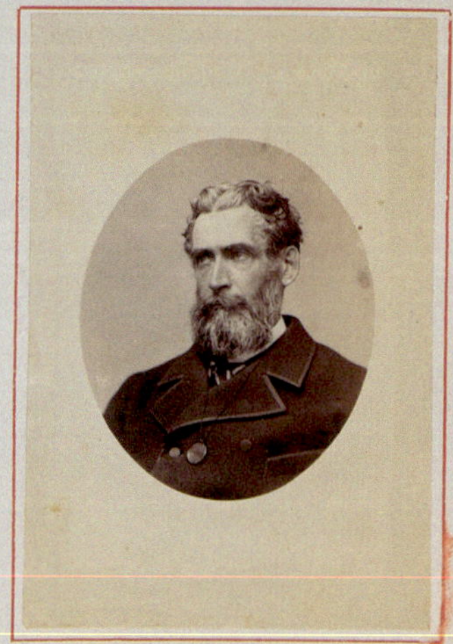

Motley

KATRIN HORN

AT HOME ABROAD

Emma Stebbins's Social and Intellectual Circles[1]

As forgotten as she might be today, even a partial list of evidence for Emma Stebbins's social and intellectual ties would suggest that she was immensely well connected among the anglophone cultural elite of the 1850s to the 1870s. When she settled in Rome in 1857 to establish herself as a sculptor, Paul Akers invited her to work in his studio. Stebbins soon shared a home with Charlotte Cushman—the most famous actress in the US at that time—and (for the first five years) Harriet Hosmer. Annie Adams Fields notes in her diary that Nathaniel Hawthorne praised Stebbins's sculptures *Industry* (pl. 10) and *Commerce* (pl. 11) when they all met in Geneva in 1859.[2] Harriet Beecher Stowe, author of the best-selling *Uncle Tom's Cabin* (1852), describes Stebbins in an article she wrote for the *Independent* (New York City) in 1860 as one of the "agreeable neighbors" who made living on Via Gregoriana so pleasant.[3] British poet Robert Browning refers to Stebbins as one of his "old friends" in an 1864 letter to Isabella Blagden.[4] Samuel Ward published "The Maiden's Children" in 1865, an eighteen-stanza poem with the subtitle "Suggested by Miss Stebbins' Statue of the Lotus Eater" (pl. 1).[5] Arthur Dexter took a picture of her with a range of other notable Americans for his 1866 album (fig. 1). During one of her trips to the US, Stebbins met famous astronomer Maria Mitchell and, after her retirement from Rome, evidently became a member of the first US professional women's association, the Sorosis Club, which was launched in 1868 by author Jane Cunningham Croly.[6]

These relationships shaped her life and work, especially during her active years as one of the first generation of women who went abroad to pursue sculpture professionally. This essay will trace how Stebbins built and maintained networks in Italy and the US by reading, writing, travelling, and hosting. In doing so, it will balance the understanding of her as a representative of the female expatriate artists who went to Rome "as 'travellers and pilgrims' to the famous city" by drawing out her individual approach to navigating a transnational life and career.[7]

FIG. 1 Arthur Dexter (American, 1830–1897), Photographs of Emma Stebbins (right column, center) and others. From Arthur Dexter, Roma 1866, compiled ca. 1863–69. Album; albumen prints on paper, sheet: 14 × 10 5/8 in. (35.6 × 27 cm); photograph of Stebbins: 3 9/16 × 2 1/4 in. (9.1 × 5.7 cm).

Boston Athenaeum, MA, Gift of Peter S. and Jane Dexter Coleman, July 2012, 2012.12 (no. 1)

Travel was an integral aspect of Stebbins's life. She crossed the Atlantic at least ten times, lived in New York City, Rome, Newport, Rhode Island, and Lenox, Massachusetts, and visited friends, colleagues, and physicians in England, Switzerland, Germany, Scotland, and France (see fig. 2).[8] For Stebbins and her peers, planning and taking trips together, visiting one another, serving as local guides to travelers, and delivering letters and packages to mutual friends were central modes of creating connections.[9] The days spent on board transatlantic ocean liners also allowed Stebbins to socialize with people who could help her secure public commissions, such as her most famous one, the *Bethesda Fountain* (pl. 47).[10] Meanwhile, the tradition of the Grand Tour ensured a steady stream of American tourists who were convinced that to obtain a "refined way of life one naturally had to travel to Europe."[11] Their enthusiasm for Rome and its artistic heritage was bolstered by the mass availability of travel handbooks, such as *A Handbook of Rome and Its Environs*, and the myriad newspaper columns and magazine articles that offered "gossip" from Rome.[12] These sources reported about a diverse group of expatriate Americans—artists, writers, activists, politicians—who had begun to follow the "lure of Italy" to pursue their "dream of Arcadia" in the 1820s.[13]

When Stebbins first sailed for Europe in May 1856, she was still known as an artist of "crayon portraits."[14] Shortly after arriving in Rome, however, Stebbins reinvented herself in life and art. At the age of forty-one, she was now embarking on a career as a sculptor, a field that broke with the ideals of femininity in multiple ways: it demanded hard physical labor, the management of workmen, the negotiation of prices (for marble or for bronze casting, shipping, pedestals, and payment), the public presentation of skills to studio visitors, and (at least for Stebbins) the use of nude male models.[15] The latter aspect in particular was nearly unthinkable at the time in the US, where few art academies admitted female students—and fewer still were willing to expose them to nudity. Hosmer, for example, studied anatomy to make up for a lack of access to male models in the US. In contrast, Rome, as scholar Melissa Dabakis shows, "offered women sculptors vital opportunities both to imagine and to re-create themselves as professional artists, using travel and expatriation as means to

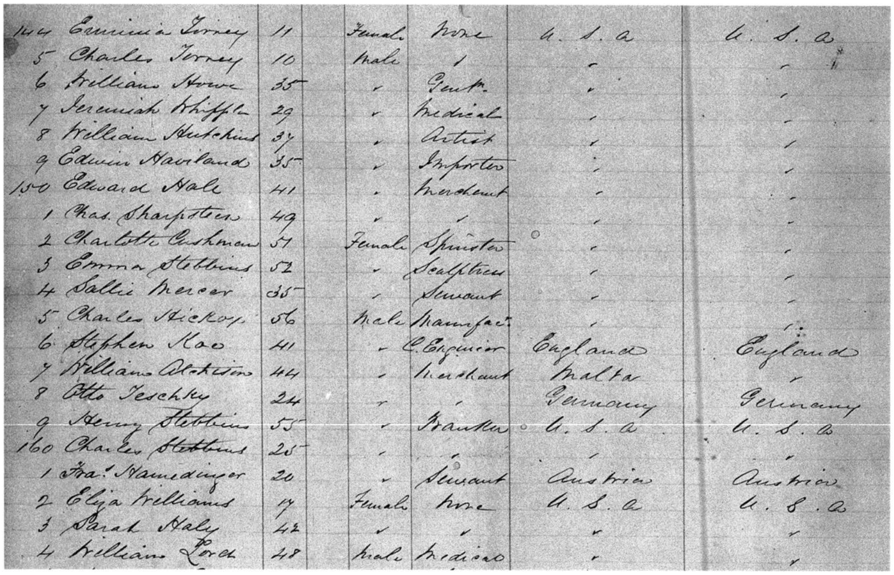

144	Emmia Torney	11		Female	None	U. S. A	U. S. A
5	Charles Torney	10		Male	″	″	″
6	William Howe	35		″	Gent.	″	″
7	Jeremiah Whipple	29		″	Medical	″	″
8	William Hutchins	37		″	Artist	″	″
9	Edwin Haviland	35		″	Importer	″	″
150	Edward Hale	41		″	Merchant	″	″
1	Chas. Sharpsteen	49		″	″	″	″
2	Charlotte Cushman	51		Female	Spinster	″	″
3	Emma Stebbins	52		″	Sculptress	″	″
4	Sallie Mercer	35		″	Servant	″	″
5	Charles Hickox	56		Male	Manufact.	″	″
6	Stephen Mao	41		″	C. Engineer	England	England
7	William Atkinson	44		″	Merchant	Malta	″
8	Otto Jeschky	24		″	″	Germany	Germany
9	Henry Stebbins	55		″	Banker	U. S. A	U. S. A
160	Charles Stebbins	25		″	″	″	″
1	Fra.s Hamedinger	20		″	Servant	Austria	Austria
2	Eliza Williams	17		Female	None	U. S. A	U. S. A
3	Sarah Haly	42		″	″	″	″
4	William Lord	48		Male	Medical	″	″

FIG. 2 Passenger list of the steamship *Scotia*, June 30, 1868, 4 (detail).

National Archives and Records Administration, College Park, MD

FIG. 3 Likely Silsbee, Case & Co. Photograph Artists (Boston, MA), *Charlotte Cushman and Emma Stebbins*, ca. 1861. Cabinet card photograph, 6½ × 4¼ in. (16.5 × 10.8 cm).

Houghton Library, TCS 2 Box 69, Harvard University, Cambridge, MA

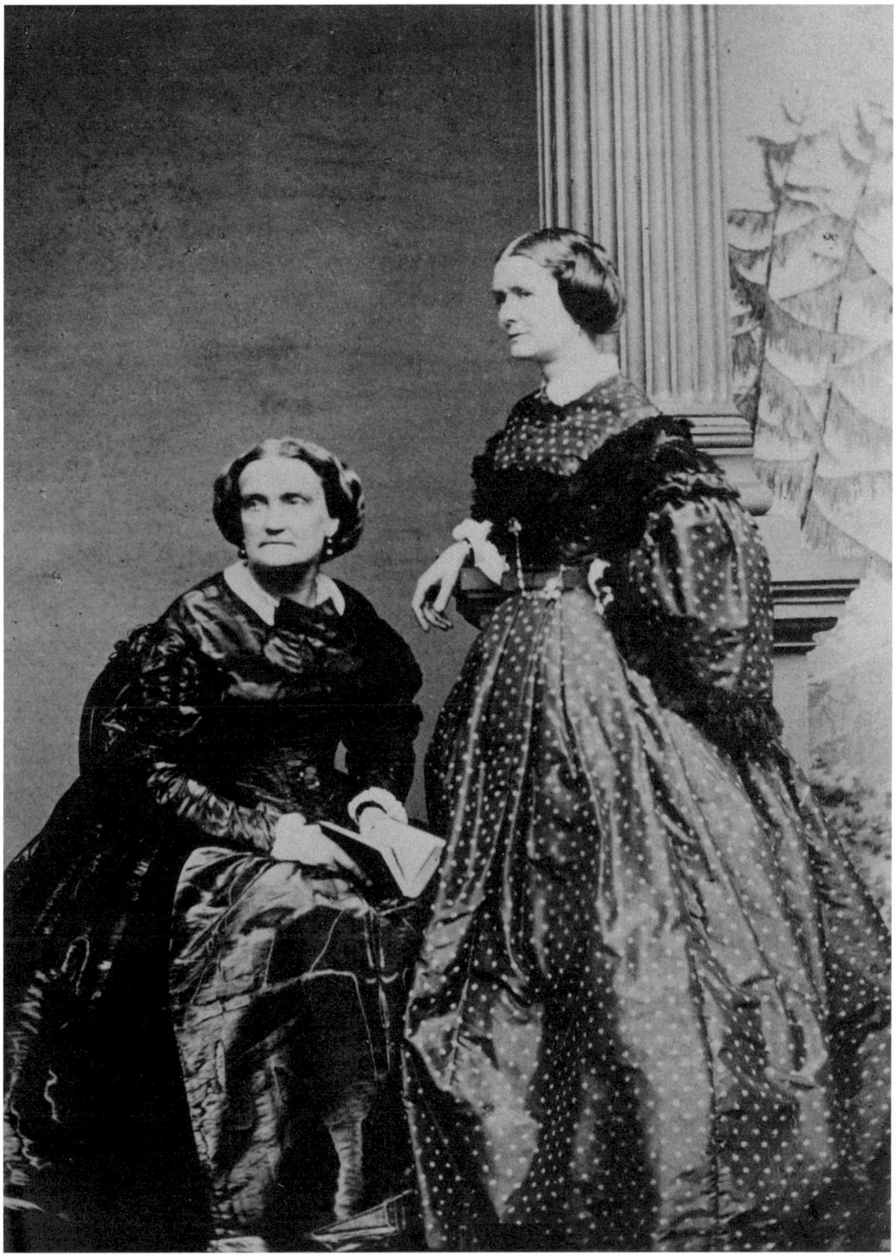

strengthen a sense of themselves as emboldened actors on an international stage."[16] Or, in the words of Frances Power Cobbe, who (like many of Stebbins's friends) combined a passion for activism with a career in writing, "American women, in particular, seem[ed] to find [Italy] a congenial sphere for the development of the more marked individuality which characterizes them."[17]

Stebbins's break with societal expectations went beyond her professional ambitions. In 1857, she "first made Miss Cushman's acquaintance" and "from that time the current of their two lives ran, with rare exceptions, side by side" (see fig. 3).[18] This marriage was another expression of the freedom afforded by the physical removal from the US, even as it demanded "a series of negotiations."[19] Cushman's letters point to the myriad compromises necessary to support two equally valued careers with often opposing demands on the couple's time and location. There were additional difficulties, some caused by familial and societal disapproval, and others by Cushman's relationship with Emma Crow [Cushman], who was twenty-three years her junior and would eventually become her daughter-in-law.[20] Yet Cushman and Stebbins remained steadfast in their commitment to each other from the late 1850s—when Cushman (despite her infidelity) prioritizes her loyalty to Stebbins and identifies herself to her lover as "already married. & wear[ing] the badge upon the 3d finger of my left hand"—to Cushman's death in 1876. Reflecting on her love for her late spouse in a letter to a friend, Stebbins states, "I lived with the embodied principle of love so many years, that it became a part of my being."[21]

Cushman was equally principled about her support of women artists seeking their professional fortunes in Italy. Her efforts, which she soon focused on Stebbins, ranged from providing free housing and financial advice to securing commissions and connecting artists with journalists and buyers.[22] Their relationship is central to understanding Stebbins's life in Italy for yet another reason, namely for how Cushman's correspondence helps us reconstruct their shared life abroad. Stebbins herself has left no diary (unlike journalist Anne Hampton Brewster or writer Sophia Peabody Hawthorne with whom she socialized in Italy).[23] Nor did anyone edit her letters for publication soon after her death (as Stebbins did for Cushman [see Stebbins's historical text in this volume], or Cornelia Carr for Hosmer).[24] In fact, most of her letters are lost, many having been intentionally destroyed by Stebbins herself.[25] What remains of Stebbins's correspondence are the letters that have been preserved in the collections of her famous addressees—primarily Anne Whitney, Sidney Lanier, and Annie Adams Fields and James T. Fields (letters to the Fields were often co-written with Cushman). These letters can be supplemented by references to her in other people's letters, primarily those of her spouse (see fig. 4). Stebbins's presence in manuscripts thus mirrors her status in life—well connected, but rarely at the center. These scattered archival sources are complemented by numerous public accounts, which

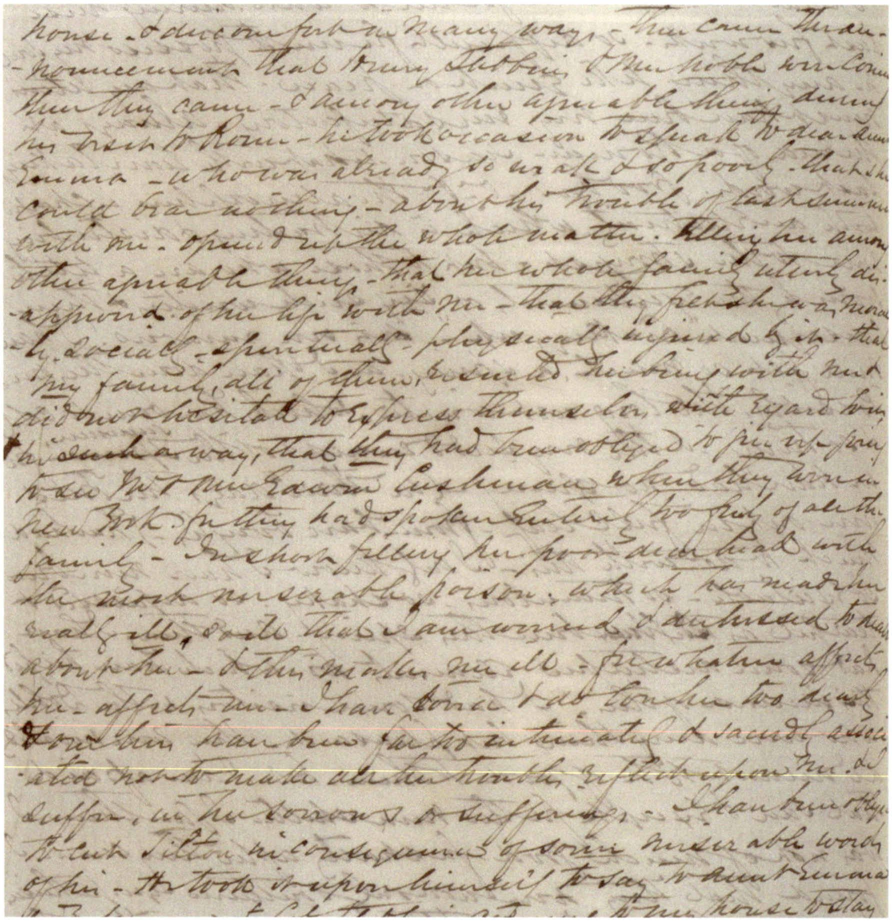

FIG. 4 Charlotte Cushman to Emma Crow Cushman, May 11, 1865 (detail).
Library of Congress, Washington, DC

rarely focus only on Stebbins but instead link her to Cushman, or compare and contrast her to Hosmer, Edmonia Lewis, and other "lady sculptors," as Henry James called them.[26] Attempts to grapple with Stebbins's social network therefore must contend with source material that is at once vast and inadequate.

This group of artists to whom Stebbins belonged, for all the possibilities afforded by transnational travel, was not entirely free of the influence of US ideals of gendered behavior since all of them relied on American (and British) customers, who "scrutinized women artists' lives and work for evidence of impurity," and required that their "life and work . . . embody the passionlessness of a True Woman."[27] Stebbins might have felt the pressure to conform even more than did some of her fellow female sculptors, given that she settled in Rome at a comparatively advanced age as a member of a well-known and highly regarded New York City family. While her art pushed boundaries from the very start—she was, after all, "the first American woman artist to undertake the male nude in sculpture" and the first woman to win a public art commission in New York City—her appearance and demeanor were perceived to be rather conventional, especially in contrast to Hosmer and Cushman, who are most often named alongside her in newspapers and private writing.[28] One illuminating article describes them as having "a strong and tireless energy, and a muscular *physique*. . . . Both are thoroughly American and patriotic, yet of strong and impressive individuality, that brings them out in striking contrast with the rest of society in Rome."[29] Hosmer, who had arrived in Rome in her early twenties as the only surviving daughter of a physician with an unorthodox parenting style, relied on her tomboy persona (even well into her forties) in order to compensate for not fitting the ideal of the "True Woman" and to disguise her artistic ambitions and sexual freedom.[30] The contemporary reception of Cushman and Hosmer contrasts with Stebbins's public image, which one article labels as "graceful, amiable, and charming."[31] Similarly, Brewster characterizes Stebbins in her private diary as "a soft gentle quite ladylike woman, a good woman too . . . a benefit to C. C. [Charlotte Cushman] most certainly I think for she grew to be more of a lady."[32]

BEING ABROAD

Stebbins's friendships with other sculptors were among her most sustained relationships, despite differences in their personal circumstances and repeated competition for the same commissions.[33] The relationship with Hosmer, in fact, might have been among her most complex in Rome. American journalist Kate Field reminisces about "a glorious day among the ruins, the mountains, and the wonderful sky" when she picnicked at Hadrian's Villa with Stebbins, Cushman, Hosmer, and John Quincy Adams Ward in 1859.[34] Hosmer herself humorously describes their views of their career prospects and gendered expectations during their time as "'the three old maids' of the Gregoriana," writing "that when everything else fails, we'll go in for lecturing. Miss Cushman will hold forth upon Dramatic Art, Miss Stebbins upon Pictorial Art and I upon the Art of Sculpture."[35] It is noteworthy that Hosmer still considers Stebbins a painter rather than a fellow sculptor in this anecdote. Similarly, in a sketch she drew of them riding across the Roman Campagna, Hosmer shows herself in the lead and with her horse in a more daring posture (fig. 5). Significant, too, is the name of Hosmer's horse: "Ivan" is one of the several animals and pets that Stebbins describes with affection and in detail in her biography of Cushman, illustrating Hosmer's embeddedness in their household.[36] Competition between

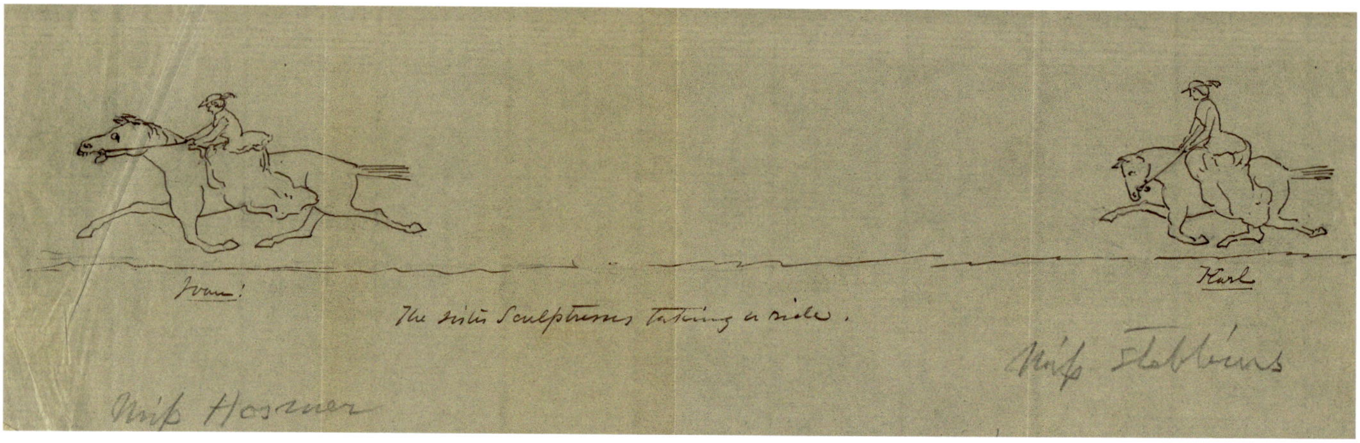

FIG. 5 Attributed to Harriet Hosmer (American, 1830–1908), *The Sister Sculptresses Taking a Ride*, n.d. Pen and ink on paper, 3¾ × 12 in. (9.5 × 30.5 cm).

Harriet Goodhue Hosmer Papers, A-162, 182, Schlesinger Library, Harvard Radcliffe Institute, Harvard University, Cambridge, MA

Stebbins and Hosmer seems to have heightened around 1862, when Cushman notes that Stebbins's *Horace Mann* statue (pl. 16) in Boston would likely be unveiled before Hosmer's *Thomas Hart Benton* monument in St. Louis (1862).[37] A year later, a visitor still notes that "Miss Hosmer & Miss Stebbins are most remarkable very dissimilar in character," but "bound together by the strongest ties of friendship."[38] Yet, when Stebbins wrote Cushman's biography in 1878, she reduces Hosmer to a "travelling friend" in a single mention.[39]

Starting in the late 1860s, Whitney—who shared her life with the painter Addy Manning and was of a social background and age comparable to Stebbins's—became (at least based on the evidence still extant) one of Stebbins's most enduring and important friends. While their lives overlapped only briefly in Rome, their correspondence extended into 1881, and encompasses their thoughts about religion, relationships, the reception of their work, and art in general. Stebbins, for example, recommends Hippolyte Taine's *The Philosophy of Art* (1873) as "well worth reading."[40] It is to Whitney that Stebbins confides that she "always love[d] best the first creation—more than the finished work," because "the soul of the work, if it is a true soul—is born and lives through it all, and an artist's eye can see it in the first effort as in the last."[41] In yet another letter from the 1870s, Stebbins offers a retrospective account of how she has long considered Whitney a trusted confidant with whom she liked to "compare notes of our experiences and our thinking" and "remember[s] in Rome the discussions we used to have . . . and how the idea of building better than we know—was laughed at" by John Gibson, Hosmer, and "that ilk" (fig. 6).[42] Even in its disparagement of these fellow sculptors, Stebbins's letter stresses that this group of artists had sustained dialogues about their respective artistic methods during their shared time in Rome. These conversations complemented the more practical ways in which these sculptors supported each other. Hiram Powers, for example, shared tools and estimates, while Margaret F. Foley and Florence Freeman accepted the invitation to stay (and travel) with Cushman and Stebbins (see the chronology in this volume).[43]

Stebbins's family, too, remained a presence in her life even after she had settled in Rome. Her brother Henry G. Stebbins regularly visited (and continued to manage her finances), while her younger sister Caroline Stebbins married painter John Rollin Tilton, who also worked in Rome.[44] Her older sister Mary Stebbins Garland later wrote a biographical sketch and collated a scrapbook that have become essential sources on Stebbins's life and work (see Garland's historical text in this volume).[45] Yet despite their sustained encouragement of her professional ambitions, Stebbins's relationships with members of her family were complex, and their support did not extend to

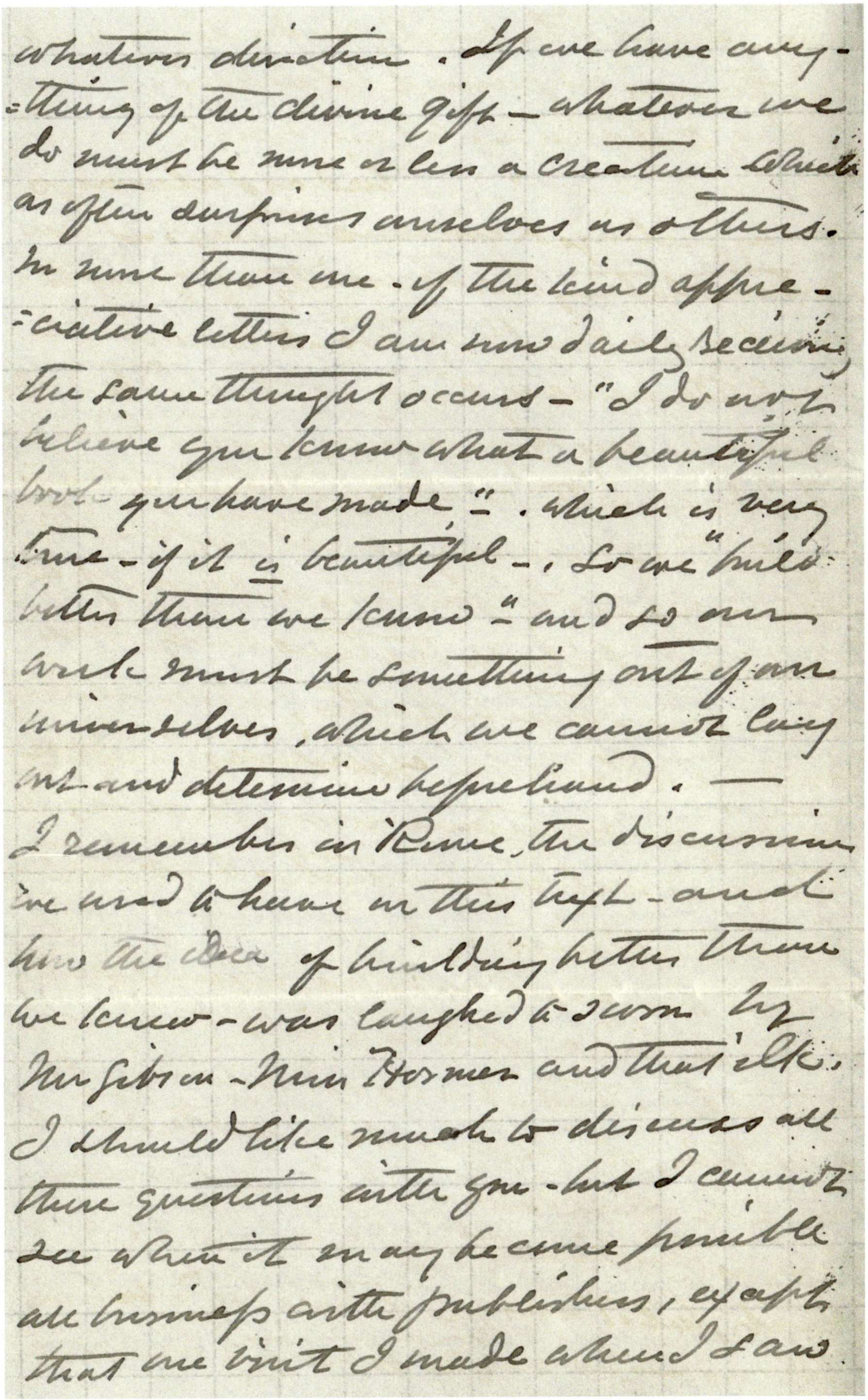
whatever direction. If we have any-
thing of the divine gift — whatever we
do must be more or less a creation which
as often surprises ourselves as others.
In more than one — of the kind appre-
ciative letters I am now daily receiving
the same thought occurs — "I do not
believe you know what a beautiful
book you have made". which is very
true — if it is beautiful —. So we "build
better than we know" and so our
work must be something out of our
inner selves, which we cannot lay
out and determine beforehand. —
I remember in Rome, the discussion
we used to have on this topic — and
how the idea of building better than
we knew — was laughed to scorn by
Mr Gibson — Miss Hosmer and that ilk.
I should like much to discuss all
these questions with you — but I cannot
see when it may become possible
all business with publishers, except
that one visit I made when I saw

FIG. 6 Emma Stebbins to Anne Whitney, June 19, 1878 (detail).

Wellesley College Archives, Wellesley, MA

how she conducted her life in Rome. After a family visit in 1865, Cushman relates with regret that Henry G. Stebbins had told his sister

> that her whole family utterly disapproved of her life with me—that they felt she was morally, socially, spiritually, physically injured by it. that my family, all of them, resented her being with me. . . . this makes me ill. for whatever affects her, affects me. I have loved & do love her too dearly & our lives have been far too intimately & sacredly associated not to make all her troubles reflect upon me. & I suffer, in her sorrows or sufferings. I have been obliged to cut Tilton in consequence of some miserable words of his. . . . & she wrote him a note bidding him be careful what he said with regard to me. . . . aunt Emma so stonily defended herself & me—& I cut Tilton completely [see fig. 4].[46]

Such gossip was not confined to family matters. The anglophone community in Rome was close-knit socially and spatially close, mostly settling within one mile of each other near the Spanish Steps (see fig. 7). As Stowe's 1860 article highlights, "Rome [was] said to be a great place for gossip."[47] And while Stowe believed that most of it did "no harm," it was, in fact, easy for such talk to ruin careers—with sculptor Louisa Lander being the most famous example of the professional damage caused by slander.[48] To avoid similar attacks on their characters, it was essential, as Lisa Merrill argues, that Cushman and Stebbins "enacted an 'idealized view' of women's loving relationships, which, paradoxically, appeared to many people to exemplify conventional societal values rather than challenge them."[49]

STAYING CONNECTED

A crucial aspect of this was their participation in various networks that sustained them privately and shielded them publicly. Networks, as Sharon Marcus argues, are particularly relevant to understanding "the social position of women in female marriages."[50] In their leisure time, Stebbins and Cushman often gravitated towards other women in same-sex relationships (e.g., Hosmer, Cobbe, Blagden, Brewster, and Whitney) and others who had rejected heterosexual marriages and enjoyed the queer sociability and freedom of expression that resulted from their female friendships. On a trip to France, for example, Stebbins and Cushman enjoyed the company of painter Rosa Bonheur.[51] Kate Field playfully refers to the couple as "Romeo and her Juliet, Miss Stebbins."[52] Such distance from contemporary norms of gender and sexuality might suggest a mainly subcultural form of belonging, one that was "organized around a limited number of shared traits" and defined by its "separation from the mainstream."[53] Stebbins and Cushman, however, consciously worked towards establishing themselves as members of various networks, which differ from subcultures by the variety among their members, by their overlap with other networks, and by being much more open (that is, easy to enter and leave).[54] Thus, in addition to the protofeminist network, which was structured by their connections to Britain, Cushman and Stebbins also participated in the pro-Union efforts of expatriate Americans and the initiatives of abolitionists in the US, maintained relationships to anglophone writers and publishers across Europe, had close ties with luminaries of the stage, and enjoyed friendships and collaborations with patrons, financial advisors, and those in public office.

This embeddedness included, importantly, Stebbins's support of others. Networks, after all, are defined by "recursive interconnectivity, nodality, as well as distributed agency."[55] In other words, in order to secure her status, Stebbins had to actively contribute to her social circles. Accordingly, she promoted the literary work of others, such as Lanier (the young writer originally picked by Cushman as her biographer), whose poems she forwarded to a friend "moving in the best literary and artistic circles" in England.[56] On behalf of an unnamed friend, Stebbins wrote to Annie Adams Fields (who herself wielded editorial power) and to the editors of the *Crayon* to ask about the possibility of publishing an English translation of a French short story.[57] At other times, she patronized other female sculptors or prepared a sketch to promote their work (see fig. 8).[58]

For Stebbins, this web of social contacts mattered not only because it helped shield her private life from unwanted attention but also because her public commissions repeatedly required the intervention of supporters in the US to ensure that she did not have to go into debt to create and ship her sculptures. Among those called upon were Dr. Samuel Gridley Howe, an abolitionist and advocate for the education of people with disabilities, and the Fields, writers and editors who wanted to use their publications "to advance the liberal political beliefs [they] shared with most of their friends," including the sympathetic representation of the political and social struggles of people of color, Indigenous people, and those afflicted by urban poverty.[59]

Their correspondence with the Fields in particular highlights how closely Stebbins and Cushman followed the reviews of their respective artistic outputs and how they were willing to rely on their network of influential, progressive interlocutors to intervene if public opinion needed to be guided in different directions.[60] One striking example occurs when Cushman stepped in to defend Stebbins and her work after reading a negative review of the *Angel of the Waters* (pls. 46, 47), which speaks of the derision with which the statue has supposedly been received because the model for "the buxom deity on the top . . . must have been brought up on pork and hominy."[61] Cushman enclosed a copy of this review in a letter to the Fields, complaining

> Is this the way you suffer the paper in which ~~you~~ JTF [strike-through in original; "JTF" was inserted above the line, also in original] holds influence to deal with Emma? I think not—. . . it ill becomes a Boston paper which once had a reputation for decency & honesty to print such a libelous thing as this which I enclose. I wish you would have some thing said in The Transcript which shall stultify the effect of the enclosed vileness—which evidently has a <u>personal</u> sting.[62]

The letter is significant in illustrating Cushman's relationship with the Fields, not only because she asks James to use his powers as a magazine editor to sway public opinion, but also because in it she allows the couple to peek behind the public facade of her relationship with Stebbins. This was one of the rare occasions in which Cushman starts a letter without the usual pleasantries, and in which she speaks simply of "Emma" (not "Emma Stebbins," "Emma S.," or "our Emma"). In addition to repeatedly using this more casual form of the name, Cushman also emphatically states she "would not have Emma see this [the enclosed review] for the world." The document thus is an example of how "[l]etters differ from autobiographies partly in exerting less continuous control over the construction of a life-myth," as it does not support their usual shared dedication to presenting themselves—and by extension their relationship—as passionless.[63]

1 Spanish Steps

Many in the expatriate anglophone community lived and worked within a mile of this location.

2 38 Via Gregoriana

Emma Stebbins and Charlotte Cushman made their home here, with various friends, family members, and employees, from 1859 to 1870.

3 Via Sistina

Emma Stebbins's first studio, where she worked from 1859 to 1863.

4 11A Via di S. Basilio

Emma Stebbins's second studio, where she worked from 1864 to 1870.

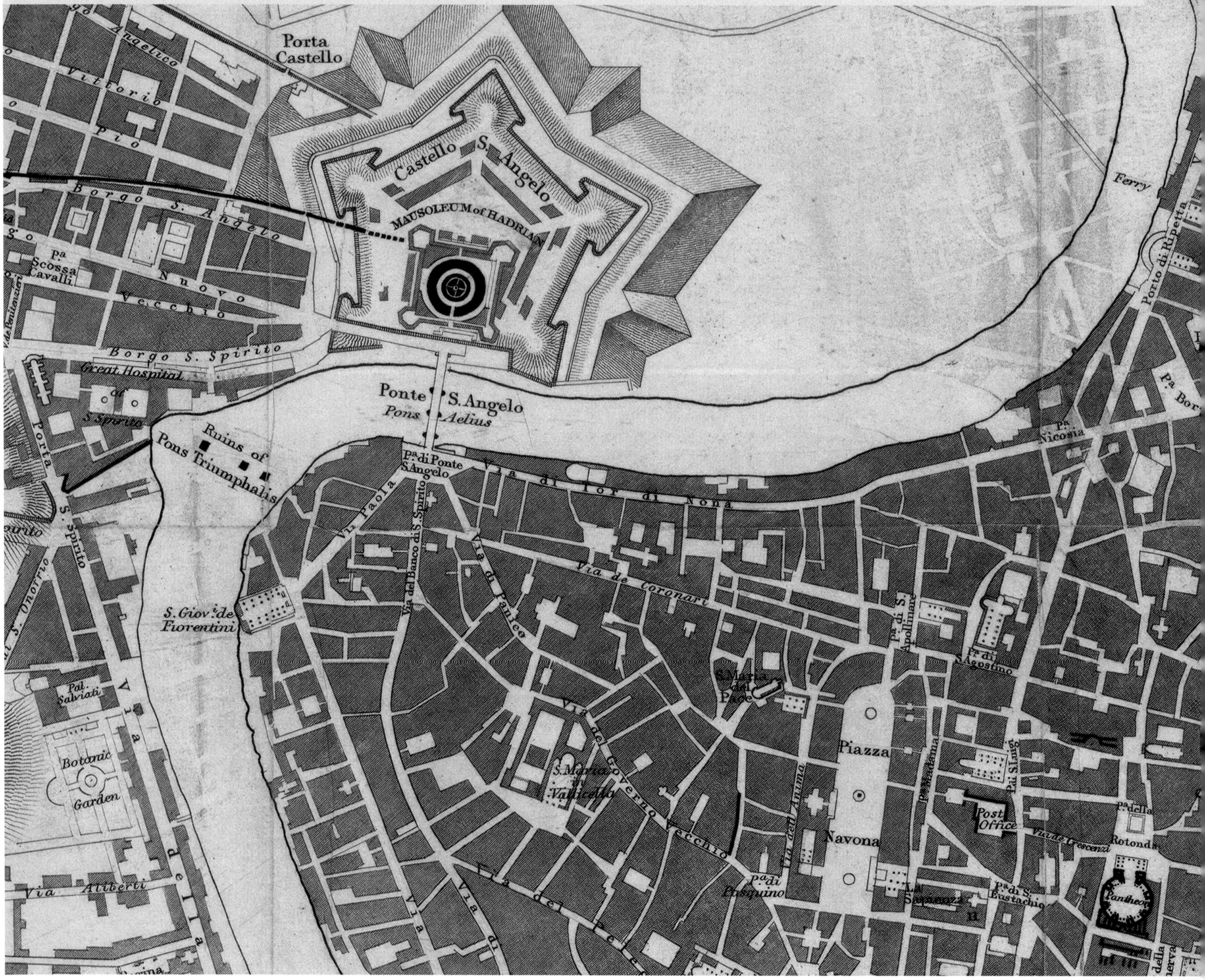

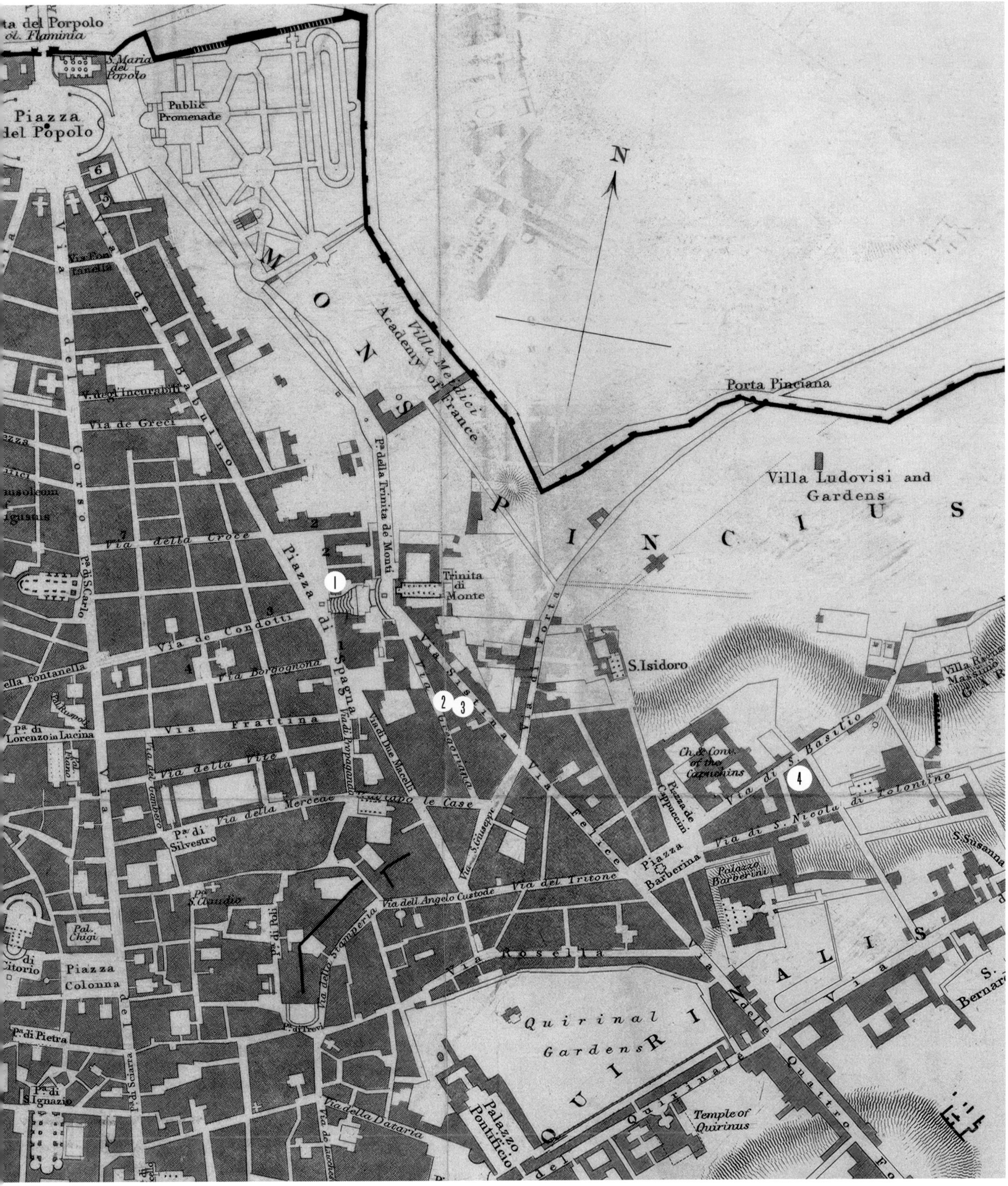

FIG. 7 John Murray (American, 1808–1892), cartographer, J. & C. Walker, engraver, *Plan of Rome*, ca. 1850–56 (detail).

Library of Congress, Washington, DC. Map annotations by Katrin Horn

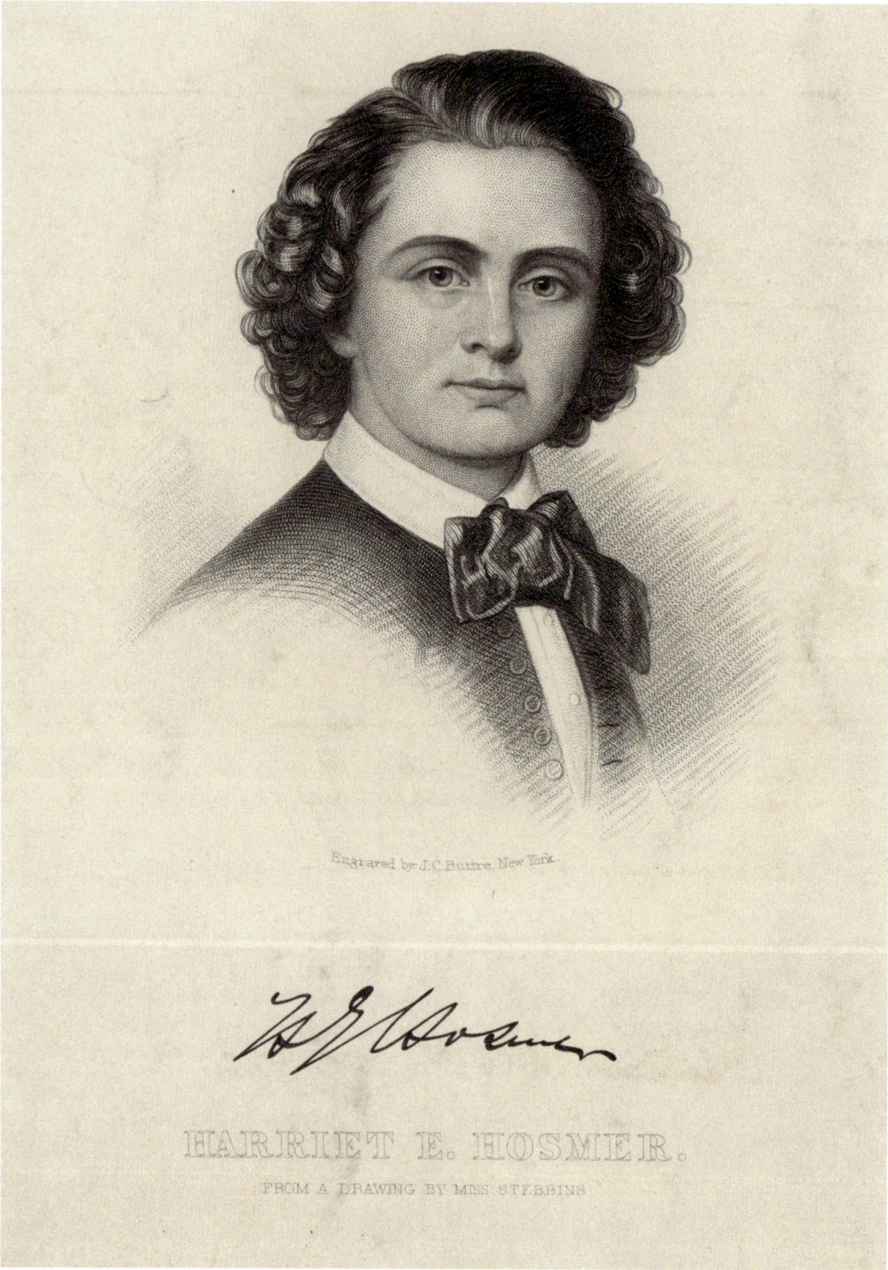

FIG. 8 After Emma Stebbins (American, 1815–1882), John Chester Buttre (American, 1821–1893), *Harriet E. Hosmer: From a Drawing by Miss Stebbins*, ca. 1861 (detail). Engraving, sheet: 9 × 6¾ in. (22.9 × 17.2 cm).

Library of Congress, Washington, DC

Besides a general sense of protectiveness for her wife, two factors might have occasioned Cushman's unusual display of emotionality. The first might be Cushman's own vanity—this, at least, is suggested by Merrill, who notes in a caption for the illustration of the fountain, "Some critics disapproved of the large, powerful body that Stebbins had given her 'Angel'—a body not unlike Charlotte Cushman's."[64] The physical similarities between Stebbins's wife and her most famous statue have also been observed in recent writing about the sculpture geared to general audiences.[65] While neither Cushman's nor Stebbins's letters explicitly address the issue of the fountain's model, a "personal sting" resulting from criticism not of the fountain's artistic merit, but its choice of female proportions, might support this assumed connection between art and life.

Another likely reason for the perception of the "personal sting" derives from the figure's symbolic meaning, namely the healing power of water (see Igoe's essay in this volume). This theme would have resonated strongly with Stebbins, whose father

(John Stebbins) and brother (John Wilson Stebbins) had died from cholera, a disease caused primarily by unclean water. Moreover, her wife—hoping for relief from the pain caused by breast cancer—was undergoing water treatment at the same time that Stebbins was working on the fountain's design. Ridicule of the *Angel of the Waters*, therefore, would have been extremely personal to both Stebbins and Cushman.

Despite their otherwise successful efforts to conceal their personal emotions from public scrutiny, the correspondence with the Fields over the course of several years suggests that the relationship between Cushman and Stebbins was accepted on a footing relatively equal to that of the Fields' marriage: greetings are mutually extended to the noncorresponding partner and terms of endearment—such as Cushman's reference to Stebbins as "my other, & much my better half"—are employed, which seems to have made this singular slippage in facade permissible.[66] The importance of the Fields for Stebbins and Cushman also found expression in much more quotidian "services" than this somewhat unusual request to rectify bad press—namely providing them with reading material.

Reading emerges as a key component of how Stebbins spent her leisure time in Rome and how she professed her political and moral convictions.[67] Stebbins was, for example, among the first expatriate Americans to have read Nathaniel Hawthorne's *The Marble Faun* (1860), which is credited with intensifying Americans' investment in Italy. Cushman describes the enthusiasm with which she and Stebbins were reading and sharing Hawthorne's novel, noting with pride that theirs was the only available copy in Rome (see fig. 9).[68] In July 1869, while the couple stayed at the Knotsford Lodge in Malvern (England), Stebbins read *The Gates Ajar*, a soon-to-be bestseller about a woman dealing with the death of her brother (a loss Stebbins and Cushman had both experienced), written by Elizabeth Stuart Phelps and published by Fields, Osgood, & Company just the year prior. It seems to have been among the several pieces of "strong fine women's writing" that they considered superior to some of the male-authored serials otherwise available to them in the British press.[69]

Just like the US-based American readers who were trying to stay informed about American artists abroad, expatriates tried to stay on top of news from home, especially during the Civil War, when news of Union victories caused "tears of joy."[70] The Fields also regularly provided Stebbins and Cushman with issues of the *Atlantic*—one of the leading literary and political magazines of the time, which was marked by "cosmopolitan ambitions" and an "unswerving commitment to the antislavery movement and a pro-Republican political stance."[71] Cushman professed that they took "great comfort" in it.[72]

Reading was also an important part of Stebbins's artistic process (see Gustin's essay in this volume). Beyond the well-established influence of Alfred, Lord Tennyson's "The Lotos-Eaters" (1832), Stebbins drew upon various forms of writing for her extensive research in preparation for her sculptures. For the *Horace Mann* statue, for example, she read Mann's twenty-thousand-word address inaugurating Antioch College (Ohio), and inquired about the best biographical accounts of his life in order to do justice—from a distance—to this icon of women's education in the US.[73]

Stebbins's life in Rome was profoundly shaped by her physical removal from the US: waiting for books, magazines, and letters, or being rushed to finish them in time for mail day were oft-repeated concerns in her correspondence. Arrangements for travel to the US, which depended equally on Cushman's theatrical engagements and Stebbins's sculptural projects, occupied the expatriate artists frequently and intensely. Yet Stebbins was not only "abroad" but also "at home" in Rome, where her days were densely structured by professional and social commitments: rise at 7:00, breakfast at 8:00, work in the studio until lunch at 1:30, horseback riding in the afternoon, dinner at 5:00, and then "stay at home to receive visits or go out to pay them."[74] While this list of daily activities may seem mundane at first glance, it had crucial implications, both socially and financially. Her contributions to the expatriate community, in fact, not only affected her standing in Rome but were also an important step in promoting her work in the US. This is particularly true for her role as one of the key figures of those "semi-public performance spaces . . . at which Anglo-Americans entertained each other 'at home.'"[75]

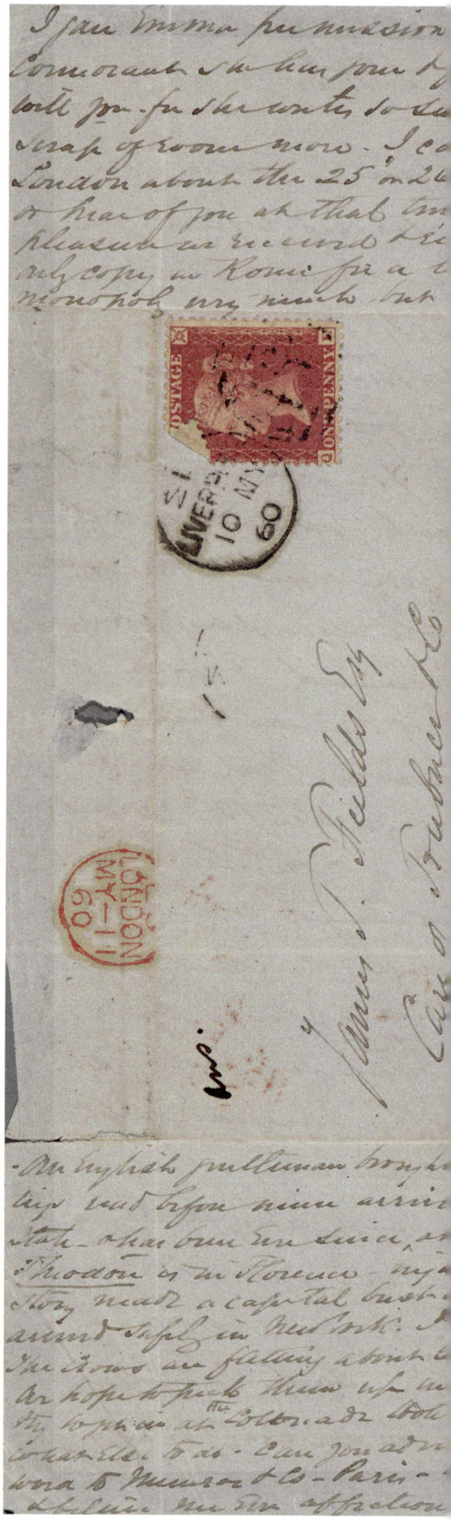

ENTERTAINING AT HOME

Stebbins's detailed description of their apartment at 38 Via Gregoriana speaks to the sentimental importance of these rooms (see fig. 10 and Stebbins's historical text in this volume).

> The reception-rooms were not large, nor were there many of them; but there was an air of *homeiness*, if one may coin a word, rarely seen in the apartments of Rome. . . . This home was a genuine one. . . . All those who have experienced the sense of strangeness and loneliness which besets one in a foreign land will readily recognize this element, and many will remember it with heartfelt gratitude.[76]

Despite the rooms' coziness, the apartment was more than a private space. Rather, contemporary newspapers and private documents attest to the popularity of Stebbins and Cushman as salon hostesses. Beginning in January 1859, their evening gatherings of up to 175 were attended by the likes of Cobbe, the Hawthornes, and sculptor William Wetmore Story and his wife, Emelyn Eldredge Story.[77] While Cushman often complained about the strain the duty of hospitality put on their household, she and Stebbins were acutely aware of its importance to maintaining their position within their transnational networks.[78]

Essential to the success of these events was Sallie Mercer, whom Stebbins praises in Cushman's biography for her "really superior administrative faculty" and describes as "a part of [their] family" (see fig. 11).[79] Mercer had begun working for Cushman at age fourteen as a maid, but soon made herself indispensable as the caretaker for Cushman's costumes and manager of travel arrangements, and later as the head organizer of the Roman household. While her presence in Rome as a Black maid who traveled with her employer was not unusual, her acknowledgment in public accounts, the greetings extended to her in private letters, the production of a carte de visite, and her status as the housekeeper to whom the Italian servants reported and turned for guidance *were* noteworthy.[80] Mercer thus constituted another central element of a household that pushed the limits of societal norms, and it was her presence in that household that allowed it to be a social hub, even as its prominent occupants continued to focus on their respective careers and other obligations. Cobbe enthusiastically recounts the "dinners of American oysters and wild boar with agro-dolce-sauce" and the "brightness, freedom and joyousness among these gifted Americans."[81] One visitor marvels at seeing Cushman in conversation with Franz Liszt and describes how she passed "on to the second, third, and fourth salons, stopping to admire tasteful collections of ornaments, statuary, paintings, and photographs" and "mingle[d] with such ordinary names as the Count Cenci, Princess Doria, Lady Montague, with

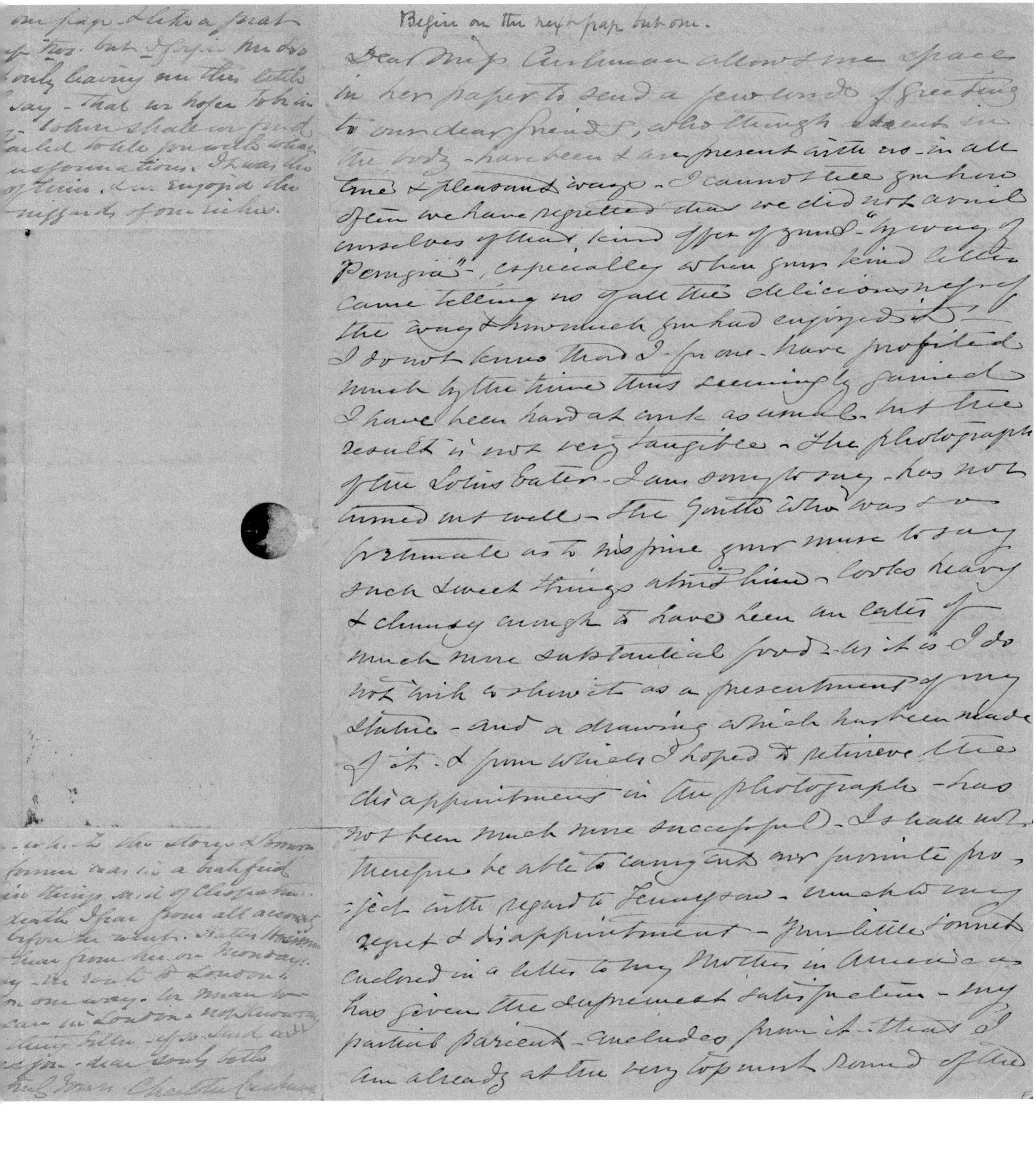
Begin on the next page but one.

Dear Miss Cushman allows me space in her paper to send a few words of greeting to our dear friends, who though absent in the body - have been & are present with us - in all time & pleasant ways. - I cannot tell you how often we have regretted that we did not avail ourselves of that kind offer of yours - by way of "Perugia" - especially when your kind letter came telling us of all the deliciousness of the way & how much you had enjoyed it. I do not know that I - for one - have profited much by the time thus seemingly gained. I have been hard at work as usual - but the result is not very tangible - The photograph of the Lotus Eater - I am sorry to say - has not turned out well - the youth who was so fortunate as to inspire your muse to say such sweet things about him - looks heavy & clumsy enough to have been an eater of much more substantial food - as it is I do not wish to show it as a presentment of my statue - and a drawing which has been made of it - & from which I hoped to retrieve the disappointment in the photograph - has not been much more successful - I shall not therefore be able to carry out my favorite project with regard to Tennyson - much to my regret & disappointment - Your little sonnet enclosed in a letter to my Mother in America has given the supremest satisfaction - my partial parent - concludes from it - that I am already at the very top round of the

FIG. 9 Emma Stebbins and Charlotte Cushman to Annie Adams and James T. Fields, May 3, 1860 (detail).

The Huntington Library, San Marino, CA

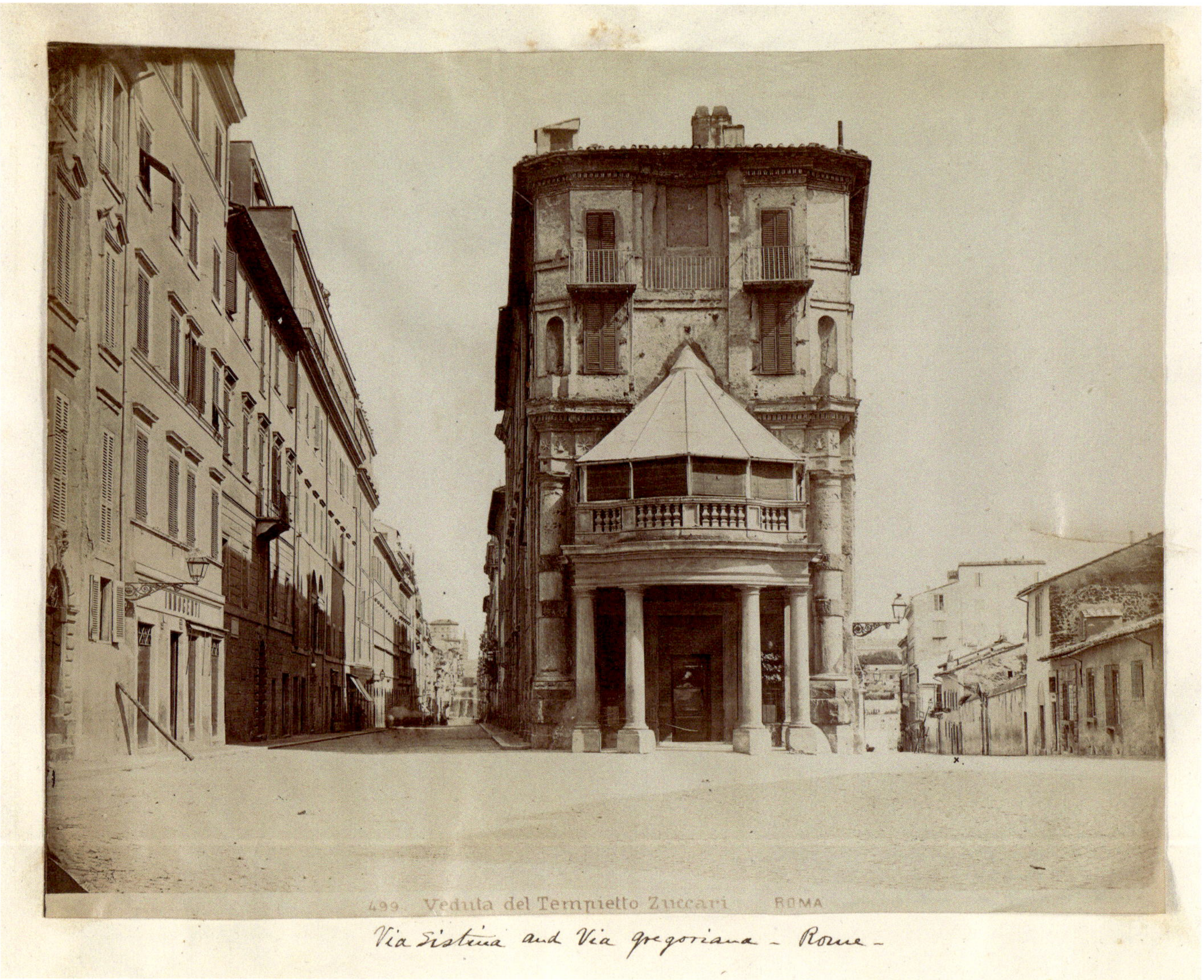

FIG. 10 Romualdo Moscioni (Italian, 1849–1925), *Via Sistina, Palazzo Zuccari, and Via Gregoriana, Rome*, ca. 1885–93. From the John Neal Tilton scrapbook, ca. 1860–80. Albumen print from a glass negative.

Archives of American Art, Smithsonian Institution, Washington, DC

Hazeltine, Reade, Hosmer, Miss Elizabeth Peabody. . . . Miss Stebbins, Misses Williams and Foley, Mr. Mozier, Rogers, and other honored Americans."[82] Another guest indicates how these gatherings could strengthen the shared national identity of American expatriates, writing that his "most pleasant recollections of my visit to Rome [were] associated with the home of Miss Cushman and her friend, Miss Stebbins. They kept *the most agreeable American house* in those days."[83]

While some scholars have suggested that their shared receptions were mainly Cushman's chance to shine—and to receive in Italy the public recognition she would have garnered in the US and England from her stage performances—Stebbins had another semipublic space in which to entertain guests and foster connections that was all her own: her studio.[84] Studio visits, a regular part of any Grand Tour, gave an increasingly mobile and affluent middle class an opportunity to use art to signify their distinction from the lower classes.[85] Guidebooks, such as *Harper's Handbook for Travelers in Europe and the East*, informed travelers as to where and when studios could be visited and what highlights they could expect at each.[86] Stebbins herself describes the atmosphere in which visitors would find her as follows:

> The houses which bounded the back view on the Via Sistina were occupied as studios and apartments, and presented to an inquiring mind a

FIG. 11 Wenderoth and Taylor (Philadelphia, PA), *Sallie Mercer*, ca. 1860–70. Carte de visite, 3½ × 2¼ in. (8.9 × 5.7 cm).

Harriet Goodhue Hosmer Papers, A162-157-5, Schlesinger Library, Harvard Radcliffe Institute, Harvard University, Cambridge, MA

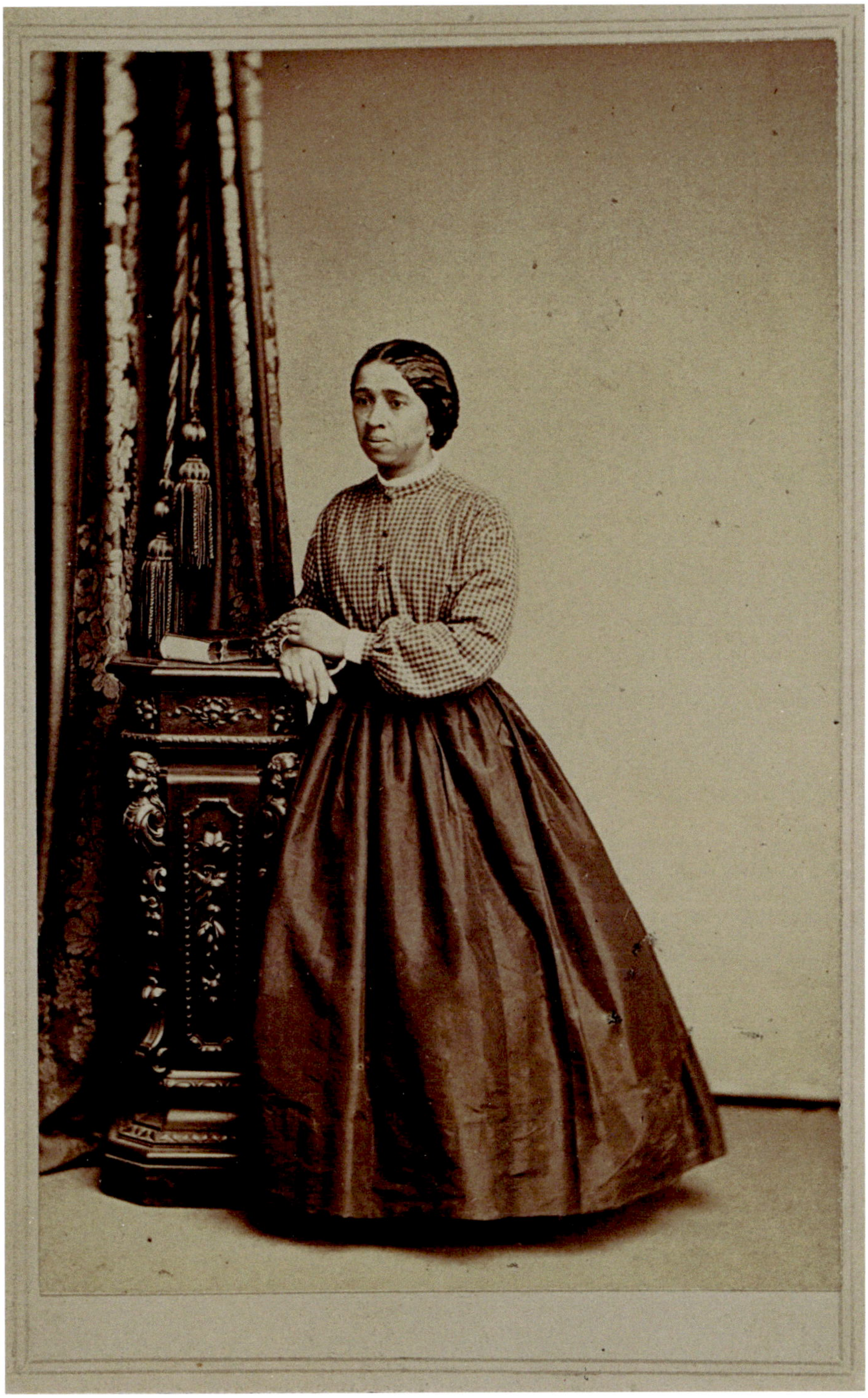

sufficiently entertaining prospect, since it is in the nature of Italians to live very much *en evidence*, and family affairs and interesting domestic events were freely discussed from window to window in the peculiar high-pitched not at all *musical* voices of the natives.[87]

The importance of studio visits for artists was at least of a twofold nature: they were a chance to find new customers and to ensure good press. An 1866 report on an insurance case relating to Stebbins's *Joseph the Dreamer* (pl. 23), for example, claims that all American tourists to Rome would have (or at least should have) seen the statue during their visits to Stebbins's studio the year prior and informs its readers that "this statue was purchased, at a large price" by a buyer "who had previously seen it in Miss Stebbins studio in Rome."[88] In addition to the financial value of receiving tourists in her workplace, *A Woman's Experiences in Europe: Including England, France, Germany, and Italy* (1872) highlights another vital function of studios, namely, to let artists guide their public image. The author remembers her visit to Stebbins's studio as a study-in-contrasts and a confirmation of the artist's adherence to standards of feminine propriety.

Through the crowd of white-powdered men and boys, who are industriously following out our fair artist's instructions . . . we reach a room where Miss Stebbins herself stands in her neat brown linen coat-dress, every part of her toilette finished with womanly care, and her gentle, delicate face expressing a satisfaction indescribable, as she looks around on her finished works, an array of lovely images that call forth an involuntary exclamation from us as we enter: "How beautiful!"[89]

Stebbins could thus use her adherence to conventional standards of dress and etiquette to make her unconventional choice of career more palatable to those venturing to Rome on the Grand Tour.

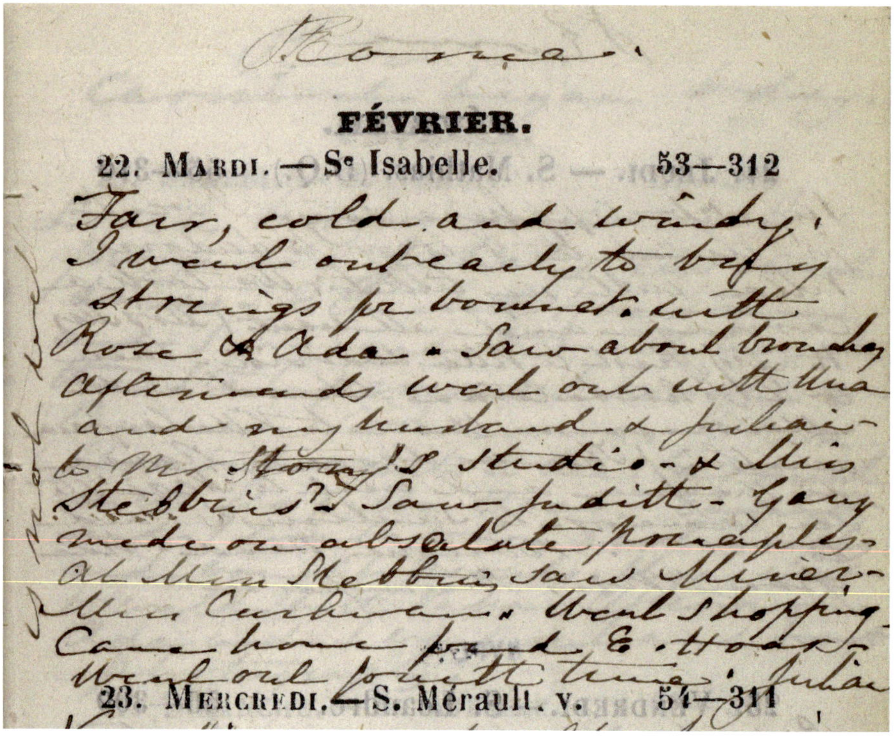

FIG. 12 Sophia Peabody Hawthorne (American, 1809–1871), Diary entry, Rome, February 22, 1859 (detail).

Henry W. and Albert A. Berg Collection of English and American Literature, The New York Public Library, New York, NY

Besides tourists, other prominent expatriates, including the Hawthornes, constituted a regular presence in her studio (see fig. 12).[90] Sculptors also paid visits to their colleagues to look at artworks and share professional advice. Whitney visited Stebbins's studio to study *The Lotus Eater*, and on another occasion relied on Stebbins for a recommendation for a stonecutter.[91] A culmination of the various functions of her "semi-public performance" in the studio can be seen in an account of journalist Brewster, with whom Stebbins was also personally acquainted. One of her articles praises the execution of the *Angel of the Waters* and explains the biblical references essential to its design to ensure that American audiences would be properly guided in their reaction to the artwork once it was installed. Brewster goes beyond that to stress her personal knowledge of Stebbins, writing: "[W]hen I was in Miss Stebbins's studio . . . I noticed with admiration some studies made by Miss Stebbins for the Central Park at the request of the managers."[92] The article thus served the double function of ensuring a positive reception of Stebbins's ambitious statue and increasing tourists' interest in her studio in Rome (where one could, Brewster suggests, gain exclusive access to models of statues already commissioned but not yet finished). At the same time, Brewster's publication served the author's own interests by presenting her as a privileged source of insider knowledge about artists whom she personally knew. The article thus highlights the mutual dependency of expatriate artists and writers, the overlap of professional and private connections among them, their shared financial dependence on the US, as well as the interest of the American public in their expatriate contemporaries.

BALANCING DEMANDS

Stebbins successfully navigated this complex field of sociability for more than a decade, while producing some of the finest examples of neoclassical sculpture from the period. The latter, in fact, would not have been feasible without the former. While it is impossible to trace the complexity of Stebbins's social relations in full—especially given the relative dearth of her own voice in archival records—the exemplary relationships outlined here make clear that Stebbins's network was as wide as it was varied, both close-knit and transnational. Studios and salons in Rome compensated for the missing infrastructure the US would have provided through galleries, art schools, and clubs, while tourists from and interlocutors in the US made up for the lack of a financially robust art market in Rome.[93] Through networking, traveling, letter writing, and her appearance in print publications, Stebbins ensured strong relations with the US even while she was living and working in Rome.

Soon after Stebbins's return to the US in the fall of 1870, interest in both neoclassical sculpture and Rome as a place of refuge was waning. Yet from the 1850s to 1870s, the glimpses we get of Stebbins's social ties, and of her maneuvering the demands of both a transnational career and a life on the margins of gender expectations, paint a highly illuminating picture of an artist both typical for her time and unique among her peers. These textual sources also give us a better understanding of the cultural context that made her work possible—and in turn, what that context demanded of her.

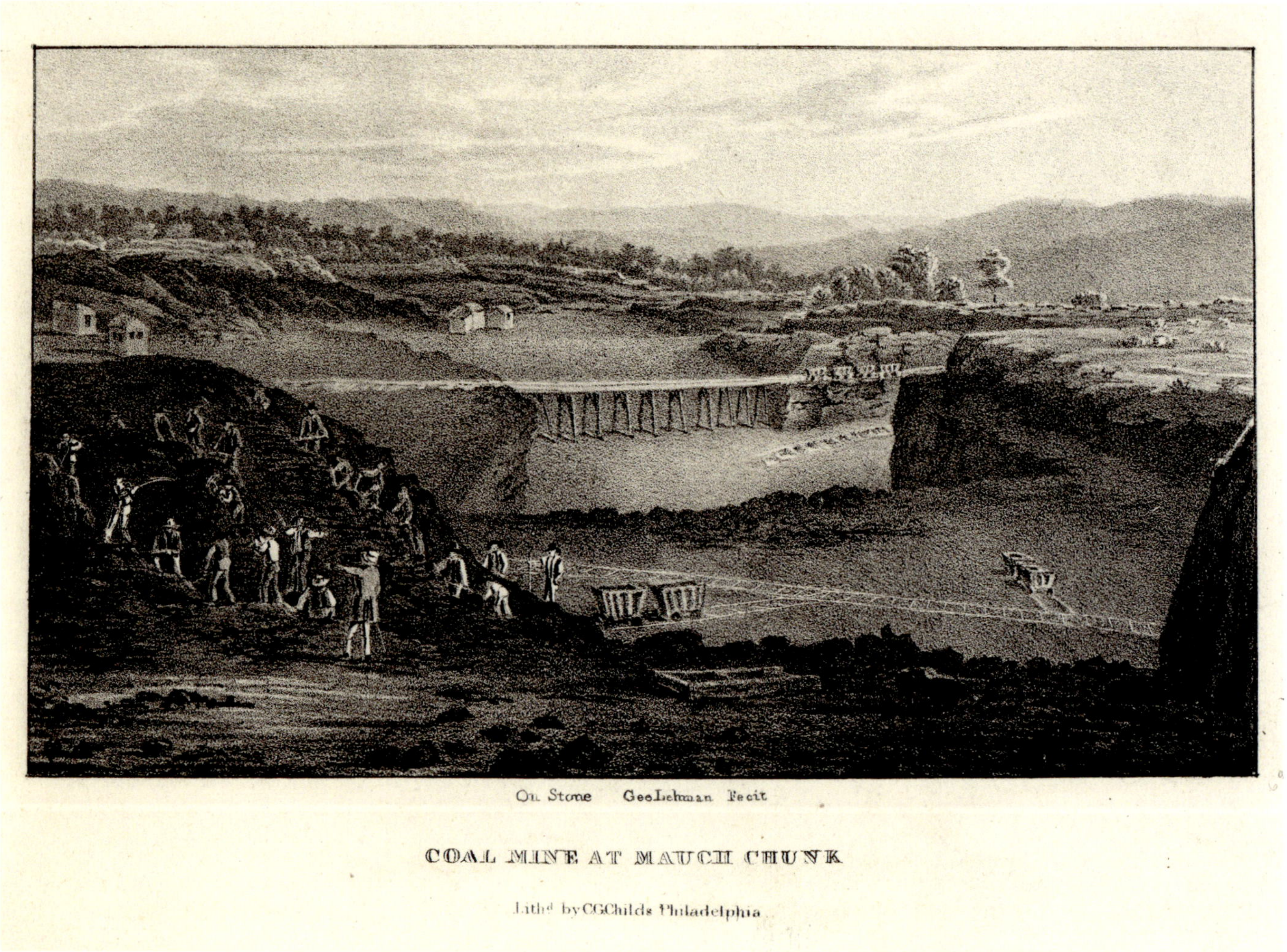

FIG. 1 George Lehman (American, b. Switzerland, ca. 1803–1870), *Coal Mine at Mauch Chunk*, 1835. Published by Cephas Grier Childs. Lithograph, image: 4 × 6³⁄₄ in. (10.2 × 17.2 cm).

The Library Company of Philadelphia, PA

LAURA TURNER IGOE

ALL THE MATERIAL THINGS

Industry, Labor, Health, and Environment in Emma Stebbins's Sculptures

In 1874, Emma Stebbins wrote to her friend, the poet and sculptor Anne Whitney, lamenting the physical toll of sculpting: "An artist ought to take the easiest groove possible—otherwise the labor of mind and body could be too severe—If there is any divine gift—all the material things should be made as easy as possible."[1] This passage speaks to Stebbins's intimate knowledge of the interconnectedness of materials, labor, and well-being, as well as her own declining health, as she struggled with an ongoing respiratory illness likely caused or exacerbated by inhaling marble dust from carving.[2] In her reference to taking "the easiest groove," Stebbins used language affiliated with carving stone, even though it was that process that was detrimental to her own health. Throughout her career, Stebbins expressed a keen interest in conceptions of work and industry and the impact of environments and materials upon the physical body. A close analysis of Stebbins's most celebrated sculptures—*Industry* (pl. 10) and *Commerce* (pl. 11) and the *Bethesda Fountain* (pl. 47)—reveals the entanglement of Stebbins's work with ecological conditions and change in the mid-nineteenth century. Through quotations of classical figures from ancient Greece and Rome, Stebbins created allegorical figures of modern labor and innovative technologies that radically transformed the natural environment and impacted public health.

Industry and *Commerce*, commissioned by industrialist Charles August Heckscher, celebrate the achievements of mining and international commerce through an ode to masculine American labor, equating miners and sailors with Greek gods and heroes. These two figures, both captured at moments of rest, stand in contrast to the actual, dangerous toil of coal miners and sailors, as well as the physical effort expended by Stebbins and quarrymen in extracting, transporting, and carving marble. The sculptures also obfuscate the significant environmental impact of both coal mining and marble quarrying.

Stebbins's best-known commission, the *Bethesda Fountain* in Central Park, commemorates the bringing of clean water to New York City via the Croton Aqueduct and reservoirs near the fountain's location. Her carefully planned suite of figural sculptures representing the *Angel of the Waters* (pl. 46) and *Temperance, Purity, Health and Peace* (pl. 45) recognizes the public health benefits of clean water following a devastating cholera epidemic in 1832. The *Bethesda Fountain* was designed, modeled, and cast when both Stebbins and her wife, Charlotte Cushman, were suffering from their own health issues and sought hydropathy, or water cures, to alleviate them, indicating the significance of clean water to Stebbins personally. Together, *Industry*, *Commerce*, and the *Bethesda Fountain* demonstrate how Stebbins both embraced and elided shifting industrial practices, public health, and environmental conditions within her work in the mid-nineteenth century.

The ecocritical approach employed here builds upon recent scholarship that interrogates the materiality and material history of artworks and their subject matter in order to relink artworks to the many hands and environments that shaped, and were shaped by, their production.[3] Stebbins, a transatlantic artist, worked in Rome and traveled frequently throughout Europe and the United States, crossing the Atlantic Ocean several times (see Horn's essay in this volume). Wealthy industrialists commissioned her work and, thanks to her own working practice and knowledge of sculptural processes, she would have possessed an intimate understanding of labor, industry, and trade, even if it was still from a perspective of extreme privilege. An ecocritical consideration of Stebbins's sculptures helps us understand them within the shifting environments that they represent, materialize, and for which they were created.

"THE WHOLE SPIRIT OF AMERICAN LABOR": *INDUSTRY* AND *COMMERCE*

By early 1859, Charles August Heckscher, a New York businessman, commissioned Stebbins to create "two small figures, representing Mining + Commerce under the forms of a Miner and Sailor."[4] The resulting sculptures, some of the earliest she carved in marble, were praised by critics who viewed the pieces in person, saw photographs, or received reports from Rome on their progress. A reviewer in the *New-York Times* noted the detail and accuracy of the sculptures while disparagingly commenting upon the perceived capabilities of female artists: "In the ideal refinement of the treatment you recognize a woman's thought and a woman's eye; but in the laborious, earnest accuracy striven for throughout, a sense appears of the supreme value of defined and logical expression which the common, and, as we heretically believe, the correct opinion of sages and scholars, refuses to the daughters of Eve."[5] The reviewer praised *Industry* and *Commerce* as patriotic and symbolic of American work ethic, writing, "The whole spirit of American labor, honest, fearless, young, high-spirited yet manly, dignified, respectful and self-respecting, speaks in these stately and graceful figures." As this review illuminates, *Industry* and *Commerce* are steeped in ideas about labor that come from a moment when the nature of work in America was radically shifting from skilled craftsmanship to industrial toil, with a seismic impact on environments and workers. These two sculptures project an idealization of the workman that ignores the actual conditions and environmental changes wrought by international commerce and the growing American mining industry.

The subjects of *Industry* and *Commerce* are representative of the trades that secured the wealth of Stebbins's patron. Born in Paris to a wealthy Jewish family of merchant bankers, Heckscher emigrated from Hamburg to the US in 1829 following a worldwide financial crash.[6] Art historian Melissa L. Gustin has speculated that

Heckscher may have been familiar with the Stebbins family and possibly met Emma Stebbins when he first arrived in New York City and she was a young debutante.[7] Heckscher and Stebbins's brother, Henry G. Stebbins, also served on the board of directors of the Dauphin and Susquehanna Coal Company and the Pequa Railroad and Improvement Company in the 1850s, providing another family connection.[8] Under the auspices of Ch. A & E. Heckscher Company in New York City, Charles August and his younger brother Edward Heckscher invested in the trade of silver from Mexico, imported tea, gunpowder, and silk from Canton (China), and exported the products of enslaved labor in the US and Caribbean, including tobacco, sugar, and cotton. The consumption and trade of these products had a devastating impact on local environments and Indigenous peoples.[9] None of these concerns are captured within the figure of *Commerce*, which does not include any details related to the goods that the sailor would have helped transport. Indeed, while at least one contemporary review described the sailor as leaning on a bulwark (or rail) of a ship, he may also be posed against a bollard (or mooring post) to which a ship is tied.[10] If it is the latter, the sailor would be positioned on the docks—not even on the ship itself—either preparing to depart or having recently arrived in port.

Through the connections of his father-in-law, John G. Coster, Heckscher next entered the coal mining industry, producing, marketing, and transporting anthracite coal from eastern Pennsylvania through the benevolently named Forest Improvement Company (FIC), which he founded in 1837. FIC entered the mining industry at a moment when surface coal was becoming scarce. Initially, the abundance of coal in Schuylkill County encouraged individual enterprise as miners could obtain coal with minimal investment in equipment or infrastructure. The author of an 1836 article in the *North American Review* agreed, "the Schuylkill region seems to have been marked by nature for individual enterprise."[11] According to one mining prospectus, "the coal is immediately perceived breaking out today in the roads and ravines in beds of streams and on the sides and summits of the mountains."[12] A lithograph of a coal mine at Mauch Chunk, Pennsylvania, by George Lehman, which shows miners excavating exposed coal from the side of a hill, seems to support this claim (fig. 1). The geological complexity of anthracite coal deposits, however, meant that once coal veins close to the surface were depleted, miners found it difficult to accurately predict the veins' passage through the earth. As demand for anthracite coal increased, the amount

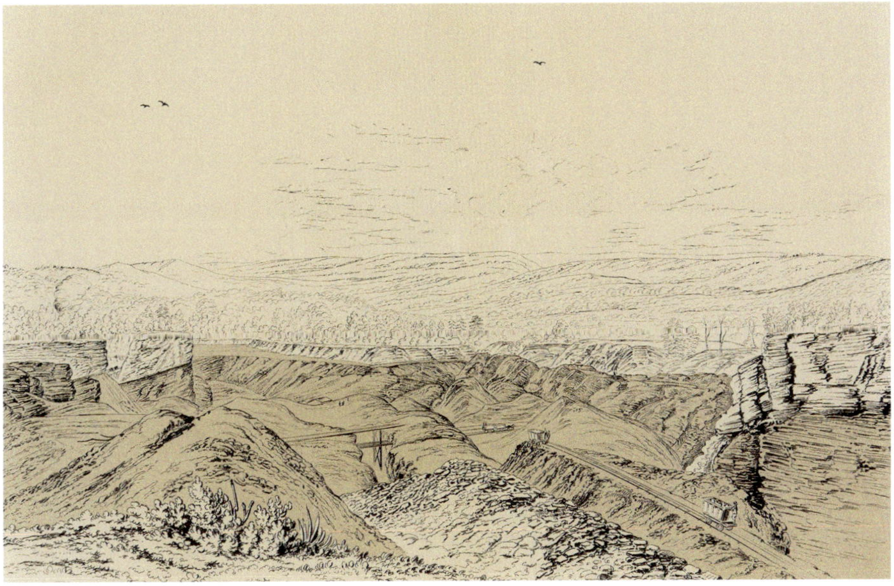

FIG. 2 William Johnston (Scottish, 1802–1888) and Alexander Keith Johnston (Scottish, 1804–1871), after George Lehman (American, ca. 1800–1870), *Part of Summit Mine of Lehigh County, Looking West.* From Henry Darwin Rogers, *The Geology of Pennsylvania: A Government Survey*, vol. 1 (Philadelphia: J. B. Lippincott, 1858).

Boston Athenaeum, MA

of coal shipped rose from 6,500 to 79,973 tons a year between 1825 and 1829.[13] Despite declarations of plentitude, anthracite coal was becoming harder to obtain by the 1830s. Illustrations in Henry Darwin Rogers's *The Geology of Pennsylvania: A Government Survey* show an area transformed by the mining industry, as carts traverse a scarred landscape (fig. 2). One 1848 publication on anthracite mining noted that mines "stripped the mountains of their gaudy foliage, and levelled the venerable and sturdy forest trees to the earth."[14]

Coal mining had a profound impact on local environments, public health, and miner safety. Waste was inherent to the mining system. Only 34 percent of the coal discovered within a vein was sent to market: miners had to leave pillars of coal behind to support the roofs of the mines, and coal was lost in the refinement process. Many mines employed children as young as eight to sort and process coal by hand.[15] These breaker boys, who worked in colliery breakers, or coal processing plants, discarded small pieces of coal, which washed into streams and local watersheds, creating acidic water conditions. Pumping ground water from deep mines dried up wells, and sinkholes formed when miners excavated coal from pillars and the ground above collapsed. The human costs of anthracite mining in Pennsylvania were also high. Scholars have estimated the death rate for miners at mid-century was 1 in 130 a year.

Improvement companies like FIC were a new form of enterprise in Schuylkill County. FIC purchased land and opened and prepared coal mines by sinking shaft mines, erecting breakers, and financing the development of mining regions. It also underwrote capital expenditures and constructed lateral railroads to transport coal to urban centers like Philadelphia. An 1846 petition criticized this corporate expansion and accused FIC of being a "monopoly highly injurious to the individual enterprises of the citizens of [Schuylkill] County."[16] By 1860, when Stebbins completed her sculptures, FIC's property extended over fifteen thousand acres and included the five largest, most productive collieries in the region.[17] As the founder and president of FIC, Heckscher's influence and land holdings in the region were so immense that he named the seat of his Pennsylvania anthracite empire "Heckscherville."[18]

Heckscher commissioned *Industry* and *Commerce* from Stebbins at a key moment of shifting perceptions of work from skilled craftsmanship to industrial labor in the United States. As art historian Melissa Dabakis has explained, tensions arose in attempts to reconcile this "friction between pride in work and estrangement from the satisfaction of productive toil."[19] As corporate monopolies like FIC amassed greater control of anthracite coal mining in the mid-nineteenth century, wage laborers did not reap the success of their efforts and industry leaders (who benefited disproportionally from the achievements of their businesses) did not engage in the actual work. While Stebbins's *Industry* and *Commerce* represent the sectors through which Heckscher made his fortune (that is, mining and trade, respectively), they also depict work that Heckscher did not himself undertake. Heckscher was not alone in his conceptualization of the sources of his wealth. According to Dabakis, the elite social class in the nineteenth century co-opted the Jeffersonian ideology of productive labor and good work ethic to contain and manage the lives of working people. This philosophy was sometimes expressed through "a sanitized and, at times, allegorical account of work," which the "middle-class and elite patronage demanded."[20]

The disparities between Heckscher and his mine employees were especially stark in the years just after Stebbins completed *Industry* and *Commerce*. At this time, miners in Schuylkill County were organizing to obtain higher wages and greater safety protections. Almost half the miners in Schuylkill County were Irish immigrants and they, along with German American farmers in the region, predominantly voted for the

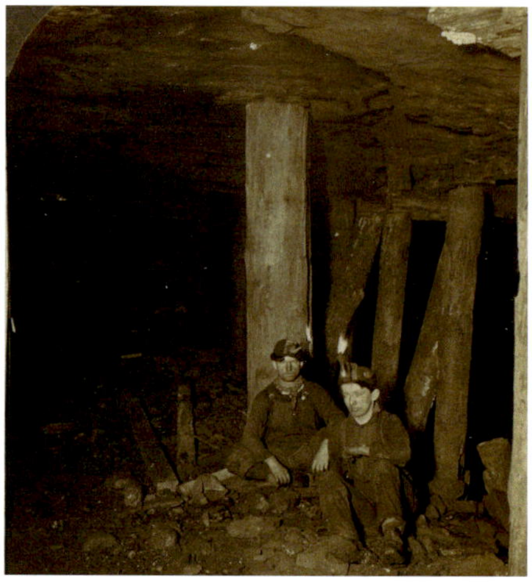

FIG. 3 Benneville Lloyd Singley (American, 1864–1938), *Abandoned Mine Showing How Prop Timber Is Used to Support Roofs of Tunnels, Scranton, Pa., U.S.A.*, 1905 (detail). Albumen print (stereograph), 3 9/16 × 7 1/16 in. (9.1 × 17.9 cm).

The Miriam and Ira D. Wallach Division of Art, Prints and Photographs: Photography Collection, The New York Public Library, New York, NY

Democratic Party, in favor of local autonomy. Industry leaders like Heckscher characterized labor unions as Civil War draft resistance in order to convince the federal government to send an army to squash unrest and protest in the region. Industrialists were therefore able to recharacterize strikes as treason.[21] Heckscher remarked at the conclusion of his presidency of FIC in 1865, "I have always said . . . that the great majority of laboring men in Schuylkill County, nay in all the mining districts are well-disposed, orderly, reasonable, and desirous to promote the true interests of themselves and their families."[22] He asserted, however, that this well-disposed majority had "repeatedly allowed itself to be over-awed and directed by the sinister suggestions and fatal advice of a designing criminal minority," who were engaged in union activity.[23]

The consumption and production of coal link the two figures of *Industry* and *Commerce*, as international trade was reliant on steamships that burned the nonrenewable energy source. Stebbins and the sculptures themselves would have traveled to the United States from Rome on a steamship, so coal also powered their transportation and eventual critical reception, which was positive. *Industry* and *Commerce*, of course, do not reference the political and economic tension, environmental degradation, and bodily harm intertwined with the mining of coal. They instead romanticize contemporary notions of labor, depicting bodies at rest, rather than bodies at toil. *Industry*, for example, stands in classical contrapposto with his left hand on an outcropping of rock and his right hand holding a pick against his shoulder. His shirt is open low on his chest and his sleeves are rolled up, alluding to the physical exertion

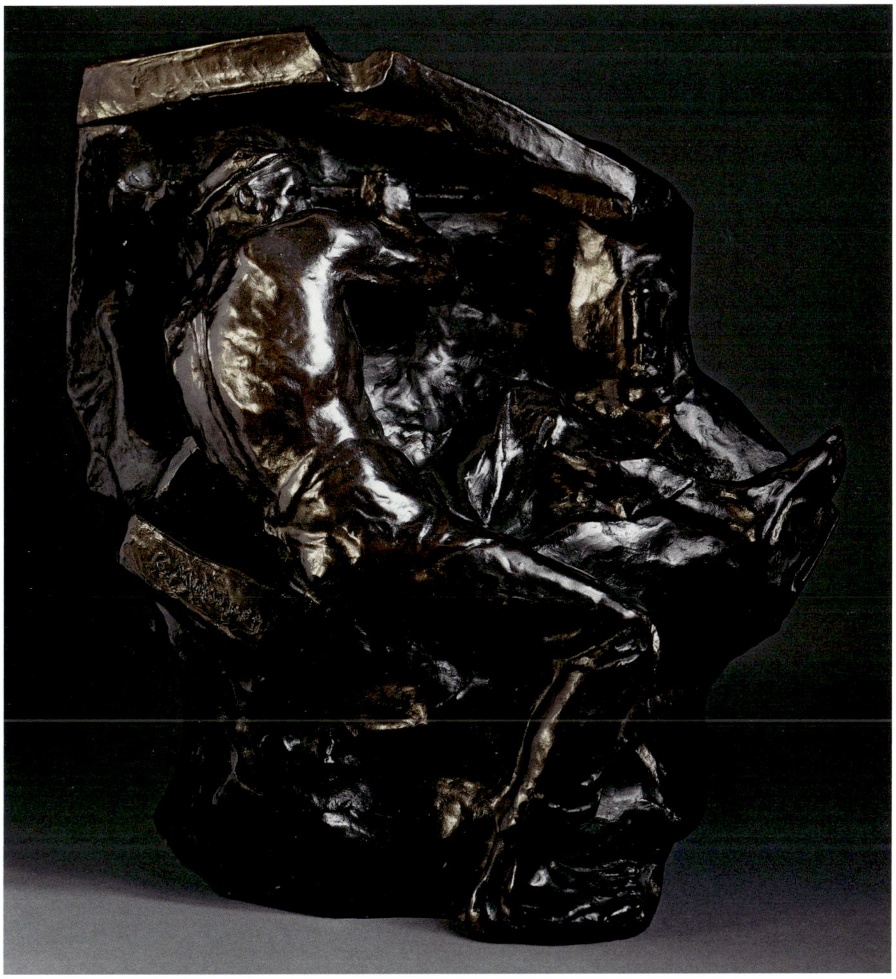

FIG. 4 Constantin-Émile Meunier (Belgian, 1831–1905), *Miner at the Vein*, ca. 1892. Bronze, 19 × 17½ × 13⅜ in. (48.3 × 44.5 × 34 cm).

Los Angeles County Museum of Art, CA, Gift of the Arnhold Family, M.82.211

of his work that is not otherwise represented. The statue stands in contrast to contemporary photographs of miners at rest (see fig. 3) that emphasize their precarious position within the anthracite mines, and later social realist sculptures by artists like Constantin-Émile Meunier, whose bronze *Miner at the Vein* (fig. 4) contorts within a tight, precarious, underground space as he pries at a vein of coal. Indeed, the material of Stebbins's *Industry*, which one critic described as "an unusually pure block of the whitest marble," does not accurately depict the dust-covered bodies of actual miners, presenting instead a sanitized depiction of the laborer removed from his working environment.[24] In her selection of smooth, refined marble, Stebbins was working within the artistic conventions and preferences of her day. As Charmaine Nelson has argued, however, uncolored, nineteenth-century marble sculptures uphold a cultural ideal of a racially pure and chaste whiteness divorced from "context, environment, and condition."[25] Despite Stebbins's sanitized view of mining, contemporary critics still found that *Industry* adhered to their romantic understanding of American labor. One writer for the *Home Journal* complimented the "natural" and "well-chosen" attitude of the sculpture and remarked that "it represents the workman in his usual dress, as he is daily seen at the entrance of the vast coal caves of Pennsylvania."[26] The *Home Journal* celebrated *Industry* as a palatable "type," heralding Stebbins as the "Priestess of the Mines."[27]

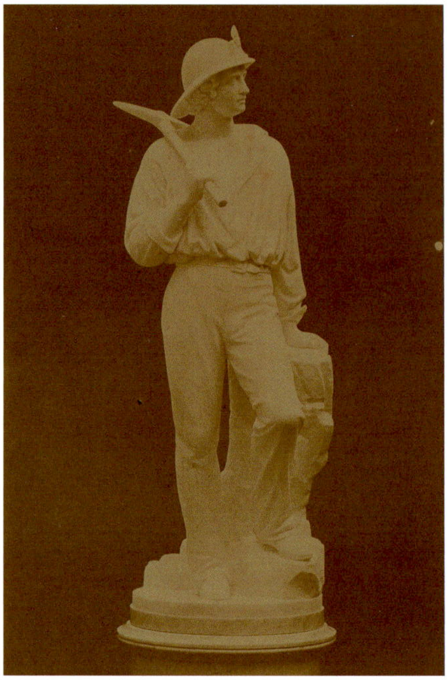

FIG. 5 Emma Stebbins (American, 1815–1882), *Industry*, 1860. Marble, 28⅞ × 10 × 10½ in. (73.3 × 25.4 × 26.7 cm). Photograph from the Emma Stebbins scrapbook, 1858–82.

Archives of American Art, Smithsonian Institution, Washington, DC

Industry wears a hat with a lamp, likely an oil-wick lamp. Although perhaps primarily intended to identify the laborer as a miner, this addition also gestures towards his actual working conditions underground. The oil-wick cap lamp, a teapot-style apparatus introduced in the 1850s, emitted light from a lit wick at the top of its spout. While these lamps burned brighter, lasted longer, and were easier to carry and wear on a hat than candles, they also were smokier and their open flames were more susceptible to igniting flammable gases present in a mine, at times creating deadly explosions.[28] A photograph of *Industry* in the Emma Stebbins scrapbook shows that the cap originally had a protruding marble flame that, along with one point of the pickax, had likely broken off prior to the sculpture's donation to The Heckscher Museum of Art in the 1920s (fig. 5).[29] This damage to *Industry* suggests it was handled, frequently moved, or perhaps in a high-traffic area in the Heckscher home, following its public exhibition. The base of the sculpture once featured a brass knob that would have allowed viewers to rotate the artwork in order to admire it from multiple angles.

Stebbins modeled *Industry* and *Commerce* after classical sculptures she likely encountered in the Vatican Museums in Rome. *Industry* closely follows the contrapposto of the Doryphoros type (see fig. 6), while *Commerce* copies the pose of the Leaning Satyr type (see fig. 7). As Gustin has argued, by quoting these classical prototypes, "Stebbins elevated the working-class subjects, giving them a heroic, noble aura and sanitizing the danger, exhaustion, and poverty actual laborers faced in order to make them fit for consideration as fine art."[30] When displayed in Heckscher's home, these sculptures projected Heckscher's possession of the bodies that earned him his fortune. While they depict a miner and sailor specifically, their titles denote that they also embody larger ideas about industry and commerce. These allegorical and classical references would have delighted and reinforced the privilege of the cultured and well traveled who would have recognized their citations.

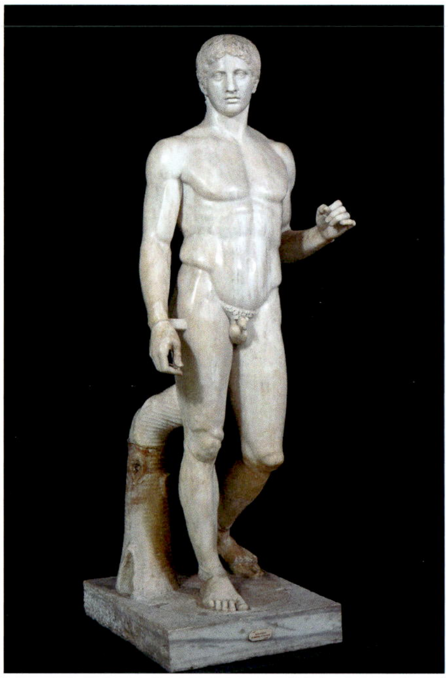

FIG. 6 Doryphoros (Spear-Bearer), first century BCE–first century CE. Roman copy of a Greek bronze statue by Polykleitos (fifth century BCE). Marble, H. 6 ft. 11 in. (2.12 m).

Museo Archaeologico Nazionale, Naples, 6011

In its classically inspired pose, *Industry* recalls another sculpture associated with mining by one of Stebbins's contemporaries: *California* by Hiram Powers (fig. 8).[31] Conceived in the early years of the 1850s and carved in 1858, around the same time that Stebbins created *Industry* and *Commerce*, *California* symbolizes the state's

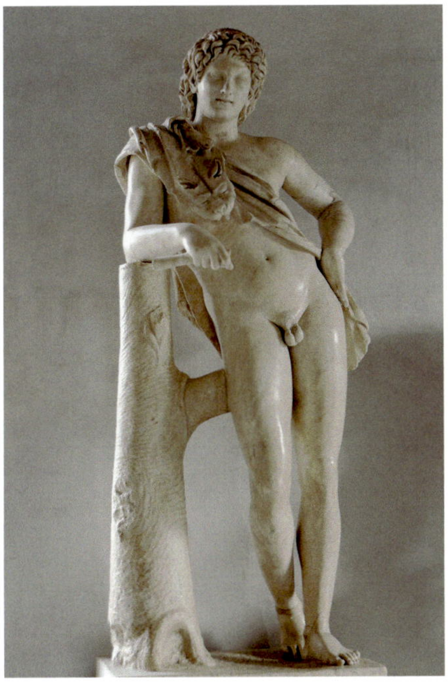

FIG. 7 Leaning Satyr, ca. 117–138 CE. Roman copy of a Greek statue by Praxiteles (fourth century BCE). Marble, H. 67 in. (170 cm).

Musei Capitolini, Rome, MC0739

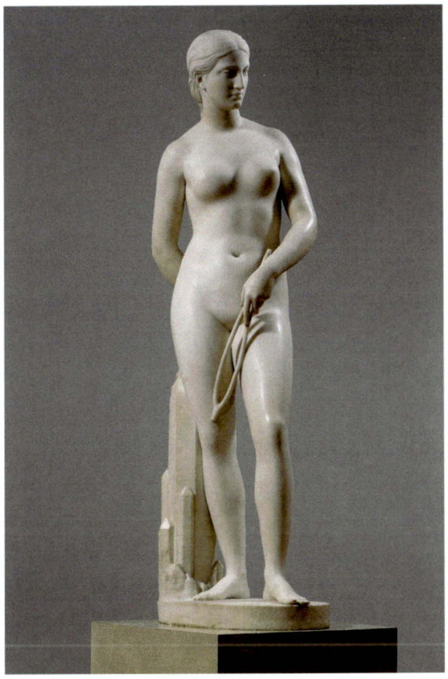

FIG. 8 Hiram Powers (American, 1805–1873), *California*, 1850–55, carved 1858. Marble, 71 × 18¼ × 24¾ in. (180.3 × 46.4 × 62.9 cm).

The Metropolitan Museum of Art, New York, NY, Gift of William Backhouse Astor, 1872, 72.3

famous gold rush. This allegorical, nude female figure suggestively holds between her thighs a divining rod (or miner's wand) believed to help identify precious metals like gold in the earth. She leans against an outcropping of oversized, faceted quartz, among which gold deposits were sometimes found. The figure holds a thorned branch behind her back, symbolizing the perils of gold prospecting. Art historian Christine Garnier has described Powers's *California* as a contested, denuded body that embodies the financial, social, and environmental realities of the mining district in central California, a site of speculation, risk, and ecological devastation.[32] Stebbins corresponded with Powers when both artists were in Italy. The familiarity between the two sculptors is demonstrated by an 1860 letter to him, in which she asked to borrow "some of the tools of your invention for working on plaster."[33] Stebbins, significantly, however, chose not to portray *Industry* and *Commerce* as nude, female allegorical figures, nor did she intend the sculptures to project a moralizing message about greed and the dangers of pursuing wealth. Instead, Stebbins's two male figures, while idealized, are clothed in contemporary dress in a nod to actual miners and sailors. A photograph of a clay maquette in the Emma Stebbins scrapbook demonstrates that she had conceived of her own California gold miner (pl. 12). In this sculpture, the miner is dressed similarly to *Industry* and also leans against a rock outcropping and holds a pickax. This figure is bearded and more masculine in his build and features than is *Industry*, however, as if Stebbins had intended to present a more rugged embodiment of Manifest Destiny in this character of the American West. Unlike Powers's *California*, Stebbins's sculptures of miners heroize her subjects without conveying any warning about the folly and risk inherent in their pursuit of valuable metals and fuel.

For the contemporary dress and poses of *Industry* and *Commerce*, Stebbins may have looked to other visualizations of labor and the workingman. The figures' clothing and stances are very similar to the frontispiece portrait of the author Walt Whitman from the first edition of his *Leaves of Grass* (1855) (fig. 9). In the portrait, Whitman takes on the persona of a day laborer or common man, wearing workingman's trousers, a shirt unbuttoned to reveal an undershirt, and a hat cocked to one side.[34] A catalogue of a posthumous sale of Cushman's belongings lists a "LARGE photograph of Walt Whitman. Framed," suggesting that Cushman and Stebbins were admirers of the author.[35] In *Leaves of Grass*, Whitman, like Stebbins in her sculptures, romanticized notions of work, praising both traditional craft and industrialized labor as moral and noble.

Industry and *Commerce* acknowledge labor not just through their subjects, but in the very materiality of the sculptures themselves, as attested to by the *New-York Times* review that described them as "laborious."[36] *Industry*, in particular, can be viewed as a declaration of Stebbins's own labor in transforming the marble block into a refined, finished piece. The figure leans upon a tall rock that we (as viewers) are meant to imagine as an impediment to, or perhaps the container of, the anthracite coal the miner seeks with the pickax slung over his shoulder. Unlike Stebbins's meticulous delineation of the miner's satiny skin and clothing, she left toolmarks on the rock and base. Stebbins prominently signed her name directly underneath the rock, firmly declaring her authorship. The juxtaposition of the smoothly and roughly worked surfaces calls attention to the mechanical process by which she transformed a rough marble block into a classically inspired figure. The statue therefore invites viewers to associate the act of mining coal with that of carving marble. Indeed, one contemporary critic noted this connection, writing that the figure's left hand rests "with the carelessness of manly strength upon a block of marble, drilled and hewn in the manner of a mass of coal."[37]

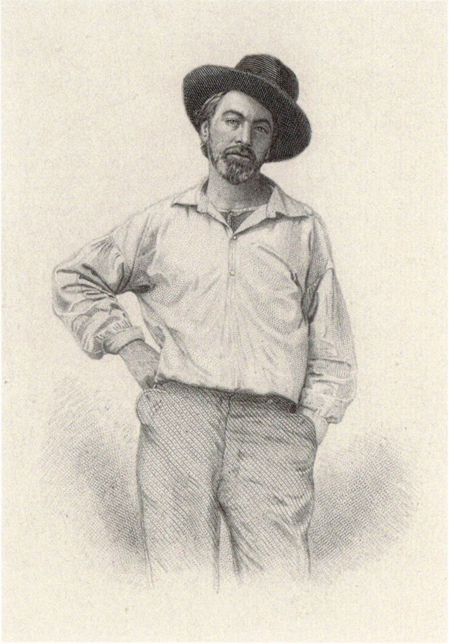

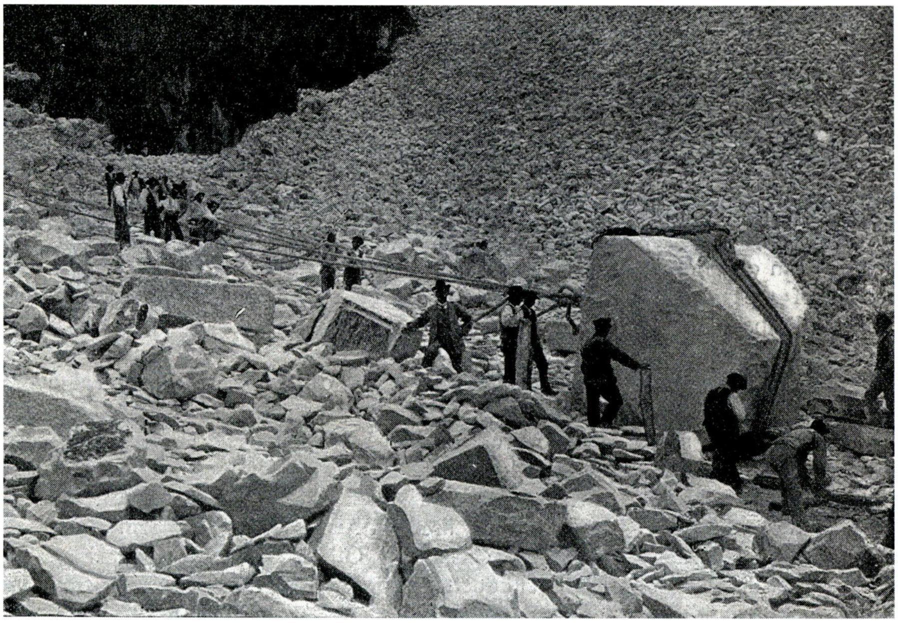

Left: FIG. 9 Samuel Hollyer (American, b. England, 1826–1919), *Walt Whitman*, 1854 (detail). From Walt Whitman, *Leaves of Grass* (self-published, 1855), frontispiece. Steel engraving, 8½ × 6¼ in. (21.6 × 15.9 cm).

Library of Congress, Washington, DC

Right: FIG. 10 *Lowering a Block from High to Low Level*, ca. 1903. From E. St. John Hart, "A Marble World," *Pearson's Magazine* 9, no. 2 (February 1903): 142.

Stebbins, notably, often refused assistance in her studio in order to control the creation of her marble sculptures from initial idea to finished product, and to thwart the questioning of artistic authorship that plagued her professional rival, Harriet Hosmer. Like the majority of male sculptors in Rome, Hosmer relied on the assistance of Italian stone carvers, who carved larger works from the artist's preliminary clay sketches. Unlike her male counterparts, however, Hosmer was scrutinized for this practice.[38] To avoid being subjected to similar accusations, Stebbins insisted on carving most of her marble sculptures herself, which may be why she only produced a few sculptures larger than tabletop size. She likely learned to carve marble from the British sculptor John Gibson, who apprenticed as a stone carver in Liverpool early in his career and with whom she studied after arriving in Rome.[39] In 1864, Cushman complained about the toll that carving took upon Stebbins's body: "That she should be classed among those who would be believed to have their work done for them makes her too miserable . . . and to struggle along without the material help which all sculptors *must have* has become so entirely a necessity to her that she is assuming labor for which she has neither physical nor mental strength."[40] Many years of carving her own sculptures and inhaling marble dust aggravated Stebbins's lungs, causing recurring respiratory illness.[41]

Prolonged inhalation of marble dust also affected those workers who quarried the Carrara and Seravezza marble in Tuscany's Apuan Alps, which was used by Stebbins and her peers in Rome and elsewhere. Marble quarries in Italy had a profound socio-ecological impact on the region. Quarries predominantly relied on the labor of humans and animals to excavate and transport marble to local rail lines, as shown in a photograph published in a 1903 *Pearson's Magazine* article on the quarries entitled "A Marble World" (fig. 10). Explosives used to dislodge large quantities of marble from the quarries produced prodigious amounts of marble waste, filling the landscape with pulverized debris.[42] In "A Marble World," author E. St. John Hart explained, "the air is grey with marble dust."[43] Workers in sawmills labored twelve-hour days, breathing a fine marble dust that permeated the workplace, irritating eyes, noses, throats, and lungs, and causing bronchitis, emphysema, pleurisy, silicosis, and pneumoconiosis.[44] In his 1846 travelogue *Pictures from Italy*, Charles Dickens remarked upon the massive amount of labor required to extract and transport large blocks of marble from the famous Carrara quarries. Dickens struggled to reconcile the seductive surfaces of finished marble statues with the crushing work he witnessed: "Standing in one of the many studii of Carrara that afternoon . . . full of beautifully finished copies in marble, of almost every figure, group, bust, we know—it seemed, at first, so strange to me that those exquisite shapes, replete with grace, and thought, and delicate repose, should grow out of all this toil, and sweat, and torture!"[45]

Stebbins may not have directly connected her own labor to that of the quarrymen who excavated the material she later refined in her Roman studio—even though American sculptors in Rome were frequently involved in the assessment and procurement of marble and sometimes visited the quarries to make their selections.[46] Besides the roughly textured base and the stone outcropping upon which the miner leans and rests his left hand, *Industry* elides any direct reference to the strenuous work of excavating coal and marble or Stebbins's own efforts (and corresponding poor health) in shaping and manipulating the hard stone. The resulting figure, along with his mate, *Commerce*, projects a classicizing, clean, and domesticated visualization of labor for Stebbins's patron, reassuring Heckscher and his peers of their wealth while distancing them from the environmental and social exploitation upon which they built their success.

"BLESSED GIFT OF PURE AND WHOLESOME WATER": THE *BETHESDA FOUNTAIN*

While Stebbins both explored and elided issues of extraction and labor in *Industry* and *Commerce*, she harnessed symbolism to project ideas about water and public health in her design and creation of the *Bethesda Fountain* in New York's Central Park. Stebbins's best-known and largest sculpture, the landmark anchors a sprawling terrace at 72nd Street. At the fountain's apex, the *Angel of the Waters*, a robed angel with raised wings, alights on a stone spouting cascading water. Inspired by a biblical passage from the Gospel of John (5:2–9) that describes an angel blessing the Pool of Bethesda in Jerusalem and giving it healing powers, Stebbins's angel holds a lily (symbolizing purity) in one hand, while stretching out the other to bless the water below. In the fountain's lower register, four cherubs representing *Temperance, Purity, Health and Peace* stand in front of tall bulrushes. Through these figures, Stebbins promoted temperance and commemorated the newly constructed Croton Aqueduct, which supplied clean drinking water to the city. This celebration of health and healing through potable water was particularly poignant to Stebbins at the time that the fountain was cast and installed, as she struggled with her own ailments and Cushman's diagnosis of breast cancer.

Proposed in the early to mid-nineteenth century when the population of New York City was quadrupling, Central Park was envisioned as a place for recreation and as a retreat from the noise and chaos of the city. Frederick Law Olmstead and Calvert Vaux designed a natural landscape composed of meandering pathways and picturesque vistas.[47] The city's Common Council selected the area between 59th and 106th Streets and 5th and 8th Avenues as the site for the park in part because a thirty-five-acre reservoir for the Croton Aqueduct would be in its geographical center, as illustrated in an 1863 map of the park (fig. 11). It is notable that the construction of Central Park displaced the inhabitants of the site, including settlements of Irish immigrants and the thriving, free Black community of Seneca Village. All were evicted under eminent domain.[48]

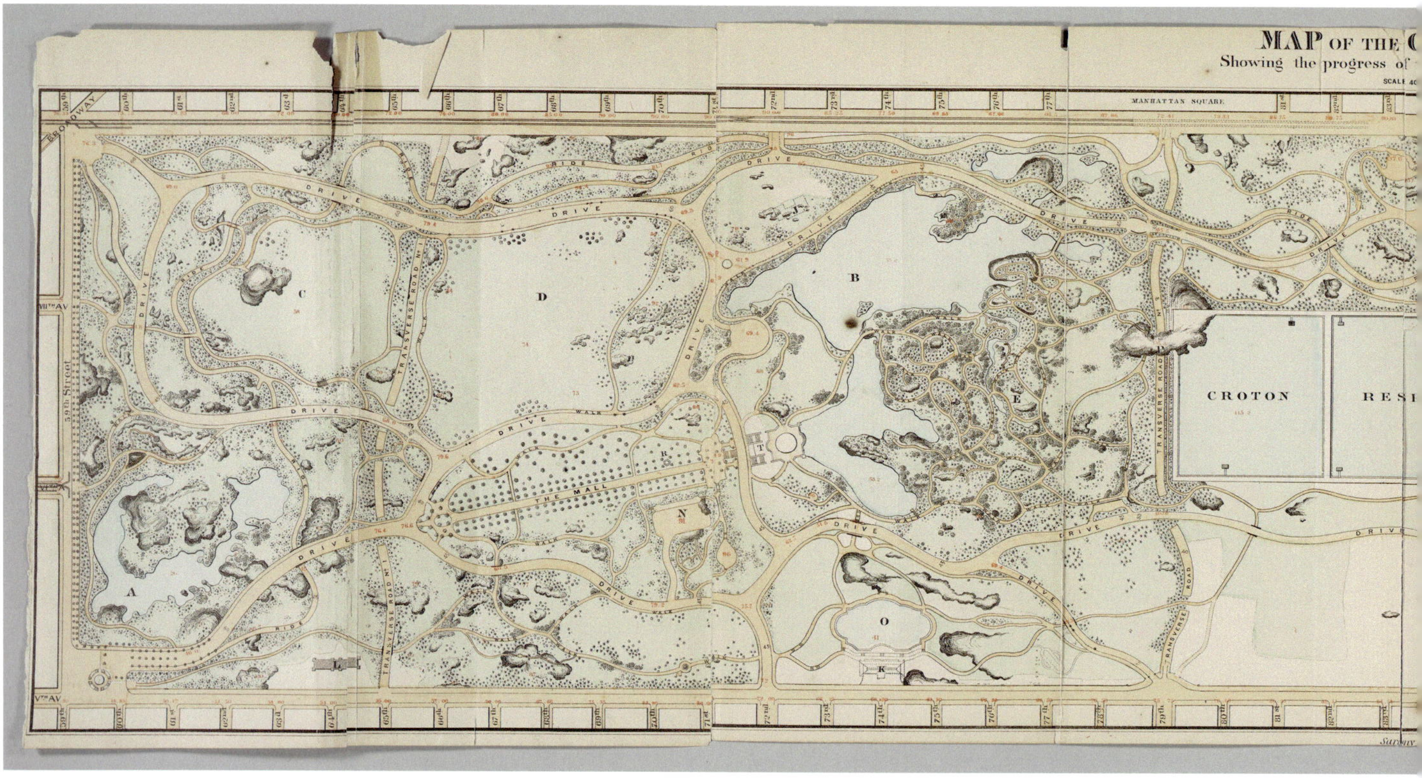

According to Cushman, Stebbins submitted sketches for a fountain sculpture for the new Central Park in 1861, only a few months after the critical success of her public exhibition of *Industry* and *Commerce*.[49] At that time, Stebbins's brother Henry G. Stebbins, a successful banker and stockbroker, was chairman of Central Park's Committee on Statuary, Fountains, and Architectural Structures. A supporter of Stebbins's artistic career, he undoubtedly lobbied for the commission of her fountain and other park sculptures that were never realized.[50] Even with this familial support, the committee did not officially award Stebbins the commission until the fall of 1863.[51]

Stebbins created these drawings for the fountain at the same time that Vaux, along with designer Jacob Wrey Mould, conceived of an ornate terrace with a vaulted arcade, through which pedestrians could walk under the 72nd Street carriage path to a skating and boating pond.[52] Despite his overall emphasis on natural features in the park, Vaux included sculptural ornamentation within his design, providing clear, thematic direction by recommending that sculptures of the four seasons be installed on the north stairs and allegories of science and art at the pond.[53] Even though Stebbins was not officially contracted by the commission, a rendering of her fountain sculpture was included in a lithograph of the terrace and pond that accompanied the Park Commissioners' *Sixth Annual Report* in 1863 (fig. 12). In this lithograph, the *Angel of the Waters* faces the pond instead of the steps (as it was ultimately oriented), perhaps for dramatic effect. Images preserved in the Emma Stebbins scrapbook show studies of the four seasons "ordered by the Park Commissioners," suggesting that the commissioners intended to have Stebbins complete additional sculptures for the terrace that were ultimately never realized (pl. 28).[54] For the lower terrace fountain, Vaux did not mention the biblical passage that inspired the *Bethesda Fountain* and instead vaguely noted that the planned decoration was intended to express "both earnestly and playfully the idea of that central spirit of 'Love' that is forever active, and forever bringing youth and age, day and night, into harmonious accord."[55] In a January 1862

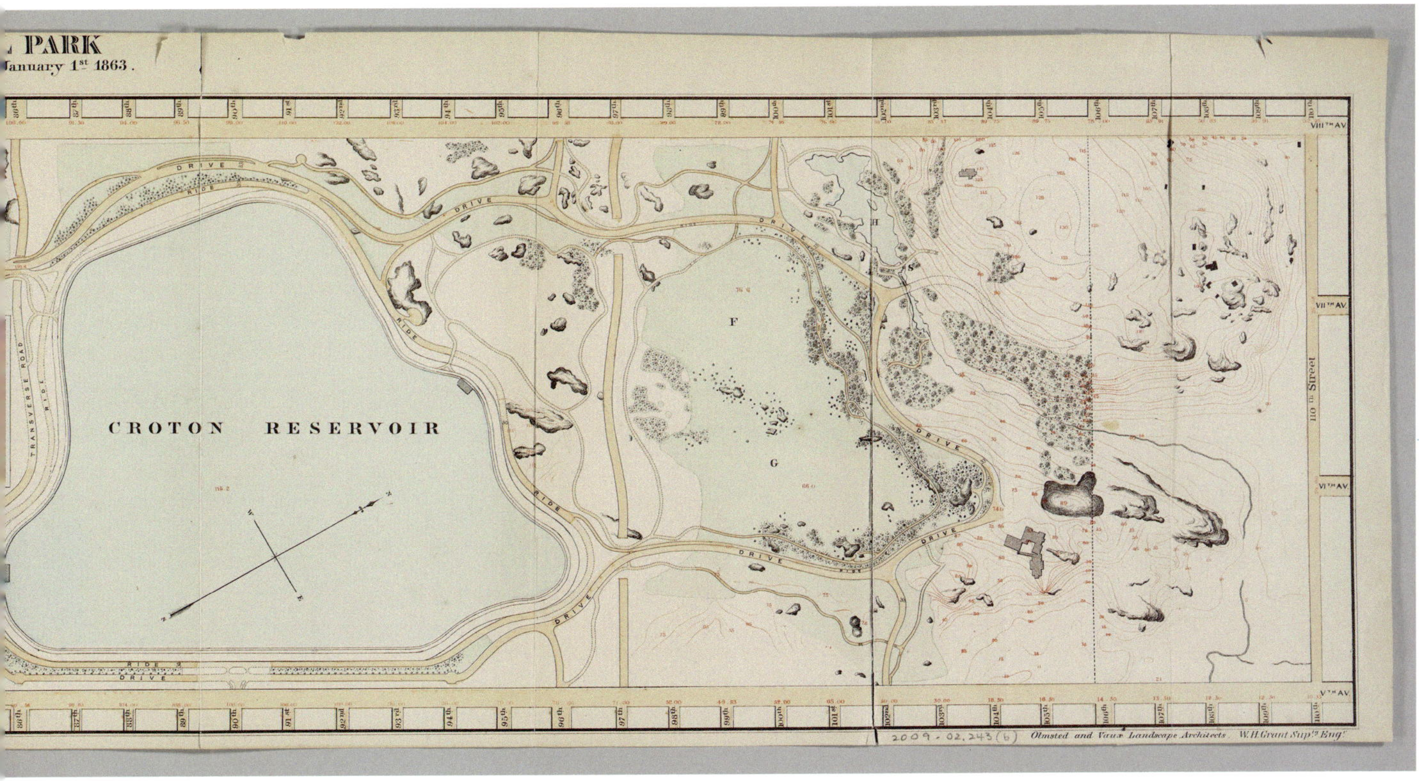

FIG. 11 Sarony, Major, and Knapp, *Map of the Central Park Showing the Progress of the Work Up to January 1st, 1863*, 1863. From *Sixth Annual Report of the Board of Commissioners of the Central Park* (New York: Wm. C. Bryant, 1863). Map, 7⅞ × 34⅝ in. (20 × 88 cm).

Seymour B. Durst Old York Library, Avery Architectural & Fine Arts Library, Columbia University, New York, NY

letter, Stebbins described the fountain subject to Powers as "the descent of the Angel to trouble the waters for healing—the scripture legend of the Pool of Bethesda," suggesting that she was the one who conceived of the design and theme.[56]

Large-scale fountain sculptures were rare in the United States at the time of Stebbins's commission. She would have been familiar with the many fountain sculptures in Rome, however, and Hosmer designed several fountains. At the same time that Stebbins was working on the *Bethesda Fountain*, Hosmer was working on *Fountain of the Siren* for the London home of her friend and patron Lady Marian Alford. Hosmer installed a copy of the fountain in her studio in Rome, where Stebbins likely saw it. In a photograph cheekily titled *Hosmer and Her Men*, Hosmer poses with the completed fountain and her workmen (fig. 13).[57] Over seven feet high, the fountain is topped by a siren holding a reed pipe and poised over a series of shells. On the pedestal below, three putti ride animated dolphins. This combination of an elevated figure with a lower register of putti is similar to Stebbins's fountain design. The *Bethesda Fountain* also recalls another iconic sculpture in Rome, the bronze *Archangel Michael* by the Flemish sculptor Peter Anton von Verschaffelt, sited atop the Castel Sant'Angelo (see fig. 9 in Gustin's essay and fig. 7 in Stebbins's historical text in this volume). This statue of Saint Michael is also tied to public health, since Pope Gregory I envisioned the archangel atop this castel, or fortress, sheathing his sword to end the terrible plague that was decimating the city in 590 CE.[58] While Saint Michael's arm is raised, as opposed to the lowered arms of the *Angel of the Waters*, the wing placement of both statues is similar. Stebbins certainly would have been aware of both Hosmer's fountain and the Saint Michael above Castel Sant'Angelo when she developed and refined her designs for the Central Park fountain.

Stebbins explicitly connected the symbolism of the *Bethesda Fountain* to the cleanliness and health of the city's new water system in the accompanying program for the unveiling of the fountain in 1873 (see fig. 6 in the introduction to this volume).

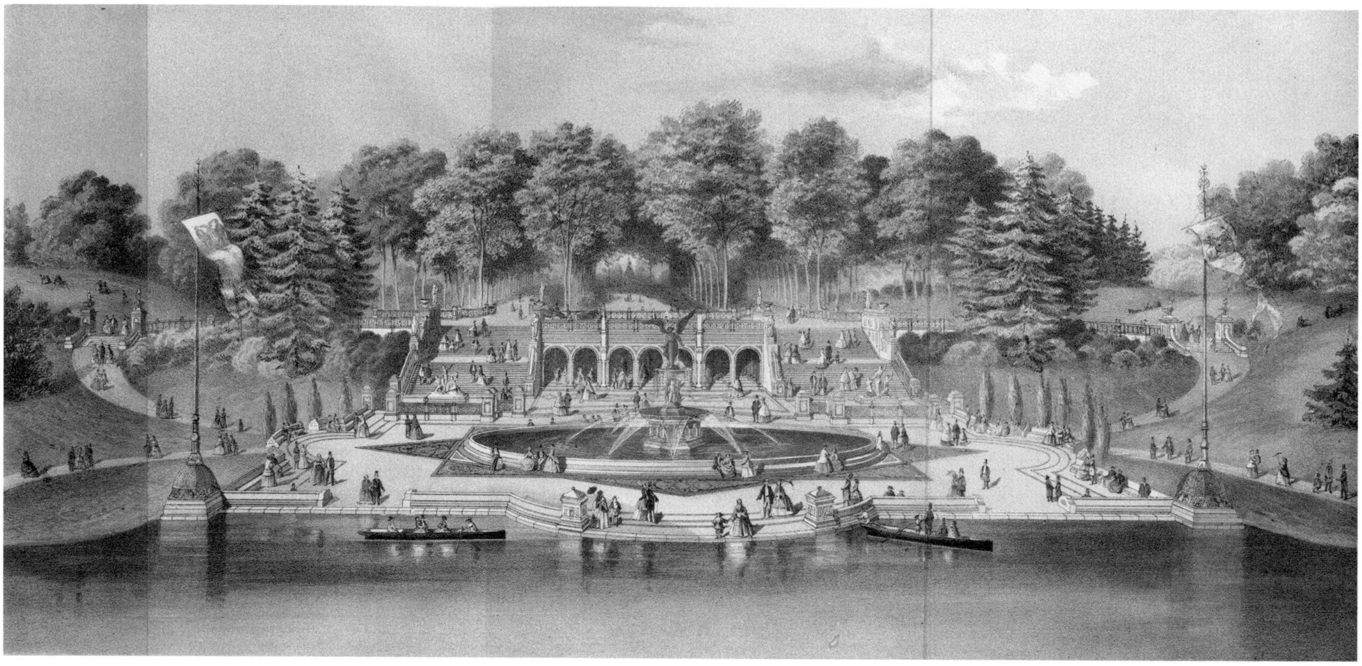

FIG. 12 Sarony, Major, and Knapp, *The Terrace*, ca. 1863. From *Sixth Annual Report of the Board of Commissioners of the Central Park* (New York: Wm. C. Bryant, 1863), frontispiece. Lithograph, 6¾ × 14 in. (17.2 × 35.6 cm).

Library of Congress, Washington, DC

> An angel descending to bless the water for healing, seems not inappropriate in connection with a fountain; for, although we have not the sad groups of blind, halt and withered waiting to be healed by the miraculous advent of the angel, we have no less healing, comfort and purification, freely sent to us through the blessed gift of pure and wholesome water, which to all the countless homes of this great city, comes like an angel visitant, not at stated seasons only, but day by day.[59]

Stebbins's description of the "blessed gift of pure and wholesome water" refers directly to the water brought to the city by the recently built Croton Aqueduct, the receiving reservoirs of which were close by in the park. Following a cholera outbreak in 1832, New York sought new ways to obtain clean water as the city's population increased and pollution contaminated local waterways. Members of the Stebbins family died of cholera in the 1830s, proving that even privilege and social standing could not protect a family from bad water.

In 1837, construction began on a massive engineering project to divert water from the Croton River in upstate New York to the city via an aqueduct. Water flowed from the Croton Dam, crossed the Harlem River via the High Bridge, and flowed into a receiving reservoir between 79th and 86th Streets and 6th and 7th Avenues, now the Great Lawn and Turtle Pond in Central Park. From the receiving reservoir, water ran to a distributing reservoir located where the New York Public Library and Bryant Park are today.[60] To celebrate the completion of the Croton Aqueduct in 1842, the new Croton Fountain in City Hall Park was turned on to much fanfare.[61] The fountain did not feature any sculpture, but instead relied on the sheer height and amount of issuing water to symbolize the strength and vitality of the Croton water supply (see fig. 14). Indeed, prior to the installation of Stebbins's artwork, the fountain on the Central Park terrace had no sculptural decoration, allowing viewers to focus on the abundance of the water supply instead of the form of the fountain (see fig. 15).

Studies of two unrealized sculptures that Stebbins prepared for the receiving and dispensing gates of the reservoir underscore Stebbins's familiarity with New York City's new water supply system and visualize the power and vitality of clean water

FIG. 13 *Hosmer and Her Men* [with *Fountain of the Siren* (1861)], ca. 1864–67. Albumen print, 9¼ × 8 in. (23.5 × 20.3 cm).

Harriet Goodhue Hosmer Papers, A162-74-2, Schlesinger Library, Harvard Radcliffe Institute, Harvard University, Cambridge, MA

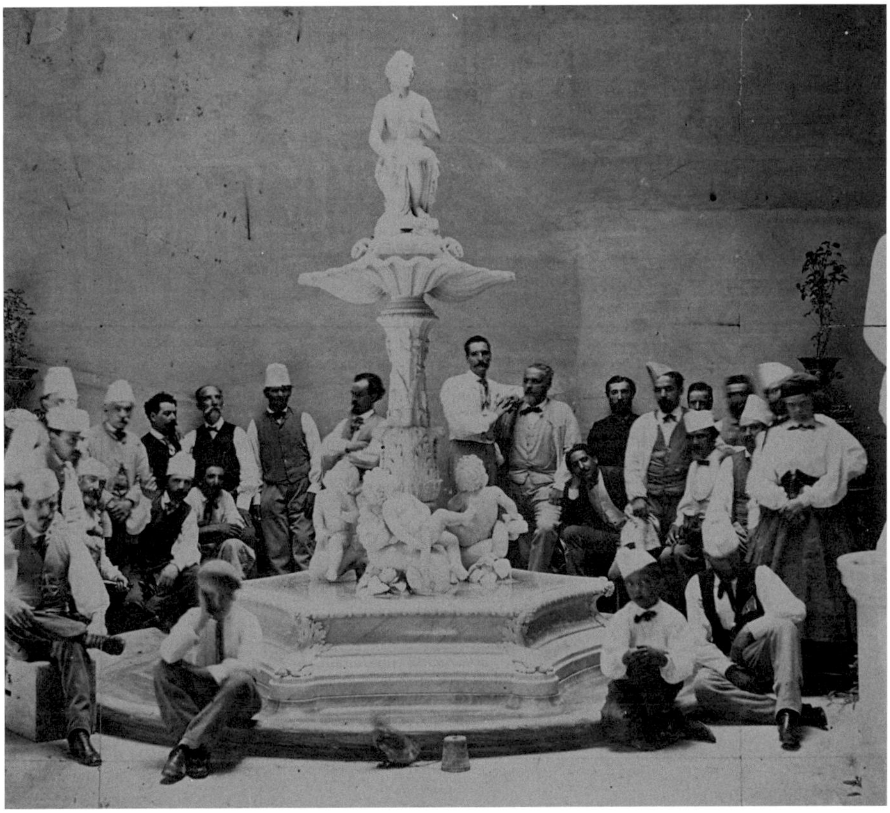

available to the city. The study for the receiving gates features the "Nymph of the River, with her attendant spirits of wood and water, putting aside the rushes in order to give the water freely to the city," according to an article by Anne Hampton Brewster (pls. 30, 31).[62] For the dispensing gate sculpture, an allegorical figure represents the "city, crowned, and bearing the emblems of commercial sovereignty, seated between her two rivers, the North and East" (pl. 32).[63] Together, these sculptures represent the power of the water tamed and disseminated via the Croton Aqueduct and Central Park reservoir.

Stebbins's *Angel of the Waters* and the allegorical figures of *Temperance, Purity, Health and Peace* encircling the lower register of the *Bethesda Fountain* are aligned with the temperance movement in the mid-nineteenth century, which believed that clean water was necessary to eradicate disease-causing filth and to provide an alternative to alcohol. In 1849, the first report of the American Medical Association's Committee on Public Hygiene emphatically stated, "the introduction of an abundant supply of water is so intimately connected with the health of a city, that the municipal authorities should rank this among the most important of their public duties."[64] Such a sentiment was visualized over two decades earlier by the artist Thomas Birch. In his *Virtue and Vice, Sobriety and Drunkenness*, a tree divides two families (fig. 16). On the right, a healthy, well-dressed couple strolls near picnickers and a child picking strawberries. The man gestures towards the Philadelphia Waterworks, providing the city with clean water from the Schuylkill River, in the background. To the left, a woman consoles a weeping child as a visibly drunk man carrying a liquor bottle faces a run-down tavern with revelers on the front porch. The right side of the tree flourishes, but its left side is bare and scraggly. The message is clear: clean water is the virtuous choice and public waterworks facilitate wholesome, moral values. At the completion of the Croton Aqueduct in 1842, Water Commission president Samuel Stevens explicitly echoed this sentiment, "The more means and conveniences for

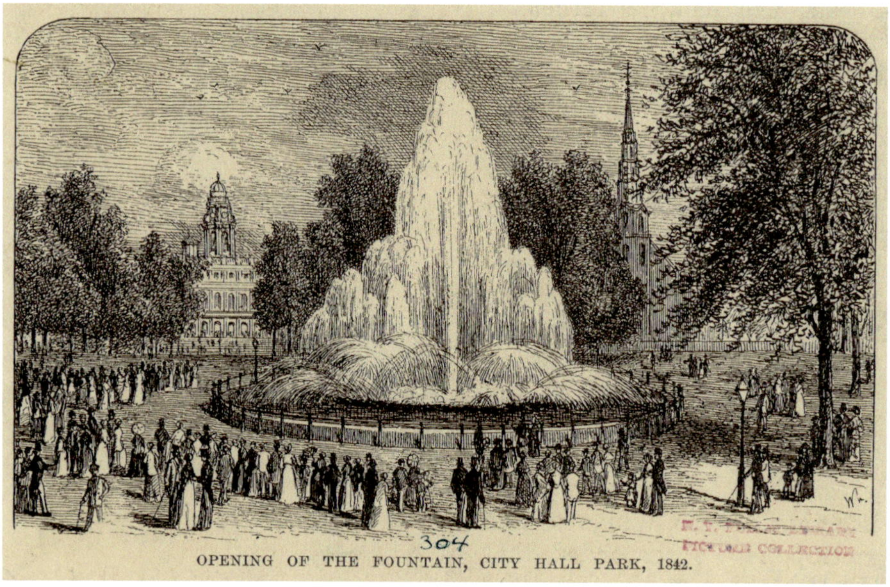

FIG. 14 *Opening of the Fountain, City Hall Park, 1842*. From James Grant Wilson, ed., *The Memorial History of the City of New-York; From Its First Settlement to the Year 1892*, vol. 3 (New-York History Co., New York, 1893). Line photoengraving, $3\frac{1}{2} \times 5\frac{3}{4}$ in. (8.9 × 14.6 cm).

The Miriam and Ira D. Wallach Division of Art, Prints and Photographs: Picture Collection, The New York Public Library, New York, NY

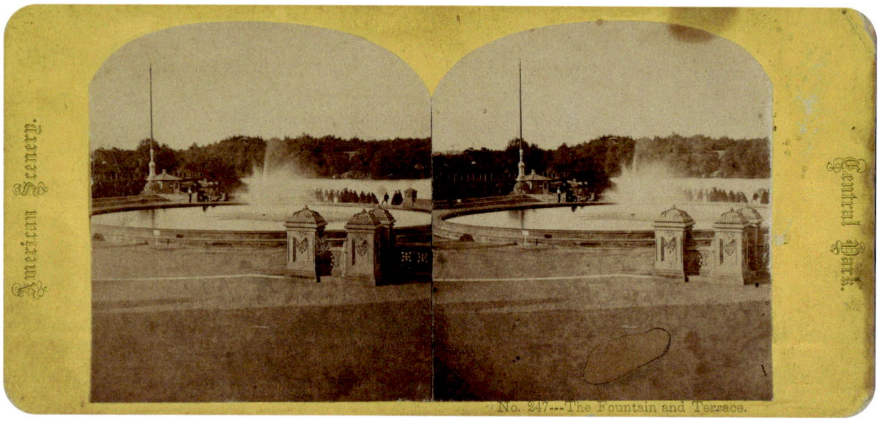

FIG. 15 George Stacy (American, 1831–1897), *The Fountain and Terrace*, ca. 1865. Albumen print (stereograph), $3\frac{1}{8} \times 6\frac{11}{16}$ in. (7.9 × 17 cm).

Library of Congress, Washington, DC

cleanliness that are furnished our population the more industrious and virtuous they will be."[65]

Notably, Stebbins's four cherubic figures representing *Temperance, Purity, Health and Peace* do not display characteristics that would identify them individually. One figure holds an upraised flower, another places a crooked finger on their chin in thought, one points upwards, and the final figure clutches at the vestments on their upper thigh. Notations in the Emma Stebbins scrapbook do not differentiate between the allegories. The final bronze figures, partially obscured by a wall of water streaming down around them, are inscrutable to public viewers. A critic in the *New-York Times* described them disparagingly as "hopelessly nondescript. They may signify Temperance, Purity, Health, and Peace, according to the programme, or any thing else that might be fished out of Lemprière [a popular reference book on classical mythology and history]."[66] In the *Bethesda Fountain*, *Temperance, Purity, Health and Peace* are interchangeable, and therefore interconnected, as Stebbins and others in the temperance movement understood them to be.

Stebbins would have additionally been supportive of the healing properties of clean water, as she and Cushman engaged in hydropathy (or cold-water treatment) for their various illnesses. In her published account of Cushman's life, Stebbins noted that the actress made her usual visit to Great Malvern (in England) "to get a little building up by water-treatment for the London season" of performances in 1854.[67] Malvern was considered the British capital of hydropathy, where patients were bathed and showered in cold water and wrapped in wet bandages.[68] According to Vincent Priessnitz, who established the practice of hydropathy in the 1820s, "cold water has a tendency to bring 'bad stuff' out of the system."[69] Like the temperance movement, hydrotherapy upheld clean living and abstinence from alcohol and other stimulants. While water treatments in Malvern and New York City enticed celebrities and intellectuals like Stebbins, Cushman, Charles Darwin, Dickens, Florence Nightingale, and Alfred, Lord Tennyson, it also drew detractors who considered it dangerous quackery.[70] Near the end of her life, Cushman expressed confidence in the benefits of water treatment; even if it did not cure her breast cancer, it alleviated her symptoms. She wrote, "I am satisfied that the treatment is doing me good, not perhaps, by any evidence in my special malady, but in my general condition. I am feeling generally much better."[71] Some have speculated that *Angel of the Waters* is, in fact, inspired by Cushman, so one wonders if Stebbins envisioned this figure of health and vitality, presiding over a continual cascade of clean water, as a type of antidote to the illnesses she and her wife struggled from.[72]

In selecting a female figure symbolic of clean water, Stebbins may have looked to one famous example connected to the water system of a nearby city: *Water Nymph and Bittern* (1809), by the Philadelphia ship carver and sculptor William Rush.[73] As recorded by painter John Lewis Krimmel in *Fourth of July in Centre Square* (fig. 17), this fountain sculpture was initially installed on the grounds of Centre Square, Philadelphia, the location of that city's first waterworks, which were designed by architect Benjamin Latrobe. Conceived to improve the health of Philadelphia residents and decrease the risk of yellow fever, which had devastated the city in the late eighteenth century, the system brought clean water from the Schuylkill River to the city's public fountains, homes, and businesses. Rush, who served as an active member of the Watering Committee, which oversaw the waterworks, designed a fountain sculpture to visually allude to the city's water source and emphasize its cleanliness and potability. The water fowl (identified by contemporary viewers as a bittern) held by the nymph and the willow branches that bound the figure's waist and hair were native to the Schuylkill.[74] The fountain water, issuing to a height of seventeen feet from the bird's upraised beak and bubbling from artfully arranged rocks at the base, also recalled the fast-moving, rocky river.[75] The Watering Committee moved *Water Nymph and Bittern* to the landscaped grounds surrounding the Fairmount Waterworks after

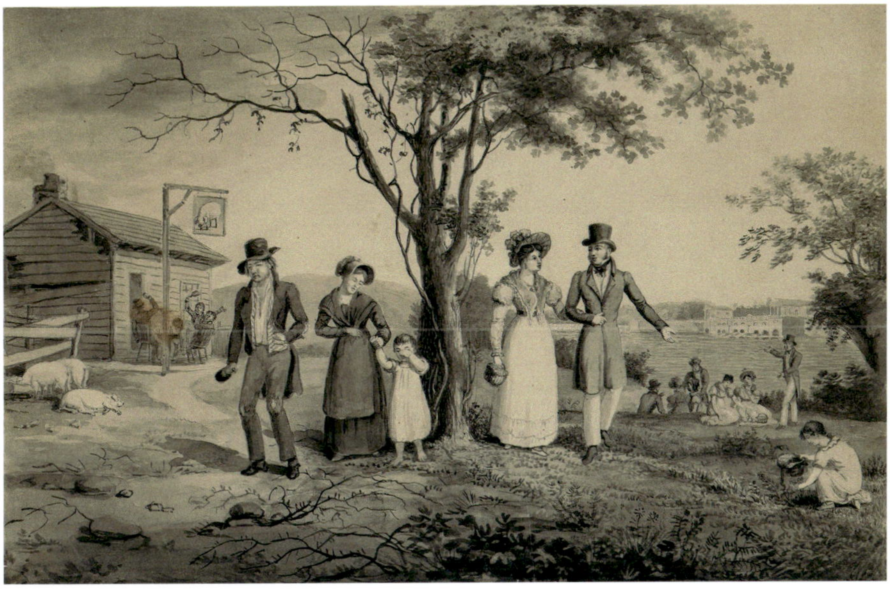

FIG. 16 Thomas Birch (American, b. England, 1779–1851), *Virtue and Vice, Sobriety and Drunkenness*, 1815–30. Ink and wash on paper, 9 × 13⁵⁄₈ in. (22.9 × 34.6 cm).

Winterthur Museum, Garden & Library, Wilmington, DE, Museum purchase, 1967.0131

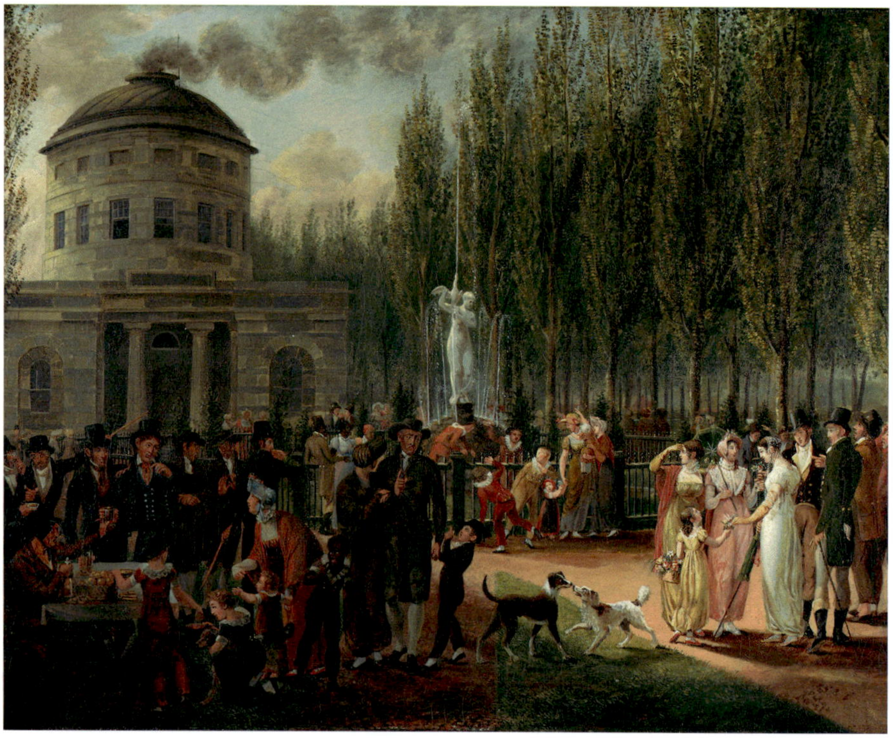

FIG. 17 John Lewis Krimmel (American, b. Germany, 1786–1821), *Fourth of July in Centre Square*, by 1812. Oil on canvas, 22¾ × 29 in. (57.8 × 73.7 cm).

Pennsylvania Academy of the Fine Arts, Philadelphia, PA, Pennsylvania Academy purchase (from the estate of Paul Beck, Jr.), 1845.3.1

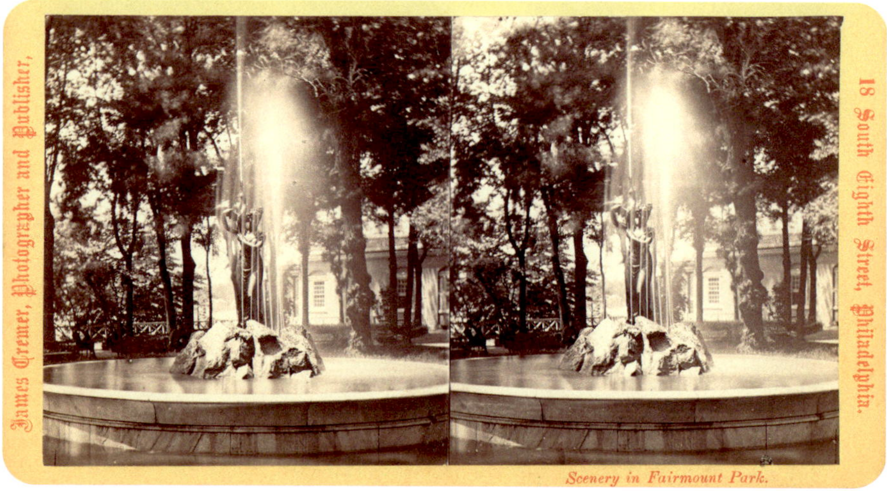

FIG. 18 James Cremer (American, b. England, 1821–1893), *Scenery in Fairmount Park*, 1876. Stereographic photograph, 4 × 7 in. (10.2 × 17.8 cm).

Cremer Stereograph Collection, Philadelphia Parks and Recreation Archive, PA

the Centre Square site was demolished in 1827. In 1872, the city elected to preserve the likeness of *Water Nymph and Bittern*, a wooden sculpture, in a bronze copy (see fig. 18).[76] Stebbins likely would have been aware of Rush's *Water Nymph and Bittern*, as the Fairmount Waterworks were a popular tourist destination, declared to be "a place wondrous to behold," by Dickens. While Stebbins's angel and Rush's nymph of course draw from different sources—the Bible and mythology, respectively—they both rely on a symbolic female figure to embody the source of clean water for an urban center. Even though Rush's nymph is not winged, the outstretched wings of Stebbins's sculpture echo the bittern's wings.[77]

When the *Bethesda Fountain* was finally installed in 1873, critical reception was mixed. The sculpture's material—bronze—became a focal point for criticism of the sculpture's quality and delayed installation. Cast by the Royal Foundry in Munich, the fountain's bronze was likely derived from copper and tin mined in Cornwall or Devon, England, the major producers of those metals in the nineteenth century. The bronze used in the *Bethesda Fountain* was, therefore, connected to the global landscape of extraction that included the marble quarries and coal mines that contributed to and inspired the creation of *Industry*. Unlike the marble-carved *Industry*, however, the *Bethesda Fountain* was cast far away from Stebbins's studio in Rome.[78] Stebbins, therefore, had to rely on others to execute the work and experienced prolonged delays due to late payments from the Central Park Commission, her limited access to her finances controlled by her brother, the Civil War in the US, and the Franco-Prussian War abroad.[79] The sculpture's casting in Munich became a point of contention for a reviewer in the *New-York Times*, who negatively compared Stebbins's *Bethesda Fountain* to a bronze statue of William Shakespeare by John Quincy Adams Ward, which had been installed in Central Park the year prior: "As for the material of the upper part, and the casting, both are infinitely inferior to the bronze of the Shakespeare." The critic noted the Shakespeare bronze had been cast in Philadelphia, and "did not come from Europe."[80] In a letter to Whitney, Stebbins theorized that this criticism may have "found its inspiration in the Bronze Casting interest here."[81] Stebbins, in other words, suggested that her patronage of a foreign foundry, even one as respected and widely used as the Royal Foundry in Munich, might have been an issue for American audiences. The *New-York Times* also appeared to blame the sculpture's casting in Munich for its delayed installation, reminding readers that the bronze sculptures arrived four years after the completion of the models.[82] While the *Bethesda Fountain* celebrates and embodies the expedient dissemination of healthy water, the reception of the sculpture itself became mired in the politics of its material casting.

Despite this criticism of the sculpture for having been cast abroad, a few reviews explicitly drew connections between the fountain, the environment, and public health. The *Evening Post* noted the symbolism of temperance and health within the sculpture, proclaiming, "what often appear the commonest benefactions of life, such as water, are among the most precious gifts of Heaven and worthy of the special and incessant ministries of the purest and noblest spirits."[83] One uncited newspaper article collected in the Emma Stebbins scrapbook explicitly connected Central Park and the fountain to a changing climate: "As the climate of New York is evidently changing, and we may reasonably hope for winters without frost if not for summers without a sun, the season does not forbid us to rejoice over a tribute of praise [for Stebbins's sculpture]."[84]

In conclusion, Stebbins's sculptures engage with environmental conditions, urban technologies, and industrial labor in a variety of ways, at times recognizing but also obfuscating these concerns and realities. Paying attention to the subjects, materials, and, in the case of the *Bethesda Fountain*, the actual function of her works connects them to a wide range of places, peoples, and conditions across the country and the globe.

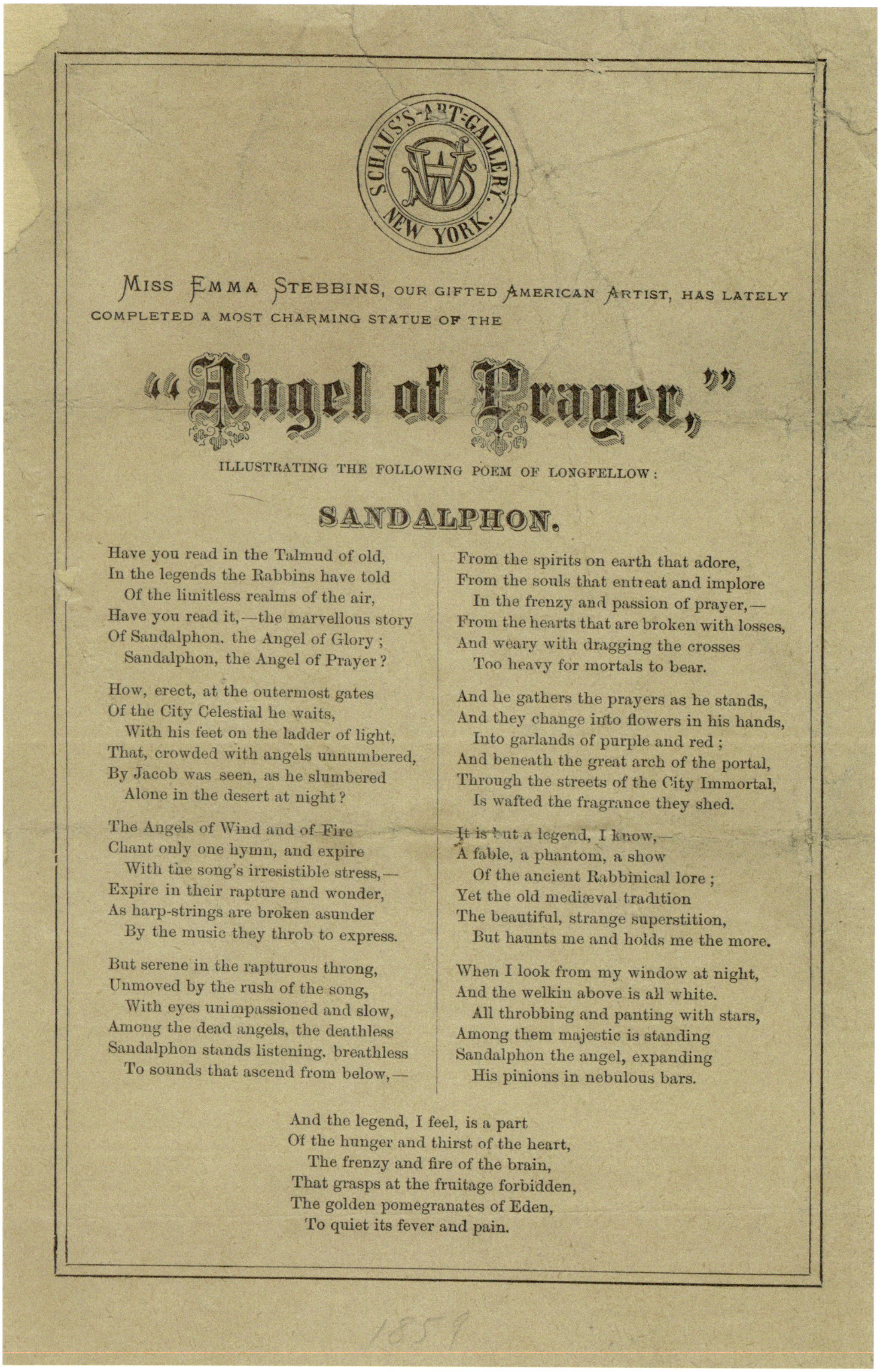

SCHAUS'S ART GALLERY. NEW YORK.

MISS EMMA STEBBINS, OUR GIFTED AMERICAN ARTIST, HAS LATELY COMPLETED A MOST CHARMING STATUE OF THE

"Angel of Prayer,"

ILLUSTRATING THE FOLLOWING POEM OF LONGFELLOW:

SANDALPHON.

Have you read in the Talmud of old,
In the legends the Rabbins have told
Of the limitless realms of the air,
Have you read it,—the marvellous story
Of Sandalphon, the Angel of Glory;
Sandalphon, the Angel of Prayer?

How, erect, at the outermost gates
Of the City Celestial he waits,
With his feet on the ladder of light,
That, crowded with angels unnumbered,
By Jacob was seen, as he slumbered
Alone in the desert at night?

The Angels of Wind and of Fire
Chant only one hymn, and expire
With the song's irresistible stress,—
Expire in their rapture and wonder,
As harp-strings are broken asunder
By the music they throb to express.

But serene in the rapturous throng,
Unmoved by the rush of the song,
With eyes unimpassioned and slow,
Among the dead angels, the deathless
Sandalphon stands listening, breathless
To sounds that ascend from below,—

From the spirits on earth that adore,
From the souls that entreat and implore
In the frenzy and passion of prayer,—
From the hearts that are broken with losses,
And weary with dragging the crosses
Too heavy for mortals to bear.

And he gathers the prayers as he stands,
And they change into flowers in his hands,
Into garlands of purple and red;
And beneath the great arch of the portal,
Through the streets of the City Immortal,
Is wafted the fragrance they shed.

It is but a legend, I know,—
A fable, a phantom, a show
Of the ancient Rabbinical lore;
Yet the old mediæval tradition
The beautiful, strange superstition,
But haunts me and holds me the more.

When I look from my window at night,
And the welkin above is all white,
All throbbing and panting with stars,
Among them majestic is standing
Sandalphon the angel, expanding
His pinions in nebulous bars.

And the legend, I feel, is a part
Of the hunger and thirst of the heart,
The frenzy and fire of the brain,
That grasps at the fruitage forbidden,
The golden pomegranates of Eden,
To quiet its fever and pain.

1859

FIG. 1 Schaus's Art Gallery (New York, NY), Printed sheet related to Emma Stebbins's *Sandalphon* (pl. 20), ca. 1871. Printed sheet, 9 7/16 × 6 11/16 in. (24 × 17 cm).

Broadsides SY1871 no.101, The New York Historical, New York, NY

MELISSA L. GUSTIN

THE BETTER ANGELS OF OUR GENDERS

Although best known today for her sculpture *Angel of the Waters* (pl. 46), which is part of the *Bethesda Fountain* (pl. 47), Emma Stebbins produced several other angelic subjects in her productive years. These works, some of which only exist in photographs of clay or plaster models, others as finished marble statuettes, are illustrative of poems or familiar texts like the Bible. Yet they are also indicative of the complications—particularly those that surround questions of gender—involved in depicting nonhuman, divine figures. The gender of angels (including fallen angels) is a troubled issue in both theology and art, and Stebbins worked in a period during which normative gender roles for middle- and upper-class women in both America and Britain were under pressure. Stebbins's peer and onetime roommate Harriet Hosmer was and is especially well known for her propriety-defying clothing, hair, and behavior.[1] Louisa Lander, a fellow American sculptor, was driven from Rome in part because she offended the gendered sensibilities of the expatriate community.[2] Stebbins's partner Charlotte Cushman made her name playing Romeo onstage (occasionally opposite her sister, Susan Webb Cushman, as Juliet).[3] Although Stebbins herself is not known for deviating from the expected presentation of proper mid-nineteenth-century American bourgeois femininity in either her dress or her sculptures, her angelic oeuvre raises questions of gender, normativity, and reception.

The works by Stebbins that have directly angelic or divine themes are the aforementioned *Angel of the Waters*, *Sandalphon* (pl. 20), *Satan* (pl. 21), a study for the *Angel of the Resurrection* (pl. 33), a study for the bracket (or plinth) for her bust of Charlotte Cushman (pl. 13), and a study for a "monument" with two young angelic figures (pl. 34), all documented in the Emma Stebbins scrapbook.[4] Of these, *Satan* is the only overtly masculine figure. *Sandalphon* and the *Angel of the Resurrection* defy easy binary gender categorization, with characteristics that can be read as masculine or feminine, or somewhere in between. *Angel of the Waters* was critiqued for being too masculine. Other sculptures of angels by Stebbins's male contemporaries

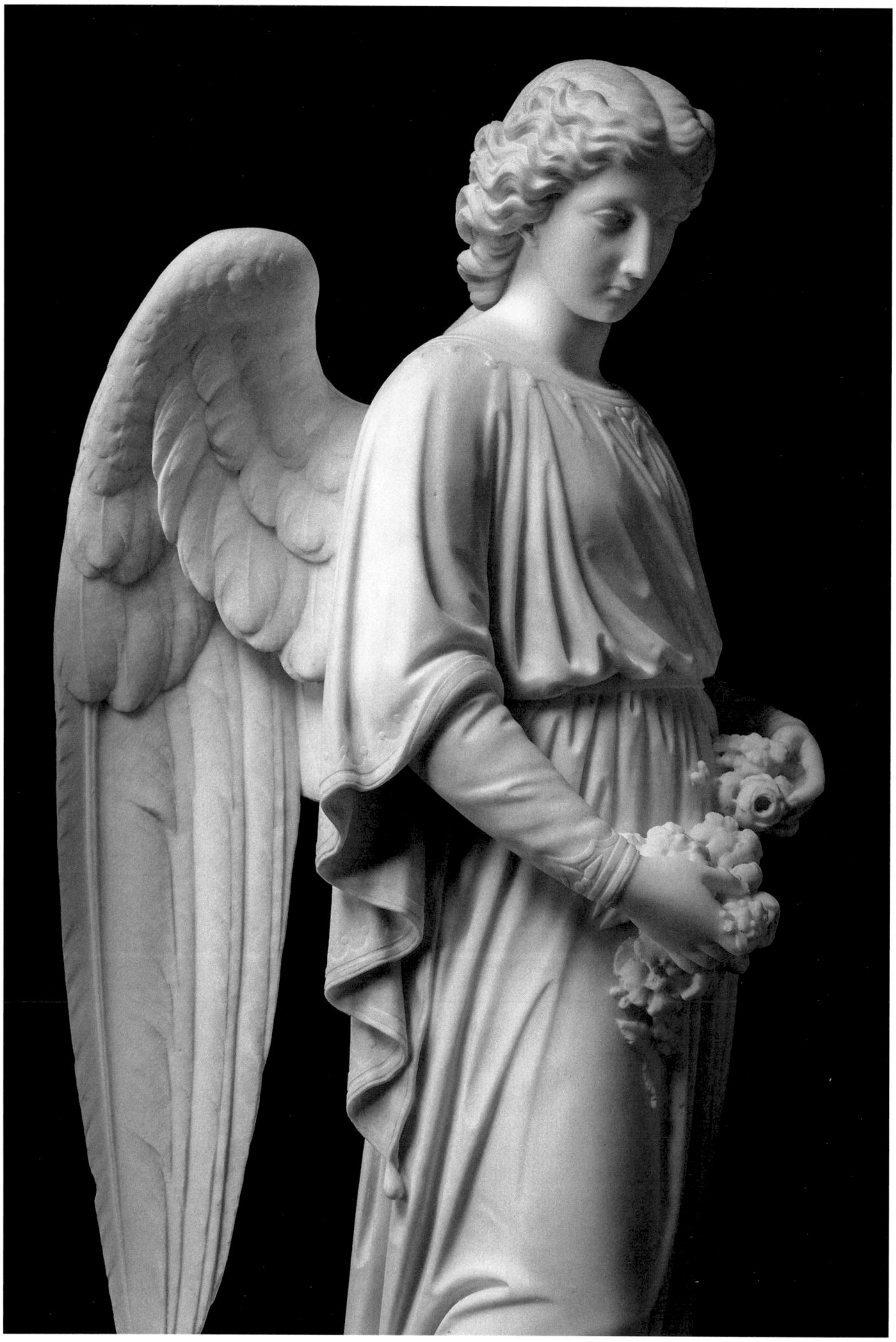

FIG. 2 Emma Stebbins (American, 1815–1882), *Sandalphon* (detail of pl. 20).

show a tendency towards a more definitive gender presentation, although, as will be seen, this was not a universal inclination. This essay will explore the relationship between Stebbins's sculptures and their sources, both literary (including poems and the Bible) and visual (drawn primarily from the Italian context in which Stebbins and her fellow Americans worked). Like the waters of the biblical Pool of Bethesda (John 5:2–9), Stebbins's angels trouble gender, especially as they were produced by a queer woman artist.

Stebbins's time in Italy exposed her to a wide range of visual references for angelic subject matter, particularly Catholic imagery in sculpture and painted media. Her literary sources were written in English. *Sandalphon* and *Satan*, with their opposing characterizations of the angelic figure, are the main focus of this essay. The *Angel of the Waters* will likewise be discussed in relation to the presentation of the figure's gender and nineteenth-century receptions of it. Like many neoclassical American artists, Stebbins was reluctant to name explicitly her artistic references from Europe. Nonetheless, these will be identified and developed through close attention to the formal similarities of Stebbins's artworks to their precedents.

SANDALPHON, "THE ANGEL OF PRAYER"

In *Sandalphon*, Stebbins repeated a formula that she had used to great success in her first ideal nude work, *The Lotus Eater* (pl. 1). She took a subject from a relatively recent poem (with an ancient origin) by a leading contemporary poet, and produced it at a scale appropriate to the parlor and with a refined, if somewhat fleshy, androgyny.[5] *Sandalphon* is inspired by Henry Wadsworth Longfellow's poem of the same name, first published in the *Atlantic* in 1858 (for the text of the poem, see fig. 1).[6] The poem describes the "marvellous story" of the angel Sandalphon, who stands at the gates of heaven and gathers human prayers; the action of the poem largely focuses on describing Sandalphon in contrast to other angels and on the narrator's hunger for mystical experiences. Under the photograph of the sculpture in the Emma Stebbins scrapbook, Mary Stebbins Garland transcribed a line from the poem, "And he gathers the prayers as he stands / And they change into flowers in his hands," and appended "Longfellow" to the quotation. In a biographical manuscript about her sister's work, Garland titled the statue, "The Angel of Prayer," which follows the language of the poem itself.[7] Cushman, however, described it as a "child's angel" to Emma Crow Cushman, writing that the statue is "sweet, pure, calm, innocent, patient, receptive. . . . The size is lovely for a drawing room."[8]

In Longfellow's poem, Sandalphon, whose gender is made explicit by the use of masculine pronouns, is referred to as the angel of prayer and of glory. Translating a poem about a religious, abstract, and nonhuman figure into something visually coherent (and commercially viable) would have been a challenge. Sandalphon as a literary or biblical character does not have a long visual tradition like that of the archangels Michael or Gabriel, who generally hold specific attributes to help the viewer identify them. Stebbins was probably the first sculptor to adapt the angel into a full-length statue. Although Garland noted the line about gathering prayers and transforming them into flowers, which is the phrase most immediately illustratable from the poem, Longfellow also described the angel as standing "erect, at the outermost gates / Of the City Celestial he waits / With his feet on the ladder of light," and as

> serene in the rapturous throng,
> Unmoved by the rush of the song,
> With eyes unimpassioned and slow,
> Among the dead angels, the deathless
> Sandalphon stands listening breathless
> To sounds that ascend from below,—

Beyond Longfellow's use of masculine pronouns, there is little else for an artist to derive specifically from the poem's verses that would aid the viewer in perceiving the subject. Indeed, Stebbins's statue could just as easily be a funerary monument as a rendition of the angel. The link between the two—that Longfellow's text is the source, not the rabbinic tradition in translation from which he derived it—is borne out by a printed sheet for Stebbins's *Sandalphon* that reproduces the poem and makes the relationship clear (fig. 1).

which shows a winged figure holding a vase in each hand and stepping forward. The robes, baring one breast, are blown back. While Stebbins's sculpture takes advantage of the material properties of bronze to create a wider wingspan and more dramatic drapery, her use of the pose of *Aurora* is clear.[22] These neoclassical sculptures in turn respond to examples in Rome and Italy more widely, including the ancient Selene of the Capitoline Museum, with drapery blown around the figure. It is worth noting that Stebbins also developed her work during the period in which the Nike of Samothrace was being conserved and restored at the Louvre. However, the Hellenistic Nike was displayed without the wings until well after Stebbins completed the *Angel of the Waters* and therefore likely had little direct influence on the sculpture's form.[23]

As with *Sandalphon*, Stebbins appears to have taken artistic liberties in *Angel of the Waters* that depart from the text, particularly regarding the visibly gendered female angel. In the Gospel of John, no pronouns are used for the angel that descends to "trouble" or stir up the waters: "For an angel went down at a certain time into the pool and stirred up the water; then whoever stepped in first, after the stirring of the water, was made well of whatever disease he had."[24] A positive review of the *Bethesda Fountain* notes, "It is scarcely necessary to say that the design for this fountain was suggested by the first few verses in the fifth chapter of St. John, where the five-porched pool by the Jerusalem sheep-market is described as being beneficently troubled by an angel, and bathed in by the blind, the halt, and the withered."[25] While in the Gospel of John, visitors to the Bethesda Pool may have bathed or submerged themselves, the *Bethesda Fountain* was purely decorative.[26] The reviewer continued, "and though we do not go quite so far as to say that the result is such an improvement on the pool of Scripture that the privilege of immersing oneself in this new Bethesda would be lavish compensation for a lifetime of suffering, yet there can be no question that the work is so chaste, so harmonious, so perfect in its combination of point, breadth, and delicacy, as to constitute one of the most attractive and elegant embellishments yet given to the park."

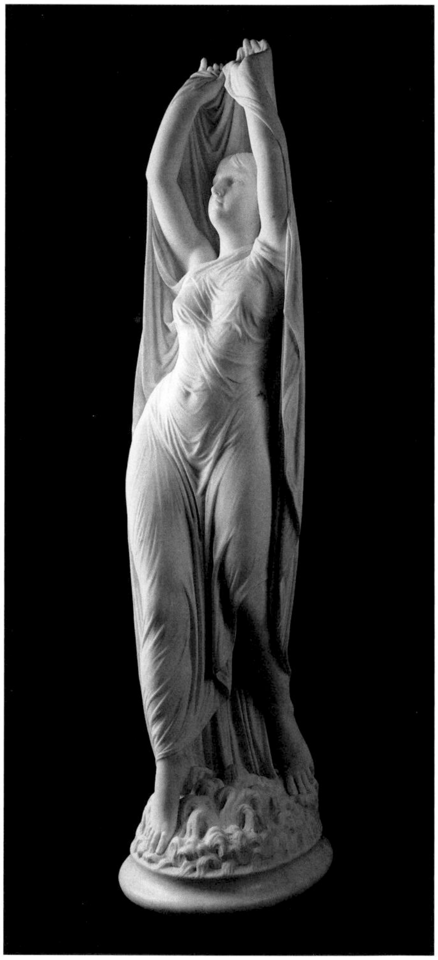

FIG. 6 Chauncey Bradley Ives (American, 1810–1894), *Undine Rising from the Waters*, after 1859. Marble, 60 × 18 × 16 in. (152.4 × 45.7 × 40.6 cm).

High Museum of Art, Atlanta, GA, Gift of the West Foundation in honor of Gudmund Vigtel and Michael E. Shapiro, 2010.67

Stebbins certainly ensured that there would be no mistaking her Bethesda angel for something more salacious and less chaste with the figure's neck-to-ankle robes and broadly spread wings. Even the crossed straps (or harness) of the angel's robes—which are more dress-like than the hieratic robes of *Sandalphon*—serve to both draw attention to the chest and create greater definition around the breasts. Compare, for example, Chauncey Bradley Ives's *Undine Rising from the Waters* (fig. 6). The *Bethesda Fountain* angel is no bathing nymph. The robes, like those of the *Sandalphon*, reveal little of the angel's body—unlike Undine, there is no clinging and sheer Greek wet drapery here, despite the splashing waters of the fountain—but they do suggest the figure's breasts and hips, thus making this statue a more feminine angel than the androgynous *Sandalphon*. The feminine characteristics of Stebbins's Bethesda angel may have been intended to reflect the healing properties of the biblical fountain; its nurturing qualities conform to ideals of the maternal figure and to the classical prototype of Hygeia, the Greek goddess of health.

However, the figure's femininity (among other things) was unsatisfactory to some nineteenth-century viewers. The *Aldine*'s reviewer felt that Stebbins's angel was a "nondescript being with a very masculine body" with "an inexpressive female face" (fig. 7).[27] This writer consistently referred to the angel as "it." Aside from the troubled gender, the reviewer also described it as "pretentious," the "least successful work in bronze," a "creature," and concluded that it "might as well be an old lady feeding her chickens, or a ball-room belle stooping to pick up a pocket-handkerchief."[28] There is a sense that the author would have preferred a saucier angel, or perhaps a work by

FIG. 7 Emma Stebbins (American, 1815–1882), *Angel of the Waters* (detail of pl. 47).

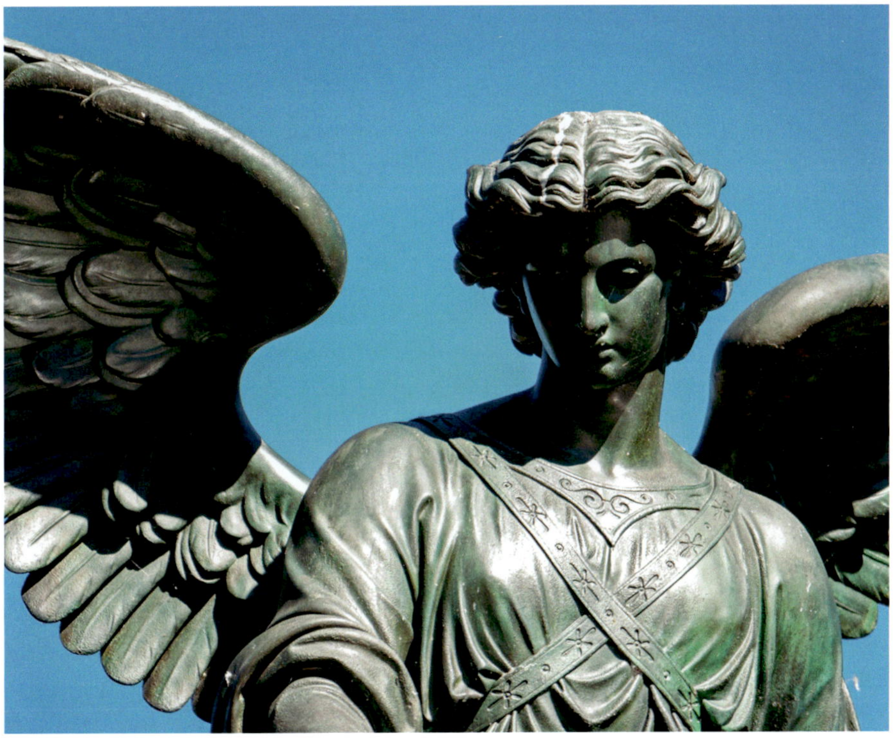

another (male) sculptor. The highly gendered criticism—that the pose is that of an old lady or a ballroom belle—combined with the apparent disdain for or discomfort with the insufficiently feminine body, indicates that there was some dissatisfaction with Stebbins's statue and, by extension, the picture it presents of femininity. There have also been suggestions, primarily made online, that the sculpture is a portrait of or at least an homage to Cushman (see Horn's essay in this volume).[29] Stebbins's portrait bust of Cushman as well as the many photographs of her certainly indicate that the angel is not a direct portrait, although Cushman was derided repeatedly for having a masculine appearance (as was Hosmer). Some reviews draw further attention to what was seen as Stebbins's failure to present either a satisfactorily gendered figure *or* a suitably angelic "neuter." For example, a critic in the *New-York Times* writes, "The head is distinctly a male head, of a classical-commonplace, meaningless beauty, the breasts are feminine, the rest of the body is in part male and in part female. Quite true it is that an angel should not be markedly of either sex, though the general reading would indicate the male. But the type is to be neuter, and not a mosaic of both."[30] This widespread (but far from universal) discomfort about Stebbins's choice to neither clearly define nor sufficiently blend the genders may reflect a similar attitude towards the women involved in its making.

GET THEE BEHIND ME, SEXY SATAN

The only overtly masculine representation of an adult angel in Stebbins's oeuvre is that of *Satan*, recorded as a plaster model in the Emma Stebbins scrapbook. The figure as photographed appears to be a parlor-sized work, similar in scale to the figures of *Commerce* (pl. 11) and *Industry* (pl. 10). Although reproduced in the Emma Stebbins scrapbook, the figure goes unmentioned in Garland's biographical sketch (see Garland's historical text in this volume).[31] The page in the scrapbook is furthermore not annotated, leaving us to assume the *Satan* is related to a reference Cushman

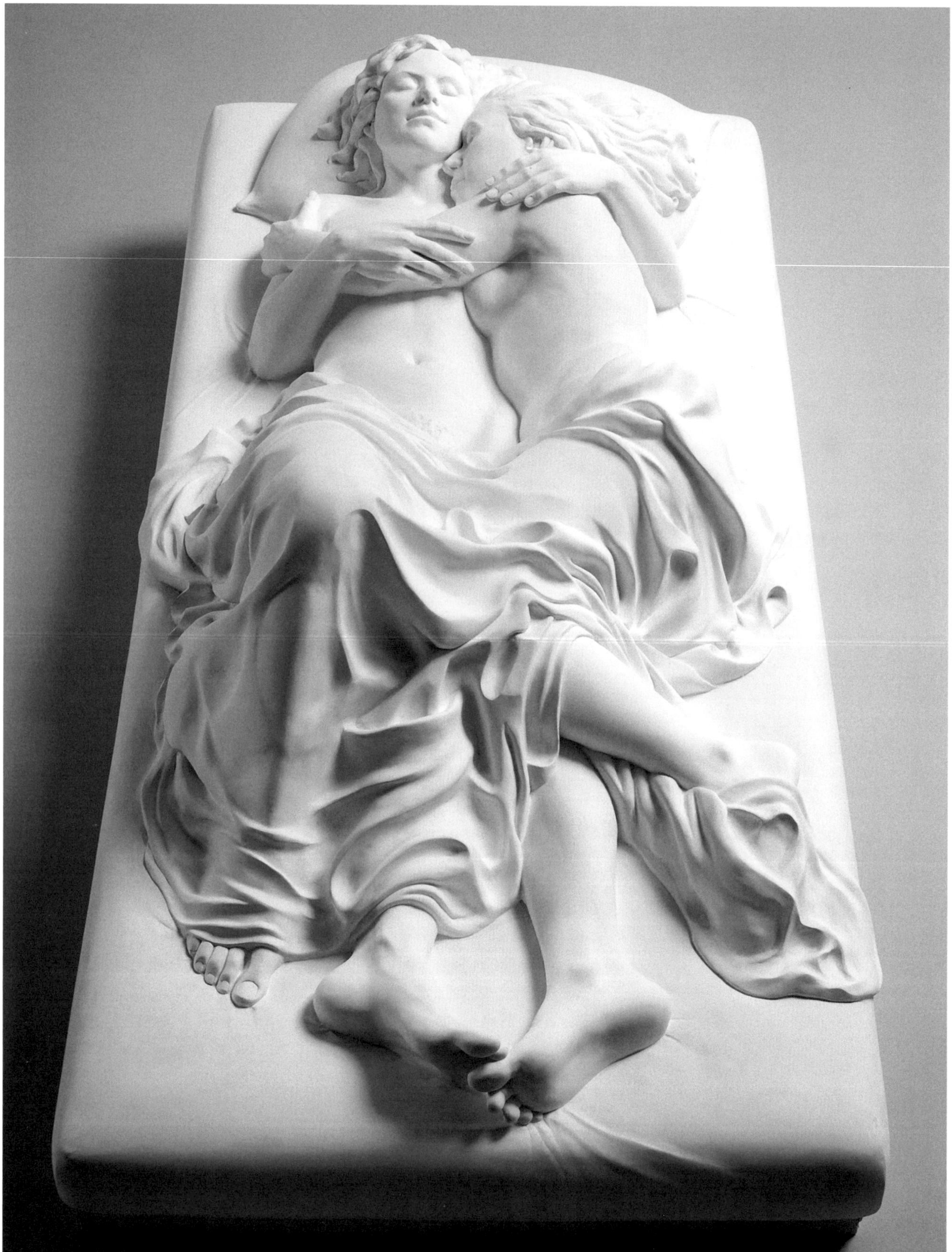

PATRICIA CRONIN

SAPPHIC ROME

American Lesbian Sculptors in the Eternal City

The rhythmic sound of wood-soled shoes tapping the *sampietrini*, the cobblestones lining Rome's streets, walking back and forth every day from Via Gregoriana down the Spanish Steps to Via Margutta. Home, to the studio, and back home. Memories of these sounds from my years in Rome at the beginning of the twenty-first century remind me of how radical it was for Harriet Hosmer, Emma Stebbins, and several other women (Margaret F. Foley, Edmonia Lewis, and Anne Whitney, among others) to walk alone unchaperoned by a male relative on Roman streets in the 1850s to 1870s. They were walking unaccompanied to work. And not just any jobs. These women in Rome were sculptors. This was highly unusual because in the mid-nineteenth century the only socially acceptable vocations for women outside of agriculture were child-care, domestic laborer, or companion of the well-to-do. The obstacles to becoming an artist were virtually insurmountable because women were prohibited from the education and training—like human-anatomy courses only offered in medical schools—necessary to become proficient in drawing, modelling, and carving the nude human form (see Gustin's essay in this volume). Equally unusual, they were all unmarried (at least to men) and child-free. The romantic partners of Hosmer, Stebbins, Foley, and Whitney were women. Author Henry James patronizingly dubbed this group of female sculptors the "white marmorean flock" because they were such an anomaly.[1] They defiantly challenged society's standards of femininity.

Rome was long known for attracting prominent British and American writers, including Elizabeth Barrett Browning, Robert Browning, Nathaniel Hawthorne, and James, and artists, like John Gibson and William Wetmore Story. Also drawn to Rome were "Independent Women," as lesbians were called then.[2] They fled the complete male control of their lives (finances, children, and property) that was legally permitted by their countries of origin. In Rome, they were free to develop and practice their artistic or literary professions while also being unconstrained by the conventional

FIG. 1 Patricia Cronin (American, b. 1963), *Memorial To A Marriage*, 2002. Carrara marble, 27 × 84 × 47 in. (68.6 × 213.4 × 119.4 cm).
Collection of the artist

gender roles for Italian women because they were considered *stranieri*, foreigners. They were liberated.

"A perfectly emancipated woman," as Elizabeth Barrett Browning called Hosmer, had to be inventive, even subversive, to navigate these gender restrictions and to live a more fulfilling life.[3] To keep within enough of society's expectations of womanhood to not offend their patrons and critics while simultaneously trying to be taken seriously as sculptors was a delicate balancing act. It required an acute understanding of behavioral norms and how to challenge them without being too overt. How to live a lesbian life in a same-sex relationship and make artwork that disrupts patriarchal world order in form and content was a persistent puzzle. And still is.

As a conceptual artist, my aesthetic strategy is to breathe new life into historic art images and forms made in time-honored artists' materials and to disrupt them by injecting my specific contemporary political views about gender equality and social justice into them. I make watercolors, oil paintings, large installations of readymade objects, monumental bronze and marble sculptures, and sometimes I write books. I rely on the seduction of the familiar to then disrupt the viewer's expectations of hierarchies and histories by insisting on feminist and LGBTQ+ representation.

While researching the history of sculpture for inspiration for my *Memorial To A Marriage* statue (fig. 1), I discovered Hosmer and her *Beatrice Cenci* (1856).[4] I was transfixed by her full-size figurative marble sculpture. I had never heard of Hosmer and wondered *Why not?* I saw the quality of her work and decided that as soon as I was finished with mine, I would research Hosmer and the nineteenth-century sisterhood of American sculptors as my next project (see fig. 2).

In 2000, when same-sex marriage was illegal in the United States and few specific women or LGBTQ+ people were honored in public monuments, I had the radical imagination to envision a world where misogyny and homophobia didn't exist and created the world's first monument dedicated to marriage equality. *Memorial To A Marriage* is a three-ton, over-life-size, double-figure Carrara-marble mortuary sculpture of my now wife and myself. It invokes the patriotic nineteenth-century American neoclassical style for two reasons. First, to critique the federal government for denying same-sex couples legal marriage, and second, to address the erasure of women and LGBTQ+ people from the public square.

Both Stebbins and Hosmer transformed American neoclassical sculpture in two major ways that I appreciate. First, they substituted the subjects: workers instead of gods, a self-portrait by a woman artist depicting herself as a man, and female sovereigns in crisis. Second, they altered the characteristic traits: contemporary clothing for male workers and dignified postures for female victims, among others. These formal decisions subverted and advanced the conventions of neoclassical marble sculpture. For example, Stebbins portrayed ordinary subjects, like the laborers in *Commerce* (pl. 11) and *Industry* (pl. 10), dressed in contemporary clothing and accessories that were appropriate for their work, elevating them as worthy subjects of art on par with Greek gods and Roman emperors (see Igoe's essay in this volume). When Hosmer selected the same narratives of female victims as did male artists, she championed women who fought back and portrayed them in a stance of moral righteousness about their wronged condition. In *Zenobia in Chains* (1859), Hosmer sculpted a tragic heroine who didn't commit suicide when captured, unlike Cleopatra, a subject favored by male artists.[5] Hosmer depicts Zenobia in a stance of dignified resignation, accepting her fate as a survivor.

Recognizing the disruptive potential of neoclassical sculpture, I have used it to address other themes in my own work, specifically in response to legal and cultural

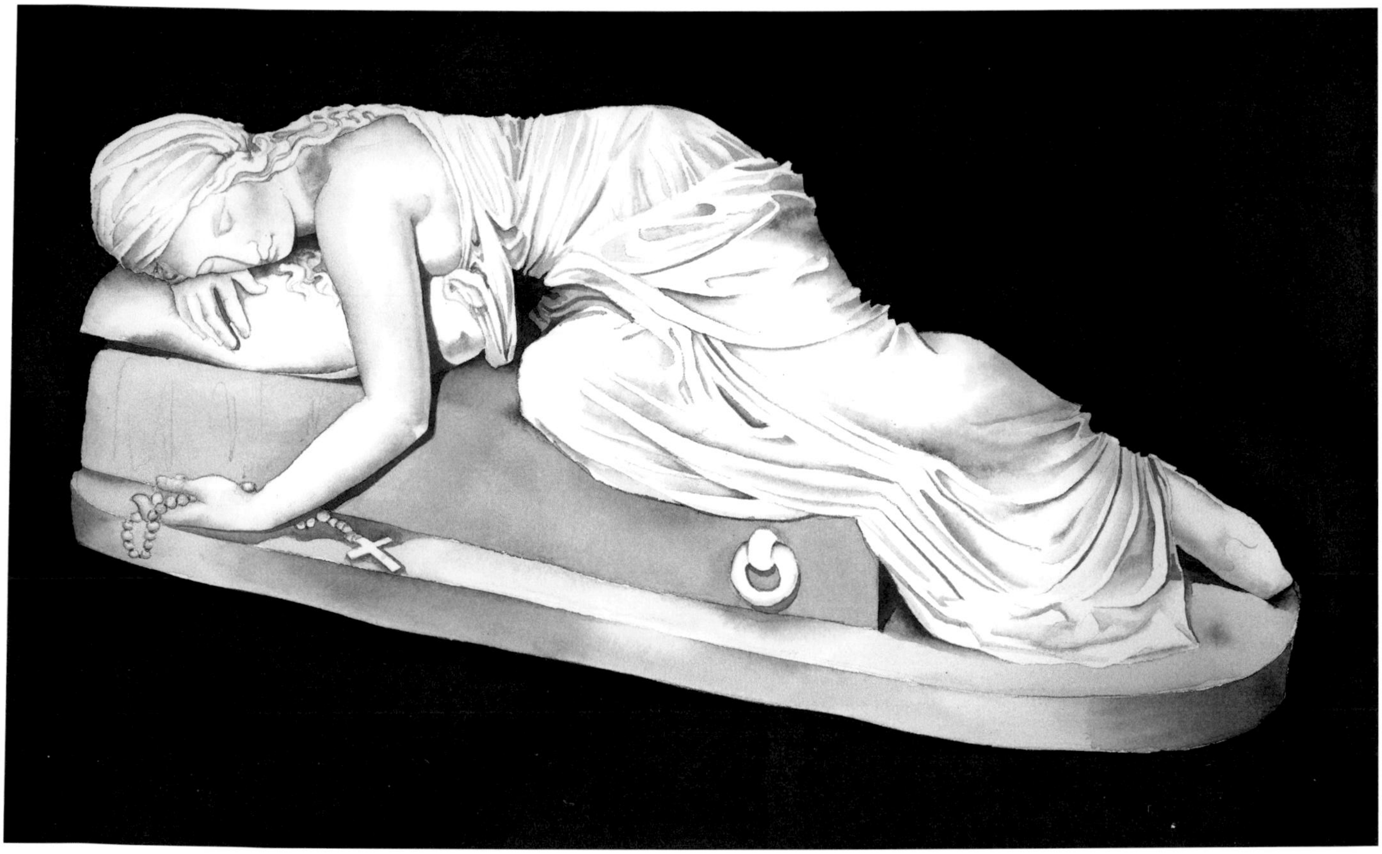

FIG. 2 Patricia Cronin (American, b. 1963), *Beatrice Cenci*, 2007. Watercolor on paper, 12 × 15 in. (30.5 × 38.1 cm).
Private collection

injustices. For centuries, since the Egyptians and the Etruscans, powerful marriages have been remembered in tomb sculptures. Yet I chose a lesbian couple—less politically and economically powerful than a heterosexual pair because of systemic misogyny—as the faces and bodies of marriage equality. Women are rarely the artists or subjects of permanent public art commissions, and the only legal remedies to simulate a few of the 1,200 benefits of heterosexual marriage were wills and other documents about the end of our lives together. So I purchased the land for our actual burial plot in Woodlawn Cemetery in the Bronx, New York—a National Historic Landmark that is a favorite final resting place for America's famous and powerful from the worlds of entertainment, finance, politics, suffrage, literature, and sports. I installed the statue of us, *Memorial To A Marriage*, among their sculptures and mausoleums, where it will be on view for eternity.

In 1852, the leading American actress Charlotte Cushman encouraged Hosmer's father to let the twenty-two-year-old artist travel to Rome with her to get a "good start" studying ancient art. Hosmer moved to Rome and lived with Cushman and her then-partner Matilda Hays. Cushman was the power center of the Anglo-American expatriate culture, and her sphere of professional influence was far-reaching (see Horn's essay in this volume). She introduced Hosmer to the prominent neoclassical British sculptor John Gibson, who accepted her as an apprentice when he saw daguerreotypes of her marble bust *Hesper, The Evening Star* (1852).[6]

After a few years Hosmer hung out her own shingle and became known as the first professional woman sculptor. She had a prominent career, was critically acclaimed and financially successful, won competitive commissions, and exhibited in the international exhibitions. Today, Hosmer's works are in the collections of prominent museums throughout the world and yet she, like the broader group of nineteenth-century American female sculptors, is still for the most part unknown.

PLATES

To provide a full picture of Emma Stebbins's body of work, this section of the book features recent photographs of most of her extant sculptures, including images of her three public monuments in situ. It also includes historical photographs, some of which document plaster casts of clay sculptures that Stebbins never translated into marble or bronze. These nineteenth-century images come from two scrapbooks compiled by Stebbins's family members. The scrapbooks contain handwritten notations about the sculptures that are not always accurate but are nonetheless interesting.

NOTE TO THE READER ON CATALOGUING STEBBINS'S SCULPTURES

Cataloguing Stebbins's sculptures, especially those documented in historical photographs, can be challenging. Museums have provided the information for the sculptures in their collections. Otherwise, the titles given in the plate captions hew as closely as possible to those found in archival sources. As outlined in the introduction to this book, the creation of Stebbins's marble and bronze sculptures often unfolded over the course of several years and involved the production of clay studies and plaster casts. Multiple marble versions of the same subject were sometimes completed years apart. For instance, two extant examples of *The Lotus Eater*, *Christopher Columbus*, and *Samuel* appear in the plates. When sources permit, the chronology in this volume tracks the development of each work. For each extant sculpture represented in the plates, the caption lists only the date that the stone carving or bronze casting was completed. For the artworks depicted in nineteenth-century images, dates, media, and dimensions are not provided, as they are sometimes difficult to ascertain with certainty.

NOTE TO THE READER ON CATALOGUING THE HISTORICAL PHOTOGRAPHS

It is unclear who created these albumen silver prints, which were likely produced in Rome between 1857 and 1870. Ranging in size from about 4 × 2 inches (10.2 × 5.1 cm) to 12¼ × 10 inches (31.1 × 25.4 cm), they are preserved within two unpaginated scrapbooks in the collection of the Archives of American Art, Smithsonian Institution, Washington, DC. Stebbins's sister, Mary Stebbins Garland, compiled the Emma Stebbins scrapbook, 1858–82. Stebbins's nephew John Neal Tilton compiled the John Neal Tilton scrapbook, ca. 1860–80. In 1981, Elizabeth Milroy donated both scrapbooks to the Archives of American Art, which has digitized them and made them available online in their entirety.

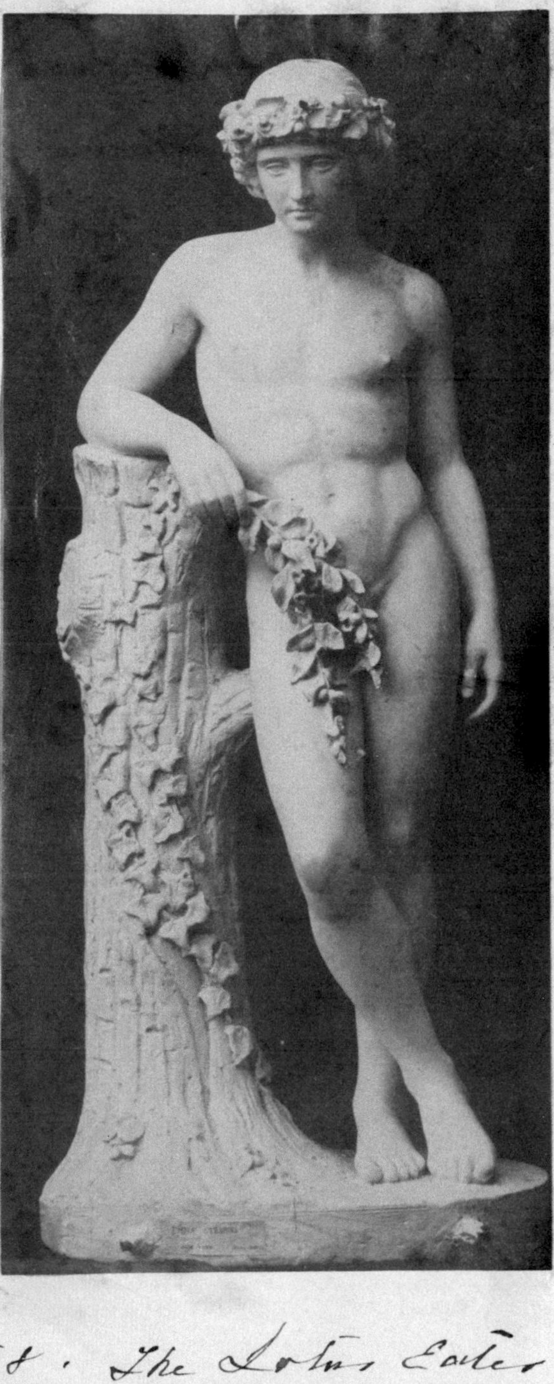

1858. The Lotus Eater (Tennyson). Put in marble for Leonard Jerome of New York –

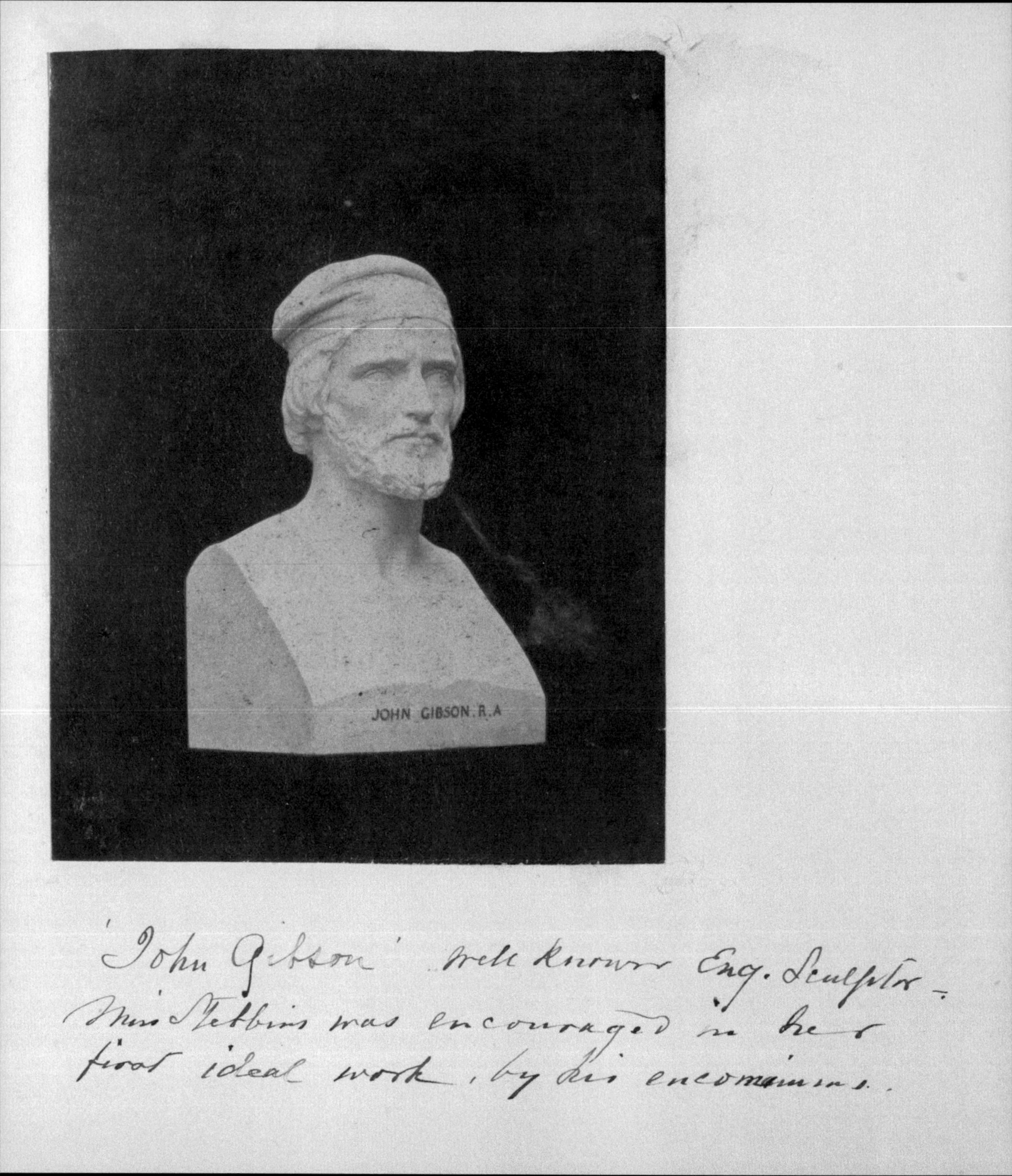

PLATE 2

JOHN GIBSON

Inscription: "JOHN GIBSON. R.A" (front)
Photograph from the Emma Stebbins scrapbook, 1858–82
Archives of American Art, Smithsonian Institution

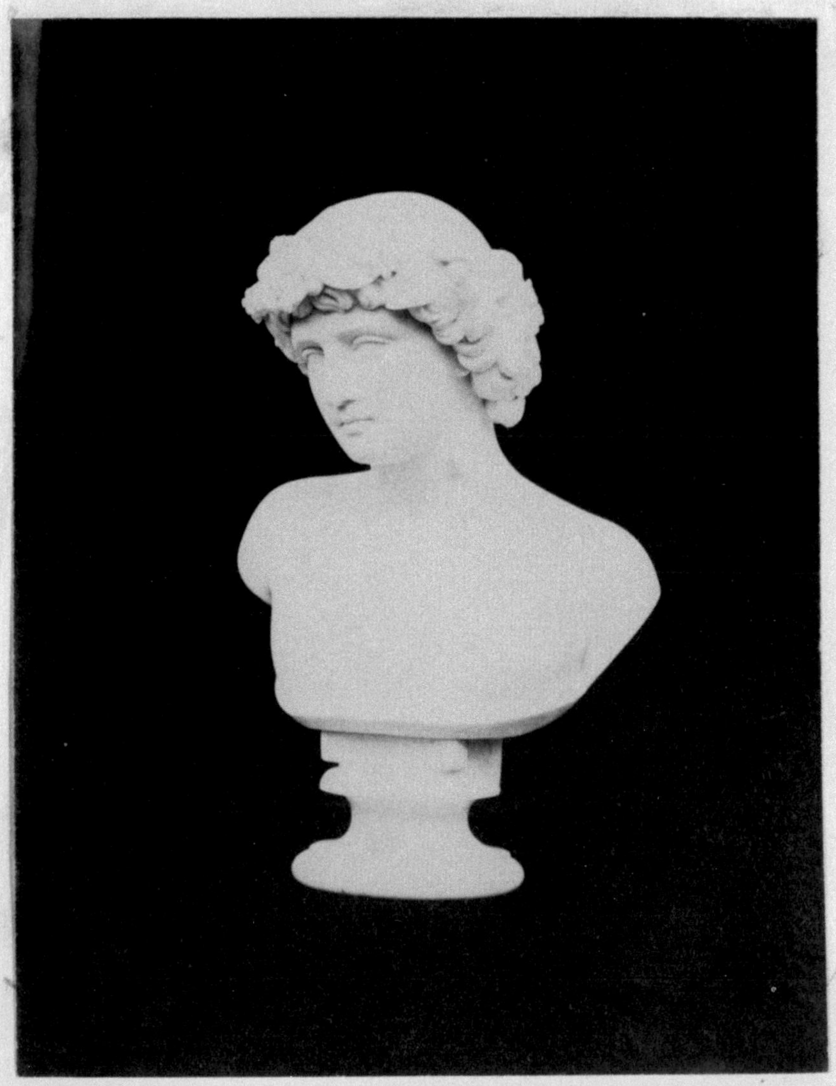

Head of 'Lotus Eater'.
frequently repeated -

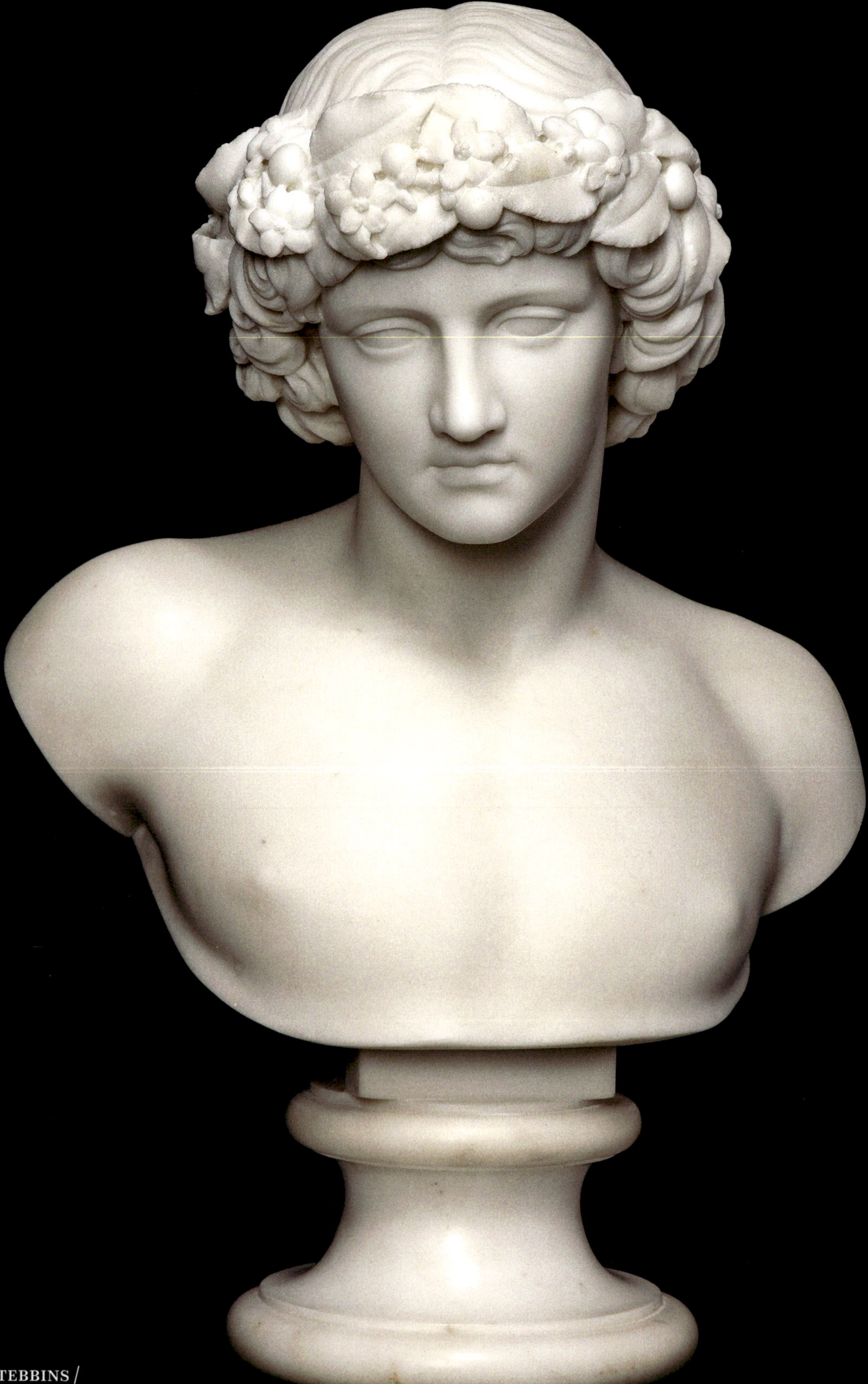

PLATE 4

THE LOTUS EATER

1863
Inscription: "EMMA STEBBINS / ROME / 1863" (verso)
Marble, 16¼ × 11 × 8 in. (41.3 × 27.9 × 20.3 cm)
The Heckscher Museum of Art, Museum Purchase, Town of Huntington Art Acquisition Fund, 2022.7.1

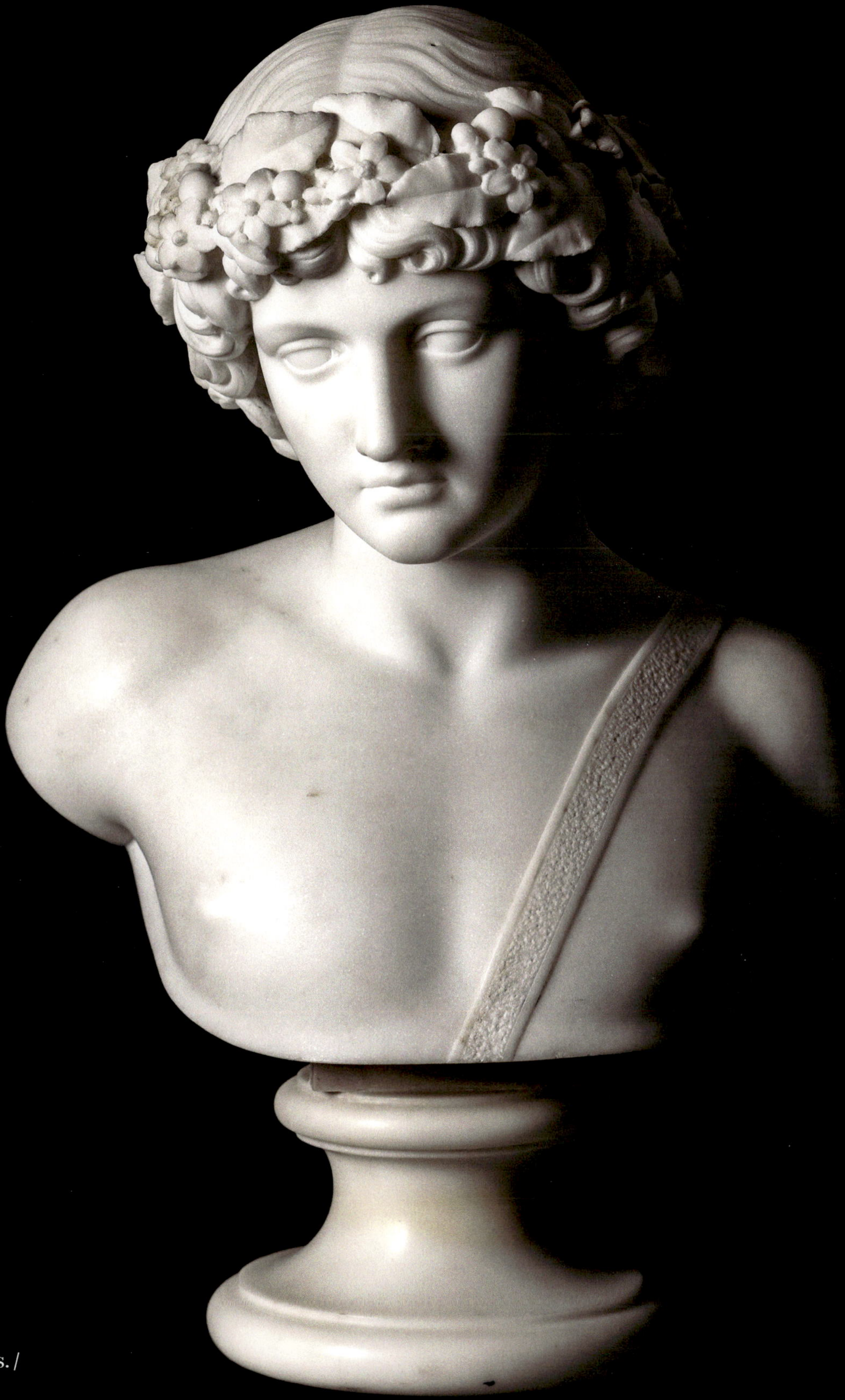

PLATE 5

THE LOTUS EATER

1870

Inscription: "EMMA. STEBBINS. / ROME. 1870." (verso)

Marble, 16¹⁄₄ × 12 × 8¹⁄₄ (41.3 × 30.5 × 21 cm)

Collection of Karen Bechtel and William Osborne

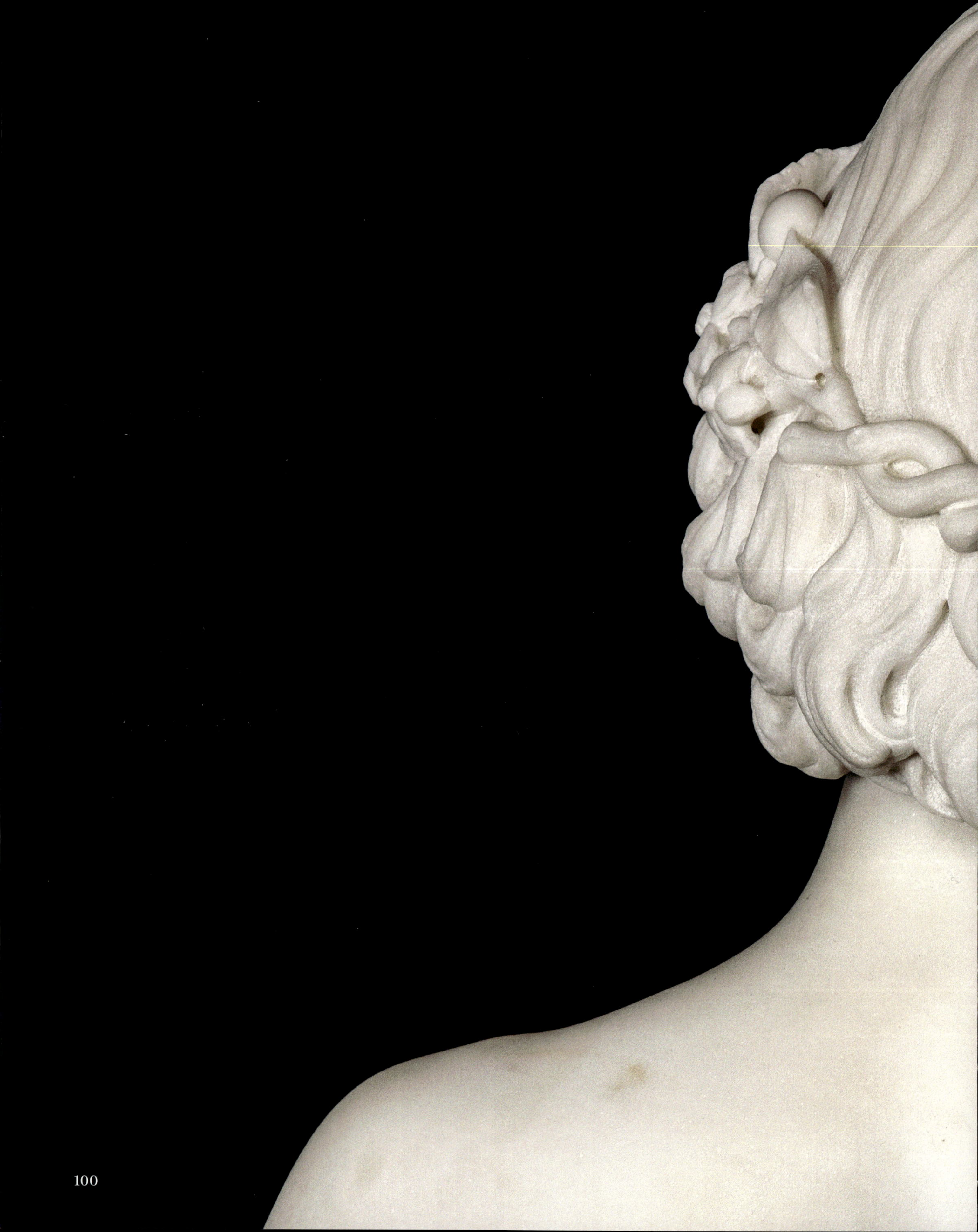

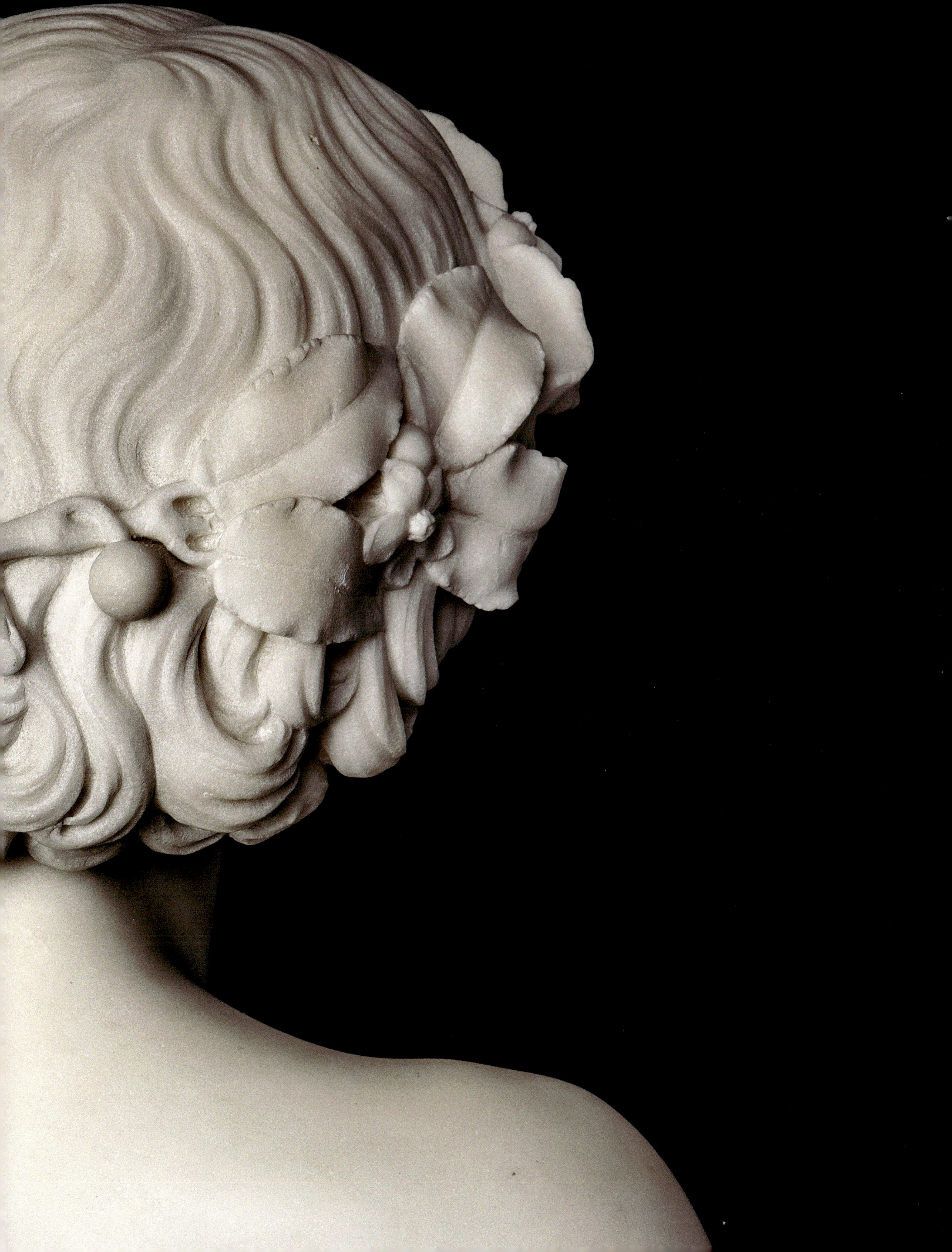

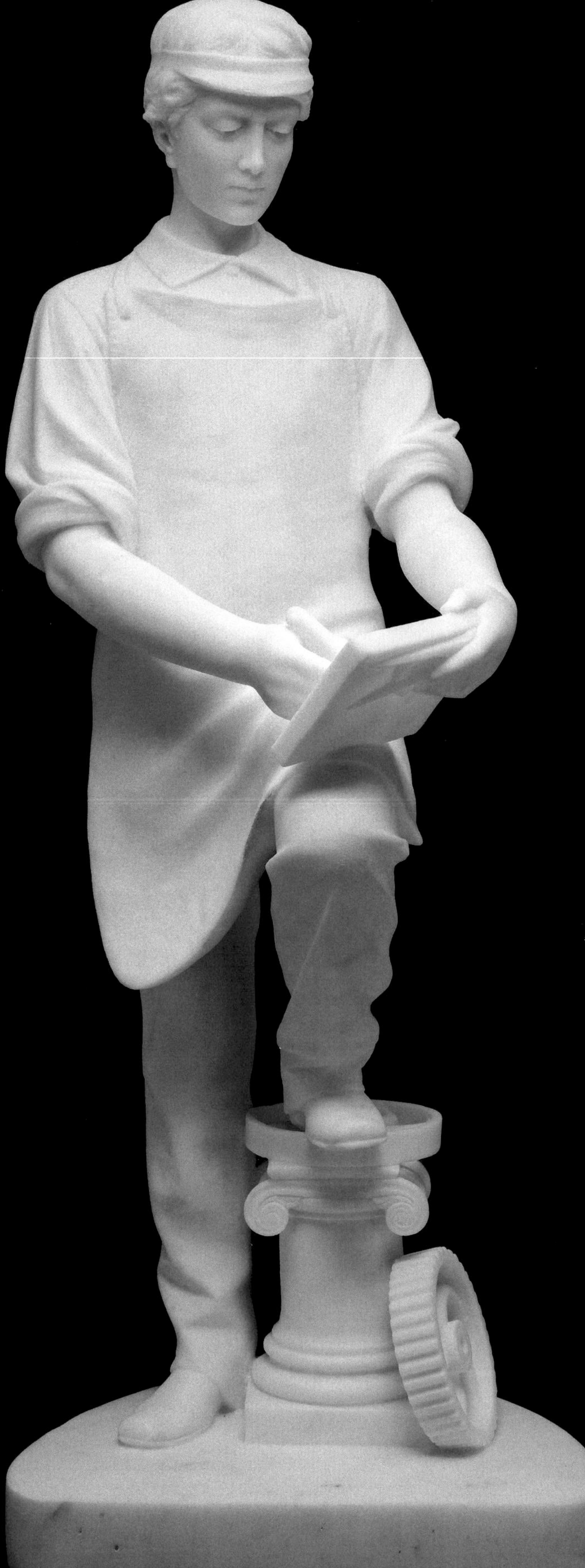

PLATE 6

MACHINIST'S APPRENTICE

ca. 1859
Inscription: "EMMA STEBBINS ROME"
(left side)
Marble, 29½ × 11¾ × 9 in.
(74.9 × 29.9 × 22.9 cm)
The Art Institute of Chicago, Gift of the Antiquarian Society, 2000.13.2

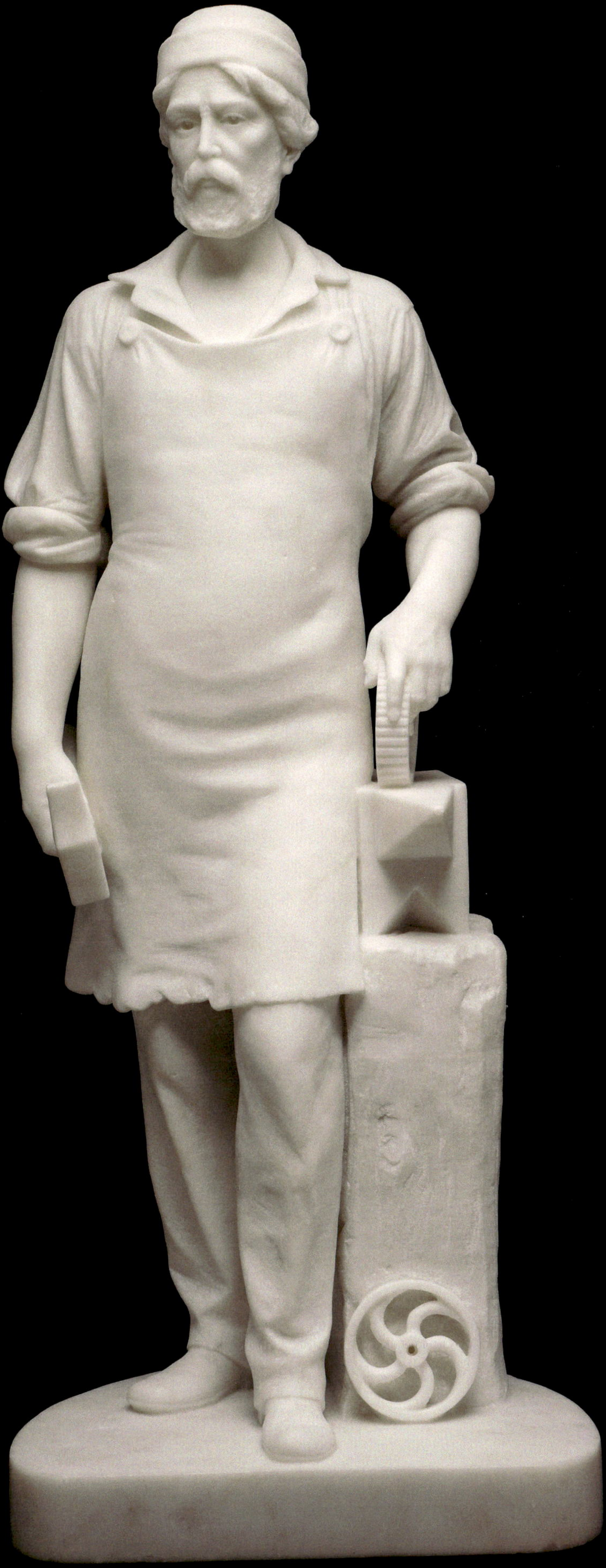

PLATE 7

MACHINIST

ca. 1859
Inscription: "EMMA STEBBINS ROME"
(left side)
Marble, 29½ × 11½ × 11½ in.
(74.9 × 29.2 × 29.2 cm)
The Art Institute of Chicago, Gift of the
Antiquarian Society, 2000.13.1

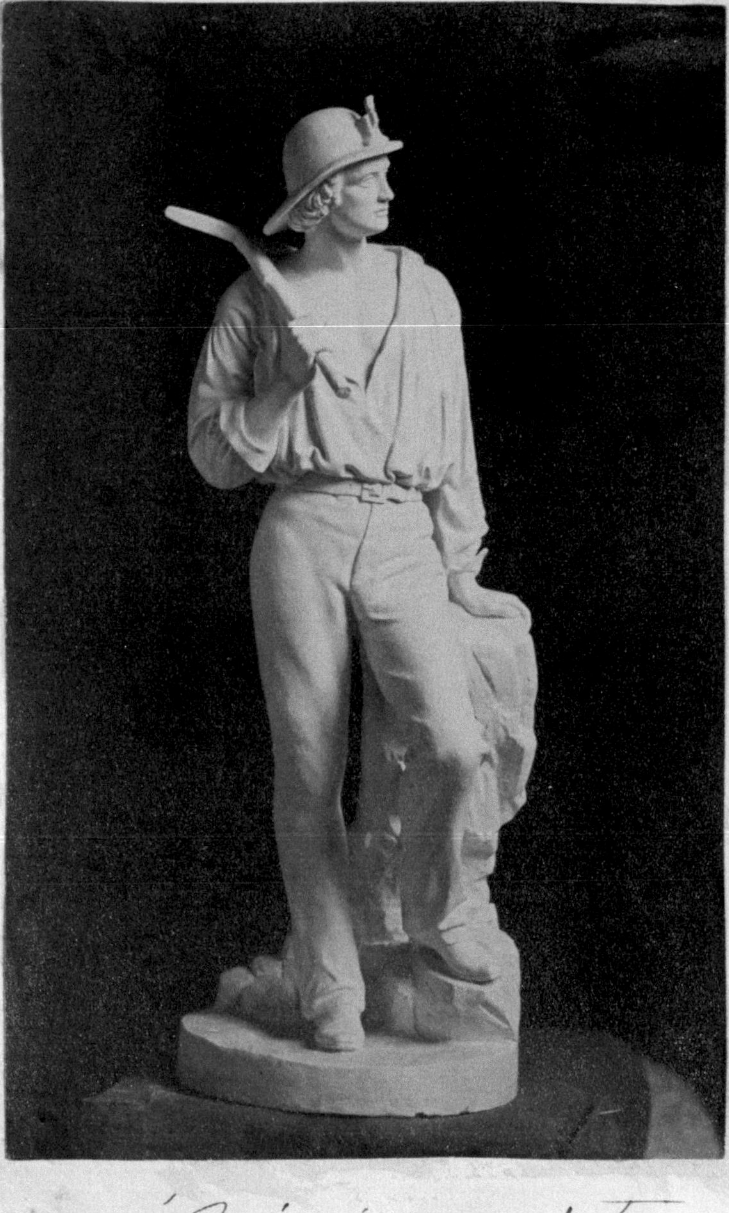

1858. 'Miner' one of two 'Statuettes' made for Mr Ch. A Heckscher, of New York.

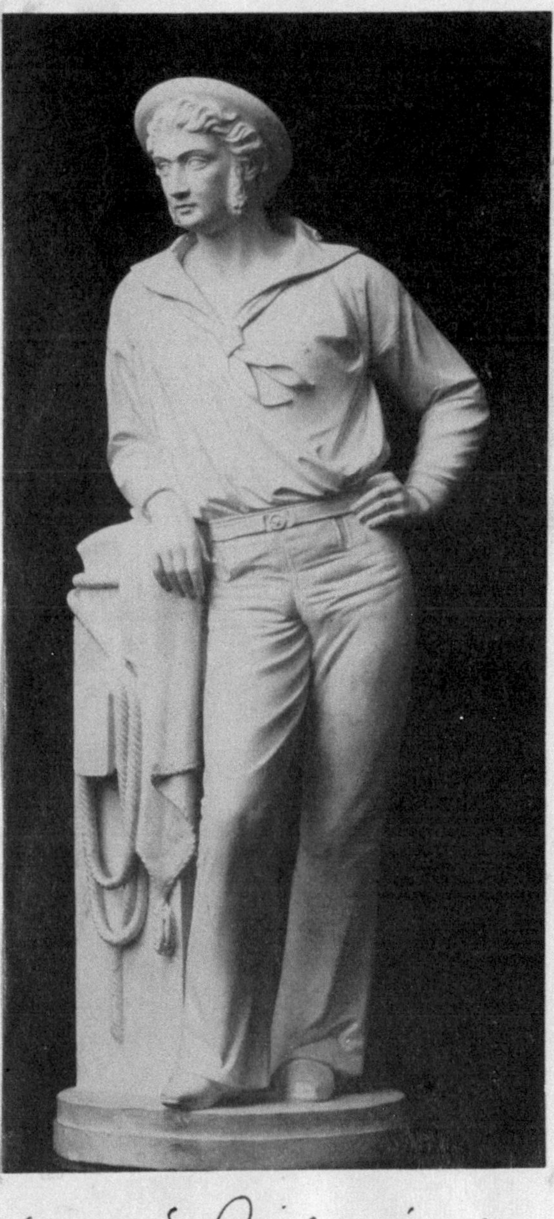

1858. 'Sailor' for
Mr Ch. A Heckscher
of New York –

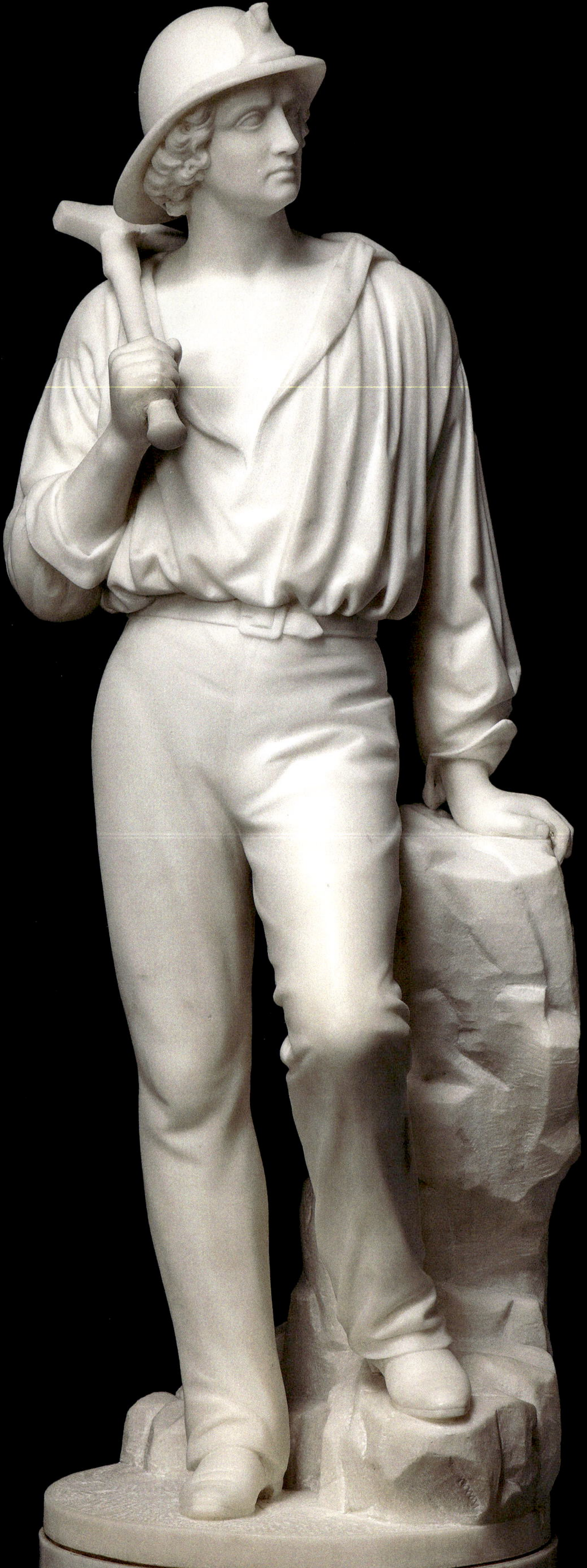

PLATE 10

INDUSTRY (ALSO KNOWN AS MINER)

1860

Inscription: "EMMA STEBBINS. ROME. 1860" (verso)

Marble, 28 7/8 × 10 × 10 1/2 in. (73.3 × 25.4 × 26.7 cm)

The Heckscher Museum of Art, Gift of Philip M. Lydig III, 1959.354

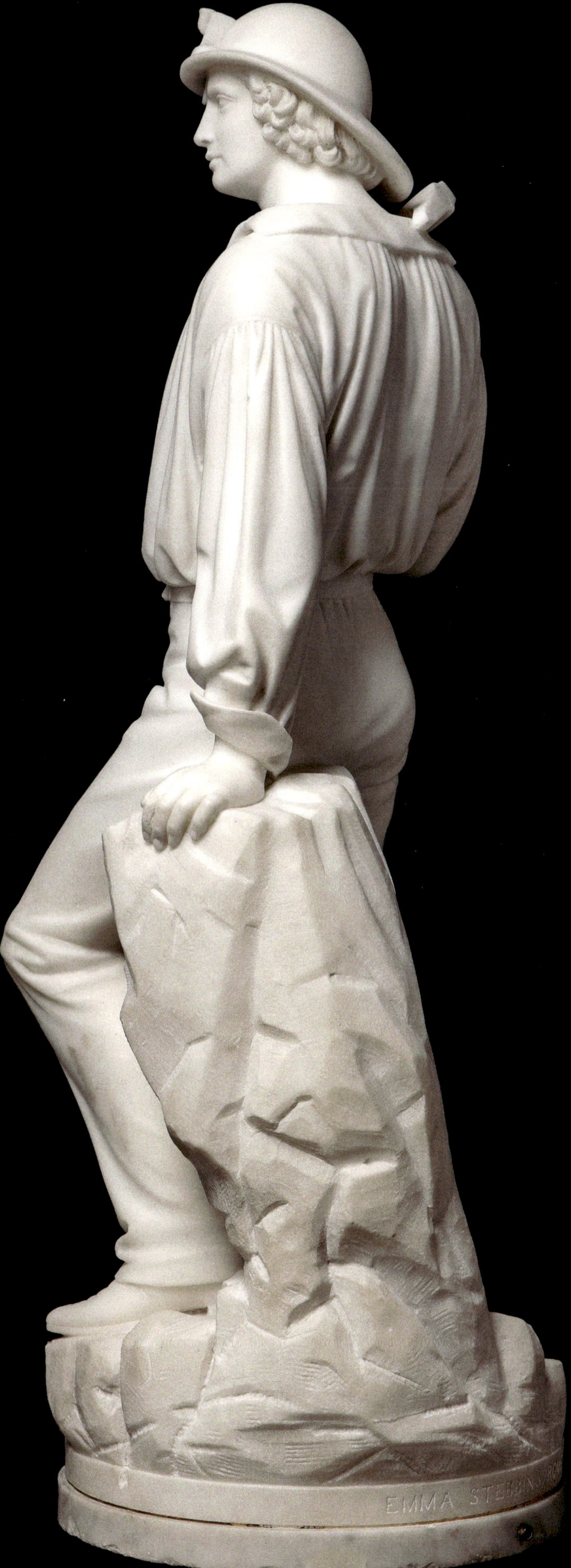

Alternate view of plate 10

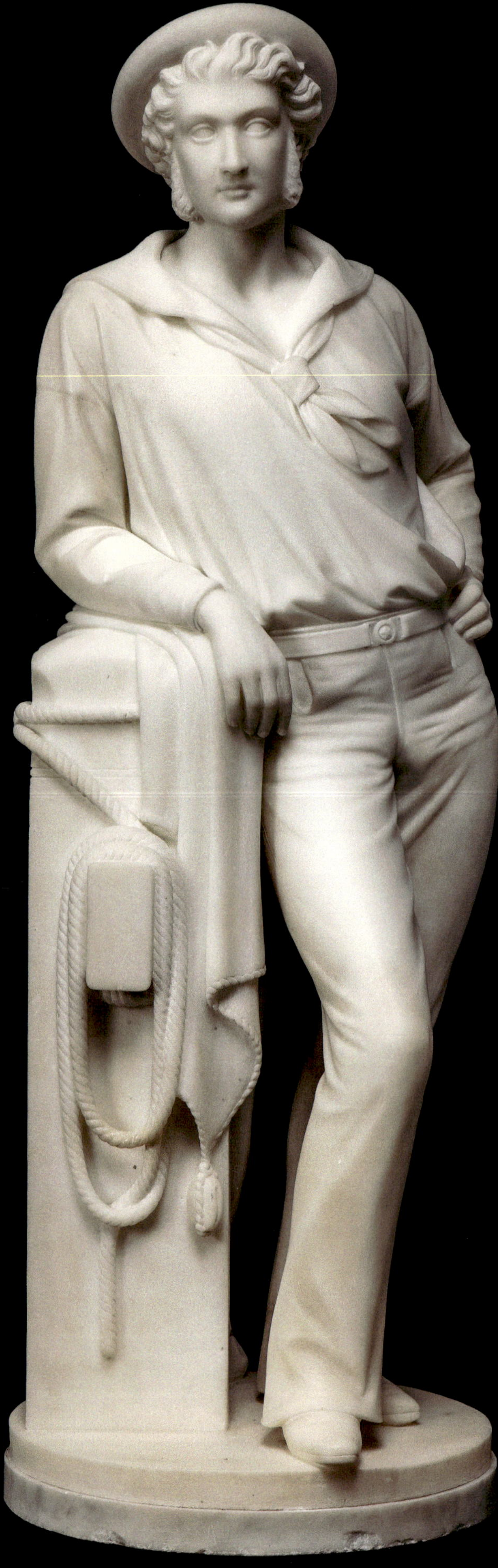

PLATE 11

COMMERCE (ALSO KNOWN AS SAILOR)

1860
Inscription: "EMMA STEBBINS. ROME. 1860" (verso)
Marble, 28⅞ × 10½ × 11 in. (73.3 × 26.7 × 27.9 cm)
The Heckscher Museum of Art, Gift of Philip M. Lydig III, 1959.355

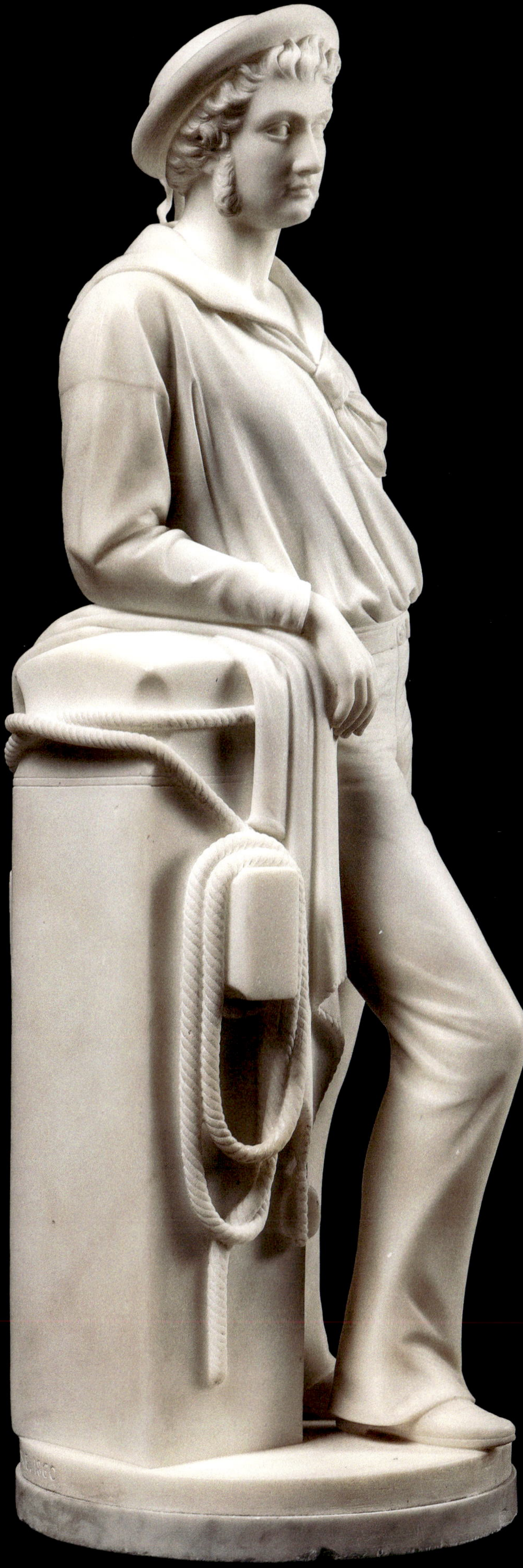

Alternate view of plate 11

PLATE 12

CALIFORNIA GOLD MINER

Photograph from the Emma Stebbins scrapbook, 1858–82
Archives of American Art, Smithsonian Institution

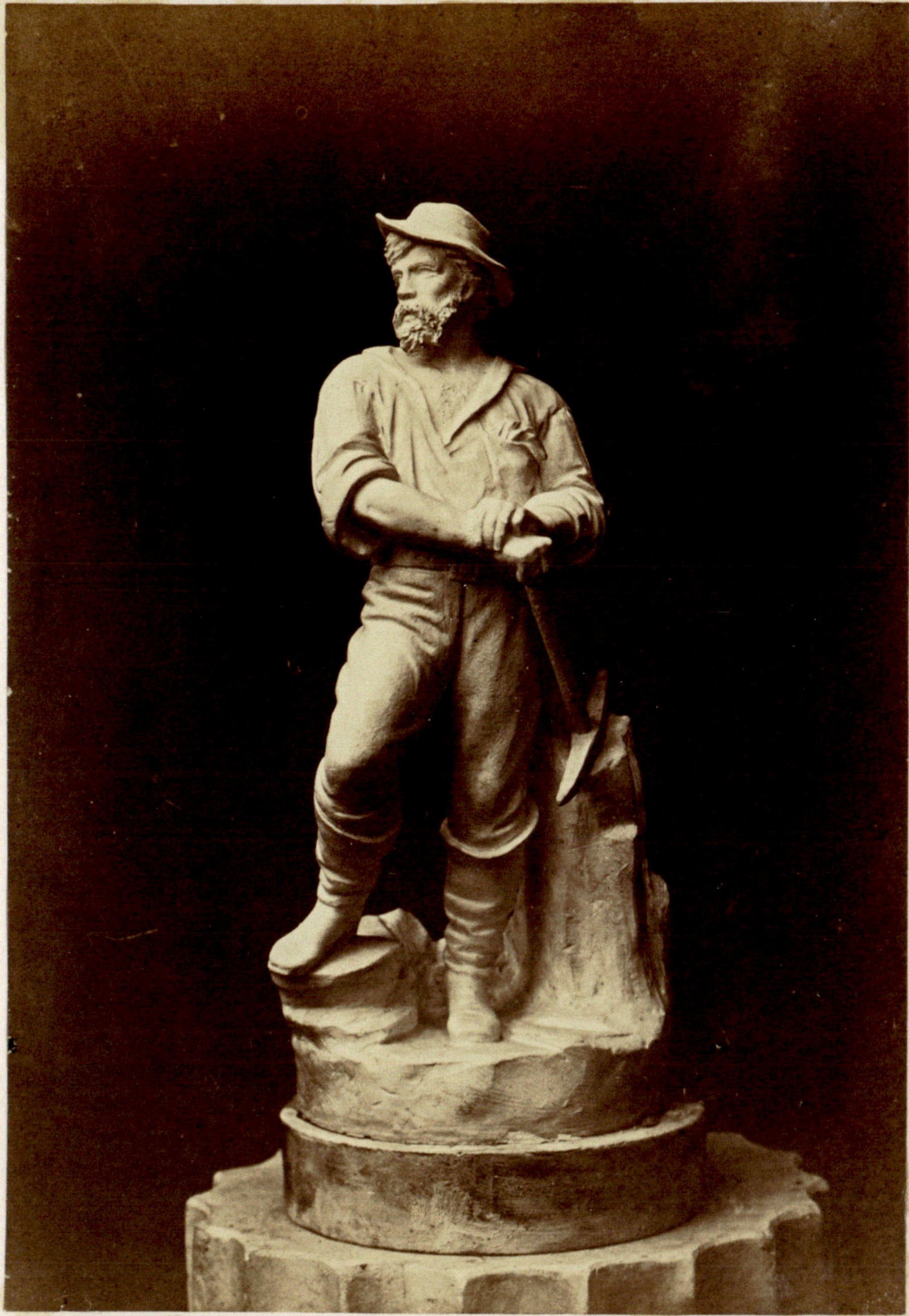

Study for a Statue of a California Gold Miner.

Emma Stebbins,
Rome

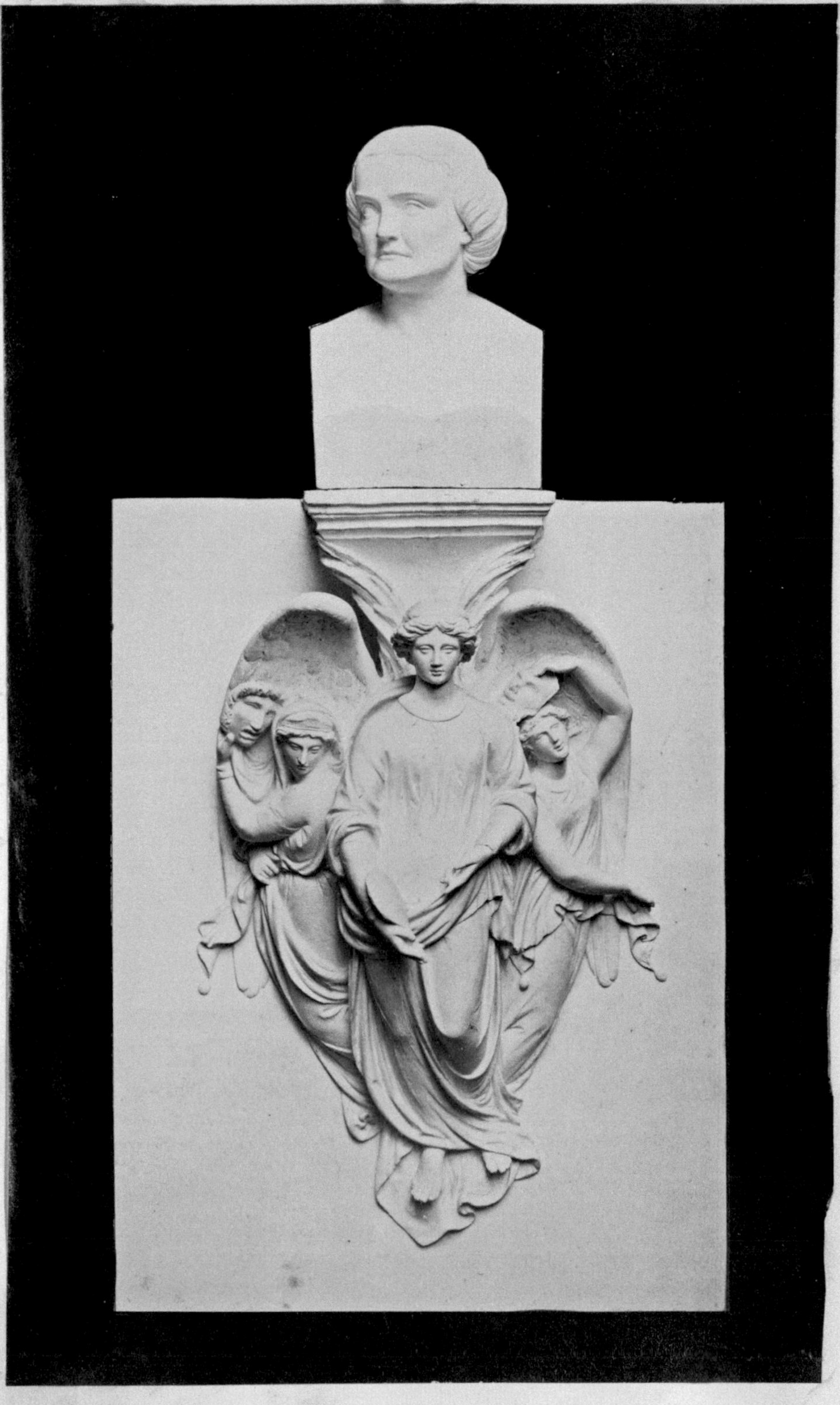

Study of "bracket" for support of Mrs C.'s bust

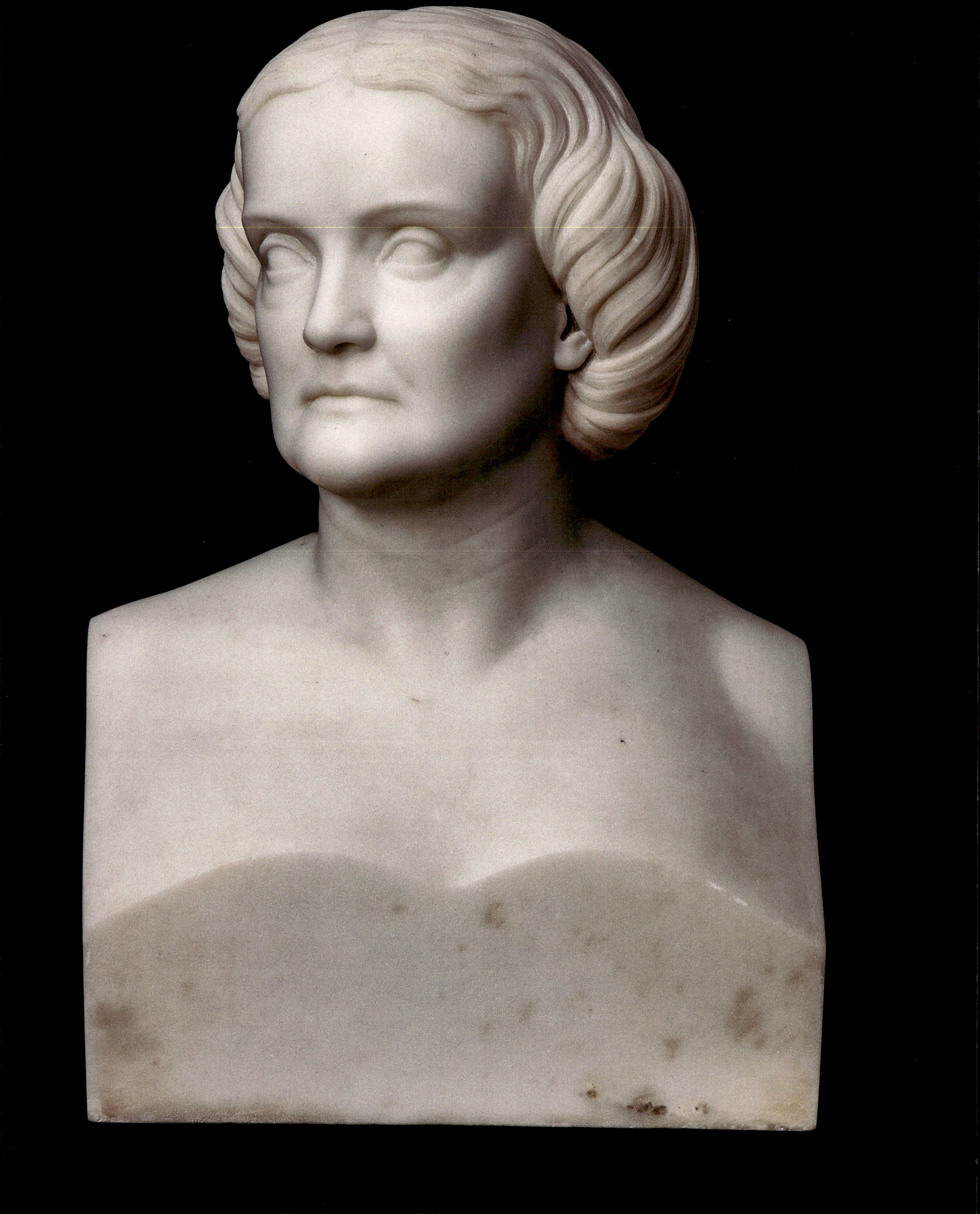

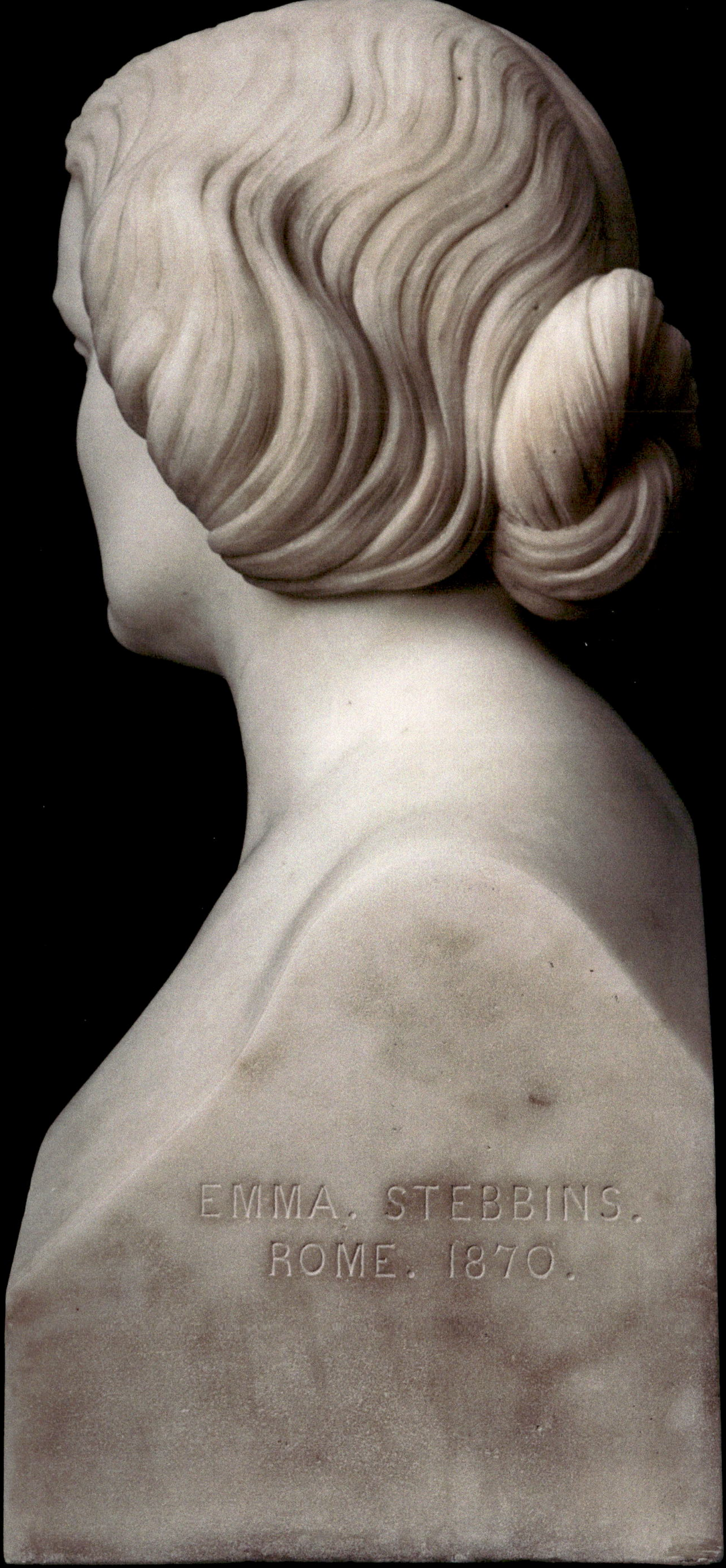

LEFT: PLATE 14

CHARLOTTE CUSHMAN

1870
Inscription: "EMMA. STEBBINS. / ROME. 1870." (left side)
Marble, $20\frac{3}{4} \times 12\frac{7}{8} \times 8\frac{5}{8}$ in.
(52.7 × 32.7 × 21.9 cm)
The Heckscher Museum of Art, Museum Purchase from the Charlotte Cushman Foundation, Philadelphia, PA, 2024.9

RIGHT: Alternate view of plate 14

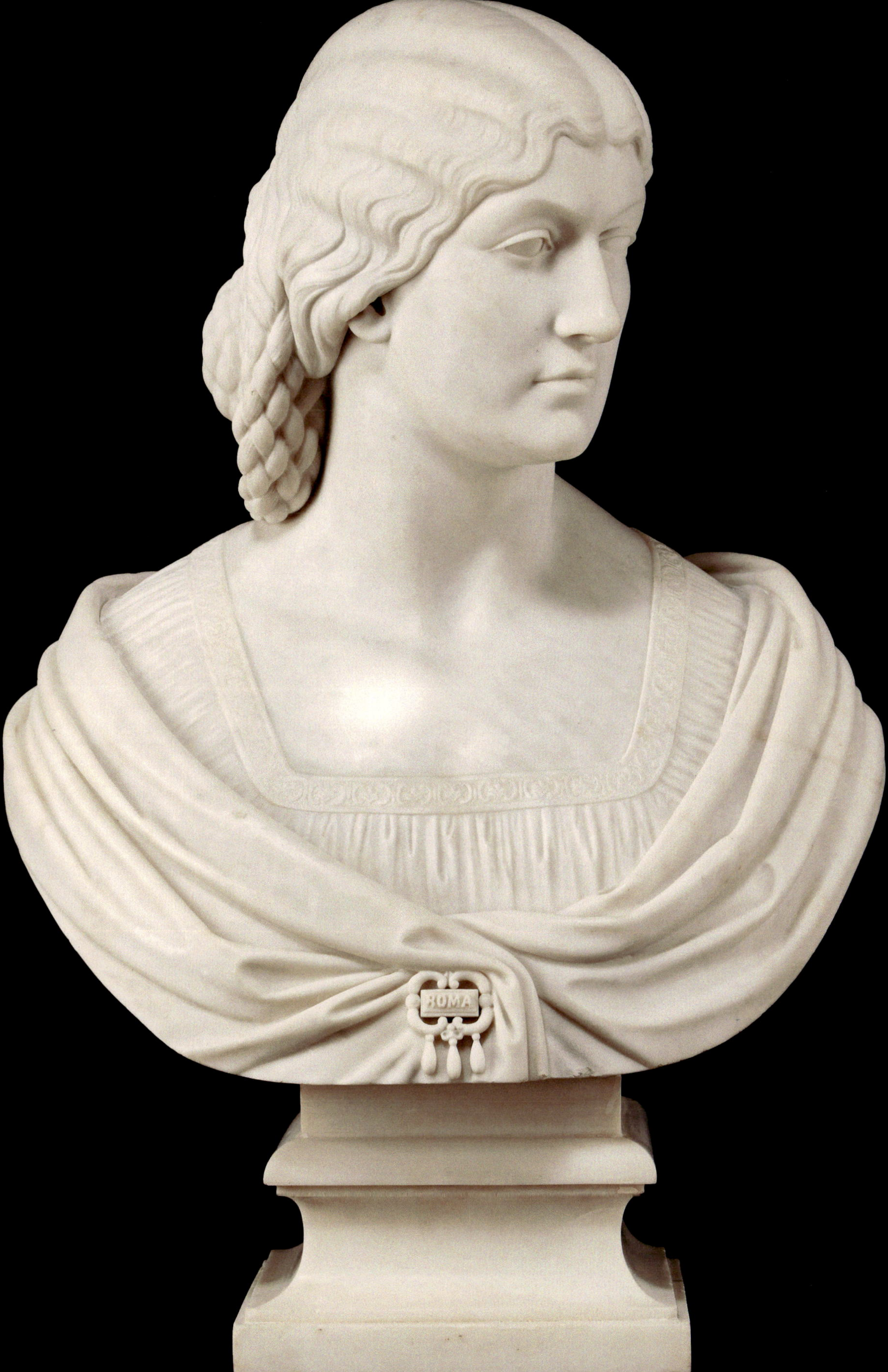
ROMA

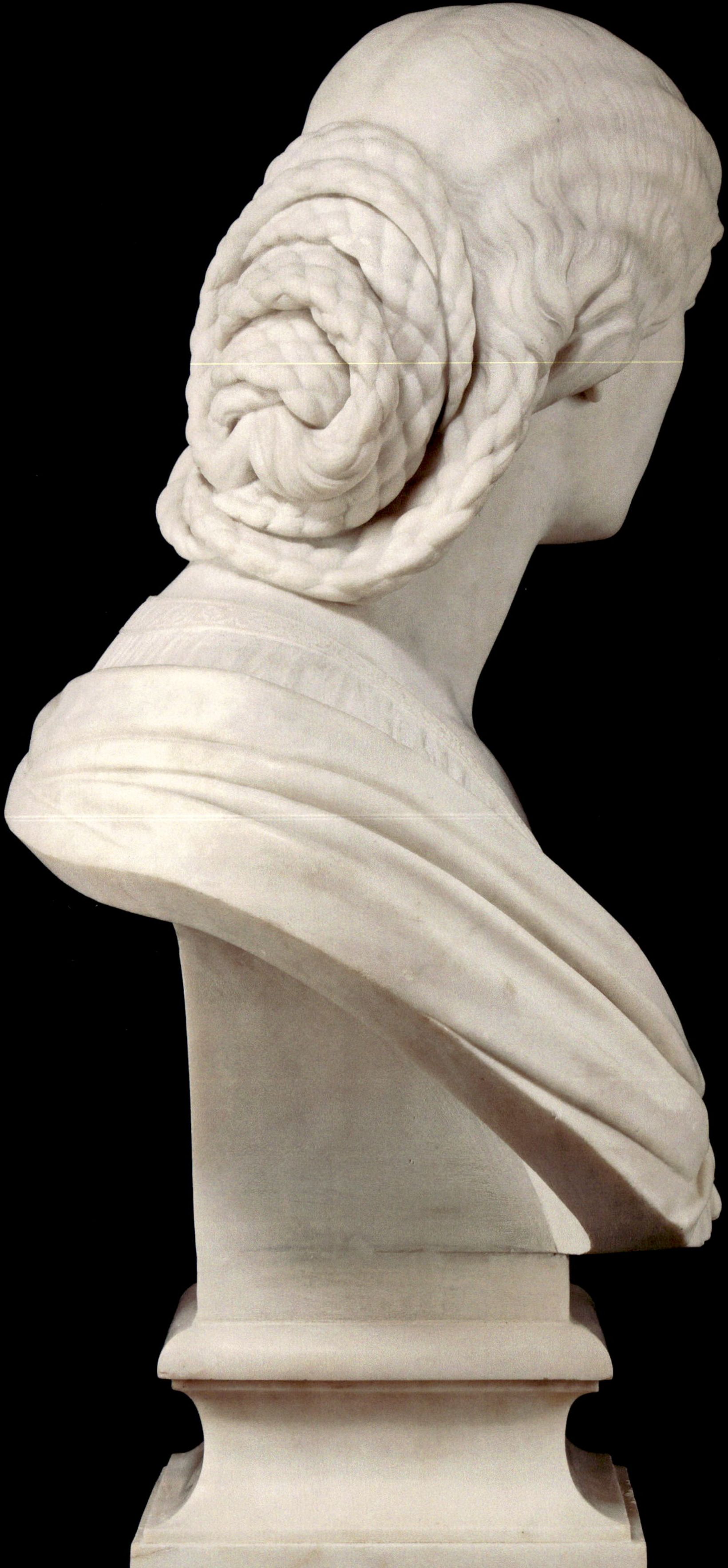

Alternate view of plate 15

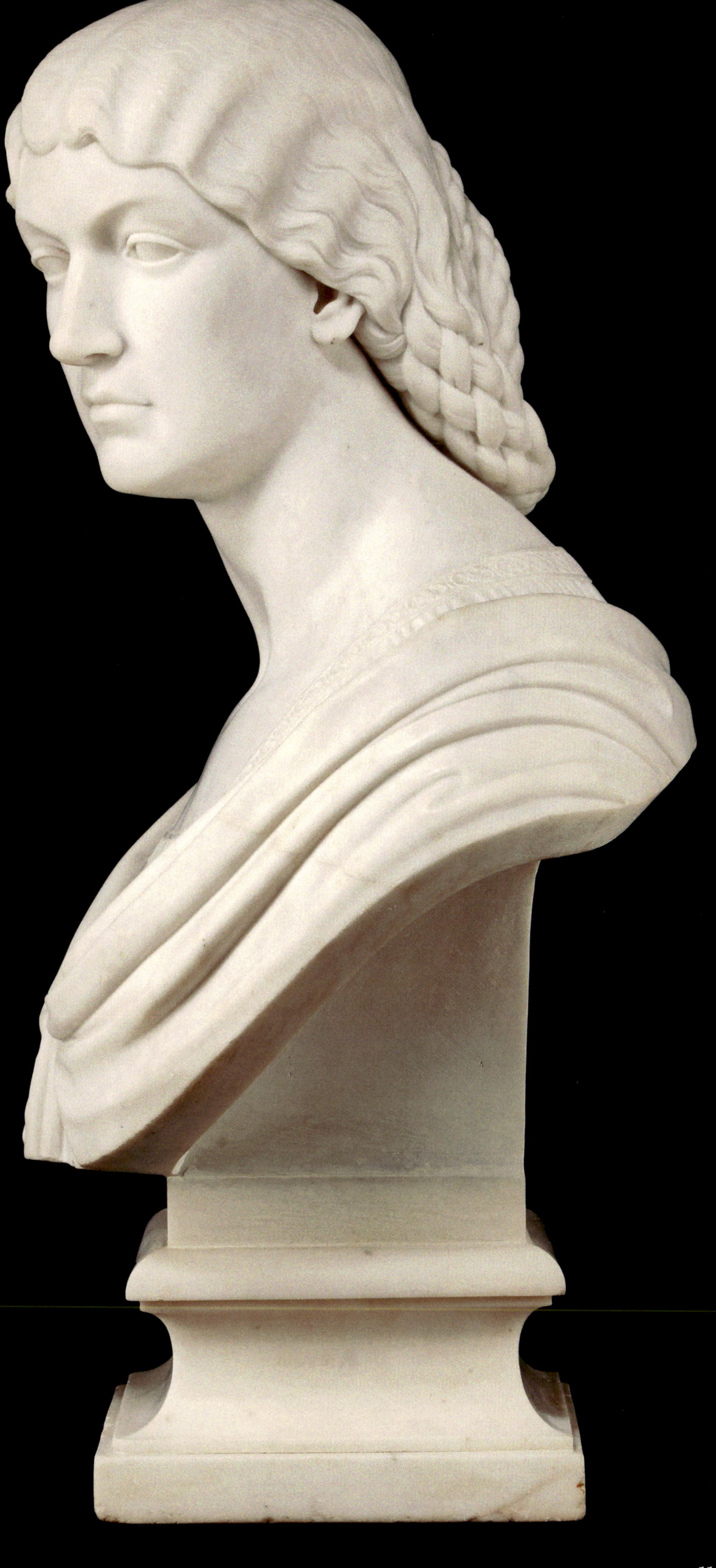

Alternate view of plate 15

RIGHT: PLATE 16

HORACE MANN

Photograph from the Emma Stebbins scrapbook, 1858–82
Archives of American Art, Smithsonian Institution

PAGES 122, 123: PLATE 17

HORACE MANN

1864
Inscriptions: "HORACE MANN" (front); "EMMA STEBBINS / ROME 1863" (right side)
Foundry mark: "FERD V. MILLER fud / MUNCHEN 1864" (left side)
Bronze, 102 × 40 × 42 in.
(259.1 × 101.6 × 106.7 cm)
Massachusetts State House Art Collection, Given by the School Children and Teachers of Massachusetts under Res. 1859, ch. 113

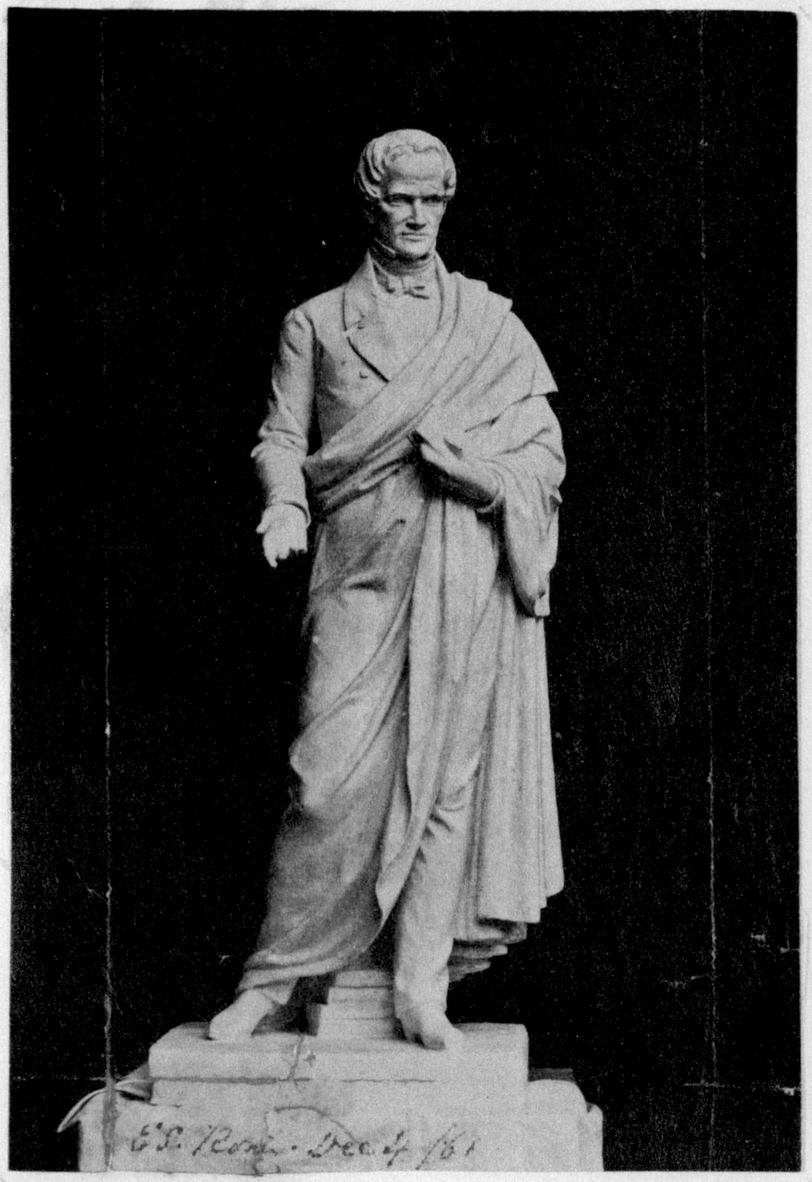

1861. Statue of Horace Mann.
for Boston - cast in bronze
at Munich -
Now in position in Boston -

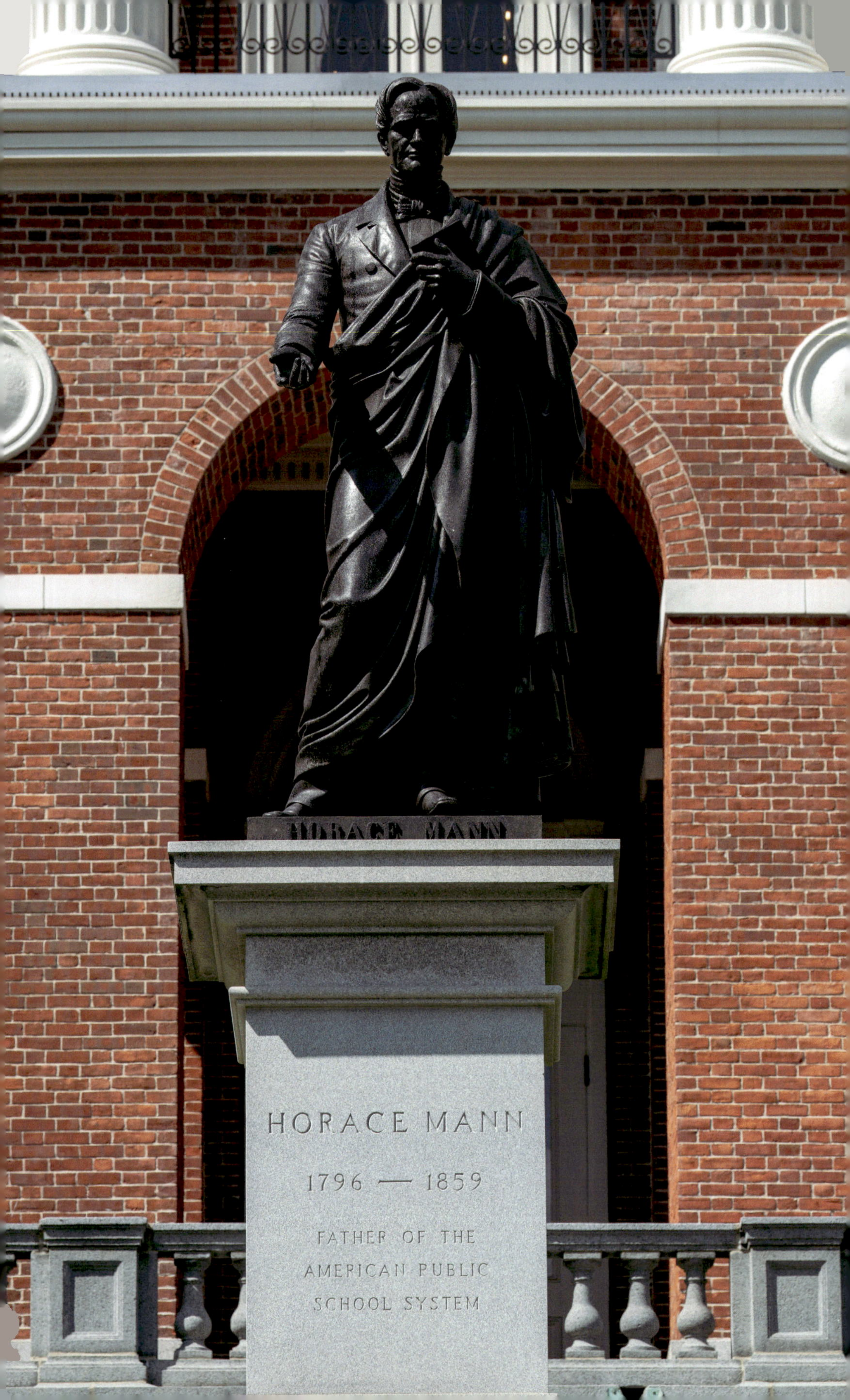
HORACE MANN
HORACE MANN
1796 — 1859
FATHER OF THE
AMERICAN PUBLIC
SCHOOL SYSTEM

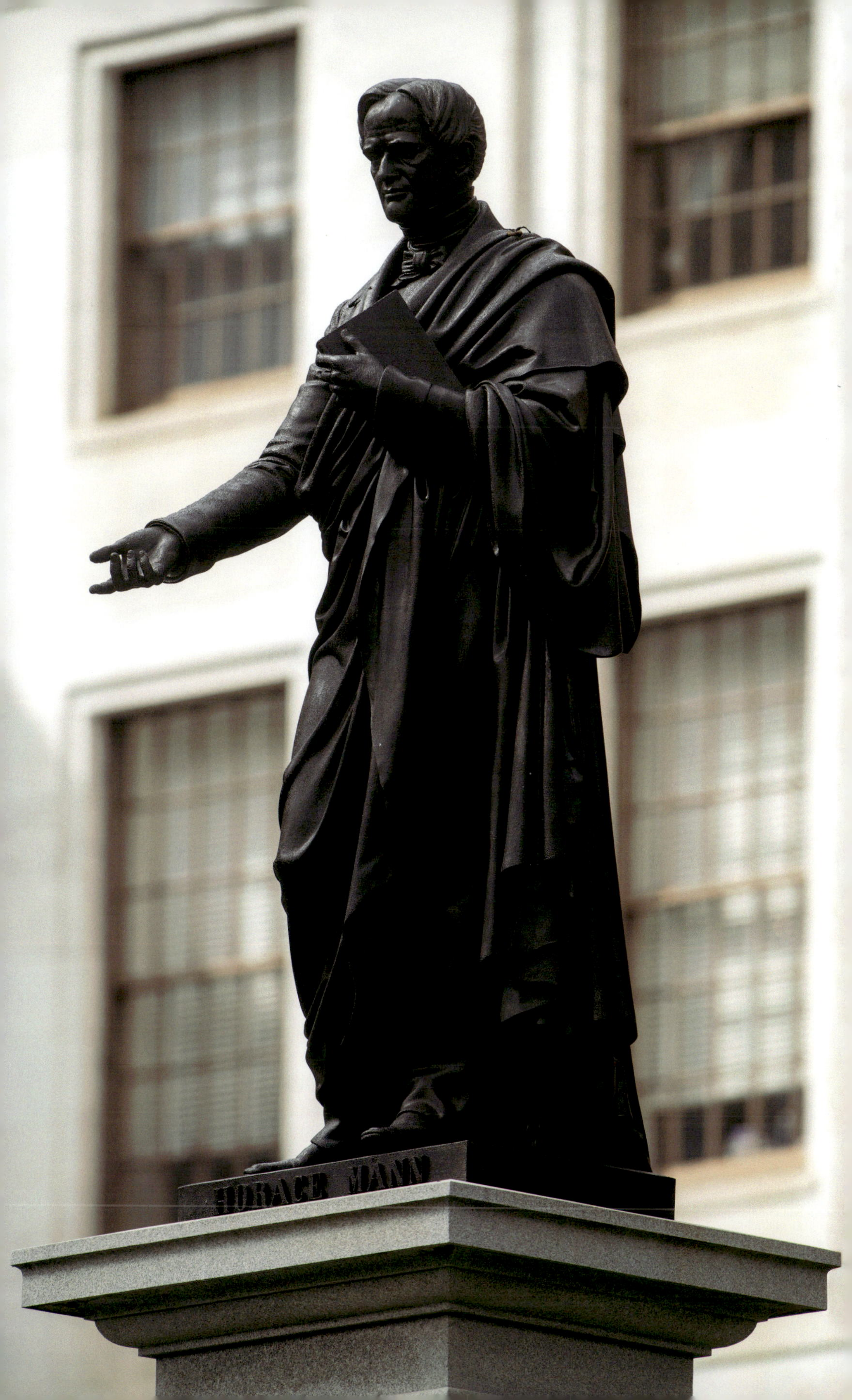
HORACE MANN

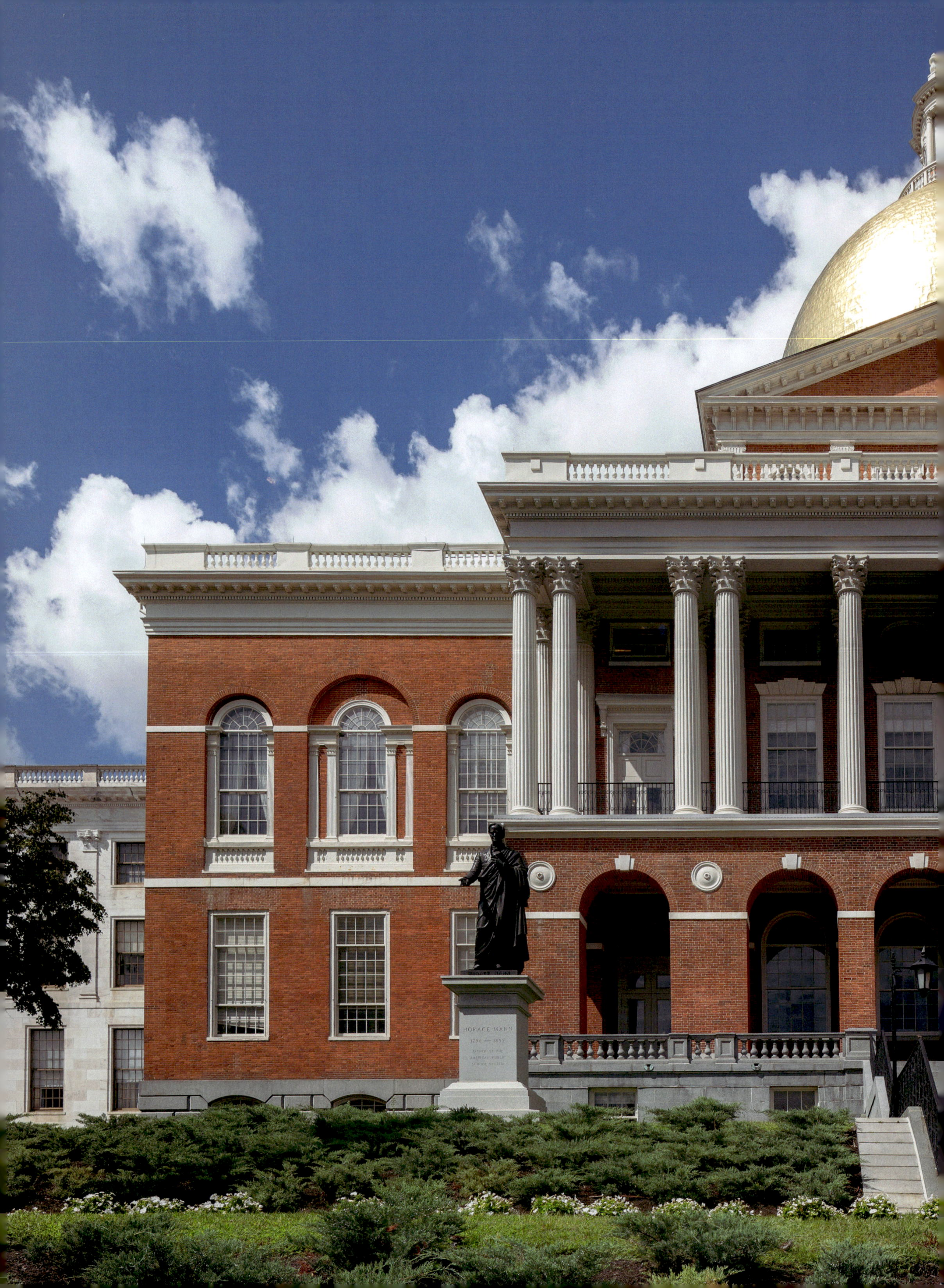
HORACE MANN

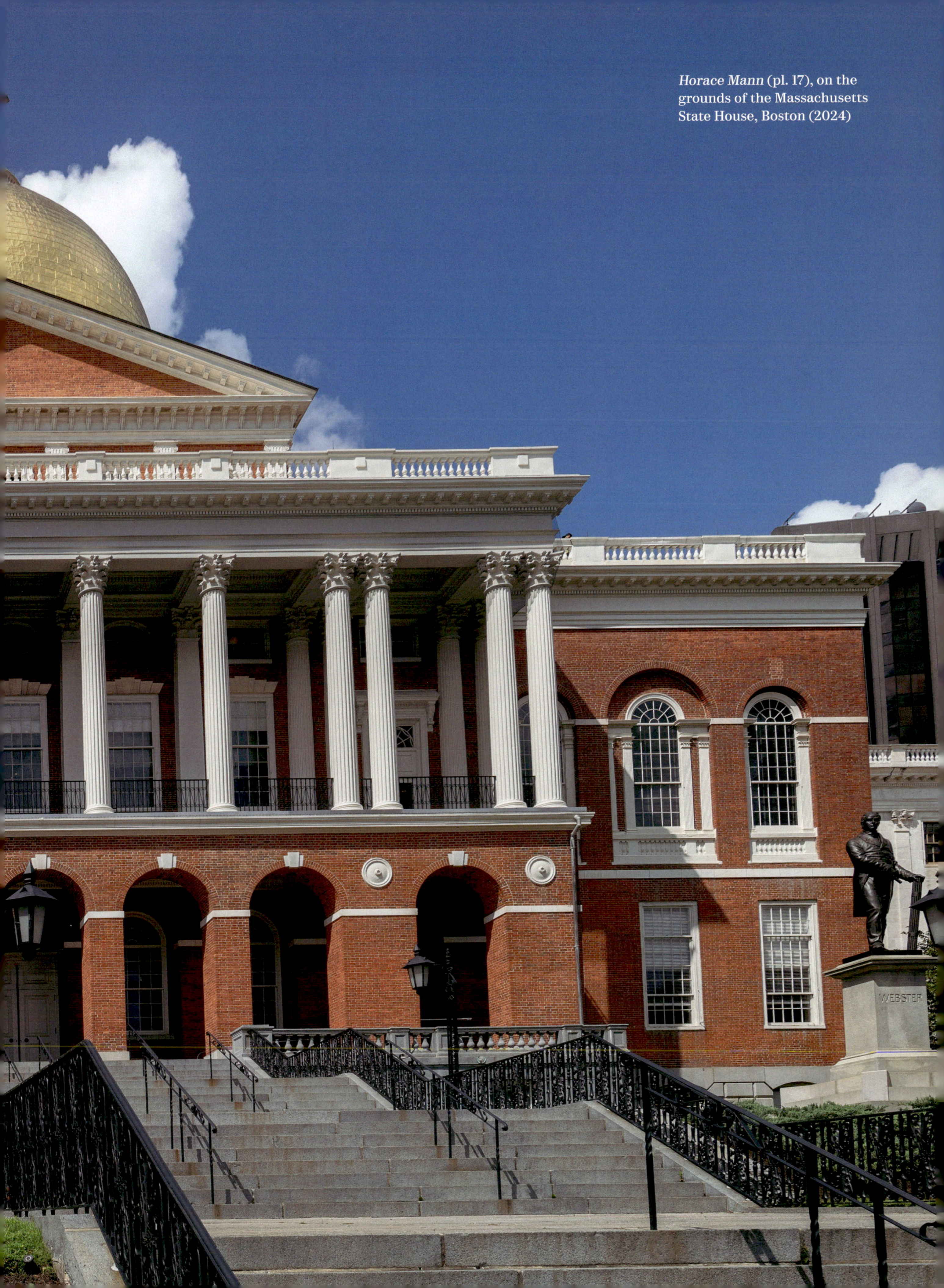

Horace Mann (pl. 17), on the grounds of the Massachusetts State House, Boston (2024)

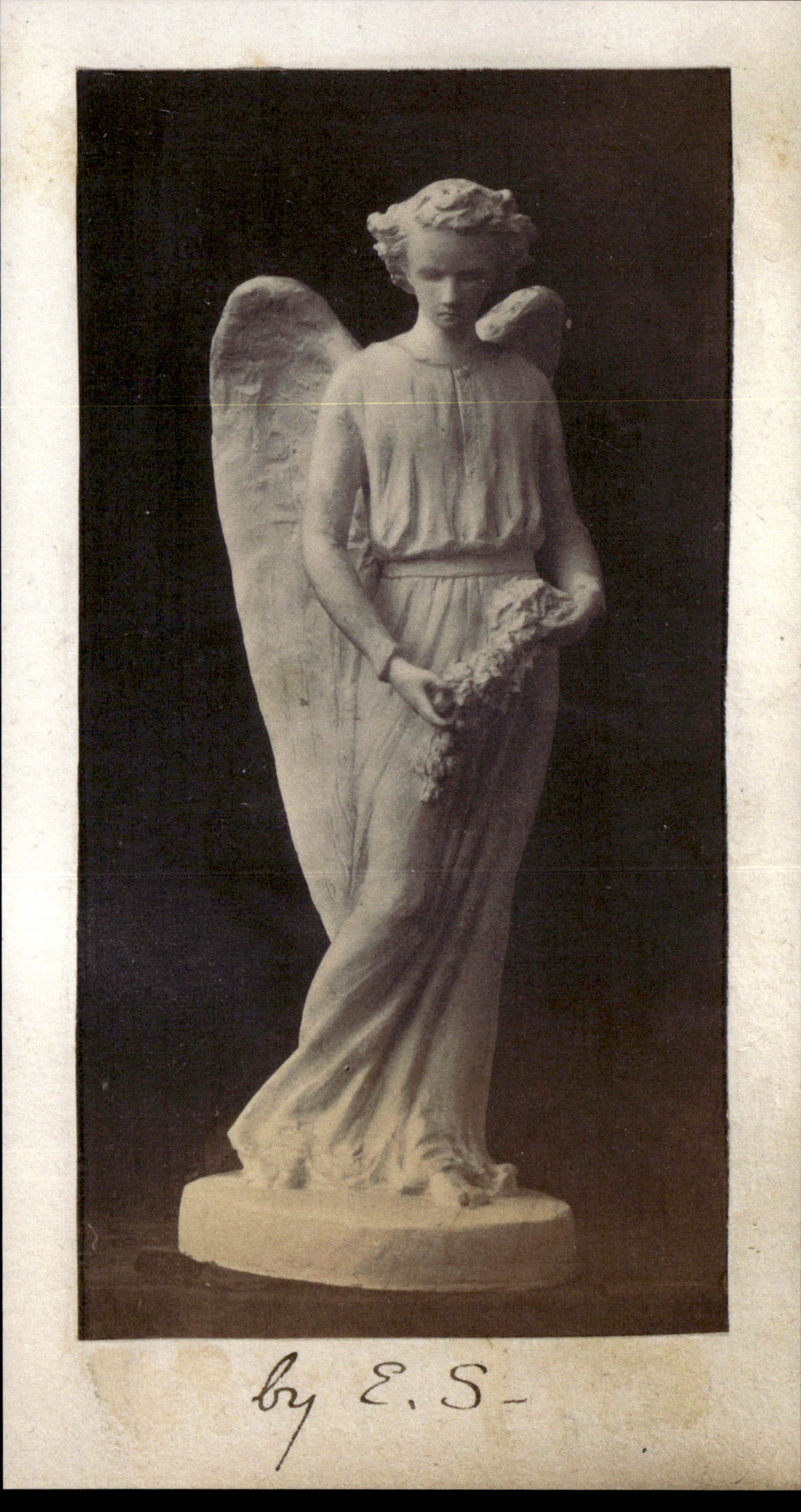

PLATE 18

SANDALPHON (ALSO KNOWN AS ANGEL OF PRAYER)

Photograph from the John Neal Tilton scrapbook, ca. 1860–80
Archives of American Art, Smithsonian Institution

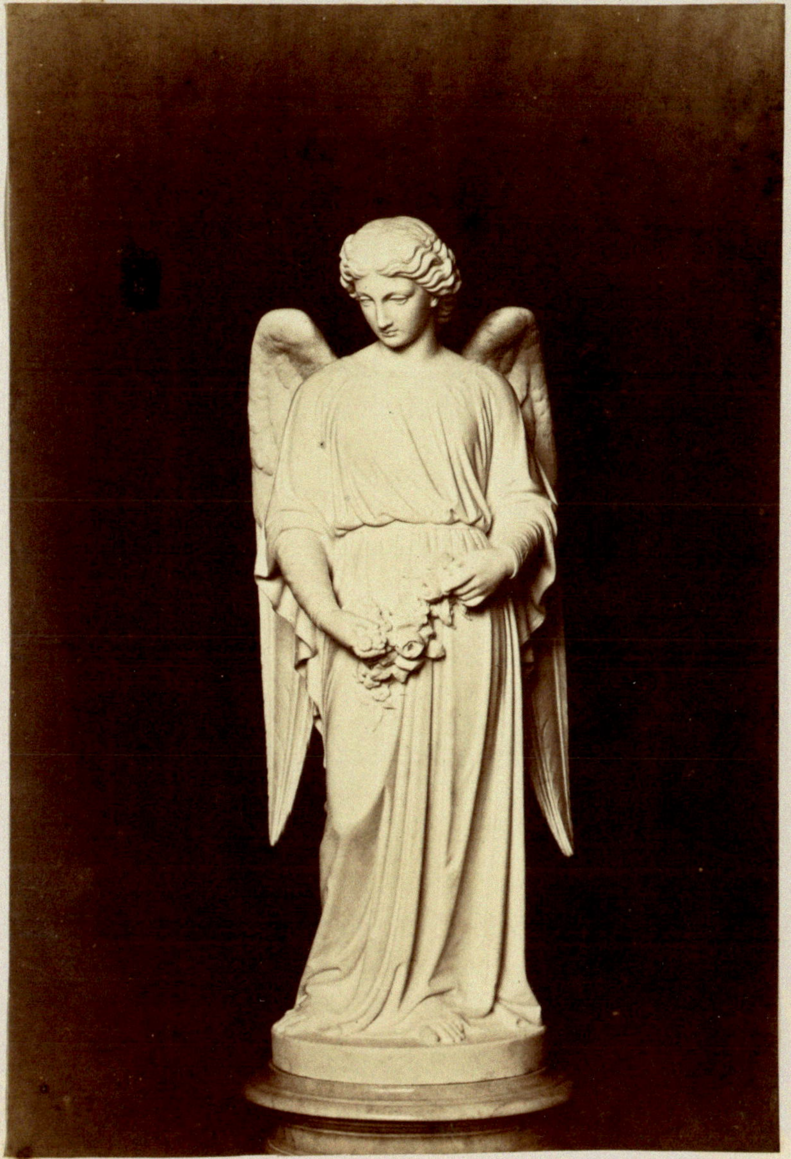

'Sandalphon'.

'And he gathers the prayers as he stands'
And they change into flowers in his hands,'
(Longfellow)

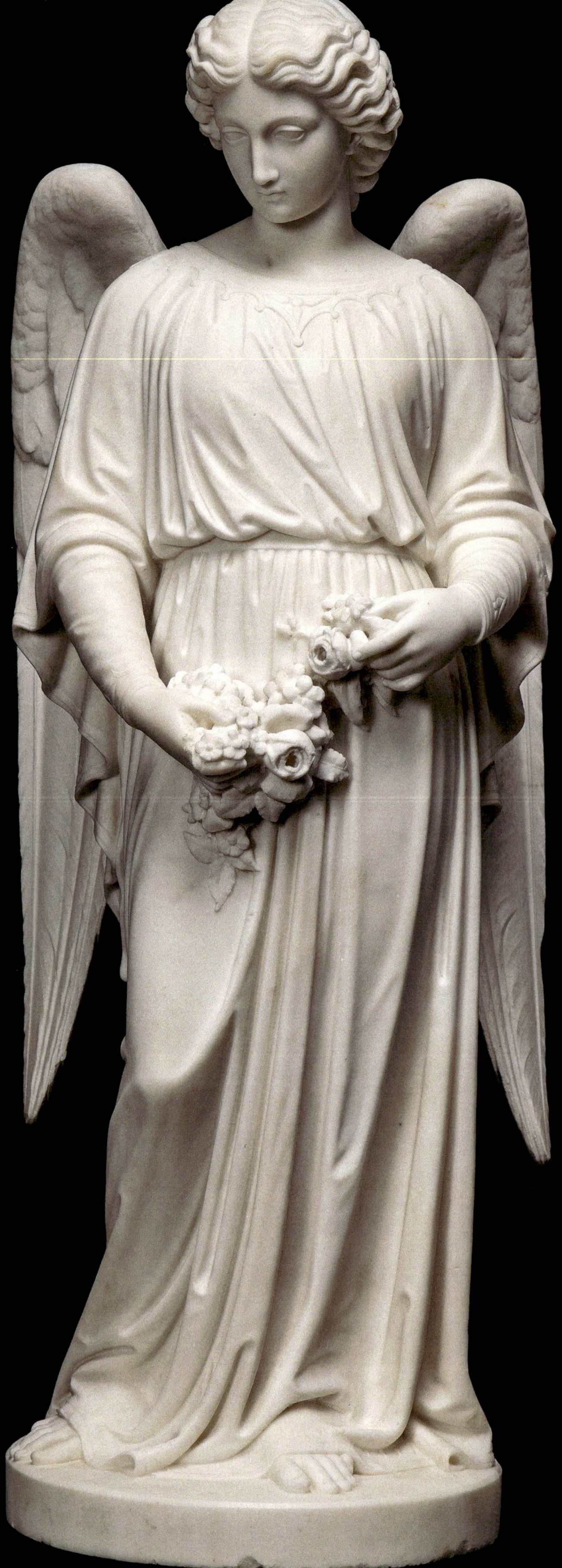

PLATE 20

SANDALPHON (ALSO KNOWN AS ANGEL OF PRAYER)

1866
Inscription: "EMMA STEBBINS ROME 1866" (verso)
Marble, 32¼ × 12 × 13 in.
(81.9 × 30.5 × 33 cm)
The Heckscher Museum of Art, Museum Purchase, Town of Huntington Art Acquisition Fund, 2022.7.2

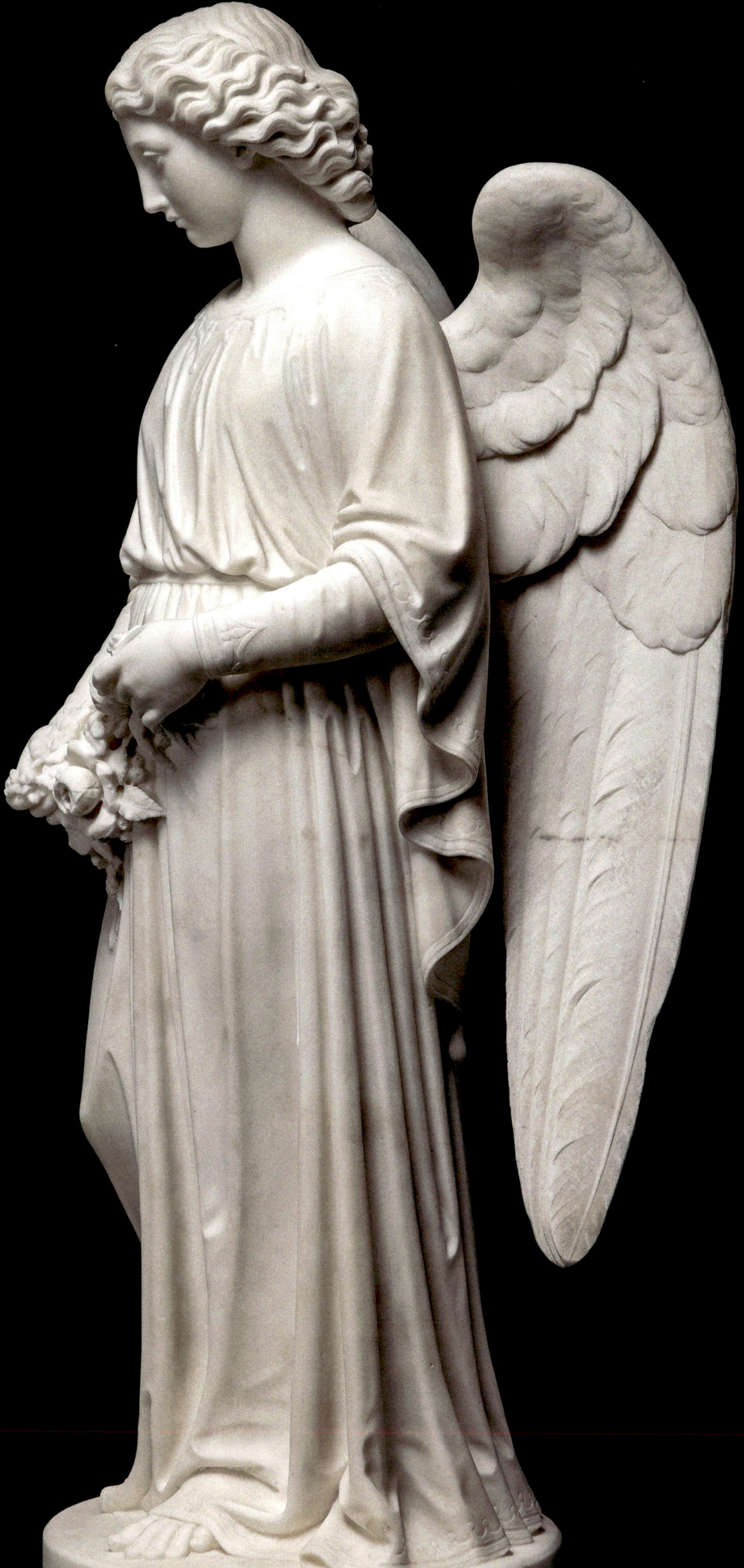

Alternate view of plate 20

PLATE 21

SATAN

Photograph from the Emma Stebbins scrapbook, 1858–82
Archives of American Art, Smithsonian Institution

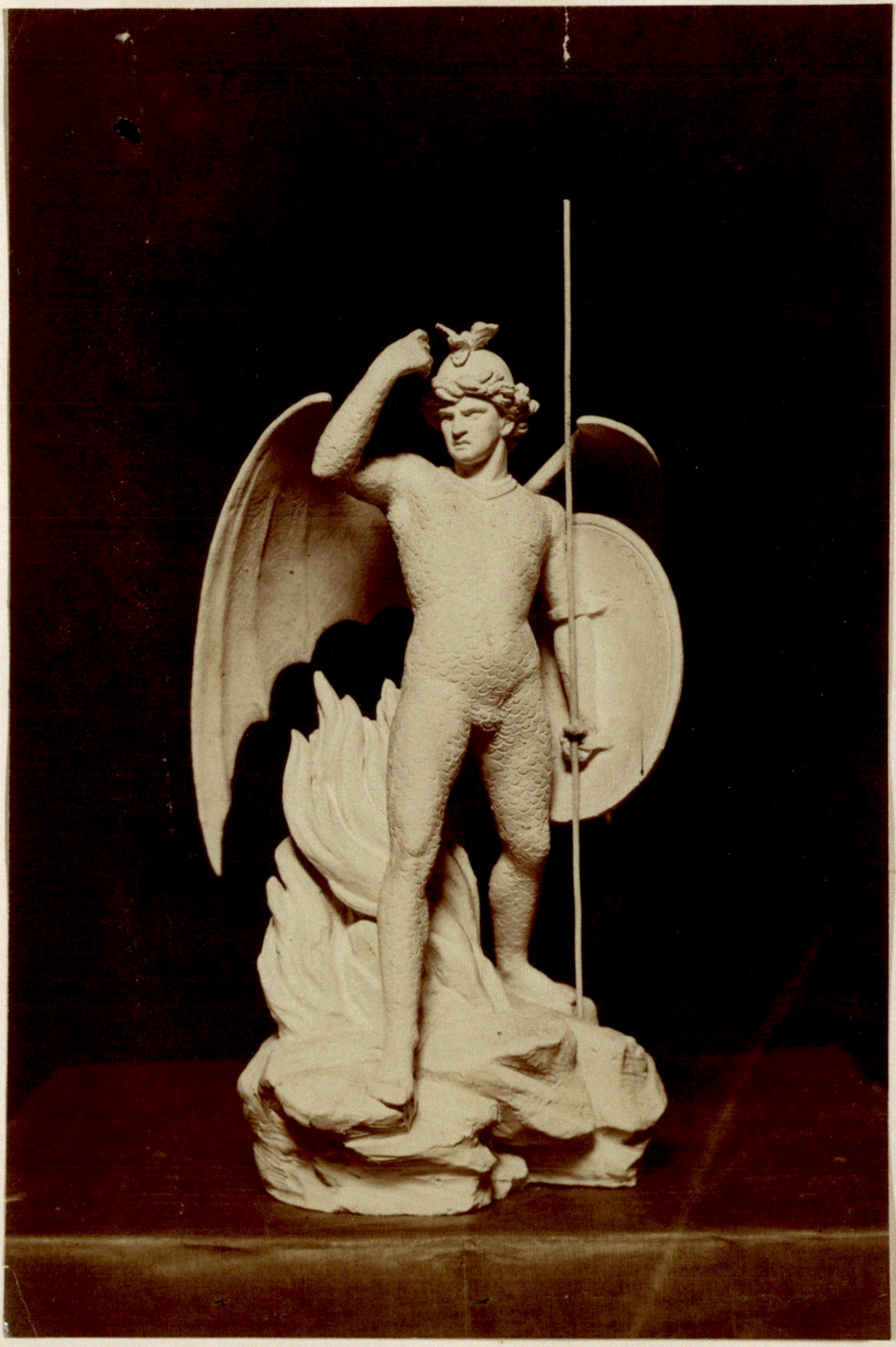

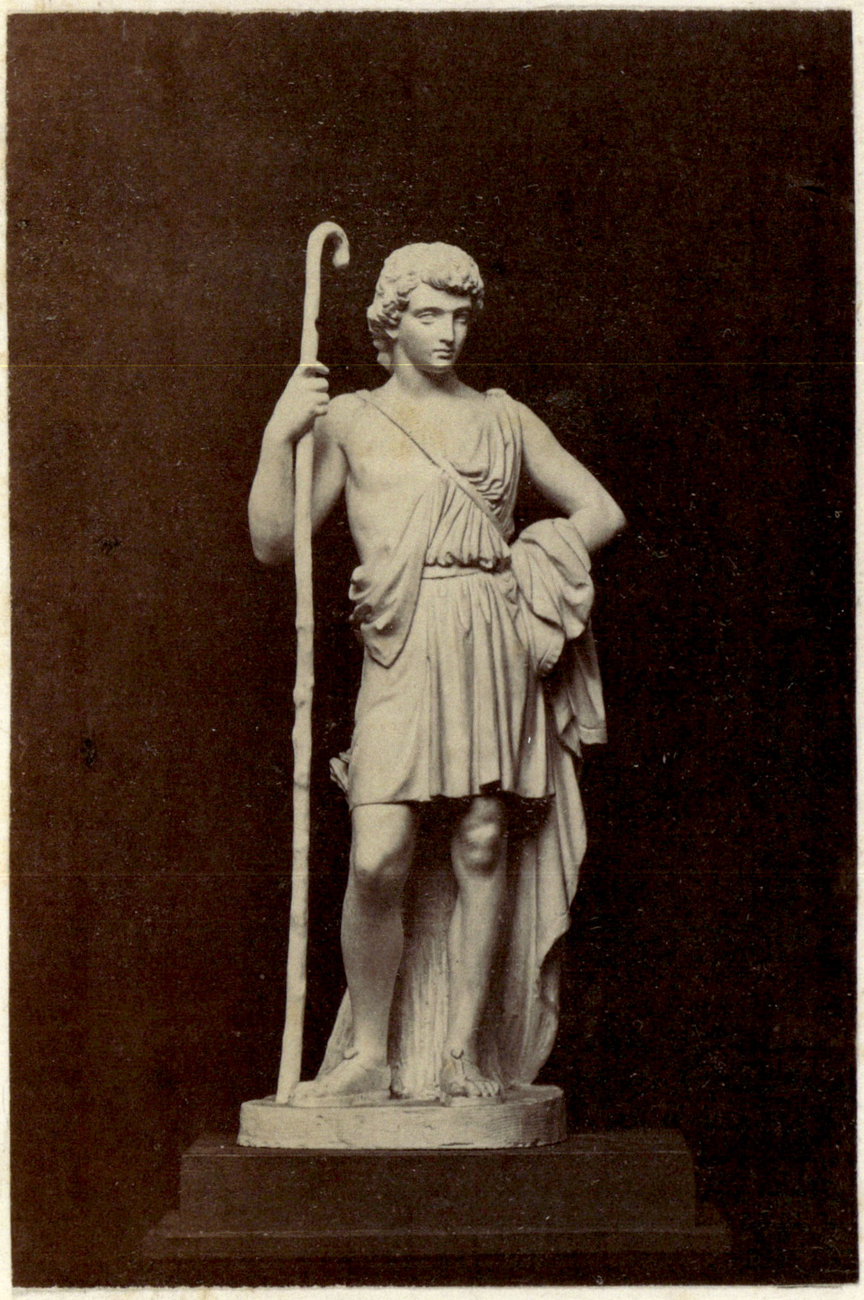

Statuettes by E.S.

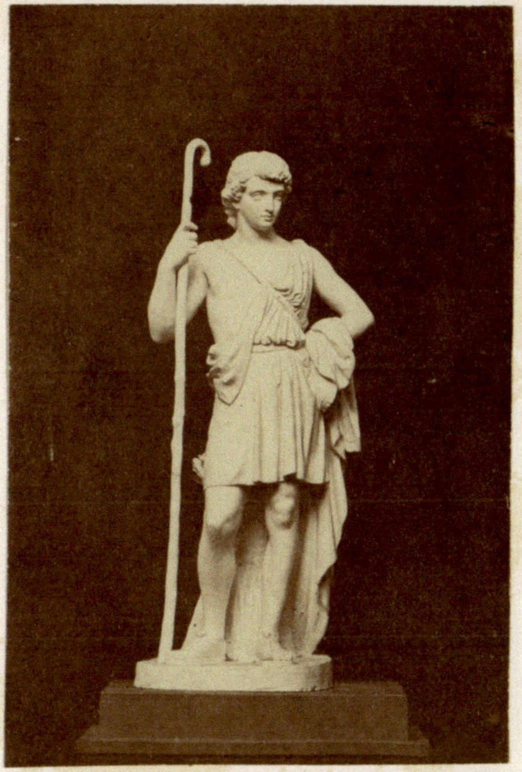

1862. Statue of 'Joseph'
called, 'The Dreamer' -
subject ordered from
the 'Old Testament'
Completed, and shipped
in a vessel, afterward
wrecked on the Mediterranean.
The figure lost - afterward
repeated for Mrs McFarland
of New York -

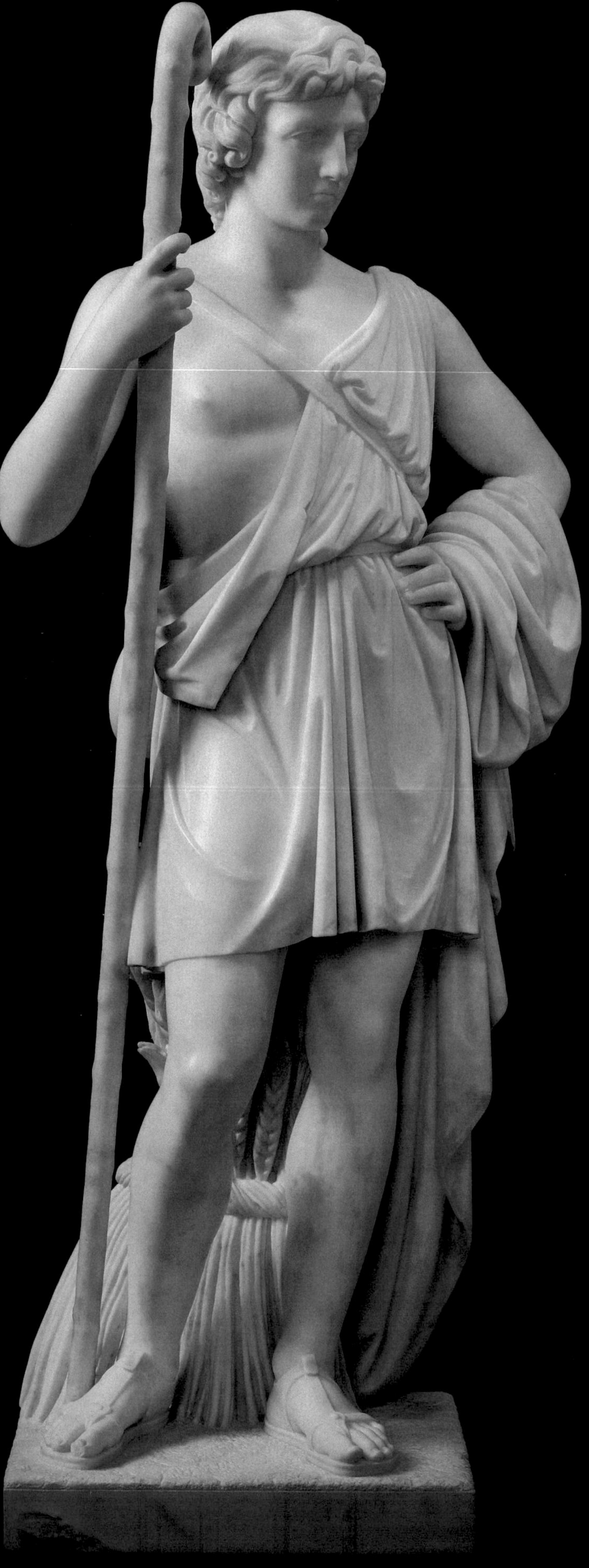

PLATE 24

JOSEPH THE DREAMER (ALSO KNOWN AS AGRICULTURE)

1864
Inscription: "EMMA. STEBBINS. ROME. 1864" (right side)
Marble, 48 × 18⅛ × 14³⁄₁₆ in. (121.9 × 46 × 36 cm)
Belfast Central Library, Libraries NI, Northern Ireland, Gift of R. G. Dunville, 1888

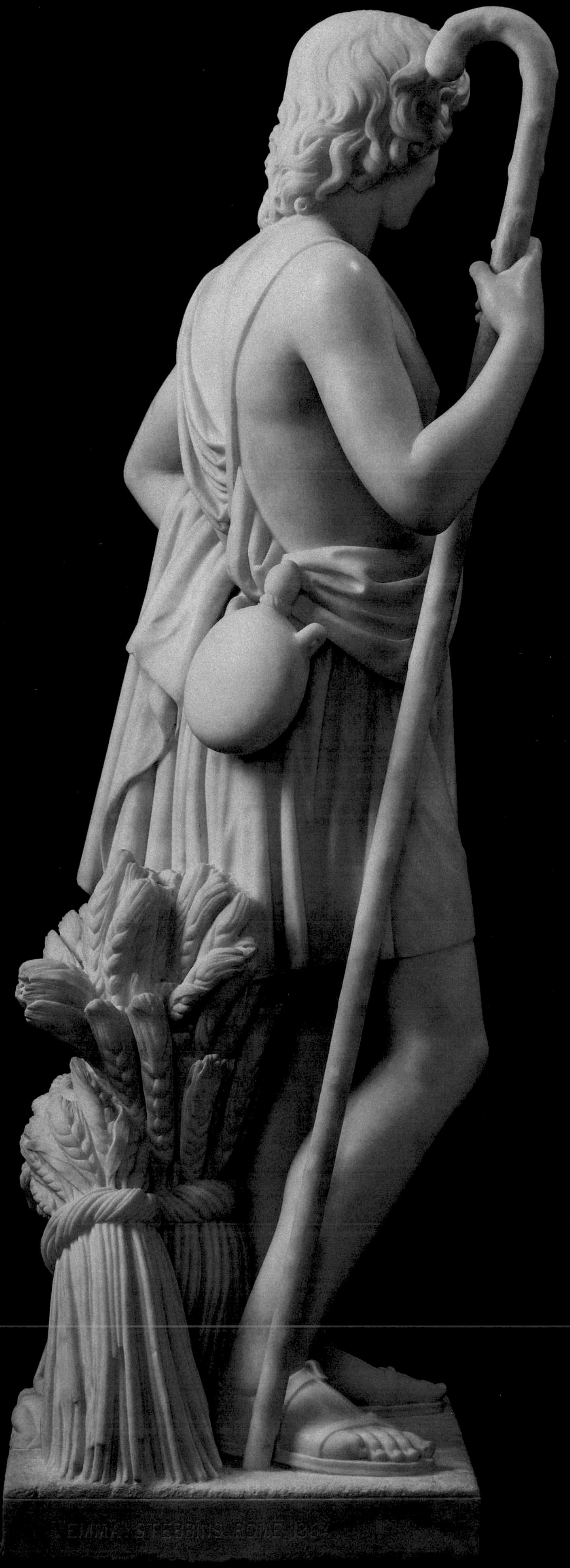

Alternate view of plate 24

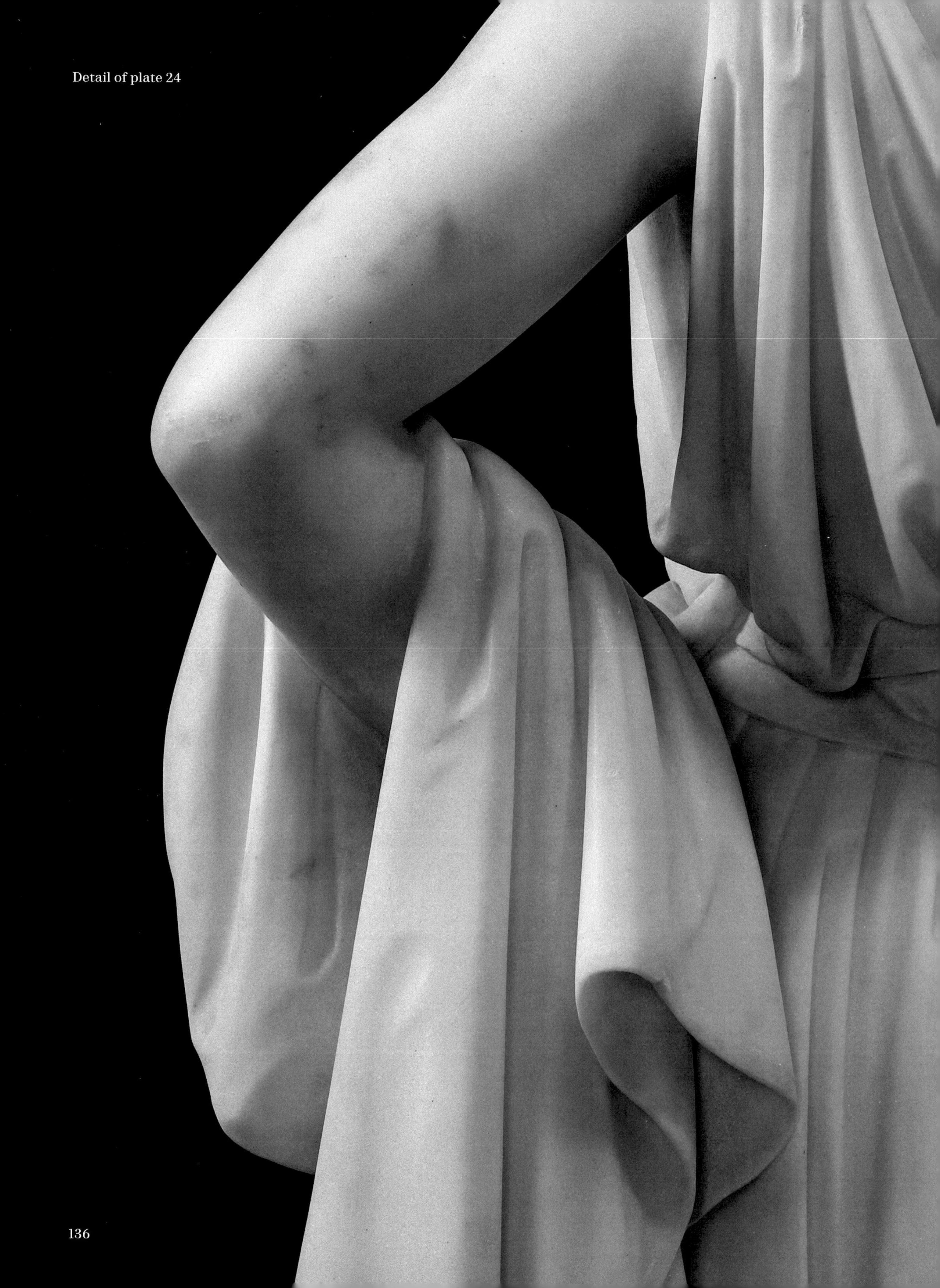

Detail of plate 24

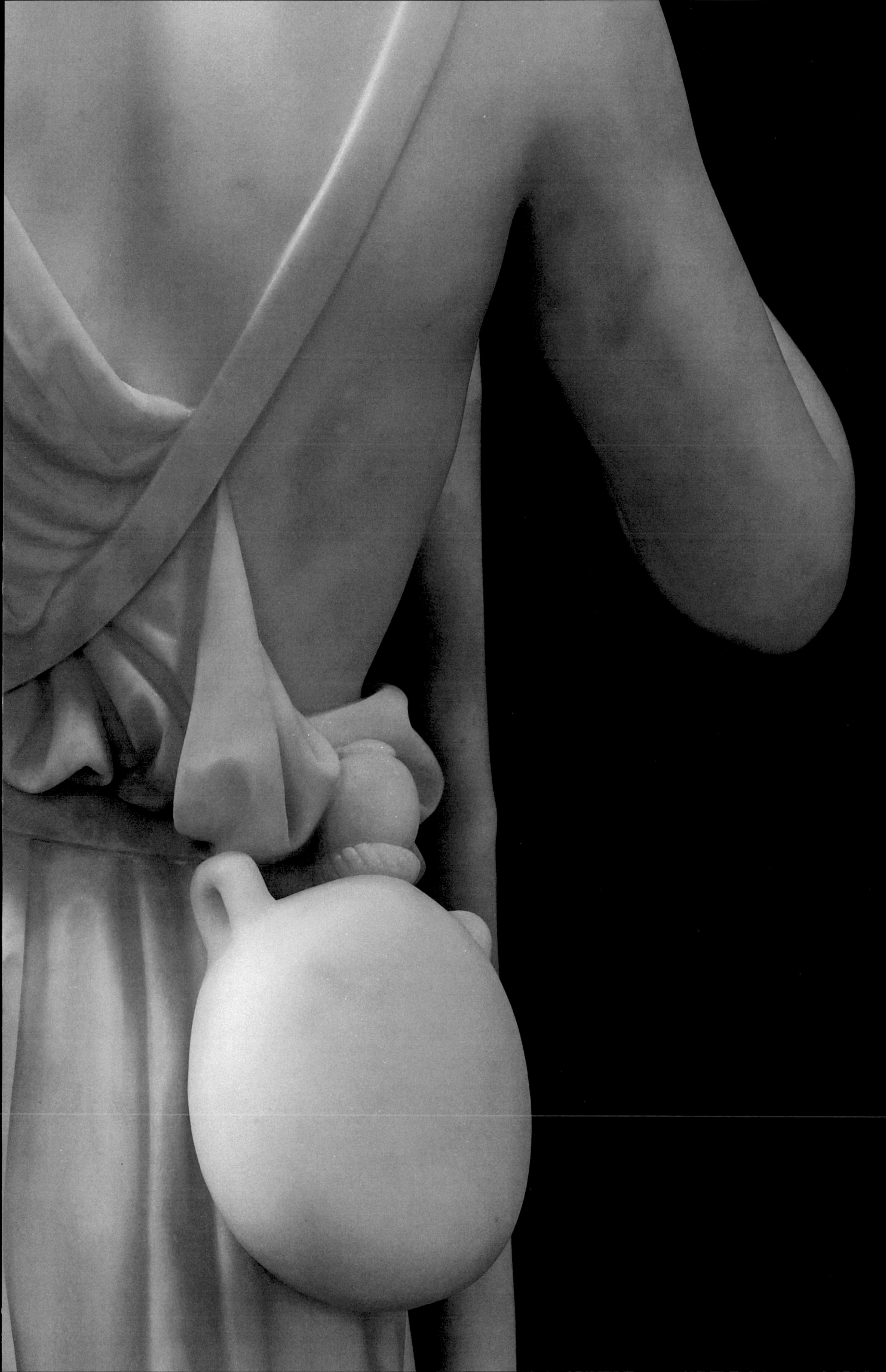

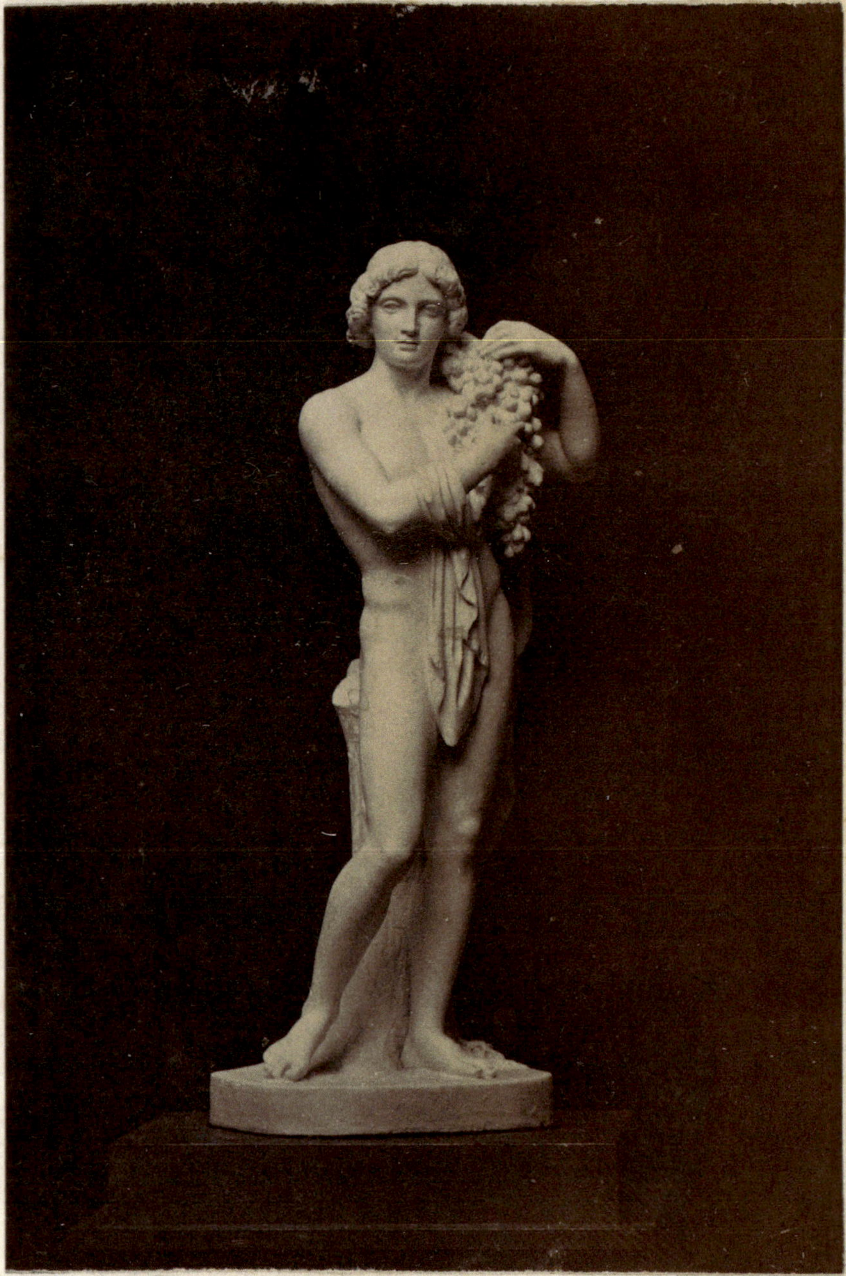

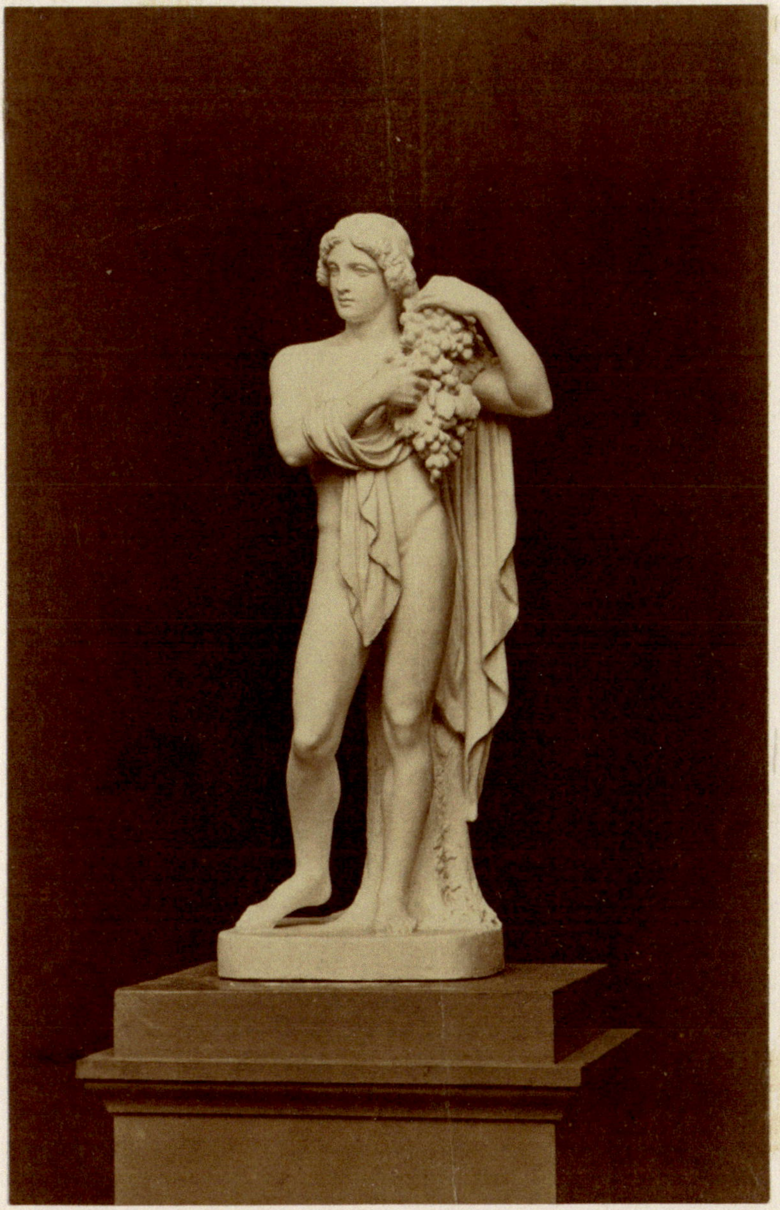

Autumn, Study -

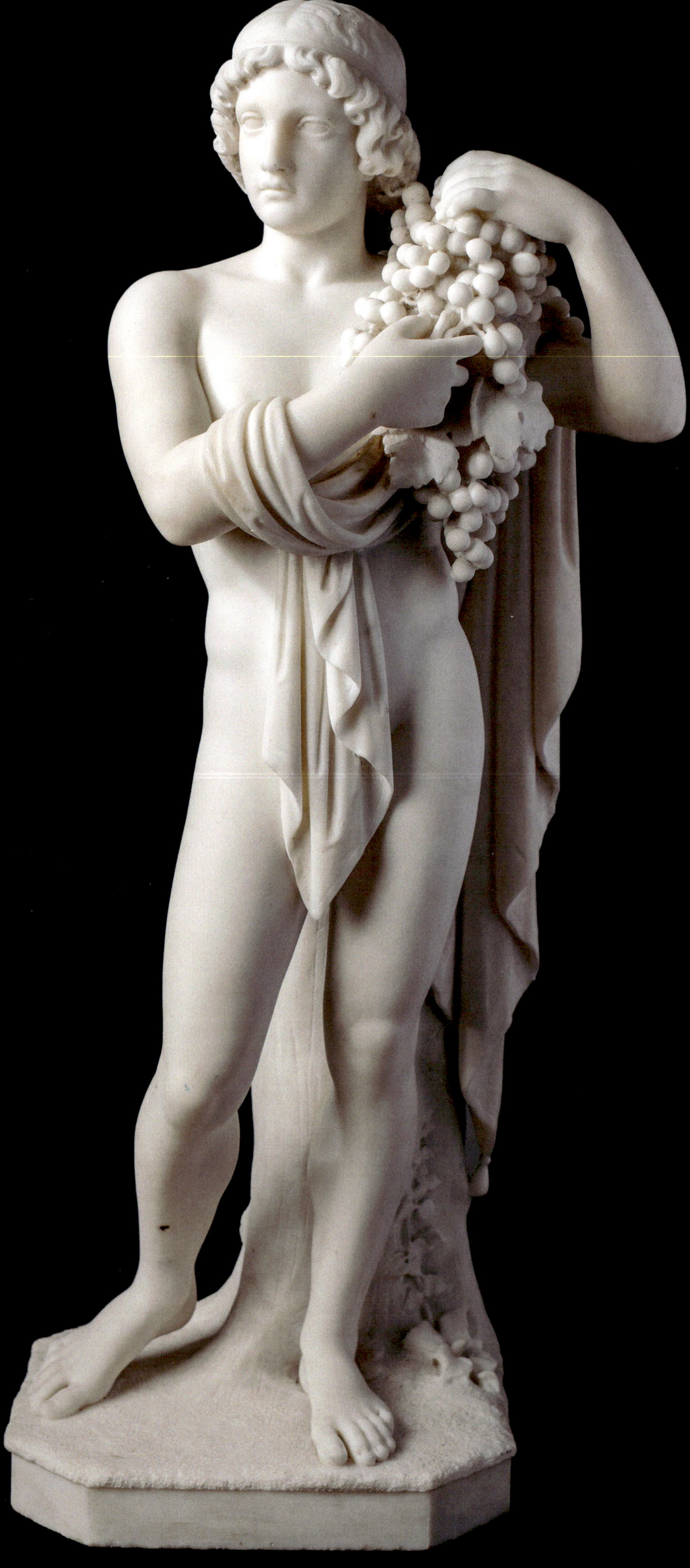

PLATE 27

AUTUMN (ALSO KNOWN AS BACCHUS)

ca. 1863–66
Inscription: "EMMA STEBBINS. / ROME." (verso)
Marble, 30½ × 13½ × 10½ in. (77.5 × 34.3 × 26.7 cm)
Collection of Tyler Elizabeth Burgess

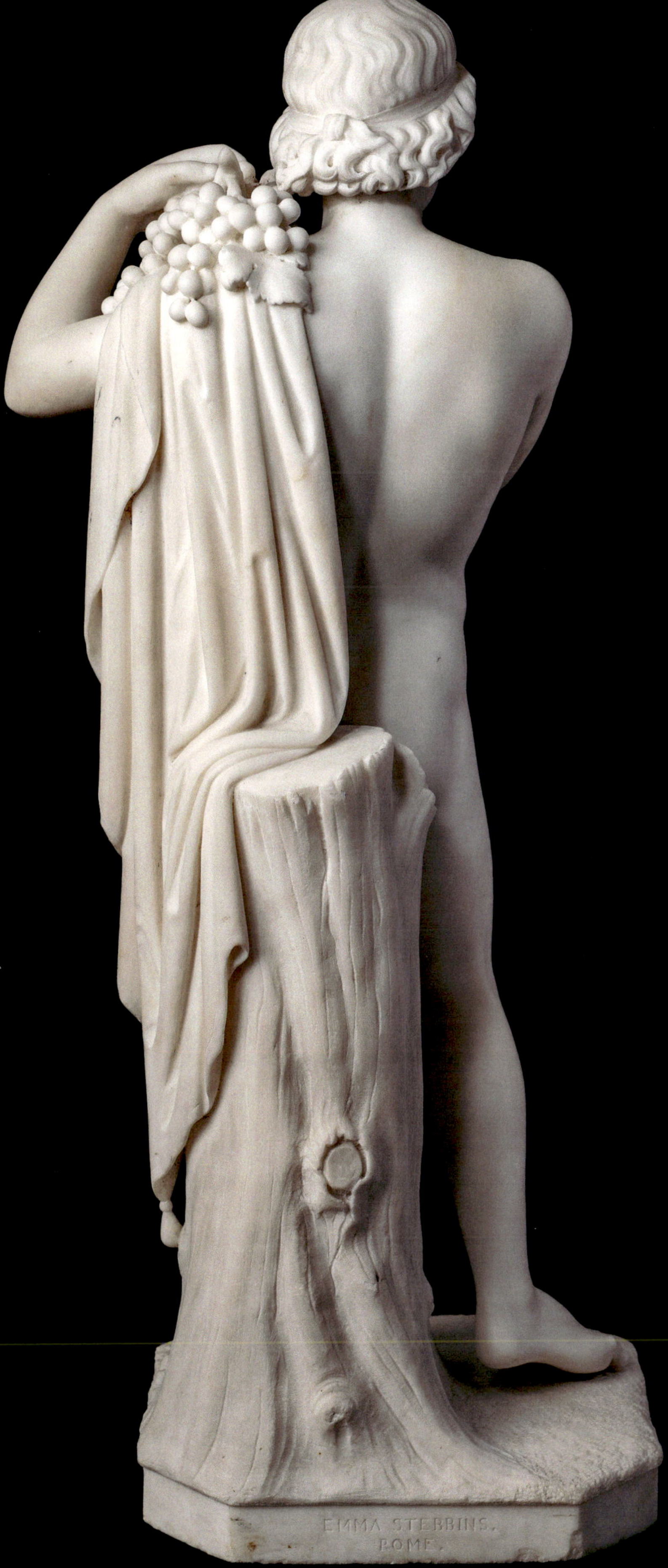

Alternate view of plate 27

Detail of plate 27

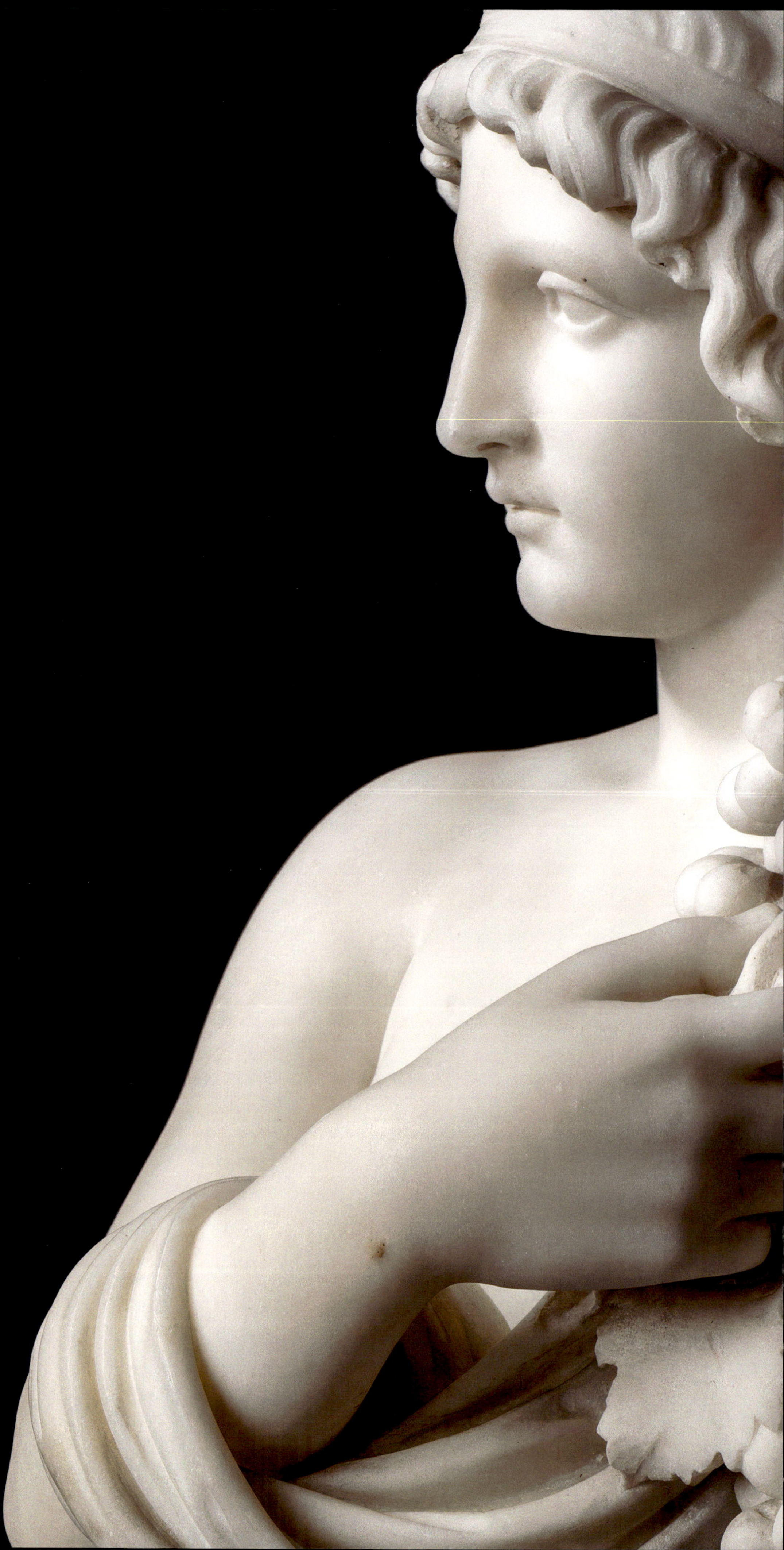

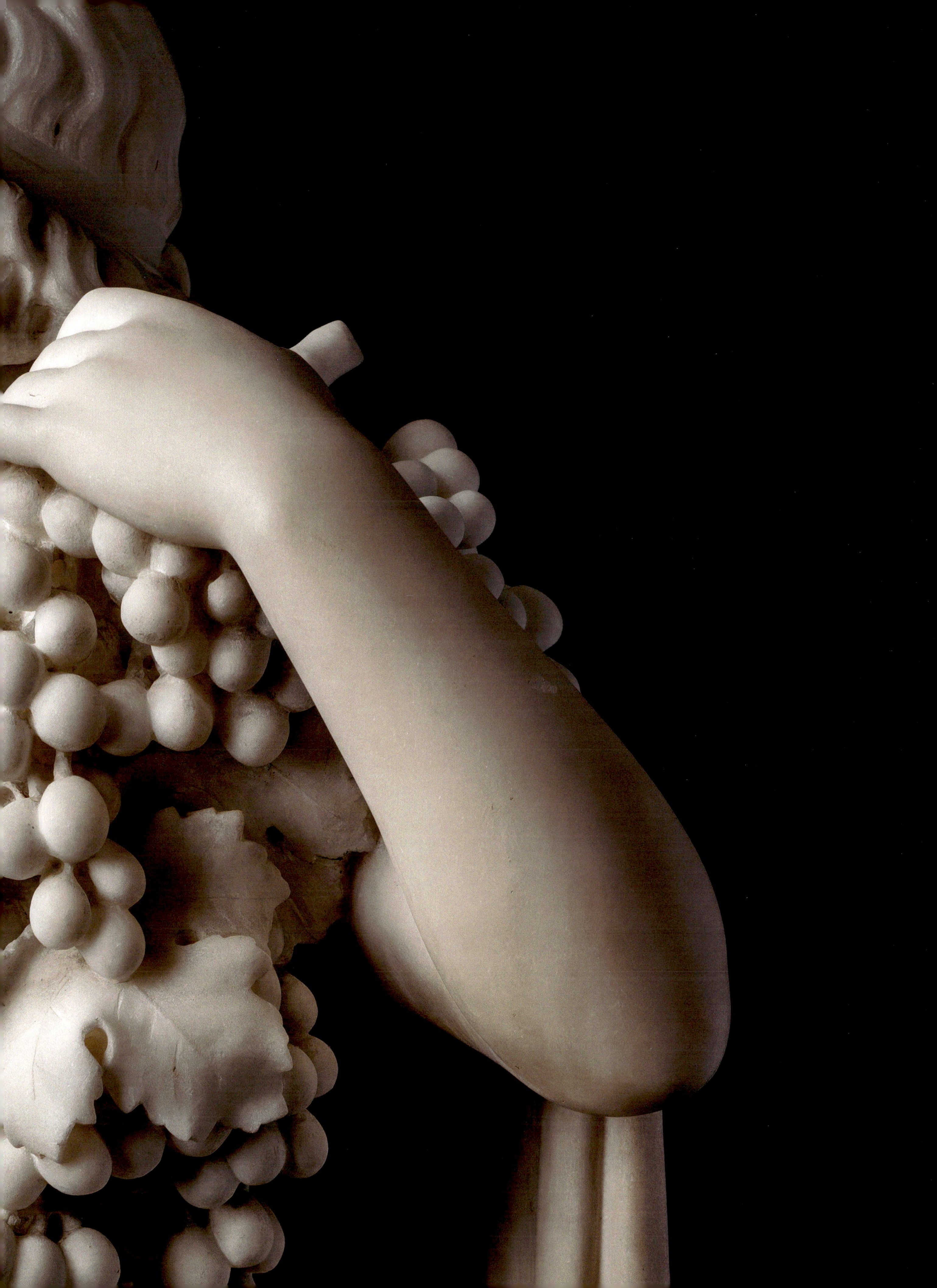

PLATE 28

THE FOUR SEASONS

Photographs from the Emma Stebbins scrapbook, 1858–82
Archives of American Art, Smithsonian Institution

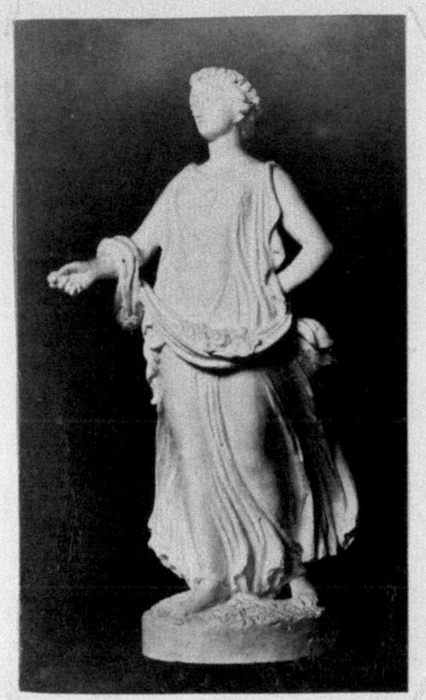

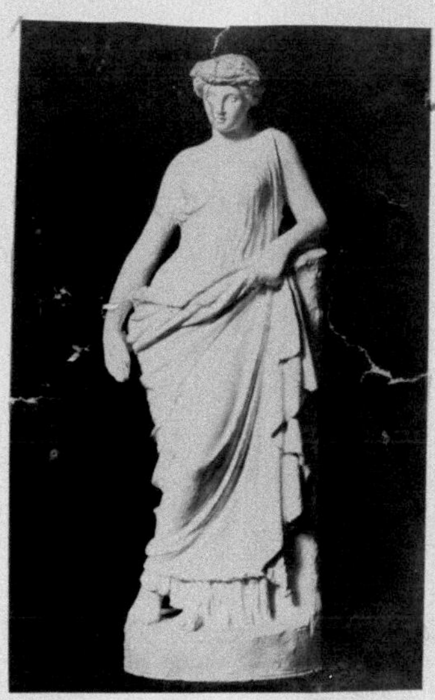

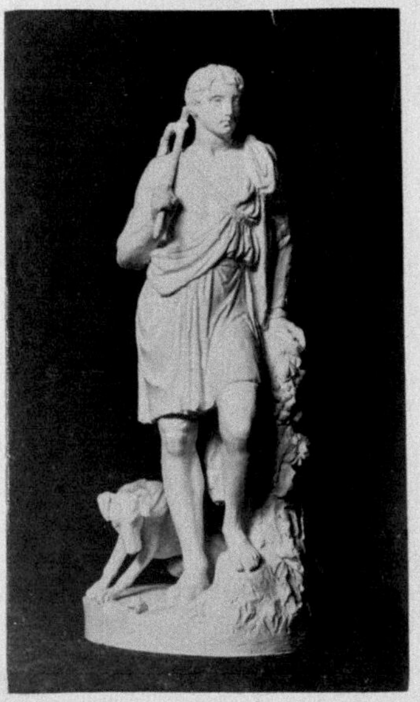

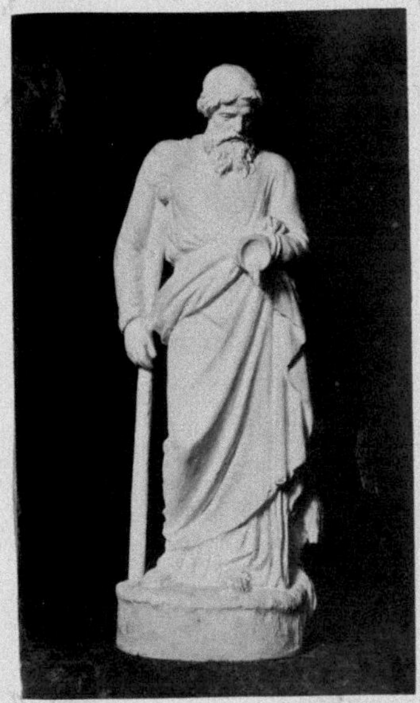

Studies, ordered by the Park Commissioners,
1863 (of the 'Seasons') to be placed on the pedestals
arranged, for such figures, on the steps,
descending from the 'Mall' in the Central Park.

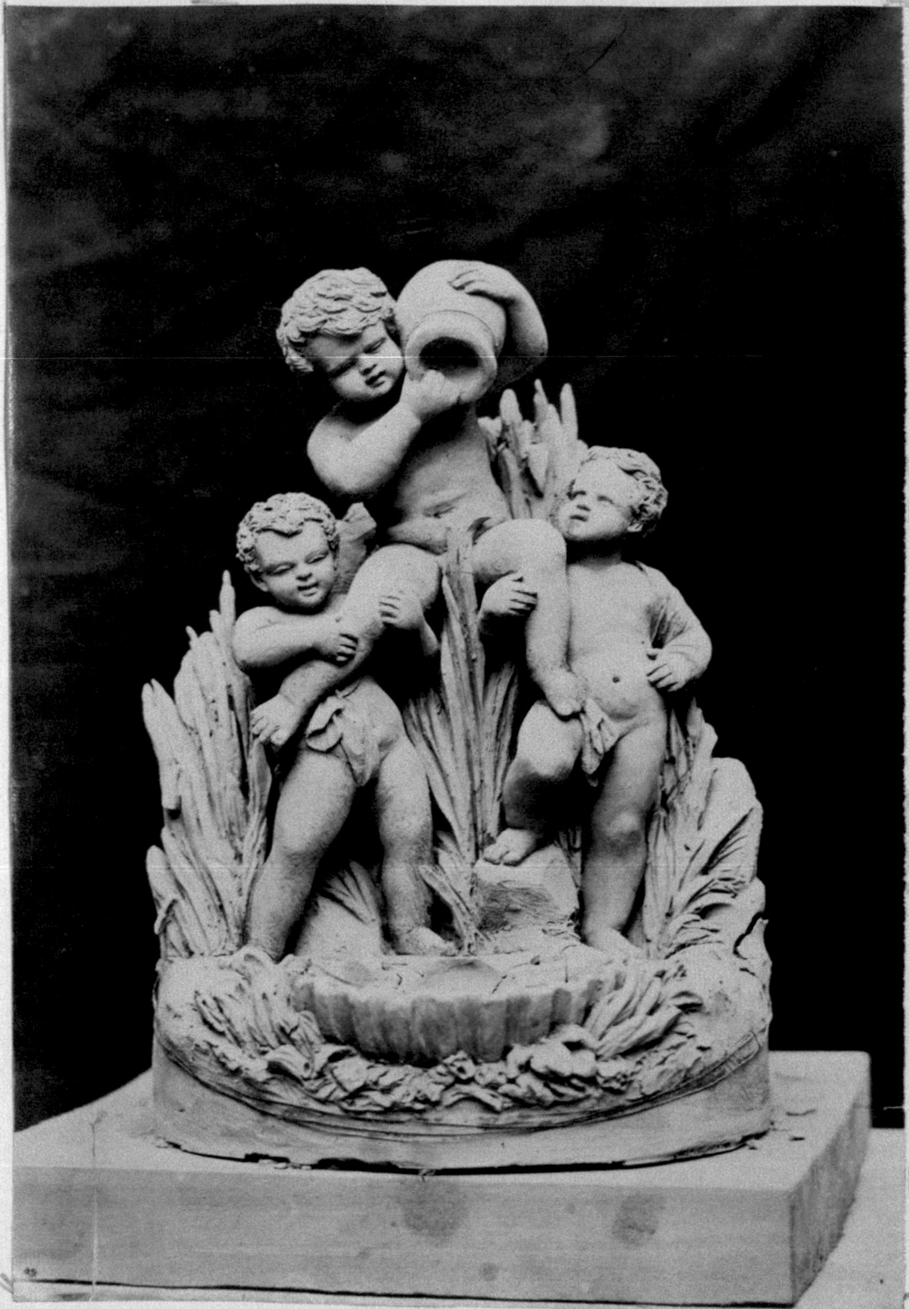

Study for fountain, made for M. G.

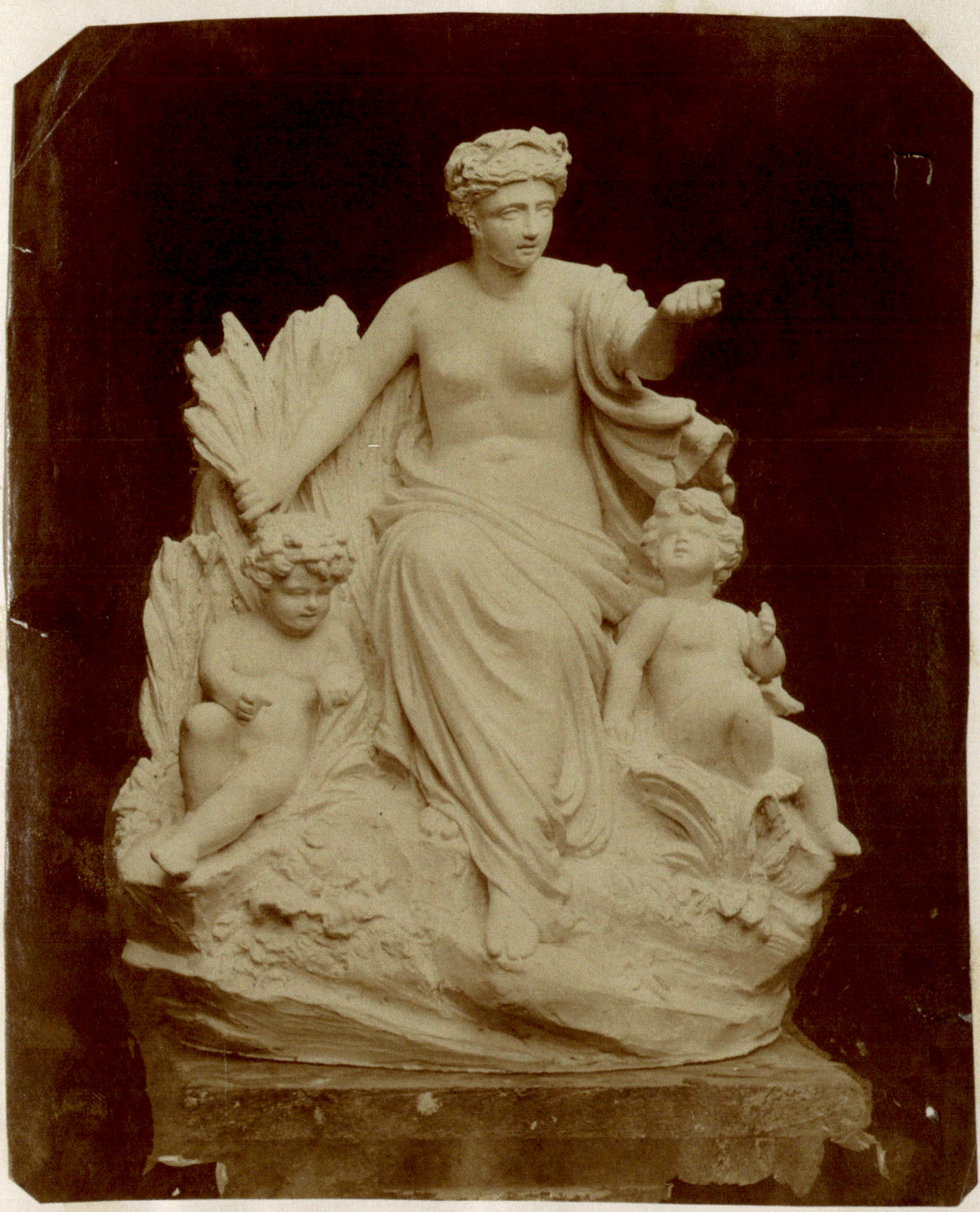

Study. Dispensing Gates of Reservoir

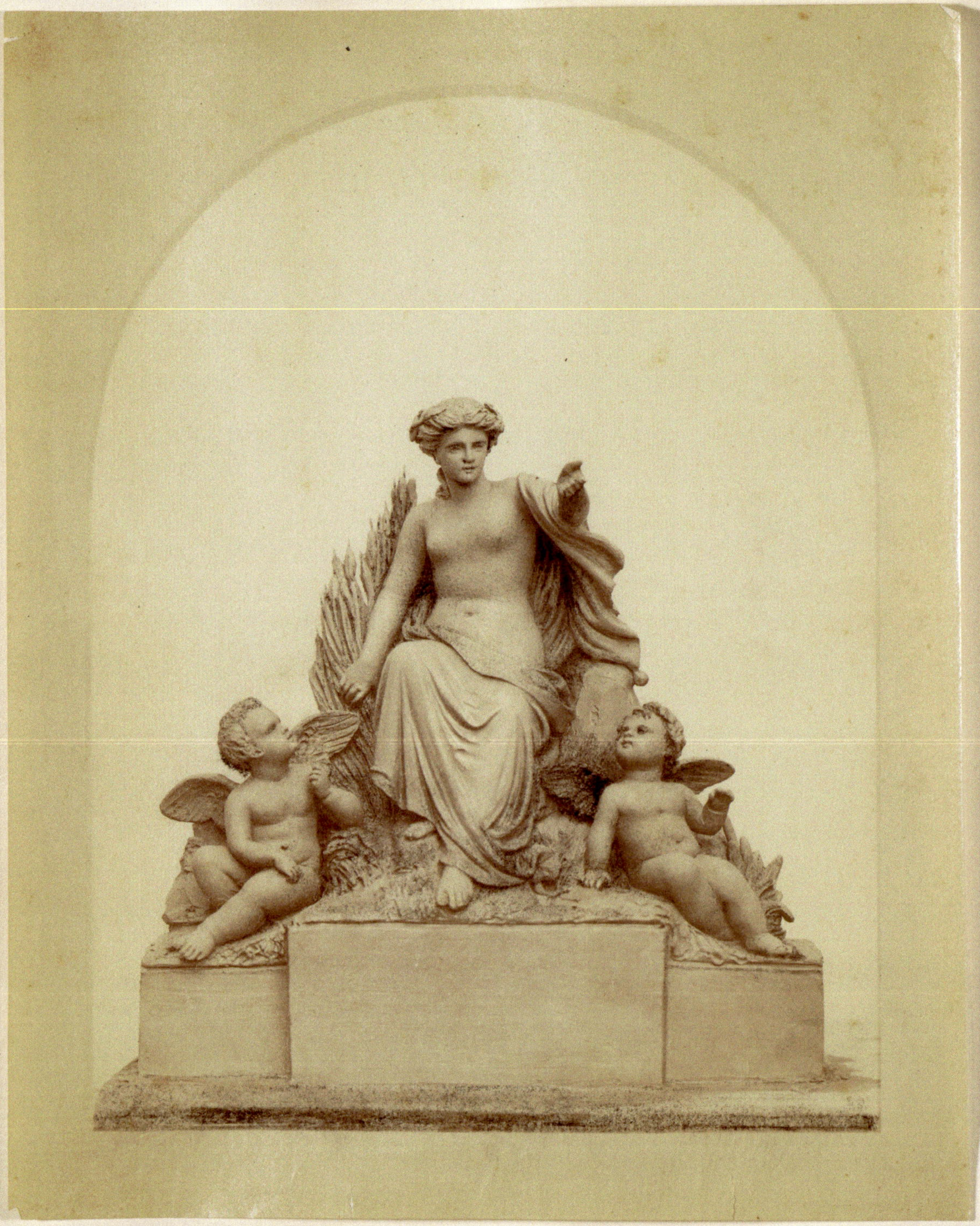

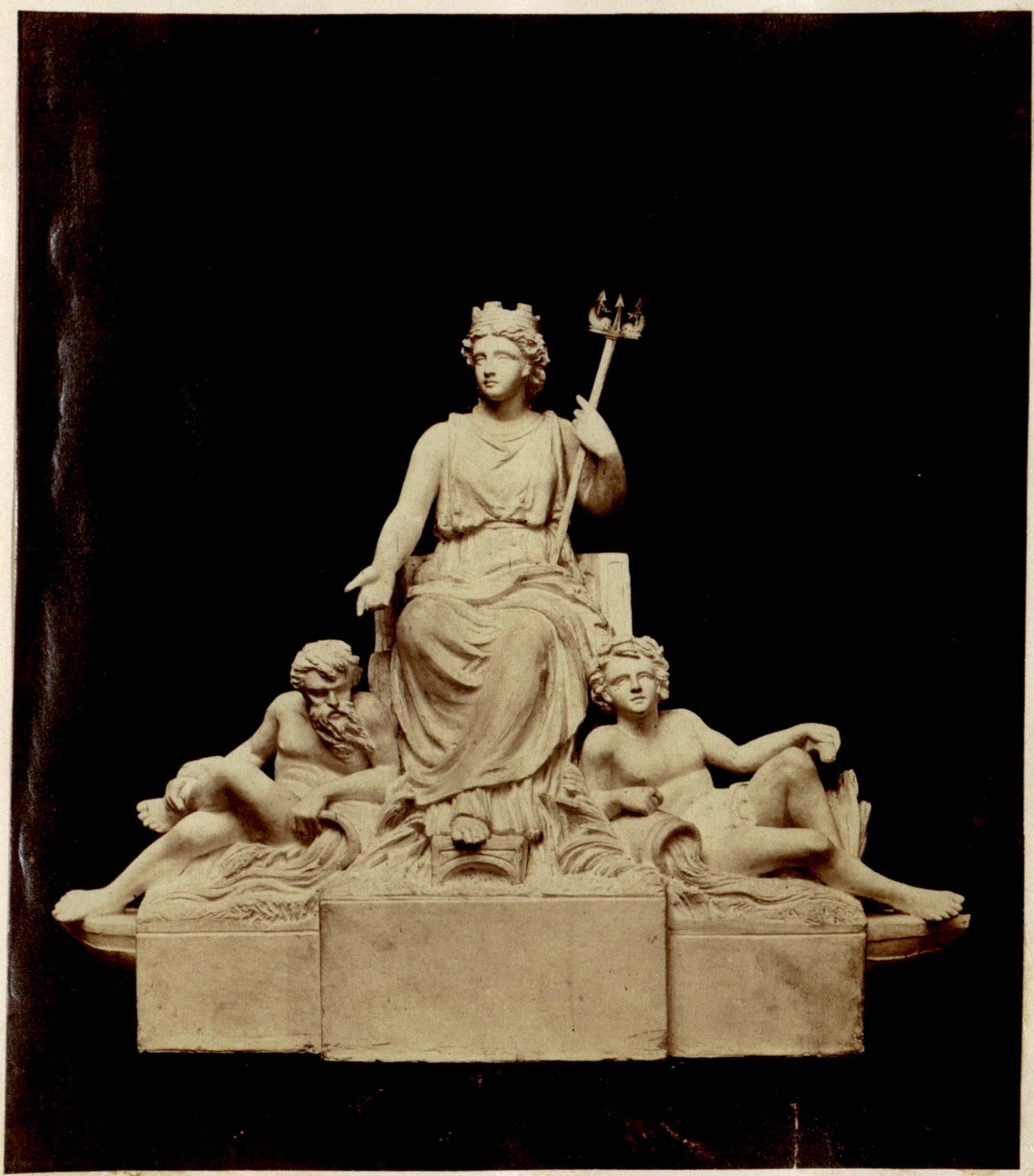

Study. Receiving gates of Reservoir.

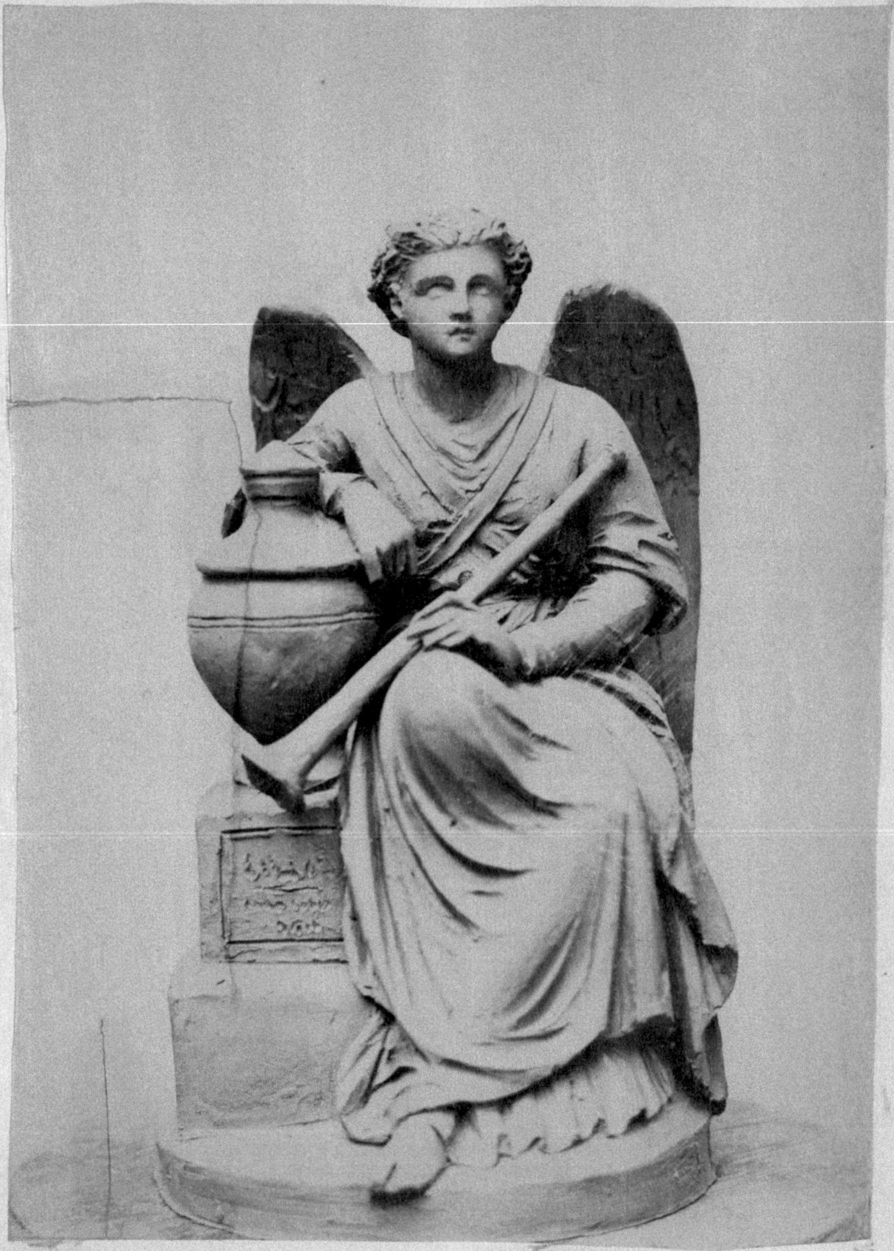

Angel of the Resurrection:
(Study)

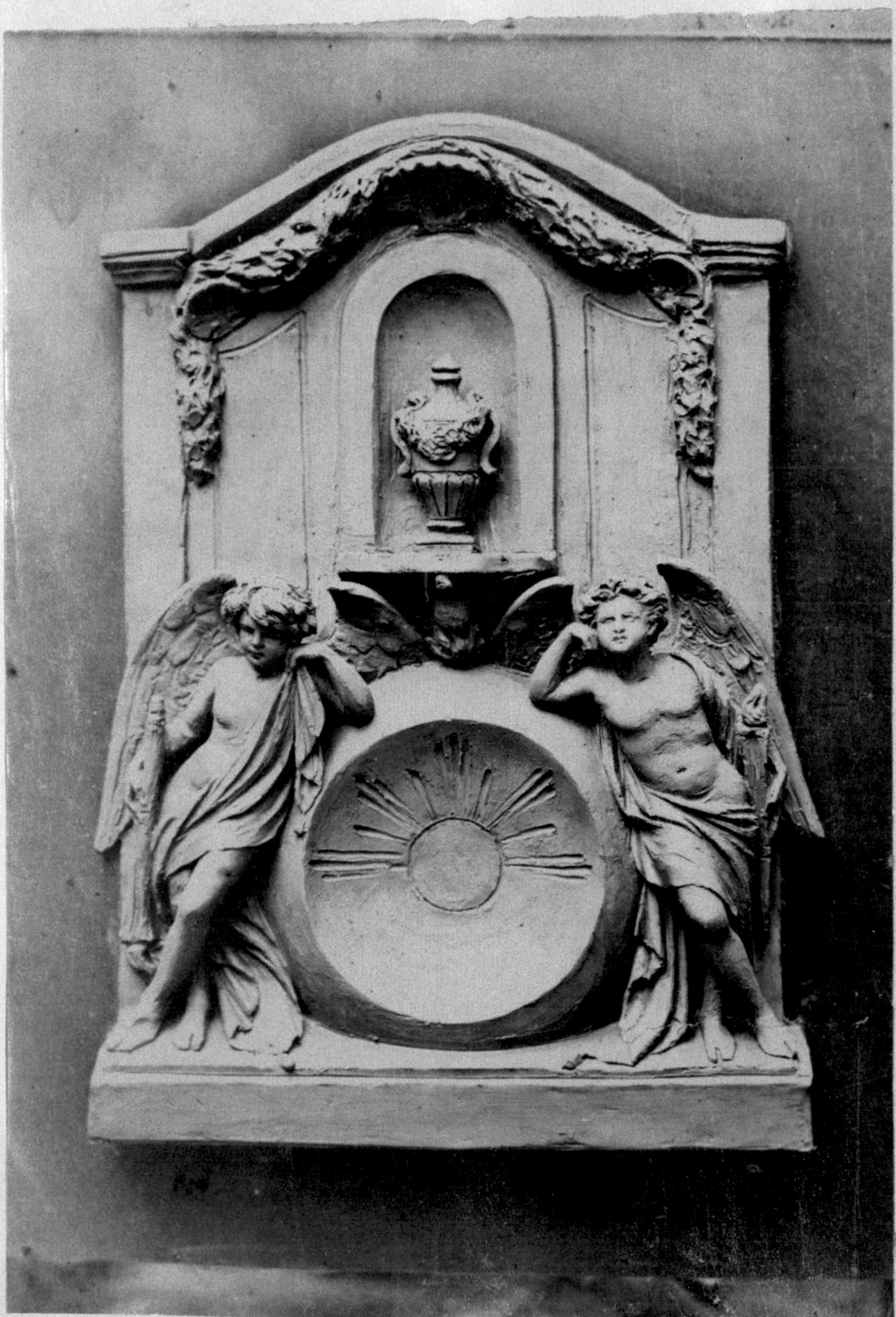

Study - for Monument

PLATE 35

TREATY OF HENDRICK HUDSON WITH THE INDIANS

Inscription: "The TREATY of HENDRICK HUDSON with the INDIANS. / for the purchase of the / ISLAND of MANHATTAN. / AD 1610" (front)
Photograph from the Emma Stebbins scrapbook, 1858–82
Archives of American Art, Smithsonian Institution

This work was completed in marble but is now unlocated. It measured 42 × 54 in. (106.7 × 137.2 cm).

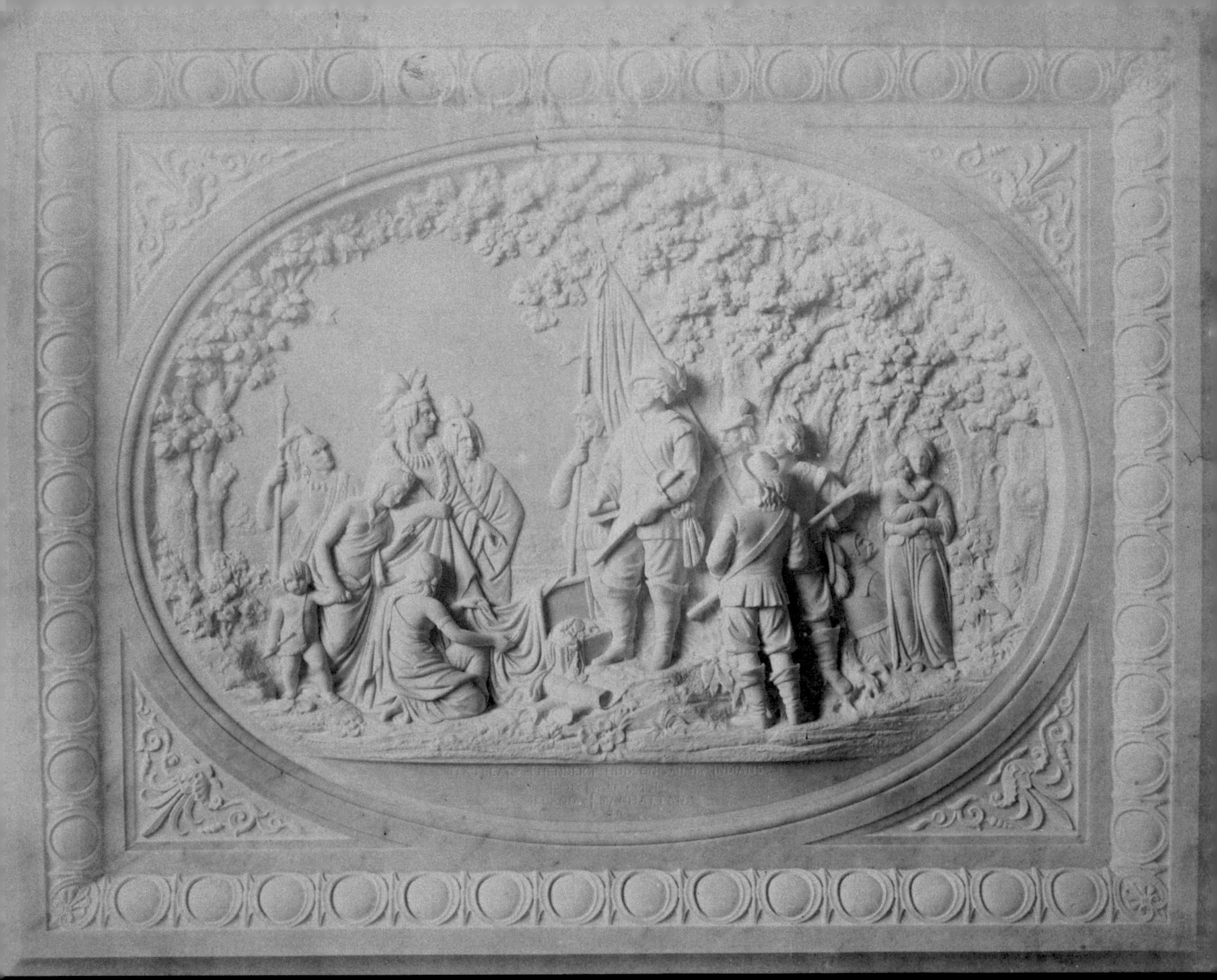

1860. Bas relief for M. C Roberts of New York. "The Treaty of Hudson with the Indians for the purchase of Manhattan Island".

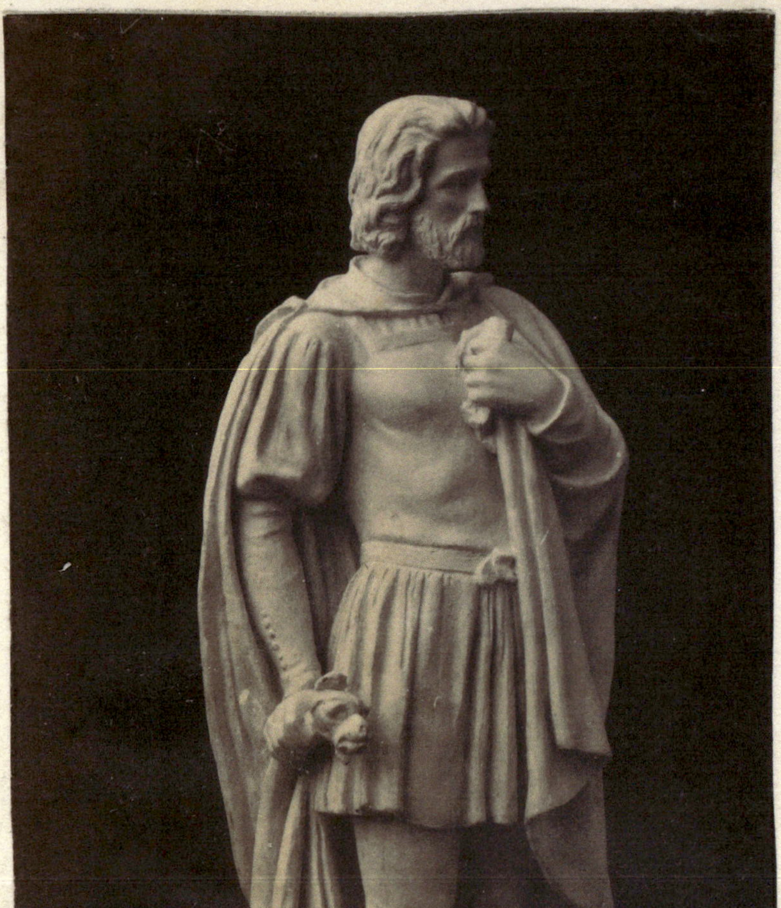

by E. S. -

PLATE 36

CHRISTOPHER COLUMBUS

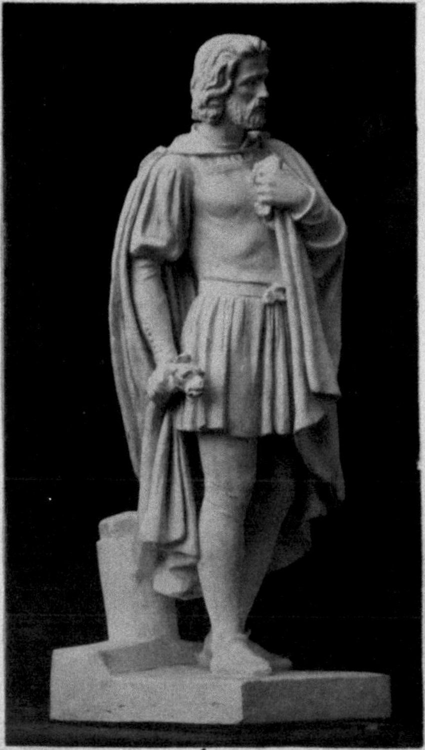

1861. Statue of "Columbus" heroic size, made for M. O. Roberts, of New York - presented by him to Central Park with agreement that it should be placed in position, and protected from the weather now in the "Museum of Natural History" C.P. New York -

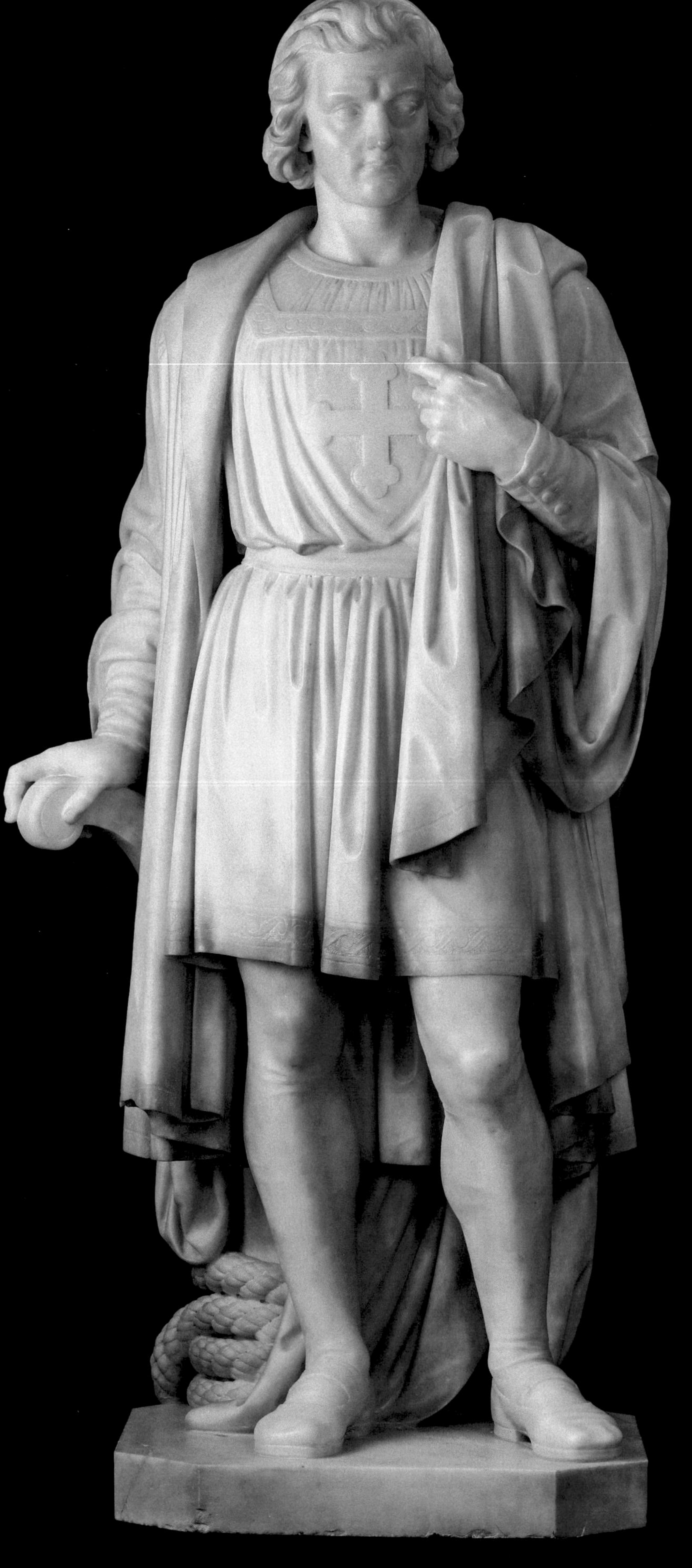

PLATE 38

CHRISTOPHER COLUMBUS (ALSO KNOWN AS COMMERCE)

1868
Inscription: "EMMA STEBBINS ROME 1868" (verso)
Marble, $48^{13}/_{16} \times 21^{1}/_{4} \times 17^{5}/_{16}$ in. (124 × 54 × 44 cm)
Belfast Central Library, Libraries NI, Northern Ireland, Gift of R. G. Dunville, 1888

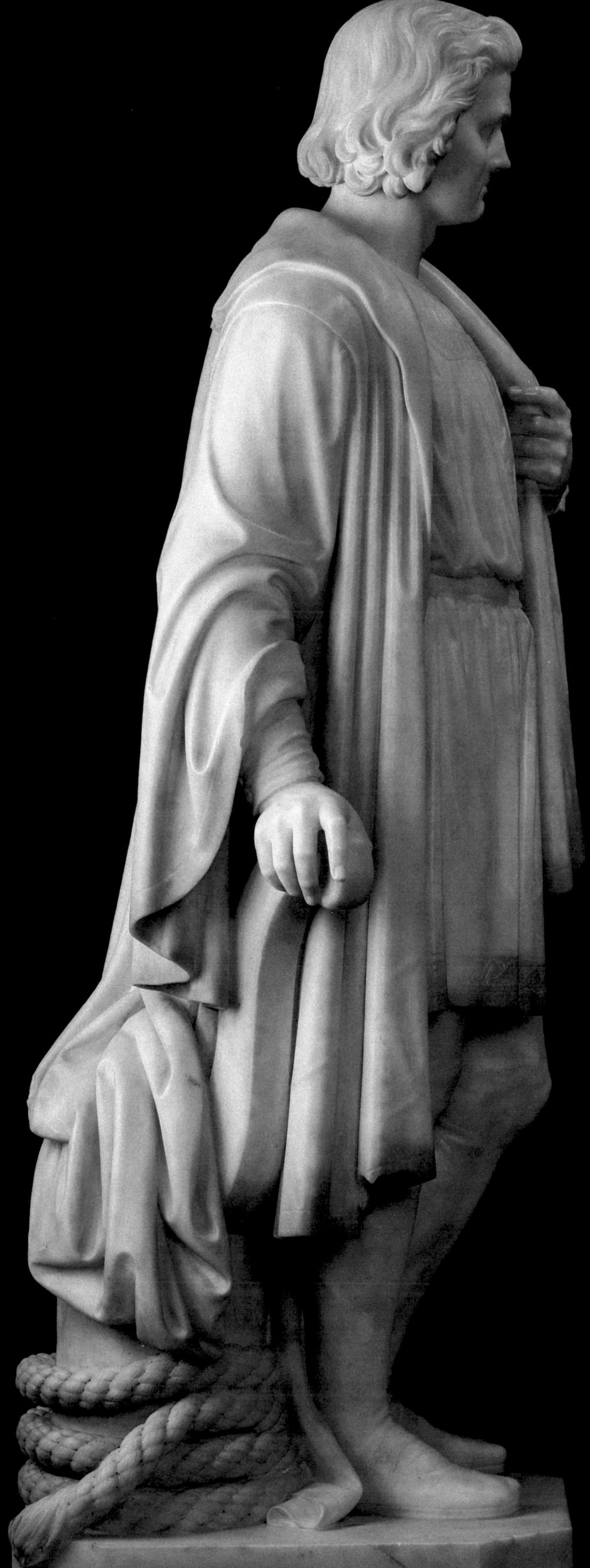

Alternate view of plate 38

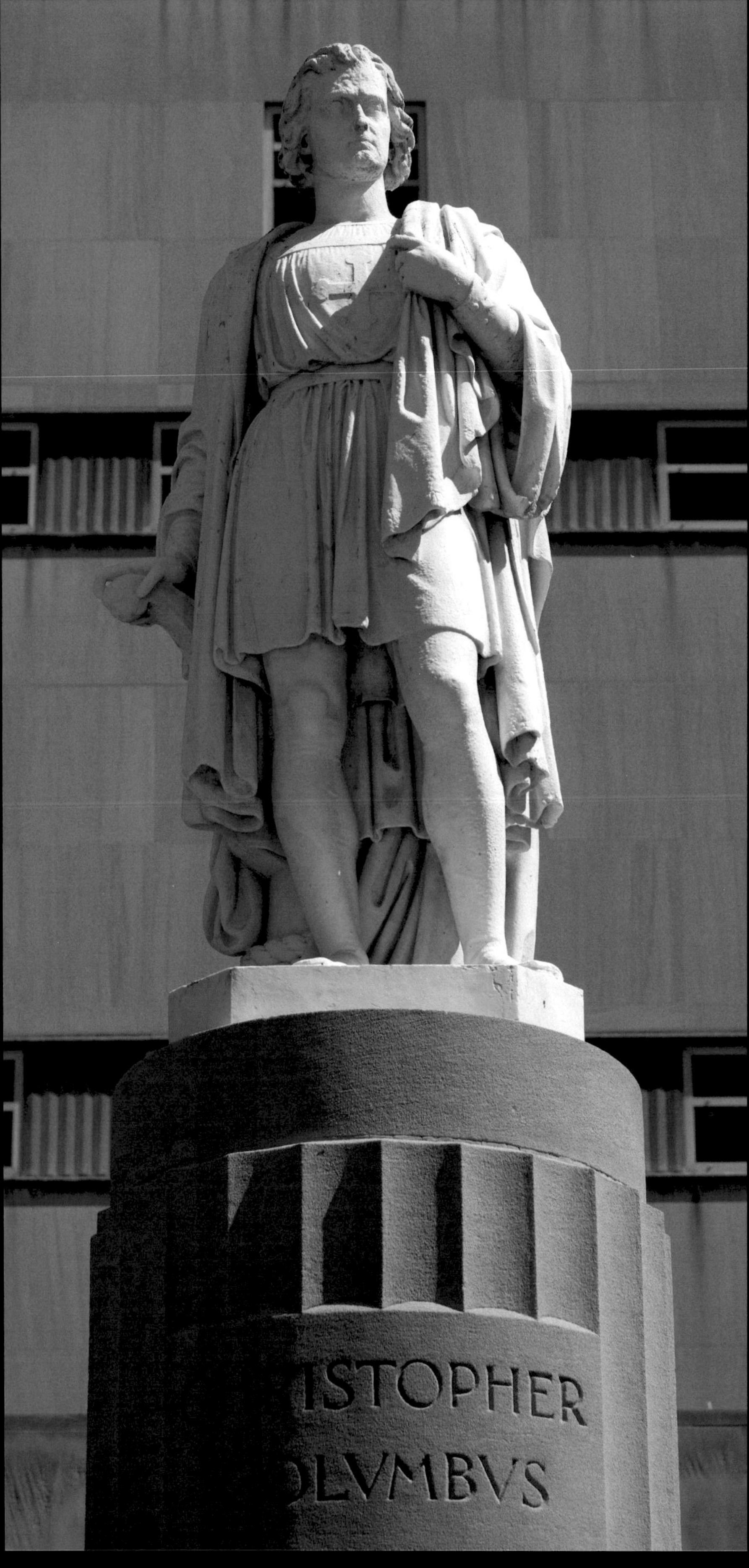

PLATE 39

CHRISTOPHER COLUMBUS

1867
Marble, H. (of sculpture) 7 ft. (2.1 m)
New York City Department of Parks and Recreation, Gift of Marshall O. Roberts, 1869

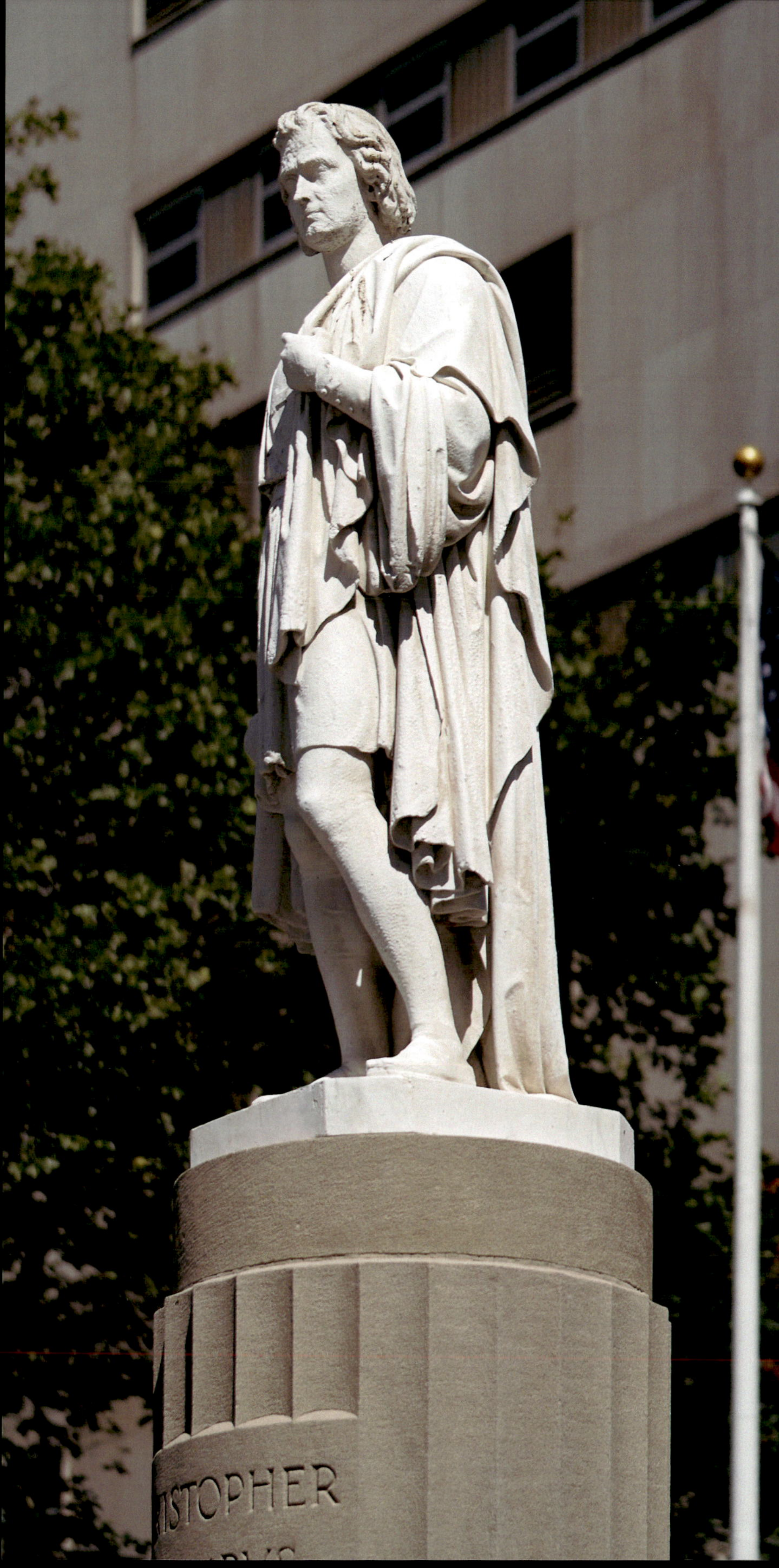

Alternate view of plate 39

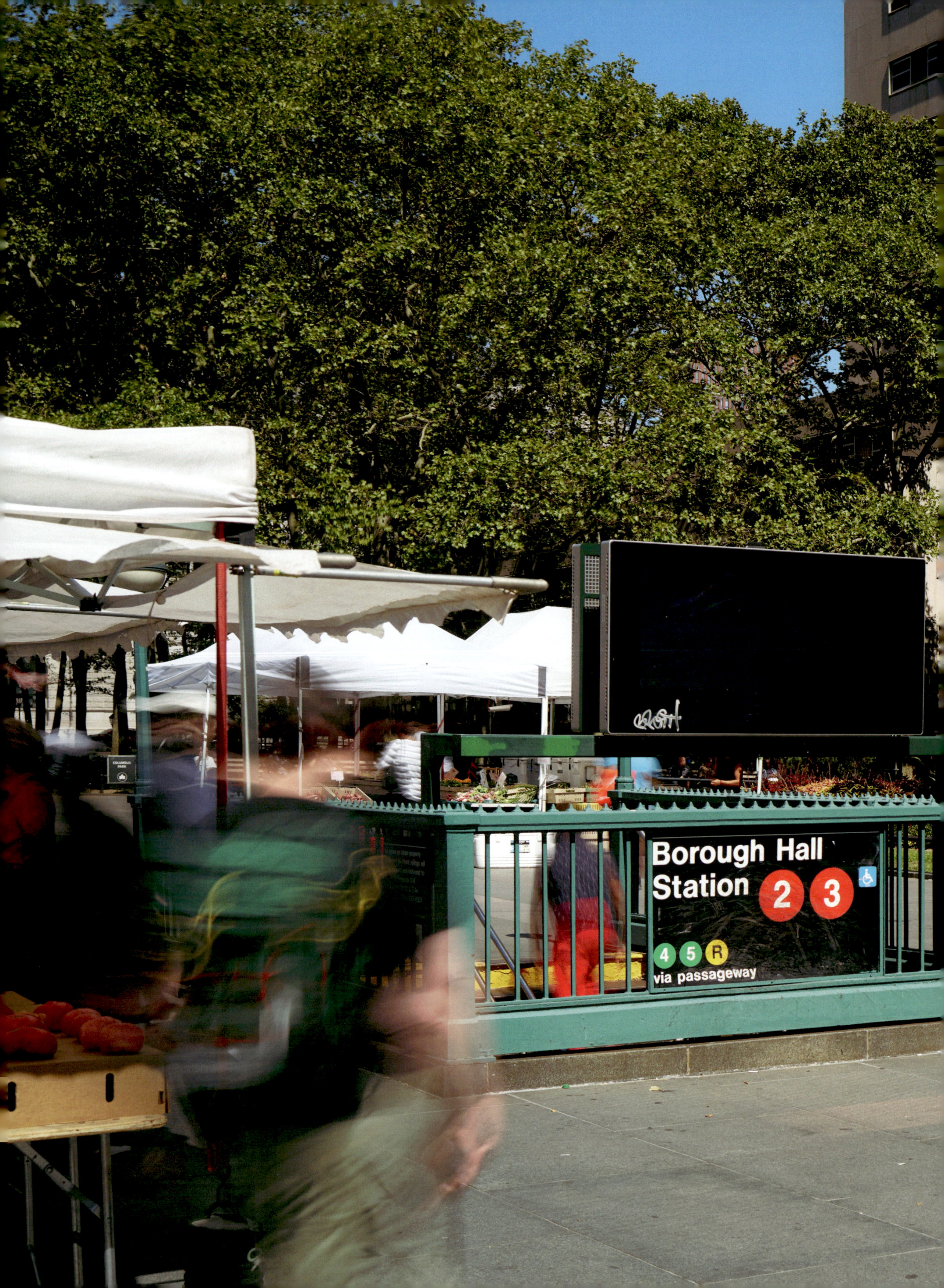
Borough Hall
Station 2 3
4 5 R
via passageway

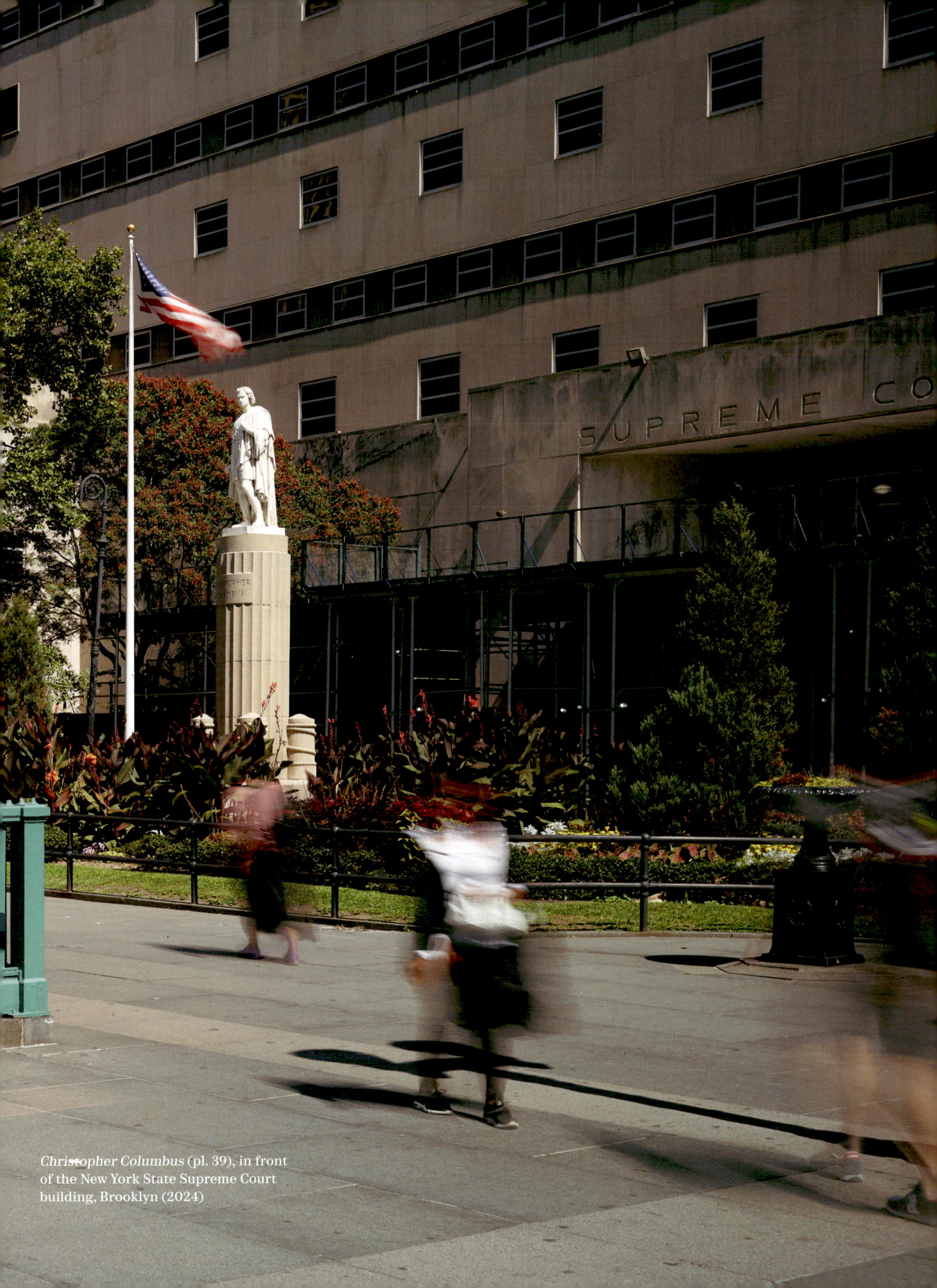

Christopher Columbus (pl. 39), in front of the New York State Supreme Court building, Brooklyn (2024)

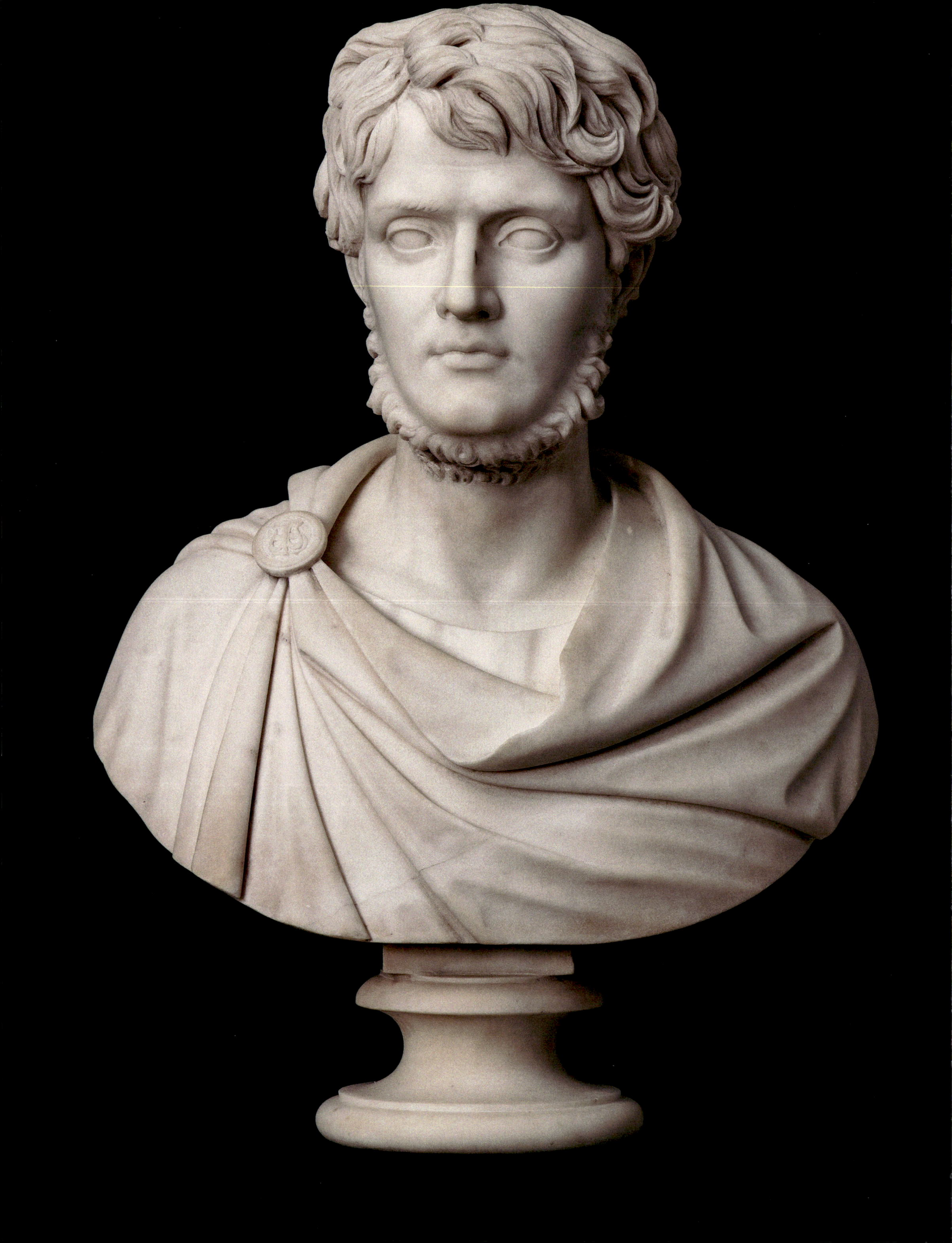

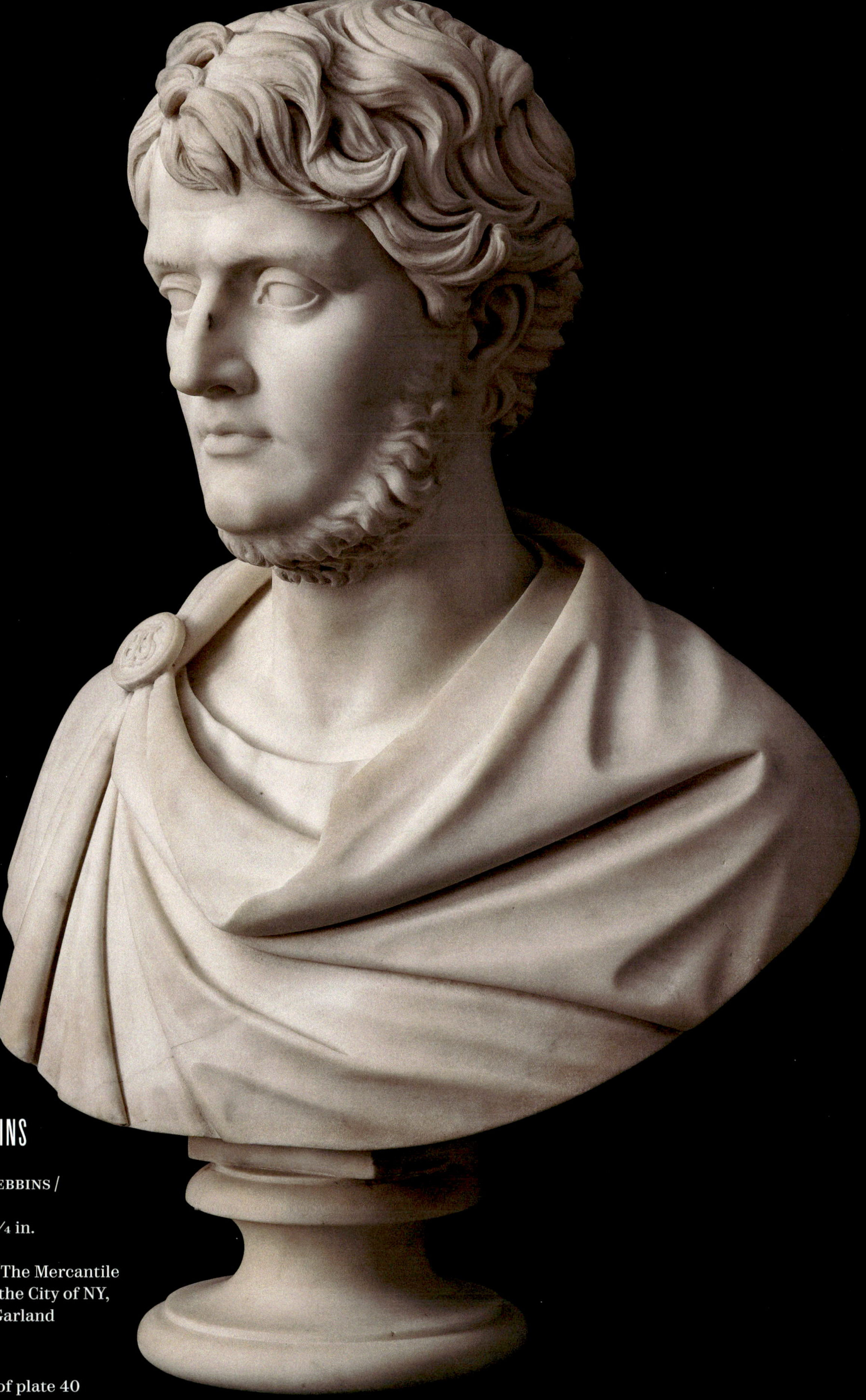

LEFT: PLATE 40

JOHN WILSON STEBBINS

1865
Inscription: "EMMA STEBBINS / ROME 1865" (verso)
Marble, 27 × 19½ × 11¾ in.
(68.6 × 49.5 × 29.9 cm)
The Center for Fiction/The Mercantile Library Association of the City of NY, Gift of Mary Stebbins Garland and Family, 1884

RIGHT: Alternate view of plate 40

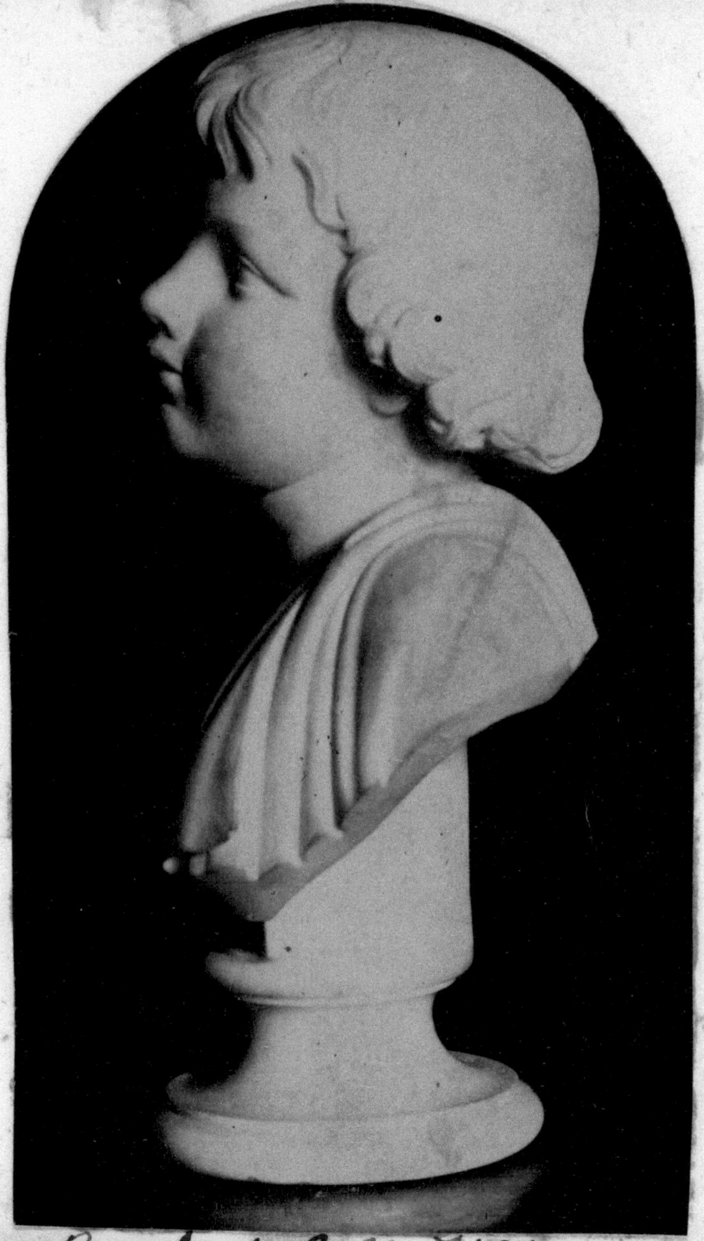

Bust of J. N. Tillon -

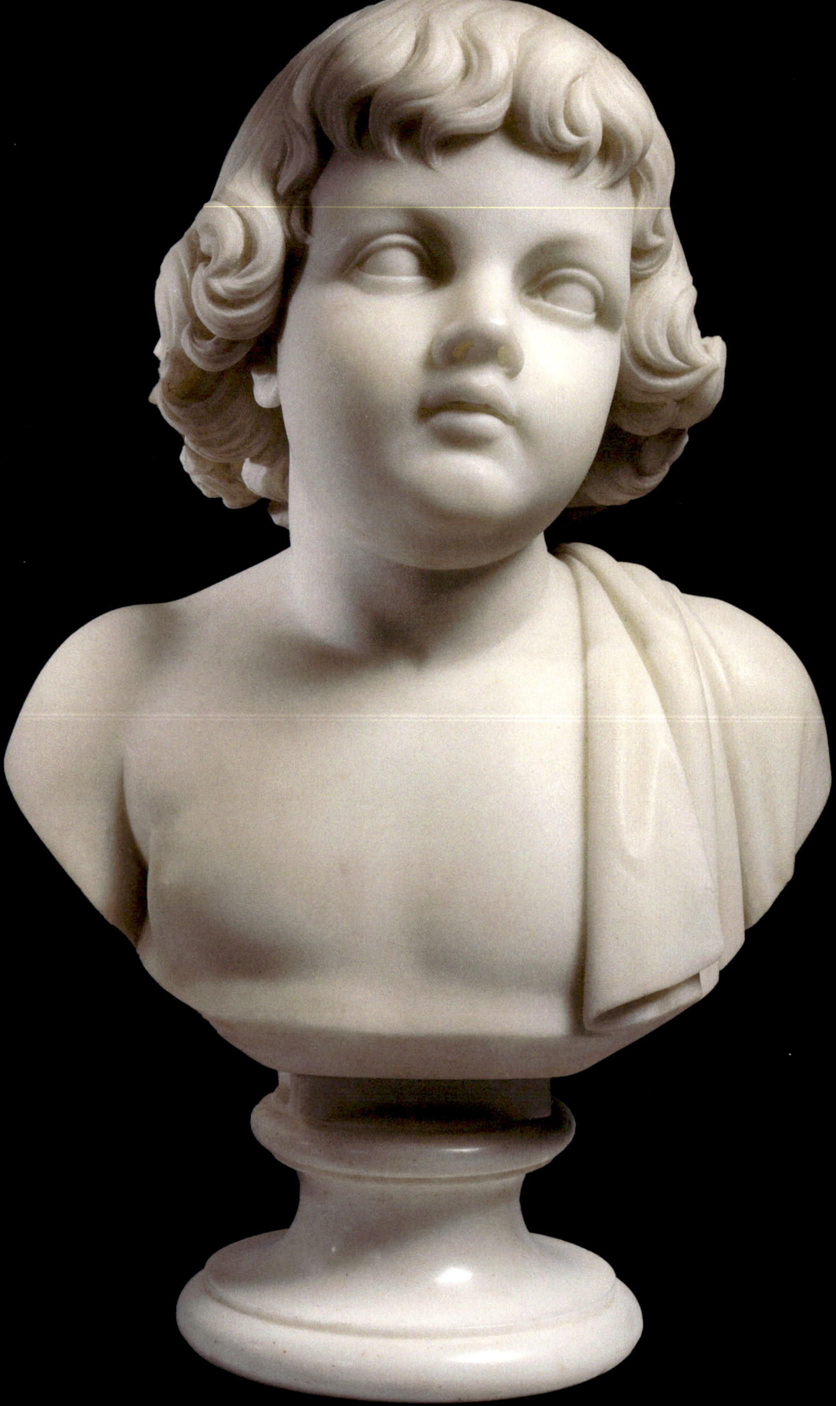

PLATE 42

JOHN NEAL TILTON

ca. 1865

Marble, $17\frac{5}{8} \times 10\frac{1}{4} \times 7\frac{3}{4}$ in. (44.8 × 26 × 19.7 cm)

The Metropolitan Museum of Art, Gift of Elizabeth Milroy, 2024, 2024.203a–c

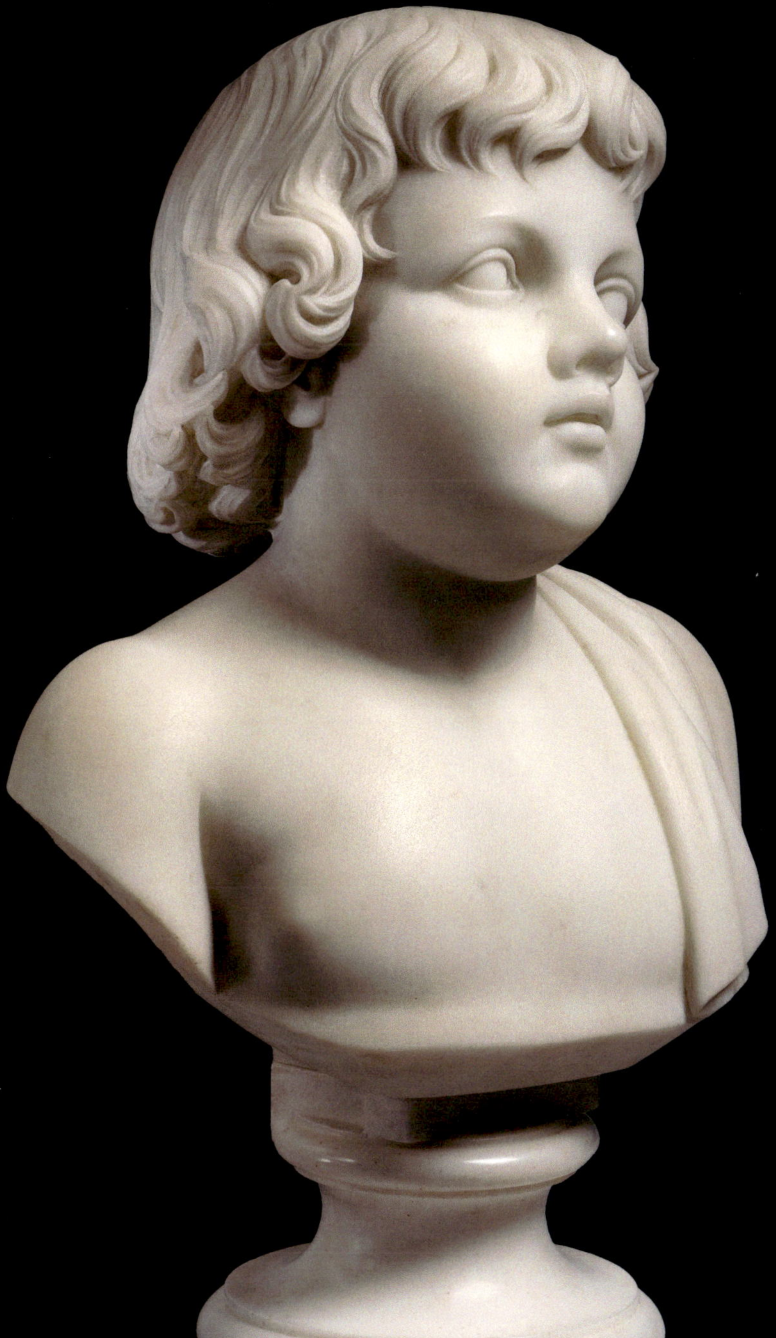

Alternate view of plate 42

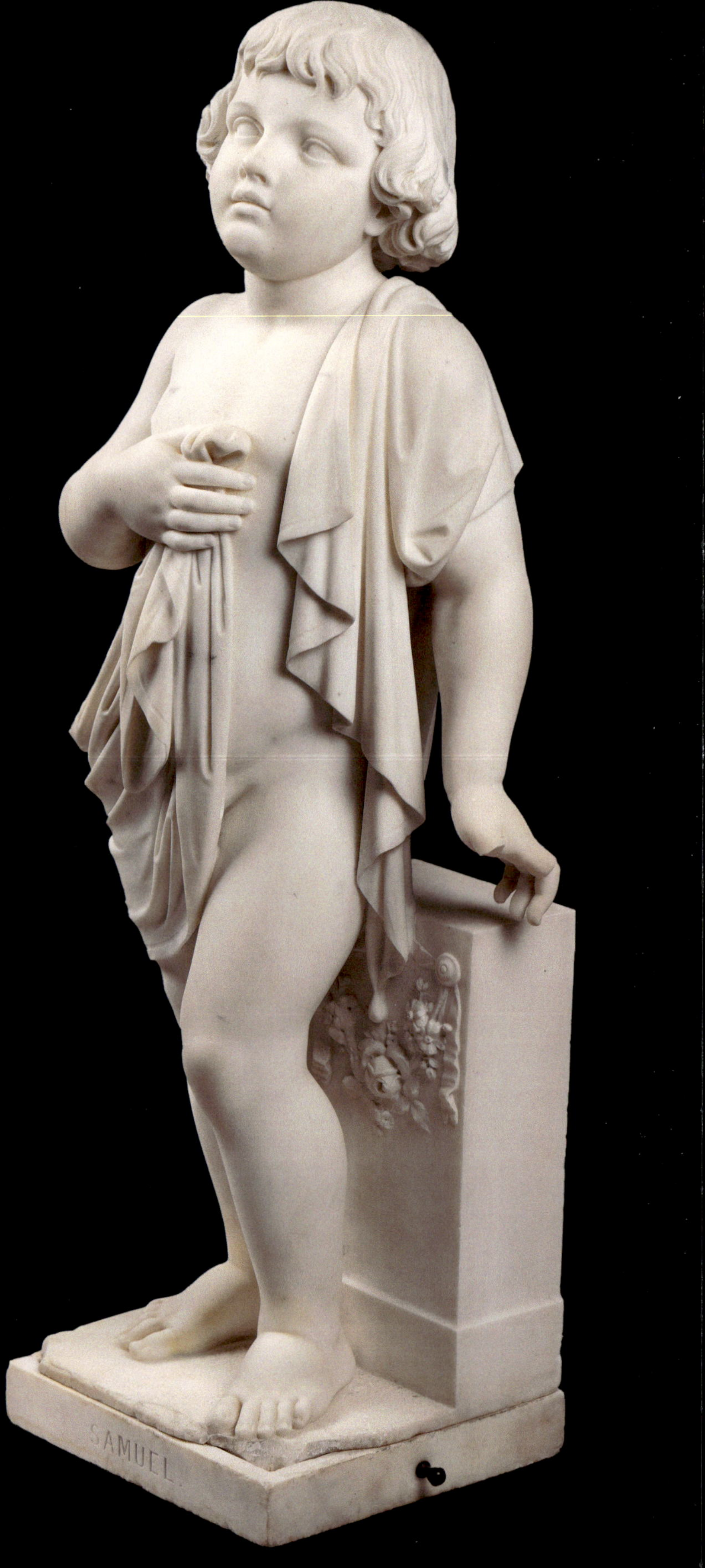

PLATE 43

SAMUEL

1868
Inscriptions: "SAMUEL" (front); "EMMA STEBBINS ROME 1868" (verso)
Marble, 39¼ × 14¼ × 10⅜ in.
(99.7 × 36.2 × 26.4 cm)
Brooklyn Museum, Gift of James Ricau, 80.191a–b

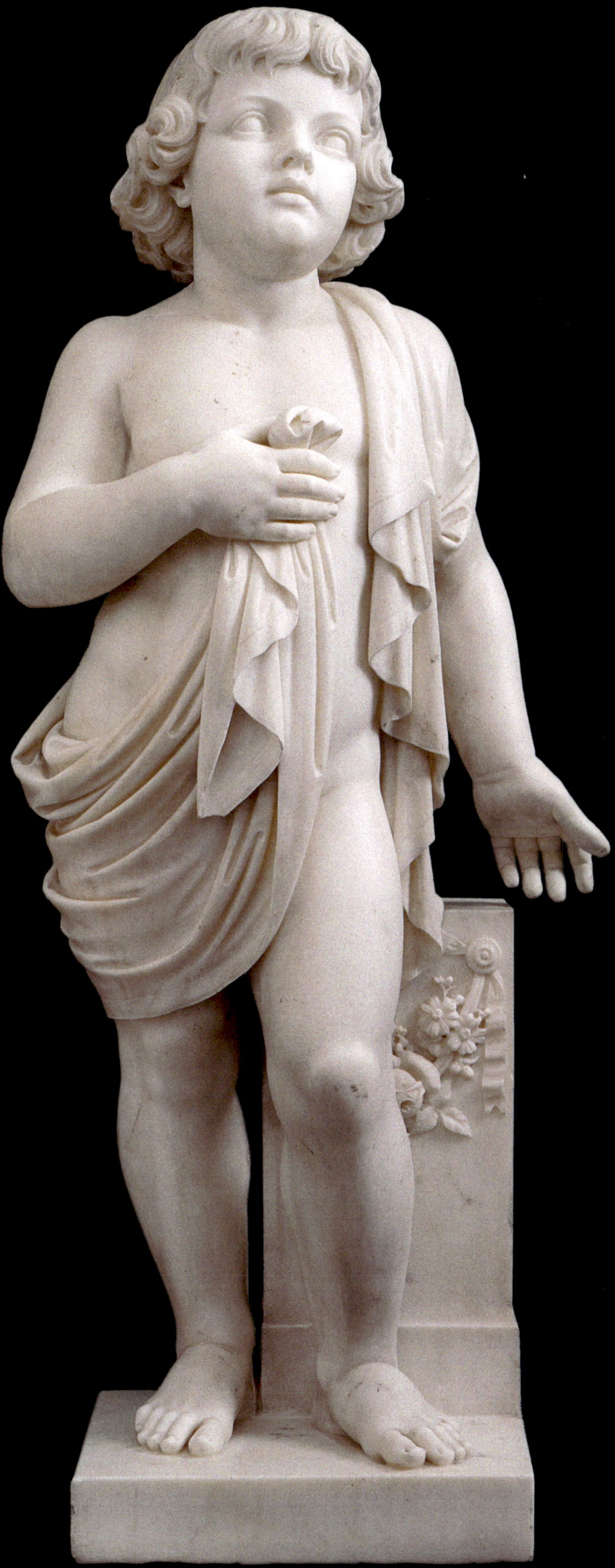

PLATE 44

SAMUEL

1870

Inscription: "EMMA STEBBINS. / ROME. 1870."
(left side)

Marble, 39 3/4 × 15 5/8 × 9 7/8 in.
(101 × 39.7 × 25.1 cm)

The Chrysler Museum of Art, Gift of James H. Ricau and museum purchase, 86.521

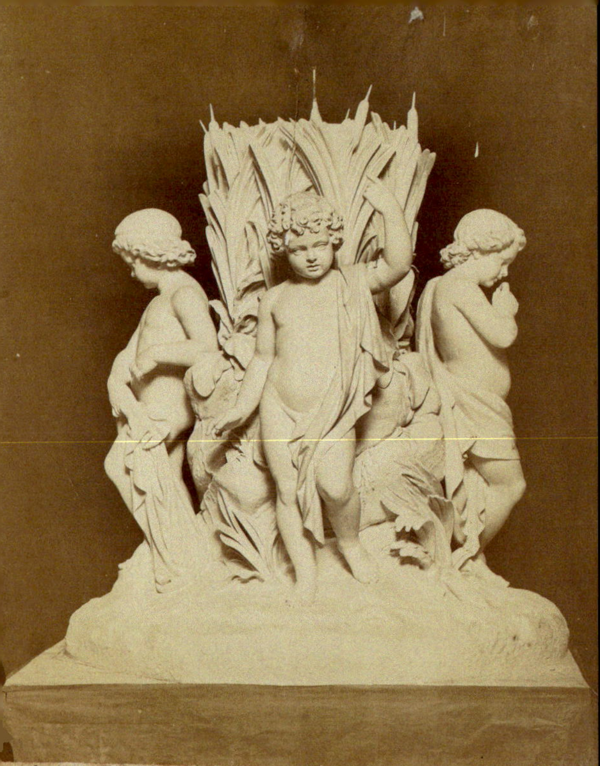

Symbols of Temperance, Purity, Peace & Health C. P. Fountain

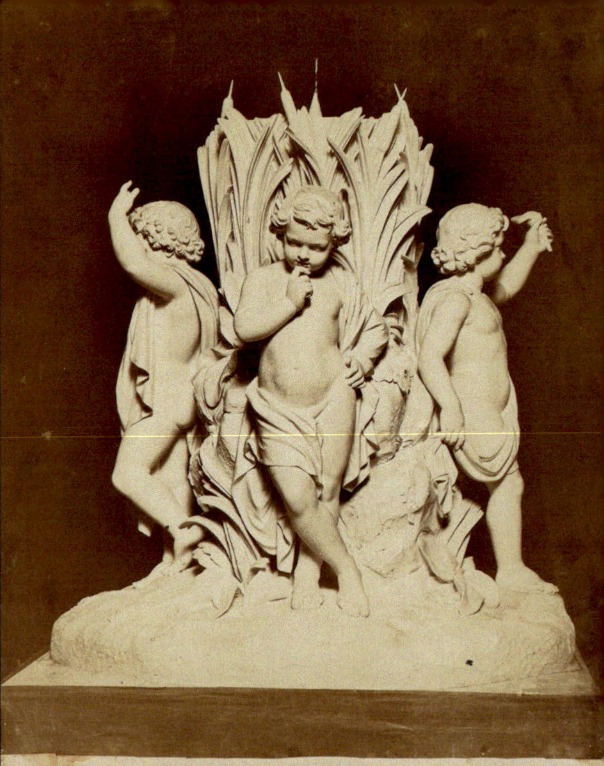

Upper Basin of the 'Bethesda Fountain'

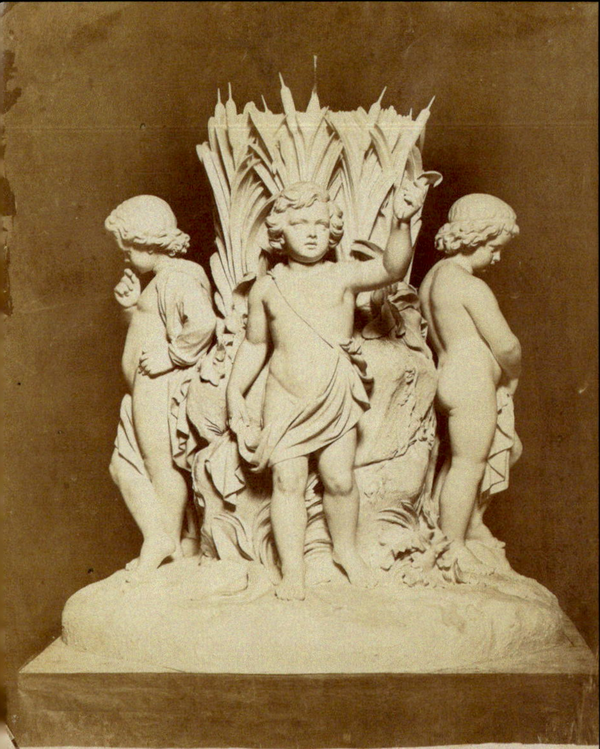

Figures placed on the upper pedestal, of the 'Bethesda Fountain
Symbolical of 'Health', Purity, peace & Temperance

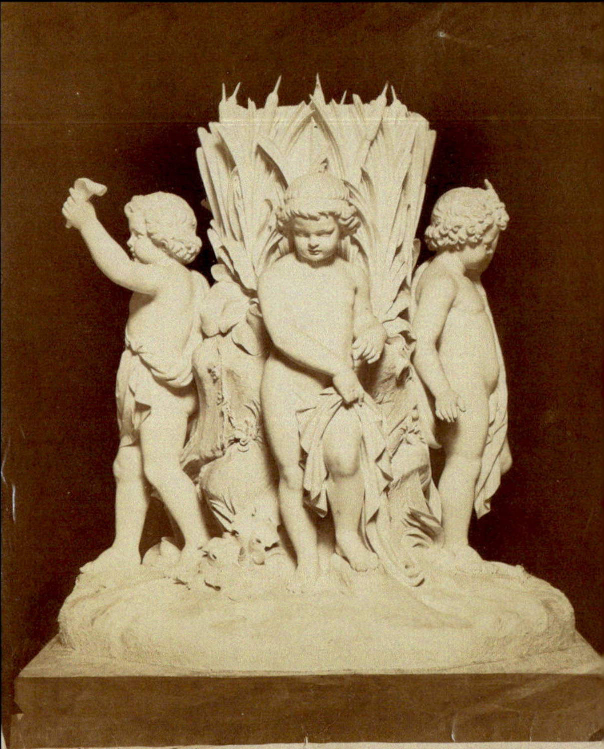

upper basin of C. P. Fountain, (Temperance, Purity, Health & Peace –

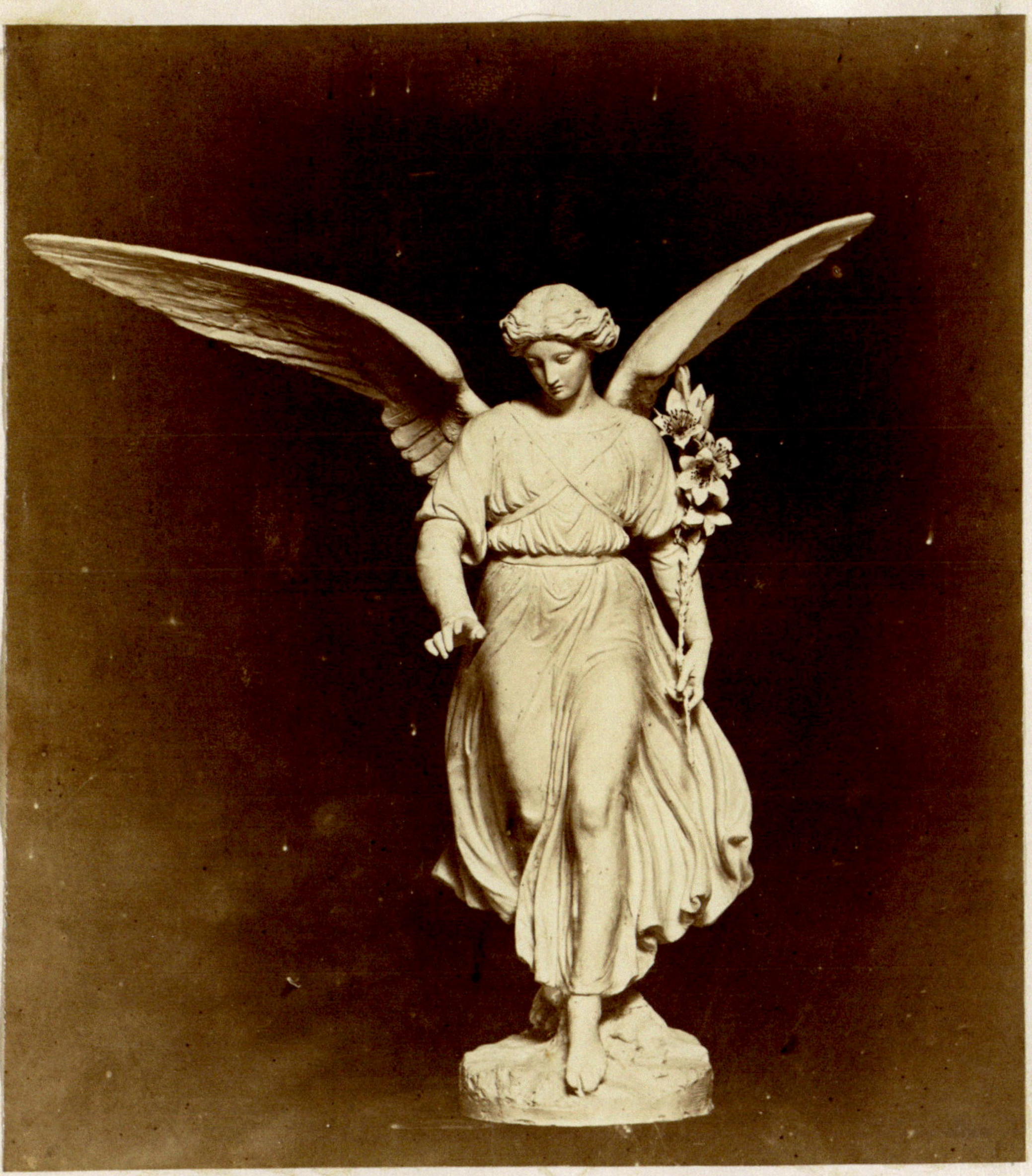

1862. 3. The Angel of the Bethesda Fountain

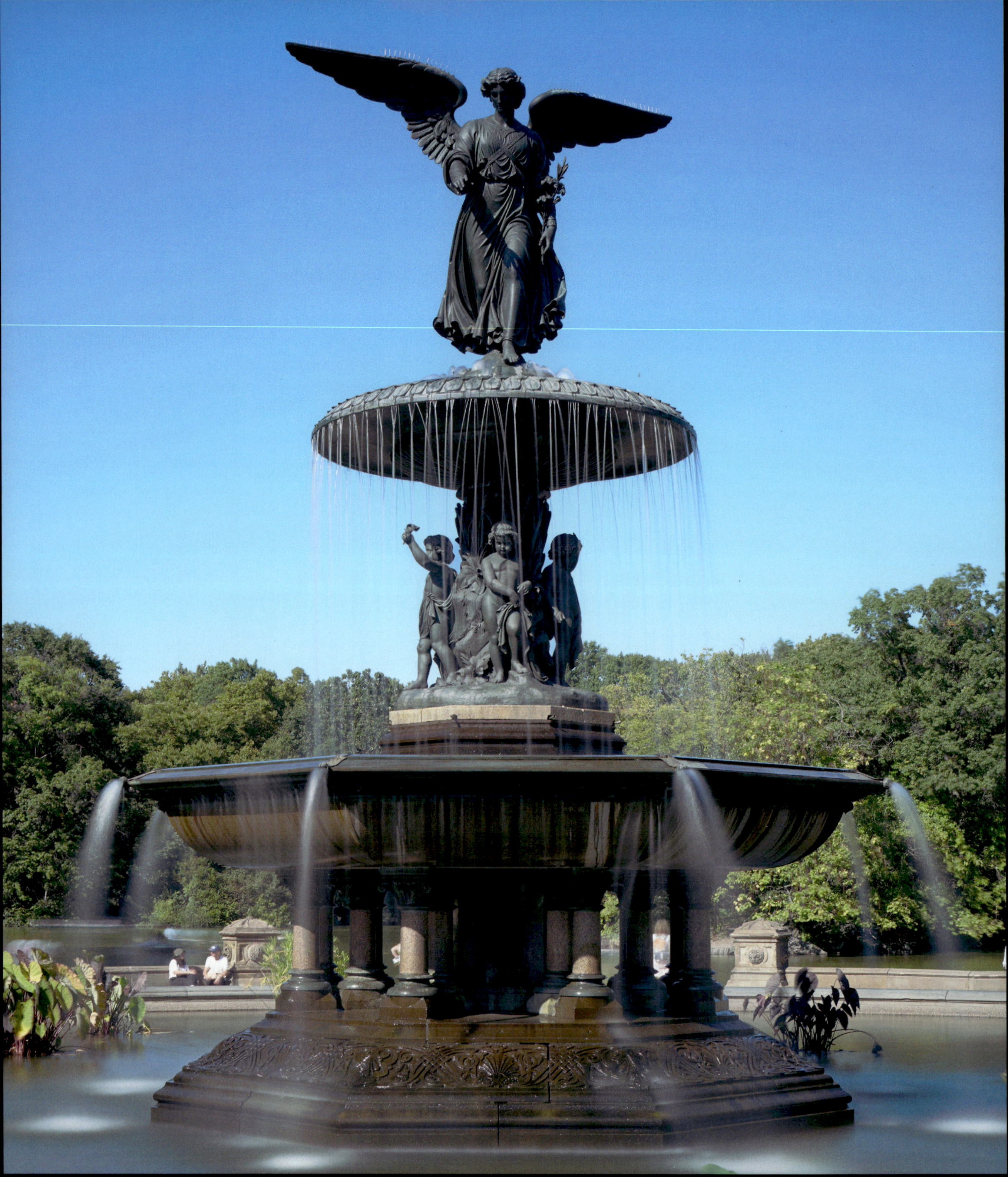

PLATE 47

BETHESDA FOUNTAIN

1870

Bronze and stone, H. overall: 25 ft. (7.62 m)

Inscription: Emma Stebbins inv.. mod. Rom. 1868 (left side)

Foundry mark: Ferd. v. Miller fudit München 1870 (right side)

New York City Department of Parks and Recreation

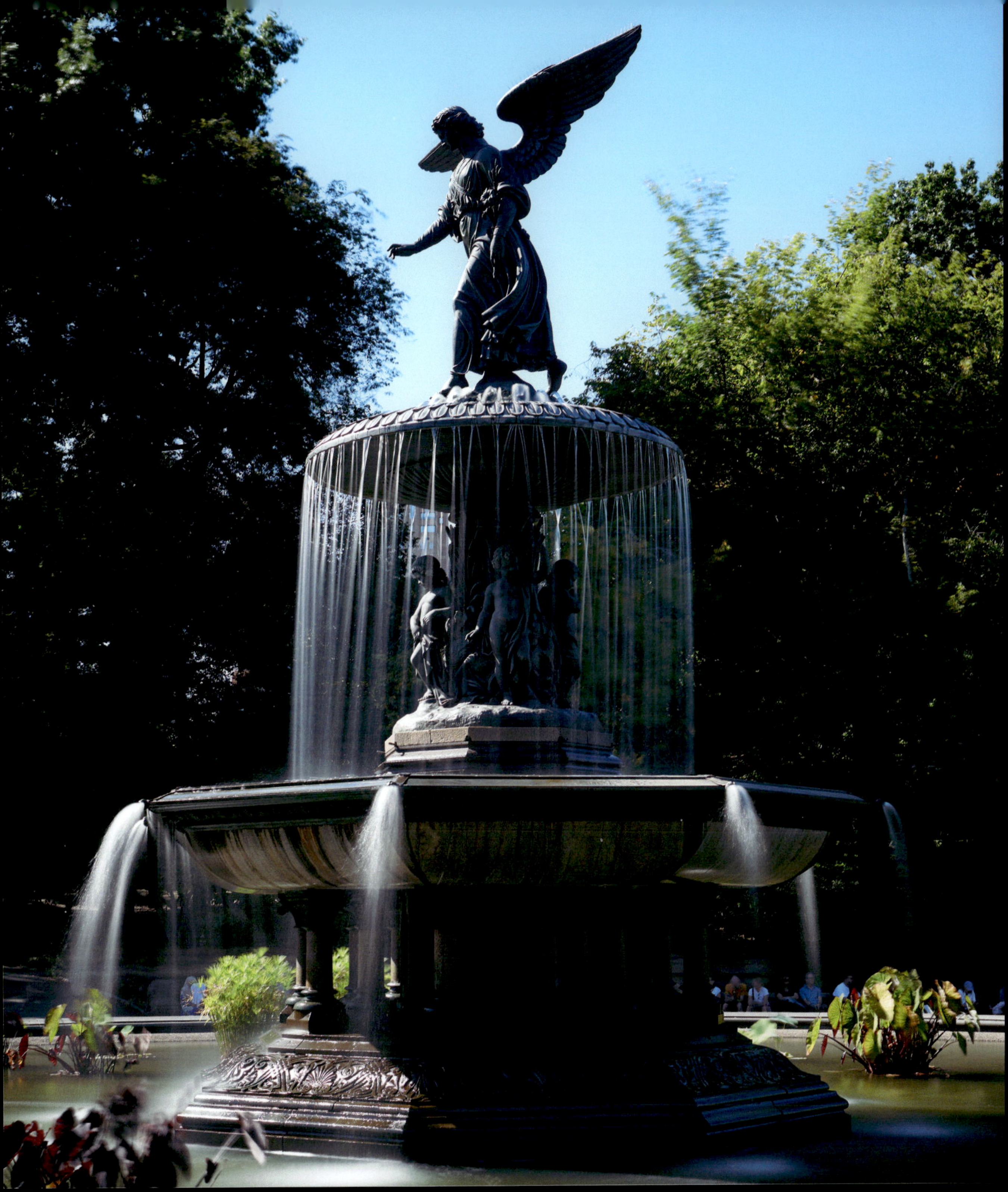

Alternate view of plate 47

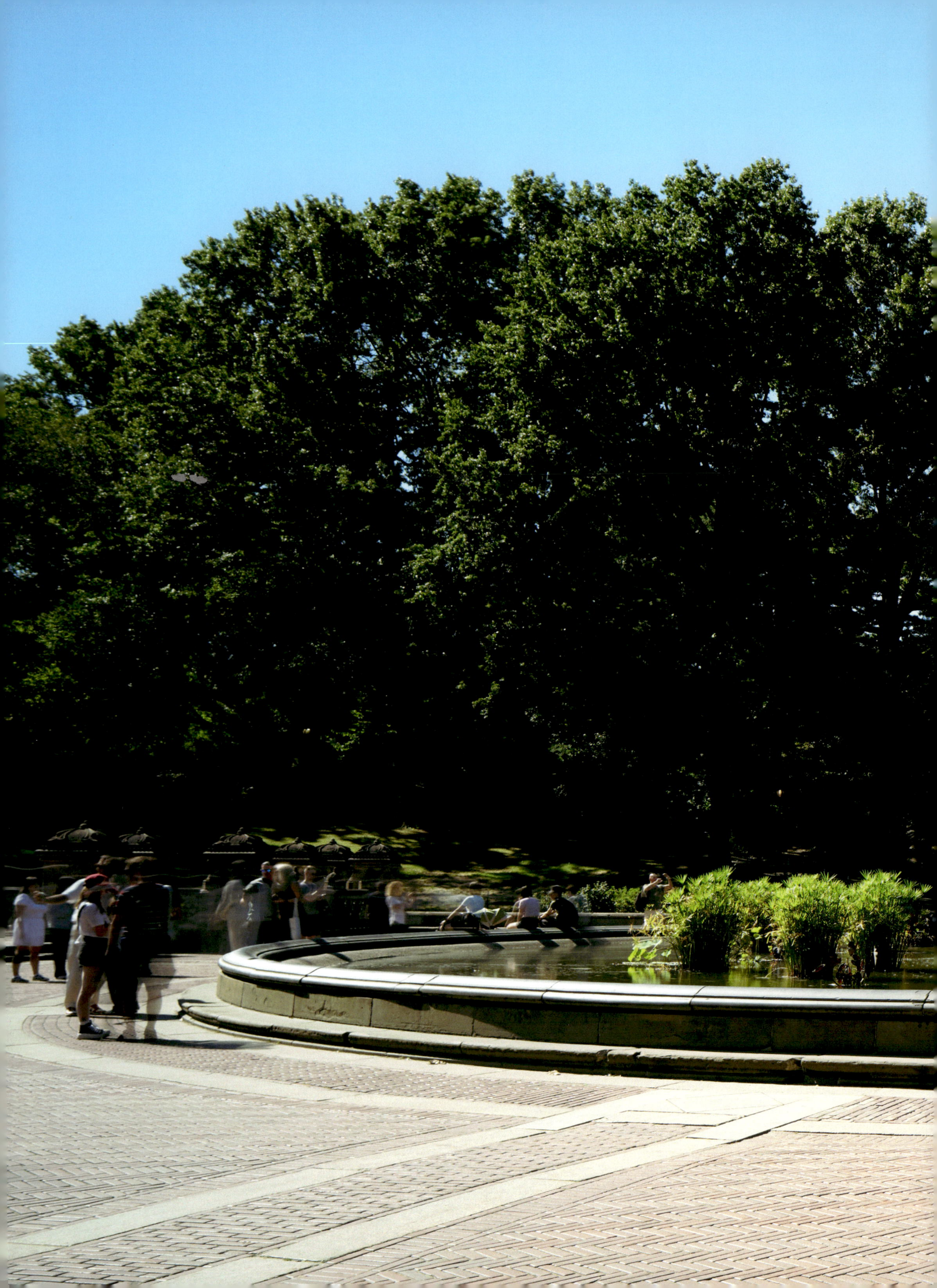

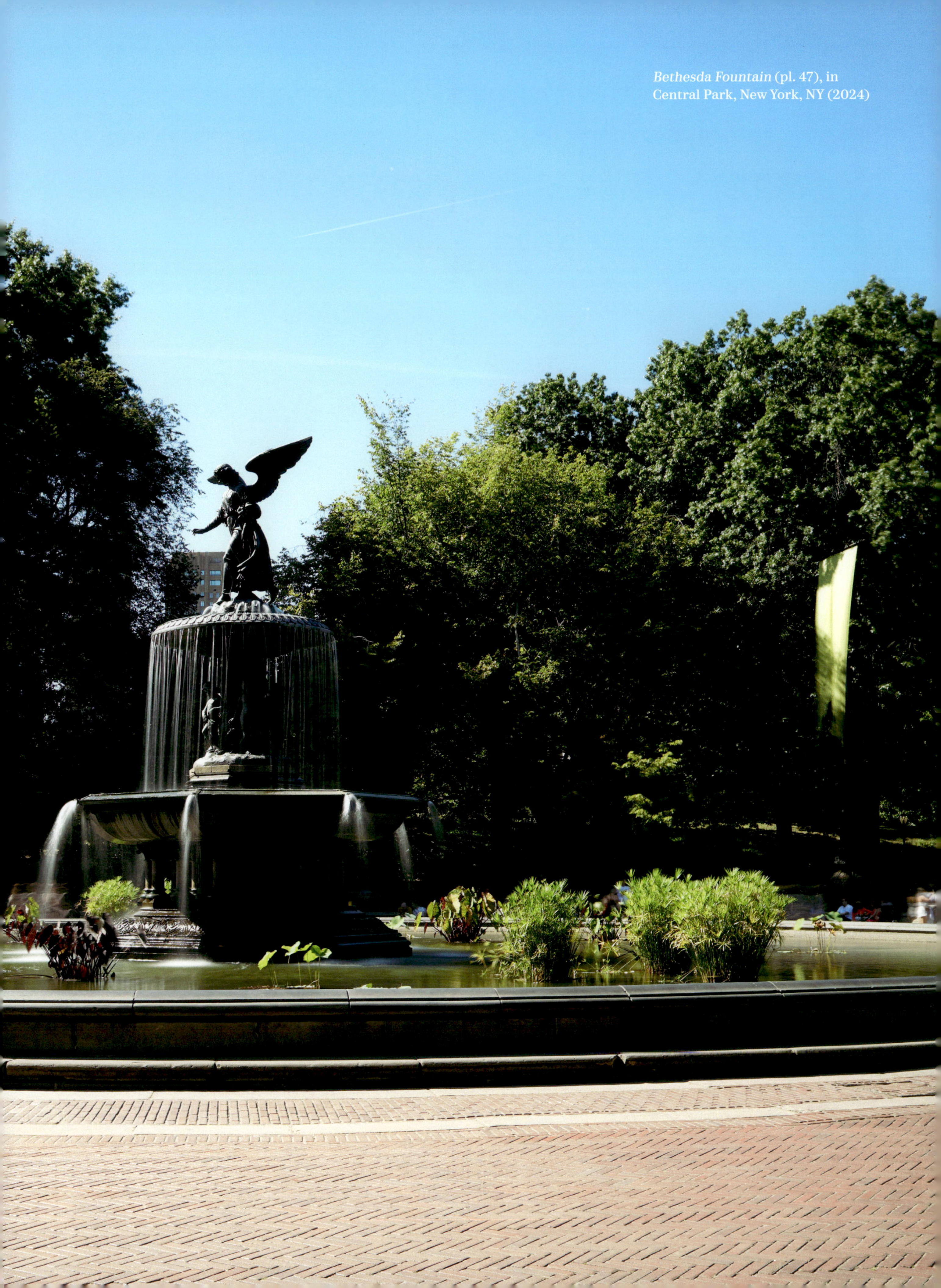

Bethesda Fountain (pl. 47), in
Central Park, New York, NY (2024)

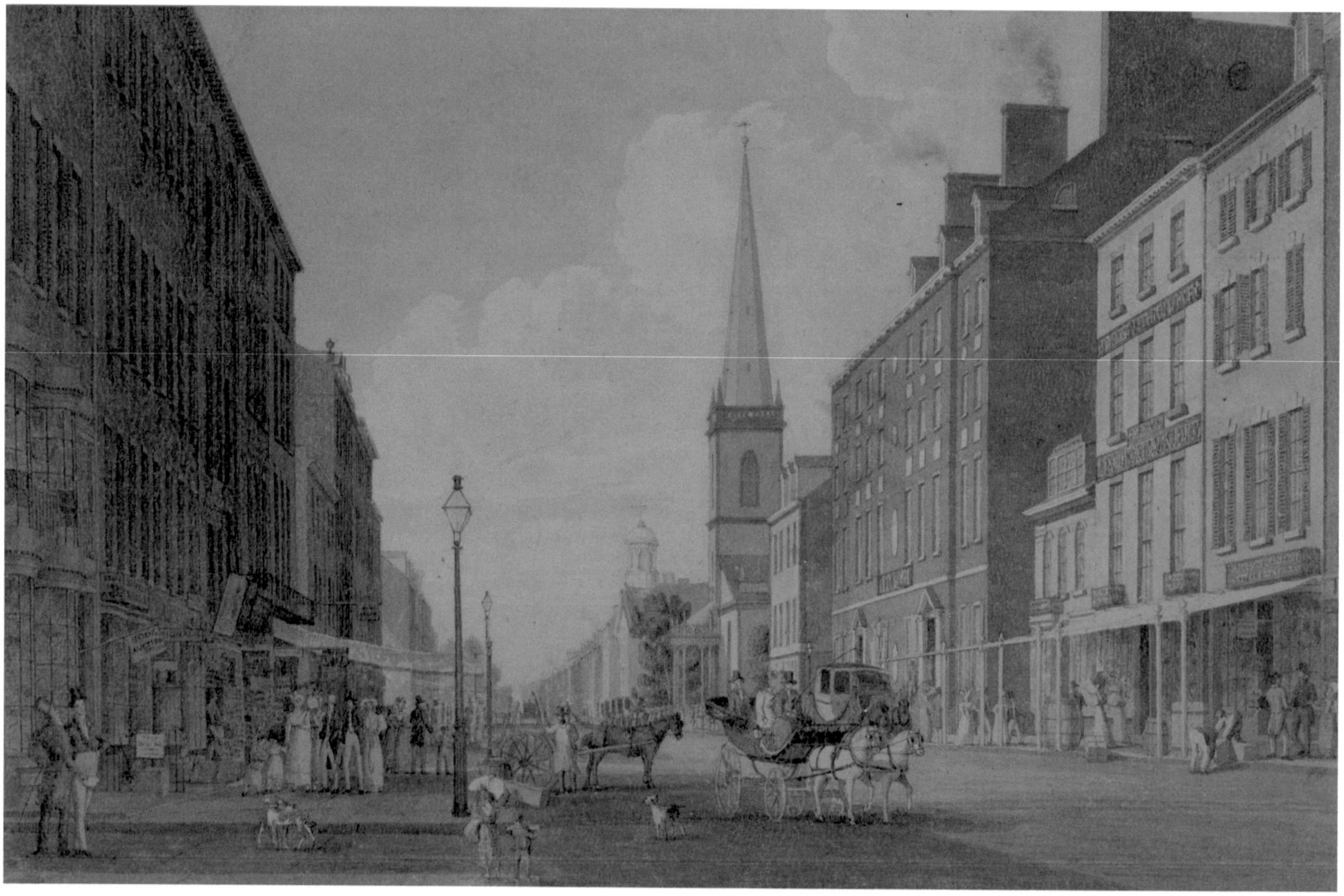

FIG. 1 John William Hill (American, 1812–1879), *Broadway and Trinity Church from Liberty Street*, 1830. Watercolor, 9 5⁄8 × 13 9⁄16 in. (24.5 × 34.5 cm).

The Miriam and Ira D. Wallach Division of Art, Prints and Photographs: Print Collection, The New York Public Library, New York, NY

KARLI WURZELBACHER

CHRONOLOGY

1815

SEPTEMBER 1 Emma Stebbins was born in New York City to John Stebbins (1783–1834) and Mary Largin Stebbins (d. 1874). Her parents had eight other children: Eliza L. Stebbins (1805–1806), John Wilson Stebbins (1807–1837), Charles Largin Stebbins (1809–1836), Henry George Stebbins (1811–1881), Mary Stebbins (1813–1906), Angelina Stebbins (1818–1898), William Augustus Stebbins (b. 1820), and Caroline Town Stebbins (1824–1903).[1]

OCTOBER 15 She was baptized at Trinity Church, which was and remains part of an Episcopalian parish (see fig. 1).[2]

1815–20

Little is known about Stebbins's childhood. She likely lived at 26 N. Moore Street. Beginning in 1813 and continuing through 1818, the annual volumes of *Longworth's American Almanac, New-York Register, and City Directory* listed a "Stebbens John, accountant" at "26 N Moore." In 1820, the directory amended the spelling to "Stebbins John, accountant 26 N. Moore."[3]

1821–28

John Stebbins, "first teller" of the United States Branch Bank, became "cashier" at the newly formed North River Bank in 1821.[4] The bank was located at 186 Greenwich Street, between Courtland and Vesey Streets, where the World Trade Center stands today.[5] He held the position through 1828, when a newspaper noted that "Mr. Stebbins the Cashier, and his family . . . occupy the dwelling part of the Banking-House."[6]

1829–30

John Stebbins resigned from the North River Bank and became a broker on Wall Street.[7] The family moved about a mile uptown, living at the corner of Hudson and Amos Streets and then at 577 Broome Street.[8]

1831

Stebbins's brother Henry G. Stebbins married Sarah Weston (1808–1893) at Saint John's Chapel on Varick Street.[9]

1832

SUMMER New York City suffered its first cholera epidemic, which left about 3,500 of Manhattan's 250,000 inhabitants dead. A large percentage of the population fled the city.[10] It is unclear how this outbreak impacted Stebbins's family, although one of her young nephews died of unspecified causes in September.[11] As detailed below, other family members later died from this disease.

1832–33

Longworth's American Almanac listed Stebbins's father at 51 Beach Street.[12]

1834

Stebbins's parents moved to 101 Varick Street.[13] On September 16, soon after she turned nineteen, her father died at age fifty-one. The record of his burial listed the cause of death as cholera and indicated that he was interred at Saint John's Burying Ground, which is now James J. Walker Park in Greenwich Village.[14]

1835–36

Stebbins and her unmarried siblings probably continued to live at 101 Varick Street, which was still her mother's address. Some of her brothers were in business together as brokers on Wall Street.[15] John Wilson Stebbins and Henry G. Stebbins both subscribed to the *Passion Flower*, a literary periodical that included blank tinted pages for "crayon sketches," an art form in which Stebbins later excelled.[16]

1836

MARCH John Wilson Stebbins obtained a passport for her and for their brother Charles Largin Stebbins. The latter was already on the island of St. Croix, which was then part of the Danish West Indies.[17]

APRIL Charles Largin Stebbins, age twenty-seven, died "at the island of St. Croix, where he had gone for the benefit of his health."[18] It is unclear when Stebbins arrived in St. Croix, and why she was there. She may have been helping to care for her brother, or perhaps was ill herself. Following her brother's death, she traveled home from St. Croix to New York City on the brig *Eliza*.[19]

1837

JUNE 4 John Wilson Stebbins died of cholera at age thirty.[20] He had been a stockbroker, a published poet, and the president of the Mercantile Library in New York City from 1832 to 1834. Stebbins would later sculpt a bust of him (pl. 40).[21]

1838–39

Stebbins likely became acquainted with Henry Inman (1801–1846) around this time, when he painted portraits of her parents and her brother Henry (fig. 2).[22] According to one period source, Inman "invited the young girl to visit his studio, and offered to give her instruction in oil-painting. She had never before taken lessons, and was pleased with the prospect of study" (see Ellet's historical text in this volume).

October 1839–Summer 1841

At some point during this period, Stebbins met sculptor Edward Augustus Brackett (1818–1908) when he was in New York City.[23] According to Mary Stebbins Garland's manuscript about her sister's career, she "was interested in his methods, received hints from him, and learned that form was the most satisfying medium of expression." Garland wrote that Stebbins created four early sculptures: "a bas relief portrait of a sister, and a statuette of another; then followed a Bust of her brother H. G. Stebbins. . . . Then boldly entering upon the ideal province, she produced a study of a boy catching a ball" (see Garland's historical text in this volume). These four works are not extant.

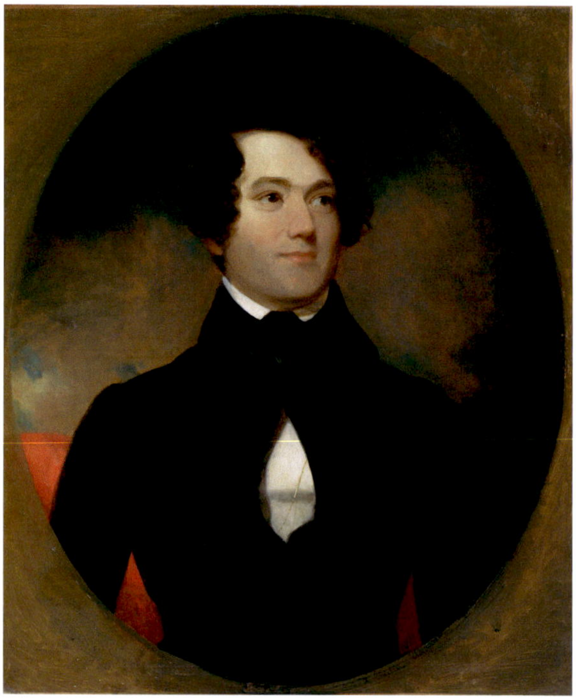

FIG. 2 Henry Inman (American, 1801–1846), *Henry G. Stebbins*, 1838. Oil on canvas, 30 × 24 in. (76.2 × 61 cm).

The Metropolitan Museum of Art, New York, NY, Bequest of Josephine S. Stebbins, 2000, 2001.269

1841

APRIL Henry G. Stebbins lent three paintings by Inman, including one entitled *Portrait of a Lady in a Riding Dress*, to the National Academy of Design's (New York City) annual exhibition.[24] This may be the same painting as the one now in the collection of The Heckscher Museum of Art (fig. 3). According to knowledge passed down within the Stebbins family, the painting portrays Stebbins.[25]

1842

New York City completed the Croton Aqueduct.

Stebbins was elected an associate member of the National Academy of Design, but her membership was later revoked on

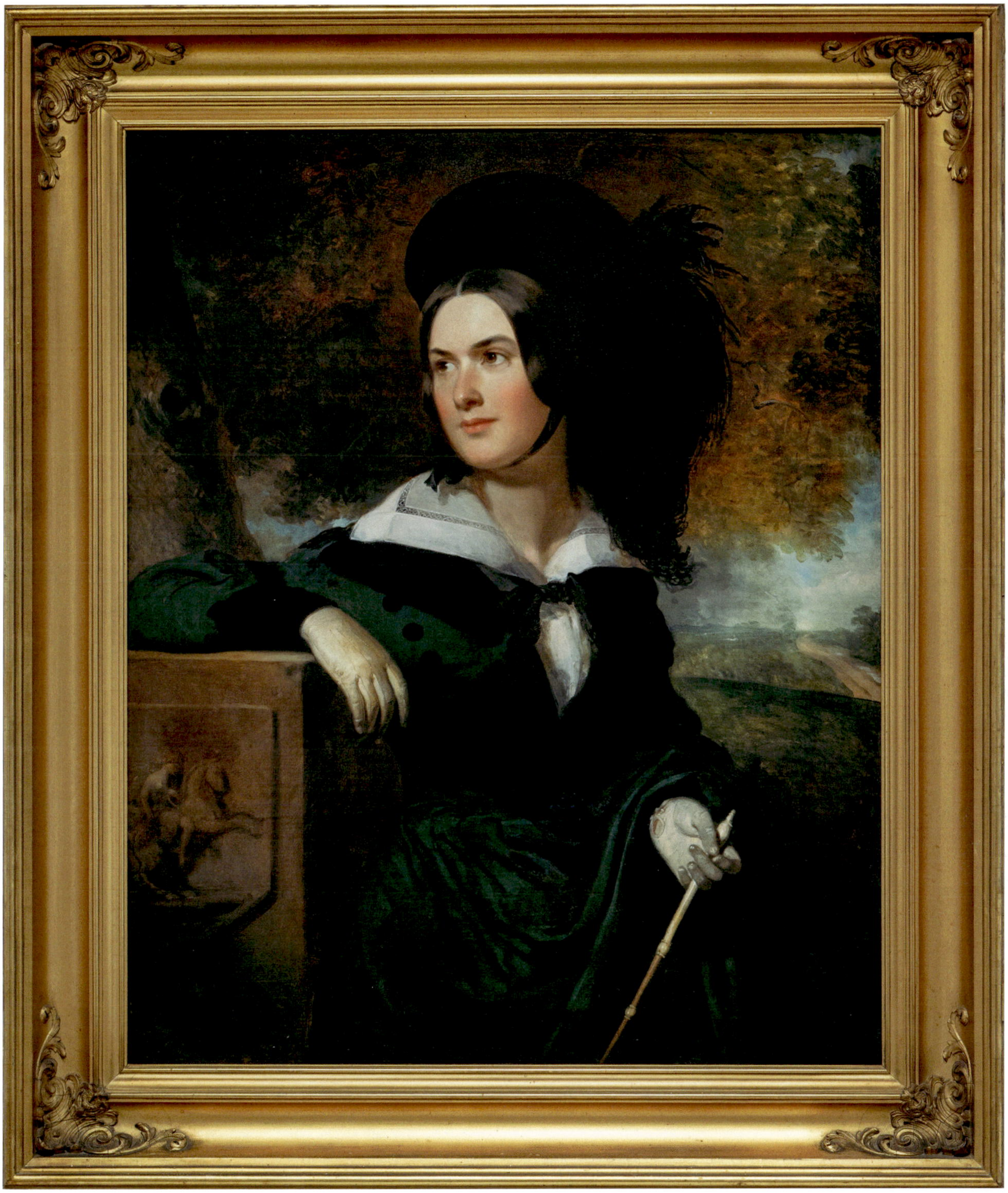

FIG. 3 Henry Inman (American, 1801–1846), *Emma Stebbins*, ca. 1839–41. Oil on canvas, 36 1/8 × 29 in. (91.8 × 73.7 cm).

The Heckscher Museum of Art, Huntington, NY, Museum Purchase: Town of Huntington Art Acquisition Fund, 2022.7.3

procedural grounds.[26] Professional artists ran the academy, which included a school and an exhibition program.

1845

Charles Macalester (1798–1873), a prominent Philadelphia-based collector, lent a work by Stebbins entitled *Portrait of a Lady* to the *Tenth Annual Exhibition of the Artists' Fund Society of Philadelphia, and the Pennsylvania Academy of the Fine Arts*.[27] It probably portrayed one of his family members.

1846–49

Stebbins likely lived with her mother and unmarried siblings on West 11th Street, north of Washington Square Park, between 5th and 6th Avenues.[28]

In 1846, the American Art-Union, first known as the Apollo Association for the Promotion of the Fine Arts in the United States, listed "Miss E. Stebbins" as a member. She next appeared on the membership list in 1849.[29] The organization presented exhibitions, held auctions, and purchased artwork to distribute by lottery. Each year, subscribers received an engraving of a painting.

1847

Henry G. Stebbins lent two works by his sister to the *Exhibition of Paintings, Statues and Casts* at the Pennsylvania Academy of the Fine Arts in Philadelphia. Entitled *John in the Wilderness* (ca. 1847) and *French Sweep Boy* (ca. 1847), both were copies after French artist Claude-Marie Dubufe (1790–1864).[30] Dubufe's *Saint John in the Wilderness* (before 1837) had been on view in New York City at the Stuyvesant Institute in 1837 and at the American Academy of the Fine Arts in 1838.[31]

1849

MARCH Poet, editor, and journalist William Cullen Bryant (1794–1878) sent Stebbins a note complimenting her on an illuminated manuscript that she had created. In one of her earliest known surviving letters, she replied, "you are so kind as to express your approbation of the manner in which I have illuminated your beautiful poem of Thanatopsis. Believe me sir, I speak from my heart, when I say, if anything could have added to the pleasure I felt in the performance of so agreeable a task, I should find it in this token of your appreciation, a proof of its merit as unexpected as it is delightful."[32] Nothing further is known about this artwork or its present whereabouts. Art historian Elizabeth Fries Lummis Ellet (1818–1877), a contemporary of Stebbins, discussed her work in illuminated manuscripts more generally (see Ellet's historical text in this volume). In the Emma Stebbins scrapbook, Garland documented a second illuminated text.[33]

1850

OCTOBER 8 The United States census recorded Stebbins's family—mother Mary and daughters Emma, Caroline, Mary, and Julia—living in the western half of Ward 15 in New York City.[34] Ward 15 was the area around Washington Square Park.

1853

Stebbins was one of seven "Lady Managers" supervising the New-York School of Design for Women, which was founded the previous year. Located on the corner of Broadway and Broome Street, its goal was "to give instruction to women, either gratuitously, or at very low rates, which will qualify them to earn a living by the practice of some of the branches taught in it, or to become teachers in other schools. Pupils are taught elementary Drawing, with reference to furnishing original designs for manufactures and other purposes where ornamental designs are required. Lessons are also given in Wood Engraving, to which will be added whatever branches may be found most advantageous and profitable."[35] Stebbins would be involved with the school through 1856.

FALL She almost certainly visited the *New-York Exhibition of the Industry of All Nations*, held at the New York Crystal Palace.[36] It included sculptures by Hiram Powers (1805–1873) and Bertel Thorvaldsen (1770–1844), among many others (see fig. 4).[37]

1855

SPRING Stebbins began to receive recognition for her crayon portraits, which were drawings executed on paper in pencil, charcoal, chalk, or wax crayon. She exhibited two at the National Academy of Design's annual exhibition—*Crayon Portrait of a Lady* and *Crayon Portrait*. The exhibition catalogue gave her address as "2 West 16th Street," which was the home of Henry G. Stebbins.[38] She may have used his address as a business address while remaining part of her mother's household just down the street, at 20 West 16th.[39]

JULY A Boston newspaper included Stebbins in a list of artists spending time in the fashionable summer resort town of Newport, Rhode Island, and noted her skill in crayon portraiture.[40] One source indicated that she charged "$50 per head" and that "her execution was said to be clear and forcible."[41]

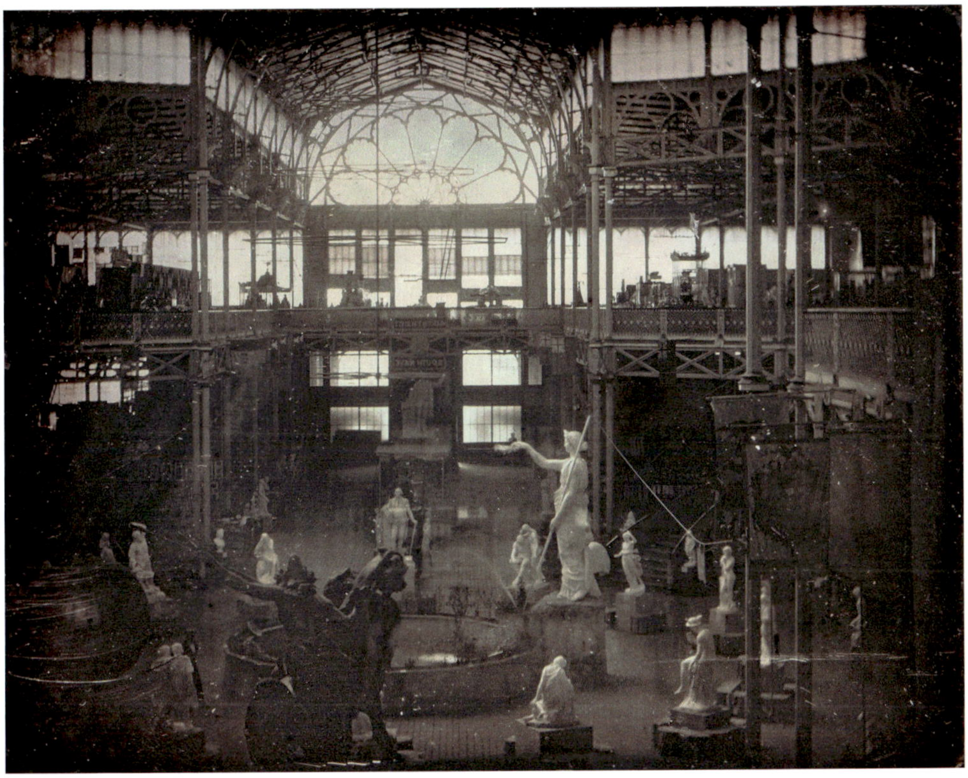

FIG. 4 *Crystal Palace Interior*, 1854. Daguerreotype.

Cased Photograph File, PR 012-2-515, The New York Historical, New York, NY

1856

FEBRUARY 16 *Home Journal* published an account of "a stroll among studios" that included artists to be found west of Broadway and between Bleecker and 13th Streets in New York City. It mentioned that "Miss Stebbins" was based further "up-town."[42]

MARCH The *Crayon* art magazine reported that Stebbins was expected to contribute a crayon drawing to the National Academy of Design's annual exhibition in April.[43] Yet she did not appear in the exhibition catalogue for that year.

APRIL Henry G. Stebbins wrote to the passport office to secure travel documents for his mother and two of his sisters (Emma and Caroline) before their imminent trip to Europe.[44]

MAY On the steamship *Arago*, Stebbins sailed for Le Havre, France, with her mother and her sister Caroline Stebbins (see fig. 5).[45] They likely traveled throughout Europe before going to Rome in the fall.

JULY *Knickerbocker* magazine wrote about "crayon-heads—a branch of portraiture more and more in vogue, and one in which Miss Stebbins . . . gained of late some enviable laurels."[46] The article mentioned that she had sailed for Europe in May.

SEPTEMBER Despite her departure for Europe, the New-York School of Design for Women continued to identify Stebbins as one of its six "managers."[47]

FALL The Stebbins family arrived in Rome and began sightseeing and socializing with American residents and other travelers.

DECEMBER They were already in Rome when actress Charlotte Cushman (1816–1876) arrived.[48] In the biography of Cushman that she would later compile, Stebbins recalled, "It was in the winter of 1856–57 that the compiler of these memoirs first made Miss Cushman's acquaintance, and from that time the current of their two lives ran, with rare exceptions, side by side. We were in Rome, as 'travellers and pilgrims' to the famous city. . . . She came late; and her advent had been heralded by many warm friends as something which would add greatly to the pleasures of the season. We soon found that the voice of fame had not exaggerated her attractions. No salon seemed complete without her, and her potent charm enhanced all the delights of the place" (see fig. 3 in Horn's essay in this volume).[49]

1857

WINTER Stebbins later remembered that Rome "was in all her glory, as the religious metropolis of the world, and passed through all her ecclesiastical phases. . . . To those who saw or two sketches, and am now pour passer le temps, modelling a bust of a bella Donna Romana . . . she is only a model, but grand and noble in the highest degree."[106]

MAY 3 Stebbins wrote to James T. Fields (1817–1881) and Annie Adams Fields about *The Lotus Eater* (see fig. 9 in Horn's essay in this volume). From her note, it is clear that one of them had written a "little sonnet" about the sculpture. She also described being unhappy with both a drawing and a photograph of the work: "the youth . . . looks heavy & clumsy enough to have been an eater of much more substantial food. As it is, I do not wish to show it as a presentment of my statue."[107]

MID-MAY Stebbins and Cushman left Rome for London, via Civitavecchia, Marseilles, and Paris. Their travel plans were interrupted when their original ship was requisitioned for troop movements in Sicily during the Risorgimento.[108]

JULY The couple's return to the US on July 5, which had been announced by the press as early as February, was widely publicized.[109] Soon after their arrival, author Harriet Beecher Stowe (1811–1896) published a much-circulated article about expatriate life in Rome, including the household at 38 Via Gregoriana.[110] Stebbins and Cushman were together for most of the summer, spending time in New York City and in Croton Falls, New York, with friends and family, including Stebbins's mother and her sister Mary.[111]

AUGUST The pair was in Newport, where Cushman's mother and her nephew Edwin "Ned" Cushman (1838–1909) joined them, as did Hosmer. The Crow family was there too, including Emma Crow Cushman (1839–1920), who was Charlotte's love interest and also Ned's future wife.[112] Stebbins must have discussed her sculptures and shared photographs of them with writers, because descriptions of her work began to appear in the press.[113] The *Hesperian* journal also grouped Stebbins with Hosmer, social reformer Florence Nightingale (1820–1910), and painter Lilly Martin Spencer (1822–1902) as examples of female achievement.[114]

AUGUST 31 The *New-York Times* published a lengthy, mostly favorable, assessment of *Commerce*, *Industry*, and *Charlotte Cushman*. Of the bust, it said, "The grander features of Miss Cushman's head are familiar to all who know the tragic artist; the womanly nature of the woman comes to us in this bust translated by a woman's intimate tenderness. . . . It is an early stage in art at which the skillful hand can reproduce what the head calmly elaborates. To carry steadily the full cup of feeling, and put into the stern and rigid categories of expression the finest and most tremulous motions, is a far higher flight of power; and it is because we recognize in Miss Stebbins' works the consciousness of this truth, and the capacity to face its demands, that we predict for her . . . a place among the elect of an art which, with Mr. Hawthorne's and Mr. Ruskin's permission, we do not believe has the slightest intention of dying, to oblige a theory" (see pl. 14 for a related work).[115]

SEPTEMBER Stebbins and Cushman visited the White Mountains (New Hampshire), Boston, and Lenox, Massachusetts, before heading to New York City, where they stayed at 20 West 16th Street.[116]

OCTOBER–NOVEMBER They each enjoyed success in their respective fields. Stebbins exhibited her sculptures in the US for the first time, showing *Commerce*, *Industry*, and *Charlotte Cushman* at Goupil's art gallery, located at 772 Broadway (see fig. 9). Multiple critical notices about her work appeared in the press.[117] Beginning October 1, Cushman performed in New York City for forty-eight straight days.[118]

DECEMBER Williams and Everett gallery in Boston exhibited *Commerce*, *Industry*, and *Charlotte Cushman*. A letter to the *Boston Evening Transcript* mentioned these works before stating, "We have seen a photograph of a better thing yet, by Miss Stebbins—a Columbus, which is the very spirit of the great adventurer himself, caught and imprisoned in marble."[119] It is unclear which version of *Christopher Columbus* the photograph depicted (see pls. 36–39 for related works).

1861

JANUARY–FEBRUARY Stebbins exhibited *The Lotus Eater* at Goupil, with a "prospectus" that quoted Tennyson's related poem (see pl. 1). The *New-York Times* described the figure as a "mournful" and "unconscious beauty," "at whose shrine worship daily many a fair dame, and all the critics of the City."[120] Critics evaluated the sculpture based on its fidelity to anatomy. For example, one writer observed, "The marble seems to have been touched into life and palpitation. All over it are traces of so severe and [conscientious a] study of the human form, that, were it not for the prospectus . . . we should be disinclined to believe it the production of a woman." This article goes on to say, "it would be a matter of extreme difficulty to determine the sex which the artist intended the work to portray—a very serious defect" (on Stebbins's figures and gender, see Gustin's essay in this volume).[121] Also worthy of praise was Stebbins's ability to expand upon the literary source material: "It requires a

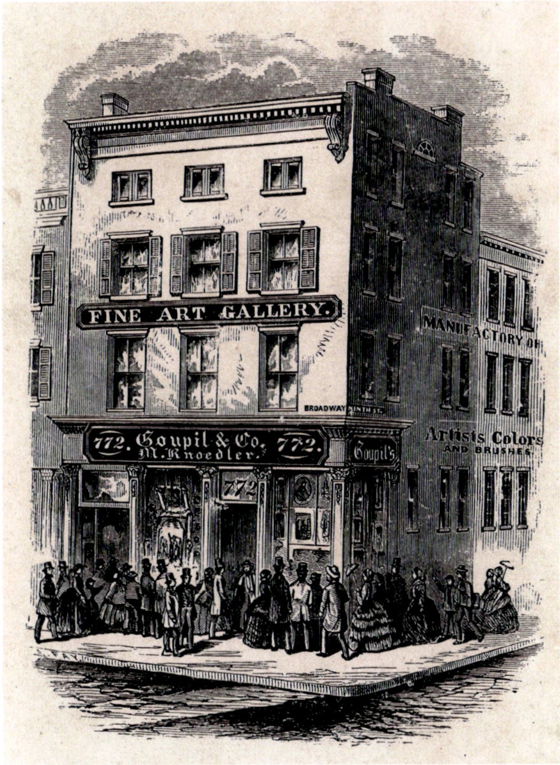

FIG. 9 Augustus Fay (American, born ca. 1824, active 1840–60), *Exterior of Goupil & Co., Fine Art Gallery, 772 Broadway*, ca. 1860. Wood engraving, 5¼ × 3¾ in. (13.3 × 9.5 cm).

American Antiquarian Society, Worcester, MA

far higher order of ability to conceive a character than to perceive it. . . . She has succeeded in conveying, in a material so hard and apparently unyielding as the cold, white stone, the half sensuous, luxurious, melancholy sentiment that Tennyson's delicate verses suggest, rather than embody. This constitutes a genuine artistic triumph."[122] Acknowledging that Homer's ancient Greek epic poem the *Odyssey* (ca. 725–675 BCE) had inspired Tennyson's poem, another paper declared Stebbins's sculpture, "the very counterpart of Homer's ideal."[123] While the *New-York Times* reported that "duplicates of this figure have already been ordered," full-length versions of *The Lotus Eater* remain unlocated.[124]

FEBRUARY Stebbins exhibited *Commerce* (pl. 11), *Industry* (pl. 10), and *Charlotte Cushman* (see pl. 14 for a related work) at Earle's Galleries in Philadelphia (where they were likely seen by artist Mary Cassatt [1844–1926] in her student days).[125]

MARCH In Boston with Cushman, Stebbins exhibited *The Lotus Eater* at Williams and Everett gallery. A critic contrasted the subject with the bustle of modern American life: "In the work-a-day world and in busy Boston, it is well to linger awhile over this form of Lotus eating, and to dream awhile with poet and sculptor. Miss Stebbins will soon return to Rome with Miss Cushman. They will take back with them another of Boston's artists, Miss Foley."[126]

APRIL 12 The American Civil War began with the battle of Fort Sumter in Charleston, South Carolina. Two weeks later, Cushman sang "The Star Spangled Banner" in Boston at a benefit for war volunteers. She added an extra verse, authored by Stebbins, which appeared in multiple newspapers: "When treason's dark cloud hovers black o'er the land, / And traitors conspire to sully her glory. / When that banner is torn by a fratricide band, / Whose bright, starry folds shine illuminated in story, / United we stand for the dear native land, / To the Union we pledge every heart, every hand!"[127]

JUNE By this time, Stebbins had begun negotiations with Samuel Gridley Howe (1801–1876), who was the chairman of a committee formed to erect a bronze statue of educator and abolitionist Horace Mann (1796–1859) to stand outside the Massachusetts State House in Boston (pls. 16, 17). Cushman was involved in determining the cost, which included Stebbins's labor, "expenses of studio," casting, and transportation. Offering to help fundraise by delivering a lecture on the character of Mann at various lyceums throughout Massachusetts, Cushman said, "In this way, women will raise the statue."[128] Stebbins and novelist Nathaniel Hawthorne (1804–1864) also corresponded about the commission.[129]

JULY 1 Stebbins and Cushman were in Washington, DC, where they saw Seward, who had become Secretary of State. Stebbins later wrote that Cushman "visited with him the entrenchments on Arlington Heights, and the various camps then in process of formation about the city."[130] It is unclear whether Stebbins joined them, although she did see President Abraham Lincoln (1809–1865) for the first time.[131] She described the trip as "a little southern excursion—to see with my own eyes before leaving the country—something of the strange and new aspect of affairs."[132]

JULY 14 By this time, Stebbins was in discussions with August Belmont (1813–1890) about creating a statue of his father-in-law Matthew Perry (1794–1858) for New York City's Central Park. Ultimately, she did not complete this monument to the US naval officer who had forced Japan into trade with the West.[133]

Hudson with the Indians, which Roberts "inserted in the wall of his house" in New York City at some point (pl. 35).[183] The "old" *Christopher Columbus* may be the work pictured in plates 36 and 37. For an image of the final marble version that Stebbins completed for Roberts, see plate 39.

EARLY FEBRUARY The controversy over the authorship of Hosmer's work was driving Stebbins "wild." According to Cushman, "That she [Stebbins] should be classed among those who would be believed to have their work done for them makes her too miserable, and to struggle along without the material help which all sculptors *must have* has become so entirely a necessity to her that she is assuming labor for which she has neither physical nor mental strength." She continued, "I never saw such crucifixion as Emma Stebbins . . . because she cannot accept these helps and tries to shuffle on to do *all* of her own work."[184]

MID-FEBRUARY Freeman visited Stebbins's new studio for the first time. Describing it as "a fine large one, with two large rooms, and one small one," she noted that Stebbins was working on the *Treaty of Hendrick Hudson with the Indians* and "a fine sketch for a statue of Columbus."[185] Guidebooks variously listed the new studio's address as "Vicolo del Basilico" or "11A, Via di S. Basilio."[186]

SPRING Howard Payson Arnold (1831–1910) published a book about his experiences in Europe. Regarding Stebbins, he wrote, "The persevering industry with which she has modelled from nature, and her study of the principles of ancient sculpture, have enabled her to produce results, which, though few, display great ability." He described her earlier take on *Christopher Columbus*, which included the face of a "monster" on the tiller under the figure's right hand (pls. 36, 37). Arnold also mentioned the following works: *The Lotus Eater* bust (see pl. 3), *Joseph the Dreamer* (see pls. 22–24), *Autumn* (see pls. 25–27), and *Horace Mann* (pl. 16). He concluded, "It is gratifying to see an earnest, persevering, faithful study of art, which does not condescend to cater for popular applause, but works quietly on, and, foreseeing the rich reward to come, is willing 'to scorn delights and live laborious days.'"[187]

APRIL The Sanitary Commission held a bazaar in New York City. Artists in Rome donated artwork and other items for sale. Cushman sent a "huge folio" of engravings of sculptures by Antonio Canova (1757–1822).[188] One paper mentioned that Stebbins gave "a copy of her famous bust of Washington."[189] It is not clear if Stebbins was the creator of this bust; the Emma Stebbins scrapbook does not contain an image of such a work, nor is there an extant marble. Their support of the bazaar is one example of their continuing involvement in the war effort. As Frances Power Cobbe stated, Stebbins and Cushman were not "so thoroughly expatriated from America and rooted in Italy, or so engrossed by their pursuit of art, as to be indifferent to the great struggles of their country. It would be impossible to respect them equally could it be so."[190]

MAY Cushman escorted Freeman to Liverpool to catch a steamer to the US, and Stebbins went to Switzerland with the Tiltons and Garland.[191] She must have completed a marble version of *Joseph the Dreamer* before leaving Rome, as the sculpture in the collection of the Belfast Central Library is inscribed 1864 (pl. 24).

JUNE A description of the *Angel of the Waters*, part of the *Bethesda Fountain* (pls. 46, 47), appeared in print: "Instead of a Naiad, Triton, Dolphin or other classical study, Miss Stebbins adopts the original idea of the 'angel disturbing the waters of the pool,' familiar to all readers of the New Testament." The article continued, "The commissioners intended to order the manufacture of this beautiful statue with the accompanying ornamental work in bronze, abroad, but the rise in gold has caused a suspension of the work, and it is now postponed, like many other good things, till 'after the war.'"[192]

JULY–AUGUST Stebbins was in the spa town of Harrogate, England, with Garland, Cushman, and Cushman's family members.[193]

SEPTEMBER–NOVEMBER The couple stayed in Bowdon, a suburb of Manchester, and then went to London.[194]

NOVEMBER 19 The Central Park Board of Commissioners met and agreed to pay Stebbins $8,000 in gold (rather than in US dollars) "for working drawings and plan of the base and first basin of the fountain, as a substitute for the base shown in the drawing presented by Miss Stebbins to the Board, and for a model of the other parts of the fountain, as shown by the above drawing referred to,—Miss Stebbins to pay all expenses of packing and transportation to such foundry . . . also to superintend the casting and shipping."[195] With this decision about the payment, Stebbins became the first woman to earn a public sculpture commission from the city of New York. According to later reports, she "designed and executed" the models for the angel, the upper bronze basin, and the four cherubs in Rome "during the winters of 1864–66 and '67" (see fig. 6 in the introduction to this volume).[196]

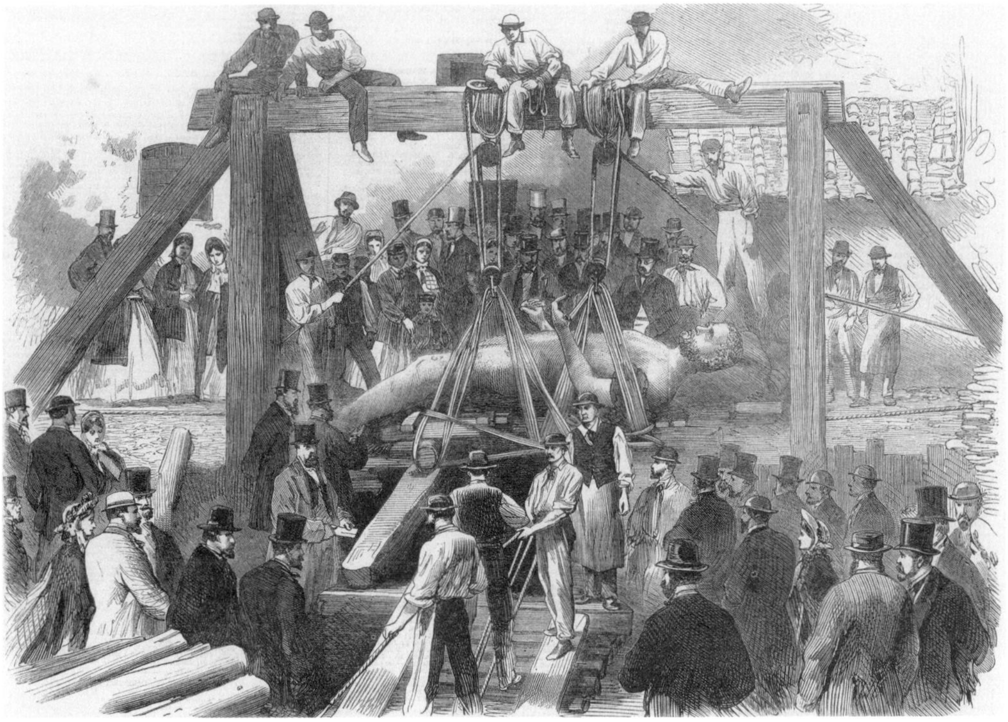

FIG. 12 *Raising the Colossal Bronze Statue of Hercules Found Underground in the Campo Dei Fiori at Rome*, 1864. From *The Illustrated London News*, October 29, 1864, 440. Engraving.

NOVEMBER-DECEMBER Hosmer published a humorous poem chastising male artists in Rome who felt compelled to "make some desperate stand, / Or else our sister artists here / Will drive us from the land."[197] She also published "The Process of Sculpture," to "correct the false, but very general impression, that the artist, beginning with the crude block, and guided by his imagination only, hews out his statue with his own hands."[198]

DECEMBER Early in the month, Stebbins, Cushman, and Mercer were still in London, staying at Cushman's townhome at 1 Bolton Row. Hosmer and Freeman were also passing through the city. They all planned to return to Rome via Paris.[199] By this time, *Horace Mann* had been cast, but had not been paid for because of the prohibitive exchange rate. Delivery to Boston was therefore delayed.[200]

1865

JANUARY Stebbins viewed the thirteen-foot-tall Roman statue of Hercules, now at the Vatican Museums, soon after it had been excavated (see fig. 12). It had been discovered in Rome the previous fall, when she was in England. Describing the experience as if it had been Cushman's alone, Stebbins wrote, "She saw . . . the great bronze statue of the young Hercules as it was lifted from its bed of oyster-shells, with remnants of the gilding which had once covered it still clinging here and there, and peered curiously into the opening in the top of the head, through which it was supposed the priests had uttered their pretended oracles" (see Stebbins's historical text in this volume).[201]

WINTER-SPRING Stebbins's main occupation seems to have been *Christopher Columbus*.[202] It was the only work in her studio to garner notice in the American press during this period.[203] One guide book listed the contents of her studio as follows: "Joseph the Dreamer [pl. 24], a colossal head of Satan [see pl. 21 for a related work], and a statue of Columbus [see pls. 36–39], with bas-reliefs from his life."[204] Stebbins likely also worked on the *Bethesda Fountain* during this period (pl. 47).[205] She may have created a bust of her nephew John Neal Tilton (1860–1921) around this time (pls. 41, 42). Tilton was the model for the allegorical figures of *Temperance, Purity, Health and Peace* (pl. 45) on the *Bethesda Fountain*. He was also the model for *Samuel*, versions of which Stebbins would complete in marble in 1868 and 1870 (pls. 43, 44). An image of *Samuel* in the Emma Stebbins scrapbook includes a quotation from the Old Testament: "Speak Lord! For Thy Servant Heareth."[206]

APRIL News reached Rome that Confederate General Robert E. Lee (1807–1870) had surrendered at Appomattox, Virginia. Word of the assassination of President Lincoln soon followed. Around this time, the bronze foundry received payment for casting *Horace Mann* (pl. 17).[207]

DECEMBER Sailing from New York City, Stebbins, Cushman, Mercer, and Freeman arrived in Liverpool and continued to Rome (with Freeman going ahead separately).[266]

1869

JANUARY Henry Wadsworth Longfellow (1807–1882), whose poem had inspired Stebbins's *Sandalphon* (pl. 20), was in Rome with his family. Stebbins, Cushman, and Hosmer were among thirty guests at a dinner given in his honor.[267]

FEBRUARY 5 Longfellow and his daughter Alice visited Stebbins's studio.[268]

MARCH 28 The *New York Herald* published a letter in which Roberts gifted Stebbins's *Christopher Columbus* to Central Park (pl. 39). It read in part, "Columbus is represented as standing upon the deck of his ship alone and at midnight, just before the land of the Western Continent burst upon his view." As a condition of the gift, he required the park commissioners to build "a suitable glass house" to protect the marble from the elements.[269] In the meantime, he stated, the statue and pedestal would remain on view at the National Academy of Design.

SPRING Cushman discovered that she had breast cancer.[270]

JUNE Writing from Rome, Anne Hampton Brewster (1818–1892) provided a detailed account of the *Bethesda Fountain* (pl. 47): "Part of it is now at Munich, nearly finished, and the support or base has just left Rome to be cut and cast in America." She continued, "The chief figure—an angel, eight feet in height—alights upon or almost seems to hover over a mass of rock which occupies the centre of the upper basin. . . . The water will play in natural jets or falls from every part of the rock, and be broken into mist or spray as it pours over the lip of the upper basin. This upper basin is ten feet in diameter, and is shaped like those in the piazza of St. Peter, here in Rome." Brewster listed the four allegories that "represent the qualities of water" as temperance, purity, health, and "contentment." She wrote that the lower basin, "octagonal in shape, eighteen feet seven inches in diameter . . . is the part that has gone lately to America; it is to be made of granite or blue stone, with bronze ornaments, or entirely of bronze, according to the decision of those who have charge of the erection of the fountain." While visiting Stebbins's studio with three other women, Brewster "noticed with admiration some studies made . . . for the Central Park at the request of the managers; four statues of the Seasons [pl. 28]. . . . Also studies for the gateways of the Croton Reservoir. . . . the Nymph of the River, with her attendant spirits of wood and water, putting aside the rushes in order to give the water freely to the city [pls. 30, 31]. . . . [The] gate at the opposite side represents the city, crowned, and bearing the emblems of commercial sovereignty, seated between her two rivers, the North and East [pl. 32]." She also wrote that while visiting Rome, "Mr. Sully Darley" had ordered a bust of Cushman (see pl. 14 for a related work).[271]

JULY A visitor to the foundry in Munich reported seeing "the new models and castings from it" for the *Bethesda Fountain*.[272]

SUMMER Stebbins and Cushman traveled to Paris, London, and Malvern, consulting with doctors and seeking treatment for Cushman.[273] Ned Cushman was recalled to the US from Rome, ending his employment in Italy and his family's stay at 38 Via Gregoriana.[274]

AUGUST 18–OCTOBER Stebbins, Cushman, and Mercer were in Edinburgh, where Cushman underwent an operation that Stebbins described as a "sad and painful event. . . . It was apparently very successful, but was speedily followed by a series of very dangerous complications."[275] Writing to Whitney about Cushman, Stebbins said, "we two have been through the valley of the shadow of death together—and by the goodness of God—permitted to return."[276]

LATE OCTOBER–NOVEMBER The trio left Edinburgh for Malvern and then started for Rome.[277] Brewster wrote, "Miss Stebbins has been quite ill. She was with Miss Cushman during all her cruel suffering, and of course, after the worst was over, Miss Stebbins's nervous system was completely prostrated."[278]

DECEMBER Newspapers reported that Stebbins and Cushman were back in Rome, the latter's "health completely restored."[279] Yet Stebbins later remembered, "in the course of the winter it became evident that the evil was not entirely eradicated."[280]

1870

JANUARY Many newspapers reported that, with the addition of Vinnie Ream (1847–1914) (who was more than thirty years Stebbins's junior), there were now seven female American sculptors in Rome.[281]

SPRING Cushman's cancer "again made its appearance," and she and Stebbins made plans to leave Rome for the US.[282] According to Freeman, they expected to rent out their furnished home, and left open the possibility of returning in fall 1871.[283] Prior to their departure, Stebbins "destroyed quantities of letters—not being able to carry them about."[284] She also completed the following in marble: at least two versions of *The Lotus Eater* (one of which is illustrated in pl. 5), *Charlotte Cushman* (pl. 14), and *Samuel* (pl. 44).[285] At some point during her thirteen-year career in Rome, Stebbins modeled *Angel of the Resurrection* (pl. 33) and *Monument* (pl. 34), neither of which were realized in marble.

MAY As Stebbins later recalled (writing in the third person), "The Roman home was abandoned to the tender mercies of tenants. All knew, though no one ever said so, that they might never see it again."[286] She and Cushman left Rome, "going by way of Venice and Munich to Paris, and from thence to England."[287] While in Munich, they visited the bronze foundry. Cushman stated that they "saw the angel, looking like an angel (can I say more?)."[288] It was likely at this time that the foundry tested the fountain in Stebbins's presence, elevating it to the proper height and running water through it.[289] Meanwhile, one of Stebbins's busts of Cushman was on view at Earle's Galleries in Philadelphia.[290]

SUMMER In Hampstead, England, Cushman endured another procedure, "severer and more painful than the first . . . namely, excision by caustic," followed by another visit to the baths at Malvern. Stebbins wrote, "the return of unfavorable symptoms induced her to make up her mind to return finally to America."[291]

SEPTEMBER 20 The Kingdom of Italy captured Rome, ending the government of the Papal States, which had been established in 756.[292]

NOVEMBER 3 Stebbins, Cushman, and Mercer arrived in New York City from Liverpool after crossing the ocean for what would be the final time.[293] They spent the remainder of the year in the city and at Garland's home in Hyde Park.[294]

DECEMBER Stebbins had shipped at least some of her work back to the US. One paper reported that *Sandalphon* had "just arrived and is to be exhibited. . . . The attitude of strength and ease, the divine pity in the downcast face are in Miss Stebbins' own characteristic vein. There are one or two glaring faults of anatomy which are unaccountable as coming from so close a student as this lady, but on the whole, the composition is excellent alike in thought and execution" (pl. 20).[295] She exhibited the work at Schaus's Art Gallery, accompanied by a printed copy of Longfellow's poem (see fig. 1 in Gustin's essay in this volume). It remained on view through at least mid-January of the following year.[296]

1871

JANUARY Newspapers reported that "Miss Emma Stebbins, the American sculptress, has announced her intention of residing permanently in New York," and that she would "probably have a studio in town."[297] While Stebbins may have continued to draw and paint, however, there is no indication that she continued to sculpt after leaving Rome.

APRIL Stebbins exhibited a bust of *The Lotus Eater* to favorable critical notice at Bigelow, Kennard & Co. in Boston (see pl. 5).[298]

JULY The *Bethesda Fountain* arrived from Germany after being "detained for a long time at Bremen, owing to the uncertainty of transportation during the Franco-German war" (pl. 47).[299] Cushman bought the corner lot at Rhode Island Avenue and Catherine Street in Newport and commissioned Richard Morris Hunt (1827–1895) to design a house for her. She moved into "Villa Cushman" the following summer (see fig. 16).[300] Stebbins would live there sporadically.

SUMMER Stebbins spent the summer with her ailing mother at Garland's home in Hyde Park.[301] One paper noted that her *Christopher Columbus* was on public view on the first floor of the museum within the Arsenal building at 64th Street and 5th Avenue in Central Park (pl. 39).[302]

FALL Cushman returned to the stage for the first time since 1863 with performances in New York City and Boston. She would continue to tour the country performing through May 1875, taking breaks during the summer months.[303]

NOVEMBER One paper reported that Stebbins had "decided not to return to Rome, which means a virtual abandonment of all artistic work, as she can get no inspiration in America, and finds it impossible to do any work here, while she does not care to leave her family and live away from them abroad."[304] At the end of the month, she and Cushman were in Boston, where Annie Adams Fields gave a dinner in Cushman's honor.[305] In New York City, Henry G. Stebbins, chairman of the Committee of Seventy, exposed the corruption of Tammany Hall, the government party that had been running New York City.[306]

1872

SPRING Stebbins remained in Hyde Park, while Cushman toured throughout the Midwest.[307]

APRIL After Lockwood died, his estate liquidated his art collection, including Stebbins's *Samuel* (pl. 43). As described

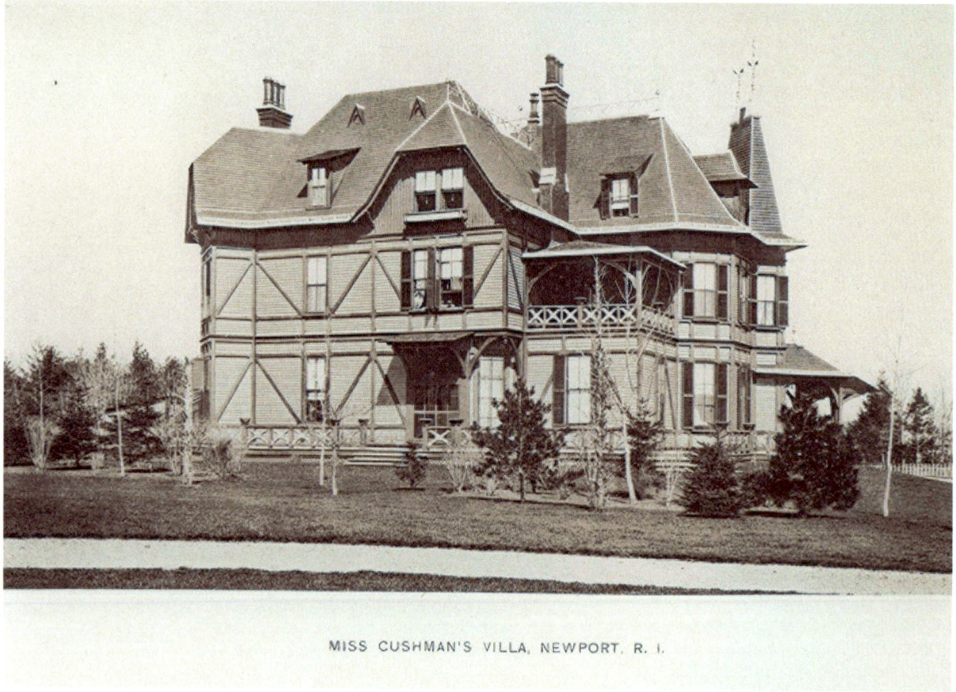

FIG. 16 *Miss Cushman's Villa, Newport, R.I.* From Emma Stebbins, ed., *Charlotte Cushman: Her Letters and Memories of Her Life* (Boston: Houghton, Osgood, 1878).

in the auction catalogue, "The pose of the figure is eminently graceful, and the modeling is done with a firm and able hand. The face most truthfully suggests the devotion of the young worshiper."[308]

SUMMER Stebbins visited Cushman and her family in Newport before going back to Hyde Park to be with her mother.[309] Cushman returned to the stage in mid-August and performed until May of the following year.[310]

1873

JANUARY On her relationship with Stebbins, a newspaper quoted Cushman as saying, "We are both spinsters . . . we love each other, respect each others [*sic*] lives and habits and opinions, and dwell together in perfect harmony." The article described Stebbins as having "gray hair that hints she has passed her meridian. An affection of the eyes has compelled her to give up her art in which she has given proofs of decided talent."[311]

SPRING Stebbins was in Hyde Park while Cushman toured.[312]

MAY 6 The *Bethesda Fountain* was installed, but remained covered with canvas wrappings (pl. 47).[313]

MAY 17 The fountain was unveiled privately "for the purpose of allowing the sculptress to test the working of the water and other mechanical incidentals."[314]

MAY 31 With Stebbins in attendance and a band playing the music of Ludwig van Beethoven (1770–1827) and Felix Mendelssohn (1809–1847), the *Bethesda Fountain* was formally inaugurated in Central Park (pl. 47).[315] The event was "without ceremony, without even any spoken words of introduction," and was attended by "many thousands . . . mostly German citizens, with their wives and children. . . . They were evidently proud of the works of their Fatherland and were profuse in their compliments of the designer of the fountain, Miss Emma Stebbins."[316] The event was covered in newspapers throughout the country, and an illustration of the new fountain appeared on the front cover of the *Daily Graphic: An Illustrated Evening Newspaper*.[317]

SUMMER Still in Hyde Park caring for her mother, Stebbins began a correspondence with Whitney, who had returned from Rome to Boston to continue her career as a sculptor.[318] Stebbins wrote to her of the "success of my fountain, after all these years of heart wearing delay & inactivity." She enclosed "a programme of the opening" and several newspaper clippings (see fig. 6 in the introduction to this volume).[319] Stebbins would correspond intermittently with Whitney until 1881.[320]

OCTOBER Cushman began her acting season, which continued until May of the following year.[321]

DECEMBER Stebbins was in Boston, where Cushman was performing. She likely visited Whitney's studio. She later described herself to Whitney as "the dilapidated individual who made such drafts upon your kindness & sympathy."[322]

1874

MARCH Stebbins traveled from Hyde Park to Philadelphia to meet Cushman, who was on tour.[323]

APRIL 21 Stebbins's mother, Mary Largin Stebbins, died.[324]

SUMMER Stebbins purchased a "cottage" in Lenox, and she and Cushman also spent time in Newport.[325]

FALL Cushman sent her nephew Ned to Rome to oversee the packing of the furnishings that she and Stebbins had left behind at 38 Via Gregoriana four years earlier. These included Stebbins's sculpture *The Roman Model (Bust of Nanna Risi)* (pl. 15), which was shipped to Newport. Three other sculptures attributed to Stebbins were also part of the contents of the Newport home: a plaster cast of the bust of Cushman, a marble portrait rondel of an unnamed sitter, and a plaster cast of Cupid and Psyche.[326] The whereabouts of these artworks are not known. Cushman returned to the stage in Boston and then performed in New York City. Stebbins traveled with her and Mercer to Philadelphia, Cincinnati, and Washington, DC.[327]

1875

JANUARY–MAY Cushman continued to perform in cities in the Midwest, in Boston and Baltimore, and throughout New York State. This was the last season in which she acted.[328]

SUMMER The Rhode Island state census recorded Stebbins living in Newport. It listed Cushman as the "Head of Family" and her profession as "Actress." Stebbins appeared as Cushman's "Companion," with the profession of "Sculptress." Emma Crow Cushman and Edwin Cushman and their four children were living in the home as well, along with "Maid" Sallie Mercer, and household staff.[329] Stebbins and Cushman also spent time in Lenox.[330] Several papers erroneously reported that Stebbins was among the artists competing for the commission to create a monument of politician Charles Sumner (1811–1874).[331] Stebbins did, however, view the public exhibition of the submissions with Annie Adams Fields, who reported to Whitney, "we saw the model of Sumner among a crowd of Sumners done in clay . . . yours was a light among them. Emma Stebbins, without knowing yours, as yours, picked it out at once as the best."[332]

OCTOBER Cushman's health was deteriorating. She, Stebbins, and Mercer moved to the Parker House hotel in Boston. Cushman began dictating her early life to Stebbins, laying the groundwork for the posthumous biography that Stebbins would edit.[333]

DECEMBER As Annie Adams Fields described, Stebbins was "utterly absorbed by Miss Cushman. . . . C. C. is very ill."[334]

1876

FEBRUARY 18 Cushman died at the Parker House in Boston at age fifty-nine. Her funeral service was held across the street at King's Chapel, and she was buried at Mount Auburn cemetery.[335] From this point on, Stebbins generally spent the winter months with her sisters Mary and Angelina in Hyde Park and New York City, and the summer months in Lenox, with occasional trips to Newport.[336]

EARLY MAY Newspapers across the country reported the contents of Cushman's will. She left Stebbins $1,500 a year and "use of her mansion in Newport." This home was to be shared with Mercer and with the family of Emma Crow Cushman and Ned Cushman.[337] However, the estate was in financial trouble, and it is unclear whether Stebbins received her full inheritance.[338]

MAY 10 The Women's Pavilion of the Centennial Exposition in Philadelphia opened to the public and remained on view through November. According to *Arthur's Illustrated Home Magazine*, "the most noticeable piece of sculpture" on display there was "a bust of Charlotte Cushman, by Emma Stebbins, of Rome" (see pl. 14 for a related work).[339] This relatively small work was the only sculpture by Stebbins in the exposition. By comparison, many of Stebbins's peers, including Foley, Freeman, Lewis, Ream, and Whitney, contributed multiple sculptures or more major works. Stebbins may have been underrepresented at this exhibition because she was no longer in Rome, where Hosmer and Brewster had secured artwork for the Women's Pavilion.[340] In addition, Cushman's declining health and death earlier in the year may have left Stebbins uninterested in participating. She may also have felt disinclined to exhibit for other reasons. Indeed, four months before the show opened, she told a friend, "I am not a bit patriotic—I don't take the slightest interest in the Centennial—I consider these great shows—thoroughly inartistic."[341]

JUNE One of Stebbins's sculptures, entitled "Angel," was for sale at auction. It is possible that the work for sale was a version of *Sandalphon* (see pl. 20).[342]

SUMMER Stebbins was in Lenox. She later described herself as "literally helpless" during this time.[343]

OCTOBER A newspaper reported that "The Angel" by Stebbins was to be auctioned as part of the sale of the belongings of "the late Collector of the Port of New York (Thomas Murphy, Esq.)."[344]

1877

NOVEMBER Stebbins was at Villa Cushman in Newport. She had finished compiling six chapters of the biography *Charlotte Cushman: Her Letters and Memories of Her Life* (1878), a portion of which is excerpted in this volume.[345]

1878

MID-APRIL Stebbins delivered the manuscript of her Cushman biography to the publishers. Writing from Newport, she told a friend, "now I feel as I used to do when I got off a statue—like a soft shelled crab—at the mercy of everything!"[346]

MAY Houghton, Osgood and Company published Stebbins's biography of Cushman. The book was widely promoted and reviewed.[347]

JUNE After a gap in the archive of four years, Stebbins resumed her correspondence with Whitney when the latter wrote to congratulate her on the Cushman book. Stebbins relayed that she had been asked by someone in Ohio to make a memorial fountain. Because her "health would not allow [her] to undertake such a work," she recommended Whitney instead.[348]

SUMMER Stebbins was in Lenox. Mercer and her nephew John Neal Tilton were her companions. In a letter to Whitney, she mentioned that the Lenox house had been closed for more than a year, and she described her declining health as "so slow but steady." Of her Cushman biography, she wrote, "upon the whole I am more satisfied than I have ever been by anything of my own doing."[349]

OCTOBER Stebbins was in New York City with her sisters.[350]

1879

AUGUST 5 Stebbins wrote Whitney from Lenox, where she was staying with her sisters and Mercer. Reflecting on her career, she said, "I did my little part as well as I could, and with some of the saving grace of truth and love to sanctify it, whatever its failures."[351]

OCTOBER 30 Writing from New York City, Stebbins told Whitney, "This summer I have felt better and higher than for three years past. . . . and if it came in my way I might even essay to work . . . the feeling is so strange to me, that I hardly know what to make of it." She also mentioned that she had plans to make her "usual autumn visit to Villa Cushman" in Newport.[352]

1880

MARCH 30 Stebbins may have attended the opening of the Metropolitan Museum of Art at its current location. Her brother Henry was one of the twenty-eight men who had incorporated the museum in 1870.[353]

DECEMBER At this time, Stebbins was living at 20 West 16th Street. As she wrote to a friend, "I am in better health than I have been for a long time, and am even able to work a little, which is a great pleasure to me."[354]

1881

SUMMER Stebbins stayed at a hydrotherapy sanatorium in Dansville, New York, called "Our Home on the Hillside." Her sisters Mary and Angelina were likely there as well.[355]

DECEMBER Stebbins's brother Henry G. Stebbins died at age seventy-one.[356]

1882

OCTOBER 24 Stebbins died in New York City at age sixty-seven.[357] She was buried in Greenwood Cemetery in Brooklyn. Her headstone reads: "Emma Stebbins / The Beloved Sister / And Faithful Friend." It also bears the phrase, "Love is the fulfilling of the law." This quotation is from Romans 13:9–10 (KJV), which reads: "Thou shalt love thy neighbour as thyself. Love worketh no ill to his neighbour: therefore love is the fulfilling of the law." Two years later, Stebbins's friends installed a simple monument to her in Lenox.[358]

LATE OCTOBER Newspapers across the country carried word of Stebbins's death with similar brief notices: "Miss Emma Stebbins, the artist, and life-long friend and biographer of Charlotte Cushman, died. . . . She had been long suffering from ill health contracted during her residence in Rome."[359] Someone close to her, perhaps her sister Mary, wrote a letter to the *New-York Tribune* to provide additional information. After stating, "a highly gifted woman has died . . . whose work as sculptor and artist deserves some notice in your paper," the letter summarized her life and career more fully.[360] The *Sun* declared: "The death of Miss Emma Stebbins . . . has removed from the world a woman of unusual mental power and brilliancy . . . and with enough genius for the sculptor's art to induce her to devote her life to its development."[361]

Miss Stebbins was interested in his methods, received hints from him, and learned that form was the most satisfying medium of expression, and was to supersede all others with her. The sculptor's passion awoke, and she saw that she had the sculptor's thumb, and the inner vision, which enables the artist in Form, to project before the minds eye a perfect image of the object to be rendered. Beginning at once to labour with enthusiasm in this new field, Miss Stebbins produced a bas relief portrait of a sister, and a statuette of another; then followed a Bust of her brother H. G. Stebbins, which was not unsuccessful. Then boldly entering upon the ideal province, she produced a study of a boy catching a ball, which was looked upon at that early date as a work of spirit and promise. There were then few facilities for the pursuit of this branch of work in New York. The figure was injured in casting, and discouragement ensued, but the passion only slumbered, and when in 1857 Miss Stebbins went with her mother and sister to Rome it awoke again.[6] There, every thing tends towards artistic production, facilities and helps of all kinds are great, the very atmosphere is Creative. She determined to remain and work in Rome. This resolution was encouraged in the kindest and most helpful manner, by her friend Charlotte Cushman who, among her many large hearted gifts, had the special one of seeing the inner needs and loving to aid and comfort them. This with the approval and assistance of her brother, (H. G. Stebbins) who had always generously fostered her talent, made it possible for the sojourn in Rome to be prolonged. Miss Cushman after her English labours and successes, established her winter home in Rome, which Miss Stebbins (and for a time Miss Hosmer) shared with her for several years.

It now became necessary to study, which was done with persistent devotion and conscientiousness, drawing from the cast and the antique, under a severe Italian master that winter, then in the studio of Paul Akers the American sculptor, anatomy and modelling from the nude.

1857: The first attempt at ideal study was made that winter and elicited encomiums from as severe a judge as John Gibson, the well known English sculptor [see pl. 2]. The subject chosen was from Tennyson's poem of the 'Lotus Eater.' This sketch was afterwards embodied in a small statue ordered by Leonard Jerome of New York [pl. 1]. The head of this statue was many times repeated, and was always a great favourite [pls. 3–5]. An order was about this time executed for 'Mr. Hecksher' of New York, for two small figures, representing Mining & Commerce under the forms of a Miner [pl. 10] and Sailor [pl. 11]. These statuettes were well spoken of at the time, though too small to be very effective.

1859: The same winter, she modelled and put in marble, a bust of Miss Cushman for Mr. Shepherd of Shepherd's Town, Eng.[7] This was three times repeated, the first copy made for Mr. James Muspratt of Liverpool, the 2^{d} for H. G. Stebbins of New York, the 3^{d} for Mr. J. Sully Darly of Philadelphia [see pl. 14]. Also during that winter Miss Stebbins executed a bust of a famous Roman model, known as 'Nana' now at Villa Cushman Newport [pl. 15].[8]

1860: The winter of 1860 was chiefly occupied in modelling for Mr. Marshall O. Roberts of New York, a bas relief, representing the Treaty of 'Hendrick Hudson' with the Indians, for the purchase of Manhattan Island [pl. 35], and also a study for a statue of Columbus, which was afterwards executed in marble, in heroic size, and presented by him, to the Central Park with the proviso that it should be protected from the weather by some suitable building; the proviso has always prevented any action being taken for the placing of the statue, and it now forms a part of the public attractions of the park in one of the buildings [pl. 39].[9]

In the winter of 1860 Miss Stebbins modelled a study for a statue of 'Horace Mann' for Boston at the request of Dr. Howe, the president of the Commission appointed for this purpose [pls. 16, 17].[10] Dr. Howe was much interested that the statue of the Apostle of Female Education should be executed by a woman. He was greatly pleased with the photograph of the study sent to him, and declared in a letter to the artist, that it was 'a resurrection of the form.' The commission followed and the statue was executed and cast in bronze at Munich and now stands in front of the state house in Boston.

During the summer of 1860 a design for a fountain had been prepared and submitted to the commissioners of the Central Park, which having met with their approbation, was accepted, and the modelling commenced in 1861 & 2.[11] It occupied four winters, and is now standing in the open square, below the mall at the foot of the steps leading to the Lake; (not the best position for a fountain, which should be looked up to, rather than down upon, but the point of view, making allowance for this defect, comprises many picturesque features). The idea of this Fountain was suggested by the scriptural pool of Bethesda, the descent of the Angel to trouble the waters for healing. It should rightly be called the Bethesda Fountain [pl. 47]. The small figures supporting the upper basin symbolize the Temperance, Purity, Health, and Peace, which flow from the blessing of the water [pl. 45].

Miss Stebbins principal artistic work ended with this group. She had also made studies, ordered by the park commissioners to complete the artistic unity of the Fountain square, of statues of the Seasons, to be placed on the pedestals designed for such figures on the steps descending from the mall, towards the Fountain [pl. 28]. The studies were submitted, but no action taken upon them.

Besides the above mentioned works completed in Rome, there are several others of great beauty, the dates of which I do not now remember, one which has been several times repeated, in statuette, and three quarter size, represents: 'Joseph,' the shepherd, and dreamer, the beloved above all his brethren [pl. 24], another 'The Angel of Prayer' [pl. 20] and another a fine Bust of Mr. W. Stebbins (Miss Stebbins elder brother) which is now in the hall of the Mercantile Library Building [pl. 40]. (Mr. Stebbins was the first president of the M. L. Association, and was largely instrumental in establishing the beginnings of that valuable Institution.)[12]

1870: In 1870 Miss Stebbins returned with Miss Cushman to America, and afterward her life was given with devotion to her friend, then suffering with a fatal disease, which terminated her life in the winter of 1875.[13] Then her own health had failed, but she succeeded in compiling and publishing, the memorial of her friend Miss Cushman, in which much of the story of their Roman life may be found. This is her only literary work of any note, made at the request of her departed friend. It has been commended by the best critics, especially by Miss Cushmans friends. Those who knew and loved her best, find in the memorial the truest portrait of that admirable and remarkable woman.

It may be said that Miss Stebbins looked upon her art life with a mixture of pleasure and pain; pleasure in the effort, which indeed was a second nature, pain in its incompleteness. She was never satisfied with her work when it arrived at the point of [completion]. The aim was high, the ideal unattainable, so there appeared in her a modesty and want of self assertion which surprised her friends, but the interpretation of this was in the high artistic standard toward which she ever strove, too high to attain to the fruition of the soul and be satisfied.

Emma Stebbins died in New York, Oct 25th 1882.[14] She was born in that city 1st September, 1815.

AFTERWORD

DAVID J. GETSY

The principal challenge for most audiences of nineteenth-century sculpture—then and now—arises from the conventions, rules, and limitations of the neoclassical style and format. Hewing closely to a monochromatic and uninflected surface treatment, these statues render in minute details clothing and musculature seamlessly but not individually. Whether it is a hat, a belt, a face, or a foot, it is often a "type" that receives the sculptor's labor rather than a unique prototype (be it an object or a person) with its own history. Even neoclassical portraits reach for likeness without specificity.

The medium of sculpture is further limited by its material and logistical confines. Unlike painting, sculpture has fewer genres and options. For instance, there are no freestanding sculptural depictions of landscape, and any sculpture of an object (say, a basket of flowers or a hammer) raises questions about its relation to the everyday world of objects—questions almost never posed to most still life paintings. Statues, busts, and monuments often have to stand alone, with little depicted context other than the occasional object in the hands or laying at the feet. Nineteenth-century sculpture was often limited to the representation of the human face and body (and the occasional horse). Mythologies, histories, allegories, eroticisms, and memories were all embodied in the human figure, usually solitary or in a pair or small group.

For all these reasons, much nineteenth-century sculpture was dually constrained by the aesthetics of the neoclassical legacy and the narrow range of sculptural formats, such as the stand-alone figure. Hemmed in by these conventions, sculptors worked in accordance with a set of restricted options. Their contemporaries, in turn, judged their success by the sculptures' adherence to those rules. These conventions needed to be learned and mastered, and cultivation was gauged by the viewers' comprehension and application of their criteria. However, we also need to remember that most people who encountered public monuments—as well as some viewers of freestanding sculptures (in salons, studios, and houses)—did not know those rules, did not care to know them, or questioned how they came to be. In the century and a half since, that distance from neoclassicism's priorities has only widened, leaving many twenty-first-century viewers uncertain just how to look closely at these nineteenth-century marbles or bronzes that, after all, often do look a lot alike at first glance.

I am not concerned with denouncing or defending these restraints; there are plenty of subsequent artists and art critics who staked their own claims to originality on such arguments. Rather, I recall these conventions (and their limitations) as a means of introducing these sculptures afresh. Rather than see their style as distant, outdated, or cold (all common reactions over the last two centuries), what if we see the constraints as a game to be played by the artist (and the viewer?). Rules are often the conditions for creativity—think of the rules by which we play games or sport.

They are constraints, but their limits produce the occasions for strategy, skill, and problem-solving. Let's think of nineteenth-century sculpture's conventions in that way: as an adopted set of rules to be enjoyed and beaten.

One benefit of this perspective is that it allows us to value the choices of the artists who sought to work within the rule systems of nineteenth-century sculpture. Read any sculptor's memoir or journalistic account of a studio and you will find that artists devoted their lives to this work with passion, integrity, and a belief that they were doing something unique and important. A too-quick dismissal of the neoclassical format disrespects those lives devoted to art and—for the sculptors of monuments—to the public and to history. As a reflection on this exhibition and the deep scholarship that this catalogue presents, I am brought again to the very human, daily life of the artist. In other words, how can we look past the distant rules of the nineteenth century to see that excitement of *living through sculpture*?

While she was an innovator, Emma Stebbins wasn't a rule breaker. She mastered the conventions for her own self-realization as an artist and because she (like other female-identified sculptors) had to work twice as hard to overcome her day's sexist presumption that only men, not women, could make art. Stebbins knew the rules, and she found ways to work within them—both in her life and her work. Stylistically, she proved herself expert at playing with the conventions of neoclassical sculpture, with her delicately carved marbles that are chock-full of detail and anecdote while maintaining an even keel. Viewers could well look to the manner of Stebbins's sculptures as exemplars of style and handling. She undoubtedly demonstrated mastery of the rules and adhered to them; this move was an important way of saying that she not only belonged but also could be judged against any competitor.

Tactically, however, Stebbins also introduced traits that bent, rather than broke, those rules. She inhabited conventions as a means to expand them from within, ultimately showing what alternatives those constraints might also hold. Let's not forget that she created the first heroic depictions of laborers in American sculpture, she was the first woman to defy sexist expectations and sculpt the male nude that had been a standard of neoclassicism, and she was the first woman to create a public monument in the US. This exhibition restores those "firsts" to the historical record, and we can see her unprecedentedness as the result of her gaming the expectations for sculpture in her day.

Stebbins's creative adaptation of rules (and the consequent expansion of the language of American neoclassical sculpture) was not limited to her profession as a sculptor. She also adopted conventions in her life, most importantly when she took on the custom of marriage as a means of defining herself through her partnership with Charlotte Cushman. Their marriage was their identity, and it used the expectations of that institution to give shape and legibility to their lives together. Twentieth- and

ENDNOTES

INTRODUCTION

Carving Out History

1. As detailed in the chronology in this volume, the Central Park commissioners ordered the fountain in 1863. They recorded their decision to pay for it with public funds in 1864. The *Bethesda Fountain* is the earliest sculpture by a woman documented in the *Catalogue of the Works of Art Belonging to the City of New York* (New York: Art Commission of the City of New York, 1909).
2. For an overview of early public monuments in Boston, see Arthur Dexter, "The Fine Arts in Boston," in *The Memorial History of Boston, Including Suffolk County, Massachusetts, 1630–1880*, vol. 4, *The Last Hundred Years, Part II*, ed. Justin Winsor (Boston: James R. Osgood, 1881), 383–414. Harriet Hosmer's *Thomas Hart Benton* was commissioned, sculpted, and cast around the same time as Stebbins's *Horace Mann*, but it was not installed in St. Louis, Missouri, until 1868. See Patricia Cronin, *Harriet Hosmer: Lost and Found, a Catalogue Raisonné* (Milan: Edizioni Charta, 2009), 62.
3. On nineteenth-century female marriage, see Sharon Marcus, *Between Women: Friendship, Desire, and Marriage in Victorian England* (Princeton, NJ: Princeton University Press, 2007).
4. "An American Prima Donna," *Chicago Evening Post*, May 14, 1867, 2; "Fine Arts," *Evening Post* (New York City), October 31, 1860, 2.
5. Henry T. Tuckerman, *Book of the Artists: American Artist Life* (New York: G. P. Putnam, 1867), 602–3.
6. Jennifer Harlan, "Overlooked No More: Emma Stebbins, Who Sculpted an Angel of New York," *New York Times*, May 29, 2019, https://www.nytimes.com/2019/05/29/obituaries/emma-stebbins-overlooked.html; "2 O'Clock Edition," *Brooklyn Daily Eagle* (NY), October 26, 1882, 3.
7. F., "The Late Miss Emma Stebbins: To the Editor of the Tribune," *New-York Tribune*, November 2, 1882, 7.
8. See Ronald G. Pisano and Carol Forman Tabler, *Catalogue of the Collection: Paintings and Sculpture* (Huntington, NY: Heckscher Museum of Art, 1979), 71–72.
9. See Lorado Taft, *The History of American Sculpture* (New York: Macmillan, 1903), 69, 211; Albert TenEyck Gardner, *Yankee Stonecutters: The First American School of Sculpture, 1800–1850* (New York: Columbia University Press, 1945), 50, 71–72; Margaret Farrand Thorp, "The White, Marmorean Flock," *New England Quarterly* 32, no. 2 (June 1959): 147–69; Wayne Craven, *Sculpture in America* (New York: Thomas Y. Crowell, 1968), 333. It is unclear if Stebbins's sexuality might have contributed to the lack of scholarship on her. For a historiography of how changing understandings of Cushman's expressions of gender and sexuality influenced historians' views of her, see Lisa Merrill, *When Romeo Was a Woman: Charlotte Cushman and Her Circle of Female Spectators* (Ann Arbor: University of Michigan Press, 1999), xix–xx, 243–66.
10. Joseph Leach was the first to publish new information about Stebbins in his biography of Cushman, *Bright Particular Star: The Life and Times of Charlotte Cushman* (New Haven, CT: Yale University Press, 1970). Lennox Strong reviewed the book in the February/March 1971 issue of the lesbian periodical the *Ladder*. Stebbins received brief mention, as Cushman's partner, in: Jonathan Katz, *Gay American History: Lesbians and Gay Men in the U.S.A.* (New York: Thomas Y. Crowell, 1976), 654; "Lesbian Art and Artists," *Heresies: A Feminist Publication on Art and Politics* 1, no. 3 (1977): 96.
11. William H. Gerdts, Nicolai Cikovsky Jr., Marie H. Morrison, and Carol Ockman, *The White, Marmorean Flock: Nineteenth Century American Women Neoclassical Sculptors* (Poughkeepsie, NY: Vassar College Art Gallery, 1972); William H. Gerdts, *American Neo-Classic Sculpture: The Marble Resurrection* (New York: Viking, 1973). Gerdts included Stebbins's *Samuel* (pl. 43) in two exhibitions at the Newark Museum in New Jersey: *A Survey of American Sculpture: Late 18th Century to 1962* (1962) and *Women Artists of America, 1707–1964* (1965).
12. The acquisition by the Chrysler prompted one of the first art historical analyses of an individual sculpture by Stebbins, *Samuel* (pl. 44): H. Nichols B. Clark, *A Marble Quarry: The James H. Ricau Collection of Sculpture at the Chrysler Museum of Art* (New York: Hudson Hills, 1997), 156–60. As this text explains, the version of *Samuel* now in the collection of the Brooklyn Museum (pl. 43) was bequeathed to the University of Michigan in 1884 and sold by the university in 1950.
13. Elizabeth Milroy, "The Public Career of Emma Stebbins: Work in Marble," *Archives of American Art Journal* 33, no. 3 (1993): 2–12; Elizabeth Milroy, "The Public Career of Emma Stebbins: Work in Bronze," *Archives of American Art Journal* 34, no. 1 (1994): 2–14.
14. Emma Stebbins scrapbook, 1858–82, compiled by Mary Stebbins Garland, Archives of American Art, Smithsonian Institution, Washington, DC.
15. Melissa Dabakis, *A Sisterhood of Sculptors: American Artists in Nineteenth-Century Rome* (University Park: Pennsylvania State University Press, 2014); Melissa L. Gustin, "Culture Capitalism: Emma Stebbins' Allegories from the Braccio Nuovo of the Vatican," *Nineteenth Century* 39, no. 2 (Fall 2019): 12–17; Melissa L. Gustin, "'This Lotus Spell Is Intenser': Sources and Selections in Emma Stebbins's *The Lotus-Eater*," *Word & Image* 38, no. 4 (2022): 478–98; Maria Teresa Cometto, *Emma and the Angel of Central Park: The Story of a New York Icon and the Woman Who Created It* (New York: Bordighera, 2023).
16. Nineteenth-century neoclassical sculpture was disdained, and therefore not studied, for most of the twentieth century. See Gerdts, *American Neo-Classic Sculpture*, 7–10.
17. Dabakis, *Sisterhood of Sculptors*, 5–7.
18. Allison Lee Palmer, *Historical Dictionary of Neoclassical Art and Architecture*, 2nd ed. (Lanham, MD: Rowman and Littlefield, 2020), 12–13. Palmer discusses neoclassicism's origins in the Age of Enlightenment, the French Revolution, and the Grand Tour. See also Dabakis, *Sisterhood of Sculptors*, 5–8.
19. See, among others, Karen Lemmey, "'Fragile Fictions' and 'Hard Truths' in American Sculpture," in *The Shape of Power: Stories of Race and American Sculpture*, ed. Karen Lemmey, Tobias Wofford, and Grace Yasumura (Washington, DC: Smithsonian American Art Museum, 2024), 35–97; Dabakis, *Sisterhood of Sculptors*; Charmaine A. Nelson, *The Color of Stone: Sculpting the Black Female Subject in Nineteenth-Century America* (Minneapolis: University of Minnesota Press, 2007); Joy S. Kasson, *Marble Queens and Captives: Women in Nineteenth-Century American Sculpture* (New Haven, CT: Yale University Press, 1990).
20. Kushner finished the first draft of *Angels in America, Part One: Millennium Approaches* in 1988 and the first draft of *Angels in America, Part Two: Perestroika* in 1990. Subsequently, he revised both

works, which are collectively known as *Angels in America: A Gay Fantasia on National Themes.* See Tony Kushner, *Angels in America: A Gay Fantasia on National Themes* (New York: Theatre Communications Group, 2013).

21. Unless otherwise noted, the information in this introduction is supported by the facts and citations in the chronology. Stebbins's father was born in Ridgefield, Connecticut, to a prominent farming family of English descent, and her mother was born in Shelburne, Nova Scotia, to a father who served with the British during the Revolutionary War. See Ralph Stebbins Greenlee and Robert Lemuel Greenlee, *The Stebbins Genealogy* (Chicago: privately printed, 1904), 496–97.
22. A letter from John Wilson Stebbins to his paternal grandfather indicates that following Stebbins's father's resignation from the North River Bank, a "habit" was threatening his health, mind, reputation, and character. John wanted to remove his father from New York City to separate him from "the sphere of former associates and temptations." John states that his promising career, and those of his brothers, will keep the family solvent. John Wilson Stebbins to Samuel Stebbins, May 3, 1829, private collection of Caroline Welling VanDeusen. VanDeusen holds other Stebbins family papers, including several letters from the artist to family members.
23. For example, John Wilson Stebbins published poetry and served a term as president of the Mercantile Library. Henry G. Stebbins, who collected art, served three times each as vice president and president of the New York Stock Exchange from 1836 to 1863. See *History of the New York Stock Exchange* (New York: Financier Company, 1887), 15–16. Like her sister, Caroline Town Stebbins moved to Rome in the late 1850s. She married painter John Rollin Tilton, was a noted salon hostess, and translated several books from Italian to English. The Stebbins family does not, however, appear in Moses Yale Beach's *Wealth and Pedigree of the Wealthy Citizens of New York City*. Published by the *Sun* newspaper (New York City) in the 1840s and 1850s, it listed those estimated to be worth $100,000 or more.
24. April F. Masten, *Art Work: Women Artists and Democracy in Mid-Nineteenth-Century New York* (Philadelphia: University of Pennsylvania Press, 2008), 3.
25. Elizabeth Blackwell to "the Reform Club" [Barbara Leigh Smith and Bessie Rayner Parkes], June 3, 1856. Quoted in Merrill, *When Romeo Was a Woman*, 186.
26. On New York City as an art center, see Catherine Hoover Voorsanger and John K. Howat, eds., *Art and the Empire City: New York, 1825–1861* (New York: Metropolitan Museum of Art, 2000). Annie Adams Fields once noted an occasion on which Stebbins quoted the Old Testament from memory. See Annie Adams Fields, diary entry, March 29, 1860, *The Brownings' Correspondence: An Online Edition*, https://www.browningscorrespondence.com/fields-diary/1860/3/29/.
27. Cushman described herself as an actress. This book uses the word "actress" to refer to Cushman's profession. Contemporary scholars, including Merrill and Marcus, also refer to her as such.
28. Emma Stebbins, ed., *Charlotte Cushman: Her Letters and Memories of Her Life* (Boston: Houghton, Osgood, 1878), 100. For more on Stebbins and Cushman's relationship, see, among others, Merrill, *When Romeo Was a Woman*, 171–242; Marcus, *Between Women*, 197–202.
29. "Lesbian" and "queer" do not have the same meanings now as they did in the mid-nineteenth century. See Marcus, *Between Women*, 2, 6, 13, 20. For a summary of shifting understandings of gender, of women's sexual desire, and of same-sex sexual desire in the nineteenth century, see Merrill, *When Romeo Was a Woman*, 245–66. As David J. Getsy outlines, the current usage of "queer," as formulated in the 1980s, undercuts the stability of identity and is "a self-declaration and a political stance" defying the "normal" and resisting inclusion in it. David J. Getsy, "Introduction: Queer Intolerability and Its Attachments," in *Queer* (Cambridge, MA: MIT Press, 2016), 12–23.
30. For examples of the ways in which Stebbins and Cushman described their love for each other, see Horn's essay in this volume. Cushman also once described Henry G. Stebbins as her "brother-in-law" in a letter to him. See the letter quoted in Cometto, *Emma and the Angel of Central Park*, 137. In addition to the language of marriage, the two used what Marcus describes as "hyperbolic references to passion, exclusivity, idealization, complicity, private language, and mutual dependence." See Marcus, *Between Women*, 54.
31. Marcus, 193–226; Merrill, *When Romeo Was a Woman*, 265. Scholars debate to what extent mid-nineteenth-century culture understood and accepted female marriages and homosexuality.
32. With the exception of the statement by Stebbins, all the quotes in this paragraph are from Harriet Hosmer, "The Process of Sculpture," *Atlantic Monthly* 14, no. 86 (December 1864): 734–37. For a more detailed explanation with images and videos, see Karen Lemmey, "From Skeleton to Skin: The Making of the *Greek Slave*(s)," *Nineteenth-Century Art Worldwide* 15, no. 2 (Summer 2016), http://www.19thc-artworldwide.org/summer16/lemmey-on-from-skeleton-to-skin-the-making-of-the-greek-slave.
33. Emma Stebbins to Anne Whitney, June 19, 1878, MSS.4, Anne Whitney Papers, Wellesley College Archives, Wellesley, MA. Stebbins expressed this belief when discussing Cushman's acting as well. She wrote, "Her first and instinctive creation was always her best. But of what art may not this be said? Human effort must be more or less imperfect. In a bright, creative moment comes *a flash*, as it were, of influence from some God-given source; the hand, the pen, the tool, works with power, something far beyond our ordinary efforts,—it may be crude, incomplete; the common eye cannot see its value; we ourselves hope from it still unutterable things; but there is in it something not to be improved upon; all the care and work and study in the world will not add to that intangible something; labor only weakens it, what is called finish only disguises it, it is lost in the handling, it is spiritual and immortal." Stebbins, *Charlotte Cushman*, 214.
34. Anna Frasca-Rath, "Via della Fontanella 4: John Gibson's Workshop in Rome," *Tate Papers*, no. 29 (Spring 2018), https://www.tate.org.uk/research/tate-papers/29/john-gibson-workshop-rome.
35. William H. Gerdts, "Celebrities of the Grand Tour: The American Sculptors in Florence and Rome," in *The Lure of Italy: American Artists and the Italian Experience, 1760–1914*, ed. Theodore E. Stebbins Jr. (Boston: Museum of Fine Arts, Boston, 1992), 66–93.
36. The plates section of this book includes images of thirty different sculptural compositions (which would have begun as clay models), some of which exist in multiple marble copies and in different sizes, and others of which are known only through nineteenth-century photographs: pls. 1, 2, 6, 7, 10–15, 17, 20, 21, 24, 27, 28 (which pictures four different sculptures), 29–30, 32–36, 38, 40, 43, 47. I am not counting the bust versions of *The Lotus Eater* (pls. 3–5) or the bust version of *John Neal Tilton* (pl. 42) as separate from their full-length counterparts. In addition to the thirty compositions represented in the plates, there is textual evidence, cited in the chronology of this volume, that Stebbins also modeled a statue of Matthew Perry, a head of Satan (which may have been a variant of pl. 21), a marble portrait rondel of an unnamed sitter, and a plaster catalogued as *Cupid and Psyche*, which may have been after Antonio Canova's late eighteenth-century sculpture of the same subject. For information on a work entitled *Il Cacciatore—The Hunter*, which is likely one of the seasons represented in plate 28, see

(New York: Columbia University Press, 2022), 277.
12. Longworth, *American Almanac* (1832), 627; Longworth, *American Almanac* (1833), 567.
13. Longworth, *American Almanac* (1834), 645.
14. "Died," *Evening Star* (New York City), September 17, 1834, 2; John Stebbins burial record, Trinity Church Wall Street Registers Database.
15. Longworth, *American Almanac* (1835), 619; Longworth, *American Almanac* (1836), 628.
16. Anna Johnson Reid, "Subscribers Who Have Paid," *Passion Flower*, no. 26 (June 15, 1836): 14. On the pages for crayon sketches, see Reid, "Subscribers Who Have Paid," *Passion Flower*, no. 2 (May 15, 1835): 1. For a discussion of working with crayon, see M. B. Odenheimer-Fowler, "Crayon Drawing," *Art Amateur* 9, no. 1 (June 1883): 8–9; Katie Scott and Hannah Williams, "Crayon," in *Artists' Things: Rediscovering Lost Property from Eighteenth-Century France* (Los Angeles: Getty Research Institute, 2024), 86–92, getty .edu/publications/artists-things/.
17. John Wilson Stebbins to John Forsyth, March 12, 1836, United States Passport Applications, US National Archives and Records Administration Database. The author used familysearch.org to access all records from the US National Archives and Records Administration Database.
18. "Died," *Christian Intelligencer* (New York City), April 23, 1836, 155.
19. "Passengers," *New-York Spectator*, April 25, 1836, 3.
20. "Died," *Evening Post* (New York City), June 5, 1837, 2; "The Late John W. Stebbins," *New-York Mirror*, July 8, 1837, 11; Miller, *Before Central Park*, 277.
21. "Presidents of the Association," *Thirty-Fifth Annual Report of the Board of Direction of the Mercantile Library Association of the City of New York* (New York: Baker and Godwin, 1856), 3.
22. See Elizabeth Milroy, "The Public Career of Emma Stebbins: Work in Marble," *Archives of American Art Journal* 33, no. 3 (1993): 3–4, 11. Henry G. Stebbins lent three Inman paintings, entitled *Portrait of a Gentleman*, *Portrait of a Lady*, and *Portrait of a Young Naval Officer*, to the National Academy of Design's annual exhibition in spring 1839. See [Mary] Bartlett Cowdrey, *National Academy of Design Exhibition Record, 1826–1860* (New York: New-York Historical Society, 1943), 1:259.
23. Mary Sayre Haverstock, Jeannette Mahoney Vance, and Brian L. Meggitt, eds., *Artists in Ohio, 1787–1900: A Biographical Dictionary* (Kent, OH: Kent State University Press, 2000), 108. Stebbins's study with Brackett is not mentioned in Ellet, *Women Artists*.
24. Cowdrey, *National Academy of Design Exhibition Record*, 259.
25. Another version of the portrait is in the private collection of Alison Heydt Tung, a descendant of Henry G. Stebbins. See Maria Teresa Cometto, *Emma and the Angel of Central Park: The Story of a New York Icon and the Woman Who Created It* (New York: Bordighera, 2023), 14–16.
26. The five other artists elected with Stebbins were also disqualified, although four of them were reelected years later. It is unclear why this happened. Milroy, "Work in Marble," 4.
27. Peter Hastings Falk, ed., *The Annual Exhibition Record of the Pennsylvania Academy of the Fine Arts, 1807–1870* (Madison, CT: Sound View Press, 1988), 214, 333.
28. Stebbins's mother is listed as "Stebbins Mary, widow of John, 74 Eleventh," in *Doggett's New-York City Directory* (New York: John Doggett Jr., 1846), 371. The same entry appears in *Doggett's New-York City Directory* (1847), 387, and *Doggett's New York City Directory* (1848), 386. Mary Stebbins moved to 102 West 11th Street in 1849. *Doggett's New York City Directory* (1849), 398.
29. "Names of Members, with their Places of Residence, 1846," *Transactions of the American Art-Union* (New York: G. F. Nesbitt, 1847), 67; "Names of Members, with their Places of Residence, 1849," *Transactions of the American Art-Union* (New York: George F. Nesbitt, 1850), 98. Henry G. Stebbins subscribed throughout the 1840s.
30. Falk, *Annual Exhibition Record of the Pennsylvania Academy of the Fine Arts*, 214.
31. Dubufe's originals and Stebbins's copies are unlocated. It is unclear where she would have seen his *French Sweep Boy* (unlocated; before 1847). See Carrie Rebora Barratt, "Mapping the Venues: New York City Art Exhibitions," in *Art and the Empire City: New York, 1825–1861*, ed. Catherine Hoover Voorsanger and John K. Howat (New York: Metropolitan Museum of Art, 2000), 56.
32. Emma Stebbins to William Cullen Bryant, March 16, 1849, Bryant-Godwin Papers, Manuscripts and Archives Division, New York Public Library, New York, NY.
33. Emma Stebbins scrapbook, 1858–82, compiled by Mary Stebbins Garland, Archives of American Art, Smithsonian Institution, Washington, DC. It seems that Garland later took the illuminated text with her to Italy in 1863. See Florence Freeman to Frances Freeman, October 2, 1863, Florence Freeman Letters, Boston Athenaeum Mss. .L840, Boston Athenaeum, MA (hereafter FFL).
34. "Population Schedules of the Seventh Census of the United States, New York City, Ward 15," 1850, 197, US National Archives and Records Administration Database. Not all of the data matches that of the Stebbins family. For example, Emma is listed as thirty-one years old, when she was actually thirty-five. She had a sister named Angelina, not Julia.
35. "New-York School of Design for Women," advertisement, *New-York Daily Times*, March 19, 1853, 8. For more on the school, see April F. Masten, *Art Work: Women Artists and Democracy in Mid-Nineteenth-Century New York* (Philadelphia: University of Pennsylvania Press, 2008).
36. The students of the New-York School of Design for Women visited the exposition to study the works of art. See "New-York City: School of Design—Pleasant Correspondence," *New-York Daily Times*, July 22, 1854, 6.
37. William C. Richards, *A Day in the New York Crystal Palace and How to Make the Most of It* (New York: G. P. Putnam, 1853).
38. *Catalogue of the Thirtieth Annual Exhibition of the National Academy of Design* (New York: Sackett, 1855), 24, 26, 32.
39. H. Wilson, *Trow's New York City Directory* (New York: John F. Trow, 1855), 787. For the history of this building, which would remain in the Stebbins family throughout Emma's life, see the National Register of Historic Places Registration Form for 20 West 16th Street, received April 20, 2007, available at the National Archives, http://catalog.archives.gov/id/75319608.
40. "Correspondence of the Transcript," *Boston Evening Transcript*, July 16, 1855, 2.
41. Virginia Penny, *The Employments of Women: A Cyclopaedia of Woman's Work* (Boston: Walker, Wise, 1863), 82.
42. "Studios of American Artists," *Home Journal* (New York City), February 16, 1856, 1.
43. "Domestic Art Gossip," *Crayon* 3, no. 3 (March 1856): 92.
44. Henry G. Stebbins to William Marcy, April 14, 1856, United States Passport Applications, US National Archives and Records Administration Database.
45. "Departures," *New York Herald*, May 4, 1856, 1.
46. "New-York Artists," *Knickerbocker* 48, no. 1 (July 1856): 28.
47. "New York School of Design for Women," *Crayon* 3, no. 9 (September 1856): 280–81.
48. For the timing of Cushman's arrival in Rome, see Joseph Leach, *Bright Particular Star: The Life and Times of Charlotte Cushman* (New Haven, CT: Yale University Press, 1970), 270. Cushman had visited Rome once before, from fall 1852 through spring 1853. See Leach, *Bright Particular Star*, 248–58.
49. Emma Stebbins, ed., *Charlotte Cushman: Her Letters and Memories of Her Life* (Boston: Houghton, Osgood, 1878), 100.

50. Stebbins, *Charlotte Cushman*, 101.
51. Leach, *Bright Particular Star*, 272.
52. Stebbins, *Charlotte Cushman*, 108.
53. This is the itinerary that Stebbins and Cushman followed in 1865. At that time, Cushman wrote that she had also visited these places in 1853 and 1857. See Stebbins, *Charlotte Cushman*, 195.
54. Stebbins, *Charlotte Cushman*, 108.
55. Leach, *Bright Particular Star*, 272.
56. Hosmer embarked for the US in early August and sailed back to Europe on October 24. See Dolly Sherwood, *Harriet Hosmer: American Sculptor, 1830–1908* (Columbia: University of Missouri Press, 1991), 147–48, 155.
57. Stebbins described Mercer as Cushman's "faithful maid" and as "the friend and companion of all her wanderings, the sharer of her trials and her triumphs, the good, devoted, faithful Sallie Mercer." Stebbins, *Charlotte Cushman*, 29, 37. For more on Mercer, see Horn's essay in this volume; Leach, *Bright Particular Star*, 127; "Personal," *New-York Tribune*, August 21, 1894, 6.
58. *Arago* passenger manifest, July 14, 1857, New York Passenger Lists, US National Archives and Records Administration Database.
59. Arthur W. Bloom, *Charlotte Cushman: A Biography and Performance History* (Jefferson, NC: McFarland, 2023), 78; *Persia* passenger manifest, September 15, 1857, New York Passenger Lists, US National Archives and Records Administration Database. Mercer and Stebbins do not appear on the list.
60. See, for example, Leach, *Bright Particular Star*, 277.
61. Charlotte Cushman to the Chase Family, October 8, 1857, quoted in Lisa Merrill, *When Romeo Was a Woman: Charlotte Cushman and Her Circle of Female Spectators* (Ann Arbor: University of Michigan Press, 1999), 205. There is a chance that the letter was misdated, or that the "Miss Stebbins" Cushman referred to was not Emma Stebbins but one of her sisters.
62. See the Emma Stebbins Art and Artist Files, Smithsonian American Art and Portrait Gallery Library, Smithsonian Libraries, Washington, DC.
63. Harriet Hosmer to Wayman Crow, December 9, 1857, Harriet Goodhue Hosmer Papers, Schlesinger Library, Harvard Radcliffe Institute, Harvard University, Cambridge, MA (hereafter HGHP). See also Sherwood, *Harriet Hosmer*, 161, 166. On some of the possible meanings of Hosmer's statement, see Merrill, *When Romeo Was a Woman*, 189.
64. The identity of the Italian master is not known. On this topic, see Mary K. McGuigan, "'This Market of Physiognomy': American Artists and Rome's Art Academies, Life Schools, and Models, 1825–1870," in *America's Rome: Artists in the Eternal City, 1800–1900*, ed. Paul S. D'Ambrosio (Cooperstown, NY: Fenimore Art Museum, 2009), 39–71.
65. I. E. C., "Benjamin Paul Akers, Sculptor," *Evening Post*, August 2, 1861, 1. Two newspapers from fall 1858 state that Stebbins had entered his studio as a student "last winter." See "Personal and Political," *Chicago Daily Press and Tribune*, September 1, 1858, 2; "Personal," *Home Journal*, September 18, 1858, 3.
66. See Emma Stebbins to Elizabeth Akers Allen, July 28, 1865, Collection of Elizabeth Akers Allen Materials, Colby College Special Collections, Waterville, ME (hereafter CEAAM); Emma Stebbins scrapbook.
67. Leach, *Bright Particular Star*, 281.
68. Charlotte Cushman to Paul Akers, February 21, 1858, CEAAM. Stebbins and Cushman also exchanged letters (later destroyed) while the latter was on tour. In her own correspondence, Cushman referred to the contents of Stebbins's letters. See Sherwood, *Harriet Hosmer*, 166.
69. Letter from Paul Akers, quoted in Leila Woodman Usher, "Benjamin Paul Akers," *New England Magazine* 11, no. 4 (December 1894): 463–64. See also Arlene Palmer, "Forgotten Fervor: Paul Akers in Rome," in *American Latium: American Artists and Travelers in and around Rome in the Age of the Grand Tour*, ed. Christopher M. S. Johns, Tommaso Manfredi, Karin Wolfe (Rome: Accademia Nazionale di San Luca, 2023), 257–68. The pose of Stebbins's *Sandalphon* (1866; pl. 20) is similar to that of Akers's *St. Elizabeth* (1860).
70. "American Artists in Rome," *Daily Exchange* (Baltimore), March 23, 1858, 2; "Rome, February 25th," *Crayon* 5, no. 4 (April 1858): 112.
71. Charlotte Cushman to Emma Crow, April 27, 1858, Charlotte Cushman Papers, Manuscript Division, Library of Congress, Washington, DC (hereafter CCP). The author would like to thank Katrin Horn for sharing her extensive original research at archivalgossip .com/collection, where many of Cushman's letters appear as scans and transcriptions. For more on this resource, see Horn's essay in this volume.
72. Stebbins must have had the clay or plaster model photographed before she left Rome for the summer. In August, the *Home Journal* published a letter that read in part, "The model of her first work, (the Lotos-Eater,) of which we have seen a photograph, is one of the most exquisite ideal creations we ever gazed upon." N. P. W., "Letter for the Ladies: Female Genius—Its History and Prospects, Idlewild, Aug. 9, 1858," *Home Journal*, August 21, 1858, 2. For an analysis of this work, see Melissa L. Gustin, "'This Lotus Spell Is Intenser': Sources and Selections in Emma Stebbins's *The Lotus-Eater*," *Word & Image* 38, no. 4 (2022): 478–98.
73. Bryant wrote that Stebbins was absent from Rome. See William Cullen Bryant to James P. Cronkhite, June 11, 1858, in *The Letters of William Cullen Bryant*, vol. 4, *1858–1864*, ed. William Cullen Bryant II and Thomas G. Voss (New York: Fordham University Press, 1984), 55.
74. Charlotte Cushman to Emma Crow, May 11, 1858, CCP.
75. Leach, *Bright Particular Star*, 281–82.
76. Bloom, *Charlotte Cushman*, 86.
77. In this letter, Stebbins mentions that she wrote to her siblings as well. Almost none of this family correspondence survives. Akers was meant to deliver this letter to her mother, but never did so. It is preserved with his wife's papers. Emma Stebbins to Mary Largin Stebbins, July 29, 1858, CEAAM.
78. Stebbins, *Charlotte Cushman*, 111. Susan Muspratt and James Muspratt (1821–1871) were with them at Malvern taking the water treatment. See Bloom, *Charlotte Cushman*, 86.
79. Bloom, *Charlotte Cushman*, 87.
80. "Domestic Art Gossip," *Crayon* 5, no. 11 (November 1858): 329.
81. Charlotte Cushman to Emma Crow, November 26 and December 24, 1858, CCP.
82. Charlotte Cushman to Emma Crow, January 22, 1859, CCP. Hosmer did not pay rent, but she did give Cushman a sculpture, *Puck* (1855), as a form of compensation. See Charlotte Cushman to Emma Crow Cushman, March 13, 1862, CCP. See also "Miss Hosmer," *Albany Evening Journal*, January 21, 1859, 2; "Miss Hosmer," *Farmers' Cabinet* (Amherst, NH), February 2, 1859, 2. On *Puck*, see Patricia Cronin, *Harriet Hosmer: Lost and Found, a Catalogue Raisonné* (Milan: Edizioni Charta, 2009), 37–38.
83. Stebbins, *Charlotte Cushman*, 112.
84. "An Interesting Letter—Art in Rome—The American Sculptors," *Charleston Daily Courier* (SC), March 9, 1859, 1. This was a reprint of a letter sent from Rome to the *Boston Courier*, dated January 29, 1859.
85. Sophia Peabody Hawthorne, diary entry, February 22, 1859, Sophia Peabody Hawthorne Collection of Papers, Henry W. and Albert A. Berg Collection of English and American Literature, New York Public Library, New York, NY.
86. Jane Tunis Poultney Bigelow, diary entry, March 20, 1859, John Bigelow Papers, Special Collections and Archives, Schaffer Library, Union College, Schenectady, NY.
87. J. B., "Rome, Editorial Correspondence of the Evening Post, March 24, 1859," *Evening Post*, April 19, 1859, 1.

88. Samuel Joseph May, diary entry, March 23, 1859, May Anti-Slavery Collection, #4601, Division of Rare and Manuscript Collections, Cornell University Library, Ithaca, NY.
89. J. B., "Rome," *Evening Post*, April 19, 1859, 1. This was excerpted in other periodicals, including in "Progress of Science and Art," *Harper's Weekly*, April 23, 1859, 258; and "Domestic Art Gossip," *Crayon* 6, no. 5 (May 1859): 162.
90. Hiram Fuller, *Sparks from a Locomotive* (New York: Derby and Jackson, 1859), 288–89; Leach, *Bright Particular Star*, 294.
91. Stebbins, *Charlotte Cushman*, 159–60.
92. Stebbins, *Charlotte Cushman*, 160.
93. Annie Adams Fields, diary entry, September 30, 1859, *The Brownings' Correspondence: An Online Edition*, https://www.browningscorrespondence.com/fields-diary/1859/9/30/. The "farmer" mentioned in this diary entry is in fact a sailor.
94. "Personal," *Evening Post*, October 10, 1859, 2.
95. Harriet Hosmer to Cornelia Crow, November 12, 1859, HGHP. The first portrait of Hosmer by Stebbins reached the Crow family in September. See "Letter from Newport," *Boston Daily Advertiser*, September 12, 1859, 2. For another mention of Stebbins's crayon portraits, see Charlotte Cushman to Wayman Crow, July 25, 1860, CCP, via archivalgossip.com. An auction catalogue of Cushman's possessions lists a "Carrara Marble. Medallion Portrait of Emma Stebbins. By Harriet Hosmer. Diameter 16 inches." The whereabouts of this object are unknown. There is also a small possibility that this sculpture was incorrectly catalogued. See C. F. Libbie, Boston, *Catalogue of the remaining portion of the private library of the late Charlotte Cushman of Newport, R.I., the celebrated American tragedienne . . . together with art objects from Miss Cushman's villa at Rome: Oil paintings, engravings, marbles, terra cotta figures, Roman bronzes and lamps, vases, chairs, etc.*, sale December 14 and 15, 1909, 156. A copy of this catalogue is accessible today at the Grolier Club, New York, NY.
96. See for example, L. Maria Child, "Harriet E. Hosmer: A Biographical Sketch," *Ladies' Repository*, no. 21 (January 1861): 1–7; S. W. Williams, ed. *Queenly Women, Crowned and Uncrowned* (Cincinnati: Cranston and Stowe, 1885), illustration 27.
97. A Bostonian, "Foreign Correspondence of the Transcript, Rome, December 20, 1859," *Boston Evening Transcript*, January 17, 1860, 2.
98. Prior to 1878, Rezin Davis Shepherd's daughter gave the bust to the Handel and Haydn Society, Boston. Copies also went to Stebbins's brother Henry G. Stebbins, to Cushman's brother-in-law Muspratt, and to Frances Sully Darley (1833–1914) of Philadelphia. See Stebbins, *Charlotte Cushman*, 161.
99. Sarah E. Kelly, "Machinist and Machinist's Apprentice," *Art Institute of Chicago Museum Studies* 30, no. 1 (2004): 10–11.
100. "Literary and Artistic," *Constitution* (Washington, DC), February 2, 1860, 2. See also "Fine Arts," *Evening Post*, February 9, 1860, 2.
101. Bostonian, "Correspondence of the Transcript, Rome, March 3, 1860," *Boston Evening Transcript*, March 28, 1860, 4.
102. Annie Adams Fields, diary entry, March 12, 1860, *The Brownings' Correspondence*, https://www.browningscorrespondence.com/fields-diary/1860/3/12/.
103. Emma Stebbins to Hiram Powers, March 15, 1860, Hiram Powers Papers, 1819–1953, bulk 1835–83, Archives of American Art, Smithsonian Institution, Washington, DC (hereafter HPP).
104. Charlotte Cushman to Emma Crow, March 26, 1860, CCP.
105. See Garland's historical text in this volume; Cherry Sandover, "Risi," in *Dictionary of Artists' Models*, ed. Jill Berk Jiminez (Chicago: Fitzroy Dearborn, 2001), 453–54.
106. Charlotte Cushman and Emma Stebbins to Annie Adams and James T. Fields, May 3, 1860, James T. Fields Papers and Addenda, Huntington Library, San Marino, CA (hereafter JTFP).
107. Charlotte Cushman and Emma Stebbins to Annie Adams and James T. Fields, May 3, 1860, JTFP.
108. Charlotte Cushman and Emma Stebbins to Annie Adams and James T. Fields, May 23, 1860, JTFP.
109. The passenger manifest records Stebbins with an incorrect first name. *Persia* passenger manifest, July 5, 1860, New York Passenger Lists, US National Archives and Records Administration Database. For the press coverage of their trip, see, among others, "Literature and Art," *Press & Tribune* (Chicago), February 9, 1860, 3; "Personal Intelligence," *New York Herald*, July 8, 1860, 1.
110. H. B. S., "Mrs. Stowe and Her Neighbors in Rome," *Boston Evening Transcript*, July 13, 1860, 4. First published in the *Independent* (New York City), it appeared in the *Lowell Daily Citizen & News* (MA), *Manufacturers and Farmers Journal* (Providence, RI), *New York-Daily Tribune*, and *Wisconsin Daily Patriot* (Madison).
111. Charlotte Cushman to Emma Crow, July 15, 1860, CCP; Charlotte Cushman to Wayman Crow, July 25, 1860, CCP.
112. Bloom, *Charlotte Cushman*, 95. For more on Emma Crow Cushman, see Horn's essay in this volume.
113. "The Watering Places," *New-York Tribune*, August 27, 1860, 5.
114. "Our State and County Fairs," *Hesperian* 4, no. 6 (August 1860): 332.
115. "American Art—Recent Works of American Artists," *New-York Times*, August 31, 1860, 5.
116. Charlotte Cushman to Wayman Crow, September 12, 1860, CCP; Charlotte Cushman to James T. Fields, September 20, 1860, JTFP.
117. Advertisements for the show, which titled the pair of artworks "Labor and Commerce," appeared in multiple New York City newspapers throughout the month of October. See, for example, *New-York Daily Tribune*, October 6, 1860, 12. The works were still on view on November 10. See "Art," *Weekly Day-Book* (New York City), November 10, 1860, 4. For reviews, see "Fine Arts," *Evening Post*, October 31, 1860, 2; "Domestic Art Gossip," *Crayon* 7, no. 11 (November 1860): 323.
118. Bloom, *Charlotte Cushman*, 95.
119. H. M., "American Art: To the Editor of the Transcript," *Boston Evening Transcript*, December 7, 1860, 2.
120. "Art Gossip," *New-York Times*, February 11, 1861, 2. It is unclear why *The Lotus Eater* was not exhibited when Stebbins debuted *Commerce*, *Industry*, and *Charlotte Cushman* several months earlier.
121. "Fine Arts," *World* (New York City), January 31, 1861, 5. A similar observation about gender appears in "Art," *Methodist* (New York City), February 9, 1861, 35.
122. "Art," *Express*, January 28, 1861, in Wendy Jean Katz, *Katz's Unofficial Index to Antebellum New York City Newspapers*, http://katzsnewspapers.org/items/show/837. See also "Art Items," *New-York Tribune*, January 31, 1861, 7.
123. "Art," *Methodist*, February 9, 1861, 35. Stebbins's work, in turn, inspired a poem. See S[amuel] W[ard], "Literature: The Maiden's Children; Suggested by Miss Stebbins' Statue of the Lotus-Eater," *Albion* (New York City), January 19, 1861, 1.
124. "Art Gossip," *New-York Times*, February 4, 1861, 3.
125. Advertisement for Earle's Galleries, *Philadelphia Inquirer*, February 5, 1861, 5; Nancy Mowll Mathews, *Mary Cassatt: A Life* (New Haven, CT: Yale University Press, 1994), 20.
126. H., "The Lotus Eater," *Boston Evening Transcript*, March 22, 1861, 2; "Personal Items," *Boston Evening Transcript*, March 15, 1861, 2.
127. Leach, *Bright Particular Star*, 308; "Military Movements," *Daily Evening Traveller* (Boston), April 29, 1861, 2. The extra verse also appeared in *New England Farmer* (Boston) and *True Democrat* (Lewistown, PA). Oliver Wendell Holmes (1809–1894) contributed a new verse as well. The Library Company of Philadelphia holds sheet

music with the verses, catalogued as "Sheet Music Star 5782.F.6a."

128. Charlotte Cushman to James T. Fields, June 26, 1861, JTFP. Lyceums were volunteer organizations for adult education that hosted visiting speakers. For more on how the commission unfolded, see Leach, *Bright Particular Star*, 305, 309–10, 317–18; Elizabeth Milroy, "The Public Career of Emma Stebbins: Work in Bronze," *Archives of American Art Journal* 34, no. 1 (1994): 2–14.
129. Scott Sanders, "Songs from the Stacks: Emma Stebbins to Nathaniel Hawthorne 1861," *Antiochiana—Songs from the Stacks* (blog), Antioch College, January 8, 2022, https://antiochcollege.edu/2022/01/08/songs-from-the-stacks-emma-stebbins-to-nathaniel-hawthorne-1861/.
130. Stebbins, *Charlotte Cushman*, 162; "Personal," *New York Evening Express*, July 1, 1861, 4.
131. Stebbins made some brief observations about Lincoln that several newspapers reported. See, for example, "A Pen Portrait of Mr. Lincoln," *Cincinnati Daily Commercial*, July 17, 1861, 4.
132. Emma Stebbins to Nathaniel Hawthorne, June 29, 1861, quoted in Sanders, "Songs from the Stacks."
133. For more on this unrealized commission, see Milroy, "Work in Bronze," 2–6.
134. "Passengers Sailed," *New-York Times*, July 18, 1861, 9; Bloom, *Charlotte Cushman*, 100. On Freeman, see Jacqueline Marie Musacchio, "Finding Florence Freeman," *Nineteenth-Century Art Worldwide* 21, no. 1 (Spring 2022), https://doi.org/10.29411/ncaw.2022.21.1.4.
135. Charlotte Cushman to Emma Crow Cushman, July 26, 1861, CCP. In the letter she also said of Stebbins, "I love her very very much, she is the finest nature I have ever been thrown in contact with—the very truest . . . of human beings."
136. Stebbins, *Charlotte Cushman*, 164.
137. Charlotte Cushman letter, September 21, 1861, quoted in Stebbins, *Charlotte Cushman*, 167.
138. Charlotte Cushman to Jane Welsh Carlyle, November 16, 1861, accessed via archivalgossip.com/collection; Margaret Howitt, "A Memoir of the Sculptor Margaret F. Foley," *Art Journal* 17 (1878): 101.
139. On Foley, see Melissa Dabakis, *A Sisterhood of Sculptors: American Artists in Nineteenth-Century Rome* (University Park: Pennsylvania State University Press, 2014), 22–25, 87–90.
140. Charlotte Cushman to Emma Crow Cushman, November 23, 1861, CCP.
141. The Perry commission had initially gone to Akers. After his death, it passed to Stebbins. Ultimately, John Quincy Adams Ward (1830–1910) completed the statue. See Milroy, "Work in Bronze," 2–6.
142. Emma Stebbins to Hiram Powers, January 5, 1862, HPP. It seems his reply was delayed or lost in the mail. See Emma Stebbins to Hiram Powers, March 26, 1862, HPP.
143. Milroy, "Work in Bronze," 7.
144. Harriet Hosmer to Wayman Crow, March 15, 1862, HGHP. In the Hosmer papers, this letter is misfiled with letters from 1863. The contents of the letter clearly relate to 1862.
145. Charlotte Cushman to Emma Crow Cushman, March 13, 1862, CCP. According to Milroy, "Mr. Nathan of New York" had commissioned *Sandalphon*. Milroy, "Work in Bronze," 14.
146. Charlotte Cushman to James T. Fields, March 15, 1862, JTFP. On Cushman's views of the war, see Stebbins, *Charlotte Cushman*, 176–77.
147. See, for example, "Rebels Caught in Their Own Trap," *New-York Times*, January 26, 1862, 3.
148. Samuel Gridley Howe to Emma Stebbins, March 15, 1862, CCP. The letter would have reached Stebbins about two weeks after Howe posted it.
149. On the sculpture, see Richard P. Wunder, *Hiram Powers: Vermont Sculptor, 1805–1873*, vol. 2, *Catalogue of Works* (Newark: University of Delaware Press, 1991), 105, 117.
150. "Fine Arts: The Roman Studios II," *Spectator* (London), July 5, 1862, 746. While published in the summer, the text was based on earlier visits. The author was likely Stebbins's friend Frances Power Cobbe (1822–1904). The quotation within the article is from *Paradise Lost* (1667) by John Milton (1608–1674).
151. *International Exhibition 1862: Official Catalogue of the Fine Art Department*, corrected ed. (London: Truscott, Son, and Simmons, 1862), 152.
152. F. P. C., "Fine Arts: Sculptors at Rome and the Great Exhibition," *Spectator*, February 1, 1862, 129. Cobbe was likely the author.
153. Harriet Hosmer to Wayman Crow, May 15, 1862, quoted in Cornelia Carr, ed., *Harriet Hosmer: Letters and Memories* (New York: Moffat, Yard, 1912), 187.
154. A., "Statue of Horace Mann," *Boston Evening Transcript*, June 14, 1862, 2. Similar text appeared in papers including the *Belvidere Standard* (IL), *Daily Sentinel and Times* (Bath, ME), *National Anti-Slavery Standard* (New York City), and *National Republican* (Washington, DC).
155. Charlotte Cushman to Annie Adams and James T. Fields, July 25, 1862, JTFP.
156. These events are alluded to in later letters. See, for example, Florence Freeman to Frances and Peter Freeman, November 2, 1862, FFL.
157. "Congressmen Elected," *New-York Times*, November 6, 1862, 8; "The Resignation of Hon. Henry G. Stebbins, M. C.," *New-York Times*, October 26, 1864, 4.
158. Charlotte Cushman to James T. Fields, November 21, 1862, JTFP. Cushman's quotation is from the book of Genesis.
159. Charlotte Cushman to Emma Crow Cushman, December 5–6, 1862, CCP.
160. James Hubbard Weeks, journal entries, December 8 and 17, 1862, Boston Athenaeum Mss. .S193, Boston Athenaeum, MA (hereafter JHW). In the entry for December 18, 1862, he mentioned seeing "a fine head of Mr. Tilton in crayon by Miss Stebbins."
161. Charlotte Cushman to Emma Crow Cushman, December 18, 1862, CCP.
162. Charlotte Cushman to Emma Crow Cushman, December 26, 1862, CCP.
163. "Art and Artists in Rome, Correspondence of the New York Evening Post, Rome, Dec. 28," *Boston Daily Advertiser*, February 7, 1863, 2.
164. Florence Freeman to Frances Freeman, January 8, 1863, FFL.
165. "December 11, 1862," in *Minutes of Proceedings of the Board of Commissioners of the Central Park* (New York: Wm. C. Bryant, 1863), 49.
166. Milroy, "Work in Bronze," 8. For a summary of a letter from Cushman to one of the board members, see Cometto, *Emma and the Angel of Central Park*, 116–17.
167. James Hubbard Weeks, journal entry, March 18, 1863, JHW.
168. Milroy, "Work in Bronze," 14. Milroy states that Samuel Courtauld (1793–1881) bought a fifth copy of the bust.
169. Florence Freeman to Frances Freeman, April 11, 1863, FFL. She also addressed the fact that Cushman and Hosmer occasionally smoked cigarettes.
170. Leach, *Bright Particular Star*, 320–25; Bloom, *Charlotte Cushman*, 103.
171. Florence Freeman to Frances Freeman, May 16, 1863, FFL.
172. On Hosmer's monument, see Cronin, *Harriet Hosmer*, 62.
173. See the letters Florence Freeman sent to her family throughout the months of July, August, and September in the FFL.
174. "Mr. Alfred Gatley," *Art-Journal*, September 1, 1863, 181; see also Cronin, *Harriet Hosmer*, 54–57.
175. See Dabakis, *Sisterhood of Sculptors*, 83–87.
176. "The Institution of Fine Arts: Second Notice," *Liverpool Mercury*, September 26, 1863, 6.
177. Florence Freeman to Frances Freeman, October 18, 1863, FFL.
178. "The Bethesda Fountain" (program for the 1873 unveiling) in the Emma Stebbins scrapbook. A later annual report also indicates that the commissioners ordered the *Bethesda Fountain* in 1863. See *Third General Report of the Board of Commissioners of the Department*

of Public Parks (New York: William C. Bryant, 1875), 7–9.

179. Milroy, "Work in Marble," 9–10. While in Washington, DC, in 1863, Cushman suggested to the US Secretary of the Interior that Stebbins create a statue of Columbus for the Capitol Rotunda. See Leach, *Bright Particular Star*, 323.
180. "The Grand Russian Ball," *Boston Daily Advertiser*, November 7, 1863, 1.
181. Leach, *Bright Particular Star*, 326; Stebbins, *Charlotte Cushman*, 189.
182. Charlotte Cushman to Emma Crow Cushman, January 30, [1864], CCP. Cushman misdated the letter "1863." She also noted that Garland remained in Rome.
183. F., "The Late Miss Emma Stebbins: To the Editor of the Tribune," *New-York Tribune*, November 2, 1882, 7.
184. Charlotte Cushman to Emma Crow Cushman, February 4, 1864, CCP, quoted in Milroy, "Work in Marble," 10.
185. Florence Freeman to Peter Freeman, February 24, 1864, FFL.
186. "Vicolo del Basilico" appears in W. Pembroke Fetridge, *Harper's Handbook for Travelers in Europe and the East* (New York: Harper, 1865), 331. Though published in 1865, the information was likely accurate for the previous year. Later guidebooks list the address as "11A, Via di S. Basilio." See, for example, *A Handbook of Rome and Its Environs* (London: John Murray, 1867), xliii. Editions of this handbook published in 1869 and 1871 place her at the same address. Her neighbors included Luigi Bienaimé (1795–1878), from Carrara, Italy, at number 16.
187. Howard Payson Arnold, *European Mosaic* (Boston: Little, Brown, 1864), 273–74.
188. J. S. F. and E. S., *A Record of the Metropolitan Fair in Aid of the United States Sanitary Commission, Held at New York in April 1864* (New York: Hurd and Houghton, 1867), 144.
189. "Our Sanitary Fair in Rome," *Methodist*, April 2, 1864, 100. Milroy included the bust of Washington on her list of works by Stebbins. Milroy, "Work in Bronze," 14.
190. Frances Power Cobbe, *Italics: Brief Notes on Politics, People, and Places in Italy, in 1864* (London: Trübner, 1864), 415.
191. Musacchio, "Finding Florence Freeman"; Florence Freeman to Frances Freeman, May 22, 1864, FFL.
192. "The Central Park Fountains: From the New York Journal of Commerce, June 22," *Boston Daily Advertiser*, June 23, 1864, 2.
193. Leach, *Bright Particular Star*, 328; Anne Hampton Brewster to Mary Howell, December 4, 1864, Anne Hampton Brewster papers, 1777–1892, Library Company of Philadelphia, PA, via www.archivalgossip.com.
194. Charlotte Cushman to James T. Fields, August 27, 1864, JTFP.
195. "Saturday, November 19, 1864," in *Minutes of Proceedings of the Board of Commissioners of the Central Park for the Year Ending April 30, 1865* (New York: Wm. C. Bryant, 1866), 42. See also *Eighth Annual Report of the Board of Commissioners of the Central Park for the Year Ending with December 31, 1864*, (New York: Wm. C. Bryant, 1865), 6–7.
196. "The Bethesda Fountain" (program for the 1873 unveiling) in the Emma Stebbins scrapbook.
197. "The Doleful Ditty of the Roman Caffe Greco," *Boston Evening Transcript*, November 17, 1864, 1. Florence Freeman to Frances Freeman, December 6, 1864, FFL. See also Carr, *Harriet Hosmer*, 193–97.
198. Harriet Hosmer, "The Process of Sculpture," *Atlantic Monthly* 14, no. 86 (December 1864): 734–37.
199. Florence Freeman to Frances Freeman, December 1, 1864, FFL. Cushman's London townhome was usually rented to others, so she and Stebbins rarely stayed there. The two did not arrive in Rome until December 21. See Florence Freeman to Frances Freeman, December 22, 1864, FFL.
200. Charlotte Cushman and Emma Stebbins to James T. Fields, December 31, 1864, JTFP. This letter states that "the statue is ready to come," which suggests that it had been cast in 1864, in keeping with the foundry mark. Early the next year, Howe wrote that the work was "approaching completion." S. G. H., "Statue of Horace Mann," *Worcester Daily Spy* (MA), January 26, 1865, 2.
201. See also Florence Freeman to Marion Freeman, January 3, 1865, FFL; Florence Freeman to Frances Freeman, January 11, 1865, FFL. Chips of marble, which Stebbins apparently mistook for shells, surrounded the sculpture. By the time Freeman saw the statue on January 3, it had been fully removed from the ground and was lying on its back indoors, being cleaned. This is likely how Stebbins and Cushman saw it.
202. As Cushman wrote from Rome, "I cannot leave here until June when I hope Aunt Em will have finished her Columbus." Charlotte Cushman to Emma Crow Cushman, January 26, 1865, CCP.
203. See, among others, "American Art and Other Items from Rome," *Manufacturers and Farmers Journal* (Providence, RI), May 15, 1865, 4; "American Travelers and American Artists in Europe," *New-York Times*, October 15, 1865, 4.
204. Fetridge, *Harper's Hand-book for Travelers in Europe and the East*, 331.
205. "The Bethesda Fountain" (program for the 1873 unveiling) in the Emma Stebbins scrapbook.
206. For more on these works, see, H. Nichols B. Clark, *A Marble Quarry: The James H. Ricau Collection of Sculpture at the Chrysler Museum of Art* (New York: Hudson Hills, 1997), 156–60.
207. Milroy, "Work in Bronze," 9.
208. Charlotte Cushman to Emma Crow Cushman, May 6, 1865, CCP.
209. Charlotte Cushman to Emma Crow Cushman, May 11, 1865, CCP. This letter is also a key source on their relationships. It is available in full online via www.archivalgossip.com. See also Cometto, *Emma and the Angel of Central Park*, 133–39.
210. "Loss of a Fine Work of Art," *New-York Times*, January 28, 1866, 4. Exhibition catalogues listed the work (priced at £370) as "The Patriarch Joseph" or "Joseph Keeping His Father's Sheep." See *Dublin International Exhibition, 1865: Official Catalogue*, 2nd ed. (Dublin: John Falconer, 1865), 118; Henry Parkinson and Peter Lund Simmonds, eds., *The Illustrated Record and Descriptive Catalogue of the Dublin International Exhibition of 1865* (Dublin: John Falconer, 1866), 479.
211. Harriet Hosmer to Wayman Crow, May 26, 1865, in Carr, *Harriet Hosmer*, 211.
212. Florence Freeman to Marion Freeman, May 29, 1865, FFL; Stebbins, *Charlotte Cushman*, 194–95.
213. Florence Freeman to Frances Freeman, June 7, 1865, FFL.
214. Emma Stebbins to Henry G. Stebbins, June 30, 1865, quoted in Cometto, *Emma and the Angel of Central Park*, 137.
215. "Inauguration of the Statue of Horace Mann," *Boston Evening Transcript*, July 5, 1865, 2; *Inauguration of the Statue of Horace Mann* (Boston: Walker, Fuller, 1865).
216. "The Statue of Horace Mann," *Springfield Weekly Republican* (MA), July 8, 1865, 4.
217. Charlotte Cushman to William F. Bridges, August 23, 1865, Charlotte Cushman Letters, 1840–1941, Massachusetts Historical Society, Boston, via www.archivalgossip.com.
218. "The Mann Statue," *Daily Evening Traveler*, July 7, 1865, 2.
219. "Boston Statues—Mann and Franklin," *Cleveland Leader* (OH), July 18, 1865, 2. For an analysis of the poses and drapery of monuments at this time, including Stebbins's *Horace Mann*, see John Stephens Crawford, "The Classical Orator in Nineteenth Century American Sculpture," *American Art Journal* 6, no. 2 (November 1974): 56–72.
220. Sea Urchin, "A Talk about Boston," *National Anti-Slavery Standard*, December 16, 1865, 4. A similar critique appeared in "Art Notes at Home and Abroad," *Round Table* (New York City), September 23, 1865, 37.
221. "Dedication of the Statue of Horace Mann," *Liberator* (Boston), July 7, 1865, 2.

222. Emma Stebbins to Elizabeth Akers Allen, July 28, 1865, CEAAM; Charlotte Cushman to Emma Crow Cushman, August 21 and September 17, 1865, CCP.
223. Naurice Frank Woods Jr., *Race and Racism in Nineteenth-Century Art: The Ascendency of Robert Duncanson, Edward Bannister, and Edmonia Lewis* (Jackson: University Press of Mississippi, 2021), 42, 57.
224. James Jackson Jarves, *The Art-Idea: Sculpture, Painting, and Architecture in America*, 2nd ed. (New York: Hurd and Houghton, 1865), 276.
225. Leach, *Bright Particular Star*, 333; Charlotte Cushman to Emma Crow Cushman, October 4, 1865, CCP.
226. See *Christie's Interiors, South Kensington, Style and Spirit* (auction catalogue), November 17, 2009. Lot 521 (catalogued as "An American Marble Bust of Antonius as Dionysus") was a bust of *The Lotus Eater*, inscribed "1865."
227. "The Bethesda Fountain" (program for the 1873 unveiling) in the Emma Stebbins scrapbook.
228. Florence Freeman to Frances Freeman, December 25, 1865, FFL. On Lewis, see Kirsten Pai Buick, *Child of the Fire: Mary Edmonia Lewis and the Problem of Art History's Black and Indian Subject* (Durham, NC: Duke University Press, 2010).
229. See "The Great Storm," *New-York Times*, January 27, 1866, 1.
230. "Loss of a Fine Work of Art," *New-York Times*, January 28, 1866, 4.
231. Underneath the photograph of *Joseph the Dreamer* in the Emma Stebbins scrapbook, Garland wrote, "afterward repeated for Mrs. M Garland of New York" (pl. 23).
232. Florence Freeman to Frances Freeman, April 9, 1866, FFL.
233. Stebbins, *Charlotte Cushman*, 203.
234. Cushman quoted in Leach, *Bright Particular Star*, 334–35.
235. G. D. M., "Scenes in the Old World.—37. Munich," *Pittston Gazette* (PA), August 16, 1866, 1. The author stated that they had previously seen the finished statue in Boston, and had also visited Stebbins's studio in Rome. For another account of a visit to the foundry that mentions *Horace Mann* but not *Bethesda Fountain*, see "Notes of Foreign Travel," *Chicago Tribune*, December 1, 1867, 2.
236. Stebbins application, September 10, 1866, United States Passport Applications US National Archives and Records Administration Database.
237. Florence Freeman to Frances Freeman, November 16, 1866, FFL. Freeman notes that Caroline Stebbins Tilton did not immediately return to Rome with her family because she had just given birth.
238. "The Bethesda Fountain" (program for the 1873 unveiling) in the Emma Stebbins scrapbook.
239. "Art Items: Sculpture," *Evening Post*, December 13, 1866, 1. See Millard F. Rogers Jr., *Randolph Rogers: American Sculptor in Rome* (Amherst: University of Massachusetts Press, 1971), 98; Wunder, *Hiram Powers*, 151–53, 207–11. Durant's wife, Heloise Hannah Timbrell Durant (1824–1901), had ordered the two busts by Powers. Perhaps she, and not her husband, was responsible for purchasing Stebbins's work as well.
240. "Personal Intelligence," *New York Herald*, January 14, 1867, 6.
241. "Art Gossip," *Milwaukee Daily Sentinel* (WI), February 13, 1867, 2.
242. Florence Freeman to Frances Freeman, February 14, 1867, FFL; Florence Freeman to Frances Freeman, February 27, 1867, FFL.
243. Suffolk, "France," *Boston Daily Advertiser*, April 26, 1867, 2.
244. See Dabakis, *Sisterhood of Sculptors*, 110–16; Jacqueline Marie Musacchio, with Jenifer Bartle, David McClure, and Kalyani Bhatt, "Mapping the 'White, Marmorean Flock': Anne Whitney Abroad, 1867–1868," *Nineteenth-Century Art Worldwide* 13, no. 2 (Autumn 2014), http://www.19thc-artworldwide.org/autumn14/musacchio-introduction.
245. On the sculpture, see Buick, *Child of the Fire*, 77–132. For more on the gift, see Woods, *Race and Racism in Nineteenth-Century Art*, 161–62; Leach, *Bright Particular Star*, 335–36.
246. Charlotte Cushman to James Holland Beal, May 23, 1867, quoted in Leach, *Bright Particular Star*, 335.
247. "An American Prima Donna," *Chicago Evening Post*, May 14, 1867, 2. For a similar article that lists Stebbins alongside writers Hawthorne and Stowe, see, among others, "Clara Louise Kellogg," *Daily Morning Chronicle* (Washington, DC), September 25, 1868, 2.
248. Suffolk, "Paris," *Boston Daily Advertiser*, August 1, 1867, 2.
249. Stebbins, *Charlotte Cushman*, 208.
250. Lucy Riall, *Garibaldi: Invention of a Hero* (New Haven, CT: Yale University Press, 2007), 350.
251. Florence Freeman to Frances Freeman, October 27, 1867, FFL.
252. Florence Freeman to Frances Freeman, November 14, 1867, FFL.
253. Henry T. Tuckerman, *Book of the Artists: American Artist Life* (New York: G. P. Putnam, 1867), 602–3. Some of Tuckerman's text was out-of-date. He wrote, "She is now at work on a statue of Horace Mann," even though the statue had been completed years prior.
254. "Personal," *Harper's Bazar*, November 30, 1867, 67.
255. *Catalogue of the First Winter Exhibition of the National Academy of Design* (New York: Sackett and Mackay, 1868), 17.
256. See, for example, "The News in Brief," *Daily Morning Chronicle* (Washington, DC), November 29, 1867, 1; "Fine Arts," *New-York Times*, November 29, 1867, 4. For an image of the sculpture on its original pedestal, see *Thirteenth Annual Report of the Board of Commissioners of the Central Park, for the Year Ending December 31, 1869* (New York: Evening Post Steam Presses, 1870), 55.
257. *Daily Ohio Statesman* (Columbus), January 11, 1868, 1.
258. Charlotte Cushman to Annie Adams Fields, February 26, 1868, JTFP. See also Florence Freeman to Frances Freeman, January 29, 1868, FFL, in which Freeman said the angel was "just finished in plaster."
259. Clark, *Marble Quarry*, 158–60. On the Bierstadt painting, see Mark D. Mitchell, *St. Johnsbury Athenaeum Handbook of the Art Collection* (St. Johnsbury, VT: St. Johnsbury Athenaeum, 2005), 50–51.
260. Wanderer, "Letter from Paris," *Portland Daily Press* (ME), June 15, 1868, 1. The letter itself is dated May 26, 1868. A similar account later appeared in "Paris," *Evening Post*, June 20, 1868, 1.
261. *Scotia* passenger manifest, June 30, 1868, New York Passenger Lists, US National Archives and Records Administration Database; "Passengers Arrived," *New-York Tribune*, July 1, 1868, 7.
262. Charlotte Cushman to James T. Fields, July 15, 1868, JTFP.
263. "Personal," *Harper's Bazar*, August 22, 1868, 675.
264. "Brief Jottings," *Boston Daily Evening Transcript*, September 7, 1868, 2.
265. See, for example, "News and Miscellaneous Items," *Worcester Daily Spy* (MA), October 29, 1868, 2.
266. Florence Freeman to Frances and Peter Freeman, December 6, 1868, FFL; Florence Freeman to Frances Freeman, December 20, 1868, FFL.
267. "The dinner given by Mr. G. W. Childs," *Daily Memphis Avalanche* (TN), February 17, 1869, 1. The dinner was on January 12. Stebbins, Cushman, and Hosmer are the only guests listed by name in this article.
268. Anne Longfellow Pierce, "Vol. 6: Rome," journal, Henry Wadsworth Longfellow Family Papers, Series 7, Anne Longfellow Pierce, box 24, folder 9. Thanks to Kate Hanson Plass, archivist, Longfellow House-Washington's Headquarters National Historic Site, Cambridge, MA, who shared this reference.
269. "The Statue of Columbus," *New York Herald*, March 28, 1869, 7. This news was picked up by papers in other states. See also *Thirteenth Annual Report of the Board of Commissioners of the Central Park*, 55–56, 146–48.
270. Stebbins, *Charlotte Cushman*, 229.
271. Anne Hampton Brewster, "American Artists in Rome," *Boston Daily Evening Transcript*, June 16, 1869, 1. For more

Miss Emma Stebbins: To the Editor of the Tribune," *New-York Tribune*, November 2, 1882, 7.

5. Emma Stebbins scrapbook, 1858–82, compiled by Mary Stebbins Garland, Archives of American Art, Smithsonian Institution, Washington, DC. The scrapbook is available online.
6. Stebbins traveled to Rome in 1856. See the chronology in this volume.
7. Shepherd was originally from Shepherdstown, West Virginia, not from England. See the chronology in this volume.
8. Stebbins began the bust in 1860. See the chronology in this volume.
9. Other sources suggest that Stebbins did not begin these artworks until 1863, at the earliest. See the chronology in this volume.
10. Stebbins started work on this statue in 1861. See the chronology in this volume.
11. Other archival information indicates that Stebbins submitted drawings for the *Bethesda Fountain* in 1861, and that she "designed and executed" it from 1864 through 1867. See the chronology in this volume.
12. John Wilson Stebbins was president of the Mercantile Library of New York from 1832 to 1834; he was not its first president. See the chronology in this volume.
13. Cushman died on February 18, 1876.
14. The date on Stebbins's headstone is October 24, 1882.

CONTRIBUTORS

Patricia Cronin is an award-winning visual artist and a Distinguished Professor of Art at Brooklyn College, the City University of New York. She is the author of *Harriet Hosmer: Lost and Found, a Catalogue Raisonné* (2009) and *The Zenobia Scandal: A Meditation on Male Jealousy* (2013). Cronin's work focuses on the international human rights of women, girls, and LGBTQ+ people. In 2002, she created *Memorial To A Marriage*, the world's first Marriage Equality monument, in Carrara marble. Many bronze versions are in museum collections in the US and abroad.

Ricky Flores is a photojournalist who has worked for publications including the *Journal News*, the *New York Times*, and the *Village Voice*. He is a three-time winner of the New York Press Publishers Award for Spot News. His book *South Bronx Family Album* (2024) is available from the Culture Crush. He teaches photojournalism at Lehman College, the City University of New York.

David J. Getsy has written about sculpture from the nineteenth to the twenty-first centuries, and his books include *Body Doubles: Sculpture in Britain, 1877–1905* (2004); *Rodin: Sex and the Making of Modern Sculpture* (2010); *Abstract Bodies: Sixties Sculpture in the Expanded Field of Gender* (2015); and *Queer Behavior: Scott Burton and Performance Art* (2022). He teaches at the University of Virginia, where he is the Eleanor Shea Professor of Art History.

Melissa L. Gustin is a curator of British art at National Museums Liverpool, where she has curated exhibitions on women and nonbinary artists, J. M. W. Turner, and changing collection displays. Her research focuses on nineteenth-century sculpture and receptions of historic art. She has published widely on Emma Stebbins, Harriet Hosmer, Antonio Canova, John Gibson, and G. F. Watts.

Katrin Horn is a professor of gender studies at the University of Greifswald's Institute for British and North American Studies. She publishes on issues of gender, feminism, and queerness in popular media, and the literature and culture of the late nineteenth century. She is the author of *Women, Camp, and Popular Culture: Serious Excess* (2017) and co-editor of *Speculative Endeavors: Cultures of Knowledge and Capital in the Long Nineteenth Century* (2025), among other publications. Her research on expatriate artists grew out of her work as principal investigator for *ArchivalGossip.com*, funded by the German Research Council.

Tony Kushner is a playwright, screenwriter, and activist. In 1993, he received the Pulitzer Prize for Drama for *Angels in America: Millennium Approaches*, the first part of his epic play, *Angels in America: A Gay Fantasia on National Themes*. He wrote the screenplays for *Angels in America* (2003), *Munich* (2005), *Lincoln* (2012), and the remake of *West Side Story* (2021). Among other honors, Kushner has received an Emmy Award, two Tony Awards, and a National Medal of Arts.

Laura Turner Igoe is the Gerry and Marguerite Lenfest Chief Curator at the James A. Michener Art Museum in Doylestown, Pennsylvania. She has published widely on materiality and the environment in nineteenth-century American art.

Karli Wurzelbacher is the chief curator at The Heckscher Museum of Art. She has organized numerous exhibitions on American art and has published on the sculpture of Courtney M. Leonard, Louise Nevelson, and Jack Whitten.

INDEX

Figures and plates are indicated by page numbers in italics.

IMAGE CREDITS

PLATES

Plates 1–3, 8–9, 12–13, 16, 18–19, 21–23, 25–26, 28–37, 41, 45–46: Archives of American Art, Smithsonian Institution

Plates 4–5, 10–11, 14, 20, 40: Photo by John Halpern

Plates 6–7: The Art Institute of Chicago / Art Resource, NY

Plate 15: McGuigan Collection

Plate 17: © Tony Rinaldo

Plates 24, 38: Photo by Rory Moore

Plate 27: Photo by Jonathan Smith

Plates 39, 47: Photo by David Almeida

Plate 42: The Metropolitan Museum of Art

Plate 43: Brooklyn Museum

Plate 44: The Chrysler Museum of Art

FIGURES

Page 7, figure 1: © Joan Marcus / Photofest

Page 8, figure 2: Donald Cooper / Alamy Stock Photo

Page 14, figure 1; page 28, figure 6; page 48, figure 10; page 58, figure 5; page 183, figures 6–7: Archives of American Art, Smithsonian Institution

Page 27, figure 5: The New York Times / Redux

Page 30, figure 9: © The Estate of Garry Winogrand. Courtesy of Fraenkel Gallery, San Francisco

Page 31, figure 10: © 2025 Martha Edelheit / Artists Rights Society (ARS), New York. Courtesy of Eric Firestone Gallery. Photo by Sam Glass

Page 34, figure 2: Photo Courtesy of American Family Immigration History Center

Page 39, figure 6: Wellesley College Archives, Library and Technology Services, Wellesley College

Page 50, figure 12; page 56, figure 3; page 66, figure 14; page 176, figure 1; page 216, figure 1: From The New York Public Library

Page 57, figure 4: © Museum Associates / LACMA

Page 58, figure 6: Courtesy of the Ministry of Culture, National Archeological Museum of Naples. Photo by Giorgio Albano

Page 70, figure 1; page 181, figure 4: © The New York Historical

Page 74, figure 3: Photo by Stefan Bauer, CC BY-SA 2.5, via Wikimedia Commons

Page 75, figure 4: Courtesy of the National Park Service, Longfellow House-Washington's Headquarters National Historic Site

Page 78, figure 6: © High Museum of Art / Bridgeman Images

Page 79, figure 7: Victor Moussa, https://stock.adobe.com

Page 81, figure 8: Hugh Olliff / Alamy Stock Photo

Page 82, figure 9: UlyssePixel / https://shutterstock.com

Page 82, figure 10: Bryan Busovicki, https://stock.adobe.com

Page 84, figure 1; page 87, figure 2: © 2024 Patricia Cronin / Artists Rights Society (ARS), New York

Page 90, figure 1: Courtesy of Ricky Flores

Page 179, figure 3: Photo by John Halpern

Page 182, figure 5: Courtesy of National Archives at College Park

Page 187, figure 9: Courtesy of American Antiquarian Society

Page 189, figure 11: © The Board of Trustees of the Science Museum

Page 193, figure 12: Antiqua Print Gallery / Alamy Stock Photo

Page 194, figure 13: National Gallery of Victoria, Melbourne

Page 210, figures 2–3; page 211, figures 4–5; page 212, figures 6–7; page 214, figures 8–9: Digital image courtesy of Getty's Open Content Program

This book is published in conjunction with the exhibition *Emma Stebbins: Carving Out History*, presented at The Heckscher Museum of Art from September 28, 2025, to March 15, 2026.

Library of Congress Control Number: 2025937940
ISBN: 979-8-9925162-1-0

Published by The Heckscher Museum of Art, Huntington, New York
heckscher.org

Distributed by The Pennsylvania State University Press
psupress.org

Produced by Marquand Books, Seattle
marquandbooks.com

Edited by Laura Lesswing
Designed by Pure+Applied
Typeset in Parmigiano and Yuni Grotesque by Brynn Warriner
Proofread by Carrie Wicks
Color management by I/O Color, Seattle
Printed and bound in China by Artron Art Group

Cover: Detail of plate 4.

Front endpapers: Sarony, Major, and Knapp, *The Terrace*, 1869 (detail). Lithograph, 8 × 14½ in. (20.3 × 36.8 cm). Via Wikimedia Commons.

Frontispiece: Detail of plate 24.

Back endpapers and back cover: *Bethesda Fountain* (pl. 47), in Central Park, New York, NY (2024).

This book was made possible through support from the Terra Foundation for American Art and the Henry Luce Foundation.

Major support provided by exhibition campaign co-chairs Richard T. Cunniff Jr. and Robin T. Hadley, and leadership gifts from Priscilla and Robert Hughes and Andrea B. and Peter D. Klein.

Additional support provided by The Deborah Buck Foundation, The Stebbins Fund in memory of James F. Stebbins and Jane Stebbins Greenleaf, the Wyeth Foundation for American Art, the Every Page Foundation, and The Gladys Krieble Delmas Foundation.

Public support provided by the National Endowment for the Arts, the New York State Council on the Arts, and the Town of Huntington, New York. Community engagement and public programming support provided by a distinguished Museums for America grant from the Institute of Museum and Library Services.

The 2024 conservation of the artwork illustrated in chronology figure 3, and the 2023 conservation of the artworks illustrated in plate 4 and plate 20, were supported through the NYSCA/GHHN Conservation Treatment Grant Program administered by Greater Hudson Heritage Network. This program was made possible by the New York State Council on the Arts with support from the Office of the Governor and the New York State Legislature. Additional support was provided from the Robert David Lion Gardiner Foundation.

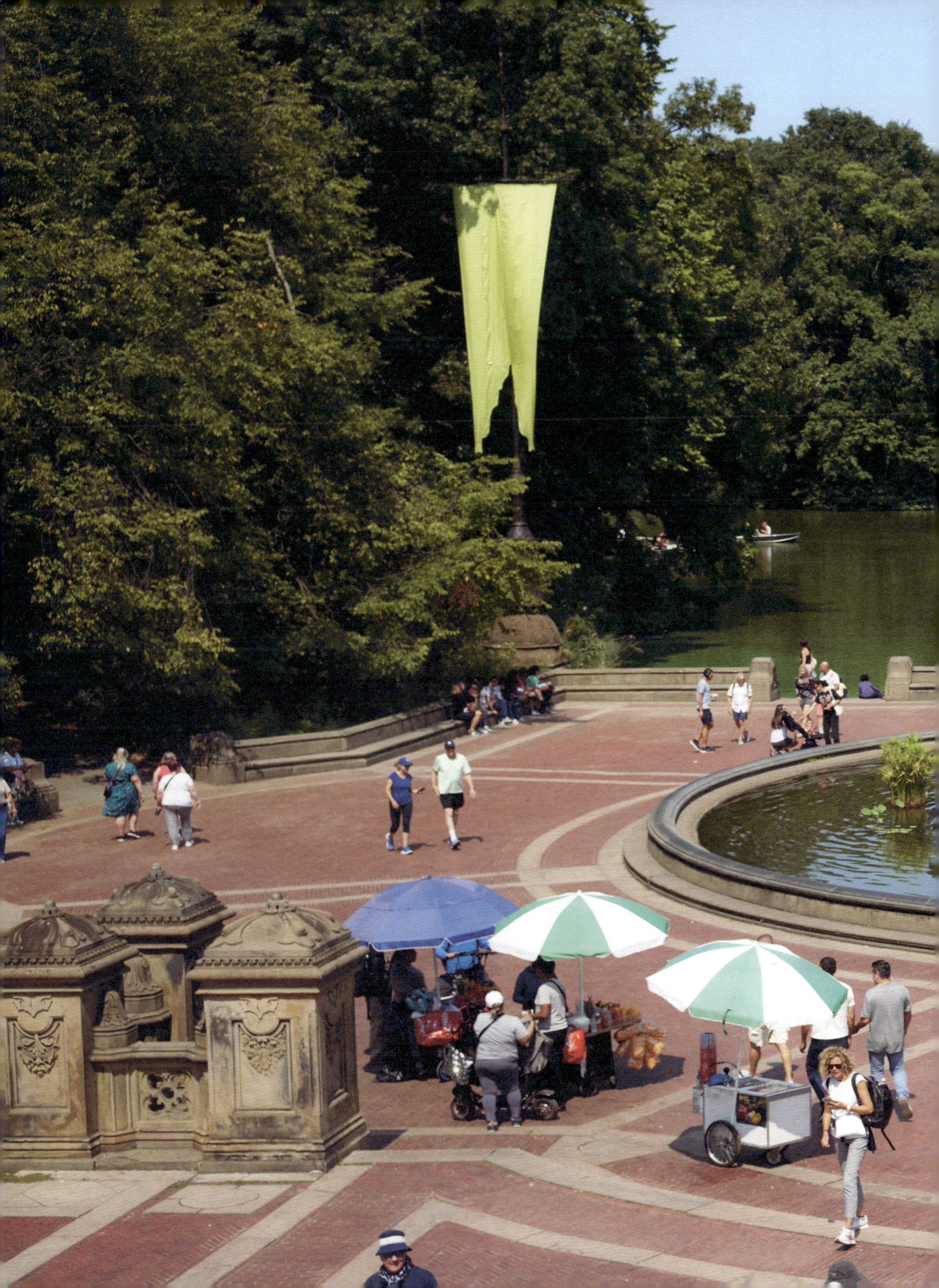

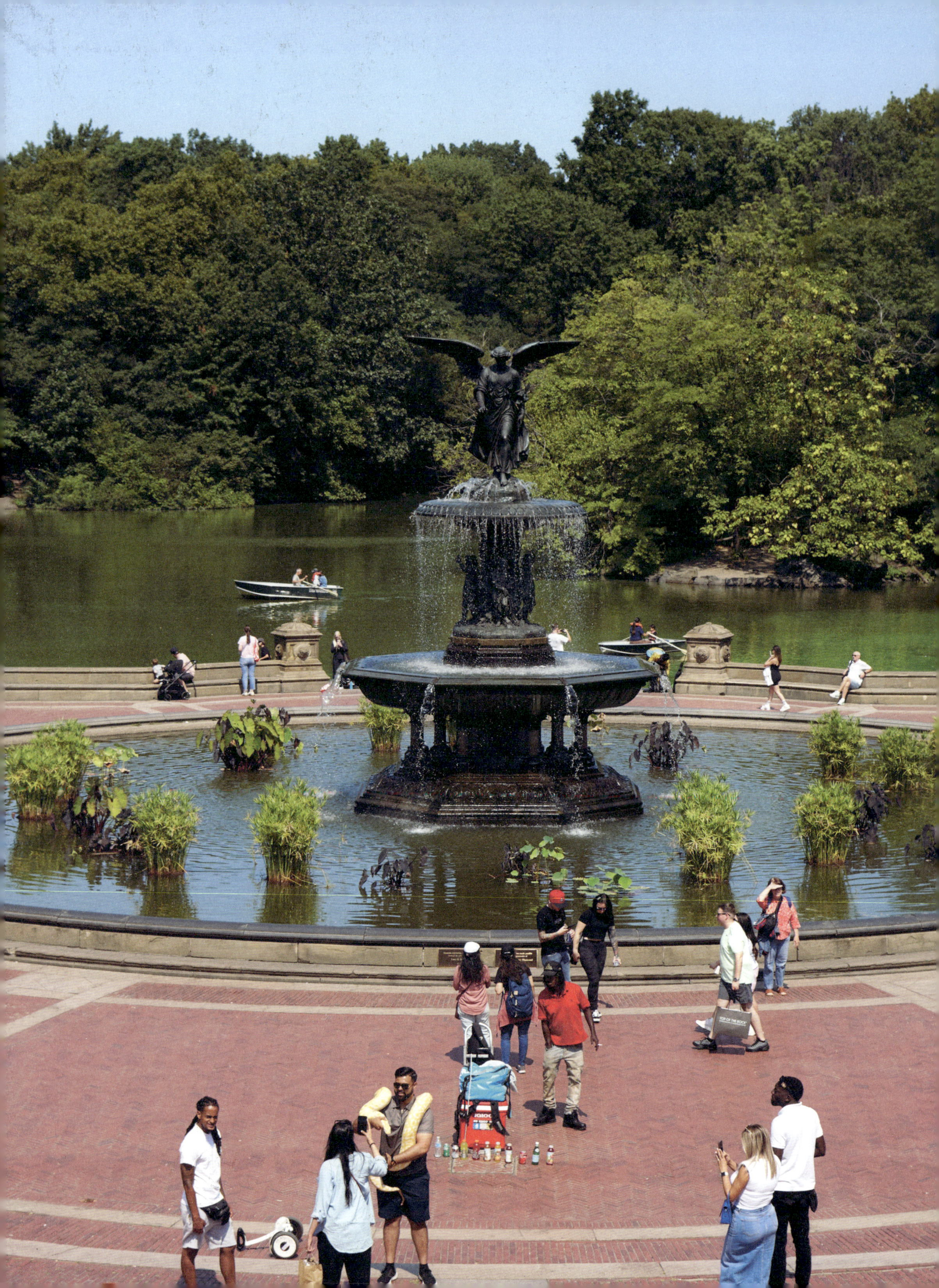

Why Someone Had to Die

By Jan Roffman

WHY SOMEONE HAD TO DIE
A DYING IN THE NIGHT
A MAZE OF FEARS
GRAVE OF GREEN WATER
ASHES IN AN URN
A PENNY FOR THE GUY
DEATH OF A FOX
WITH MURDER IN MIND

Why Someone Had to Die

JAN ROFFMAN

PUBLISHED FOR THE CRIME CLUB BY
DOUBLEDAY & COMPANY, INC.
GARDEN CITY, NEW YORK
1976

All of the characters in this book
are fictitious, and any resemblance
to actual persons, living or dead,
is purely coincidental.

ISBN: 0-385-11153-3
Library of Congress Catalog Card Number: 75-13393

Printed in the United States of America

Why Someone Had to Die

ONE

She was an unnoticed segment of humanity in the tidal wave of commuters who surged into the forecourt of Charing Cross Station: a girl in a rubbed grey flannel skirt, crinkled nylon blouse, drab out-of-shape navy cardigan draped crookedly over her shoulders, chain-store plastic shoes and a run in her tights. No one cast her a first glance, let alone a second. Yet she warranted attention in that she was committed to a life-sentence of seeking, of unwinking vigilance that at the day's end drained her emotionally and physically to a sack of flesh and bone. After five and a half years her eyes performed their appointed task automatically, sliding from face to face: each day's total adding to the tens of thousands she had already scanned.

And yet, when her eye suddenly locked itself on one individual, it was not a face that mesmerised her, but the outline of the shoulders of the man ahead: one slightly lower than the other, both hunched into the neck in an effort to camouflage the imbalance of bone. After five seconds the effect was as though a charge of electricity had shot through her body, leaving her suspended between belief and disbelief. Disappointments beyond count that had tossed her back into limbo preached caution. When the shock had diminished sufficiently to restore mobility, eel-like she forced a passage through the rush-hour crowds. He was making for the bookstall, and only seconds before he joined the queue for evening papers, she was shielded from his sight by a magazine rack.

Her body rigid, breath hardly moving in and out of her lungs, she checked off each facet of his physical appearance. Height and build? Yes. The beard? In imagination she peeled it off, her eyes raking the naked face. Yes. Hair? Nearer to black than brown, with a crisp wave, interwoven on the temples with grey. There'd been no grey when she had seen it last, but yes. She waited for the eyes to lift after he'd pocketed his change. Grey, shallow in their sockets, eyes that never mirrored even a transient reflection of the false bonhomie that was an essential component of the evil mask. Yes, yes. There was no means of checking the hated voice of deceit, so cross it off. Next match the hands to those indelibly photographed on her memory: pale-skinned, supple, the nails manicured. With one folded round the newspaper, the other holding a brief-case at the side away from her, both were invisible. Without warning, her concentration failed and her limbs began to shake. As he moved to by-pass the bookstall, she found strength to wheel, stare blind-eyed at the gaudy magazine covers.

It *was* him. The years of hit and miss dredging, from which her trawl had come up empty, lay behind her, to be obliterated from memory. The long search was at an end. She stood utterly possessed by the hatred that had become a life-force ruling heart and mind. But there was love too, a depthless well of it that would never run dry as long as breath remained in her body.

Unable to calculate how much time she had wasted, panic touched her in case in the lost moments he had been swallowed from sight. But, no, he was sprinting for a barrier. As she reached it, a whistle blew, the gate was slammed against her and, down the platform, she glimpsed him leaping into a carriage, reaching behind to close the door.

As the train moved towards vanishing point, she read its destination on the sign above her head, then involuntarily her brain began to tabulate what she must do.

First she checked the train on the departure boards. The 5:25 made five stops before it reached the coast: six stations at any one of which he could leave it. She wrote the place-names on a crumpled envelope in her shoulder-bag and, for safe-keeping, tucked it inside her notecase. She then continued her interrupted journey home, down the iron steps leading into Villiers Street and the Underground station. Rain had coated them with a film of grease. She trod with exaggerated care, holding the hand-rail to make sure she did not slip, incapacitate herself by a wrenched or broken limb. She had not a day, not an hour, not a second to waste on enforced inactivity.

Wedged against the door by the pressure of human bodies, her brain continued its tabulating. His behaviour pattern—the last minute rush for the train—labelled him as a commuter, on a journey so familiar he could gauge it in split seconds. She fixed the day of the week: Thursday, which left only one before two blank days when commuters stayed home.

In her bed-sitting-room on the outer fringe of Fulham, with a rusty gas-ring and a cracked sink poked behind a curtain dragging from its rail—the bathroom shared with three other tenants was up a flight of stairs—she went immediately to a shelf, took down a tattered school atlas, and with a pen inked in the railway line, underlining the stopping places.

Then she walked to the fire-place, above which was suspended a mirror, cracked across one corner, its scalloped edges mildewed. She stood in the hearth so that her head and shoulders were no more than six inches away, struggling to resurrect, for comparison, the self of five and a half years ago. She had ten pounds less flesh on her body, her chin was a sharp peak, her cheek-bones visible arcs. And surely her eyes were paler, as though the strain of peering into a myriad of faces had drained their colour. But the silky fawn hair, though shorter now, was unchanged in shade and texture. She raised lengths of it, draped it in different patterns about her head, over her forehead, behind her ears. It was a battle that lasted half an hour before she swallowed the bitter truth: whatever discipline she subjected it to, in ten minutes it would be hanging in limp strands about her ears. She longed savagely to tear it out by its roots.

She stared with such intense absorption that her eyes momentarily glazed, and out of the temporary blindness the solution exposed itself, so simple to contrive that she laughed aloud, a sound that hadn't left her throat for five and a half years.

New clothes too! Though any expenditure triggered off a series of alarm bells in that it depleted her precious hoarded capital, when she was poised on a narrow watershed between defeat, which amounted to a species of death, and victory, she accepted stoically that some reserves of money must be spent. She paced about the room, occasionally catching her toe in a raggy strip of carpet, building in her head an image of herself as different from the old as she could contrive. It emerged first in shadow outline and then gradually settled into a detailed portrait.

She scribbled a list of what she must buy, roughly estimated the cost. The total appalled her. It was as though she were guilty of squandering money that did not belong to her—which was partially true.

First thing in the morning she would telephone the secretarial agency, announce she was unable to finish out the week on her current temporary job. Plead illness, a family bereavement? Either, whichever excuse slipped most glibly off her tongue when she lifted the telephone. The agency's reaction was a matter of indifference to her since she intended to have no further contact with it.

When it was dark, supper too onerous a chore to contemplate, worse, an intolerable interruption of the thought patterns she wove in her head, she sat at the window and gazed blank-eyed at the street scene below. She could have summoned aid; walked into the nearest police station. In a crucifying flash-back she saw the self of five and a half years ago screaming at the faceless men, reduced to an army of book-keepers chained to the task of checking and cross-checking a mountain of statements from crooks and cranks and mischief-makers, strangled by their self-manufactured red-tape. As if, she thought with bitter scorn, she would give them a second chance.

Yet curiously, unsought, as she lay on the sagging divan bed waiting for sleep, the face of one police officer sidled into her memory; stranger still, she remembered his name: Cornford. She'd screamed at him too: "You've given up. You've failed. Why won't you admit it?"

The calm, deliberate voice echoed in her head. "Because it would not be true. We will never give up."

She hadn't believed him then and she certainly didn't now. Not that it mattered; the ferocity of her pride, total commitment to her mission was such that she scorned allies, all except one: the little gun, wadded in cotton wool she kept in her shoulder-bag. She had not even begrudged the exorbitant price demanded by the owner of the back-street pawn shop, nor the five pounds he had charged her for one minute's instruction on how to fire it. It was her most precious possession. Even in bed she looped the strap of her shoulder-bag twice round her arm and, drifting upwards out of sleep, her first conscious act was to place her hand over the hard bulge.

At 5:10 on Friday she stationed herself at a point immediately behind the barrier, so transfigured in appearance from the self of twenty-four hours ago that she felt as safe from detection as though she were huddled inside a suit of protective armour. As the passengers streaming through the barrier thickened and there was only five minutes before the train left, tremors of doubt began to torture her. Maybe he wasn't a regular commuter! Or had she, as had happened a thousand times, deceived herself? Panic rolled over her in muffling black waves, eroding hope, tossing her back into a wasteland. Half a minute later, when he came thrusting through the barrier, panic dissolved, and in its place was an anguished revulsion, a heaving sickness in her stomach at the nearness of his physical presence.

This time there was another man at his elbow. They kept abreast talking until they entered a carriage two ahead of the point at which she was standing. She climbed into the one behind. At each station she pushed her way to the door and checked the passengers who left the train. The two men alighted at the fourth stop, the name of which was Larksbridge, and joined the lemming-like stampede of passengers to the car park.

It was he who unlocked the car, held open the passenger door, which suggested it belonged to him, not to the other man, before he joined the long queue filtering through the automatic pay-gate. By running she was on the other side of it when the bright blue car, the make of which she did not know, but the number plate of which she memorised, turned left, added itself to the stream that was fast disappearing from sight.

When the last car vanished, she stared about her. The five and a half years of seeking had made her an expert in all forms of public transport; she had envisaged herself arriving at a railway station on the fringe of a town—a re-enactment of hundreds of such journeys' end. Instead she was at a level-crossing halt set down in rolling fields in which cattle grazed, the only bricks and mortar within sight the high structure of the signal box. For a second she was jolted off balance by the gap between assumption and reality, and then with a quick stride she too turned left, followed in the track of the blue car. The main road was a winding gradient bisected by side-roads and curving driveways at the end of each presumably stood a house she could not see, any one of which the blue car might have taken. After a mile she reached a cross-roads straddled by a mill, a coal depot, strings of terrace houses and a pub. A sign pointed to Larksbridge Town Centre. It was another half-mile, with more side turnings to the left and right than she could count before she reached the shop-lined streets.

Her spirit did not crack, the rock-hard certainty that her goal was within sight did not dim, but the cold realism inbred in her by the past dictated she must evolve some practical scheme if she was ever to track the blue car from the station car park to its home garage.

She went into a coffee-bar, took her cup to a table that afforded her a wide-angled view of the High Street, and weighed in her mind the various courses open to her. Only one was fool-proof: to post herself within sight of every turning and driveway she'd passed, and so by a process of elimination arrive at his home base. But the time consumed, weeks, maybe months, was such a monstrous burden on her patience that she knew she could not endure it. Somehow she must devise a short-cut.

Alongside her was a telephone, the directory on a shelf above. Her hand stretched out for it and with fear ticking she turned the pages until she reached the appropriate initial. The name wasn't listed. He'd changed it as she'd changed hers. If he hadn't; if he'd been prepared to stand before the world under the name by which she'd known him, the years of seeking would have been reduced to a sterile wasteland, the future no more than a slow progression towards death.

Staring through the bow window at the supermarket on the opposite side of the High Street, open late on Friday night, her thoughts moved in endless overlapping circles, inspiration dead until the periphery of her vision took in the window display of a small, dingy shop hemmed in between the glittering plate glass of the supermarket and a chain-store chemist. She jumped up, hurried across the street, and put her face hard against one of the window's small panes. She hadn't ridden a bicycle since she was fifteen, but wasn't there a saying that, like swimming, the knack once acquired was never lost? She noted the shop hours displayed on a card suspended from a piece of string inside a glass panel in the door: 9:30 A.M. to 1 P.M., 2 P.M. to 5:30 P.M., with half-day closing on Wednesday.

As she waited for the London train, beside her on the platform was a concrete stand with runnels, four of which supported bicycles, their front wheels padlocked. A waft of something near to happiness skimmed through her, as she stared at the ready-made parking place where she could leave hers overnight. It was as though, at last, a malignant fate had relented, cast her a half-apologetic smile. By working ahead, following a system of lying-in-wait for the blue car, making a quick getaway, she would, she calculated, halve the time expended in tracking him down.

"You're a bit rusty, miss, but it'll come back, you see. Confidence is what you need. Here, let me lower the saddle another inch. And you've not quite got the hang of the gears."

They were in a yard at the rear of the shop. After half an hour's practice her knees were reduced to jelly. Twice the bicycle had tipped her off, raising the terrorising spectre of personal injury.

"Tell you what," he suggested, "I'll go and brew us a pot of tea. That'll give you a breather. Strikes me you're trying to run before you can walk. Slow and easy does it."

A meagrely built old man, with sparse white hair and pebble-glasses that magnified his rheumy eyes, he sat her down in the back of the shop and disappeared into a cubbyhole.

"Know who set up this shop?" he asked as he placed two thick mugs before them. "My grand-dad, nigh on sixty years ago, when bicycles were a challenge and an adventure, apart from horses, the only vehicles on the road. Bit different now, eh, with juggernauts breathing down your neck, and cars bouncing you into the gutter! 'Bout time I packed it in, I reckon. Wouldn't wonder if you turned out to be my last customer."

He gave her ten minutes and then he urged her back into the saddle. This time she managed not to tumble off.

"See," he exclaimed as proudly as though it were his own triumph, "you're getting the hang of it. Remember you're the master, not the bike. Keep it steady. Come on, round you go."

Though the price of the bicycle was double what she'd expected—another theft from her capital—she wrote out the cheque, and the old man wheeled the cycle as far as the kerb. "Now don't get on till you're clear of the traffic; right wicked it is on a Saturday morning. You'll be all right once you get as far as the Wheatsheaf, that's the pub on your left, a bit of a ways down the hill. There's an open space in front of it where you can mount and get your balance."

He stood at the door of the shop watching her wheel the cycle. Nice young lady, skirts to her knees, sensible shoes. Not much to say for herself, but what she said was polite. Made a welcome change from big bottoms in skimpy shorts and indecently wobbling bosoms. With a sudden alarm he hurried to confirm she'd written her address on the back of the cheque. Mind like a sieve he had these days, and with being so taken up with teaching her how to handle the bike, he'd clean forgotten. But he needn't have worried. There it was: Helen Jones, 19 Cullington Street, London S.W.10. Helen, he thought, now there was a coincidence. It had been his dear wife's name, though she'd always been Nellie to him.

It took her eleven days to track him to his front door, the cat-and-mouse game agonisingly prolonged by confusing switches among a group of drivers who obviously worked a rota system. On two days he wasn't on his normal train, nor on the later ones for which she waited, leaving her to guess whether he had stayed home or caught an earlier one. Her sole gain from the hard labour of ticking off each turning was she was now certain he lived somewhere on the northern perimeter of the town farthest from the railway station in an area where new building developments were sprouting in enclaves of green countryside.

In the end it was an overturned tanker in the High Street that reduced traffic to a crawl and a long vehicle loaded with timber on a no-overtaking stretch that brought her to her goal.

The blue car swung down a side road marked by a general shop huddled at the corner. Pedalling frantically, she was in time to see it make a second left turn no more than twenty yards ahead of her. She dismounted, bent over her bike as though testing the tyre-pressure, while covertly taking stock of her surroundings. The road was in the initial stages of development. There were a few old houses, some new ones, foundations laid for more, but separating them and the one or two groups of cottages were margins of open land and patches of copse. After five minutes checked by her watch, she wheeled her bicycle level with the drive down which the blue car had disappeared, dawdled past. It led to a detached, three-storey, neither new nor old solidly built house, lying back from the road behind a low hedge and a lawn flanked on both sides by shrubberies. The double garage doors were open, the blue car and a smaller white one inside. With her eyes photographing the details, she walked on. Once beyond the drive, she mounted and pedalled half a mile, turned round and, before she reached the house, dismounted, crossed the road and examined it for a second time. Beyond the shrubs on one side there was a paddock in which two ponies grazed and, on the other, an area of scrubland. She thought, although she could not be sure, that there were fields to the rear. Pausing to take a final oblique view down the drive, she saw the windows were close-curtained with pleated net, screening the interior from view except for the shadow outline of a flower arrangement on a window-sill. A radio was playing, but however hard she strained her ears she could not catch the sound of a human voice.

It was not until she was level with the corner shop that a giant wave broke inside her, half pitching her off the bike, and she felt the scald of tears gushing down her cheeks. Half-blinded, struck rigid by shock at the unaccountable weakness in herself, she clung to the handle-bars. Then, when a fragment of control returned, as a punishment, she dug her knuckles hard into her eyeballs until the sheer physical pain staunched the emotional havoc that had struck her.

An old woman, walking with a stick, touched her arm. "What ails you? Fall off your bike?"

She shook her head, had to struggle to make her voice audible. "No. I felt sick for a moment. I'm all right now."

"You'd best sit down. You're the colour of a lump of old cheese. Mrs. Harris keeps a chair by the counter. She won't mind you using it."

"Thank you. But I'm quite recovered." She climbed on the bike, somehow found the pedals.

By the time she was in the train she had banished from memory the lapse into a shameful weakness she could not afford, began to savour the victory that was hers. Now she could watch without dread the dusk thicken behind the train windows. Henceforth dusk, even darkness, would be her ally. She allowed herself ten minutes to exult, and then folded the local paper she had bought to the small ad. section. Her first move must be to find herself a room in Larksbridge, cut out the time-wastage of train journeys. There were five ads. offering furnished rooms and, as a bonus, a boxed ad. for typists and book-keepers in a modern toy factory, with staff canteen, sports facilities and variable working hours to suit applicants. A temporary job would pay the rent of a room, perhaps even recoup some of the money she'd spent on clothes, so stop the drain on her capital. A half-smile formed on her lips, as her mind ordered and reordered the pattern of her vengeance.

That night she slept soundly, with none of the labyrinthian dream sequences of pursuit and escape in which her only weapons were a refusal to admit defeat and the little gun from which she was never parted.

TWO

Her first sight of the house, its size and style, doused her hopes, the more so as it was the last of the current newspaper ads. Two of the rooms had already been let, the third was a double-room for which the landlady demanded double rent. The fourth had been so stained and begrimed with other people's living, it had revolted her. The fifth ad., not for a room but a small top-floor flat, was the last remaining prospect until next week's edition of the local paper appeared. Not, she told herself, that it was even a remote possibility.

Three-storeys, white, its walls flush with the pavement, its paintwork gleaming, the brass dolphin door knocker a note of bright gold, it was the middle one of three identical houses. Maybe she'd got the wrong address. She propped the cycle against the kerb, checked. 6, St. Stephen's Piece. The name that struck her as peculiar matched the ad.

She twisted round, gazed at the railed-in oblong of grass, set with trees, shrubs, where a little fountain played, and for a moment its serenity was like a calming hand laid on her shoulder. At a slow pace she walked past a doctor's, a dentist's, an antique gallery, an herbalist's and, tucked into an alleyway, a dress shop with a single garment draped over a chair, at its foot a jade vase supporting one perfect rose.

The base of the square was filled in by a stone church, its

squat tower rising from the roof like a medieval look-out post. St. Stephen the Martyr. So that's why it was called St. Stephen's Piece. But why Piece?

Though she didn't know it, she was in the old and deeply prized heart of Larksbridge, with ancient rights jealously guarded, the preservation of which had been fought over by residents in a series of battles not yet at an end. Without being able to define it, the orderliness, the symmetry of her surroundings tucked snugly away behind the noisy High Street, evoked a response in some sensual depth of herself she had not known existed, plus a hopeless yearning for the unattainable that must be instantly scotched. All she needed was one room, not the extravagance of a flat to herself. One single room. Yet she found herself lingering, hanging over the rails of the square, listening to the fountain that whispered in the air, fabricating excuses, making pleas to herself. Maybe it was only a tiny flat. And wouldn't living in such a house provide her with an indemnity against intrusion and suspicion? In the end sheer animal curiosity propelled her across the road. It cost nothing to look. She was not committing herself. On the step she brushed a flick of dust from her skirt, smoothed straight the collar of her blouse, set her new image to rights and with a spiralling excitement she could only dimly remember feeling once before, long, long ago, lifted the dolphin knocker and let it fall. That's all she was doing, having a look at the inside of a house and coming straight out again.

When the knocker sounded, Georgina Latham thrust her reading glasses back over her forehead, rose from her desk. At the foot of the stairs she looked up at Mrs. Clownes who was descending as fast as her bunions permitted. "All right, Mrs. Clownes, I'll answer it. You get on with your vacuuming."

She had a quick, almost swinging walk, a slim body that, in early middle-age, still retained much of the fluid grace of youth. Her short ink-black hair, sculptured in wings framing fine-drawn but strong features was marked by only a few threads of grey. Her ultramarine eyes were direct, shrewd, her mouth both sensuous and gentle, as though each were in conflict with the other. She wore the classic garments of a country-town woman: tweed skirt and toning cashmere sweater.

She smiled at the girl she found on the other side of the door: short, so slight in build as to suggest a child-like fragility, dressed with extreme neatness in a navy-blue suit and a white blouse. Her light brown hair was cut in a long bob which, with the half-fringe and heavy-framed glasses gave her an appearance both waifish and owl-like.

"Mrs. Latham?" she queried jerkily.

"Yes. Georgina Latham."

"It's about the flat."

"Oh, the flat. Of course. Come in, Miss . . ."

"Jones. Helen Jones."

Georgina took off her glasses, swung them from her hand. "I'll lead the way, shall I?"

Mrs. Clownes, ignoring Georgina's suggestion, was posted on the bottom stair. With one major exception a nonsecretive person with nothing to hide, Georgina wished that Mrs. Clownes didn't assume that cleaning the house on two mornings a week gave her the right to make herself privy to every detail of the Lathams' professional and social life.

She held open the door of her den, shut it behind the girl, gestured towards a Chippendale chair set before a desk spread with a disorderly collection of charts, accounts, letters, and clips of papers.

But it was the wallpaper that claimed the girl's instant attention: a barbaric blast of colour, the background crimson, on which exotic long-tailed birds whirled through gaudy trumpeting flowers and tropical foliage.

Georgina laughed. "I know. It stuns people. But I love it. It's such a dark room it needed something to cheer it up. And, as it's my private den, other people don't suffer too much."

Helen wondered why she needed a den, which as a description of a room was unknown to her, but she said nothing, only pressed her knees tightly together, waited.

"First of all," Georgina began briskly, "I should warn you that it's not a self-contained flat, just two rooms, kitchen and bathroom on the top floor. Because this house is so old, late eighteenth century, it comes under a preservation order which means you have to obtain permission from all sorts of learned societies before you can undertake structural alterations. Also, if the flat were closed off with its own front door, we'd be compelled by law to erect a fire-escape and that would ruin the back of the house. But, of course, you'd have your own keys and, except for rare visits to the boxroom, no one in the house uses that floor." She paused, to test the reaction on the pale tightly set triangular face, found none, except extreme tension, as though the girl were caught up in some crisis. She continued: "I'm afraid it's only suitable for a single tenant. Was that your idea, or were you intending to share it with someone else?"

"No. There would only be me."

The voice was low-toned but not weak. The girl sat forward, perched on the edge of the chair, as rigid as though her whole body were clenched. Well, accommodation in Larksbridge, which was a popular commuter town, wasn't easy to find, which was why Georgina could afford to be choosey about her tenant. "Where are you moving from? London?"

"Yes. Fulham." When Mrs. Latham made no comment, she added: "In a flat, but as I've found a job in Larksbridge, it would be more convenient to live here than in London."

"Where's the job?"

"At Benbow's, the toy factory, as a private secretary."

Georgina was startled. Surely Annie couldn't have retired at last! She had been Joe Benbow's private secretary for twenty-five years, what he described with a groan as his infernal boss-woman! And with Annie in command other female staff were demoted to typists, book-keepers and runabouts.

All she said was: "They're an excellent firm to work for." She picked up a ball-point pen, executed one of the doodles for interlacing pyramids she drew while setting her thoughts in order. "There's something I should explain. My husband works at home. He writes television scripts." Her smile was an advance flash of apology. "I'm afraid he's a fanatic about noise. Anyone forever rushing up and down stairs, talking for half an hour on the telephone, playing pop music on a transistor after midnight, late parties, well, to put it bluntly he can't take it. For the last three years the flat was let to a schoolteacher, who's retired to live in Somerset. She was a perfect tenant except that, periodically, she suffered from insomnia and was given to making herself tea during the small hours, using a whistling kettle!"

As fervently as though she were affirming an oath the girl declared: "I haven't got a whistling kettle, or a transistor, and I never give parties."

Georgina, who had meant her remarks, even if they did impose limitations on a tenant's freedom, to be mildly humorous, was jolted. Such an emphatic disclaimer of what amounted to normal behaviour in the young suggested idiosyncrasy beyond the norm that might not make for easy living. It crossed her mind to wonder if the girl were studying for a degree in the evenings. She looked the dedicated type. Or was it no more than she lacked a sense of humour? Georgina hoped not, and in an effort to put her more at ease, added: "I'm afraid there's a reverse side to the coin. Normally my husband works regular hours, but sometimes there are fraught periods when he'll leap out of bed in the middle of the night and make straight for his typewriter. Since his study is directly below, he might give you insomnia! Anyway, shall we go and look at it and see how you react!"

Mrs. Clownes emerged from a doorway on the first landing.

"What do you want me to do about all the posters his lordship has pinned to the wall? Half of them are hanging off."

"Leave them," Georgina said, as Mrs. Clownes' slightly bulbous eyes minutely examined the girl. "As soon as I have time, I'll get busy with sticky tape."

On the top floor she opened a door leading into a low room with two dormer windows overlooking the garden. "Sitting-room. The kitchen is through the door on the left."

Helen breathed in the airy room, with its honey-coloured fabrics and carpet, the simple but extravagant comfort of the two low upholstered arm-chairs. With a sleepwalker's pace she advanced to a window, stood with her back to Georgina, as removed from her normal habitat as though she'd been set down in a Persian palace. She had lived isolated inside her hate-walled cell for so long that most of the time she observed the world through a dark glass that filtered out irrelevant matter. But, very occasionally, as now when she turned her gaze back into the room, a face sprang out of the blur, seized hold of her consciousness, as Georgina Latham's did: relaxed, waiting, communicating good-will. At the moment the dream was born, a smile came spontaneously to her lips, reciprocating the warmth offered. "Oh, it's beautiful!" And for a moment her face bloomed, as though the texture of the skin changed and beneath it instead of deadness life pulsed. The room's grace had acted on her like the first dawn glow in a sky after the blackness of night, a promise that here would be conceived the final stratagem that would mark the end of loneliness for ever.

Georgina laughed with pleasure and a certain amount of relief. So she was human! "What a nice compliment! I'm glad you like it." She gestured towards the radiators. "The heating isn't on up here, but they are large ones so they keep the flat warm even when we're buried in snow. Have a look at the kitchen. It's minute but adequate for one."

Helen took in the stainless steel sink, the Moorish pattern wall-tiles, the baby fridg., and totally absorbed in spinning a dream for the future, followed Georgina out on to the landing and through the opposite door.

The bedroom was small, with a single bed, built-in white cupboards and dressing-table. The bedspread was cherry, with a matching shade on the bedside lamp. The bathroom fittings were sea-green, the floor fitted with a shaggy white carpet.

When Miss Jones, apart from that single rapt exclamation, made no further comment, but appeared to retreat back into herself, Georgina suggested: "If you've seen all you want, shall we go downstairs?"

They had to squeeze past Mrs. Clownes who was vigorously brushing the stair-carpet.

When they were seated on either side of the desk, Georgina said: "I suppose we should get down to basics. The rent includes the central heating and rates, but there is a meter for the electricity for which the tenant is responsible." She named the rent per calendar month.

Helen stared at her finger-nails that were bitten to the quick, then curled their ugliness out of sight. The sum would absorb well over half the salary she would receive from Benbow's. To one conditioned never to waste a penny that proportion amounted to a wicked profligacy. But even as her mind accepted that irrefutable fact, it was counter-balanced by an emotional need over which she could exercise no control. She told herself that the extravagance was justified. The flat would form not only a perfect temporary base, but a pattern for the future. If she memorised, even sketched, the groupings of colours and textures, of furniture and fittings, the like of which she'd never seen except in vague shadows in shop windows without relevance to herself, she could reproduce them in the home that eventually she must build, one that until now, had been no more than a blur in her mind, but on the turn of an instant had been transformed into a glowing, beckoning reality. A home! The word symbolised joy beyond measure, reducing a few weeks' rent to a paltry sum when set against the return it would yield. It was, she thought—her early religious training had been based on a narrow literal translation of the Bible—like catching a glimpse of the Promised Land. She said primly: "I'd like to take it."

Georgina's reactions were mixed. On the whole the girl gave promise of being as near an ideal tenant as she was likely to find, especially as she'd already turned away three applicants on different counts, but a few niggling misgivings persisted. That curious set, almost dead-pan expression, except for that momentary lapse into a spasm of natural joy in the sitting-room, bothered her a bit, as though the girl were unwilling, or unable, to reveal a vestige of herself, so must constantly be on guard. The near speechlessness, for instance, might be no more than chronic shyness, though surely such extreme reticence was unusual in a girl in her mid-twenties—unless she had something to hide. Yet an obsessive chatterer, a breezy matiness would have been a worse alternative. So what was she quibbling about! "Good," Georgina said, not sounding too enthusiastic. "Rent paid monthly, in advance, with a month's notice if you decide to leave. Oh, one other thing. I'd prefer a reasonably long let, say a year at least. Would that suit you?"

Helen lied without a qualm. "Yes."

Georgina drew a pad towards her. "I'm afraid, though it sounds horribly untrusting, I must ask you for references. One from your bank and one from your present landlord."

Helen dictated the name of her bank.

"And your present landlord?" Georgina prompted.

A faceless corporation located in the City who sent the rent bill a week before it was due, followed it up by a reminder printed in red if the cheque was not in the process of being computerised by the first of the month. Who never acknowledged complaints, let alone investigated them. "Mrs. Barker, who owns the property, lives on the premises." She added the address, and then blurted out a shade too quickly: "If you like I could ask her to send you a reference. It would save time."

Again Georgina was conscious of a stab of unease. Of course it could be no more than Miss Jones was extraordinarily naïve in business dealings and also genuinely anxious to get settled in as soon as she could. "Better," she said with deliberate casualness, "to do it in the orthodox way. I'll drop her a line tonight. You sound as if you're in a hurry to move in."

"Yes, I am. I want to cut out the train journeys."

"Very sensible. If you leave me your telephone number I'll ring you as soon as I hear from the bank and Mrs. Barker."

Helen gave the number of the pay-box in the hall. "If you could phone me after six I'll make sure of being in."

As Helen rose, she added: "I have a bicycle. Would there be anywhere for me to keep it?"

"Yes, in the old coach-house that has been converted into a double garage. There's no entrance from the front, only from the back lane, but it's quite simple when you know the way." In a flight of compulsive joy Georgina's glance skimmed the pastel drawing of a boy above the fire-place. She nodded towards it. "My son keeps his cycle there. He was five then, now he's fourteen, away at boarding-school."

The girl took a long absorbed look. "What's his name?"

Georgina, faintly startled, gave it. "Simon."

The girl appeared to mouth it silently to herself, stared for a full half-minute at the pastel sketch, seeming loath to withdraw her eyes from it.

At the door, as Georgina promised to get in touch with her as soon as the references arrived, the only words the girl uttered were "Thank you" before she turned round, walked to her bicycle propped against the kerb. As she shut the door, the pearl-glimmer of her set, near-expressionless face lingered in Georgina's head.

"You've got a sly one there," Mrs. Clownes pronounced as Georgina walked back down the hall. "Boy friends traipsing in and out all hours of the night."

"Oh, I don't know," Georgina replied, purposely vague. It

was a precise truth. She did not know. She had a niggling feeling that the girl was too good to be true, that somewhere there was a streak of fake in her. She checked her watch. 12:15. She should be in time to catch Joe before he went out to lunch.

"Joe," she said when he answered, "I've just been interviewing a prospective tenant for the flat. Helen Jones. She says you've taken her on as your private secretary. Whatever happened to Annie?"

"God damn it, nothing. What could! The woman's indestructible."

"So what's Miss Jones?"

"A temporary typist to cope with the Christmas rush. Strictly Annie's minion."

"Did she ask her for references?"

"I wouldn't know. Hang on, I'll ask Annie."

She hung on. "The answer's no. Annie put her through a shorthand and typing test, which proved she could spell, even punctuate, which is a rare virtue. According to Annie, references are a dead loss. Most of them are forged on the firm's notepaper before the applicant left or was fired."

"Okay, Joe. Sorry to have been a nuisance."

"You're never that. But you are apt to use up time I haven't got."

She wrinkled her nose, executed another doodle of interlaced triangles. A lie or a bit of false pride? But didn't the majority of girls claim the higher status of secretaries when, in fact, they were no more than typists? The nebulous doubts persisted until, impatient with herself, she thrust them away, picked up her pen and wrote notes to Mrs. Barker and the bank in Fulham.

Lucy Burrows, a natural blonde, plump, with a rose and pearl complexion, bit into a coffee éclair, mopped up a drip of cream with her tongue. "It must be heaven to be a professional cook, know precisely how everything will look when you open the oven door, not getting the jitters. After the kids were here when Simon was home, they plagued me into having a go at some éclairs. They were the most ghastly flop; result disastrous loss of face!"

"I've been cooking ahead for the Jessop wedding reception. I'll give you a dozen from the deep freeze."

Lucy grinned. "I should protest. I'm on a diet . . . again! But I'm not going to. When is it?"

"Saturday week. Then I've got a lull before a couple of cocktail parties."

"You've certainly built yourself a terrific reputation as a Cordon Bleu cook! Where's Richard?"

"In town. There's a series hanging in the balance. They've filmed the pilot, for which Richard wrote the script. The next stage is when the producer and series editor pull it apart frame by frame, reach a verdict."

"Never mind, he's got you to come home to, plus a super meal. My three will have to make do with liver and bacon."

Except that coming home meant Richard leaving Amanda behind. As she refilled Lucy's cup, Georgina wondered with the undercurrent of fear that exists when you stare into a future without shape or certainty, whether the situation was eased or exacerbated by her awareness of Amanda's existence. Since she did know, the question was irrelevant. Laura, a relation by marriage of her father's Cousin Maude, an earnest, literal-minded girl who worked as a research assistant for the B.B.C., had not shirked what she counted her duty.

Her small muddy brown eyes held a tiny lick of pleasure. Georgina did not resent it; Laura, singularly unblessed by charm and looks, was competent, industrious, persevering and seemingly content with the narrow slot into which life had poked her. But maybe, Georgina thought, not so content that she didn't obtain a vicarious throb of excitement by revealing to Georgina that her husband kept a mistress.

Breathing heavily, she underlined what she had already said in case its enormity had escaped Georgina. "You see, it's so convenient, it gives him a permanent alibi. When Richard stays in town he's supposed to be sleeping in Max's flat. But he isn't, he's with Amanda Grey in the flat above. I can't name names, but I swear it's no gossipy rumour, but the truth. And I can't bear for you to be cheated by a common little tart, no better than a call-girl who's played around at modelling and now fancies herself as an actress." She gasped, pressed her hand to her mouth. "Oh, dear, would you rather I hadn't told you?"

Georgina said no, treated the matter so lightly that Laura, robbed of melodrama, had been visibly deflated. Georgina decided that Laura's tale was as likely to be a blown-up tid-bit of gossip as the truth. The only fact she knew for certain was that she never wished to set eyes on Laura again.

A month later she and Richard had been invited to a party Max gave to celebrate the hundredth performance of *Over the Precipice,* a play in which he had a minor part.

Behind the bar, helping Max with the drinks was a willow-wand of a girl, a crimson rose pinned at the base of the slit in the black jersey dress that plunged to her navel, the natural motions of her shoulders high-lighting the delectable breasts, the shimmering silver-gilt hair, the single layer of clinging silk that teased and promised infinitely more seductive than full nudity. As Max dodged round the bar to kiss her, Georgina received a long stabbing glance from sapphire eyes as Amanda Grey caught her first sight of Richard Latham's wife.

Pointedly no one introduced them; Richard and Amanda did not exchange a word. Only her name on other people's lips confirmed her identity. Assessing the girl's looks, in which she could not find the slightest imperfection, a part of her marvelled that Richard had won such a prize. On her way out she checked the row of brass name-plates beside the three bells. The top one meant nothing to her, but above Max's name was that of Amanda Grey. As dear Laura had suggested, a perfect set-up. If, in an emergency, she needed to telephone Richard, Max could, so to speak, retrieve him smartly from the upper flat.

"What I've been wondering," Lucy said, "is whether you've made up your mind about Madeleine Hurst. I ran into her in the supermarket yesterday and she sort of hinted. It's a bit mean, since she offered, to keep her in suspense. Sort of throwing her good intentions back in her face."

"There's more to it than good intentions," Georgina insisted, referring to the voluntary organisation called "Friends in Need" which she and five others had set up two years ago after an exceptionally severe winter in which one old woman had been found dead from hypothermia, and a young abandoned wife had shooed her two young children on to the streets while she put her head in a gas oven. The aim of Friends in Need was to provide a safety net under the yawning gaps left by the Welfare State. "The most important single factor is staying power, and never taking offence no matter what sort of reception you get." She cited old Mrs. Pritchard who would slam the door in your face if you didn't carry a shopping bag with a couple of tins—preferably filled with meat—poking out of the top. Colonel Langton, with only shreds of flesh on his arthritic bones, who kept a cut-glass decanter of sherry on the table, alongside another of gin as proof that he was in need of no one's charity, only the gin was tap water, the sherry cold tea, and the one bar of the electric fire was switched on when the bell rang, and switched off as soon as the visitor was outside the front door.

"You've met her. And that's what you've decided, that she hasn't got staying power?"

"Lucy, I'm not sure. Perhaps it's unfair to judge her on that one time I saw her at your house."

Lucy accused: "You're put off by the bleached hair, over-trendy gear. Shame on you! She had a kid late on, and naturally she doesn't fancy looking ten or fifteen years older than the other mums who ferry their tiny-tots to and from kindergarten. She's mobile, cheerful, easy to talk to and she wants to do the job. And honestly with Betty moving to Slough, we do desperately need a sixth member. Five is too few to cover the ground. Who would you suggest?"

"I don't know. So many women are taking jobs as soon as their children are at school. I'm wondering if Madeleine Hurst is well enough briefed on the welfare services." That was one of the basic planks in Friends, making sure that anyone in need claimed every benefit to which they were entitled, helping them to translate into basic English the printed forms couched in the tortuous official jargon of Civil Servants. "Why is she so anxious to volunteer?"

"My guess is that now she's got the boy to school, she's lonely and at a loose end. I honestly believe she wants to put some roots down, contribute something to the community. After all, we do. So why distrust her motives? And, love, do remember it's October. We didn't have a flu epidemic last winter, so the odds are we'll have one this. If she's to find her feet, learn the ropes this side of Christmas, well, I think you should make up your mind one way or the other."

Friends in Need had no officers, but since Georgina had initiated the scheme, and the monthly meetings at which they pooled their problems were held at her house, she was virtually chairman, and the final selection of a new member her responsibility.

Lucy said: "I'd take her on."

Georgina laughed. "Then you're a sucker, the nicest, softest sucker I know."

Lucy, unabashed, grinned. "And you're an over-exacting perfectionist. Look, I've an idea. Supposing I took her under my wing, chaperoned her for a couple of weeks, taught her to tell the difference between the scroungers and the 'don't you dare offer me charity' types. Would that make you feel easier about her? A trial run?"

"A lot. Just tell me where you're going to find the time!"

Lucy waved an airy hand. "Phooey! I'm a genius at manufacturing time." She giggled. "I'll start by introducing her to Mrs. Parker, who flies for her hat and coat as soon as I hove into sight, and demands to be taken to the shops. But never to the ones that are handy, oh dear me, no. The one she wants is never nearer than five miles! And when we arrive, it's clean gone out of her mind what she intended to buy. Well, wouldn't we all cheat to win ourselves a country drive if we were buried in a basement bed-sit-kitchen and considered ourselves a cut above our neighbours! Let me take on Madeleine Hurst, and I'll have her clued up in no time."

"Okay, you win." Not for the first time Georgina suspected Lucy had got her priorities blurred. Friends in Need did not operate to provide a bored middle-class housewife with the diversion of do-gooding. Could it be, she wondered, that Mrs. Hurst needed Friends in Need more than they needed her!

On the doorstep Lucy asked: "Have you let the flat?"

"I'm not sure until I see her references. A girl who's come to work at Benbow's."

"Girl!" Lucy queried. "I thought you were after a desiccated middle-aged spinster, guaranteed neither to be seen nor heard."

"She looks the quiet sort."

"Young and quiet! They don't breed that type any more. Noise is their intoxicant. They get high on it. See you!"

The critical hour was between six and seven when, if Richard were spending the night in town, he telephoned. At five minutes past seven when it had not rung, she put the lamb casserole in the oven, laid the dining-room table, set out the drinks. Then she sat and waited until she heard the car running into the garage. She switched on the garden light and when he opened the kitchen door went to meet him.

In the last eighteen months she had developed to a fine art that light, seemingly unconcerned glance at his face that told her instantly how his day had gone. Sometimes they exchanged a light cheek-kiss. Tonight she did not reach up for it, merely took his coat and hung it in the hall wardrobe.

His six-foot form that had once been as lithe as an athlete's now had a slight bulge beneath the waist, and there was a sag to his shoulders. But his darkly brooding face was as compellingly handsome as when she'd seen him across a room and, in the first flood of romantic passion, had described it to herself as Byronic! His chestnut hair, worn longer now, was still abundant; nor had he lost that indefinable quality of presence. From the drinks table, he asked: "What are you having?"

"Gin and tonic, I think." She waited until he handed her the glass, and then, although she knew already, asked: "How did it go?"

"It didn't. Back to square one, with Alan working on the new pilot." He drained his glass, scoffed lightly. "No surprise. He's the new rising talent. Only a bloody waste of my time."

She looked into his face that was morose and stained by the bitterness of disappointment he could not admit. She longed for a magic salve that would heal his wounded pride, release his dammed-up talent. At the same time she allowed herself to wonder why he had not spent the night with Amanda. Did it spell a tiny victory or was Amanda, whom Georgina had glimpsed in a television ad. a month ago, seemingly flying angel-like towards the sky supported by a giant packet of breakfast cereal, working? She said: "I'm sorry."

He shrugged, and as a lever to hoist himself out of the pit asked: "What's been going on here?" His mouth relaxed. "Any letter from Simon?"

"No. It will probably arrive tomorrow. If he misses the first post they take two days. Lucy looked in, and we enrolled a new member for Friends. Oh, and there was a letter from Dada." She pulled it out of the pocket of her dress. "I'm worried about him."

"Why?"

"It's so short, only half a page instead of the two or three he usually writes."

"Ring him up, talk to him, or have a word with Mrs. Forbes."

"I did. Mrs. Forbes maintains he's fine. And when I spoke to him, he said the same, but towards the end he sounded breathless, and it was he who rang off."

She saw him in the big stone house rooted into the fabric of the Yorkshire moor, in which she had been born and in which, since her mother died ten years ago, he had lived alone except for a housekeeper.

"How old is he now?"

"He'll be seventy in November."

"Well, then," he said reasonably, "you can't expect him to be as spry as he used to be."

But she did, anything less was a cold hand reaching for her heart. She thought of the morning, a month or so before her wedding, when he had put the deeds of the house into her hands. "It's the one you set your heart on; what's more important, it's a sound investment, not likely to depreciate in value. It means, come what may, you'll always have a roof over your head." As she'd kissed him, she'd forgiven him for his lack of faith in the man she was about to marry. Time would restore it.

"Damn it," Richard had raged. "He didn't have to provide you with a home. If you were so set on that particular house, we could have swung a mortgage." The gift accepted, in the early days the fact that the deeds were not in their joint names but in hers, hadn't rankled over-much. The festering resentment had only built up in the last non-productive year and a half during which she had extracted from the post the bills for rates, fuel oil, telephone and electricity. To preserve the precious last fragment of his master-image, he continued to pay the gardener. The knock-out blow to his self-esteem had been contained in a joint letter to them from her father asking if he might have the pleasure and privilege of assuming responsibility for his grandson's school-fees. Richard had unjustly suspected connivance between Georgina and her father. Though he could not bring himself to deny his son the education he could not provide for him, Georgina knew there was a particle of him that would never forgive either Dada or herself.

"I think maybe I ought to go up and see him."

"It's not all that long since you were there."

"Three months. I've got a horrible feeling he's failing. Mrs. Forbes would never admit it because she knows I'd fly up there, and she literally can't stand another woman around the house." She'd not announce her visit beforehand, just walk through the front door that was never locked during the day and find him absorbed in one of his books on archeology or cleaning his beloved guns. He'd not even appear surprised, only illuminated with depthless joy at the sight of her. "As soon as the Jessop wedding is behind me, I'll go." The ice of distaste that any mention of her professional cooking evoked closed on his face. She wanted to shout: "It costs money to live," but of course she never allowed that horny little word to insinuate itself into any conversation. Act as though it grew on trees! To do him justice, though he squandered money when he had it, he was both orthodox and honourable, belittled to himself by his failure to support his wife and son.

"If it'll ease your mind."

She debated whether she should tell him about Miss Jones. It was tempting in that at a nadir of disappointment, he might be less incensed at having to endure another stranger within the house. She couldn't be certain. In the end she decided that she would hold her tongue until she'd settled the references. If they were unsatisfactory the deal would fall apart.

After they'd eaten, he retrieved his brief-case, went up to his study. At eleven she tapped, waited half a minute to allow him time to hide the glass in the drawer of his desk alongside the bottle of whisky, then popped her head round the door. "I'm going to turn in. In case I'm asleep when you come to bed, I'll say good-night."

He looked up from his typewriter, into which a clean sheet of paper was slotted, began to type so that he had to speak above the tapping. "Tony has been pressing me to try for this thirty-minute drama slot on B.B.C.2. I may as well draft an outline."

"Don't stay up too late."

Tony Cowell was his agent, a highly successful one, who cosseted writers whose names flashed up so regularly on the screen they even won a place in viewers' memories, but who developed a blankness of mind towards those who dropped out of the main-stream. Not unnaturally, he preferred to exploit a rich talent rather than waste time and effort fostering one that showed signs of running dry. If Richard had seen him, even spoken on the telephone, the page would not have been blank, nor would he have lingered over supper. As she opened their bedroom door the typewriter ceased to tap, proof, if she'd needed any, that month by month the habit of lying became more deeply ingrained in him.

THREE

Standing at the window, squinting obliquely up the street, Miss Jones checked the postman's progress. Squat, heavy-footed, given to discursive chat, the operation dragged on her patience. When he disappeared into the next portico, she ran downstairs, was waiting to retrieve the envelopes as he thrust them through the letter-box. She extracted the one addressed to the non-existent Mrs. Barker, laid the remainder on the rickety hall table and hurried back up three flights of stairs.

A lined envelope, thick white paper with an embossed heading, plus a stamped-addressed return envelope. Ten lines of firm, instantly legible script.

Dear Mrs. Barker,

Miss Helen Jones, who I understand at present leases a flat from you, wishes to become a tenant of furnished accommodation in my house. I would be grateful if you would confirm that she is a satisfactory and trustworthy person. I am enclosing a stamped addressed envelope for your reply, and thank you in advance for your courtesy.

Yours faithfully,

Georgina Latham

She opened the pad of writing paper she had bought on her way home the previous evening, tested the nib of the old-fashioned fountain pen, and with the design of each letter clear in her head before she committed it to paper, painstakingly began her task. She was not satisfied until she had completed the sixth draft, and then she practised the signature another half a dozen times. When she had copied out the final draft, with its thick downstrokes and capitals more elaborately formed than her natural handwriting, she knew that unless it were studied by an expert in calligraphy—and Mrs. Latham was surely unlikely to be one—she was safe.

Dear Madam,

Thank you for your letter. Miss Helen Jones has occupied a furnished flat in this house for two years. During that time she has proved herself an entirely satisfactory tenant, very quiet and always most considerate in every way. I am sorry that circumstances have obliged her to vacate the flat.

Yours faithfully,

Mary Barker (Mrs.)

Georgina placed the two letters side by side on her desk. The one from the bank consisted of three typed lines confirming that Miss Helen Jones was, in their opinion, creditworthy for a flat at the rent Georgina had quoted.

She read the reference from Mrs. Barker twice, vaguely speculating whether or not it was genuine. That she should question it puzzled her—she had no grounds except that it had reached her by return of post and the writing appeared laboured. The only other evidence was that blink—a sort of visual gasp—when she'd had to prompt Miss Jones to supply her landlady's address, followed by that naïve suggestion to deliver the letter personally!

The answer from the bank removed any doubt that Miss Jones was likely to default on the rent. So what remained? Vague, unsubstantiated misgivings. It could be, *if* the letter was forged, that she was on bad terms with the landlady and didn't trust her to supply a satisfactory reference. Against her will, imagination widened its scope. Released from prison? On the run? Practical, with a logical mind, she scoffed at her forays into melodrama. In her experience most decisions left in abeyance formed themselves. True enough, at six o'clock, with no effort on her part it did, its base a memory of that split second when Miss Jones had turned from the window transported into near rapture. Jail birds, girls on the run!

When she telephoned Miss Jones she sounded breathless. Georgina said both references had arrived and were satisfactory. When would she like to move in.

"Could I . . . would it be possible . . . tomorrow?"

The hint of desperation in the disjointed plea breathed new life into Georgina's misgivings. Furthermore, she was being hustled in the job of going over the flat, checking the inventory of china and linen, preparing two copies of the agreement. "Well . . ."

"If I could. I start work at Benbow's on Monday morning."

Georgina conceded it made sense. The work involved wouldn't take her more than a couple of hours at the most. So why quibble. "All right, as long as you don't arrive until tomorrow afternoon." If the weather held, Richard would be playing golf, so spared a spectacle he found unbearably humiliating, that of a stranger's luggage being moved into his home, as though it amounted to occupation by an enemy force.

That evening she waited until he'd finished his second drink. "Oh, by the way, I've let the flat. To a single girl who looks and sounds like an ideal tenant."

Across half the room his wounded glance accused her of a monstrous betrayal. She saw the shameful word that rang in his head: "lodger," and was divided between contrition at the hurt she'd inflicted and exasperation at the self-deceit he practised.

"Do we have to?"

Surely he knew the answer: Even with what she earned, Simon's school-fees paid by her father, his generous birthday and Christmas cheques, with none of Richard's scripts appearing on any of the three channels for nearly two years, the fees for the odd repeats were his sole income. But it was no moment to pierce a hole in the armour of his pride. She left the plea unanswered. "She's a quiet girl, a bit mousy. My guess is that you'll hardly know she's there. I've briefed her on whistling kettles, transistors and the telephone. She'll be working at Benbow's, so she'll be out all day."

"Signed and sealed?"

"Yes. But if I'm wrong about her I can always give her a month's notice to quit."

"When is she moving in?"

"Tomorrow afternoon."

The flesh on his face turned as cold and withdrawn as if it had been chiselled out of stone. "If it's a *fait accompli* there's nothing more to discuss, is there?" he pronounced in a voice that put a million miles of space between them.

As soon as Frank Henning picked Richard up to drive him to the golf club, where they would lunch, Georgina whipped over the top flat with a duster, ran a vacuum over the carpet, checked the inventory and, as a gesture of good-will, picked a bunch of late Peace rose-buds, arranged them in a bowl on the sitting-room window-sill. By 3:30 she had prepared two copies of the tenancy agreement for Miss Jones to sign, a rent book, and added a key to the garage to the ring Miss Patterson had left behind. Perversely, after a perfect autumn morning, the clouds were congealing to form a grey ceiling from which rain was beginning to drip, which meant that either alone or with Frank Henning Richard would be home for an early tea.

When, almost immediately the bell rang, tension eased out of her. With luck Miss Jones would be tucked away on the top floor before Richard returned.

On the step Tom Stokes who ran a mini-cab service made his usual friendly greeting of tipping his peaked cap farther back on his scalp. "Afternoon, Mrs. Latham. Young lady asked me to dump her luggage with you."

"Miss Jones. Yes, I'm expecting her. But where is she?"

"Somewhere half-way up Pennet's Hill, would be my guess. Biking!" He cast his eyes heavenward at the idiocies of the female sex. "Wanted me to load it on the car, but I mean to say you can't, can you! One bike into one mini won't go."

"I see what you mean." By his side rested a medium-size suitcase and a canvas holdall. It struck her as sparse luggage for a long-staying tenant. "If you could heave the case into the hall for me, Tom."

"Carry it upstairs for you if it would be any help."

"It certainly would. Straight up to the top landing." When Tom came down she asked as she tipped him: "Did she pay you in advance?"

"Yes. Just. But this makes it okay. Thank you, Mrs. Latham."

"On the scrounge, Georgie," Frank Henning apologised. "Mollie's in town taking the kids to some sort of cultural exhibition. So the alternatives were wishy-washy tea and stale madeira cake at the club, or an empty house and brewing it for myself. But you're welcome to throw me out if you want."

"As if I would!" Frank Henning was an endearing creature; besides which she prized him as one of Richard's few friends in Larksbridge. "I had an idea you might turn up." She divided her smile between them. "There's a fire in the drawing-room. Go and make yourselves comfortable. Tea coming up."

She had poured three cups when the bell rang. "Sorry. I'm afraid that means I'll have to leave you to look after yourselves while I instal the new tenant in the top flat." Richard's glance studiously avoided meeting hers, every muscle in his body braced against the assault on his privacy.

Miss Jones, supporting the bicycle, wore a beige mackintosh cape, a waterproof jockey cap. Both were streaming with rain.

"Poor you, you're drenched!" Georgina exclaimed. "I wonder if it would be a good idea to put the bicycle to bed first. That way you won't have to get wet a second time."

"Which way do I go?"

"It's a little complicated. I'll come with you the first time. Wait a second while I grab a mac and a head scarf."

A hundred yards past the house there was an arch over an entrance into an alley fenced in by walls that emerged into a lane backing on to the gardens of the three houses. Georgina opened the second pair of double-gates, crossed a tarmac drive, unlocked and flung back the doors of what had originally been a coach-house. Their two cars left wide margins of space at either side. She pointed to a bicycle swathed in polythene that leant against a wall. "Why don't you put yours in front of Simon's?"

Without a word Miss Jones did as instructed, took a duster from the saddle-bag, wiped the handle-bars, mud-guards and saddle.

Georgina locked the garage doors. "We can take the short-cut back to the house through the garden. Not that you could be much wetter than you are."

As they reached the end of the stone path skirting the rockery she saw Richard's face within a few inches of the window. Too late, she realised, it would have been better if she'd warned him about the bicycle.

In the kitchen, with the rain dripping off on to the floor, her face under the tight clamp of the jockey cap, the look of waifishness was emphasised. Yet, a stoical waif, Georgina decided, inviting neither pity nor comfort, her demeanour suggesting a steel-bound self-possession. All at once she was moved by a compulsion to coax a smile out of that young, disciplined face. "If you like you can leave your cape and hat down here, save taking them upstairs to dry, then pick them up when you next go out."

No smile and Miss Jones's reply was no more than perfunctorily polite. "If they won't be in your way."

"Of course not." Georgina peeled the cape off her shoulders in much the same manner as she would have divested Simon of a wet garment. When she'd hung up the dripping clothes, she took a ring containing five labelled keys off the dresser. "One for each of your rooms, the front door, back door and garage. You will find two copies of the tenancy agreement upstairs. You have to sign both, and let me have one copy back. Also your rent book. To keep it straight, I've made it up for the last three weeks in October, and then we can go on from there on the 1st of each month."

Miss Jones took the keys, thanked her. She was, Georgina decided, inordinately poor at communication, as if speech were a penance or so precious she couldn't afford to squander a word. A little clam.

At the bottom of the stairs Georgina paused. "My husband has brought a friend home to tea, so I wonder if you'd excuse me. You know the way, don't you? Your luggage is upstairs. I do hope you'll be comfortable. If there's anything missing, let me know. Oh, as it's Sunday tomorrow and I wasn't sure whether you'd arrive before the shops shut, I left you a pint of milk and half a dozen eggs in the fridg. and a small loaf."

Miss Jones scrabbled for her purse. "How much do I owe you?"

"Oh, don't bother now. Tomorrow will be time enough to settle up. The milkman doesn't call on Sunday. You can leave him a note on Monday if you want him to deliver your milk."

When Helen found the right key for the door of the sitting-room and kitchen, she kicked off her wet shoes, leaned back in one of the feather-cushioned arm-chairs. You can lay down an exact plan, construct in your head a solid edifice of the future, but there remains a small basis of doubt, not of the ultimate objective being achieved, but of a delay so protracted it may spell defeat. Now it was lifted, and as she lay supine in the chair, her flesh and bones were light, the pulse of her heart steady, and all the stored-up energy and purpose a burning radiance within her. With no regard for promises made, she calculated the approximate time required for the preparatory stage, then reached for her shoulder-bag made heavy by the gun, and in her diary counted off the days and enclosed them in an inked square. This was the beginning; the ultimate end a home as near a replica of this as she could contrive within the limits of her capital. A richly embroidered dream that encompassed her every wish. She laid aside the spectacles and allowed herself the luxury of sleep.

When he had seen Frank Henning off, Richard returned to the drawing-room, where Georgina was working on her third *petit-point* seat for the dining-room chairs. Though he acknowledged within himself a wound inflicted in childhood that would never heal, it did nothing to assuage the fires of his resentment. When he'd been six years old, to keep them housed and fed, his widowed mother had been forced to take in lodgers, subjecting her son to the shame of a home to which he was not allowed to invite his school friends. His mother, worn to a permanent state of desperation by cooking, cleaning and laundering for eight assorted males, once she had assured herself he was clean and decently clothed, had literally not a spare second to waste on him. Admittedly, those early years had won him a bonus: an unquenchable determination to excel that had earned him success. Now trapped in the dreary labyrinths of non-success, there padded round his head a terrorising spectre that life was back-tracking, bent on repeating itself. Acclimatised to an overdraft, he could see no reason why it shouldn't be increased to cover the pittance the lodger paid. If there was a clamp-down, all right, they could sell the house, buy a smaller one. Except that Georgina would never sell.

He poured himself a drink, swallowed half of it. "Why did you have to take Miss What's-her-name into the garage?"

"Jones. Helen Jones. She rides a bicycle. I don't want it cluttering up the scullery. Better to house it in the garage."

"So presumably you gave her a key to the garage?"

"Yes."

A hot gush of anger exploded from him. "What check is there that she'll remember to lock it? In addition to two cars, there's a complete set of electrical tools, a couple of spare tyres, gallons of paint, two lawn mowers, and enough valuable oddments to keep a petty thief in luxury for months! Not to mention Simon's bike."

The eruption of that blast of fury was so dreadful in her ears that momentarily she could not lift her eyes from her needle. It raised hideous memories of Dennis and Jason, of a frenetic, mindless fury that was not subject to reason. She had to work hard to quench her fear, persuade herself it simply could not happen a third time. "She seems a responsible young woman, I wouldn't imagine she'd be careless about locking the garage. The bike's to take her to and from Benbow's. But if you're uneasy, I promise that before I go to bed, I'll check that the garage is locked."

"Thanks," he said. "I'll do it myself."

She woke early. As Richard rarely went to bed before one, and thereafter slept heavily, she had no fear of disturbing him by getting out of her bed, half drawing the curtains to admit the light that was beginning to spread itself across the room. Her glance raked through the garden, allotting to it sections of a day that, for once, held no outside commitments. An hour after breakfast before she had to start preparing lunch, another while it was cooking and, with luck, a couple more this afternoon. With the one-day-a-week gardener laid up with sciatica there was the rockery to weed, odd shrubs to prune and maybe, if the wind was in the right direction, a bonfire.

She was turning away, when she heard the lightest barely audible creak of a board on the landing, as though someone was tip-toeing across it. With her own bathroom and kitchen, no post on Sundays, why on earth should Miss Jones be creeping downstairs at 6:45 A.M.?

Or had she imagined the creaking? There was a fitful breeze that tossed the tails of the wisteria across the window-panes and disturbed thc pockets of dried leaves that rustled in crevices on the terrace. And the sound of those delicately treading footsteps—if her ears hadn't deceived her—had ceased. Then, directly below, she heard the key being turned in the lock of the back door. A moment later Miss Jones was walking down the flagged path, a slight, boyish figure in a bottle-green trouser suit, with a briskness that suggested some definite objective ahead.

Mystified, Georgina watched until she disappeared round the coach-house, and then the explanation hit her. Miss Jones was a Catholic, off to early mass.

At four o'clock Georgina was heaving up the stones of the rockery in a last-ditch attempt to defeat her enemy: the fibrous roots of ground-elder, when she heard a step behind her. "Oh, hello, Miss Jones. Sorry to look like a witch, a muddy one too. Everything is still soaked after yesterday's rain." She raked her hair out of her eyes with a gloved hand caked with earth. "Thanks for the cheque and for signing the agreement. I've left the receipted rent book on the hall table and your change from the shopping."

Helen, after years of self-inflicted isolation, found it beyond her to respond to a casual, friendly approach—she'd had no friends on whom to practise. Furthermore, the gains of the day had been off-set by a thrust of harsh reality warning her that though the initial stage was comparatively simple, the later ones demanded infinitely more guile and expertise, plus a precision of execution. As soon as the first stage was complete she must embark on the second. That it was not yet an exact pattern in her head was like being at the mercy of an inner chaos she could not subdue. Even so, the third stage, the beautiful promise, hung in her mind, like treasure to come. As though it were a talisman, she put her hand under the base of her shoulder-bag, felt the weight of the little gun. She found Mrs. Latham's presence an unwelcome distraction. But the smile, the deep calm voice, the mud that streaked her chin, pulled her a fraction out of her inner world. "Thank you for the roses. They're lovely."

"About the last, I'm afraid." Georgina, still smiling, studied the taut face, the blue-green eyes behind the spectacles, found curiosity and concern evenly balanced. Apart from church-going, driving to the coast or pub-crawling, Larksbridge offered no distraction on a Sunday. "Have you friends in Larksbridge?"

Miss Jones's reply was a mute shake of her head, accompanied by a near-visible shrinking, as though a single question had sent her scurrying for the safety of her shell. She turned and hurried towards the house. Georgina watched her, puzzled rather than offended by the abrupt gracelessness. Brought up in a small Yorkshire village, the habit of befriending, even mothering strangers was instinctive. Well, in this case both were unwelcome. Even so, she wished she knew the reason for the girl's pathological shyness.

On Monday morning she automatically opened her eyes and checked her watch when she heard the creaking board on the landing betray that would-be silent departure. Could it be that Miss Jones was a physical fitness enthusiast? Instead of doing a daily dozen—which Georgina herself managed about once a week—did she go pedalling miles on her bike? It was one theory.

Georgina was whisking potatoes for supper when Miss Jones

entered the kitchen. Deliberately she made no attempt to molest her, merely smiled and said hello. When she'd gone Georgina found the word she'd used odd; even so, she was certain it was the correct one.

On Wednesday afternoon when she was driving Mrs. Fennis back from hospital where she had visited her husband, Georgina's eye was caught by the sight of Miss Jones on foot crossing the road a hundred yards ahead.

Tears were washing Mrs. Fennis's cheeks. "But he isn't himself, Mrs. Latham. I swear it, and his breathing is ever so much worse than when he went into hospital, and not a morsel of food has he swallowed. He's going down, I know it."

Certainly Mr. Fennis, suffering from chronic bronchitis, blue-lipped and wheezing, had indeed been an alarming sight. The ward sister, whom Georgina had contacted after she'd deposited Mrs. Fennis by her husband's bed, admitted: "Well, he's not too good, poor old chap, but at least he's not on the critical list. Also, it's too early for the anti-biotics to have had much effect."

"It's partly the hospital atmosphere," Georgina soothed, checking the turning down which Miss Jones had disappeared. "It's always depressing until you become acclimatised to it. Also the special course of drugs he's on take away his appetite. He'll be through with them by the end of the week, and then he should begin to pick up."

While she alternately consoled and commiserated, she was calculating that Miss Jones, to be where she was, must have clocked off from work soon after three, a privilege that wouldn't have pleased Annie. With Mrs. Fennis's cottage half a mile ahead there was no chance of following her. Suddenly, the absurdity—and the sheer effrontery—of the idea hit her. What right had she to check on Miss Jones's movements, even speculate on where she was going?

Mrs. Fennis sobbed: "I keep wondering what's going to happen if . . ."

Georgina lifted one hand from the wheel, squeezed Mrs. Fennis's woolly glove. "Nothing's going to happen, Mrs. Fennis, except that in ten days or a fortnight, he'll be sitting beside me going home, and you'll be waiting on the doorstep to welcome him."

By the time Georgina had got her indoors by a fire, with a cup of tea and some toast by her side, she had decided that Miss Jones was a natural loner; their number was legion, and as one she had a perfect right to have her privacy respected. Tomorrow morning, she swore she wouldn't even glance at her watch when the landing boards creaked under those stealthy footsteps. Just thank heaven they were stealthy!

FOUR

Though it required an effort, Georgina stuck to her resolve, not even allowing her thoughts to pry into Miss Jones's hyper self-sufficiency. When they met in the hall or on the stairs she limited herself to hello and some conventional remark on the weather. Miss Jones's response was good-morning or good-evening, as fitted the time of the day, before she passed on with that inimical look that hid her inner self from sight. But Georgina's eyes betrayed her resolve: they registered that Miss Jones was thinner, her face peakier than when she had first met her on the doorstep, as though she were being consumed by some inner force that would, given time, reduce her to a ghost that would dematerialise into nothingness.

When Richard, without fail, checked the garage each night before he went to bed, he found it locked. That he could not fault Miss Jones as a tenant was, Georgina knew, more a source of irritation to him than relief.

The Jessop wedding reception was on Saturday; on the following Monday Georgina planned to travel to Yorkshire, pay a surprise visit to her father.

When the bride and groom had driven away, Georgina slipped into the kitchen to pay the three domestic science students who'd served drinks and waited at table. Mrs. Jessop, crowned with a hat of purple roses, ran after her. "Georgie, dear, Richard's on the phone. In the library." She kissed Georgina's cheek. "Oh, it's been quite perfect. You're a genius. That salmon mousse was out of this world." She turned to the students. "And you were all marvellous too."

Richard had spent the previous night in town, excused himself from the wedding function on the plea that he didn't know what time he'd arrive home. She'd assumed, with the stoicism she assured herself she'd acquired, he'd spent it with Amanda. Now she wondered whether he'd decided to make a weekend of it. Then, as she lifted the receiver, she knew with an unerring, almost unearthly sense what he was about to say, and that for the rest of her life she would live with a blighting sense that she'd been too late.

"Mrs. Forbes telephoned five minutes ago. She's been trying to get through since ten this morning, but I've only just arrived home. Your father's been taken to hospital. I thought you'd want to travel up tonight instead of waiting until Monday."

"Yes." For a moment that was the only word she could force through her lips. "I'll leave right away. How bad is he?"

"A coronary. Apparently they have to wait for the results of certain tests before they can judge how serious it is."

"I'll be home in ten minutes. Would you look up the late afternoon trains to Bradford? I only know the morning ones."

"I'll have them ready for you."

He'd also dug out her small suitcase, and his car was parked outside the front door. "There's a 5:04 from King's Cross, arriving Bradford a few minutes after nine. I'll drive you to London."

"You don't have to."

"I want to. There's plenty of time and it will cut out the tedious business of taxi-ing between the two main-line stations. While you pack, I'll get you a drink. Tea, coffee, alcohol?"

"Tea, please." She thought how perfectly he reacted to crises apart from those that hinged on his own powers of creation. They lifted him out of himself, revealed a highly perceptive kindness that was only fired by such an emergency. As she raced upstairs Amanda's status in their lives was reduced to that of a distraction: akin to his Saturday's game of golf.

They arrived at King's Cross twenty minutes before the train was due to leave. He guided her into the buffet, ordered scotch for them both. "I could come with you, if it would help."

She shook her head. "Not at this stage. There'll be nothing to do except wait, wheedle the truth out of consultants and doctors." She extracted from her handbag a note she'd scribbled coming up in the car, passed it to him. "Would you phone Lucy? She was taking over from me on Monday for four days, but I'll probably be away longer, and I ought to let her know. That's her number. Mrs. Clownes won't be in until Tuesday. She's not on the telephone but you could slip round and see her if you need her on Monday. That's her address."

"Tuesday will be fine. Anything else?"

"You could mention to Miss Jones I'm away."

He made a grimace of distaste. "I will if I see her, but she isn't around much, is she! Creeps about the place like a scared rabbit. We'd better be moving if we're to find you a corner seat facing the engine in a non-smoker."

In the carriage, he said: "Try not to worry more than you can help. He's a tough old guy."

"I'll telephone you tonight after I've had the hospital report."

She telephoned him from the big room in which she'd pictured herself surprising her father, watching the deep joy bring radiance to his bony, deeply seamed face. "He died an hour before I reached the hospital." That was all she was able to put into words.

"I'm sorry." His voice was gentle. "I'll be up in the morning."

"No." For twenty-four hours she desperately needed to be by herself with no witnesses to whatever grief was about to do to her. "Sunday trains are vile. Wait till Monday. I'll telephone Simon in the morning. I'm afraid he'll be upset. They were very fond of one another. When I know when the funeral will be, I'll see if he wants to come."

Richard drove up, made a diversion to collect Simon who'd been granted two days' leave from school.

Even in those two days which were locked in a cold segment of time, Simon, desolated by the loss of the old man, comforted Georgina. And, as always, when they were transformed from a couple into a trio, life took on a smoother rhythm. Scholastically and at sport Simon was a middle-runner. Except for his burnished copper hair, he was not even good-looking. His single gift was for happiness and for loving, plus an instinctive compassion for any creature less fortunate than himself. "He'd give his head away if someone asked for it," Richard had declared when Simon was five, but uncomplainingly, much as she'd fed the filthy, often alcoholic tramps Simon had brought home.

Sitting before the log-fire on the evening of the funeral, Simon said: "I wish I'd done something to make him proud of me, like Jameson who's just been made captain of the second eleven, or Gladwell who's a dead cert to win the prize for Latin verse."

Richard smiled reassurance. "Your grandfather was proud of you. For instance, the way you handled a fishing rod." Getting up to toss another log on the fire he'd touched his son's shoulder. "You'll do. You may surprise us yet, but if you don't it's okay with me."

"And me," Georgina echoed.

"You're sure it's all right about bringing Nick home for Christmas. He can't fly to Nigeria to be with his parents because he's used up his free air ticket for this year."

Richard said: "I told you, we're looking forward to having him."

"It'll be fun for all of us," Georgina added.

Next morning when she walked with them to the car, Richard said: "Don't tire yourself out. When is Langley coming?"

"Ten o'clock. The main job is sorting through a life-time's accumulation of letters and documents. Nobody but me can cope with them. And there are the possessions he was particularly attached to, like his fishing rods, guns and books. I'd like to distribute them among his friends. Also I must find a few mementoes for Cousin Maude. They were very close when they were young. His death will hit her hard. That done, I can hand over the house to Langley, and he'll deal with the estate agents and moving the furniture to the salesroom. We haven't room for much, but there are a few pieces I'd like. The small Queen Anne writing desk in Mother's room, and the brass-handled tea-chest. And half a dozen pictures, his Lowry for instance. I'll ask Langley to have them crated and sent on."

"Well, take care of yourself." He kissed her mouth, and Simon hugged her, pleading: "Do what Dad says, Mum."

It took her until Sunday to strip the stone house in which she had been born of its personal and private treasures. On Monday, with a copy of her father's will tucked into her handbag, she travelled back to Larksbridge.

It wasn't until they were drinking their after-dinner coffee that she asked with a sharp prick of concern: "How is Miss Jones getting along? Have you seen much of her?"

He chose his words with precision, relishing each one of them. "Your Miss Jones has turned out to be a snooper and a potential thief."

"A thief! Are you serious?"

"One morning last week, Thursday, I think, that blasted dog next door woke me up soon after six and I went downstairs to make tea. The door of your den was open and I caught her in the act of opening your centre drawer." He laughed cynically. "Gave her the shock of her life. I thought she was going to faint."

"How did she explain it?"

"How indeed! She mumbled some dumb excuse that she'd lost her pen and wanted to borrow one of yours. Then she vanished in one of her terrified mouse-acts and except in the distance, I haven't set eyes on her since. I suggest when you've finished your coffee, you check your desk to make sure she didn't help herself to anything she fancied."

There were three deep drawers on either side of the desk, a shallow one in the centre. She riffled through the not-too-tidy contents that were a miscellaneous hoard reaching back over years: cheque-book stubs, balls of string, receipts, shopping lists, old diaries, and snapshots that had never been put into albums. The pretty enamelled brooch-watch of her mother's with a broken pin she'd intended taking for repair and forgotten, was in its kid box, also the emergency £5 note she kept handy in case she ran out of cash after the bank closed. And the last two letters from her father.

The web of grief had the effect of dulling her reactions. It seemed a fuss about nothing, based on Richard's neurotic prejudice at having a stranger literally tucked away under the roof. With a suspicion that he had deliberately blown up a tiny incident to incriminate Miss Jones, she couldn't work up any indignation.

Collecting a letter from Simon that must have arrived that morning, she returned to the drawing-room. "I can't find anything missing. Anyway, I don't keep any valuables in my desk."

Incensement still smouldering, his look accused her of not trying very hard. He waited until she'd read Simon's letter, then shot at her: "Do we have to keep her . . . well, now?"

Part of the answer lay in her father's will, a copy of which she handed to him. It was probably, she thought, the shortest will on record, simply: "I leave all my worldly possessions to my beloved daughter Georgina Anne Latham." When he looked across at her, she explained: "He bought Mrs. Forbes an annuity six months ago, before I saw him in the summer." Which meant he'd foreseen at some not too distant date his death, and shielded her from the knowledge. "There is a Trust Fund for Simon, and he'd already made gifts to charities with which he'd been associated." Knowing Richard was poised on a knife-edge of suspense she didn't list them, but gave him the single fact he yearned to know. "After death duties, Langley's approximate estimate of the value of the estate is £75,000. So the answer is no, we don't *have* to keep her."

His smile was a brilliant expression of tumultuous relief. "So you'll get rid of her quick?"

"Under the terms of the agreement, she is entitled to a calendar month's notice. On the 1st of November."

"She's invalidated any such agreement." He stared at her in a deep, pounding rage. "Are you saying, for God's sake, that she'll be creeping and prying round the house for nearly another five weeks?"

"Yes."

He bent forward, speaking so fast his words ran into one another. "Listen, Georgie, please. We could fix up those rooms for Simon. Put another bed in the bedroom, turn it into a flat for him with room for a visitor. He and Nick free to make all the din and mess they want, and blessedly outlawed from our bathroom. For a Christmas present we could buy him his own stereo. Georgie, don't you see!"

"Yes, of course I do. It's a marvellous idea. I'm all for it. But even if she stays on until the end of November, you'll still have nearly a month to get the job done before Simon and Nick arrive for Christmas. Richard, I am not prepared to throw her out without the notice to which she is legally entitled."

He raged, his voice shooting out of control. "I've told you, she forfeited that right by spying, meddling with our property. I can't for the life of me understand why you took her in! To put it mildly, she's not normal."

She said, trying to placate him: "I admit she's neurotically shy . . ."

"Not shy," he interrupted. "A sneak thief!"

For a second she experienced that curdle of fear that never quite died in her, the dread of the past repeating itself: Richard possessed by a crescendo of hate for someone who existed merely on the periphery of his life, when false and violent images multiplied themselves in his brain, drove him to . . . She lopped off the memory. Not again, she thought, it couldn't happen again.

With an immense effort, she forced herself to laugh. "You know what you're doing, don't you? Writing her into a script. You're brilliant at women with a past, unmasked five minutes before the credits roll! Remember *The Soul of Comfort?* That nail-biting thriller about the devoted companion who bludgeoned her mistress to death and then did a masterly cover-up?"

The play was three years back in time. It was painful from this distance to reflect on the acclaim it had brought him. He jumped to his feet, resentment stiffening his body. "Take my advice and get that screwy little bitch out of this house fast."

"I'll ask her to go, but with a month's notice." She forced a smile. "I thought I'd take off for Cousin Maude's tomorrow morning, spend Tuesday and Wednesday nights with her, drive home on Thursday. In her letter she sounded well, pretty down. Will that be all right with you?"

"Sure, give Miss Jones another opportunity to go through your drawers. I suggest you either lock up your jewellery or take it with you."

On Tuesday morning Georgina was not woken by the stealthy progress across the creaking board. But when she was collecting a few items from the refrigerator to take to Cousin Maude, she felt rather than heard a presence behind her. On the threshold of the kitchen Miss Jones was standing poker-stiff.

"Hello, Miss Jones. How are you?"

The girl's look was one of such blanched intensity that Georgina thought: Oh, no, she's going to complain that Richard accused her of stealing! But what Miss Jones actually said in a small, hesitant voice was: "I wanted to tell you how sorry I am that your father died."

Georgina breathed again, but as she still found sympathy hard to take, worse to acknowledge gracefully, she said: "Thank you. I'll miss him very much," and to break one of those stifling silences into which Miss Jones withdrew, asked: "Do you still have your parents?"

"No. They are both dead."

Georgina did not speak, but gave the girl a look of mingled concern and enquiry, inviting her confidence. It was, she reflected, like painstakingly coaxing a small child or a wild animal in whom faith has been destroyed to trust again. But Miss Jones's lids were lowered to shield her eyes, and she was on the point of turning away.

On an impulse Georgina reached for the only bait at hand, a pottery jar. "Do you happen to like *paté?* Up in the North where I come from they call it potted meat."

Miss Jones looked startled, as though it were a trick question. In her primmest tone she said: "I've never tasted it."

Georgina grinned. "Why not try it and see if you like it? It's good spread on toast, or if you don't want to bother making toast you can make a sandwich with it."

Miss Jones mutely shook her head, not sure whether she was being offered a present or an act of charity and prepared to accept neither, to have her self-made sanctuary breached. For nearly a week she had lived with a vague sense of fright in that she was running late on her time-table, encountering more obstacles than she had anticipated, one particularly that had so far proved insurmountable. In her dreams she overcame it effortlessly; in reality it was a block that imposed upon her an agonising delay before she could move on to the second stage. "No, thank you."

"Oh, come on," Georgina wheedled. "I make pounds of it.

You're not robbing me or anyone else. I'd love you to try it and tell me what you think of it. See, it's only a midget pot." Coaxingly, she extended her arm. "Please."

Completely at a loss to frame a blank refusal, Miss Jones reluctantly accepted it, gazed at the eau-de-nil pottery jar. Its colour, the smoothness of its shape within her palm, Mrs. Latham's voice and smile did nothing to lower the barrier between her and the whole human race, but she was conscious of the pleasantness of the unexpected. It brought a sketch of a smile to her mouth. "All right," she said as though taking a momentous decision. "If you're sure you can spare it. And I won't forget to return the pot."

Relishing her microscopic triumph, Georgina did a quick check on her supplies for the Clarkson cocktail party, then packed into a wicker basket the mementoes she had selected from her father's house for Cousin Maude: a carriage clock, a mohair shawl that had been her mother's, and a small Queen Anne silver tea-pot.

At breakfast Richard made no further reference to Miss Jones. His mood was one of deep inward brooding, of being set at a far distance from the events around him. As the aged with their petty, repulsive infirmities offended him—as though he saw in them an advance vision of himself—he did not mention Cousin Maude, as much as send her a perfunctory greeting. It was doubtful if he took in details of the food Georgina had laid on for him.

The kiss with which he brushed her cheek as she said goodbye, promising to be home by tea-time on Thursday, was no more than an abstracted gesture. For the first thirty miles she was accompanied by a tension of unease, a feeling that it might have been wiser to put off the visit to Cousin Maude for a day or two, an impulse to turn back. Then determinedly she shook it off. She had written ahead giving the old lady the date of her visit. To have postponed it would have disappointed and upset her.

She was later in arriving home on Thursday than she'd planned. After six. The house was in darkness. On the hall table was an envelope addressed in Richard's handwriting, inside it a scrawled note. "Tony telephoned, asked me to go up and see him. Should be back some time Friday. R."

Relief like an unexpected warmth expanded within her. Tony was not a man to waste a second of his valuable time on a failing writer. It followed there must at least be a prospect of a script in the offing.

She went to bed at ten, only remembering when she lay there that she hadn't checked that the garage door was locked, though Miss Jones's bicycle had not been visible when she drove in. She listened to the rain drumming on the windowpanes, told herself that Miss Jones must be home by now, and as she listened became aware of the trancelike silence within the house, so absolute that it was impossible to believe another mortal shared it with her. Not a footstep, not a gurgle of plumbing. Lying waiting for sleep, the small self-sufficient figure that stubbornly refused to move outside the orbit of her self-imposed isolation, was the pivot of her thoughts. What made a girl in her mid-twenties, which Georgina estimated Miss Jones to be, recoil from every-day human contacts? Hurt, grievous hurt was the only answer she could come up with before she fell asleep.

On Friday morning she seized the opportunity to vacuum and dust Richard's study, a room from which Mrs. Clownes was barred since she'd burnt the contents of a waste-paper basket into which he'd accidentally dropped a couple of pages of a script on which he'd been working. The vacuuming completed, the overflowing ashtrays emptied, the windows opened, she embarked on dusting and polishing, stamping in her mind the exact placing of any object she temporarily moved.

She pulled out the deep side-drawer, looked inside. Two bottles of whisky, one full, one half empty, and a glass that had been used but not washed so many times that it was stained.

She put it back, not daring to rinse it out. She wondered if a resurgence of success—even one thread of hope of it—would lessen his craving for drink, the sipping between sentences in which he had no faith, and which he typed out of compulsion rather than inspiration. But even if it did, there was Amanda. And there was Simon.

She was in the middle of drinking a cup of coffee at the kitchen table, when Annie Marchant telephoned. "I'd be much obliged, Mrs. Latham, if you could inform me when Miss Jones proposes to be back at her desk. I presume she's sick. If she is, she must abide by the firm's rules. A doctor's certificate to be provided after an absence of two days. There was a printed slip to that effect inside her first week's pay packet, so she can't plead ignorance."

"Sick!" Georgina repeated, alarm flooding her as she imagined Miss Jones lying ill and helpless on her bed, incapable—or unwilling, knowing Miss Jones—of summoning help.

"Annie, I'd no idea. I've been away for a couple of days visiting an elderly cousin. I only got back last evening. Can you hang on while I go up and see what's wrong with her?"

"If it's not too much trouble, I'd rather you rang me back, Mrs. Latham. Mr. Benbow has a trade delegation arriving from Holland in half an hour and there are some revisions to be made on the price lists."

Both doors were locked. Georgina rattled the knobs, rapped on the panelling. There was no response. She even bent her ear to the bedroom keyhole, expecting what? Heavy bronchial breathing seemed the likeliest guess. Dead silence, not even the rustle of a sheet as a sick, feverish girl tossed and turned.

She raced downstairs and grabbed her duplicate set of keys. There was no sick girl lying in bed. Bed and room were in immaculate order. In her initial flying examination of the four rooms she could not see that a single possession had been added to her furniture and fittings. Then, under the flap of one of the chairs, she spied a pair of needles stabbed through a ball of dark blue wool. Less than half an inch completed of what, from its width, suggested an amateurish attempt at a scarf.

She examined the four rooms a second time, each as unmarked by Miss Jones's tenancy as though she had never taken the flat. She found it incredible that a human being had lived there and except for a ball of wool and a pair of knitting needles left no faintest imprint of herself.

Baffled, alarm beginning to twitch at her nerve-ends, she flew downstairs to telephone Annie. "You're saying," Annie retorted, cutting corners, "that she's done a moonlight flit, left owing you rent?"

"No," Georgina corrected firmly. "Her rent is paid until the end of the month. The last time I saw her was on Tuesday morning. And you say she wasn't at the office on Wednesday, Thursday, or this morning?"

"That's right. And not the decency to telephone. Not that that surprises me."

Georgina made a determined attempt to deal positively with a situation that baffled her. "It could be that she's been involved in an accident. I'll phone the hospitals and let you know if I get any news."

"My guess is that you'll be wasting your time, Mrs. Latham. Wasn't a stayer, that girl, never had her mind on her work."

Annie's prophecy was proved correct. Neither the General Hospital in town, nor the one ten miles distant had admitted a Miss Helen Jones. The local police station had no record of any accident involving a young woman of that name.

Already late for delivering Mrs. Paine's jig-saw puzzle she ran to the garage. The bicycle! Surely a key factor? It wasn't propped against the wall, so wherever she'd gone, Miss Jones had taken it with her. No part of Georgina was prepared to accept the theory that Miss Jones had walked out of the flat without giving her an hour's warning—not unless the remoteness in which she sealed herself had suddenly exploded, induced some species of mental collapse. The triangular face with its over-large glasses, the heavy frame of hair imprinted itself on the windscreen as far as Mrs. Paine's door. A withdrawn secret face but one which, for all its determined non-acceptance of friendliness, had touched off in her a liking and warmth. And creeping up on her was a suspicion that at some key moment she'd been blind, and on its heels a stiletto thrust of guilt, though for what, since Miss Jones had repulsed her overtures, she couldn't imagine.

After leaving Mrs. Paine, she hurried through her shopping, promising herself that she'd find the bicycle propped up against the garage wall, some perfectly reasonable explanation on hand for Miss Jones's absence. The bicycle wasn't there, but Richard's car was. He walked down the path to meet her. Acutely sensitive as she was to his mercurial moods, with her mind absorbed in Miss Jones, it took her a few seconds to become aware of the serenity merged with hope that lay on his face, as though a smoothing hand had passed over it.

He kissed her cheek, encircled her shoulders with his arm. "Well, how was Cousin Maude?"

"Herself. Coping magnificently, but ageing terribly, mainly through loneliness. She misses Stuart badly. I counted a dozen photographs of him in her tiny sitting-room. But she was delighted to see me and to have what she called her last presents from Dada. Did you see Tony?"

"I had dinner with him last night. There's a vacant slot in a drama series Anglia is putting on in the New Year. Apparently, on the off chance he sent them a story-line I did a year ago. They're inclined to like it. Anyway, the series editor wants a full treatment by today week."

The transformation, as though the humiliations of the last two years had been expunged from memory, moved her. "Do you know him?"

"No," he said blithely. "I'm a new broom, and itching to get to work. Make me a sandwich and I'll take it upstairs. But first, let's have a drink."

She debated whether to break his concentration that was beginning to cohere, or wait, and decided now was better than the evening when he'd be physically and mentally played out.

"Something rather odd has happened. Miss Jones has disappeared. She hasn't shown up at Benbow's since Tuesday. Annie assumed she was sick and telephoned me. That's how I knew. The last time I saw her was in the kitchen on Tuesday morning. Did you come in contact with her while I was at Cousin Maude's?"

He considered briefly, then shook his head. "Had you told her that you wanted her to move out?"

"No. I intended to have a word with her on Monday."

He said with the crisp satisfaction of one who has been proved right: "You can't say I didn't warn you that she was a little crook. Up to no good in this house or any other. Taking her in was an error of judgment on your part. You do sometimes make them, darling! Stems from this obsession of yours for taking the whole world under your wing. You were duped, my soft-hearted do-gooder, duped. What do you imagine she was up to riding round in the dusk, often in the dark? When you've found the answer to that, if you ever do, you may solve the mystery of her disappearance."

"It may not have been a voluntary disappearance. She could have met with an accident."

"Oh, I doubt that."

"Then what is your theory?"

"There are several. The most likely that she was a scout for a gang of house-breakers. Pros. Information on antiques, silver, jewellery, pictures in likely houses, plus detailed time-tables of owners' exits and entrances, number of staff employed, efficiency of locks, position of safes and visibility of premises from the road. Provided the burglars have all the gen beforehand, 95 per cent of the risk is eliminated. So it's worth paying handsomely to have the joint expertly cased. Miss Jones was obviously lining her pockets and now, with the job completed, she's moved out to operate on a new territory." He raised his glass, grinned. "Meanwhile we should congratulate ourselves that she has vanished from our lives and that I in particular am never likely to set eyes on that creepy midget again."

His state of mild euphoria had set his imagination running wild. Fine, when he got upstairs to his typewriter, but an infeasible and ridiculous theory when applied to Miss Jones. She curbed her inclination to protest, said mildly: "That sounds a bit over-dramatic to me. I'll go and make you a sandwich. Coffee?"

"Yes, please. A big pot."

FIVE

Georgina bit into a sandwich, found she couldn't swallow it, and consigned it to the rubbish bin. She climbed the stairs to the top floor. Now she was over the initial shock of Annie's announcement she would make a calmer and more detailed search of the flat.

She started in the kitchen. Marooned in the gleaming interior of the fridg. was a single egg, the remains of a half-pint carton of milk and a knob of margarine wrapped in a screw of greaseproof paper. On a shelf to itself stood the eau-de-nil *paté* jar, empty and washed out. The vegetable drawer and freezing compartment were also empty. In the built-in cupboard there was a canister containing a few ounces of tea, a midget jar of instant coffee, and in the bread-bin the heel of a brown loaf. The meagreness of the food, at bare subsistence level, raised a harrowing picture of Miss Jones going hungry to bed in her house! She jerked herself back to sanity. Benbow's ran an excellent staff canteen and she could have eaten her evening meal out. Maybe, too, she just hated to cook.

She walked into the sitting-room. Every drawer she opened was empty, not so much as a crease or a smudge of dust on the lining-paper. No letters, newspapers, not so much as a ball-point pen. A room in which the occupant had made no effort to establish herself, but behaved like a guest who had alighted in a hotel for a single night.

With a slow tread that kept pace with her pondering, she went into the bedroom, flung open the doors of the built-in wardrobe and was struck by a tingle of shock, as she heard herself swallow her breath. Staring down at her from a shelf was a wig on a block, the blank-eyed, rough shape of the chalk-white polystyrene face mocking her with its sly, blind-eyed smirk. For heaven's sake, wigs, hair-pieces were commonplace! Lucy, for example, possessed a whole range. It was simply that she didn't associate the excessively neat Miss Jones with minor vanities. She pulled the wig off the block, turned it inside out to read the stitched-in label, from which she learned it was fashioned out of genuine human hair and had been purchased from a store in Oxford Street. Had Miss Jones owned two identical wigs—which Lucy maintained was essential—or only one which she had left behind her? Gone out with her own hair stuffed inside the jockey cap? Robbed of the wig, Georgina found herself thrown by not being able to picture how Miss Jones would look without it—what colour her own hair was. She fitted the wig back on the block, picked out each coat-hanger in turn.

The green trouser suit, a blue gabardine coat, a short camelhair jacket, a brown and cream check dress, a tweed skirt and toning blouse—the mackintosh cape and the navy suit were missing. All the garments were as lightly worn as though they'd come straight from a shop rail. On a shelf she found a small pile of underwear: one bra, two pairs of panties, two pairs of tights and a shortie nightdress, shabby and faded by laundering. The contrast between upper and under garments puzzled her. Like the food, it suggested a miserliness towards what wasn't on show, a minor act of deceit. On a higher shelf was the jockey cap which suggested, with her hair uncovered, she'd been wearing a wig. Alongside it were the suitcase and kit-bag. On the floor of the wardrobe was a single pair of shoes. No dressing-gown, no slippers.

On the dressing-table lay a modest range of chain-store cosmetics, a blue plastic hair brush and a comb, clean but with three broken teeth. In the top drawer she found a small box of tissues and a nail file. In the second a japanned cash-box, locked. Georgina weighed it in her hand, moved it from side to side. There was no answering rattle. Not large enough for documents, it presumably contained letters, perhaps paper money —if it contained anything at all. She replaced it, and opened the last drawer. Empty. In the bathroom, tucked away under a towel, was a faded flannel. On the middle shelf of the cabinet a tooth-brush, a tube of paste and a sliver of soap. That the total sum of one human being's possessions could be so meagre suddenly became painful to her.

She returned to the sitting-room, sat down in the arm-chair and deliberately, as her father had taught her when she was a teen-ager, relaxed one limb at a time, drove the tremors of fear, the beating concern from her mind, in the hope that, left unburdened it would, of its own accord, straighten out the mystifying facts and cohere them into an acceptable pattern.

The reverse happened. The freed mind composed for her a gallery of pictures conveying desolation and desperation, of loneliness so insupportable that she jumped from the chair, found herself shaking her head in furious denial at the shocking word that rang in her ears: suicide.

She was rescued by the hands of her watch. She was due to pay two visits, both urgent. To young Millie Andrews, widowed three months ago and still so cemented in grief and loneliness she was in danger of mental collapse. To Mr. Sparling, a semi-crippled despot who, if his middle-aged spinster daughter wasn't to crack under the strain of an eighteen-hour nursing day, must be coaxed temporarily into an Old People's Home while Ethel took a holiday.

Millie showed a slight improvement in that she summoned up sufficient energy to make two cups of tea, to speak her husband's name twice and to say, as Georgina left: "I do try, Mrs. Latham. I try ever so hard."

"I know you do, Millie. A job really would help. I'll drop in next week and we'll talk about it, just run over the possibilities, don't worry."

Mr. Sparling stonewalled. She left Ethel, guilt-ridden at abandoning her father, yet threatening hysterically to walk out on him. Georgina promised to contact Dr. Lewis, persuade him to add the weight of his authority. Privately she doubted whether he'd be prepared to do so. Dr. Lewis was young, monstrously overworked, with such a meagre ration of spare time he'd no inclination to expend any of it on middle-aged spinsters suffering from stress. She could hear him demanding: "What about my stress, three emergency night calls in a row, two from young mothers who panicked because their babies yelled. The third a simple case of gluttony, not an appendix about to burst. I wish to God someone would remember there are only twenty-four hours in my day as well as everyone else's."

Her route home took her past the police station. A few yards farther on she drew into the kerb. She examined the idea that had flashed unprompted into her mind, decided it was not only realistic and sensible but obligatory in that no one else, certainly not Annie, would embark on it.

The young constable behind the counter enquired, parrot-fashion: "Yes, madam, what can I do for you?"

Fair-skinned, tight curling blond hair, he looked like a well-scrubbed seventeen-year-old—the corny joke about policemen growing younger as a sure sign that you were ageing rang sourly in her ears. "I'm Mrs. Latham. I'd like to see a senior officer if he can spare a moment."

She'd offended him: she was sorry but unrepentant.

"Inspector Donaldson is engaged. I've no idea how long he'll be tied up. If you don't mind waiting. It's up to you."

"Thank you, I will." She retreated to a row of plastic-backed chairs set against the wall. The waiting-time lasted thirty-five minutes.

A woman constable escorted her to an office in which there were two empty desks and a third from behind which Inspector Donaldson made a perfunctory gesture of rising. A slim, straight-backed thirty-five-year-old, with sharp-edged features and a glance that barely touched her, he emitted a brisk professionalism. "Now what's the trouble," he consulted a note on his desk, added: "Mrs. Latham?"

"I wish to report that a tenant of mine, a young girl, is missing."

"Missing?" His glance evinced no concern, merely requested clarification.

"She's disappeared, vanished, leaving her clothes and all her belongings behind her."

"But not, I hope," he said with a slight rise of interest, "taking any of yours with her?"

She said with emphasis: "She was not a thief."

His glance expressed mounting boredom. "Perhaps you'd better give me the particulars. To start with her name, and when she went missing." He opened a notebook, took down the facts she supplied, then summed up: "Two days, three counting today. Not long, is it? Young people go to rave-ups, smoke pot, or worse, bed down for the night, maybe two nights and wander back to base when they're capable of making the effort. How old was she?"

"I don't know precisely. At a guess about twenty-five."

He gave her a belittling smile. "Old enough to take care of herself, wouldn't you say? How long had she been your tenant?"

"Three weeks."

"Left owing you rent, did she?"

"No. Her rent is paid to the end of the month."

"Who else lives in the house besides you and . . ." He had to consult the notebook to remind himself of the name. "Helen Jones?"

"My husband, and in the holidays my son who is away at boarding-school."

He checked the dates. "You say you last saw her on Tuesday morning. Did your husband have any contact with her after then?"

"No. He's as mystified as I am."

He leaned back in his swivel chair, his look cool and unpromising. "Mrs. Latham, what exactly are you asking us to do?"

"I've checked the hospitals. They have no record of admitting her. I also telephoned you, and was told that no young woman answering to her description had been involved in any accident. But that doesn't mean she's not in need of help. For instance, she could be suffering from amnesia and . . ."

"Mrs. Latham," he interrupted in the tone of one hanging on to his patience, "over 90 per cent of the cases of amnesia are self-induced, a home-made hidey-hole to escape from trouble. But the psychic boys are pretty clever at spotting the phonies. I wouldn't put too much faith in that theory if I were you. Genuine amnesia is pretty rare unless it's induced by drugs."

"But she's missing. So shouldn't she be added to your Missing Persons list?"

He sighed. "According to you, she's around twenty-five, a woman, not some kid in her teens in moral danger, to be hauled back to Mum and Dad. And teen-agers, together with absconding husbands, are our prime concern. Get the kids back home, locate the husbands and lean on them to contribute to the support of the wives and children they've deserted." He paused. "And it's not as though you were a relative, is it? You can't know her all that well after such a short acquaintance. It could be as simple as she accepted a lift from a handsome young man in an even handsomer car, is now snogged up in his flat somewhere, and wouldn't thank you for breaking up the party."

"She wasn't the type. Officer, I feel very strongly that some effort should be made to discover what has happened to her. Are you prepared to take any action or not?"

Georgina could, when she chose, which was rarely, make herself formidable; she did so now, holding the pose until, with an off-hand shrug, he conceded with audible reluctance: "I suppose we could make some enquiries. Give me a description of her."

"About 5 feet 2 inches, slightly built. She wore glasses with dark tortoise-shell rims, and from the clothes she left behind I'm pretty sure she was wearing a beige mackintosh cape over a plain navy suit with a white blouse. She had short, light brown hair with a half-fringe, but I'm afraid that's not much help because she wore a wig, and I've no idea whether it matched her real hair or was a different colour. She left one wig on a block in her wardrobe, but if you wear a wig all the time, you need two, so I'd guess she was wearing one, but I can't swear to it."

His glance accused her of deliberately adding complications. "Where did she live before she took your flat?"

"In London. Fulham." She added the address.

"Probably back there. Anything else you can add?"

There was: the nature of Helen Jones, her pathological shyness, a clenching up as though if she were accidentally touched she would shrink physically. But as she doubted whether, even if she could convey it, the nature and behaviour of Miss Jones would light a glimmer of interest in Inspector Donaldson, she said: "No," then added: "She rode a bicycle. That's disappeared too." So much for his theory that Miss Jones had been picked up by a kerb-crawling Bentley!

For the first time since she'd entered the room, he concentrated his gaze on her person, assessed her status. "And you're absolutely sure she didn't help herself to any valuables, your jewellery, for instance? I take it you've checked?"

"Yes. Nothing is missing." She rose. "Thank you for your time, Inspector."

The dart of sarcasm by-passed him. "I'll pass on the information to Missing Persons but, as I said, I can't hold out too much hope that we'll run her to ground, especially if she doesn't wish to be found. After all, provided she didn't remove any of your property, cheat you out of rent, she hasn't committed any indictable offence. But if anything turns up, I'll telephone you."

She sat in the car, made an effort to subdue the fumes of her anger. All right, she'd been given the brush-off by a police officer who'd as good as accused her of over-reaction and panic. She granted the police were way under strength and the force of his argument that missing teen-agers and absconding husbands had priority. Even so . . . When she was calm what remained was that drag at the heart, a feeling that the near-mute girl had been vulnerable to something or someone, but to what or whom?

By the time she'd put the car away, it was dark, and she had to thread her way carefully down the unlit garden in the dark. Richard threw open the kitchen door, showering her with light. "Where on earth have you been? I was beginning to have visions of you engaged in another round of fisticuffs with the bailiffs!"

It was a reference to her involvement in the forcible eviction of a couple in their mid-eighties. It had taken place three years ago, but he had never forgotten or forgiven the spread of pictures in the local paper.

She laughed. "I don't make a habit of arguing with bailiffs! I've never set eyes on one from that day to this. It's filet steak and a fruit pie that's already made for supper. I'll have it on the table in half an hour."

He took her coat to hang up in the hall, and then followed her into the kitchen. "What did keep you out this late?"

"It seemed a sensible idea to report Miss Jones missing to the police. They kept me hanging about for over half an hour."

She turned from switching on the grill to see rage contort his features, re-drawing them into an ugly shape. "I don't believe it. I just don't believe that even you . . ." Rendered speechless by anger, he shook his head in silent denunciation.

He was tired, nerves taut after a six-hour session of work the success of which was crucial to him, even so the outburst came as a shock. "Richard, she's been missing for three days. She took nothing but the clothes she stood up in and her bicycle. For all we know she could have skidded on a wet road, been pitched into a ditch, be lying there unable to summon help. In the circumstances I decided the police should be told."

"Are you out of your mind? She did a bunk. When she'd got whatever she'd come for she left. She was a snooper and in all probability a thief. That's the beginning and the end of the saga of your Miss Jones."

In an effort to slake that self-destructive rage, she said placatingly: "Then she'll have a record, and the police will turn it up."

He laughed scorn in her face. "Jones! You don't imagine for a moment that's her real name, do you!"

"Thousands of people are called Jones."

"But not *your* Miss Jones." For a moment his lips shook, then he steadied them, demanded: "Well, now you've fulfilled your duty as a citizen, informed the police, what action do they propose to take?"

"Very little would be my guess. A police officer took down her description, promised to add her name to the Missing Persons list. He certainly didn't hold out much hope of finding her."

His anger flew higher. "That doesn't mean we shan't have a squad of them crawling all over the house." His voice broke into a paean of anguish. "Georgie, how could you? You know I've got exactly six days to get the treatment done . . ."

She put her hand on his arm. "Darling, that won't happen. I swear it. If by a remote chance one policeman turns up, I'll keep him out of your hair. Anyway, what would be the point of them coming here? Miss Jones came to no harm in this house, but she may well have done somewhere else. And I refuse to write off a human being as though she were an animal that had strayed."

He looked at her in silence, his breath so heavy that his chest moved. The emotion that ruled him was no longer pure rage. Another element was added, one she couldn't define. "Richard," she urged, "I do promise you that you won't be involved."

He pulled his arm from her touch, and in the second he turned away, the emotion defined itself: fear, sheer animal fear. After dinner, he went straight up to his study. As she piled the silver and china into the dishwasher, she felt a sliver of ice lodge itself in her consciousness. She would not admit to herself what had caused it to form.

Across the Lewises' crowded drawing-room Georgina spied Joe Benbow edging towards her. When she had first met him he was in his forties, he'd looked sixty, now, having reached that age, he appeared to fit it comfortably. Long before sideburns had become fashionable, he had sported a luxuriant growth of Victorian-style mutton-chop whiskers. Stubby and heavily fleshed, with a high-starched collar and a gold watch-chain draped across his middle, there was a Dickensian air about him.

In character, his first words were a compliment. "Dear Georgina, a very pleasing sight, as always. A long frock makes even a plain woman look elegant, but on you it's positively ravishing."

"Thank you, dear Joe. Blatant flattery, but none the less a nice boost to my ego."

"Richard not here?"

"No. He's working on a script with a tight deadline so he had to cry off."

He sipped from his glass, confirmed that hers was full. "That girl, who lived on your top floor, Annie reports she not only left the office without so much as an hour's notice, but without telling you she was moving out. What do you make of it?"

"I'm completely at a loss. Because I was frightened she might have been involved in an accident I reported her missing to the police. So far they haven't come through with any news. Frankly, I'm completely baffled."

He eyed her shrewdly. "And bothered. I don't wonder." He helped himself to a chicken vol-au-vent from a passing tray. "She was strictly Annie's department, but I caught stray glimpses of her when I passed through the general office and on a couple of occasions when we were rushed, she did a batch of letters for me. Remarkable, not a spelling mistake or a rub-out. In fact she was so exceptionally efficient it made me question what she was doing working as a typist in a small outfit in Larksbridge when she could have earned three times the salary as a top West End secretary."

"Her last address was in London. But London's changed, Joe. People are fleeing from the rat race, the traffic jams and the astronomical cost of keeping a roof over their heads. She's quite likely to have been one of them."

He stared obliquely across the room, seemingly absorbed in a picture on a distant wall, then collected himself, pinned his shrewd blue eyes on hers. "You know how she struck me? Like someone playing a part. Know what I mean?"

"I'm not sure." She remembered the wig. "You mean she adopted some form of disguise?"

"I haven't got that far. Only an idea, maybe nothing in it. More likely she was too good to last. Ah, there's Alice making her private signal to me that she's stood on her feet long enough. Anyway, if Miss Jones should contact you, get her address so that Annie can post on her insurance cards and the two days' salary that is due to her."

Lying in bed, gazing at the needle-thin streak of moonlight that pierced the narrow gap in the curtains, she pondered on Joe's summing-up. The wig, the glasses a disguise? It could be. Equally the glasses could have been prescription lenses, the wig no more than a fancy for a change of hair style. The nag that kept her awake was the dread that two floors above her bulging caterer's size deep-freeze Miss Jones had gone to bed hungry. Finally, as a sedative she lured herself into sleep by planning the tea menu for the Friends in Need monthly committee meeting the next afternoon.

It was strictly informal, with no minutes though each of the six members brought along a jotting pad for notes. Its purpose was an exchange of views, a pooling of advice on the queries arising from the two-way system of communication they'd established with the Social Services. Friends in Need coaxed or coerced them into speedier action; the overworked officials offloaded borderline cases on them.

Members arrived promptly at two, had an early tea and departed in time to collect children from school. At 2:15, the five of them disposed about the drawing-room, Georgina asked Lucy: "What about Madeleine Hurst? Isn't she coming?"

"I ran into her on Friday and reminded her. Oh, there's the bell; maybe that's her."

Madeleine Hurst launched into profuse and over-elaborate apologies for her lateness. Georgina, murmuring that it didn't matter, had a distinct feeling her misgivings had been justified. Madeleine Hurst's nerves were strung as taut as fiddle-strings. Words, barely coherent, tumbled out of her mouth. Since one of their prime duties was to act as a listening post, she wondered if Madeleine Hurst was capable of bridling her tongue for long enough to allow the aged and inarticulate space to air their griefs and deadliest fears. Noting her dyed strawberry-blonde hair so scented with spray it shouted she had come direct from the hairdresser's, her too formal town suit with a mink collar, Georgina's initial doubts doubled. Among the casually dressed members, including Lucy in slacks and a polo-necked sweater sprawled on the hearth, she looked as out of place as a visiting lady mayoress. The smile that seemed glued to her mouth was tense with strain and before she had even sat down in the chair Georgina pulled forward, she was reaching inside her handbag for cigarettes.

While Georgina paid attention to the discussion in which Madeleine Hurst joined more frequently than became an inexperienced newcomer, a part of her mind was scrupulously totting up a balance sheet, taking into account her prejudice against brittle high-voiced women, so basically unsure that they had to dominate any scene of which they were part. The elderly and house-bound had no complaint against an over-dressed visitor; rather the reverse; the smartness was taken as a compliment to themselves. And though many needed to unload their woes, there were others who would relish having an hour moving at a snail's pace whiled away by a flow of chat. Catching a mute beseeching look from Lucy, she smiled, cocked an ironic eyebrow.

It was when Madeleine Hurst interrupted Mrs. Stokes in mid-sentence that Prue, the most senior member in age, quenched her with an authoritative: "If you would be kind enough to allow me to finish, Mrs. Hurst. Thank you."

As Prue continued, Madeleine Hurst's face and throat were first suffused with scarlet, then, as the fire drained away, a sickly pallor. She leaned towards Georgina, whispered: "I'm sorry to be a nuisance, but could I use your bathroom?"

"Of course. The cloakroom is down the hall, on the right."

Georgina turned round to check if her footsteps were steady, and then gave her attention to Prue. After a show of hands, she announced: "Tea, I think."

The eatables were spread about and she was returning to the drawing-room with the tea when she heard a sound on the stairs. Madeleine Hurst, one foot poised in mid-air, was half-way down.

Georgina's reaction was one of mild exasperation. "The cloakroom is downstairs. I did explain."

The initial acute embarrassment had been expunged from Madeleine Hurst's face before she reached the stair-foot, and the switched-on smile was back in its place. "Oh, I do apologise. The truth is that I felt faint, and I must have been too muzzy to take in your directions. I had to find some cold water to throw over my face before I passed out."

"How do you feel now?" Georgina was aware she should have sounded more concerned but since Madeleine Hurst's make-up had not been dabbed with water, much less splashed, she felt disinclined to make the effort.

"Fine. A bug struck me down over the weekend. I thought I was through with it, but it seems I was over-optimistic."

"Would you like to go home straight away, or have a cup of tea first?"

"Oh, a cup of tea would be heaven."

Lucy stayed on after the others left. "Come on, out with it. I don't want you to choke on your righteous indignation. Admit it, you can't stand her."

"I'm not terribly enthusiastic. What I most resent is that she spent ten minutes prowling round my bedroom and bathroom, despite my having directed her to the cloakroom on the ground floor."

Lucy grimaced. "Ugh, sneaky! But admit it, if they can get away with it, most women can't resist poking round other women's houses. The first time I came here, while your back was turned, I opened the kitchen door, took a peek. Look, I'm not excusing her. I don't know why, but obviously she worked herself into a fine old state of nerves this afternoon; probably felt herself on approval and that always brings out the worst in anyone, me included. Are you going to throw her out?"

"No. With your promise to keep an eye on her, I'll give her a month. If she's no good we'll soon hear from the customers! Anyway, she's only got a small case-load, and most of it involves car ferrying."

Richard's mood when he came downstairs at six, was one of limpid satisfaction that acted as a tranquilliser on mind and nerves. One more day, he told Georgina, and he'd be through with the treatment. On Thursday he would deliver it to Tony.

Instead of gulping his drink, he savoured it slowly, and when a silence fell between them, he cast her a look that glowed with pleasurable anticipation. "I'll probably get a few days' gap before the series editor okays the treatment and I can get going on the final script. I'd like to use them to take measurements upstairs for the extra shelving and flat-tops, order the hardboard, check through colour charts and wallpaper samples. That way, I can put the order in and have the stuff delivered by the time I'm through with the script. Oh, and I'll need an extra outlet point for the stereo. Charlie Rawlins will fix that." His smile was akin to one used on a child to coax it to see reason. "In law Miss Jones's tenancy has run out. So what about clearing the rooms, stowing her belongings in the box-room?"

The half-suppressed urgency in his voice set up a warning thrum. It was the first time Miss Jones's name had crossed his lips since the evening Georgina had returned from seeing Inspector Donaldson—who had not contacted her. Also the finality signified by the removal of Miss Jones's clothes from the flat struck her as a callous act in that it offered a choice between two stark alternatives: Miss Jones had either, under some extreme pressure, abandoned the flat and her wardrobe, or she had come to some harm.

She said in a casual voice: "I think we should give it a few days longer."

"Georgie!" He feigned patience. "What's the point of dilly-dallying? She is not coming back."

"How do you know?" She stared into his face. "How can you be so absolutely sure?" And in an instant she knew his answer was immensely important. "Richard, how do you know?"

"Know!" A little of his patience slipped out of control. "Of course I know. Anyone would, except you who have an inborn bias towards the odd bods in society. Come on, darling, admit it. That butter-ball that serves you as a heart has let you down, and not for the first time. Accept the fact that you're never likely to set eyes on Miss Jones again, and let me get ahead with fixing up the flat for Simon."

She'd got an answer that was no answer at all. She had to choose—operating her mental balances—between further protest which would crack his temper, and peace, a joint peace between the two of them, and a private peace for him while he finished the treatment, endured the nerve-cracking suspense of its acceptance—or non-acceptance.

She gave her assent grudgingly, guiltily, as though she were betraying herself and, more important, Miss Jones. "All right. There isn't much to do. I'll pack her clothes in the suitcase and kit-bag, put them in the boxroom, and then if you're wrong and I'm right, they'll be there for her when she comes back."

His laugh was joyous, either with triumph or relief. "Not a hope, darling. Not a vestige of it."

SIX

The next morning, submerging feeling under a skin of stoicism, armed with swathes of tissue paper, Georgina packed Miss Jones's clothes into the suitcase, the wig-block and toilet articles into the hold-all. It was only when she opened the third drawer of the dressing-table that she saw the cash-box. She balanced it in the palm of her hand, undecided as to what she should do with it. Bury it in the kit-bag? Force the lock? She found both alternatives unpalatable. It took her a while to reach a decision: since there was a possibility the cash-box might contain a letter or a paper that would provide the name and address of a relative or a friend, she would pack it up and leave it with a note at the police station for Inspector Donaldson. The forcing of a lock by officialdom seemed a lesser violation of privacy than if she'd attempted it herself.

She put the suitcase and kit-bag in the boxroom, protected them against possible damp with thick brown paper and then she went on a final pilgrimage through the four rooms, discovered she'd overlooked the few rows of knitting with the needles stabbed through the ball of blue wool. Reluctant to unlock the boxroom, unzip the kit-bag, she left it where it was, half under a cushion on the chair. At the door of the sitting-room, she looked back, wondered if, remodelled to a schoolboy's taste, the memory of Miss Jones would gradually cease to haunt the flat, and so no longer remain a drag on her conscience.

She wrote the explanatory note, packed and labelled the cash-box and delivered it to a girl police-cadet—which probably amounted to dropping it in a hollow tree!

The Golf Club Committee, of which Richard was a member, met on the first Wednesday of the month, and meant them having their evening meal early. When she took him a cup of tea at four, not knowing how near he was to the end of the treatment, she enquired if he intended going.

"Sure!" He gazed at her with an innocent wonderment she hadn't seen on his face for a couple of years, pointed to the stapled typed sheets. "What do you know! The old brain box still works, is as crafty as ever. I'll deliver it to Tony tomorrow and if he exerts a bit of pressure, I may be lucky and get a final decision before the weekend."

"Clever! Oh, very clever."

He nodded and laughed in a way that touched her heart. "You'll stay overnight at Max's?"

His glance dropped to the stapled sheets. "Thursday night definitely and if there's a hope of a decision, Friday too."

The blindingly beautiful figure of Amanda materialised in her imagination. Even if Richard's career took an upward leap, would such a ravishing sexual prize be willing to bind herself in marriage to a forty-two-year-old, hamstrung with an overdraft, whose only source of income depended upon the inventiveness of his brain? Or was she just playing him along as a human stepping-stone in her own career? Guess, she thought, guess and guess again. Any of them could be right, all of them wrong. Sometimes she longed to know. Others she didn't. It was an ambivalence in herself she despised. "By the way, I've cleared out the top flat. Not that there was much to do. So you can get Charlie in to fix the electric point any time you want."

"Fine. I'll telephone him now."

"After dinner I'll be out too. The Merediths are throwing a

party to celebrate their twenty-fifth wedding anniversary, and she needs his moral support before she commits herself to the menu. So I promised I'd look in on them about half-past eight. But I should be back before you're home."

To her surprise the expression of distaste that normally gripped his face when she mentioned what, with a derogatory emphasis, he termed her "cooking," was absent. A second later she realised he hadn't heard her.

"Georgie, I appreciate you've got a sentimental hang-up about that damned girl. That, well, you feel responsible for her. God knows why, but you do, don't you?"

"Yes. Apart from the fact I don't care for real-life mysteries when they happen under my own roof, I'm old enough to have been her mother. And she had no parents of her own, she told me so. Consequently I'm not prepared to write her off, not care a hoot what has become of her."

His smile was tolerant, forbearing. "The exact reaction you'd have to any normal girl living under your roof: to cosset, befriend, act as a stand-in foster-mother." He leaned towards her, the timbre of his voice suddenly urgent. "But Miss Jones wasn't normal, Georgie. The last thing in the world she wanted was to be mothered, petted, even talked to." He repeated remorselessly: "Georgie, she was not normal. No criminals ever are, basically. And if I'm wrong and she wasn't a criminal or a potential one, she was a nut-case. So what about putting her clean out of your mind?"

"How can you be sure she was either a criminal or a nutcase? Or, for that matter, that we'll never see her again? How can you be so damned positive? What proof have you got? You can't have exchanged more than half a dozen sentences with her . . . not much more than good-night or good-morning."

"Except twice I found her snooping round the house. I told you about her hanging over your desk. Well, there was another time when I caught her in the drawing-room that first evening you spent with Cousin Maude."

For a moment her heart emptied and a second later began to thud in slow beats of panic, as appalled, she counted up the eight days she'd been in Yorkshire, plus the two she'd spent with Cousin Maude. Ten blank days and ten blank nights on which nothing was recorded except that Richard had twice surprised Miss Jones snooping round the house. She'd assumed that Richard and Miss Jones had, by mutual consent, avoided one another. Only now, when it was too late, did she accept that she had under-reacted to Richard's paranoiac resentment of the girl's presence in the house. A tiny segment of her mind reproduced a horror picture of that volcano of hate erupting. . . . No, she thought, no, and stamped it out. She quoted Lucy. "You wouldn't know, but women can't resist looking round other women's houses. That's all she was doing. She stole nothing."

"Maybe," he retorted, "she didn't find what she was looking for!" He leaned back in his typing chair, spoke cajolingly. "Georgie, things are at last moving our way. Good times ahead. Your father's money, for you, *not* me; the treatment, please heaven, accepted, and making over the flat for Simon. Do you have to spoil it?"

She said nothing, thinking how blinkered he was against love to suppose she preferred her father's money to having him alive.

He went on: "I'm not going to nag you about it, but you could even give up cooking for other people's parties."

"I shouldn't," she said softly, "nag, I mean."

He grinned and it brought back the youth to his face. "Okay, but for God's sake accept that we've seen the last of that little creep! Don't keep the issue on the boil, behave like a mother-hen who's lost her only chick."

"I'll try," she answered, without much confidence that she'd keep her promise. Anyway, why should she? Hadn't she a human right to know what had happened to the girl!

As Georgina drove home along the back-lane, later than she'd anticipated, she automatically checked the windows for lights that would signal whether Richard was home. The blast of astonishment was such that she jammed her foot on the brake, shot forward in her seat-belt. Lights in Miss Jones's sitting-room! A huge uprush of relief surged through her, making nonsense of Richard's cloak and dagger theories, and banishing for ever that black, hideous moment when a single word had tolled like a knell in her head. Miss Jones was home, explanations for her absence only minutes ahead. She'd probably gone on a visit. Why not! She was under no obligation to notify them when she left the house. Then, on the turn of a second, joy and relief were swept away as she saw Miss Jones returning to a flat picked clean of her belongings and, for all she knew, thrown out. Dispossessed! She drove the car into the empty garage and then ran, tripping once to her knees in a desperate urgency to reassure the girl, to drag the suitcase and kit-bag out of the boxroom as positive proof that nothing had been moved from the house. In her haste she left her pocket torch in the car, and it took her an age to locate the back door lock, insert the key.

Switching on lights as she ran, she called: "Miss Jones. Miss Jones . . ."

The top floor was shadowy, only the upflow of light from the lower landing revealing the open door to the sitting-room and kitchen. Breath pumping in her lungs, she leant against the door-frame, lifted her finger to the switch. The room was precisely as she'd left it at three o'clock except that she had closed and locked the door. The action of doing so was lodged firm in her memory. Methodically and minutely she examined the four rooms. A reproduction of a Fantin-Latour flower print was slightly askew on the sitting-room wall. The third drawer in the dressing-table in which she'd found the cash-box was open an inch. Nothing else had been disturbed. No possession of hers had been stolen; except for the knitting there were none of

Miss Jones's to steal. And the needles and wool had not been moved. In the boxroom Miss Jones's shrouded suitcase and kit-bag stood where Georgina had placed them.

Had she mistaken the lights on the top floor for those of the Buchanan house next door, used as living quarters by an elderly housekeeper? No, the angle was wrong. In winter the birch tree by the wall threw a lacy pattern over the Buchanans' top windows, while hers were unimpeded by shadow. Besides, there was the open door she had left locked, the not-quite shut drawer. She tried to calculate the time-interval between her driving into the garage and entry into the house—not many minutes, but enough to alert the intruder, enable him to make his escape through the front door.

Eyes downbent she trod the stairs. Faintly marked with hers and Richard's footprints, there was no hope that any others would be markedly discernible. But on the third tread from the bottom she picked up a flake of mud so dry that it crumbled to dust in her fingers. Miss Jones creeping back into the house when she had made sure it was empty? But why? She pressed her powers of invention to the limit but no reason that was remotely logical came to her mind. Then someone else? A burglar? She ran through the downstairs rooms making a lightning check. She could find no object missing, no means of a forced entry.

Richard came through from the kitchen. "You forgot to switch on the garden lights." He rubbed his shin. "I damn nearly broke my ankle on the corner of the rockery. Why you have to turn the garden into an obstacle course I can't imagine." His tone was less querulous than his words.

"Sorry. I forgot."

The muted, disassociated voice caught his attention. "Something up?"

She found herself suspended between the truth and a lie. Congenial company, plus a drinking session had temporarily released him from the prisonlike thraldom of his inner world.

He'd fall asleep the instant his head touched the pillow. Catapult him back into the subject of Miss Jones and there was a high risk that the near-paranoia would erupt and the state that passed for peace between them would be destroyed. The system of checks and balances by which her life was ruled, as though she kept a pair of scales in her head, exasperated her. Nonetheless, she took the easy way out. "The Merediths were a bit tiresome. She opts for silver foliage and white roses, Scotch salmon for the main course. He's for autumn tints and beef stroganoff. In the end I came away giving them three days to make up their minds."

"Ah, well," he said good-naturedly, "if you will get yourself involved in other people's bean-feasts! I'm going up. Coming?"

"In a minute. I forgot to take a casserole I'll need out of the deep freeze."

When he'd disappeared round the curve in the stairs, she checked the front door. It was locked, the mechanism of the new locks fitted a year ago was guaranteed burglar-proof, so they had got out of the habit of bolting it. Tonight she did and the back door. One fact stood stark clear in her mind. Somewhere outside in the dark was a man or a woman who possessed a ring of keys that would admit him or her to the house.

Lying awake in the heightened state of consciousness that attends sleeplessness, she found it oddly out of character that Richard had never once raised the question of Miss Jones's keys. Keys she had lost, that had been stolen from her, or keys that had never left her possession?

On Thursday morning, after Richard had left, Mrs. Clownes arrived ten minutes early, gloated: "So I wasn't wrong about that young miss, was I? Stood out a mile she was up to no good. Your trouble, Mrs. Latham, if you'll pardon my saying so, is that you're much too easily taken in."

"I don't mind your saying so, even though I don't agree with . . ."

Mrs. Clownes broke in: "I expect now she's done a bunk

you'd like me to give the top flat a good turn out, let some fresh air into it?"

"I'd rather you turned out the drawing-room and my den." She decided the source of Mrs. Clownes's information was a contact with one of Benbow's cleaners.

Confirming her guess, Mrs. Clownes ran on: "Miss Marchant has checked all the books but except for twenty pence missing from the petty-cash she can't find she pinched anything, but it's early days."

Georgina edged backwards. It was either that or diversionary tactics, and those she must reserve for the eleven o'clock cup of coffee that she drank with Mrs. Clownes, who counted it one of her perks to be entertained, waited upon; left to reach for as much as the sugar bowl, she sulked.

Facing her across the table, Georgina struck first. "How's Samantha these days?" Samantha was Mrs. Clownes's youngest who for a year had attended ballet classes, while her mother had indulged in an ecstatic vision of her dancing on the stage at Covent Garden with "that Russian young man Samantha is wild about." When that dream faded, Samantha opted condescendingly to fill in an application form to be an air-hostess. Currently she was a check-out girl in a Larksbridge supermarket, who zombie-eyed punched keys and only with the utmost reluctance consented to put frozen food into bags.

Mrs. Clownes bridled with pleasure. "Oh, didn't I tell you, she's got a new feller, an army man! Guardsman type. Comes from an old army family. Well, you can't beat the Services, can you!"

"Indeed not," Georgina murmured, relieved that all she need do was sip her coffee, look rapt as Mrs. Clownes's phantasies built themselves to the pinnacle of a church wedding, complete with a guard-of-honour with crossed-swords, bearskins and a few of the trappings that graced royal weddings.

On Friday afternoon the telephone was ringing when she arrived home from a visit to Millie Andrews.

The male voice was low-toned, formally courteous. "Mrs. Latham? This is Det. Inspector Cornford of Larksbridge C.I.D. I wonder if it would be possible for you to look in and see me about Helen Jones? I understand she was a tenant of yours. Also you left a cash-box belonging to her addressed to Inspector Donaldson. As I am now in charge of the investigation it would be very helpful if we could have a chat."

"Have you found her?"

"I'm afraid not."

"Of course I'll come. What time would you suggest?"

"As soon as possible."

She glanced at her watch: 3:30. Richard had not telephoned so she had no indication of whether he'd be home tonight or stay on until tomorrow. Say an hour with the inspector and she'd be home before 5, which was about the earliest he'd be likely to arrive. In any case the fire of her impatience would stomach no delay. "I can be with you in ten minutes."

"That's fine. Thank you, Mrs. Latham."

He occupied a small office made dim by a window that faced a brick wall. His raincoat had fallen from the coat-rack to a heap on the floor, presumably because the collar tape had snapped. She guessed his age at fifty, though he might be younger; the circle of tight-curled grey hair surrounding the bald pate was ageing. He stood up, leant across the desk to shake her hand and revealed himself as paunchy and overweight, wearing a suit that should have been handed in at a dry-cleaner's weeks ago. His thick-fleshed, jowly face was wholly bland, except for bright hazel eyes reduced to slits by down-drooping eyelids, which shrewdly examined her as he murmured: "Good of you to come."

"I'm desperately anxious to know what has happened to her. You say you've no idea where she is?"

"I'm afraid not." He opened a thick file. "Tell me, Mrs. Latham, does the name Susan Bates mean anything to you? Have you any recollection of reading it in the press around five and a half years ago?"

"No. Is there some link between her and Miss Jones?"

"They were the same girl." He lifted the cash-box from a drawer, opened it and handed her a slip of paper. "Her birth certificate. Susan Jane Bates, daughter of Alfred and Elizabeth Bates, born in Loughbridge 21st September 1949, now twenty-six years old. She changed her name after it had been spread in headlines across every newspaper in this country and a good many others."

Her voice surprised her by its total lack of emotion.

"What had she done?"

"Nothing. Susan wasn't the guilty party. She was the victim. Her six months' old son was stolen from her, never found. The file on the kidnapping of Simon Bates is still open."

Simon! She recalled the intent, almost worshipping gaze Miss Jones had fastened on the pastel drawing. "I see." And that was an exact description of her reaction. The revelation made by Cornford temporarily blinded her to his presence, the seedy, box-like office. Suddenly, spectacularly, the opaqueness in which Miss Jones had imprisoned herself dissolved. "Yes, I see," she repeated, and to give herself a short breathing space, side-tracked from the main issue. "I'm trying to remember. It must have been that spring my son was ill. When he was well enough we went to Corfu for a month. While we were there we didn't see an English newspaper, and our transistor radio broke down."

"The boy was kidnapped between the 2nd and 6th March. By the end of the month the Bates baby had been wiped out of the headlines, was reduced to a few paragraphs on the inside pages."

She handed him back the birth certificate, breathed: "Could you . . ."

"Give you the facts? Yes, of course, at least a summary of them. Susan Bates was an only child. Her father held a medium-grade job in Local Government. Both her parents were Plymouth Brethren, a strict chapel sect, the members of which do not mix with outsiders and maintain a rigid code of moral conduct. Susan's childhood, while not unhappy in the sense she was deprived, was lonely, in that she was forbidden pleasures and activities that children take for granted. She was never, for instance allowed to go to a cinema or, when she was older, to visit a dance-hall. When she left school she was employed as a typist in the Town Hall.

"On the morning of her eighteenth birthday, instead of going to work, she walked to the station and took a train to London." He paused, retrieved a bitten-stemmed pipe from an ashtray, made a gesture with it. "Would my pipe bother you?"

"No," she said, impatient of the delay.

"She was a well-trained, efficient typist and experienced no difficulty in finding employment, though in fact she rarely stayed in the same job for more than six months. She lived in Earl's Court in a succession of bed-sitting rooms. Every time she changed her address she notified her parents, presumably from a sense of duty inculcated in childhood. Consequently when the tragedy occurred the police were able to contact her. A skidding tanker crashed into their terrace house, totally demolished it. Mr. Bates was killed instantly; Mrs. Bates survived twenty-four hours. After the funeral Susan went straight back to London. The house was leased, but if she had engaged a solicitor she would undoubtedly have been entitled to compensation from the company who owned the tanker for the wrecked furniture, maybe even some payment for the loss of her parents. However, she chose to take no such steps."

"Had she *no* friends?"

"One. Just one. A girl of her own age who lived in the same street. Sandra Murphy. By then she had married and moved away. We were never able to trace her, and she never contacted us." He picked a small leatherette book from the cash-box. "Susan had £2,000 to her credit in a building society into which she made monthly payments." He pointed to a bank statement. "There is £500 in her current account and £1,000 on deposit, making a total of £3,500. To accumulate that amount she must have skimped on everything but the bare essentials of living." He paused, as though inviting comment from her.

She stayed silent, seeing the midget jar of coffee, the nut of margarine, the heel of a loaf. Miss Jones had denied herself food, yet paid a rent that must have made a large hole in her salary from Benbow's. A front? Just as the top clothes had been new, the underwear worn and washed out of shape. But a front for what?

When she did not speak, he went on: "A year after the death of her parents Susan became pregnant. So far as I know she never divulged the name of the father to anyone; certainly not to us. She was not a promiscuous girl. There must have been an attachment on her side, if not on his. Maybe he was married, went back to his wife, without even being aware that Susan was pregnant. It could even be simpler: that she wanted a child." He lifted a second birth certificate from the cash-box. "Her son was registered in her name. Simon John Bates, born the 10th October, 1969. Three months previously she had moved out of London to Croydon and was later admitted to the maternity wing of a local hospital. In the next bed was a Mrs. Kathleen Jackson who, a few days before, had given birth to a still-born son. She was forty years of age, with a history of miscarriages and unlikely, in the opinion of the doctors, to bear another child. She was not unnaturally suffering from severe depression, and her mental state was giving rise to anxiety. It was her husband, Anthony Jackson who, as he sat beside his wife, became aware that the girl alongside received no visitors, wore no wedding ring and was the only patient in the ward without fruit or flowers. He supplied them, coaxed his wife to make friends with the girl—maybe he confided his hope to her; we don't know. Certainly in the last week she was in the maternity wing, Mrs. Jackson's mental health improved dramatically.

"The Jacksons lived in comfortable circumstances in Carshalton, a few miles from Croydon. When both women left hospital, Mr. and Mrs. Jackson maintained close contact with Susan. When Simon was three months old, Susan had to return to work. Mrs. Jackson pleaded to be allowed to look after him in the day-time but Susan, not one to accept favours, refused. She found a job, put him in a day-nursery. But he lost weight, developed a succession of small ailments and finally, distressed at his deteriorating condition, she agreed that Mrs. Jackson should care for him during the day-time. Mrs. Jackson drove to Croydon, collected Simon before Susan left for her office and returned him after she arrived home. Then, in early February, there were heavy snowfalls resulting in treacherous icy roads. The Jacksons suggested, to save the child being moved around in the late evening, when he would be better in his cot, they should keep him during the week and he should spend the weekends with his mother. Susan reluctantly accepted the offer. Thereafter, for three weeks Mrs. Jackson collected Simon on Monday morning. On Friday evening, after she left her office, Susan went by bus to Carshalton, and Mr. Jackson drove her and Simon home.

"On Friday the 6th March when she arrived at the Jacksons' house she found it in darkness, no one at home. She waited for an hour and then, desperate, she threw a brick through a window, forced an entry. The sound of the breaking glass alerted the next door neighbour, who telephoned the police.

"At this point I should explain that at that time I was attached to the local C.I.D. and later that evening I entered the house, met Susan. It soon emerged as a straight case of kidnapping. The Jacksons had taken nothing from the house, except maybe a change of clothes. Next day we found a pile of ash in the garden. When this was analysed it told us that, before leaving, they had burnt a large collection of documents, letters, account books, records and also photographic prints and colour slides. That left us without a photograph of either of them. We never traced any relatives. Mr. Jackson, who was due a period of leave, had not been at the City offices of the firm of computer manufacturers by whom he was employed for a week. Neighbours supplied us with contradictory statements as to when the Jacksons had last been seen. The latest date for Wednesday morning.

"Their car was found abandoned in a parking area near Dover, suggesting they had made for the continent. The attendant remembered it had been there for some days, but couldn't swear how many. We appealed to passengers on Channel ferries and hovercraft who had seen any couple resembling the Jacksons with a young baby, to come forward, if only for purposes of elimination."

He leaned back in his chair, gazed into the smoke spiralling from his pipe. "Simon Bates's kidnapping received maximum coverage in the newspapers and on television. Police, not only in this country, but in Europe, later Australia, America were alerted. Interpol were asked to help. To use a cliché, Mrs. Latham, no stone was left unturned to run to earth the baby and its kidnappers. Once we believed we'd found the Jacksons in Hawaii, another time in Auckland. We were mistaken. We never found them." He tapped the folder with his pipe-stem. "We're still looking."

"And Miss Jones . . . I mean Susan?"

"After she had recovered from the initial shock, her behaviour was exemplary." He gave a wry smile that chided himself. "Older, wiser, or at least more experienced, I realise that she was suffering from second-degree shock that is often more severe than the initial one. There were even some officers working on the case who suspected her of lack of feeling for the child. That, of course, was not so. The calm was a cover-up. One theory she refused to entertain: that the child had been taken out of the country. She insisted that Mrs. Jackson had a phobia about flying, had hated the only foreign holiday her husband had persuaded her to take, and sworn she'd never go abroad again. Well, we never proved her wrong or right. Over the previous months, Anthony Jackson had been selling out his investments, life-insurance, closing his bank account, so we were able to estimate he'd accumulated a capital sum of somewhere in the region of ten thousand pounds, either in money or negotiable portable valuables such as jewellery and rare stamps. The house, furniture, clothing, all personal possessions they abandoned. One of the newspapers dubbed it "The Marie Celeste house."

"Hardly a day passed when I or one of my superiors was not in contact with Susan. Then, two months after Simon was kidnapped she walked into the station and demanded to see me. I was out; she had to wait over an hour before I returned." He paused, sucked on his pipe-stem and riveted his gaze at a point beyond her head. "I recall her face as she made her announcement. Except for the colour of her lips it was pale, absolutely rigid. She said she no longer had any confidence in our ability to find her son. We were entangled in red tape and files; we had spread our net too wide, so that the chances of our catching the Jacksons were nil. From now on she proposed to search for Simon herself and, to use her precise words, 'we needn't bother any more.' Of course she had no authority to dictate to me or my superiors. It made no difference whether she retained any faith in the police or not. The search would continue. I told her so. I doubt if she heard me.

"All our efforts to trace her failed. She had moved from her lodgings, leaving no forwarding address. The first news we had of her from that day to this was when Inspector Donaldson, who vaguely remembered the case, handed over to me the cash-box you deposited with him."

The tension of listening had left her bones aching; her brain spinning with questions most of which cancelled one another out; reduced her to a state of semi-stupor. Then like a rocket the truth blazed in her. "She was looking for him in Larksbridge. She'd found him."

He said pedantically: "It's one theory."

"What other one is there?"

"There's always more than one." He studied a typed sheet in the file. "I have here the dates of Susan's arrival at and departure from 6, St. Stephen's Piece. Bare bones. Could you put a bit of flesh on them? For example, the opinion you formed of her habits, behaviour. In fact, anything at all about her that would be helpful."

She collected in her mind and passed on to him, in as coherent a pattern as she was capable of, Miss Jones's comings and goings, the self-imposed isolation, the evasion of any contact that could be avoided. "Sometimes she left the house as early as 6 A.M., and often she wouldn't return until after dark. Isn't that proof she was looking for the boy, knew where he was?"

His nod was so vague that it neither confirmed nor denied her suggestion. "Now I wonder, Mrs. Latham, if you would allow me to see the flat Susan occupied?"

She'd given Richard a promise, but Inspector Cornford could hardly be described as a horde of policemen! She glanced at her watch: 4:15, said quickly before he could sense her hesitation: "Yes, of course. When would you like to come?"

Without replying he took a colour photograph from the file, handed it to her. "Would you recognise that as your Miss Jones?"

Fair, shoulder-length hair, with a centre parting above a high brow, thin hair that hung in separate strands, the eyes without the glasses revealed as wider-spaced than the ones she had known. The delicately formed nose, the set mouth and the stalk-like white throat were the only familiar features. "No, not unless I heard her voice. The wig, the glasses . . ." She shook her head, handed back the print.

"I thought so. That means I'll have to beg another favour, your co-operation in building up a photo-kit picture of her, which we can circulate. In the hope that you'd agree, I laid on the man who specialises in them. Shouldn't take too long. And then, if I may, I'll come and look over the flat."

She hadn't counted on the delay, but it was too late to protest.

The composition of the picture took three-quarters of an hour. When the policeman had thanked her, another one met her in the corridor, gave her a message. Detective-Inspector Cornford had been unexpectedly called out of the station, but he hoped to be at 6, St. Stephen's Piece, within half an hour.

SEVEN

Inspector Cornford moved in a leisurely pondering manner round the top floor, stopping occasionally as though to commit some particular detail to memory. When his task was completed he gave Georgina a commending nod. "A very charming flat if I may say so."

She unlocked the boxroom, indicated the suitcase and kitbag. "Would you like to examine them?"

"I'll send someone round to collect them in the morning. Would it be too much trouble if I asked to look over the rest of the house?"

"No, of course not."

He paused on the threshold of each room until she said: "This is my husband's study." Then he walked forward, easing his pear-shaped body between Richard's desk and a filing cabinet to the window, and stared at the garden which, except for the glow from a single lamp in the lane, was shrouded in dusk.

Downstairs, he opened the back door, took a second look into the darkness, and then followed her as she opened the other doors. When they reached the drawing-room, the drinks table was directly in view. Partly out of basic courtesy, partly because his opening of the back door had triggered off a memory that had been temporarily eclipsed by the afternoon's events, she asked: "Inspector, won't you have a drink before you go?"

"No, I don't think . . ." He changed his mind. "Thank you, a glass of sherry would be very acceptable."

She took the worn, stained Burberry, draped it over a hanger in the hall. As she handed him his sherry, he asked: "And your husband, Mrs. Latham, where is he?"

"At a script conference in London. That's his job: television scripts. He writes them at home, but the debates and decisions take place in London. He may be back tonight, or not until tomorrow."

He gave her that look of slightly hooded consideration with which she was becoming familiar. "Mrs. Latham, the flat, indeed the whole house, is completely out of character as a base for the Susan I knew. Would you tell me what rent you charged her?"

She named the amount. He appeared to do a sum in his head. "After tax deductions that would account for a large proportion of her salary at Benbow's." He sipped delicately at his sherry. "Her clothes, could you give me an idea of their quality? I mean the price range. Cheap or moderately expensive?"

"Neither. Middle-grade. On the conservative side. Skirts to her knees; serviceable clothes that would last through a couple of seasons, maybe more." Since a policewoman would presumably examine the contents of the suitcase and kit-bag, she made no mention of the pathetic pile of shabby underwear.

"When I knew her, her clothes appeared to have been bought from jumble-sales. Except as an essential covering they meant nothing to her. It's my experience that people don't basically change in five and a half years. That wig . . ."

"It was a disguise," Georgina burst out. "And probably the glasses. She'd found him, or believed she had, and for that she needed to make herself unrecognisable. Inspector, what other explanation is there?"

Ignoring the question, he reached in his pocket for his pipe, thought better of it. "Simon Bates is now six. By law, forced to attend school. In Larksbridge there are four private kindergartens, three state primary schools, six more in villages within a five-mile radius of the town. We're checking the registers, investigating every case of a child being absent from sickness or any other reason within the last three weeks. The kidnappers of Simon Bates worked for months to perfect their plans, sacrificed their home, tore up roots, to possess a child. Such a couple, even five and a half years later, aren't likely to leave him unguarded, to be snatched back by his mother."

She said, she hoped reasonably: "If it had happened they'd hardly have been likely to report it to the police, would they?"

"No. But young children have friends. There are also neighbours . . ."

His slowness of approach began to exasperate her. "If the neighbours had queried his absence, they could have said he had been sent to stay with relatives."

"Indeed yes. But there is one fact we have to bear in mind: Susan was a compulsive bolter."

"A what?"

For the first time the smile on his jowled face expressed genuine amusement. "Ah, I see I've used an archaic word. I mean time and again she upped stakes and vanished. Turned her back on the past, made a fresh start: new lodgings, new job. It had become a deeply ingrained, almost a compulsive habit." He set down his empty sherry glass. "That was most acceptable. Now I've kept you long enough. . . ."

"Inspector," she broke in, "there was an incident I haven't mentioned. On Wednesday evening both my husband and I were out separately, and when I drove into the garage, about ten, I saw lights in the sitting-room of the top flat. I assumed Miss Jones had returned. She hadn't. The flat was empty, in darkness. But someone had been there; I knew because that afternoon I had locked the sitting-room door and it was ajar."

He said, totally alert: "A break-in?"

"No. Definitely not. Not a sign of it. Whoever it was must have used Miss Jones's keys. Hearing the car driving into the garage they'd know that I'd come in through the back door, which gave them time to make their get-away through the front. One drawer that I'd shut was open, as though they'd been searching for something. But there was nothing for them to find. I'd stripped the flat earlier in the day, packed her clothes and put them where I showed you, in the boxroom."

"Where was your husband? Was he home?"

"No. He came in later." She paused, slightly embarrassed by the admission. "Actually, I didn't tell him. He'd been working under pressure on a treatment for a script with a deadline. It would have upset and worried him when he urgently needed a good night's rest."

His glance lay on her for a moment, the eyes bright and searching between the drooping lids. "And it didn't occur to you to report it to the police."

"It didn't cross my mind. Nothing was missing."

He brooded for a moment. "It would be helpful if you'd jot down the date, exact time of entry and any detail that comes back to your mind, and hand it to the constable who'll collect Miss Jones's luggage in the morning. And I'd advise you to have the locks changed. In the circumstances it is a sensible precaution to take."

As he rose, she heard the kitchen door bang, and couldn't for the life of her think how she'd missed the sound of the car driving into the garage. In the frantic hope that she could dispose of Inspector Cornford in the wink of an eye, she held out her hand.

He had moved one pace forward, and she was at his shoulder when the drawing-room door, left ajar, was thrown wide by the thrust of Richard's palm. In the crook of his arm was a bottle swathed in white tissue-paper, its gold-foil cork arresting her eye like a semaphored message: the treatment had been accepted. Richard's minutely-observing glance that by-passed her rested on the figure of Inspector Cornford, his face so expressionless that it resembled that of a wax dummy.

Remaining no more than two steps inside the room, his voice was impersonal to the verge of insolence. "I don't think we've met."

Cornford gave a nod of acquiescence. "I think not, Mr. Latham. I'm Det. Inspector Cornford of Larksbridge C.I.D."

When Richard made no response, Cornford elaborated: "I'm in charge of the investigations into the disappearance of the tenant known to you as Miss Jones. Mrs. Latham very kindly permitted me to see over the flat she occupied."

As he moved towards the door, Richard stood well back, as though to avoid contagion with a police officer. He remained there, keeping them within sight as Georgina handed Cornford the grimy raincoat. On the doorstep he said formally: "Thank you, Mrs. Latham. Naturally, if there are any developments, I'll be in touch. I appreciate your concern. And meanwhile, if you would jot down those notes and hand them to the constable who will collect her bags in the morning, I'd be grateful."

For a few seconds she stood with her back braced hard against the closed door, then with a fast tread she returned to the drawing-room, the words that must be said bursting from her tongue. As Richard opened his mouth, she spoke with a passion that made her voice unrecognisable in her ears. "Please, for once, listen. Five and a half years ago Miss Jones's baby was kidnapped. He's never been found. She was still searching for him. Her behaviour wasn't odd; she wasn't a nut-case or a criminal, she stole nothing from this house or any other. She was a mother searching for her lost child." She began to jabber. "He was called Simon, and all she was doing in my den was looking at the crayon sketch of our Simon when he was the same age as her Simon is now. And in this room she'd picked up the colour picture of him on the mantel."

She watched him, still cradling the bottle of champagne,

walk to the window over which the curtains were not drawn, stare into the blacked-out garden. As the silence deadened, she took a deep breath to quench the hysteria in her voice. "Before he moved to Larksbridge, Inspector Cornford was attached to the Surrey police. He worked on the case when the baby was kidnapped from a house in Carshalton." It was the utter impassiveness of his back, a total uncaring that made her shout: "For God's sake, Richard, her son, a baby of six months was kidnapped. . . ."

He wheeled to face her. "All right. I get the message. Miss Jones had a baby, maybe legitimate, maybe not. No one seems to mention a father. She lost it, which suggests she didn't take too good care of it. Some five years later she comes to look for it in Larksbridge and chooses our house as a base for her operations. She vanished. So, one would suppose, she either found the child, kidnapped it back, so to speak, or she failed, and moved on somewhere else." He came forward, and his dead-level voice that assumed absolute omnipotence ran an icy finger down her spine. "And, since you saw fit to call in the police, our house was searched, you were interrogated, and in all probability they will arrive on the doorstep, note-book at the ready, to interrogate me. They'll be out of luck. Miss Jones and her lost child are no concern of mine. I have precisely ten days in which to complete the script. I do not propose to waste five minutes of them on Miss Jones." His smile was wry, without a shading of compassion. "Heartless? Callous? Where she is concerned I'm guilty. Whether she has succeeded in kidnapping back her own child, or got pitched off her bicycle into a ditch, however much it offends or shocks you, Georgie, I choose to keep my priorities straight. And top of the list is that I don't want Simon to have a failed writer as a father, or you as a husband. Can you understand? Am I getting through to you?"

"Yes. You're saying you don't care whether Miss Jones is dead or alive."

"Precisely. So I do not propose to have my concentration blasted to hell by a posse of policemen. And now I'll go and chill the champagne. For once, we do have a cause for celebration. Not only was the treatment accepted without a quibble, but I've been asked to submit an outline for a second play in the series."

"Congratulations."

He grinned. "Don't overdo the enthusiasm!" At the door he looked round. "By the way, was her name really Jones?"

She licked her lips that were so dried they felt as if they might crack. "No. It was Susan Bates. She changed it to Helen Jones after the baby was kidnapped."

He smiled benignly at her.

Preparing supper, Georgina's normally dexterous movements were made clumsy by the echo of her voice spiralling into hysteria in a passion of grief. The effect was to leave her feeling undermined, diminished in her belief that she was a woman of sense and reason. In the first months of marriage she had been forced to come to terms with the inhuman egotism of writers, who counted work-time filched from them as a mortal crime for which there was no forgiveness. She had accepted a regimen that for days, maybe weeks reduced her to a moving blur in Richard's sight. But a stolen child . . . she half choked on her anguish, her helplessness to pierce the armour in which he insulated himself.

Richard was relaxed as he opened the champagne. His smile was no more than slightly quizzical as he handed her a glass. "I've a suggestion to make: that we call a ten-day truce on the subject of Miss Jones-Bates. By which time, with a bit of luck the police will have solved the mystery, if mystery there is, without any help from us. What do you say?"

She said cryptically: "I'll promise not to mention her name, and if the police come asking more questions, I'll do my best to keep you from being involved. By the way, Inspector Cornford said it would be a good idea to change the locks."

"For heaven's sake, why?"

"Because she didn't leave her keys behind." Once again she found it odd that he'd never once raised the matter of Miss Jones's keys. "So, if she lost them, or if they were stolen from her . . . someone may have them."

He considered. "I suppose he's got a point. Though it seems likely that anyone wanting to shed their identity, as presumably the Jones-Bates girl did, would have thrown them down the nearest drain. All right. Tell Charlton's, the locksmiths in the High Street, to get cracking." He cocked an amused eyebrow at her. "I suppose you realise the job will cost more than the rent you received from her!"

All she said was: "Charlie fixed the plug this morning."

That pleased him, and during the meal he dwelt happily on the transformation of the top flat. He was an excellent craftsman, who had taught himself carpentry and decorating; moreover absorption in physical work released tensions, acted as a balm upon temper and spirit. For which, she supposed she should be thankful.

The two glasses of champagne that were her limit did not blur her senses, rather extended and clarified them, so that temporarily every facet exposed in depth, became brilliant, precise. The pattern of Miss Jones's years of search to recover the stolen baby drew itself on her own heart. She felt, as deeply as if they were her own, the conflicts at war in Richard: the dread that he was doomed to mediocrity, even failure, a fear that made him blind to any need but his own.

Strangest of all, though she had no belief in life after death, it was as if, during that small span of time, she had only to reach out her hand to touch her father's.

Yet, as the extension of her senses dwindled, she found herself wondering when the commitment to work would be overthrown by Richard's compulsion to see and touch Amanda. Because it would. For nearly two years he had never been separated from her for longer than a week.

Next morning, before she left the house, she went through the routine of plugging in the electric coffee percolator in Richard's study, leaving a note on his desk of her estimated time of arrival back at the house.

Her first call was at the school outfitters to replace two pairs of Simon's pyjamas of which the laundry disclaimed all knowledge. She had made her selection, was dictating the postal address to old Mr. Dunning, when a voice behind her struck a familiar note. Madeleine Hurst was watching as the senior assistant set a fuchsia-pink cap on the head of a small boy.

"That seems to be the size." Madeleine Hurst tested it. "Yes, the next size would be too large. It might blow off. Darling, this is the second cap I've bought you in two months. So do try hard not to lose it. Caps cost a lot of money."

"I didn't lose the last one. Faulks threw it into a ditch and though we hunted we couldn't find it. I expect a squirrel carried it off and made a nest out of it. So it's not really wasted."

Georgina thought he was an engaging child, articulate and self-possessed, with thick blond hair, well-sculpted features. She walked towards them. After a visible start, Madeleine Hurst smiled. The shaky nerves seemed under better control than on the last occasion they had met, and the simple grey flannel trouser suit was vastly more becoming than the mink-trimmed outfit, as was the hair that was no longer back-combed into an old-fashioned puff-ball.

"Oh, hello, Mrs. Latham. This is my son Dominic. As you heard, prone to losing items of his school uniform."

He held out his hand, corrected his mother. "They lose themselves."

Georgina laughed as she shook the small hand. "As I well know. I have a son, a lot older than you are now, but when he was your age, in some mysterious fashion, he never had two socks that matched." She turned to his mother. "Now the school laundry has mislaid two pairs of his pyjamas: seemingly vanished without trace."

After Georgina had asked Dominic's age, which he informed her was five years and three months, the two women left him examining a rail of scarlet wind-cheaters while they returned to the counter: Georgina to claim her receipt, Madeleine to write her cheque.

"He's not at school, then?"

"No." For the first time Madeleine switched on the blatantly artificial smile. "He's had a bad throat, been on anti-biotics. I hope he'll be fit to go back on Monday."

To Georgina's experienced eye, he looked perfectly fit now. Above average-tall for his age-group and, it struck her, mentally more mature. She and Madeleine Hurst murmured goodbyes, and it was only when Georgina was pressing the lift button that an hysterical scream hit her in the back. "Dominic! Dominic! Where are you?"

Madeleine ran, reeling and stumbling through the rail of wind-cheaters, then blundered into a rack of blazers. "Dominic . . . Dominic . . . Come here, I tell you, come here." The elderly woman assistant took hold of her arm. "Really, Mrs. Hurst, he can't have gone far," as Mr. Dunning scurried behind a curtain.

With the triumphant smile of a conjurer producing a rabbit out of a hat, he pushed Dominic forward. In his hand were the remains of a sugar biscuit. "Our modest tray of elevenses acts on them like a magnet."

Madeleine sagged against the rail, drawing audible breaths, the skin-tone of her face so blanched that her mouth in contrast was a brilliant scarlet. Wordlessly she held out a shaking hand. Dominic said to Mr. Dunning: "Thank you for the biscuit. I was sure you wouldn't mind my taking one when you had a whole tin-full."

"Certainly not." Mr. Dunning bowed. "You're most welcome." He steered Dominic towards his mother, who when he was within reach grabbed his wrist and jerked him out of the show-room, by-passing Georgina who was waiting by the lift, dragging Dominic after her down the stairs.

Georgina diagnosed panic based on terror that induced a physical and mental disablement. But what was the reason for Mrs. Hurst's hysteria? The only threat to Dominic's safety was the traffic in the High Street, two floors below the out-fitting show-room. A toddler, yes, but a self-possessed five-year-old who had presumably learned his kerb-drill. Unless the mother was neurotically possessive it didn't make sense.

When she'd served Richard his salad lunch, which he ate at his desk and then, according to the weather, either napped on the divan, or drove the car out to the common and took an hour's walk, she telephoned Lucy. "I want to look in on Mrs. Fennis, make sure she's coping now her husband is home from hospital, and I wondered if I could drop in on my way back before Chris and Nina arrive home for tea. But say if it's a bad time."

"Couldn't be better. Chris is staying on for a rehearsal. He's been cast as Pharaoh in the school nativity play. And Nina's on a diet, and quite capable of poaching herself two eggs with a garnish of lettuce. Come when you like." She paused. "It's about Madeleine, isn't it?"

"Yes. See you."

On her way back from visiting Mrs. Fennis, the left turning ahead triggered off a memory of Miss Jones walking purposefully towards it the afternoon she had driven Mrs. Fennis back from hospital. On an impulse she swerved left and reduced her speed to a crawl. A century ago when City tycoons had felt the urge to breathe country air, they had built themselves an assortment of turreted and towered mansions, insulated themselves from the unwelcome sight of neighbours by acres of grounds. The majority of the houses had been converted into separate apartments, the intervening land covered with modern, compact dwellings, but a few of the grandiose mansions still remained. One was a convalescent home, another an institute for the blind, a third a private clinic, and at the far end, at the point where Georgina reversed the car, she was faced by two impressive stone pillars topped by a curved board on which was inscribed: St. Christopher's Primary School for Boys. It was one of two they had considered for Simon just before he reached his fifth birthday. There had been little to choose between it and Bennett's Primary School, except that Bennett's was five minutes' walk from home, and Simon had been outraged by the idea of wearing the pink blazer and cap of St. Christopher's. "Pink's a girl's colour. They'll be a lot of sissies."

At 3:45 the pupils were either spurting or dawdling through the gates, the smaller ones to be met by mamas in cars, the older to shove and push one another into the gutter. In her head she pictured Miss Jones leafing through directories for the names and locations of boys' schools in Larksbridge, hanging round the entrances, searching desperately for a boy of six she hadn't seen since he was a few months old! She visualised Simon at the same age: a pudgy-faced baby in a pram, hair so tardy in growing it was no more than fuzz, compared him with the lean five-year-old, with burnished chestnut hair who had complained bitterly at being taken and fetched from school. Ah, but the eyes that were a double heritage from his grandfather and mother had not changed: a dense blue, with what Richard had dubbed cow-lashes, and the trick, even at six months, of using them to gain advantage over authority. Had Miss Jones haunted the gates of St. Christopher's and a half a dozen other boys' schools to recognise her son's eyes in the faces of a milling horde of little boys? Or was she guilty of letting her imagination run riot?

Lucy took her into the sitting-room that ran from the front to the back of the house. "I'll fetch the tea. Sorry it's all a bit messy, but it's been one of those days. How's Richard?"

"Doing ten days' hard on the script of a tele-play."

"Goody. I can't wait to see him back on the box. Nothing I enjoy more than an hour of murky suspense with my feet up and a glass in my hand. Shan't be a tick."

"Okay," she said as she handed Georgina a cup. "Madeleine Hurst was an error of judgment on my part. She has fallen down on the job. No excuses. Though she was sick for over a week with some bug, and then Dominic caught it and she's been tied to the house nursing him. Anyway, it would have come to an end soon. They're off for a holiday in the sun, lucky devils. Morocco, or is it Bermuda? Anyway, my idea of heaven for Christmas. Meanwhile, I'll cope until we find someone to fill the gap."

"I'll help. Parties tend to fall off from about now until mid-December, so I'll not be tied up cooking and freezing. I'll telephone or write and thank her. I've got her address and number. She lives in Meadow Lane, doesn't she?"

"Yes. Third house on the left, red brick set back from the road."

"How long have they lived there?"

"At a rough guess around nine months. That's when I had my sister's youngest boy Jonathan staying while she was in hospital. He and Dominic got chatting over the gate, and she brought him along once or twice."

"Where did they live before they came to Larksbridge?"

"I haven't a clue." Lucy's glance was puzzled. "Does it matter?"

"No. I was curious about her background." Georgie described the extraordinary scene in the school-outfitter's.

"Um, she does tend to keep him tied to her apron strings. When he and Jonathan were playing, she more often than not hung about too, instead of parking him and picking him up later."

"What's her husband like, what does he do?"

Lucy protested: "Lovey, she isn't a bosom pal! Like half the husbands in Larksbridge he commutes to London, but what he does there I wouldn't know. We went for a drink once. He looks forty-five to fifty, like her older than the norm for parents of a primary school kid. All right, but a bit tense, again like her. We asked them back but they couldn't leave the boy and when I suggested Maureen Phillips who used to sit for us, she made some vague excuse. So they came along one Sunday morning, brought him with them, and that's when she told me she'd heard of Friends in Need and could she help." Lucy wrinkled her nose. "Since we've written her off, why the vetting? I don't get it."

Georgina shrugged. "I suppose the scene in the shop triggered off my curiosity."

Lucy reached for her cup. "What I'm bursting to know is all about your Miss Jones. I mean what's behind her being 'missing'?"

"Who told you?"

"It's common knowledge. Couldn't be otherwise with a picture-drawing of her on the bill-board outside the police station and another by the town hall. Two different names. The police asking for information as to her whereabouts. Honestly, Georgie, I think you might have come clean about her. You've been here over half an hour, and never a word about it!" She glared in indignation. "And my guess is that you wouldn't have mentioned it, if I hadn't brought it up."

"She's just disappeared. That's all there is to it. Nine days ago. I only knew because Annie Marchant telephoned me and, assuming she was ill, asked me to remind her to get a sick certificate. When I went to look for her, she wasn't there. I reported it to the police." She gulped. "It knocked me out. . . ." Which was the nearest she could get to the acute sense of loss she felt for a girl she had hardly known. And the guilt.

Nina, fourteen years old, despite the disadvantages of a school uniform and puppy-fat, did her best to float gracefully into the room. Between the curtains of hair, that was now blonder than when Georgina had last seen it, she gazed soulfully at her mother's guest. "Oh, Mrs. Latham, I prayed last night that I would see you. Do you think Simon would come to my Christmas party on the 27th December? It's a late one; we'll probably finish up with bacon and eggs at five o'clock."

Behind her daughter's back, Lucy who could never hold a grudge, winked at Georgina.

"Why don't you write and ask him? He is bringing a friend home for the holidays, so . . ."

"Oh, he'd be welcome too. I think we might even be short of a man. I'll send him an invitation for two." Suddenly, the sophisticated pose became too hard to sustain, and she blurted out: "But if he has another invitation for the 27th, I thought maybe you would . . . well, you know, tell him what a super party it's going to be. Not kids' stuff. Mummy and Daddy aren't coming near. Mummy, you did swear . . ."

"A couple of ancient old crocks like us? Even if we could stand the wear and tear on our ear-drums, we wouldn't dream of it." Lucy smiled sweetly. "Nor can we be expected to have strength left in our old bones to clean up after you next morning."

Georgina rose. "I'll be sure and mention the party to Simon when I write."

"Oh, thank you, Mrs. Latham. You see, I think he's super."

"See what you've given birth to," Lucy murmured, as she saw Georgina to the door. "Flies round a honey pot. He'll be the beau of the ball. Not that it's going to be quite the rave-up Nina has in mind. Don't lead him to expect belly-dancers."

Georgina laughed.

On the doorstep Lucy took hold of her elbow. "I'm sorry about the mess or mystery, whichever it is, over the disappearance of your Miss Jones. Being you, of course, you feel bad about it. That's your Methodist conscience working over-time, as usual. But, lovey, it's the police's job to find her, not yours. Try not to let it get you down."

"You're right. I'll try." Georgina hesitated a moment, debating whether she should tell Lucy about the stolen baby, then found the emotional effort beyond her.

EIGHT

Inspector Cornford was wearing the same out-of-shape suit; his desk was still in what, Georgina guessed, must be a permanent state of disorder.

"I thought," he began, explaining his telephone call, "you would like to be kept up to date. We've so far been unable to trace a child missing from any Larksbridge primary school. Attendance registers have been checked and those children absent through sickness or other causes have been accounted for. If Susan found her son in Larksbridge she made no attempt to claim him, that is so far as we have been able to trace. She could, of course, have made an abortive one."

"Surely if she'd tried to get him back and failed, she would have gone to the police? That would have been her only hope, wouldn't it?"

"She wasn't, as I have explained, a predictable girl."

He was, she supposed, competent at his job, but the manner in which he operated with no suggestion of urgency, of reacting to a crisis situation, exasperated her. He seemed to obtain satisfaction from dealing in enigmatic ambiguities. "I have remembered a school in which Miss Jones took a particular interest. One afternoon, soon after she'd moved into the flat, while I was driving down Meadow Lane, she crossed in front of the car, and walking, not on her bicycle, went along King's Crescent. At the far end there is St. Christopher's Primary School for Boys."

He shuffled the papers in the file, extracted one. "St. Christopher's. Ten children absent on the relevant dates. Five on holiday with their parents; five at home sick. All checked, and with the exception of one boy of eight, all back at school. Did you actually see Susan waiting outside the school?"

"No. But surely there was no other reason she should walk down that particular road?"

"Not one that we know of." He reached for a typed report from the file. "Now, Mrs. Latham, I would be grateful if you would clarify a point for me. During the two days you spent visiting a relative in Dorset, was your husband at home?"

She was conscious of a small shock, as though she had made a mistake she could not correct, but not even to herself would she admit the menace contained in the quietly spoken question. "He spent Thursday night in London. You were there on Friday evening when he got back."

"Where did he spend it?"

"With a friend, Max Allstead, at his flat in Clemens Street, Chelsea." He had, she thought with a flash of anger, been questioning Mrs. Clownes, who would have been in her element at being invited to inform on her employers; Richard had probably left with his overnight case while she was still in the house. Watching Cornford writing down the name and address, indignation, what she assured herself was righteous indignation, offered a temporary haven of refuge: "Why have you been checking on my husband's movements?"

He expressed no contrition. "We've checked on yours too. The approximate time of your arrival at and departure from Dorset. It is customary, I assure you. Oh, and one further point, in the statement you made to Inspector Donaldson, there is no mention of the death of your father, your departure for Yorkshire and return to Larksbridge nine days later?"

Again, Mrs. Clownes could be the only source of his information. "Why should there be! I didn't consider my movements were of any concern to the police. Only Miss Jones's. It was she who was missing."

"Yes, indeed. But you were not actually at home when she disappeared, which is a fact of some relevance. During your two absences did your husband, when you returned, mention any contact he had had with Susan?"

"No." She lied with reluctance but without a qualm of conscience. "I've explained how she went to great pains to avoid contact with both of us. At the time I didn't understand why; now I do."

He lifted out another typed sheet from the folder. "Now I wonder if we could go back a bit, to an incident that occurred at your house eighteen months ago, when a window-cleaner, Dennis Bridestone, fell off a ladder propped up against the window of your husband's study, sustained a broken leg and a fractured collar-bone."

She thought simply: Oh, God! and was conscious of the bright hazel eyes under the down-drooping lids studying her in the seconds she needed to marshal her words, tune her voice to a note that expressed concern but no alarm. "He lost his balance and fell on to the stone terrace. When the police examined the ladder they discovered the base was uneven. In fact, it was dangerously unsafe."

"Yes, that was the case. Even so, Dennis Bridestone charged your husband with deliberately pushing the ladder away from the window, proposed to take the matter to court, claim compensation for malicious injury. Later, he withdrew the charge. Now why was that, Mrs. Latham?"

"My husband certainly did not push Dennis off the ladder. But while Dennis cleaned the windows he liked to chat to whoever happened to be in the room. Even I, when I was busy, found it irritating. Also, it amused him to play jokes, suddenly pop up at the window and startle anyone inside the room. This, well, rather childish habit annoyed my husband intensely; it interrupted his writing, disturbed his train of thought. So I asked Dennis to leave the study window uncleaned unless my husband was away. That particular morning I was out, and presumably he forgot. When he pushed up the window, which was immediately in front of my husband's desk, he ordered him to clear off. When Dennis did not do so, my husband slammed the window. Perhaps too violently, which could have jolted the ladder, dislodged it from the wall. Assuming there was blame on both sides, my husband was not injured, but Dennis was. It seemed only reasonable to make up Dennis's wages to their normal level until he was fit to work, which we did."

"A wise course, especially in view of the cost of litigation today. I hope you will forgive me, Mrs. Latham, if I enquire if your husband's temper is on the quick side, a little explosive, say?"

Not when he was wreathed with the sweet airs of success, but frustrated by talent running to waste, yes. But she could hardly ask Inspector Cornford to understand the chasm separating the two states of mind. "Not in the least, except that he doesn't suffer fools gladly." She gestured towards the small window. "Would you welcome a window-cleaner thrusting his head through that when you were hard at work?"

"I take your point. During the eight days you were in Yorkshire, did anyone you know speak to Susan? Say your cleaning woman, neighbours?"

"My cleaning woman who comes two mornings a week, doesn't arrive before 9:30, after Miss Jones would have left for work. The Durrants who live on one side are away on a cruise. Mr. and Mrs. Buchanan on the other, are elderly. She is a semi-invalid and he is very deaf. They neither entertain nor go out, except on very rare occasions. They have a resident housekeeper, also elderly. I wouldn't imagine that any of them would even be aware Miss Jones was living next door." She paused, softened her voice to mild irony. "Inspector, if you're thinking that while I was away, my husband established some sort of relationship with Miss Jones, you're mistaken. He is not the type; and far more important, she hadn't a sideways glance to waste on anyone, man or woman, until she'd found her son."

For a few seconds that stretched out to a small eternity, they sat in an eyeball to eyeball confrontation. His alert probing, at odds with the fleshiness of his face that lent it a permanent shape of amiability. She broke first. "What possible grounds have you for suggesting that my husband was in any way concerned with Miss Jones's disappearance?"

"I suggested nothing of the sort. But it is my duty to check not only live ends but dead ones, Mrs. Latham. A tedious business. In every case we handle, shoplifting, murder, hooligans ripping out telephones for the hell of it, or a girl who disappears without trace, the bedrock of our investigations is a timetable of the incident. In this case, I'm sure, unintentionally, some confusion has been created. So it would be helpful if your husband would provide us with details of his movements, both while you were in Yorkshire and during the two days you were visiting your cousin. I don't think he will find that an unreasonable request."

"You're saying you want to call and question him?"

"I'd prefer him to come here, make a formal statement. I suggest that you tell him this when you get home and ask him to telephone and make an appointment for some time this evening. That way, it will not interrupt his day's work. Will you do that, Mrs. Latham?"

"Yes, of course." As he rose, held out his hand, she said: "It was you who said she was a bolter. Wouldn't that imply that she might, if she hadn't found her child, have been so cruelly disappointed that she literally fled?"

"This time when she bolted she left behind her cheque book and a building society account book. Also her own and her son's birth certificates. Clothes, she might have abandoned, particularly if they'd served her as a disguise. But not the contents of the cash-box. A girl on a bicycle can't travel long distances, and we know it was never put on any train at Larksbridge station. Therefore, there would seem to be some grounds for the assumption that, in this instance, she didn't bolt of her own free will."

"You're saying . . ."

He interrupted her with a calm she found maddening. "Merely that we must explore every possibility."

Richard was in the drawing-room a glass in his hand, the television on but the sound off, as he waited through the last children's programme before the news at 5:45. Hearing her step, he peered round the wing of the arm-chair. "Ah, you're home. Nice!" He poured her a drink and went forward to switch on the sound.

She watched him covertly during the news, noting the air of languor, of repleteness that spelled out a good day's work behind him. When the weather report flashed up on the screen, he switched off.

"What have you been up to? I should have thought most of your old biddies were tucked up in bed by dusk."

"I looked in to see Lucy, ran into Nina who is panting to have Simon at her Christmas party. I promised to add a bit of pressure." She sipped her drink. "When I got home Inspector Cornford telephoned, asked me to go round and see him. They haven't found Miss Jones; there's no child of the right age missing." She improvised to cushion the impact of Cornford's message. "Maybe they're back to the accident theory. I honestly don't know."

"Accident," he took the word from her lips, savoured it. "Or foul play. The technical nomenclature for being beaten to death, thrown into the sea with legs tied together and weighted with bricks, strangled, shot in the back. Take your choice."

She swallowed her revulsion. "You're not plotting a piece of fiction."

He grinned. "Come on, let's have the rest of it. And don't look scared out of your wits. What does that bumbling old copper want from me? Obviously something."

"He's compiling a time-table of every contact Miss Jones made from the time I saw her on the Tuesday morning until Annie rang up and said she hadn't been at Benbow's since Tuesday afternoon. I hadn't, because it didn't seem relevant, mentioned my visits to Yorkshire and Cousin Maude, nor that you'd spent Thursday night in town. I can only suppose the police questioned Mrs. Clownes who knew where I was, and who probably saw you drive off with an overnight bag. He wanted to know where you'd spent Thursday night, so I gave him Max's address."

She waited for the explosion of anger. It didn't come. He gazed with mild amusement into his glass, then slowly lifted his head. "So I take it that Inspector Cornford is due to hammer on our front door any minute now?"

"No. He wants to see you at the police station, this evening if you can manage it. He asked if you would telephone him and let him know what time you could make it."

He leaned back and laughed in sly glee. "Softly, softly, catchee monkey! Dear me, with all respect to Inspector Cornford, he's a few decades behind the times." He rose. "I imagine an hour should suffice to bring Cornford's time-table of the incident up to date. So I'll be off to do my duty as a responsible citizen. Instead of telephoning, I'll give him a pleasant surprise."

His show of nonchalance did not surprise her. Writers were as adroit at slipping into the characters they had created as actors. It bothered her that she couldn't nail down the fictional rôle he was playing. How had that particular tele-play ended? Was he acting-out the hero or the villain? She gave a mental shrug; surely what mattered was that he had complied with Cornford's request? But she'd have felt easier if she could have guessed what prompted the swing-round.

To use up time, she went to his study, threw the window open a foot, and sat down to wait for ten minutes when it would have completed its job of air purification, still trying to recapture the name of the character into whose skin Richard had slipped, and failing. Her final action, after closing the window, was to open the deep drawer in his desk. The whisky was less than two inches below the level where it had been when she had last examined it.

He was gone for less than forty minutes. "Okay?" she queried, nerves twitching.

He gave her a sardonic smile. It suited him, lifted a few years from his face. "Who's to know! I mean what ticks beneath that balding pate! And frankly, who cares! Oh, one footnote, he politely requested permission to look round the garden tomorrow morning. I gave it, on one condition, they don't start digging it up. I said you'd object."

"Why on earth should they?"

"Presumably to find a body!"

She snapped: "Richard, must you!"

He either did not hear or chose not to heed her protest. "Or maybe they'll employ a divining rod, if one exists that twitches like mad over a decomposing corpse!"

"That's enough of the Grand Guignol. Let's eat. After supper I want to ring Matron, let her know that Simon's pyjamas were posted today. I'll ask her if we can have a word with him." This was a privilege, not a right; sometimes it was granted, sometimes refused. The likeliest time was 8:15 when school supper was over.

Matron proved agreeable. They each talked to Simon for a couple of minutes. His team was top of their league in the Rugger table. If his mother could send some jars of *paté* and black currant jam, they'd be super for evening snack parties.

Just before ten o'clock Max telephoned. After speaking to him for over a quarter of an hour—and for all she knew Max might have summoned Amanda to the phone—Richard came back, slumped into his chair, his airy nonchalance dissipated. "He's got a bad attack of the jitters. It seems a local constable had been ordered by Telex or phone to call and confirm the date of my last visit. It's a throw-back to the night the flat was raided, and some junkie was found with a few shags of cannabis in his jeans, so the police hauled the lot of them to the station to turn them over. Ever since Max has had a phobia about the police. The pig syndrome. He's practically hysterical." He sighed petulantly. "I'm afraid, damn him, I'll have to slip up and either smooth his shattered ego, or dose him with tranquillisers. But I'm not wasting time on him for a day or two."

She wondered if Amanda had been thrown into a panic, doubted it. Amanda wasn't the type to crack even under pressure.

She was late falling asleep and woke to instant consciousness when the illuminated hands of the clock pointed to 2:10. Lying in the darkness, she realised it was the depth of silence, undisturbed by Richard's breathing, that had broken her sleep. The bedroom door was ajar and an ethereal wash of moonlight from the uncurtained landing window lay across the empty bed. She waited ten minutes by the clock and then, throwing her dressing-gown about her shoulders, she stepped barefooted on to the landing, so silvered with brightness the moon must be full, the sky cloudless. She leant over the banister, her eye running down the curve of the stairs to the wide hall and the closed doors. Then across to Richard's study door, so tight a fit that, like all the others in the house, there was no tell-tale hair-line of light to be seen at the foot; the key on the inside blocked even that tiny window.

She pressed her ear against it, conscious of a stealth that was ludicrous. Yet surely there was a basis for concern? Drawn from his bed long before dawn, the house with the automatic heating off until six, it was natural she should reassure herself that Richard was not stricken by one of his vicious headaches that made lying down a purgatory. Her ear against the thick mahogany, detecting no sound, her glance ran up the silvered stairs to the top floor. The sitting-room door was half-open. As though she were a thief in her own house, she crept upwards, pausing to test her weight on each stair.

Richard was standing in front of the window, looking into the garden, his back to her, a dense black silhouette, apparently staring at the miniature domes and pyramids of plants and shrubs, clearly identifiable in the lunar brilliance.

Her body was reduced to a degree of catalepsy wherein no breath seemed to pass through her lungs, her mind becalmed. She had a curious sense of stepping outside herself, being reduced to a pair of watching eyes that transmitted a message that her brain refused to accept. For a time beyond calculation she stared at the silhouette, and then on feet that were numbed to insensibility, clinging to the banister for support, she propelled each stump from one step to the next. In bed, the coldness attacked her like an ague, sent her teeth clashing against one another. When her feet came to tingling life and she could order her teeth to silence, she was swept with a rocking desolation of body and spirit. For a period of time that the clock told her had lasted over half an hour, she had stood spying on a man to whom she had been married for fifteen years, in whose innermost nature she acknowledged the existence of a faulty seam, and who had receded so far from her that he was virtually a stranger. By an act of will she forced herself to sleep, avidly hugging it closer and closer as the first shrouds muffled and then blacked out thought.

When she woke in the morning, her head automatically turned to look at the other bed. Richard was asleep in his customary pose, forearm across his face as though to hide it from sight while he slept. Her dressing-gown was a heap on the floor, his hung on its hook on the door; his slippers were neatly in place beneath the tallboy. It came to her that the eerie venture into the moonlight had been a dream . . . or a nightmare. Even her dressing-gown was not firm evidence. Each night she laid it across the foot of the bed, ready to grasp it before she went downstairs to fetch the papers. It could have been tumbled off by the restless tossing of her body.

Before she descended to the ground floor, she glanced upwards. The door of what was still to her Miss Jones's sitting-room was closed.

There were no marks on Richard's face at breakfast to prove or disprove that long vigil at the window. He wore the withdrawn expression of a man who is concentrating on the hours ahead rather than the passing minutes. He made no mention of Inspector Cornford's inspection of the garden. His sole plea as he gulped down his egg was that she should route Mrs. Clownes away from the first landing, so spare him the excruciating ordeal of her tuneless singing.

Mrs. Clownes walked into the kitchen as Georgina at the back door was handing Inspector Cornford the key of the garage. After the brilliant frost-hard night, the morning was dulled with an opaque cloud and a light, sticky drizzle. Through it Georgina could just make out the shape of a man standing by the rockery holding in his hand an object that she could only vaguely identify as a rod, or even a pike. "Sergeant Jones," Inspector Cornford explained. "I do assure you we shan't make a nuisance of ourselves. I merely want to see the lie of the land, the exits and entrances, and also look round the garage. It shouldn't take long."

"Now what?" Mrs. Clownes demanded as soon as Georgina closed the door on him. "Ferreting round the garden, only one reason the police do that . . ." For once the expression on her face was genuinely aghast. "Digging . . ." she whispered.

Georgina said sharply: "The garden is not about to be dug

up, Mrs. Clownes. Since Miss Jones took her bicycle with her, the police naturally wish to see where she kept it."

Mrs. Clownes gave her a pitying look, then pointed through the kitchen window. "Then why are they sticking a pole into the rockery?"

"I've no idea. They have my permission to do anything they wish." She issued precise orders as to the work she wanted done, to which Mrs. Clownes, as usual, took exception. She preferred to select her own jobs. "Kitchen, scullery, pantry and hall, if you please, Mrs. Clownes." Though it would afford her an unimpeded view of the police activities, it was preferable to her off-key rendering of "Top of the Pops" on the first floor landing. As Georgina left the kitchen, as a gesture of independence, Mrs. Clownes switched on the radio, tuned it to her favourite disc-jockey, turned up the sound to maximum.

Lucy telephoned at ten. "Care to give me a cup of coffee? And bring me up to date on Miss Jones. The rumours flying around get more dramatic by the hour."

Georgina said she could come when she liked. Plugging in the percolator, setting Mrs. Clownes's solitary place at the kitchen table, she did not allow her glance to stray towards the window. Mrs. Clownes assumed her most injured air.

The cloud was lifting, and as Lucy walked into the drawing-room, Inspector Cornford and his sergeant were plainly visible mid-way down the garden, bending over a rose-bed.

"What the hell's going on?" Lucy demanded. "You're not relaying the garden, are you?"

"They're police, plain-clothes. Inspector Cornford and a sergeant he's brought along. Miss Jones kept her bicycle in the garage, used the back door into the garden, so they want to check over the ground."

Lucy said nothing, but curled herself up on the end of a sofa, stirred her coffee and waited. When Georgina did not speak, she suggested: "Start at the beginning."

"It didn't start here. It began five and a half years ago."

"God!" Lucy whispered, when she'd finished. "Enough to drive her nuts. Maybe that's . . . well, it would only be natural, wouldn't it? Having a kid stolen from you, you'd never be completely normal again, would you?"

"No," Georgina said and watched Inspector Cornford's pear-shaped figure retreat down the garden. Mrs. Clownes, handed the garage key, must have been disappointed that though the rockery and borders had been prodded, they had not been dug up. She wondered if Richard had watched or, glance down-bent on his typewriter keyboard, had blinkered himself to the unspeakable intrusion.

Lucy began again. "What's their theory? What do they think has happened to her?"

"It's impossible to tell. Cornford's not the confiding type. Hugs his opinion to himself. The first time I saw him I got the impression that he'd been, well, fond of her, because he'd been in on the kidnapping of the baby. Now I don't know what to make of him. My guess would be that his outside doesn't match up with his inside, but I could be wrong."

"But if no child is missing, it means she can't have got her hands on him, doesn't it?"

"I don't know." Georgina stared at a picture that had suddenly lit up in a corner of her mind. Dennis screaming on the terrace, the broken ladder lying across his shoulders, and Richard shouting: "Stop squealing like a pig." Memory slotted in another tape. Jason, the boy who delivered the morning papers, leaving them on the doorstep where they'd been reduced to pulp by a fall of sleet, instead of putting them through the letter box. Richard lying in wait behind the door next morning to berate Jason and, when he stubbornly refused to apologise, boxing his ears, after which Jason had refused to deliver to the house again. His mother, taking him to hospital, claiming he was deaf, though the tests by the ear, nose and throat specialist had proved his hearing was unimpaired. And when Georgina had placed her order with a different newsagent, the woman behind the counter had stonewalled. "Well, I don't know, I'm sure, Mrs. Latham. We've a girl on that round. Nancy Fenton, nice-mannered, small for her age. What I'm saying is that I wouldn't like her to be subjected to any unpleasantness. In fact, to be honest, I wouldn't stand for it."

"There won't be any. I'll give you my word. If she'll knock I'll come down and collect the papers from her myself."

With doubt written across her face, the woman had grudgingly taken the order, and thereafter Georgina had run downstairs at 7 A.M. to take in the newspapers.

Suddenly a dark, chilling thought shot across Georgina's mind. Wasn't it odd that Lucy had not mentioned either incident? Jason's slapped ears had never reached the local paper though gossip had broadcast the affair, but there'd been half a column about Dennis's accident, his statement to the police. Lucy being uncharacteristically tactful, pretending out of the lovingness of heart to be unaware of both bouts of a temper spiralling out of control? And if Lucy, how many others? She had the sense of the ground no longer solid under her feet, and the temperature of the air about her dropping.

Lucy asked: "What about parents? Any other relations?"

"Her parents are dead and there don't appear to be any other relations."

"There's the boy's father. All that publicity when he was kidnapped, I vaguely remember it happening, you'd have thought he would have surfaced, or maybe he didn't know it was his."

Georgina shook her head. "God knows! You guess and guess and you get nowhere. He was called Simon."

Lucy's smile was gentle. "The last straw! It's tragic, heartbreaking and the hell of a thing to have happened to her . . . and you. But honestly, Georgie, do you have to break *your* heart? It wasn't as if she was a kid."

"According to the police she was twenty-six. That seems pretty young to me!"

"What I'm saying, is please stop crucifying yourself. For

heaven's sake, you hadn't even got to calling her by her Christian name. Always Miss Jones!"

"I know it sounds odd, but that's what she was to me: remote, wanting desperately to keep her distance, terrified of even the simplest friendly gesture."

Lucy wheedled: "Now the coffee's cold, you wouldn't care to offer me a drink? Say a thoroughly decadent brandy and soda?"

"I just might."

When they'd sipped half, Lucy said, partly as a diversion: "Oh, your Millie Andrews, I went to see her while you were away. Looked to me as though she was teetering along the edge of a precipice. You know you asked me to keep my eyes open for a suitable job for her. Well, I heard of a possible one. José, my hairdresser, not a pricy one like yours, but with a little salon down Benton Road. She told me when I was in yesterday that the girl who mans the telephone, sweeps up, unpins the curlers, is leaving to get married, and she's looking for a replacement for mornings. She's got a girl for the afternoons. What do you think?"

"The job must be so simple and undemanding there's no risk of Millie falling down on it. It would be fatal if she did."

"There are only a couple of assistants and José. If they were briefed on Millie's background they'd be tactful and understanding."

"Sounds hopeful. I'm not too sure about the telephone. Millie doesn't find it easy to talk. She dries up. I'll drop in this afternoon, sound her out and let you know. How long has she got to decide?"

"Not long. Betty leaves at the end of next week, and Millie ought to overlap her by a couple of days."

Millie hadn't drawn the curtains over the front windows, which was a good omen, and though she hadn't put on any make-up, her hair was brushed and she had shoes not scuffs on her feet.

Though she accepted in principle the idea of a job, the mention of a specific one terrified her to the extent that she had to replace her tea-cup in the saucer before it spilled its contents. "Oh, I don't know, Mrs. Latham. Maybe in a little while. I still get these shaking fits. . . ."

Her eyes implored. Georgina wanted to soothe and comfort, defer the decision, but it was over three months since Cyril's car had spun off the road, burst into flames. "You have to make an effort, Millie, or the shaking will only get worse. Mrs. Burrows will pick you up in her car at 9:30 tomorrow morning, and take you along and introduce you to Madame José and her two assistants. No one will ask any awkward questions, or make you attempt any job you can't cope with. And, best of all, it's only for half a day."

Millie began to cry. "Oh, I don't know, Mrs. Latham, I really don't."

"Give it a week's trial and if you find it's too much, you can give it up." She rose. "Put on that smart red dress and make up your face. That'll give you a boost, and Mrs. Burrows will be with you. You like her, don't you?"

Millie blew her nose. "She's nice, ever so kind, but . . ."

"That's settled then. 9:30 tomorrow morning. I'll be keeping my fingers crossed for you."

Outside Millie's terrace house, she reversed the car, drove it in the opposite direction from home. The decision had made itself or, more correctly, had been taken by her subconscious, predetermined by two incidents that had left black query marks in her head. Also by fear. She admitted the fear, but not the reason for its existence.

Though the long driveway, with the double garage door closed, was free, she parked at the kerb. The house, for an urban area on the fringe of a town, was comparatively isolated, with a deep front lawn, shrubberies protecting its privacy on each side, and as far as she was able to make out there was open land to the rear. She was almost, but not absolutely sure, that the sketch map from the past her memory had retained, was correct and to scale.

Her excuse for calling rehearsed in her head, she walked up the drive, rang the bell.

NINE

The door, guarded by a chain-lock, parted a bare four inches. Through the slice of space three quarters of Madeleine Hurst's face was visible. Her lower lip drooped which made her look slightly stupid.

When she did not speak or unlatch the chain, Georgina said: "I hope I haven't caught you at an inconvenient moment, but Mrs. Burrows told me that you were going abroad for a long holiday, and before you left, I wanted to thank you . . ."

She was interrupted by Dominic's ringing enquiry: "Mummy, who is it? Who's come?"

Madeleine smiled but her eyes remained curiously blank. "Oh, do excuse me. There have been so many break-ins around here my husband insists I keep the chain on the door."

She closed the door, reopened it to its full width. "It's Mrs. Latham, darling. You remember, we met her the other day when we bought you a new cap."

"I remember." His wide-spaced blue eyes had an overtone of green, his gaze was direct, his voice scathing that anyone should suggest he would not remember.

"Do come in?" Madeleine Hurst moistened her lips. "It's nice to see you."

With Madeleine leading the way, Dominic following at her heels, Georgina walked through a door Madeleine held open, found herself in a square graceless room with a high ceiling and an unmistakable air of disuse. The carpet was a conventional beige, the sofa, two chairs were upholstered in mid-green rep. There were two nests of small tables, a mirror over the fire-place and two reproductions of seascapes hung on the wall. An elaborate arrangement of artificial flowers stood on the window-sill. All the rest was space. Georgina found it unbelievable that there were still women, of whom Madeleine Hurst must be one, who reserved a room for the reception of visitors.

Madeleine Hurst bent and switched on the electric fire. "Do sit down." Her hand plunged into the pocket of the soiled pinafore she was wearing over her jersey and skirt for a half-crushed packet of cigarettes which she extended to Georgina. When Georgina refused, she lit one, had to search around for the solitary ashtray in the room.

She said, in a rush of words that tangled with one another: "I'm sorry, I've let you down, haven't I? I didn't mean to. It was rotten luck we all got ill one after the other. First my husband was home with his ulcer that is always flaring up, then I went down with a bug and Dominic caught it from me. I feel dreadfully guilty about forgetting to see that old lady to help her fill up her Supplementary Allowance form when Mrs. Burrows had explained it all to me. It simply went out of my mind."

Georgina smiled. "Forget it. Lucy coped. She's filled in so many forms, she can practically do them blindfold." With no make-up, Madeleine Hurst's face was pallid and drawn, the fine net-work of lines about the eyes plainly visible. On her temple Georgina thought she could see a vein throbbing. In confirmation Madeleine pressed it hard with two fingers. "Lucy said you were going abroad for a long holiday?"

"Yes. My husband is badly in need of a break, and Dominic's so chesty we decided not to risk the worst of the winter in England."

"Where are you going?"

"North Africa."

Dominic, who had stayed leaning against the door, demanded: "Why do we have to come in here? Why can't we be in the other room?"

"You can go in the other room if you want, or you can fetch your aeroplane kit in here."

"There's no table big enough and the glue might drip on the carpet. Besides, I want to show Mrs. Latham my swimming pool."

Madeleine emitted a high-pitched laugh. "Darling, a swimming pool isn't worth looking at until it's filled with water, and that won't be until the spring. Anyway, it's too cold for you to be standing about in the garden."

"I haven't coughed for three whole days. I've kept count." With the tenacity of a child accustomed to exercising its will, he demanded of Georgina: "Wouldn't you like to see my swimming pool?"

"Yes, I would." She looked questioningly at his mother. "Maybe through a window?"

"Really, there's nothing to see. Darling, don't be so tiresome."

"But there is. It's finished except for the water, and some of the tiling round the edge that Daddy is going to do at the weekend." He went to his mother, tugged her hand. "And Mrs. Latham wants to see it. She said so. And she's a visitor."

"Oh, very well," she snapped, and mashed her cigarette out on the tarnished silver ashtray. "He's so excited about it. I suppose because, except for the excavation, my husband designed and built it, with Dominic playing builder's mate." She rose, led the way into a living room that, in reverse of the one they had left, was a shambles of disorder.

"Forgive the mess. My cleaning woman failed to turn up today."

"She comes on a Friday. Today's Tuesday."

Madeleine ignored her son's correction, stooped and picked up the odd pieces of the construction set strewn between them and the french window looking on to the rear garden. With a sleight of hand she spread a newspaper over the remains of a snack lunch, that included a gin bottle.

Dominic pulled on Georgina's hand until they reached the window. "There!"

"My goodness, what a beautiful pool." It was on the south side, separated from the house by a lawn. The displaced earth had been used to landscape a high bank to the north.

Dominic boasted: "It's eighteen feet long and twelve feet wide. On Saturday it will be finished."

Georgina smiled into his upturned face. "Aren't you lucky to have a father who can build you a swimming pool!" She turned to his mother. "There must have been an awful lot of muscle power involved in all that digging and heaving."

"My husband employed a labourer to do the excavation; and he hired a concrete mixer which saved him having to do the job by hand. The skilled part, of course, is installing the heating and filtering systems, which he did himself."

"I helped," Dominic insisted. "And if the water is warm, I don't see why we can't swim even if the air is cold."

"Darling, don't argue. I'm going to make Mrs. Latham a cup of tea." With a firm grasp on her arm she escorted Georgina back to the show-room. Georgina sat down in the chair she'd left three minutes previously. "Please don't make any tea for me. I've promised to collect Mrs. Cathers' radio from being repaired, and she doesn't like opening her door after dusk." Despising the cliché, she murmured: "It's a charming house. Have you been here long?"

"Nearly a year."

"Where were you before you came to Larksbridge?"

"Quite a few different places." She added as though justification were needed: "My husband's job keeps us moving around."

"He commutes to London every day?"

"Yes." She snatched for a cigarette.

Dominic, bored, gave a faint cough. His mother rounded on him. "There, you can't say now you haven't coughed today."

"That wasn't a cough, I was only clearing my throat. Daddy says you fuss, and it's true."

Children, particularly only ones, could be devastatingly logical, but this was a deliberate condemnation of his mother, embarrassing to her in front of a visitor. Quickly Georgina rose, held out her hand. "Thank you. I do really have to go now. Good-bye, Dominic."

"Good-bye. Will you be coming again?"

"If you ask me, say when your swimming pool is filled."

Madeleine Hurst did not speak. Half a dozen steps down the drive, Georgina turned about, her hand raised to wave to the boy, but the door was already closed.

Driving home, after delivering old Mrs. Cathers' radio, she reviewed the scene behind her. Madeleine Hurst was an overpossessive mother—not unusual in a woman who'd borne an only child when she was within sight of middle-age. But Lucy, warm-hearted and impulsive as she was, was no fool. She'd never have campaigned for Madeleine Hurst to be co-opted into Friends in Need if she'd witnessed her fly to pieces in Carlin's, or reduced to the nerve-racked, twitchy woman Georgina had visited that afternoon.

So wasn't it within the bounds of possibility that she'd only lately been brought to her present state, say in the last fortnight? Many householders had chain-locks on their doors, but unless they were elderly and living alone, few of them used them in daylight hours. And the boy's eyes, blue except when they reflected direct light, and then the green overtone was stronger than the blue. A perfectly healthy child kept from school because his mother had suffered a fright and could not bring herself to let him out of her sight?

She manipulated a jig-saw of suspicions into a pattern she

knew would convince no one but herself. Or was it more a need to extinguish a fear so deep buried in her subconscious that she dare not admit its existence even to herself? The father, she thought with a flash of inspiration, if she could devise some way of seeing, talking to, even looking at him.

During the two days while she prepared and served the Merediths' anniversary party, her mind, whenever it was disengaged, was absorbed in concocting a plan where this would be practicable. It came to her late on Friday afternoon a few minutes before Richard finished work.

He came into the drawing-room moving his arms in their sockets to ease the ache in his shoulders. "I'm a day ahead of myself, so with Max fast working himself into a permanent state of hysteria, because a police constable made a second call on him this morning to query a sentence in his statement, I better take tomorrow off and talk some sense into him before he goes completely round the bend." His glance was suddenly sharp, demanding. "No worries this end? Cornford hasn't been dropping in again, has he?"

"Not a word. I'd imagine he'd have told me if there'd been any developments. Though I can't be certain."

"Time's getting on. I'd doubt if there'll be any now."

On Saturday morning there was a light fog. If it followed the pattern of the last three days it would lift by mid-morning, descend again by early evening. After a day with Max, laced with drink, she decided she would prefer Richard spent the night with Amanda than driving too fast—he was incapable of driving slowly except in heavy traffic—and risking a crash. It was a decision that struck her as a trifle bizarre.

Over breakfast she said: "If it's foggy in London, remember it will be thicker when you leave the motorway. Better stay overnight."

The startled, naked look he gave her ripped a hole in the protective camouflage with which they covered themselves. "It'll have to be pretty thick. One day's all I can spare Max."

He went to collect his coat and returned to the kitchen where she was piling china and silver into the dish-washer. She wiped her hands, turned to say good-bye.

His expression, even the angle of his body, set off an alarm bell: familiar but deep buried in the past. A penitent, bent on baring his soul, receiving expiation: a throwing of himself upon her mercy.

"Georgie . . ." He flicked his eyes out of range and she thought with a heave of revulsion that he was about to confess to Amanda. She found her hands rising as though to fold them over her ears, block out his voice.

"You think . . . Well, I know what you're thinking. That comes of knowing one another. Holding up mirrors that tell tales. What's tormenting you is that you're scared that on the Tuesday night when I found Miss Jones snooping round the drawing-room, I had a row with her, threw her out of the house. To a degree you are right." Georgina dropped her hands, waited. "She was touching one of the blue lustres on the mantel, for all I knew about to pick it up, make off with it." He shrugged. "Okay, I lost my temper. I accused her of creeping into rooms where she had no right to be. I may even have called her a thief. I certainly ordered her out of the house, told her never to show her face again, or I'd put the police on her. Maybe she obeyed, and the reason for her disappearance is as simple as that."

Her voice was so casual that she might have been asking him about the weather. "You didn't touch her, shove her out of the drawing-room?"

His smile was wryly condemning. "I did not strangle her. I didn't, in fact, lay a finger on her." His tone softened. "Georgie, I wanted you to know, to stop you worrying yourself to death."

"Did you tell Cornford?"

"For God's sake! In this town I've got a record of violence and assault." He closed his eyes for a second, beseeched:

"Georgie, why don't we get out, out of the house, out of the town?"

She disregarded the question. "A record of losing your temper, not of murder."

He obviously found the comfort she offered inadequate. "I doubt if the police would draw any fine distinction between the two."

He walked past her, out of the kitchen, not even closing the door behind him, and down the garden to the garage. She thought it unlikely that fog, or no fog, she would see him that night. And for that she had no one to blame but herself. She believed he was telling the truth because, years ago, she had learned to detect with her nerve-ends—or maybe her heart—when he was lying. That's what she told herself: that she believed him.

She used the morning to plan and type three alternative menus for a buffet supper Mrs. Calthorpe was giving for her sister who was paying her first visit to England since she'd sailed away to become a G.I. bride. Mrs. Calthorpe having, on a visit to Connecticut, sampled American hospitality, was jittery in case hers should fall short of the high standard set before her. Georgina sifted through old tried menus, juggled them about, added dishes she hadn't so far considered likely to appeal to the conservative taste of Larksbridge hostesses. Every so often her concentration failed, and she found her fingers resting motionless on the typewriter keys, and when she checked the spaced items they were as meaningless as though they had been composed by someone else.

After dropping the envelope through the Calthorpes' letter-box just after three, she sat in the car getting her bearings, checking up on the ordinance survey map, pin-pointing the spot where, years ago, she had picnicked with Simon and two school-friends: an open space of meadowland where there was a pond in which the boys had fished hopefully but without success while she had sat nearby shielded from a blustery wind by a copse. They'd approached it by a lane, climbed over a stile. That much she remembered. The rest was a bit blurred.

The first stretch of the lane had been widened; a pavement laid down on one side, beyond which a carefully screened private housing development was half visible. But as she progressed the road dwindled into the curving lane unchanged from the image her memory had retained. There was the farm on the left, with its scattering of barns and tied cottages, where frolicking lambs had drawn the boys like a magnet. And there, a hundred yards farther on was the stile, by its foot a square stone engraved: Right of Way.

The grass was spongy and clogging, from which the heels of her boots released themselves with a squelching sound. The track had vanished, probably from disuse, and either she had forgotten the exact location of the pond or it had silted up. To the right lay a wilderness of scrub; to the left the dividing hedge in the shelter of which she kept. The morning fog had dissolved leaving a pearl-grey sky that matched itself to the air about her; an afternoon of such unbroken stillness that the sucking note of her boots pulling themselves free of the sodden ground made her uneasy, and she proceeded at a slower pace, choosing high tufts of grass, odd stones or rubbish that would support her weight.

When she came to the second stile, with its right of way stone, she proceeded with even greater caution. Now the harsh-brick twin gables were in sight. Though it was unlikely that anyone was looking out of the top windows, she had to accept the risk that, if they were, she would be intermittently visible as she dodged in and out of the protection of the overhanging hedge. In one respect she was in luck: the window in the left-hand gable was either blacked out or covered with a thick blind. A hundred yards from a second hedge, running at right angles to the first, that formed the boundary of the Hursts' garden, she heard voices: Dominic's with its clear pitch, precise enunciation, isolated words of which reached her, and the lower tones of a man's speech that was no more than a background murmur.

At the apex of the triangle between the two hedges she squatted down, her slacks, even her sheepskin jacket dipped in the water-filled ditch. The hedge was mixed, mostly hawthorn and privet. She found a spy-hole in the leafless hawthorn, so low that she was forced to lie on the ground, her legs spread-eagled across the ditch. She had to widen it by breaking off isolated twigs to by-pass a garden shed that threatened to block her view.

Now the dialogue between man and boy was audible. They were arguing as they completed tiling the edge of the pool. Dominic pushing a small wheel-barrow of tiles, boasting about how many he'd loaded, and the man telling him not to take too many. "Four at a time. That's plenty. If you overload the wheel-barrow it's likely to tip up. Now give me those, and you sit down there and watch me. If you're good I'll let you lay the last tile."

Dominic squatted on his heels on the rim. "When we've finished, why can't we turn the tap on?"

"Because we don't want the pond to freeze in the winter while we're away."

The blond head and the black one were close together. In the intensity of her anxiety for Norman Hurst to lift his and reveal his face, she lost the thread of the conversation. The minutes dragged interminably until he stood up. In dungarees over a woollen sweater, with the sleeves rucked to his elbows, he was roughly six feet tall, lean, thin-faced, with a close mat of dense black hair cut into his neck, the temples and side-burns grey, the well-trimmed beard that covered the lower half of his face as black as the crown of his head. His eyes were some neutral shade. There was no visible physical likeness between him and his son. As he stood up, his hand twisted backwards to massage his spine, she decided he was between forty-five and fifty.

When his father lifted the last tile out of the wheel-barrow, Dominic jumped up, seized the handle. His father took it from him. "You've hauled enough. I'll fill it."

With his father the boy didn't argue back, but followed dog-like at his heels. The barrow was full and they were jointly wheeling it to the pool, when Madeleine Hurst shouted from the back-door. "Dominic, it's getting cold. I want you to come in."

Dominic hunched his shoulders. Man and boy stubbornly ignored the summons. An anorak thrown over her shoulders, Madeleine came hurrying down the garden.

"Norman, I've made the tea. You're both to come in and have it, and then you can come out and finish the job, but Dominic's been out long enough. You should know that, for heaven's sake, without my having to tell you!"

He did not glance up from his kneeling position. "The fog's coming down. In half an hour there won't be enough light to see. I'm keeping going."

"You can finish it in the morning."

"I prefer to finish it now, so shut up."

She seized Dominic's arm. He wrestled with her until his father ordered: "Dominic, go with your mother. She's right. It is getting cold, and it's time you had your tea."

"But you promised I could lay the last tile."

His father put his fist under his son's chin, gave it a feigned punch. "And so you shall, in the morning. I promise I won't lay the last one. Go on in, there's a good fellow."

Pulling himself out of his mother's grasp, he walked leadenly behind her.

Georgina waited the thirty-five minutes until Norman Hurst rose, again eased his back, gathered up his tools and wheeled them to the garden shed on his side of the hedge. By now dusk and a light fog was beginning to lay a gauze curtain between them. When he'd turned the key in the door, instead of walking to the house, he followed the line of the hedge, and when he reached the point behind which she lay, he ran his gaze along it, so close now that she could see the puckered line across his forehead, the doubting pout of his thin lips, and the shoulders he hunched slightly. She literally froze, flesh and bones momentarily deprived of life, as though she were a hunted animal facing extinction. Three paces from the hedge; he had only to walk forward, look over it, and there she'd be with no plausible excuse for being where she was. But he did not move forward. After a period of suspense which was timeless, he turned, walked back to the house that, except for the oblong lights in the lower windows, was now shrouded in fog, so that she lost sight of him before he went indoors.

The long motionless waiting had locked her muscles, and for the first hundred yards she lurched and stumbled as though she were drunk. Cold and tension had robbed her of all power to evaluate. She did not try to resuscitate it until she had soaked in a hot bath, and even then it operated feebly. The idea had been simple, basic, in which, oddly, Miss Jones had hardly figured: to protect and preserve what belonged to her.

The afternoon's effort had yielded three snippets of knowledge: that Dominic bore no more resemblance to his father than his mother—then what proportion of children did? That he had an easier relationship with his father than his mother; that husband and wife were either incompatible, or given to outbursts of extreme irritability towards one another. She was left with a sense of frustration but not total failure.

The early evening news forecast continuing fog in the home counties. Georgina prepared a tray-supper, ate it watching a television serial that acted as a mild soporific on the front of her mind, while leaving the deeper regions sifting through possible courses of action which one by one she rejected until her brain was drained not only of inspiration but of coherent thought.

At ten-thirty she had locked up, checked the windows, and was climbing the stairs when she heard the car drive into the garage. She raced back to switch on the garden lights, unlock the back door.

She scanned Richard's face the second it came into view. It was dulled and hardened. "I'd given you up. You must have had a wretched drive."

"I've known worse." He threw a London evening paper on the table. "I tried to telephone you, but you weren't here."

"I was out this afternoon. I missed the post with the Calthorpe estimate and as I'd promised it by Monday, I delivered it by hand." Not a lie. She'd provided one shred of truth, withheld the rest. A habit, she thought, common to both of them. A deliberate hiding of three-quarters of themselves from the other.

"Cornford must have telephoned while you were out. Not getting a reply, he took a chance of telephoning me at Max's. He wants to see me."

"Tonight?"

"No. Tomorrow morning at 9:30." He stabbed a finger at the newspaper. "Take a look at that. The name of Susan Bates must have rung a bell in the memory of some news agency reporter, who did his homework, checked with Cornford. So now we get the sob-story of the kidnapped child. Read it."

The column was headed in black caps:

KIDNAPPED BABY'S MOTHER DISAPPEARS

The two pictures that were plastered outside the police station and the town hall were reproduced. Helen Jones, alias Susan Bates, whose last known address was 6, St. Stephen's Piece, Larksbridge, missing since Tuesday, October 26th. There now followed a résumé of the kidnapping, a recap on the Jacksons. The final paragraph stated that Det. Inspector Cornford of Larksbridge C.I.D., who was in charge of the case, appealed to anyone who had seen Susan Bates alias Helen Jones, or who had any knowledge of her whereabouts to contact him at the following telephone number. Putting the newspaper down, Georgina wondered why Cornford had not seen fit to divulge the fact about the kidnapping earlier.

"Missing since Tuesday, the 26th. What makes them so damned sure of their dates?"

The answer was so obvious she couldn't account for the hard, almost desperate note of challenge. "That was the last day she was at Benbow's."

"Making me, on the police records, the last one to see her!"

"The last one who admits it," she corrected.

TEN

Though normally anti-barbiturates, Richard swallowed a sleeping pill with the last gulp of his scotch. The effect on him next morning was a heaviness of eye, a sleep-walker's lethargy of movement. He ate nothing but drank two cups of black coffee.

Georgina walked with him to the door, her hand lightly on his arm. "I know you make your living out of your imagination but that doesn't mean you have to work overtime."

He opened the door, turned his head, said half-mocking, half-serious: "Let's face it, I'm a swine. You know it and I know it."

"As men go, you're pretty run of the mill, except you've got . . ."

Suddenly he grinned. "A hair-trigger temper, plus a record of assault and battery. Jason, Dennis. Duly noted on Cornford's file." His grin widened. "But I'd doubt whether he's uncovered that greasy gigolo who made eyes at you in Venice, whom I tossed into the canal. How was I to know that a Venetian, surrounded on all sides by water, hadn't learnt to swim!"

"He survived."

"Just. So now you're asking me not to put my temper on public exhibition to Cornford, is that it?"

"If you please!"

"Point taken."

He'd been gone less than twenty minutes when the door-knocker sounded.

A man in a duffel coat stepped forward. Behind him was a companion with a camera hanging round his neck. "Mrs. Latham?" Without waiting for her assent, he edged nearer the open door. "I wonder if I might have a few words with you. I'm from the Evening *Echo.*"

"Sorry, I'm afraid not."

His toe applied itself to the edge of the door. "I understand that Susan Bates, whom you knew as Helen Jones, lived here, that you were her landlord. If you could give me a few facts."

Instead she gave him her serenest smile. "Sorry, that's not possible. The police station is only ten minutes' walk away. To your left, then right, and left again. Det. Inspector Cornford is handling the case. He'll brief you."

"Then Mr. Latham . . ."

"He's not here." And with a firmness that dislodged the toe, she closed the door on his face.

To be out of view from the downstairs windows, Georgina climbed to the top floor, skirted the stacks of hardboard and cans of paint that were piled on the landing. Looking through the bedroom window, she saw that the reporter had secured himself a grand-stand view of the house by stationing himself against the rails enclosing the gardens. From the sitting-room she watched the photographer open the double gates, focus his lens on the rear of the house. It took him five minutes to get his shots and then, omitting to close the gate, he ambled into the lane and disappeared from view.

It was not their nuisance value that unnerved her, but the significance of their presence: that a London news editor had calculated money spent in maintaining a watch on the house would pay off. The tremors started in her limbs, travelled upward like a rising tide. She made herself take slow, deep breaths, sat down in an arm-chair. She picked up the royal blue ravel of knitting and closing her eyes to regain her calm, abstractedly let her fingers travel along the three uneven rows. Gradually the press on guard outside, Richard under police interrogation—even if he kept his temper, being arrogant and non-cooperative—was no longer the central point of her consciousness. What was Miss Jones doing sitting in this chair, hunched forward so that the arms would not impede the needles, laboriously teaching herself to knit a scarf for the son who had been stolen from her.

In the absolute quiet of the Sunday morning, unbroken by a sound, a small, precise picture formed in her head: the blanked-out window at the Hursts' house. It shook and bewildered her. She had no particle of belief in any supernatural or psychic phenomenon. Her nature was such that she was repelled that she should, even for a moment, have been caught in the web of what she counted a commercial mumbo-jumbo that existed to exploit the bereft and the bereaved. She decided she was overwrought, incapable of a balanced judgment.

She carried the knitting downstairs, wrapped it carefully, as though it were precious, in tissue paper and laid it in the central drawer of her desk. Obstinately a section of her brain continued to high-light that top left-hand window, demanding an explanation. A broken pane, a shrunken, ill-fitting frame that admitted howling draughts? But surely householders with attics or unused rooms didn't normally black-out or seal up windows, if only for the reason that any closed room needed an occasional crack of air if it wasn't to become musty?

Her fear that Richard would get involved in a brawl with the reporters—there were now four at the front of the house—proved groundless. As he opened the door, he flung good-naturedly over his shoulder: "My advice to you is to buzz off. You'll only get frost-bite hanging around."

To Georgina, on the other side of the door, he said: "Don't look so jittery. They can't legally force an entry."

"Not jittery. I find it disconcerting to see strange faces peeping at me through the downstairs windows."

"Simple. We'll climb the stairs. And I promise you if one of them steals a ladder to peer into my study window, I'll knock him off, and plead unwarranted invasion of privacy!"

"I've made some coffee. I suggest we have it in my den. The back of the house seems clear at the moment."

"I've got five minutes," he warned, and tossed off his coat.

Since he showed no inclination to tell her about the interview with Cornford, she asked.

With a look of disdain, either feigned or genuine, he said: "A white Capri, letters of the number plate quoted, but the figures uncertain, was seen parked in a lay-by alongside Trensham Common between 6 and 7:30 on the evening of the Wednesday you spent with Cousin Maude. I was able to confirm it was mine." He chortled. "Put Cornford right off his stroke. He'd expected a denial."

Sometimes, either after lunch or in the evening, Richard drove to Trensham Common, parked the car and walked for an hour to ease the stiffness out of his muscles or to clear his head.

He mimicked Cornford's mild voice. "Walking in the dark, Mr. Latham! Is that a habit of yours?"

"Not in the dark, Inspector. In the dusk. And there was a rising moon. And unless someone parked it there, there was no body in my boot!"

Nausea leaped in her stomach.

"Don't look so shocked. What else did you imagine he suspected? His next move was to request permission to have forensic experts examine the car. Request granted." He laughed. "At least the inside will get a good vacuum. I've never got around to sweeping up the powder you spilled on the carpet when you dropped your compact." He stared into the whorls of his cigarette smoke. "They arrive with plastic bags, you know, collect their samples with little tweezers. Then label them neatly for the forensic lab. Spots of blood, hairs, a shred of wool or artificial fibre, a flake of human skin." He nodded commendingly. "A highly skilled process." He threw the keys of his car on to the desk. "It promises to be a merry afternoon, with the Press having a field day." He set down his half-full coffee cup. "I'll have a sandwich for lunch and work on."

When he'd gone, she was aware that she had not uttered one word.

Activity within the front office of the police station was at a high pitch. The ringing of telephones constantly overlapped and the atmosphere was one of a carefully underplayed crisis building to a peak. She had to wait ten minutes before she could see Cornford, during which three reporters cooling their heels plied her with questions as to her opinions on what had happened to Miss Jones. She had no answers to give them.

When she was eventually allowed into Cornford's office, he was ushering out two men. One was the Chief Constable of the County whom she'd met once at a cocktail party, an occasion which he appeared not to remember, and a thick-set bullet-headed man with an air of authority whom she judged to be Cornford's boss.

"Perhaps I should have telephoned and made an appointment."

He glanced at his watch. "Not at all," he said with his usual slightly laboured courtesy, "but I am due at a conference in fifteen minutes."

The number of lines on his face seemed to have increased, and the shoulders under the unpressed suit had even more sag than she remembered. Even so, her sympathy remained in a low key. "I wanted to ask you if you'd explain why my husband's car was examined by forensic experts yesterday afternoon."

He answered her question by one of his own. "Would you feel less indignant if I told you that four other cars and two vans have undergone the same treatment in the last four days?"

"Making him one of seven suspects?"

"No, Mrs. Latham. The correct term is that your husband, along with the drivers of the other vehicles, is helping us with our enquiries into the disappearance of Susan Bates." His voice took on a firmer note. "No more, no less. You feel, maybe with a margin of justification, that you have been singled out for special treatment, which you resent. But Susan disappeared from your house, Mrs. Latham. Consequently our enquiries, any police enquiries, must start there."

"From my point of view my husband does appear to have been singled out for special treatment. If I told you, would you believe me when I said you were wasting your time."

"Unfortunately, wasting time is part and parcel of a policeman's job. And until the case is closed, only the Almighty can judge what time is wasted and what spent to good effect. Have I reassured you?"

The blunt answer was no, but she held it back. "There is something else. A boy, Dominic Hurst, an only child of five years and three months, who lives with his parents at Woodlands, Meadow Lane . . ." His look on the turn of a second became so alert, that the words dried on her tongue.

"What about him?"

"His mother is literally terrified to let him out of her sight. They are also on the point of going abroad, ostensibly for a holiday, but that could be a cover."

His eyes remained on hers for several seconds. "The Hursts are known to you? Friends?"

"No. I've only met Mrs. Hurst. She recently joined an organisation to which I belong. . . ."

"Friends in Need."

"Yes. After a couple of weeks she resigned. She is obviously a woman under severe stress. I would guess on the verge of a nervous breakdown."

"Those are all the facts you have?"

"Not quite. If you remember, I told you that one afternoon when I was driving along Meadow Lane, I saw Miss Jones turn right down King's Crescent, continue in the direction of St. Christopher's Primary School for Boys. Dominic Hurst attends that school which is about ten minutes' walk from his home."

He challenged softly: "Are you suggesting that Dominic Hurst is Simon Bates?"

"I think it is a credible theory. His eyes are the same colour as hers, and it's an uncommon shade."

He delved into one of two files, drew out a foolscap sheet, ran his thumb down it. "Norman Hurst, Woodlands, Meadow Lane. Wife, Madeleine Hurst. One child, male, Dominic Hurst, born Belfast, 2nd September, 1970. Father employed by Cathers & Co., a firm of industrial chemists in the City." He looked up. "We did a second check on boys between five and six who were absent from school at the time when Susan disappeared. Dominic Hurst suffered a slight bronchial infection, is now recovered and back at school. The detective who visited Mrs. Hurst and certain other parents had been instructed to ask to see the child's birth certificate. Mrs. Hurst produced it, and . . ."

Whatever he'd been going to add was cut off by the telephone ringing. "Right. I'll be along straight away.

"I'm afraid I'll have to ask you to excuse me. Is there any other fact about the Hursts you wish to add to what you've already told me?"

He was getting to his feet, gathering up his files. She resented that he patently counted her guilty of introducing a red herring to divert their attention from her husband. While she counted him guilty of deliberate procrastination, of playing her along because he'd convinced himself of Richard's involvement in Miss Jones's disappearance. She rose. "I'm sorry to have kept you."

Clutching the insecure files under his arm, he moved towards the door. She could see him dropping the files in the corridor, sending their contents spewing over the floor. He appeared to her as inefficient and unco-ordinated. Ineffective if not utterly useless.

"No need to apologise." He held the door open for her to precede him. "We'll run another check on the Hursts and, if in the slightest degree it confirms your suspicions, we'll take the appropriate action. Anyway, I'll be in touch."

"Thank you." She walked past him, along the corridor, through the front office and out of the police station. He'd keep his word, delegate a detective sergeant, or maybe only a constable to the task of running another check on the Hursts which they, if they were the practised deceivers she suspected them of being, would effortlessly outwit.

Richard came downstairs at five, announced his intention of driving out to Trensham Common, stretching his legs in a two-mile walk. She recognised it for what it was, an act of bravado, a cocking a snook at the police. To prove her right, he added: "I'll probably be followed by a posse. Murderers are expected to return to the scene of the crime, or hang over the grave of their victim. Why, I've never been able to fathom, not unless they are mentally deficient."

"Take care."

"Why?"

"They'd love to arrest you on a charge of driving with over the prescribed limit of alcohol in your blood!"

"One drink," he lied.

She followed him into the hall as he grabbed for his coat. "Is it easy to buy a forged birth certificate?"

He turned and gave her a look of blank astonishment. "For God's sake, what a question! I suppose I heard you right?"

"Yes. Is it?"

"What possible interest could you have in buying a forged birth certificate? Come on, explain yourself."

She couldn't. "It's something I read in a thriller. The author made it appear so simple, I was curious to know if it is so in fact. Is it?"

He'd lost patience with her. "If you know where to go, have the right contacts, and you arrive with sufficient hard cash, you can buy any false identification paper you care to name."

"Thanks. I'll expect you back in an hour, and I'll have dinner for 7:15, which will give you time for a couple of drinks before."

Over dinner, she said: "Max telephoned. He still sounded het-up. I promised you'd ring him after you'd eaten."

He grunted an assent. "Probably he's going to tell me he's moving out of the flat. He was talking about negotiating a sublet when I saw him. There's a chance his agent may be able to get him a walk-on part in a Broadway play. Take him beyond the range of the British police force!"

"That would leave you without a pied-à-terre in London."

"About time that I exchanged his lumpy divan for a bed, especially if the second play script goes through. Tony was telling me about a retired butler in Knightsbridge who runs a house converted into one-room flats that sounds promising."

Amanda not instantly available up a single flight of stairs, but a taxi ride away, which signified what? That the affair was burning itself out or that small inconveniences existed merely to be overcome. She looked down an endless stretch of years during which she would be condemned to play a cruel guessing game, and never even know when she'd been released. She asked: "By the way, were you tailed?"

"Not visibly." He grinned sardonically. "Of course they may have been hiding in the bushes." When she found it beyond her power to grin back, he exploded: "Don't give me that condemned cell look. Unless she crept into the car one night, tried it for size, there can't be a hair of her head, a fingerprint of hers inside it."

"Why on earth," she asked, startled, "should she try your car for size?"

For a second he looked puzzled. "I don't know, but more than once I got the feeling that's what she was doing with the whole house, seeing herself here instead of us." He shrugged, added: "I wish to God, you'd never taken her in. She was bad luck from the start."

"It wasn't exactly lucky for her."

"She was the type that was predestined to disaster. Doomed."

"And I'm supposed not to care." She controlled the rising indignation. "Either about you or what's happened to her."

"Being you, no. But you can care too much about the wrong people. Squander pieces of your heart. It's a bad habit of yours."

The next day she never stirred from the house, concentrated on the preparations for Mrs. Calthorpe's party, her ear alert for the telephone. Three calls. One from Lucy, one from Tony asking for confirmation that the script would be finished on time, and one from Samantha Clownes, speaking from a phone box announcing in a flat voice that her mother had fallen and sprained her wrist. She rang off before Georgina could utter a word of sympathy, which meant under domestic protocol Georgina would have to visit Mrs. Clownes . . . but not till tomorrow. Surely, given a measure of priority, it should not take more than a day to run another check on the Hursts. "I'll keep in touch," Cornford had promised, but it had been casually spoken with little firm intent behind it.

"Even with those damned bobbies sniping at my heels, I've finished a day ahead of schedule. How's that?"

"Good," she said, and raised her glass. "Back on form."

"But not you. You're slipping out of that skirt, and if you don't watch out you'll turn into one of those haggard women, with haunted eyes. You must have lost pounds in weight in the last week. You pick over your food as if you suspected it of being poisoned."

His concern that was spiked by irritation and maybe self-interest—he hated her to be ill—amused her. She laughed. "Since when have you liked tubby women?"

His exasperation rose a notch. "You're obsessed with her. I didn't dig a grave for her, but probably somebody did, somewhere."

"You're guessing, phantasising. You can't possibly *know*. Why can't she be alive . . . somewhere?"

"That's what you want, is it?"

She nodded, and the blanked-out window came alive in her head. Tied up, gagged, kept prisoner until the Hursts had made their second getaway with their stolen child.

"You believe she found the kid?"

Again she nodded.

"If she did, it follows, since no child has been reported missing, that she tried and failed. So the supposed parents are hardly likely to leave her free to spread the news, are they? And the only person who can't talk is a nice cold corpse. And unless you happen to have access to a bath of acid, the handiest way to shift a corpse off your hands is to bury it, as deep as time allows."

"I don't believe she's dead."

He said with airy magnanimity: "Because you don't want to. That's what obsession is. A blindness to sense and reason."

"They could be keeping her a prisoner until they got safely away."

At least he paid her the compliment of considering her suggestion. "Where? Locked up in a garage, a shed?"

"Or in an attic?"

"Poses too many risks."

"It's been done," she insisted.

"In films, novels. It wouldn't work in real life. If the prisoner isn't to die on you, he has to be fed. That means removing the gag. They'd spit out the food and scream."

"Not with a gun digging into their ribs."

"For heaven's sake, what's all this! Go on believing that little creep is still alive if it's any comfort to you, but be realistic. If she is, and she's free, it could be she discovered the child she imagined was hers, was not. And she took off. You certainly won't find her chained to a post." He shook his head at her with good-natured disdain. "I'll make an early start in the morning, have the typescript on Tony's desk by 10:30. That should give me the weekend to begin on the top flat."

ELEVEN

The hours of the morning dragged. Georgina filled them with a fierce self-cross-examination. How did she know? How could she be certain she wasn't indulging in a wild extravaganza of wish fulfilment in her belief that Miss Jones was being held a prisoner. Her judgment wavered, then half-steadied. All right, reduce it to a possibility. A possibility that screamed out to be investigated.

When Cornford had not contacted her at two o'clock, she drove out of the garage, delivered the envelope containing her week's wages to Mrs. Clownes, who wore her arm-sling like a badge of honour, insisted that Georgina drink a glass of sherry at 2:30 in the afternoon, and when she had recited verbatim the circumstances of the accident, the doctor's diagnosis, turned with gloating tones to the subject of Miss Jones. "They've given up hopes of finding her alive, that's what I hear. They've had tracker dogs out on the common and on all the open ground round about. But then you'd know more than I would, seeing the police every day, particularly that inspector chap."

Georgina swallowed the remainder of her sherry in one gulp, rose to her feet. "Actually we know no more than you do. Thank you for the sherry. Ask Samantha to telephone me next week and let me know how the wrist is." And throwing manners to the winds, she opened the door for herself.

Mrs. Clownes had the last word. "Well, when there is any news, I mean where ever they find her, you and Mr. Latham will be the first to know. Only natural, isn't it, her living with you and he being the last person to see her alive, that night you were away visiting."

The season had temporarily shifted out of its lowering mists and drifting fog. The sky was a summer blue, and the sun, low and slanting on the horizon, dazzled her eyes as she drove along the lane, parked the car in a lay-by a hundred yards beyond the farm. The view of the window would be clearer, more precise than on Saturday. She trod exactly the same route, hugging the hedge, but when she reached the boundary, instead of the wormlike approach, she placed herself just beyond the garden shed. By projecting her head a few inches beyond it, raising the tiny pair of theatre binoculars she'd brought with her, when she got the window in focus, she saw that it was boarded up from the inside. As she slipped the binoculars back into her pocket, the suspicion that Miss Jones was imprisoned up there solidified into a hard conviction. It took her a quarter of a minute to identify the sound behind her as breathing, so close to her ear that for a second's space she didn't, couldn't, believe it was human. Her body became so rigid she was unable to turn her head.

"It's Mrs. Latham, isn't it?"

A man's voice. In slow motion, she wheeled her face towards it. Norman Hurst, smiling, extending his hand. "You know my wife, Madeleine, but I don't think we've met. Like me, I see you've decided it's a perfect afternoon for a country walk." Above the smile the slate grey eyes focused on her were peculiarly static. The inference that she had a perfect right to be where she was, inspecting his property through binoculars, injected a cold fluid into her veins, so that she had to make an effort not to shiver. Yet when she spoke, it was with a casual response that matched his. "Very welcome after all the cloud and mist. I was tempted to leave my car and come across the fields by the right of way. I hope it *is* a public footpath and that I've not been trespassing."

"Actually, you're a few hundred yards astray, but I'm sure the owner of the land wouldn't object."

She stared at the middle button of his jacket, her brain suddenly numbed so that no suitable conversational gambit suggested itself.

"As you're so near, won't you come in for a few minutes? Madeleine would be delighted to see you, especially"—he gave a semblance of a laugh—"as she was upset that you caught her the other day after she'd had a sleepless night and, her description not mine, the whole house was a shambles."

A spider cajoling a fly? And how had he been able to pin a name to her face? Indecision gripped her in a vice from which she could not release herself, as he went on: "There's a gate, you don't have to climb the hedge. Quite an inconspicuous one, home-made. Dominic and I are sometimes guilty of trespassing, as I am now."

He turned his back on her, walked to the corner, eased some paling over the tufted grass. "After you. We're off on holiday tomorrow. That's why I'm home today giving a hand with the packing."

The decision still unmade, she was drawn compulsively towards the gap. "Is Dominic home too?"

"No." He closed the make-shift gate behind her. "At school. That way he can't nag to have every toy he possesses packed. Also Madeleine and I can make do on snacks provided he has a solid school dinner."

"Where are you going?" Her glance slid to the rim of the swimming pool, where the last tile was cemented into place.

"Marrakesh."

He walked closer by her side than was necessary, and the

certainty flew through her mind that if she turned and ran, he'd grab her, hold her prisoner. He was staring at his feet as though to keep his pace matching hers, and when he felt her glance on him, he angled his head sideways, and very slowly the smile that contained no particle of warmth formed on his lips.

He opened the french window and she stepped forward into the sitting-room that was even more chaotic than when she'd stood there with Dominic admiring the pool.

Without moving from her side, he shouted: "Maddy! Maddy! We've got a visitor.

"Do sit down." He touched her elbow and guided her to an arm-chair on the far side of the room, then stood as if on guard a couple of feet away.

"Yes, what is it?" Madeleine demanded from the open door, and then drew in her breath in a tiny hiss.

"Mrs. Latham, darling. We met while we were both taking a stroll down the field. I persuaded her to come in."

"Why, yes . . ." The dyed blond hair was set in the same puff-ball extravaganza as on the afternoon she had climbed Georgina's stairs. The rest of her was an unco-ordinated mess: grease-spotted slippers, snagged tights, too-short skirt, and a shrunken sweater. She seemed lost, dazed, her glance flying to her husband for help. "Our flight leaves Heathrow so early in the morning that I'm having to . . ."

"Darling, make us a pot of tea. . . ."

"No, please . . ." Georgina interrupted.

Madeleine pleaded, wringing one hand in the other. "I must collect Dominic in half an hour and there are things I've still got to buy."

"Tea, please, darling," he said adamantly. "You can finish your shopping *after* you've collected Dominic."

She chewed her lip, then silently nodded her head, like an automated doll when a string has been jerked, and went to do his bidding.

"My wife," he explained with an attempt at delicacy, "is suffering from a *crise* of nerves. That's one of the reasons why we're getting away from it all."

Her sense of reality came and went in waves, so that it was impossible to hold it steady. She seized and held firm the one truth that was absolute. At the top of the field he had watched her raise the binoculars and focus them on the blacked-out attic window, made no reference to the flagrant act of spying, but escorted her into the house as though she were a welcome guest. A response so unnatural that it could be nothing other than a premeditated act of deceit. Through a haze she saw Miss Jones lying bound and gagged on a bed. Or maybe there was no bed, and she was lying on a cold floor.

As he continued to prowl, never withdrawing his wet-slate gaze from her for more than a couple of seconds, she murmured: "I understand you've been ill, too. Are you better now?"

For a second he looked nonplussed, then he shrugged. "A mild indisposition. Do you enjoy good health, Mrs. Latham?"

"Exceptionally good."

"And your husband?"

"He never ails a thing," and again she was overcome by the total unreality of the scene, a sense of being submerged under a nightmare.

"Good!" He gave her a patronising smile, repeated: "Good."

His prowling took him behind her back and she heard him open a drawer. She jerked her head sideways but the chair obscured her view.

When he strolled back, he was folding into place the flap of his jacket pocket. There was a bulge. A gun? With her eye she measured the space between her chair and the french window. Roughly twenty feet. As her glance lifted, she saw he was measuring it with her.

Madeleine Hurst fumbled with the knob, then opened the door wide with her knee. She set the tray of tea on the table, and with that glazed dummy look, intoned: "You'll have to excuse me. It's time I changed and went to collect Dominic from school."

"We'll excuse you, darling." He went to the door, opened it for her, and with the precise enunciation one might use to someone who was deaf said: "I'll expect you both home in an hour. Half-past four. That should give you ample time to finish your shopping."

As he closed the door on his wife, Georgina heard a click. She stared at the door, unable to remember whether or not there had been a key in it.

He said with cloying facetiousness: "I'll be mother, shall I?"

He placed a cup and a bowl of sugar by her side, carried his own tea to a facing chair, from which he lifted a pile of shirts that were presumably waiting to be packed in the three-quarters-full suitcase under the table.

He stirred his tea, then very slowly lifted his face that was wreathed in sly pleasure. "I imagine you must have known the girl who's disappeared. Helen Jones, or that's what she called herself."

Released from the charade of pretence, the salty taste of reality acted on her like a tonic. "She was a tenant of mine." She paused, added with relish: "As you well know. Your wife went on a spying trip round my house, and it was you, wasn't it, who used the keys you stole from her to search for something of hers you needed: probably her son's birth certificate. But you were too late. I'd handed it and all her belongings to the police. And, anyway, I surprised you."

"I wouldn't say that. I'm not an easy man to surprise. I prepare myself for every eventuality." He pursed his thin lips. "Naturally Susan made a confidant of you. An accessory, or might a better word be accomplice?"

"In what?" She made herself lift the cup, touch it with her lips, though she could not swallow a drop of tea.

Expression and voice changed as though he'd ripped off a

mask. "In evil," he shouted. "What else, since that is what she was, an evil young woman."

"Evil?" she queried, still light-headed with relief that deception had been abandoned. "Evil to reclaim her own child!"

"Evil," he repeated, his mouth shaking with the violence of hate. "She was incapable of being a mother to her son. Given the chance, she'd have made a parcel of him, abandoned him on the steps of a police-station or a vicarage, an illegitimate child to be brought up like a pauper. She made one attempt, which fortunately I was able to circumvent. He was a millstone round her neck from which she was determined to cut herself loose."

She laughed. "You're a bad liar! It surprises me with all the practice you've had: five and a half years of lying."

His voice spiralled unnaturally high, became manic. "What do you know about it? The love, the anguish . . ."

When he caught his breath, she interjected: "I have a son of my own. But that's not important. What is, is that I've come here to find her and take her away. Where is she?"

He feigned an expression of disbelief. "You mean, you don't know?"

"I'm prepared to make a guess. You've got her gagged and bound in your attic. You're about to bolt and leave her there to die of starvation if she isn't found. That's murder. . . ."

"Murder!" He gave a sanctimonious shake of his head. "Not one I'm about to commit, I assure you. If I may say so you appear to be given to jumping to quite preposterous conclusions." He sipped delicately from his tea, returned the cup to the saucer, said with silky triumph: "You can't murder a girl who's already dead, now can you?"

The seconds hung like lead as she was subjected to a slow torture in which she learned the margin that separated bearable fear from animal terror.

Across the length of the hearth-rug, he nodded at her. "Don't make the mistake of disbelieving your ears, Mrs.

Latham. Your Miss Jones is not only dead but neatly buried where no one is ever likely to find her." He held out his hand. "Come, I'll show you her grave."

Like an invitation to a visitor to walk her round the garden! When she did not rise, he came forward, jerked her to her feet, dragged her to the french window. "Quite a pretty grave. At the deep end. The circumstances couldn't have been more propitious. The earth had already been dug out by a labourer and banked up. After she had been snugly disposed of, all that remained was the levelling, concreting and tiling. A job requiring a certain amount of manual effort, but not beyond me. You see, I'm a very fit man, Mrs. Latham."

Standing there, she literally prayed for release from the conviction that he was lying. She brought her gaze with feeble hope to his face. It was bathed in serene pride. For a second panic seized her that she might vomit.

He went on in a light conversational tone: "She appeared to be under the illusion that she was invisible, or that a wig, a pair of glasses transformed her into a different person. Every day, either early in the morning, or after dark she prowled like an alley-cat around the place. She was even on one occasion standing outside the school when my wife collected Dominic. Not that I'm grumbling; it was an illusion that played into our hands. All we had to do, when we were ready for her, was to leave the french window unlocked, turn off the light, and wait for her to walk in. In her handbag she was carrying a little gun, a Webley-Scott 7.65 automatic. I imagine she saw herself saying 'Hands up' and our meekly obeying. Then bang, bang, and we'd be dead." He laughed hilariously. "She existed in a dream-world, disassociated from reality. A mental condition for which the psychologists no doubt have a name. But a layman like myself doesn't need high falutin' terms. The simple truth is that she was crazy, only fit to be locked up." He smiled obscenely. "The little gun and the bicycle were buried with her. It seemed appropriate.

"And do you know what she screeched, when her farcical scheme collapsed about her ears? 'Mrs. Latham knows all about me and Simon, that he's mine and you stole him, and that I'm going to get him back. She knows.' She was, of course, a congenital liar, but maybe this time she wasn't lying. Or maybe she told you and you didn't believe her . . . not until now."

Death suddenly leaping out of nowhere. The scene in the attic a mirage with which she'd deluded herself. And yet somewhere there was release from one pain that had gripped her, dim and far away but precious. A tiny portion of her heart sighed away the anguish that might have lain there, from which she had now been saved. Only one corner of her mind functioned: ticking out a warning like a Morse code. A murderer only confesses to a murder if he is cornered, or knows beyond an iota of doubt that his confession is as safe as though it were buried beyond recovery in a grave.

She took the only direct action open to her, lunged forward, butted him with her head.

She heard the crack of his laugh as he spun her round, wrenched her wrists behind her back, held them with one hand, while with the other he whipped a roll of adhesive bandage from his pocket, bound them together. She screamed, flung herself against the window. He jerked her back, and for a second scissors flashed lethal as a knife as though he were about to cut her throat, before he plastered a length of the bandage across her mouth, snipped it off, let the roll and scissors drop to the floor.

"All a bit of an anti-climax," he jeered, "not to say wasted effort on your part. By the way, that attic you were so interested in is my dark-room."

She could hear her own screams though not a sound of them could pass her lips. Jammed, they screeched insanely in her head, while the feeling of being suffocated induced mental and physical terror. She flung herself forward against the window.

One pane cracked, but didn't break. "You'll wear yourself out," he mocked. "And to no purpose." His right hand like a second vice on her wrists, with his left he stooped and retrieved the roll of adhesive bandage and the scissors which he pocketed. "For the moment I'll leave your legs. You'll need them."

In the second he opened the french window, she was through it, into the bliss of the open air where surely there was a hope of relief from the suffocation and panic. He grabbed her when, thrown off balance by her bound hands, she pitched forward.

He hauled her up, and she was conscious of a dizziness where she'd knocked her head, of images that were elusive, slipping and changing before they melted into the nothingness of horror.

He thrust her forward, past the blur of the swimming pool, over the soft texture of the lawn, before he threw her into the garden shed, sent her sprawling to the floor. He bent, wrenched off her boots, and, despite all her frantic kicking, bound her ankles as tight as her wrists. Then he went through the pockets of her sheepskin jacket, confiscated her car keys.

On his feet he was breathing hard. "I warned you," he whispered hoarsely, "not to waste your energy." He kicked the side of her head. "You've nobody to blame but yourself: you took her in, listened to her lies. Encouraged her. Then when she got what she deserved, you went running to the police. A little intelligent deduction would have revealed what she was: trash, a demented girl who would have dragged her child down to her own level if we hadn't rescued him." He took a deep breath. "Now he's a fine boy. My son. And no one, not even you, is going to steal him from me. Mark that, Mrs. Latham, because in a couple of hours you'll be incapable ever again of interfering in my life or anyone else's. If you've any prayers to say, you better get busy."

She heard the door bang, the key turn. For a while all she was conscious of was the claylike coldness of her body, an icy fear that fused into the pain that throbbed in her wrists, ankles and hammered in her temple.

Trussed like a chicken, her face rubbed into a concrete floor caked with grit and trodden-in earth, her sense of being debased and humiliated past all redemption pre-emptied her of terror. In that blackest of all moments she appeared to herself as slightly less able than Mrs. Clownes, on a par with Samantha punching keys as she dreamed of a white wedding, clashing bells and a military guard of honour. Her naïveté at visualising herself battering her way into the attic, freeing Miss Jones from bonds and gags, reuniting her with her son, and presenting them both to Cornford as some sort of trophy she had won single-handed appalled and sickened her.

Yet, paradoxically it was the self-abasement that in the end acted as a restorative. Having touched the lowest depth of self-contempt unless she was to be reduced to a wormlike acceptance, there was nothing for her to do but clamber out of the pit. It took her five minutes to heave her body over, lie on her wrists that prickled with pain and which she judged in a little while would be numbed by the restricted blood flow. There were two four-paned fixed windows, neither of which opened. One faced down the field, one looked towards the house. Even had she been able to reach them and break the glass, only a small child or an adult thin as a bean-pole could have squeezed through the opening.

On the floor were a lawn-mower, a wheel-barrow, some trugs, and a collection of hoes, rakes, spades and a yard-broom. There was a shelf, its supports plugged into the walls of the shed, stacked with small hand-tools, tins and containers of insecticides and fertilisers. By tilting her head at an extreme angle she brought into focus a pair of secateurs identical with a pair of her own: precision-turned, razor-sharp, guaranteed to cut cleanly and at the precise angle required. To reach them she had somehow to propel herself upright, a feat that demanded such a high degree of athleticism, plus the muscle control of a female Houdini that at first it seemed beyond her. Propping herself forward on her bound hands, she dug with her heels, bent her knees and lurched upward. On the seventh attempt she made it, sweat running down her forehead and neck, frightened she would choke because her nasal tubes were insufficient to pump out the breath that roared in her lungs. With the dying orb of the sun fallen out of sight, and the shed growing dimmer by the second, she calculated that in less than an hour her ration of half light would be used up.

With her head she butted the secateurs off the shelf on to the floor, but she had miscalculated the amount of force needed, and they skidded too far. To reach them she had to hop laboriously forward. Her hope had been that she could control them with her toes in which, even though her ankles were bound, there remained a degree of mobility. When her grasp on them failed to manoeuvre the catch that released the blades, tears of frustration momentarily blinded her.

There was no alternative but to spread herself face-down on the floor, chin the secateurs towards the angle of the wooden strut supporting the shelf, press against the catch. It should have given a click as the blades flew apart. When, the side of her jaw scraped raw, there was no click, she saw that the blades were jammed by a spit of wood. Close to her eye, the dying shaft of sun that pierced the dusty window on to the field, revealed they were unoiled, corroded with rust and had probably not been used for years.

She laid her forehead on the dirt-caked floor as the fact of her own death became not an event at some unspecified date in the future but an execution that would be summarily performed before lightness returned to the earth.

Like a vision Simon's face, with its angles and curves, the light that suffused it except in rare moments when he was uncertain or confused, materialised in her head. Her heart heaved and, when it steadied, she suffered a grief more profound than she had ever experienced, not on her own account but on his, of the love enduring until the end of her life of which he'd be deprived by a man who would murder the world to keep a boy he counted his son.

And rising behind Simon's face was Richard's. She studied it objectively. There was no woman but herself who, at twenty-four, had fallen so wholly in love with him that she could never totally divorce herself from that obligation of loving, who would care for and protect a consummate egotist, support him when he was hounded by the dread of professional failure, who was subject to bouts of drunkenness, whose temper ran amok, tipped over into physical violence. Certainly not Amanda, whose body would win her a more rewarding and richer provider.

And emerging, delineating itself with remorseless clarity in her head, was Miss Jones, so wholly committed to recovering her son, that there was no vestige of herself to spare, as she concentrated heart and mind on a single objective. And when she failed, flinging Georgina's name, as though it would provide her with a shield against death, in Norman Hurst's face. So there was Dominic too.

She had got, somehow, to survive. The judgment arrived at, it was with a blessed sense of calm that she made an inventory of the gardening implements. The mower, she decided. She wriggled wormlike until her feet lay horizontally alongside it, twisted her body, raised her trussed wrists, dragged them over the blades. But the blades were not straight but curved, clogged with grass, and if she exerted too much pressure they whirled away from her. Doggedly she sawed on, but the surgical bandage was tough; she could make no clean cut, and desperately as she strove to wrench her wrists apart they remained clamped together.

Lying flat, winning back her breath, she ticked off the methods that he might use to kill her. The likeliest, since he had picked the keys out of her pocket, seemed the car. Parked in the lay-by, it was plainly visible from the road so might attract the curiosity of the farmer or one of his employees if it was abandoned too long; on the other hand she was almost certain that the fields immediately beyond it were filled with winter cabbages that, unlike stock, would require no human attention.

And, with the keys in Norman Hurst's possession, would it still be there? There wasn't an answer. But assuming it was where she had left it, how did he propose to remove her, dead or alive, from the shed to the waiting car over a mile of rough field track? She stared at the now barely discernible outline of the wheel-barrow. With her legs tucked under her chin, covered by a rug or sacking, some plausible story invented if he was questioned, provided she were either dead or clubbed to insensibility, she could be trundled to the car. Then what? Suddenly her nostrils were assaulted by a phantom stench. On the outskirts of the town, in a derelict area, which was accessible by the lane at the end of the field, there was a monster rubbish-tip. She'd been among the petitioners who had harried the Council—without success—to have it made sanitary, fenced off to prevent children playing with rusting refrigerators, abandoned cars with lethal metal edges, tanks in which sufficient petrol remained to constitute a fire hazard. Was a can of petrol ignited by a flaming rag to form the pattern of her dying on a rubbish dump? Or was she to be murdered, her body left to decompose in a filthy, locked shed?

Every pulse in her body was revolted by the obscenity of either. All right, assume she was going to live, even if she did not know how.

The twilight was ebbing fast and before darkness closed upon her she must commit to memory the lay-out of the shed, fix in her mind the precise position of every implement. Unable to move the heavier ones, she must conceive a plan that would induce inanimate objects to work for her.

Once again, she began the slow, draining effort to haul herself to her feet. On the tenth heave, her head swimming, she propped her back against the shelf, waited until she regained the strength to hop two paces towards the door.

A trunk, she thought, that was what she was reduced to, a trunk without limbs, useless except as a human battering ram.

Through the window that faced the house she saw a glow. She stared hard at it, but gradually her eyelids sealed themselves together. Then in a panic they flew wide, her lungs pumping breath in snorts through her nostrils as she heard a car in the drive. Her car? Now it was dark had they brought it to the house to transport her to her grave, or were they merely reversing the parking order of their two cars?

For a moment of stark horror her brain refused to feed back to her the plan it had conceived. She panicked, and behind the bandage plastered tight over her mouth, heard with the ears of her mind the silenced screams of abject terror. Then, like a page turned, it spread itself out before her to read.

She counted off the seconds in the dark, adding minute to minute until she reached twenty, and then her ability to count in three figures deserted her. Just one to sixty and then start again.

It was a light that flashed intermittently over the four little squares of glass that alerted her to his approach. The grass over which he walked yielded no sound of footsteps, and she heard nothing until the key rattled in the lock. Her preparations made, all she had to do was to alter her balance.

The door, which opened inward, shielded her from the torch-beam he flashed. Not finding her, he slammed the door, leaving her with a single unguarded second. She leaned forward, gave herself maximum propulsion and flung herself on top of him. She bore him not to the floor, but on to the hard angles of the lawn-mower.

The torch flew out of his hand, and in the darkness she was granted a moment of pure hope when his body lay prone, unmoving beneath her own. Then with a heave, he tossed her off, bent and shook her as though she were a rat. "Bitch," he snarled. "An interfering bitch." He lit his cigarette lighter to find the torch, but the flame snuffed out.

From the house, coming nearer as she ran down the garden was Madeleine Hurst's high-pitched scream. "Norman, Norman . . . You're wanted. Norman."

He stood rock still in the darkness, bracing his foot on her spine as, nearer now, Madeleine began to screech. "Norman, it's the police. They want to see you."

He was through the door, had it shut behind him before the light of another torch hit it.

A voice, in the pedantic tone of one reciting textbook phrases learned by heart, said: "Mr. Hurst, I'm sorry to disturb you, but Inspector Cornford would be obliged if you would accompany me to the station. He understands that you are leaving for Marrakesh in the morning, and there are one or two final points he'd like to clear up before you go."

Norman Hurst's voice had an arrogant ring. "What points? I've already supplied him with all the information he asked for."

"I couldn't say, sir. If you wouldn't mind coming with me."

Georgina ceased to listen to the dialogue. She needed to gather together in one unified effort all the remnants of her mental and physical strength. To haul herself to her feet yet again was beyond her. For a second she closed her eyes, as though inner darkness would restore to her mind the memory of each implement in the shed. She arched her back, drew in her knees, kicked out with her bound feet and sent the wheelbarrow skidding into the forks and spades and hoes.

"Who's in there, sir?"

"No one. It's a dog . . ."

"If you'd open the door, sir . . ."

Spread across the filthy floor, Georgina's ears rang with the sound of a shot, a cry, a woman's anguished wail, and then with a gratitude that was almost love she accepted the black oblivion that was folding itself around her. The last sound her brain registered before it blanked out was that of a child screaming.

TWELVE

The instant her eyelids parted Georgina recognised where she was: in one of the two side-rooms off Ward 5 in Larksbridge Hospital. She'd spent hours there the previous winter during the terminal illness of Mrs. Watson, who possessed no relatives and whose irascibility and autocracy precluded her from making friends. Momentarily she recalled the spasmodic tight grasp on her hand that expressed the abject loneliness Mrs. Watson's tongue could not bring herself to acknowledge.

Under the dimmed light of the small ward, she looked for her watch. Where it should have been were clean gauze bandages, but the approach of the trolley along the corridor, the chink of cups suggested it was around six o'clock.

She pressed the bell on her pillow. Sister Bellamy materialised as swiftly as though she'd had her eye to the keyhole. Taking Georgina's pulse, she enquired: "And how are you feeling, Mrs. Latham, after that nice long sleep?"

Georgina had no intention of telling her. "Right as rain. By the way, whose nightgown am I wearing?"

"One of the reserves we hoard for emergencies. I picked out the best on offer." She plumped up the pillows. "Nurse Dickinson is bringing you a tray of tea. When you've drunk it, I'll bleep Dr. Cox and ask him to come to have a look at you. Feel a bit muzzy, I expect?"

"No," Georgina denied. "As clear as a bell. Where is my husband?"

"Dr. Cox sent him off after you'd been sedated. Told him there was nothing he could do but go home and mix himself a stiff drink. I imagine he'll be back pretty soon."

Sister Bellamy took the tray from the teen-age probationer, and firmly pushed the door closed against her blatantly inquisitive glance. "You're by way of being a bit of a celebrity. Not that that cuts any ice with me." She grinned. "To me you're a patient, no more, no less. How's the head?"

"Fine." Georgina's wrists and ankles throbbed. There was a pain in her right temple and the small of her back felt as though it had been kicked—which it had, but she was not prepared to admit to the slightest pain or indisposition.

Sister Bellamy waited until her patient had sipped one cup of tea, then said as she poured a second: "I hate to do this to you so early in the morning, but Inspector Cornford made me swear an oath I'd telephone him as soon as I'd received the okay from Dr. Cox that he could see you. After all you've been through, it's a shame."

"No," Georgina retorted. "I want to see him. Bring on a reserve toothbrush."

Dark shadows under Inspector Cornford's eyes signalled a sleepless night. Georgina brushed aside his courteous enquiries about her state of health. "Tell me what happened to the boy, Dominic. I heard him scream just as I was going under. Was he hurt?"

"Not physically. The shot woke him and he ran downstairs. He remained with his mother until we could lay on a woman P.C., and then he was driven to Fairview. As I expect you know, it is one of the most advanced child care centres in the county. Only six children to a cottage, each run by a married couple. It was the best we could do for him in the short term."

"Yes, I do know Fairview, and the head matron, Mrs. Carstairs. I heard Norman Hurst fire a gun. Was anyone hurt?"

"Det. Constable Rigby." He paused momentarily, appeared to deepen his concentration. "Mrs. Latham, there are certain background developments to the case that, in view of your close involvement with it, I feel you have a right to know. On consideration, after your last visit it was decided to run a more detailed check on the Hursts, covering a much longer period. Hurst, on being interviewed, stated that he and his wife were born and brought up in Southwark, and produced marriage and birth certificates to prove it. He'd held a wide variety of unskilled jobs after he'd left school, and was then employed as a bookmaker's clerk; also, as he had a talent for figures, he did free-lance accountancy work. This continued over some years, and then they moved to a flat in Notting Hill Gate. Again he worked for a bookie. Three months before Dominic was born they settled in Belfast, where Hurst found employment in the accounts department of a plastics firm. Nine months later the firm went bankrupt and the Hursts emigrated to Johannesburg where, after a short period as a clerk, he was promoted to a more responsible position. They returned to England in January of this year and after living for a short period in furnished accommodation in North London, he got a job as an accountant with a shipping company in the City and bought the house in Meadow Lane. The reason he gave for their return to England was that he wished Dominic to be educated in this country.

"He was asked to supply names, addresses and precise dates. These he provided with the exception of the address in Notting Hill which he said he had forgotten. Both sets of parents were dead and Hurst claimed that with being abroad they had lost touch with other members of their families and friends. However, he did give us the names of three friends who had known him in the old days in Southwark. We were only, until the time of his arrest, able to contact one, a barman in a pub, who swore he knew Hurst well from placing bets with him. The firm in Johannesburg confirmed that Hurst had been employed by them for over four years. As proof they were only leaving the country for a holiday, Hurst produced their return air tickets to Marrakesh, and a receipt for a three-week booking at a hotel there.

"Thereafter we ran into a blank wall. Southwark, as you well know, dating from the '50's onwards, was an area of high priority development. Over the years acres of sub-standard houses have been demolished, streets razed to make space for high-rise flats. The two houses the Hursts had lived in before their marriage no longer exist, neither does the one they had occupied after marriage. The betting shops have disappeared. This meant we had to contact the local authorities, ask permission to examine old records of property that had been torn down years ago. The request was granted, but it proved a somewhat laborious time-wasting process.

"In Belfast the address Hurst had supplied was in a much-bombed, now derelict street, none of the houses currently habitable. The firm by whom Hurst had been employed was defunct and, once again, time would be required to trace ex-members of the staff. Two distinct areas that had been laid waste were stretching the arm of coincidence just that much too long, suggesting that time was being employed as a deliberate delaying tactic. Time we must expend before we could confirm whether the addresses which Hurst had supplied were genuine or fake. Time that, with plane tickets booked for today, was on his side unless we could prove he was lying. At that point it was decided to put the Hursts under a twenty-four hour a day surveillance.

"Then late yesterday afternoon we received a call from the Belfast police. A detective-sergeant, who had been on sick leave and had now returned to duty, chanced to know a couple who had lived at No. 8 Belfont Street for twelve years. Hurst claimed to have occupied No. 6. The Reillys said their neighbours at No. 6 at the relevant period had been a widower and his teen-age son; those at No. 10 an elderly childless couple. It is a short street and the Reillys had known everyone in it and were adamant that the Hursts had not been among them. At that point a radio message was sent to Rigby ordering him to bring Hurst to the station immediately. He left Det. Constable Morton, who was on watch with him, in the car in the drive and went to pick him up.

"At first Mrs. Hurst refused to admit her husband was at home, but when Rigby insisted on searching the garden, she became hysterical, ran ahead of him, shouting a warning to her husband. Hurst, on being ordered to open the garden-shed, shot Rigby at point-blank range. Morton, hearing the shot, raced down the garden and, fortunately, managed to disarm Hurst." Cornford paused, looked across the bed into space. "Norman Hurst, or to give him his correct name, Anthony Jackson, will appear at the magistrates' court this morning. He will be charged with murder. Rigby never recovered consciousness."

"I'm sorry."

She doubted whether he heard her. He went on: "In fact, the bookings for Marrakesh were a blind. A husband and wife, boy aged five, were booked under the name of MacIntosh on one-way tickets to Salisbury, Rhodesia, on a plane that left shortly before the one to Marrakesh. These seats were never claimed; the address given does not exist. The Hursts would, of course, have been tailed to London airport, not allowed to board the Salisbury plane. We wouldn't have lost them, but we might have lost you." He cleared his throat. "With the Hursts' movements visible from the front of the house, with no means of exit for a car other than down the drive, I omitted to extend the surveillance to the rear, and so had no knowledge that you were on the premises. It was an error of judgment on my part which I deeply regret."

It seemed no moment to vent her pent-up anger that a large

portion of the time he mourned had been fruitlessly spent on trying to establish Richard's guilt. Maybe that was a method common to all policemen: throw their trawl wide enough and they'd catch someone. She made a disclamatory gesture with her hand. "I came to no serious harm. I'm only sorry you lost Detective Constable Rigby."

"He was a first-class man, the type we can ill afford to lose." The simple epitaph spoken, he gathered himself together, went on: "And I apologise, when you must still be suffering from the effects of last night's ordeal, to have to ask you for a statement. Merely the facts as you recall them. If necessary, we can amplify them later." The narrow hazel glance skimmed over her. "Did you honestly believe you would find Susan at the Hursts'?"

She nodded, which set up a slight throbbing in her head. "There was an attic with a boarded-up window. You could say I hypnotised myself into believing they were keeping her a prisoner there until they could make a second get-away. In fact, it was Norman Hurst's dark-room." She steadied her breath. "But he'd already killed her, hadn't he?"

"Yes. All we have at the moment is Mrs. Hurst's statement. Hysterical and inconclusive. She was moved to a psychiatric ward for treatment early this morning. Hurst refuses to make a statement until he is legally represented. His solicitor will be with him this morning. According to Mrs. Hurst, he shot Susan with her own gun, but we shan't know whether that was so until we've recovered her body which she says he buried under a layer of concrete at the bottom of the swimming pool he was in the process of constructing."

Her flesh cringed on her bones. For a long moment her tongue was rigid, speech beyond her as she strove to control her mindless, compulsive grief. Even when she could speak, her articulation was laboured. "They'd seen her, that's what he boasted to me, watching the house, waiting outside St. Christopher's. One night they deliberately left the french window unlocked, trapped her. The wig, the glasses didn't fool them."

"No. It was obvious, even in the state of near dementia Madeleine Hurst was in, that they were never off guard, always on the alert and prepared in case Susan should succeed in tracking them down."

"She never had a hope of getting Dominic away from them, had she?"

"I can't conceive of one, not unless she'd come to us, or confided in you?"

She cried out in bewildered despair: "Why didn't she?"

He brooded, staring at his folded hands. "Her childhood, the hand life had dealt her. She had retreated so deep inside herself she trusted no one. Silence, secrecy had become a prison from which she could not escape. We'll never know in what circumstances her son was conceived. All we do know for certain is that she gave birth to an illegitimate child alone and without a single friend. A child she loved, who was stolen from her.

"And that she purchased a gun. Maybe she believed she could shoot them both, make a get-away with the boy before the bodies of the Hursts were discovered. Since she left the cash-box behind her, I would think it unlikely she intended to murder them the night she entered the house. It was the only time she had effected an entrance, and her first move would surely have been to familiarise herself with its lay-out, for instance to discover the room where the boy slept. She would also have needed a safe hiding place for them both, and presumably some form of disguise for each of them. Whether she'd already made these preparations, we don't know, probably never shall."

He lapsed into silence, lifted one hand, pleated his upper lip between his finger and thumb, again concentrated his yellow-brown gaze on the space at the far side of the bed, before he made a visible effort to pull himself together. "Now if I could have your statement of what occurred from your arrival at the house until P.C. Rigby was shot, I'll leave you to rest."

When she'd finished piecing together a coherent sequence, he snapped the note-book, appeared to have some difficulty in enclosing it within a slippery rubber band. As he stood up, he held out his hand and then on the sight of her bandaged wrists withdrew it. "I'm relieved to learn from the medical staff that you'll be fit to go home today." For a moment his bland, meaningless smile took on a genuine warmth, widening a little Georgina's insight into a personality she had found maddeningly complex. She had questioned whether he cared, now she learned he did. He said quietly: "You deserved to win. I'm sorry you didn't. But at least you've nothing to reproach yourself with."

Only failure, she thought, as she watched the thick body disappear. A failure that she would never be given the chance to redeem, that would leave behind a tiny, grieving voice for ever.

When he'd left, Sister Bellamy put her head round the door. "Okay, if I let your husband in?"

"If you'd give me a hand, I'd rather get dressed first. The sight of me even mildly indisposed scares him rigid. It conjures up a macabre vision of me lying in a coffin."

"Oh, men! Babies the lot of them. He's brought you some fresh clothes. I'll fetch them."

They were a singularly ill-assorted collection, grabbed at random by someone whose concentration was shot to pieces. Georgina and Sister Bellamy made the best of them. "Not very co-ordinated, are they? Still, you'll be in the car, so it doesn't matter. I wonder why on earth he chose a pair of his trousers instead of your slacks. And all topped off by a mink jacket!"

"He gets so carried away with the phantasies that run riot in his brain, that practical common sense gets lost."

"Well," Sister Bellamy said kindly, "I suppose you've got to make allowances for writers. Now don't forget you promised Dr. Cox you'd call in your own doctor to have a look at you tomorrow morning. You could suffer from a bout of delayed shock."

Georgina saw Richard's hand shaking as it folded itself round the door. "I'm okay," she called out in her brightest voice. "No need to treat me like an invalid."

"Why, so you are!" His grin was silly with relief. "Last night you looked . . ." He gulped.

"Last night I was doped, probably looked ghastly, but I'm fine now. Did you park the car at the front or the back?"

Suddenly, as though his legs could no longer be trusted to support him, he sank into a chair. "The back."

"Good. That's nearer of the two car parks from this end of the hospital."

Without warning the tears flowed down his cheeks. He smeared them away with his hand. "God, what an exhibition!"

"It's shock. The only treatment is a cup of strong, syrupy tea. I'll make you one as soon as we get home."

He grabbed her hand. "Georgie, I thought I'd lost you . . . and I couldn't have taken it."

She savoured his words for a few seconds. They might have to last her a life-time. Then she laughed, gently, consolingly. "Not a chance. I'm a sticker, not easy to lose."

Reaction, as she'd intended, set in. "But what in hell's name possessed you? Tangling with a maniac, on your own, as though you were some species of super-woman?"

"Ah," she said, keeping his hand in hers for a few more seconds. "That's a long story. It'll keep till we get home."

He growled: "That bloody girl, she hypnotised you. Come on, admit it!"

She dropped his hand, rose and walked to the door. As he opened it, she said softly: "She's dead."

For a second his glance remained coldly outraged, and then a semblance of what she had schooled herself to accept as love returned. "Okay, I get it. Don't speak ill of the dead. But you might remember that though she may be a martyr to you, to me she was a screwy kid who came damned near to getting you murdered. . . ." He paused, then added a footnote: "Apart from leaving me number one suspect in the eyes of the police." He gave her a swift, almost squinting glance. "Did you ever think I'd done her in?"

"No," she lied, not even aware she was lying. "It never crossed my mind."

It was a week later when Mrs. Clownes on her way out—she always made her exit through the front door—trundled back to Georgina's study. "There's a young woman outside. Says she wants to see you. Inspector Cornford sent her, or that's her story. A Mrs. Sandiman. Want me to send her off?"

The name had no niche in Georgina's memory. "You'd better show her in. No, I'll come myself."

She was probably in her late twenties, short, sturdy, dressed in a thick tweed coat, serviceable flat-heeled shoes. Her dark hair, except for a few stray wisps was imprisoned inside a crocheted woollen hat, which accentuated the round, fresh-coloured face innocent of make-up.

"Mrs. Latham? Inspector Cornford told me to come and see you." She spoke in the tone of someone obeying an order rather than acting of her own free will.

"Please come in."

With an absorbed stare she examined the hall before she put a foot across the threshold, and then followed at Georgina's heels into the drawing-room.

"Do sit down. Can I give you a glass of sherry? It's a bit late for coffee."

Her refusal was firm, unequivocal, as her glance made forays about the room. "I haven't time." She sat down abruptly on the nearest chair. "It was Inspector Cornford's idea; not that I'm saying I didn't want to see you. I don't suppose Susan ever mentioned me, but I was Sandra Murphy until I married my husband a few months after she went to London."

"I'm afraid she didn't, but Inspector Cornford told me that you were about the only friend she had."

"I suppose you could say that. Then about a year after we were married we moved to Wales. You see, all Bill ever wanted was to own his own bit of land, and he thought he'd maybe have a chance of buying a cottage with a few acres of hill-farming, begin in a small way with some sheep. That's what he is, a shepherd." Suddenly a smile made near beautiful a face that feature by feature had no claim to it. "Thinks, breathes and eats sheep you could say. I can never get him to bed in the lambing season. We had a lean time to begin with, for the best part of six years. Land values had gone sky-high and there didn't seem a hope of our ever buying a farm, however small, of our own. Those were the years that taught me how little you can live on if you don't think beyond food and a cake of soap. We hadn't money to spend on stamps, but I did write to Susan a couple of times. She never replied. Maybe she never got my letters. Inspector Cornford says she moved about a lot. The only newspapers we read were those wrapped round the groceries and we didn't own a radio. Then, twelve months ago, an old bachelor farmer for whom Bill did odd jobs when he wasn't up to working himself, died and left Bill his house, sixty acres and a fine flock of pedigree sheep." She drew in her breath in exultation. "It was like a miracle, it *was* a miracle. Our own home that no one can turn us out of, Bill so happy that each morning he has to pinch himself to remember it's not a dream." The throaty laugh expressed both joy and incredulity.

"I've learnt to drive and he's bought me a second-hand car." She spread her hands wide as though to emphasise the extent of her good fortune. "Driving the children to school, taking them for a day to the sea they'd never seen. Sometimes it's me that needs to do the pinching." She doused the smile from her face. "You must excuse me for going on so long." She glanced at her watch.

"I'm glad you did," Georgina said, and wondered why Mrs. Sandiman, so obviously short of time, had been ordered by Cornford to spend some of it on her.

"We've three girls, seven, five and three they are." She looked down at her stout leather gloves to screen her eyes. "And there won't be any more. That's why, when I read about him, and talked it over with Bill, I came." Her half-defiant glance flew up to meet Georgina's. "He'd have a good home and there's no man living who's a better father than Bill."

Georgina asked, still not sure that she was guessing right: "You're saying you are going to take Dominic home with you?"

"Yes. To bring him up as our own. I spent yesterday afternoon with him. He's not an easy child; he'll take a bit of knowing, and it will be a while before he adjusts to our ways of living. But we can give him everything that matters to a child, and that's what we aim to do, give without stint for as long as it takes, for ever if need be. Inspector Cornford explained there'd be lots of paper-work and long delays while we were being vetted by the Adoption people and the Social Welfare. He said it might be a year or more before Dominic was legally our son. But we don't mind waiting, if we're allowed to adopt him in the end. That way, the only way, I see it, Susan's life won't have been wasted."

Georgina automatically said words that were, she hoped, appropriate though she didn't actually hear them, she was too deeply absorbed in studying the woman who was still poised, ready for instant flight, on the edge of the chair.

Warmth, good-will, immense capability, the best of intentions, plus a willingness to give away a piece of herself, like a sacrament, for a dead girl who had once been her friend. Could she ask for more? She told herself no. She smiled. "If anyone can wipe out . . . what happened, make Dominic happy, I'm sure you will. I don't think it's true that children have short memories. Sometimes they're very long indeed. It may be hard-going for you."

"None of it's going to be easy, but he'll be loved, and he'll be the only son we'll ever have." She glanced anxiously at the carriage clock on the mantelpiece. "I can't dawdle any longer. Inspector Cornford is having me driven to Fairview to collect Dominic and to take us to Paddington. That'll mean we'll be home for supper and Bill and the girls will be waiting at the station. But before we left, Inspector Cornford asked me to tell you about Dominic coming to us. He seemed to think you'd be pleased."

His perception, the delicacy of approach startled her, sparking off not so much gratitude as amazement. "I *am* pleased," she said and thought how inadequate the word was, "and very relieved. I was worried about him."

"That's what he said." For a moment she stared at different objects in the room. "It's so pretty, like a scene in a film, not that I see many, but we've got a television now. Susan must have enjoyed being here. In her own home everything had to have a purpose, nothing just to look at. And it was never warm. You started to shiver as soon as you were inside the front door. That's the farthest I ever got. You see, Mr. and Mrs. Bates didn't welcome visitors. And if you're never allowed to make friends while you're young, you never learn the knack. But you liked her, that's what Inspector Cornford said."

"Yes, I did."

At the front door, Georgina asked: "Do you think you could let me know how Dominic is?"

She looked doubtful, vaguely affronted. "Well, I don't know . . . I suppose there wouldn't be any harm in it, but he's sharp and I wouldn't like him to see a letter with a Larksbridge postmark. I'd rather leave it awhile, until we've made him feel thoroughly at home. Say, after Christmas. We're counting on that making him happy."

When Georgina had thanked her, shut the door, Richard

came downstairs, wearing his painting dungarees, a brush in his hand. "Who was that?"

"An old friend of Miss Jones's. She's taking Dominic back with her to Wales, and if the Courts give their permission, she and her husband want to adopt him."

Down the length of the hall their glances linked warily. "Georgie, I know what you wanted. But use your head, darling, it wouldn't have worked out. How the hell could it?"

"Oh, I agree. He'll be far better off with the Sandimans."

But common sense, the best solution that could be found, didn't stop her wanting to repay, to exorcise her guilt by loving.

Richard held out his hand. "I've just finished the last lick of paint. Come and take a look, tell me if you think Simon will be pleased."